THE LEGAL CASE FOR PALESTINE

This book critically analyzes the Palestinian legal arguments against Israeli occupation and in favor of Palestinian statehood.

For the past two decades, the Palestinians have chosen to pursue their claims against the Israeli occupation through litigation at the international courts. It is therefore appropriate, the author contends, to analyze the merits of the Palestinian legal claims separately from their political claims. To do so, the book comprises five parts:

- Part I addresses the role of international law in the conflict as well as Palestinian legal framing and lawfare.
- Part II recounts the relevant legal history, including the crucial legal implications of the Oslo Accords.
- Part III analyzes Palestinian legal claims regarding the West Bank and the Gaza Strip.
- Part IV assesses the Palestinian legal case for statehood.
- Part V analyzes Palestinian legal claims regarding Jerusalem.

Ultimately, it is argued that the Palestinian legal case is weak even though the two-state solution continues to represent the most viable long-term *political* outcome to the conflict. Moreover, the author suggests that Palestinian leaders have repeatedly opted for conflict perpetuation through lawfare and violence, rather than conflict resolution through negotiation.

Providing fresh insights into the claims and counterclaims of Palestinian legal arguments, the book will appeal broadly to anyone interested in the Israeli-Palestinian conflict and international law.

Steven E. Zipperstein is Associate Director and Distinguished Senior Scholar at the UCLA Center for Middle East Development and an Assistant Adjunct Professor at the UCLA Luskin School of Public Affairs. Zipperstein is also a Visiting Professor at Tel Aviv University Law School and a Visiting Lecturer at the Hertie School in Berlin. Zipperstein is the author of *Zionism, Palestinian Nationalism and the Law: 1939–1948* (Routledge, 2022) and *Law and the Arab-Israeli Conflict: The Trials of Palestine* (Routledge, 2020).

UCLA Center for Middle East Development (CMED)

Series Editors: Steven Spiegel, *UCLA* and Elizabeth Matthews, *California State University, San Marcos*

The UCLA Center for Middle East Development (CMED) series on Middle East security and cooperation is designed to present a variety of perspectives on a specific topic, such as democracy in the Middle East, dynamics of Israeli-Palestinian relations, Gulf security, and the gender factor in the Middle East. The uniqueness of the series is that the authors write from the viewpoint of a variety of countries so that no matter what the issue, articles appear from many different states, both within and beyond the region. No existing series provides a comparable, multinational collection of authors. Thus, the series presents a combination of writers from countries who, for political reasons, do not always publish in the same volume. The series features a number of sub-themes under a single heading, covering security, social, political, and economic factors affecting the Middle East.

20. **Zionism, Palestinian Nationalism and the Law**
    1939–1948
    Steven E. Zipperstein

21. **Elections and Public Opinion in Turkey**
    Through the Prism of the 2018 Elections
    Edited by Ali Çarkoğlu and Ersin Kalaycıoğlu

22. **The Legal Case for Palestine**
    A Critical Assessment
    Steven E. Zipperstein

For more information about this series, please visit: www.routledge.com/UCLA-Center-for-Middle-East-Development-CMED-series/book-series/CMED

THE LEGAL CASE FOR PALESTINE

A Critical Assessment

Steven E. Zipperstein

Routledge
Taylor & Francis Group
LONDON AND NEW YORK

Designed cover image: Alaa Badarneh/POOL/AFP via Getty Images

First published 2025
by Routledge
4 Park Square, Milton Park, Abingdon, Oxon OX14 4RN

and by Routledge
605 Third Avenue, New York, NY 10158

Routledge is an imprint of the Taylor & Francis Group, an informa business

British Library Cataloguing-in-Publication Data
A catalogue record for this book is available from the British Library

Library of Congress Cataloging-in-Publication Data
Names: Zipperstein, Steve E., author.
Title: The legal case for Palestine: a critical assessment / Steven E. Zipperstein.
Description: Abingdon, Oxon [UK]; New York, NY: Routledge, 2024. |
Series: Ucla center for middle east development (cmed) | Includes bibliographical references and index. | Identifiers: LCCN 2024006999 (print) |
LCCN 2024007000 (ebook) | ISBN 9781032686516 (hardback) |
ISBN 9781032686554 (paperback) | ISBN 9781032686561 (ebook)
Subjects: LCSH: West Bank—International status. |
Gaza Strip—International status. | Palestine—International status—History. |
Recognition (International law)—History. | Declaration of Principles on Interim Self-Government Arrangements (1993 September 13) | Arab-Israeli conflict—1993—Peace. | Palestinian Arabs—Legal status, laws, etc.—History—1948– | Palestine—Politics and government—1948– |
Legitimacy of governments—Middle East.
Classification: LCC KZ4282 .Z575 2024 (print) | LCC KZ4282 (ebook) |
DDC 341.4/2095694—dc23/eng/20240326
LC record available at https://lccn.loc.gov/2024006999
LC ebook record available at https://lccn.loc.gov/2024007000

ISBN: 978-1-032-68651-6 (hbk)
ISBN: 978-1-032-68655-4 (pbk)
ISBN: 978-1-032-68656-1 (ebk)

DOI: 10.4324/9781032686561

Typeset in Sabon
by codeMantra

For My Grandchildren

CONTENTS

TABLES

CASES

Ahmad et al. v. Prime Minister, Israel Supreme Court, HCJ 9132/07 (2008).
Ajuri v. IDF Commander, HCJ 7015/02 (2002).
Armed Activities on the Territory of the Congo (Democratic Republic of the Congo v. Uganda), Judgment, I.C.J. Reports 2005, p.168.
Award in Regard to the Validity of the Treaty of Limits between Costa Rica and Nicaragua of 15 July 1858, Decision of 26 July 1899, Reports of International Arbitral Awards, Volume XXVIII, 189–236.
*Beit Sourik Village Council v. Government of Israe*l, HCJ 2056/04 (2004).
Case of Certain Norwegian Loans, Judgment of July 6, 1957, I.C.J. Reports 1957, p.9.
In The Matter of The Chagos Marine Protected Area Arbitration (Mauritius v. U.K), Case No. 2011-03, Award, Permanent Court of International Arbitration (2015).
Dispute Concerning Delimitation of the Maritime Boundary between Bangladesh and Myanmar in the Bay of Bengal (Bangladesh/Myanmar) (Judgment), ITLOS 4 (2012).
Dweikat et al., v. Government of Israel et al., HCJ 390/79 (1979).
East Timor (Portugal v. Australia), Judgment, I.C.J. Reports 1995, p.90.
Elettronica Sicula S.p.A. (ELSI) (US v. Italy), I.C.J. Reports 1989, p.44.
Ffrost v. Stevenson (1937) 58 C.L.R. 528 (High Court of Australia).
Frontier Dispute (Burkina Faso/Mali), Judgment, I.C.J. Reports 1986, p.554.
Fur Seal Arbitration (U.S. v. Gr. Brit.), Proceedings of the Tribunal of Arbitration (1893).
Gaza Beach Local Council v. Knesset of Israel, HCJ 1661/05 (2005).

Georges Pinson (France) v. United Mexican States, Franco-Mexican Claims Commission, Annual Digest of Public International Law Cases 1927–28 (19 Oct. 1928).

Husseini v. Government of Palestine, High Court No. 55 (1925).

International Status of South-West Africa, Advisory Opinion, 010-19500711-ADV-01-01, I.C.J. Reports 1950, p.150.

Island of Palmas (Miangas), United States v. Netherlands, Reports of International Arbitral Awards Recueil Des Sentences Arbitrales, 2 U.N. Rep. Intl. Arb. Awards 829-871 (Perm. Ct. Arb. 1928), (4 Apr. 1928).

Judgment No. 2867 of the Administrative Tribunal of the ILO upon a Complaint Filed Against the International Fund for Agricultural Development, Advisory Opinion, ICJ Reports, 2012, p. 10.

Land and Maritime Boundary between Cameroon and Nigeria, Preliminary Objections, Judgment, I.C.J. Reports 1998, p.275.

Land and Maritime Boundary (Cameroon v. Nigeria: Equatorial Guinea intervening), I.C.J. Reports 2002, p.303.

Legal Consequences for States of the Continued Presence of South Africa in Namibia (South West Africa) notwithstanding Security Council Resolution 276, Advisory Opinion, I.C.J. Reports 1971, p.50.

Legal Consequences of the Construction of a Wall in the Occupied Palestinian Territory, I.C.J. Reports 2004, p.136.

Legality of the Threat or Use of Nuclear Weapons, Advisory Opinion, I.C.J. Reports 1996, p.226.

Mara'abe v. The Prime Minister of Israel, HCJ 7957/04 (2005).

Maritime Delimitation and Territorial Questions between Qatar and Bahrain, Jurisdiction and Admissibility - Judgment, I.C.J. Reports 1994, p.112.

Military and Paramilitary Activities in and against Nicaragua (Nicaragua v. United States of America), Merits, Judgment, I.C.J. Reports 1986, p.14.

The Minquiers and Ecrehos Case, Judgment of November 17, 1953, I.C. J. Reports 1953, p.47.

North Sea Continental Shelf, Judgment (Federal Republic of Germany v. Denmark; Federal Republic of Germany v. Netherlands), 1969 I.C.J. Reports, p.3.

Physicians for Human Rights v. IDF Commander, HCJ 4764/04 (2004).

Prosecutor v. Naletilic, ICTY Case No. IT-98-34-T, Judgment, Trial Chamber (2003).

Public Committee Against Torture in Israel v. the Government of Israel, HCJ 769/02 (2006).

Rhine Chlorides, 144 ILR 259 (2004).

Situation in the State of Palestine, No. ICC-01/18, International Criminal Court, Pre-Trial Chamber I, *Decision on the Prosecution Request Pursuant to Article 19(3) for a Ruling on the Court's Territorial Jurisdiction in Palestine* (5 Feb. 2021).

Situation on the Registered Vessels of the Union of the Comoros, The Hellenic Republic and The Kingdom of Cambodia, Public Decision on the 'Application for Judicial Review by the Government of the Comoros,' International Criminal Court, No. ICC 01-13 (2020).
South West Africa Cases (Ethiopia v. South Africa; Liberia v. South Africa), Preliminary Objections, Judgment of 21 December 1962: I.C.J. Reports, 1962, p.319.
South West Africa, Second Phase, Judgment, I.C.J. Reports 1966, p. 6.
Temple of Preah Vihear (Cambodia v. Thailand), I.C.J. Reports 1962, p.6.
Ungar v. Palestine Liberation Organization, 402 F.3d 274 (1st Cir. 2005).
United States v. Krauch, et al., Case No. 6 (United States Military Tribunal, Nuremberg), Judgment of the Tribunal (1948).
United States of America v. List et al., 8 Law Reports of Trials of Major War Criminals 38 (United Nations War Crimes Commission 1949).
Western Sahara, Advisory Opinion, I.C.J. Reports 1975, p. 12.
Yugoslavia Arbitration Commission, Opinion No. 2 (1992).

Statutes

International Criminal Court (ICC) Statute, 17 July 1998, in force 1 July 2002, United Nations T.S. vol. 2187, No. 38544.
International Court of Justice (ICJ) Statute, Charter of the United Nations and Statute of the International Court of Justice, June 26, 1945, 59 Stat. 1031 [the Charter], 1055 [ICJ Statute], T.S. No. 993.

PREFACE AND EXPLANATORY NOTE

The Palestinians solemnly promised 30 years ago in the Oslo Accords to pursue all their claims through negotiation with Israel. The Accords resulted from robust, arms-length direct negotiations between the Palestinians and the Israelis. Both sides signed the Accords knowingly, voluntarily, and willingly.

The importance of the Oslo Accords cannot be overstated. They represent the governing legal documents for the Israel-Palestinian conflict. The Accords are legally binding and remain in effect as of today. Neither side has abrogated the Accords.

The Palestinians agreed in the Oslo Accords that the Israeli occupation and settlements could remain in place pending the completion of permanent status negotiations, which would also cover issues such as Jerusalem, refugees, settlements, security arrangements, borders, relations and cooperation with other neighbors, and other issues of common interest. The Palestinians agreed to renounce terrorism and violence, to stop teaching their children hatred, and to pursue all issues between the parties through diplomacy.

Israel complied with most of its obligations, especially by acceding to the creation of the Palestinian Authority (PA) and handing civil control of the main Palestinian populated areas to the PA. The Palestinians have occasionally cooperated with Israel on security matters but have otherwise breached their obligations under the Oslo Accords.

Unfortunately, for the past two decades the Palestinians have abandoned diplomacy and the peace process, choosing instead to pursue litigation against Israel at the international courts by cloaking their political claims in legal language. Indeed, the Palestinians have so successfully conflated their political claims with their legal case that most observers and the majority of academics now view both sets of claims as interchangeable.

However, the conflation of politics and law ignores the analytical imperative that the Palestinian legal and political cases must be decoupled from each other and considered separately, each on its own merits. A strong political case does not automatically translate into a strong legal case. The annals of international and domestic law are filled with claimants who lost in court despite the political strength of their claims.

Few if any published works have subjected the Palestinian legal arguments to close or even mild scrutiny. The vast majority of scholarly and international public opinion simply accepts the Palestinian legal case as if it had long ago been proven beyond all doubt.

This study therefore fills a gap in research by conducting a critical analysis of the merits of the Palestinian legal case, separate and apart from the Palestinian political case. The Palestinian decision to abandon the Oslo process, and pursue litigation rather than negotiation, renders such an analysis both necessary and appropriate.

*****

As this study neared its final stages, the Israeli-Palestinian conflict exploded on 7 October 2023. Hamas terrorists invaded southern Israel in a surprise attack under the cover of thousands of rockets fired at Israeli civilian targets. The terrorists slaughtered more than 1,200 babies, children, women, and elderly. The terrorists murdered parents in front of their children. They decapitated infants. They raped women and girls. They burned people alive. They threw hand grenades into a small shelter where young people who had been dancing hours earlier at a music festival were hiding for their lives. The atrocities were unspeakable. The terrorists also took more than 240 hostages back to Gaza.

After a very short period of sympathy for the victims of the massacre, the world quickly turned against Israel once the Jewish State retaliated with air strikes and subsequent ground operations against Hamas targets in Gaza. The international media falsely reported Israel had bombed the Al Ahli hospital in Gaza on 17 October 2023 and killed 500 innocent civilians, when it turned out an errant Hamas rocket was to blame, that the rocket had struck the adjacent parking lot and not the hospital, and the death toll was well below 100.

The Palestinians and their supporters in the international community, following a well-worn script from prior conflicts, accused Israel of "war crimes" and "genocide." Palestinian supporters around the world marched in the streets and on university campuses demanding "justice" for the Palestinian people. Antisemitism and anti-Israelism soared.

As of this writing, the war continues in Gaza, following a week-long pause in late November 2023 when Hamas traded 81 women and child hostages, including toddlers, for more than 200 Palestinian terrorists in Israeli prisons. The war resumed after Hamas broke the terms of the pause and fired more than 50 rockets into Israel on 1 December 2023.

Israel is acting in legitimate self-defense, fighting for its very survival. But even as the physical war rages on, the Palestinians have ramped up their parallel legal war against Israel.

One would expect the International Court of Justice (ICJ) and the International Criminal Court (ICC) to have taken immediate action against Hamas and its Iranian sponsors. But those courts, dominated by anti-Israel judges, have proven less than objective in assessing the Israeli-Palestinian conflict.

The ICJ is currently considering a December 2022 request from the United Nations General Assembly to issue an Advisory ruling slamming Israel for its treatment of Palestinians. The court will likely issue a ruling in 2024 against Israel on every issue. The ruling, while merely advisory, will likely prompt further recrimination against Israel.

The ICJ is also considering a December 2023 South African request to indicate provisional measures against Israel for alleged violations of the 1948 Genocide Convention resulting from its defensive actions in Gaza in response to the 7 October 2023 Hamas attacks. In January and March 2024 the court issued rulings indicating provisional measures against Israel, finding it "plausible" that Israel's actions following the 7 October attacks implicated Palestinian rights not to be subjected to violations of the Genocide Convention. Although the court has not yet issued a final ruling on the merits, a hostile ruling against Israel seems likely at some future point, especially given the court's predisposition against the Jewish State.

The ICJ previously demonstrated its anti-Israel bias in 2004, when it ruled the West Bank separation wall illegal, even though many other countries around the world have similar barriers, and even though the wall significantly reduced terrorist attacks against Israel originating from the West Bank. Those attacks had risen dramatically during the so-called second intifada between 2000 and 2003, prompting Israel to build the wall.

Likewise, the ICC and its prosecutor have focused enormous attention on investigating and potentially bringing charges against Israeli citizens in cases such as the present war, where Israel is lawfully defending itself against Hamas atrocities and rocket attacks. The ICC prosecutor visited the Egypt-Gaza Strip border in late October 2023 and threatened Israel with legal action for its conduct of the war. In early December 2023, the prosecutor also indicated he might investigate "potential" Hamas crimes committed on 7 October 2023.

The ICC gave a huge boost to Palestinian efforts to weaponize international criminal law against Israel when it issued a legally questionable ruling in February 2021 conferring "statehood" on Palestine. In so doing, the court granted the PA formal standing to request the court's prosecutor to initiate investigations of Israeli citizens.

It is highly likely that both the ICJ and the ICC will devote the majority of their resources in the coming months and years to Israel's response to the 7 October 2023 Hamas massacres. Both courts will continue to welcome Palestinian legal claims, and they will continue issuing harsh rulings against Israel.

Meanwhile, the PA, which repeatedly has sought to invoke the jurisdiction of the international courts as part of its long-running lawfare campaign against Israel, has embraced and celebrated the 7 October 2023 Hamas massacres. Jibril Rajoub, who serves as the PLO's Central Committee Secretary in the West Bank, was quoted on the Kuwaiti news website *Al-Anba* on 26 November 2023 describing the Hamas massacres as "an earthquake, an unprecedented incident, and a war of defense full of epics and acts of heroism."

The PA's support for the Hamas massacres raises the question whether the equitable doctrine of unclean hands should bar the doors of the international courts to proponents of terrorism. Unfortunately, those courts will not be bothered by the PA's support for the atrocities.

*****

A brief explanatory note: this study mostly avoids the Latin words and phrases so appealing to professors and practitioners of international law, except for the discussions of *uti possidetis juris* in Chapter 9 and *pacta sunt servanda* in Chapter 14. Otherwise, this study largely ignores Latin legal terminology such as *jus cogens, jus in bello, jus ad bellum, erga omnes, lex lata, lex ferenda, lex specialis, res nullius, terra nullius, debellatio*, and *ex injuria jus non oritur*, which represent quaint but mostly muddled components of international legal discourse.

Accordingly, this study bypasses Latin almost entirely, preferring plain English explanations of international legal concepts, norms, and principles.

Nevertheless, *caveat emptor.*

ACKNOWLEDGMENTS

First and foremost, I offer my profound gratitude to Professors Steven L. Spiegel and Michael F. Lofchie of the University of California, Los Angeles for their tremendous support, guidance, and mentorship.

Professor Elizabeth G. Matthews of California State University San Marcos provided valuable advice and encouragement. Special thanks to Joe Whiting at Routledge for his kind support and excellent substantive suggestions, and to Euan Rice-Coates at Routledge and Anandan Bommen at codeMantra for their editorial assistance.

My close friend Ira Raphaelson read significant portions of the manuscript and provided very helpful comments. Many distinguished international legal experts, including Marlene Mazel, Natasha Hausdorff, Jonathan Turner, Andrew Tucker, and Anne Herzberg offered valuable advice and guidance regarding a variety of issues discussed in the book. I also want to thank several Palestinian and other Arab friends for their willingness to share their views with me over the past decade.

Several student members of the UCLA Center for Middle East Development research team, under the direction of my wonderful colleague Warren Fahmy, made important contributions to the chapters on Jerusalem and the Egyptian occupation of the Gaza Strip.

I am also very grateful to the three anonymous referees for their careful review of the manuscript and their excellent suggestions for improvement.

Despite the enormous help from so many people, I alone am responsible for any errors, omissions, or mistakes in this study.

As always, I would not have been able to start, much less finish this project, without the constant support and inspiration from my wife of nearly 40 years, Diane Zipperstein.

This book is dedicated to our dear grandchildren, whom Papa loves with all his heart and soul. May they grow up in a better world.

INTRODUCTION

Brief History

Following the defeat of Germany and Turkey in World War I, the Treaty of Versailles (1919) and the subsequent Kellogg-Briand Pact (1928) established a new principle of international law governing territories acquired in wartime. Eschewing the centuries-long practice of recognizing acquisition by conquest, the newly established League of Nations and the eventual Kellogg-Briand signatories declared that no longer would the victors be permitted to keep for themselves territories captured in war. Instead, the territories Britain and France captured from Germany and Turkey, including Palestine, would be treated as "Mandates" under temporary League of Nations tutelage until the local populations would be ready for self-rule.

Accordingly, in July 1922 the Council of the League of Nations voted unanimously to place the area colloquially known as "Palestine," which had been under Ottoman Turkish rule for four centuries (1517–1917), into the post-World War I Mandates system under British control.

The League of Nations treated the Palestine Mandate separately from all other Mandates. Most notably, the Palestine Mandate acknowledged Zionism as the national liberation movement of the Jewish people. The Preamble to the Mandate specifically recognized the "historical connection of the Jewish people with Palestine and ... the grounds for reconstituting their national home in that country." The words "historical connection" and "reconstitute" carry enormous legal significance, as they made clear the international community's recognition that the Jewish people would be pursuing self-determination in their indigenous and ancient homeland, where Jews had maintained a continuous presence even after the Roman expulsion two millennia ago.

DOI: 10.4324/9781032686561-1

The words "historical connection" and "reconstitute" therefore completely debunk the modern-day and baseless effort to characterize Zionism as a form of "settler colonialism."

The Palestine Mandate further supported Zionism by codifying the British Government's promise in the November 1917 Balfour Declaration to establish a National Home "for the Jewish people" in Palestine. The Palestine Mandate thus embodied a legal commitment from the international community to the Jewish people worldwide, not just to the tens of thousands of Jews already living in Palestine. The Mandate further obligated Britain to facilitate Jewish immigration and Jewish "close settlement" of the land, while respecting the civil and religious (but not political) rights of the local non-Jewish population.

The Arab leadership in Mecca, whom Britain had lured into an alliance against Turkey in the early years of World War I in exchange for promises of independence after the war, initially supported but later opposed the creation of a Jewish National Home in Palestine. By the early 1920s the Arabs argued Britain had included Palestine in the areas promised to the Arabs for post-war independence. Britain, for its part, maintained it never intended to include Palestine.

In any event, the Mandate did not confer sovereignty over Palestine on Britain or anyone else. Instead, sovereignty over the West Bank and Gaza has remained, as a matter of international law, "suspended" or in "abeyance" from the moment Turkey formally relinquished the area in the July 1923 Treaty of Lausanne, until the present day.

During the 1920s and 1930s, many local Arab lawyers and witnesses repeatedly insisted there was no such place as "Palestine." Thus, they argued, the Mandate for "Palestine" lacked any legal foundation and should be rescinded. Those lawyers and witnesses argued instead that the area the League of Nations had recognized as "Palestine" and the people living there should be subsumed within the borders of Syria.

These arguments reflected the geopolitical reality that "Palestine" did not exist as a recognized entity during the four centuries of Ottoman rule. The area was divided between the Ottoman administrative districts known as the *Vilayet* of Beirut and the *Sanjak* of Jerusalem. The concept of "Palestinians" or the "Palestinian people" was completely unknown.

Thereafter the Palestinians changed tactics, demanding statehood in Palestine. But when offered statehood they repeatedly refused. They rejected the original British two-state solution in July 1937. They rejected Britain's offer of the one-state solution in May 1939. And they rejected the United Nations' two-state solution in November 1947, launching a violent and bloody war instead.

Britain unilaterally terminated the Palestine Mandate on 14 May 1948. Israel declared its independence the same day. Every neighboring Arab country plus Iraq invaded the new Jewish state. The war finally ended in April 1949. The United Nations accorded full membership to Israel one month later. In so doing, the international community fulfilled the commitment it made to the Jewish people nearly three decades earlier in the Palestine Mandate. The United Nations not only recognized Israeli sovereignty over the area of Mandate Palestine it had allocated in November 1947 for the Jewish State, but also over portions of the areas designated for the Palestinian Arab state that Israel had captured during the 1948–1949 war.

In December 1948 a conference of Palestinian leaders in Jericho explicitly waived West Bank sovereignty and statehood, pledging their loyalty to Jordan's King Abdullah I. Following the end of the war in April 1949, Jordan occupied and purported to annex the West Bank. Egypt occupied the Gaza Strip. Both occupations, largely forgotten to history, lasted nearly two decades until the June 1967 Six-Day War, when Israel replaced Jordan as the occupant of the West Bank and Egypt as the occupant of the Gaza Strip in a lawful war of self-defense.

Significantly, the Palestinians *never* sought statehood in the West Bank and the Gaza Strip during the Jordanian and Egyptian occupations between 1949 and 1967. The PLO's May 1964 founding Charter explicitly reiterated in Article 24 the prior Palestinian waivers of statehood in the West Bank and Gaza, declaring, "[t]his Organization does not exercise any regional sovereignty over the West Bank in the Hashemite Kingdom of Jordan, or the Gaza Strip."

But following the June 1967 war the Palestinians changed direction once again and asserted rights of self-determination and sovereignty over the West Bank and the Gaza Strip, even as sovereignty remained legally unresolved. Jordan renounced its legal and administrative ties to the West Bank in July 1988, but that act was meaningless under international law, as Jordan never held sovereignty over the West Bank in the first instance. Immediately thereafter the Palestinians purported to declare "statehood," but that unilateral declaration likewise was meaningless under international law, given the unresolved status of sovereignty over the West Bank and the Gaza Strip.

The Oslo Accords

A little more than three decades ago, on 13 September 1993, following months of intensive negotiations, Israel and the Palestine Liberation Organization (PLO) signed the "Declaration of Principles on Interim Self-Government Arrangements," the first in a series of agreements collectively known as the Oslo Accords.[1]

PLO Chairman Yasser Arafat and his team, including current PLO Chairman and Palestinian Authority President Mahmoud Abbas, negotiated and signed the Declaration of Principles on behalf of the Palestinian side. Former

Israeli Prime Minister Yitzhak Rabin and his team negotiated and signed on behalf of the Government of Israel.

The Oslo Accords covered the entire gamut of the Israeli-Palestinian conflict. The opening paragraph of the Declaration of Principles states:

> The Government of the State of Israel and the PLO ... representing the Palestinian people, agree that it is time to put an end to decades of confrontation and conflict, recognize their mutual legitimate and political rights, and strive to live in peaceful coexistence and mutual dignity and security and achieve a just, lasting and comprehensive peace settlement and historic reconciliation through the agreed political process.

The United States and the Russian Federation formally witnessed the signing of the Declaration of Principles. Their respective United Nations Ambassadors jointly submitted the document to the United Nations on 8 October 1993, asking that it be circulated as "an official document of the General Assembly ... and of the Security Council." Israel's U.N. Ambassador and the PLO's United Nations Observer separately did the same.[2]

Four days before signing the Declaration of Principles, PLO Chairman Arafat pledged in a letter to Israeli Prime Minister Rabin that the PLO recognized "the right of the State of Israel to exist in peace and security." Arafat made several other commitments in his letter, including renouncing terrorism and violence. Most significantly for purposes of the present study, Arafat's letter stated, "The PLO ... declares that *all outstanding issues relating to permanent status will be resolved through negotiations*."[3]

Prime Minister Rabin responded in writing the same day. Relying on Arafat's written promises, Rabin confirmed that, "in light of the PLO commitments included in your letter, the Government of Israel has decided to recognize the PLO as the representative of the Palestinian people and commence negotiations with the PLO within the Middle East peace process."[4]

Arafat's commitments in his letter, together with Rabin's response granting Israeli recognition of the PLO in reliance on those commitments, made it legally and politically possible for both sides to sign the Declaration of Principles. The parties on two later occasions reaffirmed their adherence to the mutual commitments set forth in the September 1993 exchange of letters.[5]

The Palestinians negotiated at Oslo for Israeli recognition of the PLO as the sole representative of the Palestinian people. The Oslo Accords created a transitional governing body, known as the "Palestinian Authority," to take control of the major West Bank population centers (Areas A and B) and the Gaza Strip. In exchange, the Palestinians agreed Israel would maintain control over the remainder of the West Bank (Area C), including all Israeli settlements until a permanent status agreement would be reached.

Significantly, the Oslo Accords – the result of months of arms-length, intense negotiations, and willingly signed by both parties – expressly permitted Israeli settlements and settlers to remain in place, pending the outcome of permanent status negotiations. Moreover, the Accords contained *no* guarantees of future Palestinian statehood, nor any promises of future Palestinian sovereignty over any portion of the occupied territories.

The Palestinians and the Israelis agreed in the Declaration of Principles to reserve the thorniest permanent status issues for future negotiation, including Jerusalem, refugees, Israeli settlements, security arrangements, borders, relations and cooperation with other neighbors, and other issues of common interest.

Legal scholars generally view the Oslo Accords as binding. Watson (2000), for example, regards the Accords as agreements between "subjects of international law" – a state (Israel) and a National Liberation Movement (the PLO) – with the result that the Accords are legally binding on both the Palestinians and the Israelis.[6]

Sabel (2022) takes a somewhat different approach, characterizing the Oslo Accords as an agreement between a state (Israel) and a sub-state actor (the PLO) which at the time of signing did not control any territory. As such, Sabel argues the Oslo Accords cannot be regarded as a "Treaty" under the Vienna Convention on the Law of Treaties, notwithstanding the Convention's language in Article 3 indicating the Convention does not impact the legal validity of agreements between states and "other subjects of international law."[7] Sabel instead prefers to ground the legal status of the Oslo Accords on the notion of unilaterality, based on Israel's decision to be bound by the Accords, but only to the extent the PLO and the Palestinian Authority comply with their obligations under the Accords.[8]

The arrangements agreed upon at Oslo were contemplated to serve as an interim *status quo* pending a final deal on permanent status issues. Those interim arrangements remain in place today. Neither party has officially renounced the Accords as of this writing.[9] Contrary to the accusation that Israel has unilaterally imposed a form of "apartheid" on the West Bank, the political situation and the division of land and people in the West Bank today reflects *exactly* what the Palestinians bargained for at Oslo.

The permanent status negotiations contemplated by the Oslo Accords began in May 1996, but were suspended after a few hours. The negotiations resumed in 1999–2000, but failed for various reasons, including disagreement over the future of Jerusalem, especially the Old City and the Temple Mount. As Lapidoth (2011) recounted, "[s]ome of the Palestinian leaders, including Arafat, even claimed that there had never been a Jewish Temple on the Temple Mount in Jerusalem."[10]

The closest the parties came in recent years to reaching a permanent status agreement occurred during the short-lived efforts in 2008 of former Israeli

Prime Minister Ehud Olmert and Arafat's successor, Mahmoud Abbas to agree on final terms. Unfortunately, the talks collapsed when Abbas inexplicably rejected what Olmert later described as an unprecedented Israeli offer to withdraw almost entirely from the West Bank and the Arab neighborhoods of East Jerusalem, *and* to cede the Old City of Jerusalem to international control.[11]

In recent years the peace process and the political path to which the parties committed themselves at Oslo have lost nearly all momentum. The Palestinians and Israelis have repeatedly accused each other of violating the Oslo Accords, leaving the once-promising diplomatic track all but abandoned.

Israel, for example, has been accused of violating the Accords by failing to comply with its commitment in the 1995 Interim Agreement to "gradually transfer" Area C to Palestinian jurisdiction. Israel has also been accused of changing the status of the West Bank in violation of the Accords by building new settlements and expanding existing settlements.

The Palestinians, for their part, have been accused of a variety of breaches of the Accords.

For example, the Palestinians continue employing terrorism and violence, in direct violation of their legal obligations under the Oslo Accords. The Palestinian Authority offers "pay for slay" incentives, providing financial rewards to terrorists and their families. Palestinian schools continue teaching children to hate Israelis and Jews, despite the Palestinian pledge in the Oslo Accords to remove such content from school curricula.[12]

Hamas, which has ruled the Gaza Strip since mid-2007 following Israel's complete withdrawal in September 2005, proclaims itself committed to Israel's destruction and to killing as many Jews as possible, as exemplified so horrifically in the 7 October 2023 Hamas massacres of more than 1,200 innocent babies, children, women and elderly in southern Israel and taking more than 240 hostages to Gaza.

Palestinian Lawfare

For purposes of this study, the most important Palestinian breach of the Oslo Accords involves the Palestinians' failure to comply with their commitment to resolve *all* outstanding issues through negotiation. For the past two decades the Palestinians have abandoned negotiation in favor of litigation at the International Court of Justice, the International Criminal Court, and elsewhere. The Palestinian litigation effort has been part of a broader "lawfare" campaign against Israel, including the Boycott, Divestment and Sanctions movement, accusations of apartheid and genocide, and other strategies for delegitimizing the Jewish State. The Palestinian lawfare campaign has been accompanied by a parallel Palestinian effort to frame their political claims in *legal* terms, casting themselves at the center of the global social justice movement as perennial victims of alleged Israeli illegality.

The Palestinian litigation/lawfare campaign violates the binding Dispute Resolution process set forth in the Oslo Accords. That process, which both parties negotiated for and agreed to observe, requires in the first instance that any disputes be resolved by a Joint Israeli-Palestinian Liaison Committee. If the dispute cannot be resolved by negotiations within the Joint Liaison Committee, then the next step would be to resolve the dispute "by a mechanism of conciliation to be agreed upon by the parties." Should that not produce a resolution, then the final avenue would be for the parties to agree to submit the dispute to an Arbitration Committee *to be established by the parties themselves*.[13] In no event, however, do the Oslo Accords permit either party to commence (or to ask others to commence on their behalf) legal proceedings before the International Court of Justice, the International Criminal Court, or any other external body.

Nevertheless, the world community largely accepts Palestinian legal claims as valid, including claims that conflict with concessions the Palestinians made in the Oslo Accords.

Palestinian advocates and their supporters in academia, the media and elsewhere have succeeded in steering international opinion and international law in their favor since the turn of the 21st century, churning out an impressive array of books, articles, blogs and other publications.[14] The vast majority of scholarly and international public opinion today simply accepts the Palestinian legal case as if it had long ago been proven beyond all doubt. Few if any previously published works have subjected the Palestinian legal arguments to close or even mild scrutiny.

But the conflation of politics and law ignores the analytical imperative that the Palestinian legal case and the Palestinian political case be decoupled from each other and considered separately, each on its own merit. A strong political case does not automatically translate into a strong legal case. The annals of international and domestic law are filled with claimants who lost in court despite the political strength of their claims.

The Palestinian legal case contains four key elements:

First, the Palestinians contend the Israeli occupation of the West Bank (including East Jerusalem and the Old City of Jerusalem) violates international law. They argue the occupation resulted from an unlawful Israeli use of military force in June 1967. They also argue the more than 50-year duration of the occupation violates international law. The Palestinians have extended this argument to the Gaza Strip, from which Israel withdrew completely in September 2005, arguing Israel nevertheless continues to "occupy" Gaza, even in the face of the 7 October 2023 Hamas invasion of southern Israel and ensuing massacres.

Second, the Palestinians contend the manner of the occupation violates international law, by imposing "apartheid," by depriving West Bank residents of their international legal right to self-determination, and by violating international humanitarian and human rights laws.

Third, the Palestinians allege Israeli settlements in the West Bank violate international law.

Fourth, the Palestinians argue they are legally entitled to sovereignty and statehood in the West Bank and the Gaza Strip. They also argue, in the alternative, that Palestine has *already* achieved statehood/sovereignty over the West Bank and Gaza, with all the legal rights and privileges accorded to states.

The distinction between the Palestinian legal and political cases is of crucial importance. For example, the Palestinians hope to use litigation and the legal process to obtain court rulings condemning Israel, which they could not otherwise obtain if they were to focus purely on diplomacy and negotiations, as they committed to do at Oslo. Those rulings could then be used to isolate and pressure Israel in the political and economic spheres, and perhaps to call into question the Jewish State's very legitimacy. The Palestinians have also urged that criminal prosecutions be brought against Israeli citizens at the International Criminal Court (ICC). The Palestinians have also dramatically ramped up litigation against Israel at the International Court of Justice (ICJ).

These developments signal a troubling new phenomenon: Israel's adversaries, wary of the U.S. veto power in the United Nations Security Council, are using the international courts as their preferred fora for addressing issues of politics, war, and peace that should be the sole province of the Security Council. Rather than dismissing such efforts, the ICC and the ICJ have embraced the opportunity to play a larger role on the world stage, raising questions about their proper role as courts of law rather than arbiters of diplomacy.

Goals of this Study

The legal and political stakes are high. Therefore, it is entirely appropriate and fair to ask: *Just how strong is the Palestinian legal case, separate and apart from the Palestinian political case?*

This study addresses that question and offers a critical analysis of the merits of the Palestinian legal case. Part I addresses the role of international law in the conflict, as well as Palestinian legal framing and lawfare. Part II recounts the relevant legal history, including the crucial legal implications of the Oslo Accords. Part III analyzes various Palestinian legal claims regarding the West Bank and the Gaza Strip, including the legality of the Israeli occupation of the West Bank; the legality of Israeli settlements in the West Bank; allegations of apartheid and denial of self-determination; and whether the Gaza Strip remains "occupied" despite the full Israeli withdrawal in

2005. Part IV assesses the Palestinian legal case for Statehood, including the extent to which the Palestinians are legally entitled to statehood, and whether the West Bank and Gaza Strip have *already* achieved statehood as a matter of international law. Part V analyzes Palestinian legal claims regarding Jerusalem.

The purpose of this study is *not* to argue against the two-state solution, which continues to offer the best and fairest long-term outcome for all parties to the conflict, despite the Hamas atrocities of October 2023 and the Palestinian Authority's refusal to condemn those atrocities. Palestinian political aspirations for self-determination and statehood in the West Bank and the Gaza Strip hopefully will someday be realized as the result of the peace process to which the Palestinians committed themselves in the Oslo Accords.[15]

Instead, the purpose of this study is to cast a critical, fair and scholarly eye on the merits of the Palestinian *legal* case in its various aspects, and to attempt to recalibrate the application of international law to the conflict in a manner consistent with the traditional understandings and purposes of the key legal principles at stake. In so doing, it is hoped the international courts will reflect on their increasing tendency to intervene in the fundamentally political Israeli-Palestinian conflict, at the risk of undermining the parties' prior agreement to pursue their claims solely through diplomacy.

Notes

1 *Declaration of Principles on Interim Self-Government Arrangements*, 13 Sept. 1993, 32 I.L.M. 1525 (1993). The Palestinian leader Mahmoud Abbas (Abu Mazen) recounted the negotiations in detail in his book *Through Secret Channels* (Garnet, 1997).

2 United Nations A/48/486, S/26560, Letter to the General Assembly and the Security Council from Madeline K. Albright and Yuliy M. Vorontsov (11 Oct. 1993), https://www.un.org/unispal/document/auto-insert-180015/ (last accessed 1 Oct. 2023).

3 Letter from Yasser Arafat, Chairman, Palestine Liberation Organization, to Yitzhak Rabin, Prime Minister of Israel (9 Sept. 1993), https://www.un.org/unispal/document/auto-insert-205528/#:~:text=LETTER%20FROM%20YASSER%20ARAFAT%20TO%20PRIME%20MINISTER%20RABIN%3A&text=In%20firm%20conviction%20thereof%2C%20I,Council%20Resolutions%20242%20and%20338 (last accessed 30 Sept. 2023) (emphasis added).

4 Letter from Yitzhak Rabin, Prime Minister of Israel to Yasser Arafat, Chairman, Palestine Liberation Organization (9 Sept. 1993), https://www.un.org/unispal/document/auto-insert-205528/#:~:text=LETTER%20FROM%20YASSER%20ARAFAT%20TO%20PRIME%20MINISTER%20RABIN%3A&text=In%20firm%20conviction%20thereof%2C%20I,Council%20Resolutions%20242%20and%20338 (last accessed 30 Sept. 2023).

5 Preamble to the Agreement on the Gaza Strip and the Jericho Area (4 May 1994), 33 I.L.M. 622 (1994); Preamble to the Agreement on Preparatory Transfer of Powers and Responsibilities (29 Aug. 1994), 34 I.L.M. 455 (1994); and Preamble to the Israeli-Palestinian Interim Agreement on the West Bank and Gaza Strip (28 Sept. 1995), 36 I.L.M. 551 (1997).

6 G. Watson, *The Oslo Accords: International Law and the Israeli-Palestinian Peace Agreements* at 101–02 (Oxford Univ. Press, 2000) ("the Oslo Accords are legally binding international agreements. Thus, there is a legal basis for the assertion that the Oslo process is 'irreversible' … [c]onversely, there is no basis for the claim that the Accords are non-binding 'political' documents").

7 Vienna Convention on the Law of Treaties, UN Doc. A/CONF.39/27 (23 May 1969).

8 R. Sabel, *International Law and the Arab-Israeli Conflict* at 272–75 (Cambridge Univ. Press, 2022).

9 *Id.* at 282.

10 R. Lapidoth, *Jerusalem: Some Legal Issues* at 29 (Jerusalem Institute for Israel Studies, 2011).

11 "Abbas Admits he Rejected 2008 Peace Offer from Olmert," *Times of Israel*, 19 Nov. 2015.

12 See, e.g., Georg Eckert Institute for International Textbook Research, *Report on Palestinian Textbooks, 2017–2019* (2021), https://owncloud.gei.de/index.php/s/FwkMw8NZgCAJgPW (last accessed 4 Dec. 2023).

13 *Declaration of Principles on Interim Self-Government Arrangements*, 13 Sept. 1993, Article XV, 32 I.L.M. 1525 (1993); *Israeli-Palestinian Interim Agreement on the West Bank and the Gaza Strip*, 28 Sept. 1995, Article XXI, 36 I.L.M. 551 (1997).

14 The many published monographs and books include J. Quigley, *The Legality of a Jewish State: A Century of Debate over Rights in Palestine* (Cambridge Univ. Press, 2021); S. Adem, *Palestine and the International Criminal Court* (Springer, 2019); J. Quigley, *The Six-Day War and Israeli Self-Defense: Questioning the Legal Basis for Preventive War* (Cambridge Univ. Press, 2012); J. Quigley, *The Statehood of Palestine: International Law in the Middle East Conflict* (Cambridge Univ. Press, 2010); J. Quigley, *Palestine and Israel: A Challenge to Justice* (Duke Univ. Press, 1990); J. Quigley, *The Case for Palestine: An International Law Perspective* (Duke Univ. Press, 1990); N. Erakat, *Justice For Some: Law and the Question of Palestine* (Stanford Univ. Press, 2019); V. Kattan, *From Coexistence to Conquest: International Law and the Origins of the Arab-Israeli Conflict, 1891–1949* (Pluto Press, 2009); S. Akram et al., *International Law and the Israeli-Palestinian Conflict: A Rights-Based Approach to Middle East Peace* (Routledge, 2011); M. Mazzawi, *Palestine and the Law: Guidelines for the Resolution of the Arab-Israel Conflict* (Ithaca Press, 1997); H. Cattan, *Palestine and International Law: The Legal Aspects of the Arab-Israeli Conflict* (2nd ed.) (Longman, 1973); H. Cattan, *Palestine, the Arabs and Israel: The Search for Justice* (Longman, 1969); T.W. Mallison and S. Mallison, *The Palestine Problem in International Law and World Order* (Longman, 1986); V. Kattan, *From Coexistence to Conflict: International Law and the Origins of the Arab-Israel Conflict, 1891–1949* (Pluto Press, 2009). There have also been countless articles in academic journals. In addition, since 1984 the annual *Palestine Yearbook of International Law* has published a broad range of submissions supporting the Palestinian legal case.

15 At minimum, the future Palestinian state must be demilitarized to ensure it poses no threat to Israel's right to exist in peace and security, especially in the wake of the Hamas 7 Oct. 2023 invasion of southern Israel and ensuing massacres, rapes, sexual violence and wounding of thousands of victims, plus the kidnapping of more than 240 hostages.

PART I

International Law and the Israeli-Palestinian Conflict

1

INTERNATIONAL LAW

Aspiration vs. Reality

Introductory Note

International law is based on the concept that states have an interest in governing their relations through a rules-based system derived from international agreements and norms of international custom and practice.

As Shaw (2021) explained:

> International law aims for harmony and the regulation of disputes. It attempts to create a framework, no matter how rudimentary, which can act as a kind of shock-absorber clarifying and moderating claims and endeavouring to balance interests. In addition, it sets out a series of principles declaring how states should behave.[1]

Shaw traces the modern international legal system to the moral and ethical stance of ancient Israel, which promoted "the demand for justice and a fair system of law founded upon strict morality."[2]

Both Shaw and Sabel (2022) argue that most states observe most international legal rules most of the time, if for no other reason than self-interest and garnering third-party support and leverage.[3]

The Historic Role of the Law in the Israeli-Palestinian Conflict

As I have previously written, both the Israelis and the Palestinian Arabs (and their predecessors in Ottoman and Mandatory Palestine) have for more than a century used the law against each other as a weapon in the conflict and as a means of influencing international opinion.[4]

DOI: 10.4324/9781032686561-3

The Late Ottoman Period

During the late Ottoman period the Palestinian Arabs and Jews used the Ottoman Petition (*Arzuhal*) system as a means of taking their grievances directly to the Sublime Porte for adjudication.[5] For example, in 1891 several Arab notables from Jerusalem petitioned the Ottoman government in Constantinople, "demanding the prevention of further immigration of Jews and purchase of land by them."[6] Arab small farmers also used the petition process to complain about Jewish land purchases from absentee landowners in Rehovot and the Jezreel Valley, asking either to remain on the purchased land or receive compensation with grants of alternative Imperial land.[7]

Jews also resorted to the petition process, in one instance seeking permission from the Sultan to construct agricultural buildings in Rishon Le'Zion, Nes-Ziona, and Rehovot, and to drain swamps near Petach Tikvah.[8] The Jewish community of Jerusalem also used the petition process in approximately 1890 to obtain permission from the local Ottoman authorities to repair and replace the pavement in front of the Wailing Wall.[9]

In addition to disputes over land use, the Muslim community also petitioned in 1911 for a ruling banning Jews from bringing chairs to prayer services at the Wailing Wall in Jerusalem. The Muslim petitioners feared the Jews were bringing chairs and benches to the Wall as a first step toward asserting Jewish ownership over the entire *Haram al-Sharif* (Temple Mount area) and eventually rebuilding the ancient Jewish Temple. The Ottoman Authorities granted the Petition, ruling it "*inadmissible by Law* in all respects that there should be placed chairs, screens, and similar articles, or any innovation be made which may indicate ownership."[10]

Early British Rule

These early legal encounters established a pattern in which both Arabs and Jews, lacking military, economic, or diplomatic power, repeatedly turned to the law and legal procedure as a means of pressing their grievances and claims against each other. The parties also used the law as a means of jockeying for political leverage both with the British government and the broader international community, especially the Permanent Mandates Commission (PMC) of the League of Nations, vested with oversight authority over the British administration of Palestine.

The Jewish and Muslim practice of raising legal issues via the petition process continued following the collapse of the Ottoman Empire and the arrival of British military rule at the end of World War I. For example, a 4 November 1918 Arab petition to the British military authorities protested a Jewish celebration of the first anniversary of the Balfour Declaration.[11] Two weeks later another Arab petition protested Jewish immigration to Palestine.[12]

Following the onset of British civilian rule in 1920, Arabs and Jews in Palestine (and the British authorities themselves) increasingly relied on and invoked legal procedures and legal arguments on a broad range of issues, most notably (i) the proper interpretation of Britain's promises in the McMahon-Hussein correspondence of 1915–1916 to entice the Arabs to rebel against Turkey in return for independence, and the impact of those promises on the legality of the November 1917 Balfour Declaration and the 1922 Mandate for Palestine; (ii) the separate Arab assertion that the Mandate was unlawful because it conflicted with the Covenant of the League of Nations; (iii) whether Britain was implementing the Mandate in a manner consistent with its terms; (iv) the respective rights and claims of the parties to the Wailing Wall and the then-narrow strip of pavement in front of the Wall; and (v) the causes of violent outbreaks in Palestine during the 1920s and 1930s.[13]

The first major outbreak of violence in British Palestine occurred during the *Nebi Musa* pilgrimage in and near Jerusalem in early April 1920. The British High Commissioner for Palestine, Sir Herbert Samuel, appointed the first of a series of Commissions of Enquiry established during British rule to investigate Arab-Jewish disputes. This first Commission, a Military Court of Inquiry chaired by Major General P.C. Palin, took testimony from 152 witnesses over 50 days and issued a lengthy report.[14]

The next Commission, chaired by Palestine Chief Justice Sir Thomas Haycraft to investigate the causes of the Jaffa riots during the first week of May 1921 and subsequent incidents in June and July 1921 conducted ten weeks of hearings from 12 May to 26 July 1921, taking testimony from 291 witnesses.[15]

The British Government also realized during the 1920s that the holy places in Jerusalem, especially the Wailing Wall, represented potential flashpoints for controversy and confrontation. Article 13 of the Palestine Mandate required Britain as the Mandatory Power to preserve the *Status Quo*, essentially a legal concept governing the rights of the various religious communities at the holy sites. The British defined the *Status Quo* by reference to the pre-existing legally authorized practices of the Muslim and Jewish communities under Ottoman rule.[16] A Mandatory Government official wrote a comprehensive memorandum in July 1927 attempting to define the *Status Quo* for all Palestinian holy sites (Muslim, Christian, and Jewish), including the Wailing Wall.[17] This memorandum became the baseline legal document for implementing the Mandate's requirement that Britain safeguard the pre-existing, legally recognized rights of the different religious communities at the holy sites.

The Mandatory Government's interpretation of the *Status Quo* as an enforceable legal principle frequently led to controversy regarding the Wailing Wall, particularly during Passover 1922,[18] Yom Kippur 1923[19] and Yom Kippur 1925.[20] The most notable confrontation occurred on Yom Kippur 1928, when the British Deputy District Commissioner for Jerusalem ordered the forcible removal of a screen the Jews had placed on the pavement in front of the Wall to divide men from women during prayer services.[21] The ensuing controversy led the Jews to resort once again to a legal remedy, this time filing a Petition with the League of Nations seeking redress.[22]

The Muslims, for their part, began filing petitions "at the rate of probably one protest a month" with the British authorities from 1922 onward, objecting to "illegal Jewish activities at the Wall."[23] The British Government also responded with a legal document, issuing a White Paper in November 1928 officially defining the *Status Quo* regarding the respective rights of Muslims and Jews at the Wailing Wall.[24] In August 1929 another series of incidents occurred at the Wall, culminating in a bloody week of rioting and violence in Jerusalem, Hebron and elsewhere in Palestine.

The Shaw and Lofgren Commissions

These disputes and the accompanying violence ultimately led the British (with strong lobbying from the Zionist leadership, and over initial Arab opposition) to convene two Commissions of Enquiry. The first, known as the Shaw Commission, was formed in the fall of 1929 to determine the causes of the August 1929 violence in Palestine. The second, known as the Lofgren Commission, was tasked several months later with the approval of the League of Nations to determine the respective rights and claims of Muslims and Jews to the Wailing Wall.

The Shaw Commission conducted a total of 47 public sessions in Jerusalem between 24 October and 27 December 1929, finally issuing its report in late March 1930.[25] The report, which found fault on both sides but exonerated the Mandatory Government and the Palestinian leader Haj Amin al-Husseini, the Grand Mufti of Jerusalem, provoked bitter reactions from the Zionist leadership.

The Report of the Shaw Commission attracted the interest of the PMC of the League of Nations, responsible on behalf of the Council of the League for overseeing all Mandatories in the performance of their duties. The PMC met in June 1930 in Extraordinary Session to consider the Shaw Commission's findings, as well as a broad range of other issues the Muslims and Jews had raised via the petition process.[26] The minutes of the PMC's deliberations on the Shaw Commission report, including the manner in which the PMC grilled various British officials, provide a fascinating window into the international community's view of the Arab-Jewish conflict in Palestine at the time, contrasting sharply and quite dramatically with the modern-day United Nations approach to the conflict.

The Lofgren Commission was constituted soon after the completion of the Shaw Commission hearings, and represented Britain's attempt to comply with its obligation under Article 14 of the Mandate to determine the rights and claims of the Muslim and Jewish communities to the Wailing Wall and the pavement in front of the Wailing Wall.[27]

The Lofgren Commission conducted hearings for an entire month in Jerusalem (June–July 1930).[28] The Commission issued its report and verdict in December 1930, reaffirming the Status Quo at the Wailing Wall. Neither side was happy with the outcome, but both seemed grudgingly to accept it.[29]

The Peel Commission

Even after the Shaw and Lofgren Commissions completed their work, the British Government once again felt compelled in 1936 to appoint another Commission, this time a Royal Commission chaired by Lord Robert Peel. The Peel Commission's Terms of Reference were laden with legal language and legal inquiry. The Commission was asked to determine the causes of recent violence in Palestine, to examine how Britain was "implementing the Mandate" and "complying with its obligations" as Mandatory to both the Jewish and Arab communities, to decide whether either community had any "legitimate grievances" based upon a "proper construction" of the Mandate's terms, and, to the extent any such grievances were "well-founded," to make remedial recommendations.[30]

The Peel Commission spent months hearing testimony, both in public and in secret, from the most prominent figures on both sides, including David Ben-Gurion, Chaim Weizmann, Golda Meir, the Grand Mufti Haj Amin al-Husseini, as well as Winston Churchill and David Lloyd George. The Commission issued a report in July 1937 recommending the original version of the two-state solution for Palestine.[31] But the Peel Commission recommendation was never implemented.

In early February 1939 the British Government convened parallel conferences in London with the Palestinian Arabs and Jews to discuss Palestine's future.

Shortly after the London Conferences began, Britain agreed to create an Arab-British subcommittee to examine the Arab and British legal arguments involving the McMahon-Hussein correspondence of 1915–1916. The Palestine Royal Commission had previously found the correspondence, despite its ambiguous language, did not support the Arab claim that McMahon had promised Palestine to Sherif Hussein as one of the areas for future Arab independence. McMahon himself had written to the *Times* in late July 1937 making clear he never intended to include Palestine in the areas pledged to the Arabs, and that Hussein well understood Palestine had been excluded.

Nevertheless, the British Government invited and even encouraged the Palestinian Arabs during the London Conferences in 1939 to press their legal case regarding the McMahon-Hussein correspondence. The Palestinian

Arabs hired the former Chief Justice of the Palestine Supreme Court to act as their lawyer for the McMahon-Hussein issue, while the British Government had its highest legal officer, the Lord Chancellor, take the lead for the British side during the subcommittee's discussions. The Arab legal team forcefully argued the ambiguous language in McMahon's letters to Hussein should be construed in favor of the Palestinian Arabs, to avoid an otherwise unjust outcome.

The Arab legal team also utilized the 1918 "Hogarth Message" to great effect, arguing it stood as compelling contemporaneous evidence of Britain's intent to construe the Balfour Declaration as narrowly as possible.

The McMahon-Hussein subcommittee produced an extraordinary joint Arab-British legal report, in which the British Government conceded half the Palestinian Arab claim, agreeing Hussein had intended to claim Palestine among the areas of Arab independence. But Britain still insisted McMahon himself never intended to pledge Palestine to the Arabs.

The May 1939 White Paper

Ultimately, the British Government unilaterally announced its new Palestine policy in the form of a White Paper published 17 May 1939. The White Paper's key elements included a one-state solution, meaning a majority-ruled, Palestinian Arab State would emerge within ten years. During the first five of those years, Jewish immigration would be permitted to continue, but slowed to a trickle, with only 75,000 total immigrants allowed during the entire five-year period, thereby locking in a two-to-one Arab majority. Any Jewish immigration after the five-year period would be subject to Arab veto power. The White Paper also proposed banning nearly all Jewish land acquisition in Palestine, a policy the Mandatory Government codified in early 1940 with a new Land Transfers Ordinance.

The White Paper represented a sweeping verdict in favor of Palestinian Arab nationalism and a crushing defeat for Zionism. But the Palestinian Arabs rejected the White Paper, upset that it fell short of their demands for *immediate* statehood and an *immediate* halt to Jewish immigration. The Palestinian Arab leadership insisted instead on framing the White Paper as an "injustice" due to the minor inconveniences of a ten-year waiting period until full statehood and a five-year continuation of minimal Jewish immigration. Blinded by their all-or-nothing approach, the Palestinian Arabs needlessly squandered the best chance they would ever receive in the history of the conflict for statehood throughout the entirety of Palestine.

The Palestinian Arab leadership's refusal to accept the White Paper and Britain's offer of the one-state solution ended up costing their people dearly, and they continue paying the price today.

The Anglo-American Committee of Inquiry

Following the end of World War II, the British and American governments appointed a 12-member "Anglo-American Committee of Inquiry," which conducted a three-month series of courtroom-style hearings from January through March 1946 regarding the short-term plight of European Jewish holocaust refugees and the long-term future governance of Palestine. Co-chaired by British and American judges, and containing four additional members with legal training, the Anglo-American Committee heard testimony from scores of witnesses, subjecting many of them to rigorous and occasionally hostile cross-examination. The Committee also received extensive written submissions from the parties.

Despite the underlying conflict between British and American political objectives, the Committee reached a unanimous verdict following three weeks of tense deliberations in Lausanne, Switzerland in April 1946. The Committee rejected the White Paper policies restricting Jewish immigration and land acquisition as illegal under the terms of the Mandate. The Committee also disagreed with the White Paper's "One-State Solution" in favor of the Palestinian Arabs, urging instead a "No-State Solution," with the Mandate or a successor Trusteeship continuing for Palestine indefinitely.

UNSCOP and the General Assembly Ad Hoc Committee

Britain eventually handed the Palestine file to the newly-created United Nations in the spring of 1947. The UN appointed a Special Committee on Palestine (UNSCOP) in May 1947 with several lawyers among its 11 members and a Swedish high court judge as its chairperson.

In July 1947, UNSCOP conducted public hearings and various secret meetings in Jerusalem, hearing testimony from more than 30 witnesses and receiving thousands of pages of written submissions. The Palestinians boycotted the proceedings and refused to offer any witnesses.

After completing its deliberations, a majority of the Special Committee rejected both the "One-State" and "No-State" solutions, reverting instead to the Palestine Royal Commission's July 1937 recommendation for a "Two-State" solution. The Special Committee majority recommended terminating the Mandate and dividing Palestine into separate Jewish and Arab sovereign states, with Jerusalem remaining a separate body under international control. A minority of the Special Committee's members issued a separate recommendation for a "One-State" solution for Palestine, endorsing Palestinian Arab sovereignty over all of Palestine within a federal-state governance structure.

Shortly after UNSCOP issued its Report, the United Nations appointed a follow-on committee, known as the "Ad Hoc Committee on the Palestine

Question," to focus in more detail on the UNSCOP majority's two-state solution (partition) and the minority's one-state solution.

A former Australian High Court judge chaired the Ad Hoc Committee. The Palestinian Arabs abandoned their boycott, opting to participate in the Ad Hoc Committee's hearings. The leading Palestinian Arab representative, the Mufti's cousin Jamal Husseini, testified three times before the Ad Hoc Committee during the fall of 1947.

The Ad Hoc Committee was divided into two subcommittees to prepare reports on the UNSCOP majority and minority recommendations. The second subcommittee endorsed the One-State solution, issuing a detailed report containing a lengthy discussion of the legal arguments in favor of Palestinian Arab sovereignty over all of Palestine and against Jewish statehood in even a tiny portion of the country.

The legal arguments mustered by the second subcommittee reprised and expanded on the longstanding Palestinian legal framing of the conflict, and in many respects offer the best summary of the Palestinian Arab legal case as of November 1947. The second subcommittee also identified a variety of legal issues it wanted the General Assembly to refer to the International Court of Justice, including whether the General Assembly itself had any legal jurisdiction over Palestine.

The Ad Hoc Committee by majority vote endorsed the two-state solution and rejected the second subcommittee's proposals to terminate the Palestine Mandate immediately and create a single, Arab-ruled state. The Ad Hoc Committee also rejected Arab requests to seek rulings on various issues from the International Court of Justice.

The United Nations General Assembly approved the UNSCOP and Ad Hoc Committee partition proposal on 29 November 1947 in Resolution 181(II). This represented the first-ever formal international endorsement of a solution for the Palestine conflict, in which two states would be formed, one Arab and one Jewish. Both the United States and the Soviet Union endorsed the two-state solution, in a remarkable show of unity for two countries already locked in their post-War global rivalry.

The Jews accepted the General Assembly's verdict, but the Palestinian Arabs renounced the verdict and immediately launched a bloody civil war. The surrounding Arab countries ultimately joined the war when the Jews declared statehood in May 1948 in the portion of Palestine the General Assembly had allocated to them.

International Law Today: Inconsistent Aspirationalism

International law has expanded dramatically in the post-World War II era. The United Nations has ballooned to nearly 200 member states, and its various organs, including the International Court of Justice, have churned out endless proclamations addressing a broad range of subject areas (such as self-determination and human rights) that have increasingly been recognized as part of the constellation of customary international law norms. Many other international and regional organizations have sprung up in recent decades, including the World Trade Organization, the European Union, and the International Criminal Court (ICC), all of which claim the power to announce legal rules.

But the modern conception of "international" law reflects more of an aspiration than a reality. Most of the modern norms of international law – nonaggression, territorial integrity, human rights, self-determination, and so on – reflect high-minded principles that are respected inconsistently and applied hypocritically. For example, Russia launched an unprovoked war against Ukraine in February 2022 in violation of all international legal rules and norms. The Russian military launched repeated attacks on Ukrainian civilians. Nevertheless, more than half the member states of the United Nations have supported Russia's aggression against fellow UN member Ukraine.

Russia's membership and veto power in the UN Security Council guarantees there will never be any UN condemnation of Russia. The ICC's Prosecutor has issued an arrest warrant for Russian President Vladimir Putin for deporting thousands of Ukrainian children to Russia, but no one expects Putin will ever be held to account for his war crimes and crimes against humanity.

China, for its part, has violently persecuted its minority Uyghur Muslim population with impunity, while the UN and the Organization of Islamic Cooperation have remained silent. The Syrian Dictator Bashar al Assad used chemical weapons and barrel bombs on his own civilians during a civil war that took hundreds of thousands of lives and forced more than four million Syrians to flee, yet the international legal system has done nothing.

The international legal system has likewise utterly failed to address the denial of Kurdish self-determination; the Azerbaijani killings of Armenian civilians in Nagorno-Karabakh; China's denial of Tibetan self-determination rights; and the Taliban government's denial of civil and human rights to Afghani women and girls.

At the same time, Russia and China have led the vast majority of the international community in condemning Israel for lawfully defending itself against Hamas's illegal invasion and horrific slaughters, rapes, and kidnappings of hundreds of Israeli innocents on 7 October 2023. Neither the UN General Assembly nor the Security Council has condemned the Hamas massacre, which violated multiple international norms, including war crimes, genocide and crimes against humanity. The ICC Prosecutor has taken no action against Hamas as of the publication of this book. The UN has not asked the International Court of Justice to rule on the legality of Hamas's brutality. Instead, the international community has fixated on condemning Israel's military response.

The international legal system's refusal to address the Hamas massacres is only the latest example of the gulf between the aspiration of international law to govern relations between states impartially and fairly and the unfortunate reality of the international legal system's betrayal of those aspirations.

Modern International Law and the Israeli-Palestinian Conflict

The Palestinians have repeatedly weaponized international law in the modern era, evoking the memory of the early legal struggles and the key role of the law in today's conflict. For example, in October 2016 the official Palestinian news agency announced a year-long campaign marking the 100th anniversary of the Balfour Declaration, demanding the United Kingdom "atone for the big crime Britain had committed against the Palestinian people."[32] In 2017, as part of that campaign, the Palestinians increased the pressure, insisting Britain either voluntarily apologize for and rescind the Balfour Declaration, *or face litigation* forcing it to do so.[33]

The Palestinians have also continually resorted to legal formulations in expressing their opposition to the Israeli occupation of the West Bank, describing the occupation and Israeli settlement activity as "illegal" and lacking "respect for the law."[34] The Palestinians successfully challenged the legality of Israel's "Wall of Separation," obtaining a nearly unanimous advisory ruling from the International Court of Justice in 2004.[35] The Palestinian-founded Boycott, Divestment and Sanctions (BDS) movement of recent years justifies itself as a *legal* response to *illegal* Israeli settlement activity.[36]

The Palestinians also successfully persuaded the United Nations Security Council in December 2016 to adopt Resolution 2334 (with the United States abstaining), declaring Israeli settlement activity a "flagrant violation" of international law.[37] The Palestinians increased the legal pressure on Israel even further by successfully joining the ICC in January 2015,[38] and then in May 2018 formally demanding the ICC's Chief Prosecutor investigate potential criminal charges against Israeli military and civilian officials for alleged violations of international law in the West Bank and Gaza.[39] The ICC, which only has jurisdiction over disputes between *states*, nevertheless recognized Palestine as a "state" in a bizarre and highly controversial split decision in February 2021, thereby permitting the Palestinian Authority to invoke the ICC's jurisdiction to investigate various "war crimes" complaints against the Israeli government.[40]

More recently, on 30 December 2022 the UN General Assembly adopted Resolution 77/247,[41] requesting the International Court of Justice render an advisory opinion regarding the legality of Israel's presence in the West Bank and Israeli activities "in the Holy City of Jerusalem." The ICJ conducted public hearings in February 2024 in The Hague, allocating three full hours to the Palestinian side for their oral presentation, but only 30 minutes each to every other party.[42] The ICJ also permitted the Organization for Islamic Cooperation to participate fully in the proceedings, but it rejected a parallel request from the World Jewish Congress.

Meanwhile, at no time in its history has the ICJ or the ICC ever condemned Palestinian terrorism against Israelis and Jews, nor has the court ever addressed the Palestinian Authority's and Hamas's denial of human rights to Palestinian dissidents, to Christians, to members of the LGBTQ community, to women, or to any other protected groups.

The ICJ intervened most recently in the conflict by entertaining a 28 December 2023 petition from South Africa accusing Israel of committing "genocide" while defending itself against the barbaric Hamas terror attacks of 7 October 2023.[43] The Court, relying mostly on highly suspect "facts" supplied by Hamas, has issued two rulings since then (26 January 2024 and 28 March 2024) indicating so-called "provisional measures" against Israel.[44]

The ICJ's increasingly activist stance in the Israeli-Palestinian conflict raises fundamental questions about the Court's proper role in international politics. Many countries, wary of the American veto at the UN Security Council, have urged the ICJ to step into the politics of the Israeli-Palestinian conflict and issue rulings against Israel that would otherwise be unobtainable at the Security Council. Unfortunately, the Court has taken on that role with relish.

Shaw (2021) cautioned against the encroachment of international policy and politics into the realm of international law,[45] but this conflation has already pervaded the role of international law in the Israeli-Palestinian conflict. The international community overwhelmingly sides with the Palestinians as a political matter, and seeks to justify that support by molding and shaping international law to follow along.[46] The ICJ has entered the fray enthusiastically.

What are we to make of an international legal system that applies its rules selectively and inconsistently, trumpeting one set of rules for Israel and a separate set of rules for everyone else?

Brierly (1955) warned long ago that "it is unreasonable, when we are seeking the true nature of international rules, to force the facts into a preconceived theory instead of finding a theory which will explain the facts as we have them."[47] Unfortunately, in the context of the Israeli-Palestinian conflict international law has failed this test. The UN, the ICJ, the ICC, and many others have not only relied on a distorted and historically inaccurate version of the facts but have also forced those "facts" into a manufactured narrative of Palestinian victimhood.[48]

Notes

1 M. Shaw, *International Law* (9th ed.) at 10 (Cambridge Univ. Press, 2021).
2 *Id.* at 12.
3 *Id.* at 5 ("Contrary to popular belief, states do observe international law, and violations are relatively rare"); R. Sabel, *International Law and the Arab-Israeli Conflict* at 4 (Cambridge Univ. Press, 2022).

4 S. Zipperstein, *Law and the Arab-Israeli Conflict: The Trials of Palestine* (Routledge, 2020); S. Zipperstein, *Zionism, Palestinian Nationalism and the Law: 1939–1948* (Routledge, 2022).

5 *See generally* Y. Ben-Bassat, *Petitioning the Sultan: Protests and Justice in Late Ottoman Palestine 1865–1908* (I.B. Tauris, 2013).

6 Y. Porath, *The Emergence of the Palestinian-Arab National Movement, 1918–1929* at 26 (Frank Cass, 1974).

7 Ben-Bassat, *op. cit.* at 168–69.

8 *Id.* at 195–98 (Petition by Four Members of the Bedouin Group Abu-Hataba from Mazra'at Duran to the Grand Vizier Against the Establishment of the Colony of Rehovot, 15 Dec. 1890); 168–69 (Petition regarding sale in 1910 of land in the Village of al-Fula to the Jewish National Fund); 171 (Jewish petitions).

9 Wailing Wall Commission, *Minutes of the Session at Jerusalem* (unpublished typescript, hereafter "Lofgren Commission Transcript") at 83–84 (testimony of Joseph Giva Goldsmith, 26 June 1930).

10 *Report of the Commission Appointed by His Majesty's Government in the United Kingdom of Great Britain and Northern Ireland, with the Approval of the Council of the League of Nations, to Determine the Rights and Claims of Moslems and Jews in connection with the Western or Wailing Wall at Jerusalem*, 58-9096 (Dec. 1930; hereafter "Lofgren Commission Report"), Moslem Exhibit No. 7 (English translation of Decision by the *Majles Idarah* (Administrative Council) of the *Lawa* in response to a Petition filed by the *Mutawalli of the Awakaf of Abu Median al-Ghoth Shua'ib*, 12 Nov. 1911) [emphasis added].

11 J. Priestland (ed.), *Records of Jerusalem 1917–1971*, Vol. I (1917–1920) at 285 (Cambridge Univ. Press, Archive Editions 2002) (Petition filed by "inhabitants of Jerusalem and villages attached thereto, speaking for themselves and on behalf of all the Arabs, Moslem and Christian, residing in Palestine").

12 *Id.* at 291–93 (Petition dated 16 Nov. 1918, submitted to British Military Governor Col. Ronald Storrs by the "[m]embers of the Moslem and Christian Committee for all the Moslems and Christians of Jaffa District ... [i]t is surely incredible to us, that Great Britain who liberated us from the Turks, should tolerate to see us fall into the grip of the Jews.").

13 In 1925 the Executive Committee of the Palestine Arab Congress filed a Petition with the League of Nations raising 11 separate issues, including the grants of various concessions for utilities and salt mining, the conduct of elections, police interrogation practices, the Jerusalem drainage system, etc. Those issues lie beyond the scope of this study, but are illustrative of the broad range of matters pursued via the Petition process during the early years of the Conflict. *See* Letter to Chairman, Permanent Mandates Commission from Jamal Husseini, General Secretary of the Executive Committee, Palestine Arab Congress, 8 Apr. 1925, discussed in C. 405.M.144.1926 vi (C.P.M./9th Sess./P.V.), League of Nations, Permanent Mandates Commission, *Minutes of the Ninth Session held at Geneva from 8 to 25 June, 1926*, App. (19 June 1926).

14 FO 371/5121, *Secret Report of the Court of Inquiry Convened by Order of H.E. the High Commissioner and Commander-in-Chief* (12 Apr. 1920, hereafter "Palin Commission Report").

15 Cmd. 1540, *Palestine Disturbances in May 1921, Report of the Commission of Inquiry with Correspondence Relating Thereto* (Oct. 1921; hereafter "Haycraft Commission Report") at 3, 17; *see also* Weizmann Archives 5-645, Memorandum from Zionist Commission, Jerusalem to Zionist Executive, London (29 May 1921) ("no lawyers are allowed to appear" before the Haycraft Commission). Sir Harry Luke, who would later serve as the Chief Secretary of the Mandatory Government in Palestine and as the Officer in Charge (Acting High Commissioner) of

the Palestine Government during the crucial months of Sept. 1928 and Aug. 1929, was one of the appointed members of the Haycraft Commission. Dr. Mordechai Eliash, a Jerusalem-based lawyer, served as one of the Assessors for the Haycraft Commission. Dr. Eliash acted as lead counsel for the Jewish side in the Lofgren Commission trial nine years later.

16 Cmd. 1785, League of Nations, *Mandate for Palestine, Together with a Note by the Secretary General Relating to its Application to the Territory Known as Transjordan, Under the Provisions of Article 25* (hereafter "Palestine Mandate") (Dec. 1922) art. 13 ("All responsibility in connection with the Holy Places and religious buildings or sites in Palestine, including that of preserving existing rights and securing free access to the Holy Places, religious buildings and sites and the free exercise of worship ... is assumed by the Mandatory, who shall be responsible solely to the League of Nations in all matters connected herewith ... provided also that nothing in this mandate shall be construed as conferring upon the Mandatory authority to interfere with the fabric or the management of purely Moslem sacred shrines, the immunities of which are guaranteed."). The Arabs, the Jews, the British Government and the Shaw, Lofgren and Peel Commissions all spent considerable time and resources attempting to determine exactly what this and other language in the Mandate meant regarding the rights of the parties to the Wailing Wall and the narrow strip of pavement in front of the Wall.

17 L.G.A. Cust, District Administrator, Jerusalem, *The Status Quo, Its Origin and History Till the Present Time* (July 1927), original printed copy located in Chancellor Papers, MSS. Brit. Emp. S.284, Bodleian Libraries, Oxford (hereafter "Chancellor Papers"), Box 24/2.

18 CO 733/179/4, *Memorandum on the Wailing Wall*, Enclosure I to Confidential Despatch to Secretary of State, para. 10 (17 Jan. 1930).

19 *Id.*

20 Cmd. 3229, *The Western or Wailing Wall at Jerusalem, Memorandum by the Secretary of State for the Colonies*, at 4 (19 Nov. 1928).

21 E. Keith Roach, Deputy District Commissioner, Jerusalem, Despatch 10/24 (25 Sept. 1928), *reprinted in* Priestland, *op. cit.* Vol. II at 623–27.

22 Letter dated 12 Oct. 1928 from the Palestine Zionist Executive to the Officer Administering the Government of Palestine, "request[ing] that this petition may be transmitted through the proper channels to the Secretary General of the League of Nations for the information of the Permanent Mandates Commission," *reprinted in* Priestland, *op. cit.* Vol. II at 628–32.

23 Lofgren Commission Transcript, *op. cit.* at 768.

24 Cmd. 3229, *op. cit.* at 6 (Jews have a "right of access to the pavement in front of the Wall for the purposes of their devotions and also ... to bring to the Wall those appurtenances that they were allowed to take to the Wall under the Turkish regime. It would be inconsistent with [the British Government's] duty under the Mandate were they to endeavour to compel the Moslem owners of the pavement to accord any further privileges or rights to the Jewish community.").

25 Cmd. 3530, *Report of the Commission on the Palestine Disturbances of August, 1929* (Mar. 1930; hereafter "Shaw Commission Report"). The original typewritten version of the Report can be found in file CO 733/177/4 at the British National Archives.

26 League of Nations, Permanent Mandates Commission, *Seventeenth (Extraordinary) Session of the Commission* (Geneva, 3–21 June 1930), Official No. C 355. M. 147. 1930 VI and accompanying Minutes thereto.

27 Palestine Mandate, Art. 14 ("A special commission shall be appointed by the Mandatory to study, define and determine the rights and claims in connection with the Holy Places and the rights and claims relating to the different religious

communities in Palestine. The method of nomination, the composition and the functions of this Commission shall be submitted to the Council of the League for its approval, and the Commission shall not be appointed or enter upon its functions without the approval of the Council.") Neither the British Government nor the Mandatory Government took any steps to comply with Article 14 prior to seeking permission from the Council of the League of Nations in 1930 to appoint the Lofgren Commission.

28 *Id.* Appendix II.

29 CO 733/195/5, Paraphrase Telegram No. 157 from the High Commissioner of Palestine to the Secretary of State for the Colonies (16 June 1931).

30 Cmd. 5479, *Palestine Royal Commission Report* at ix. (July 1937).

31 Id.

32 Palestinian News and Information Agency (WAFA), "Palestinians Prepare to Mark One Hundred Years of Balfour Declaration" (24 Oct. 2016), http://english.wafa.ps/page.aspx?id=G8NFN5a50719869123aG8NFN5 (last accessed 4 Dec. 2023).

33 "Palestinian Authority Plans to Sue UK over Balfour Declaration," Arab News (4 Nov. 2017), http://www.arabnews.com/node/1187831/middle-east (last accessed 4 Dec. 2023) ("The Palestinian Authority plans to sue the UK over the 100-year-old Balfour Declaration, which paved the way for the creation of Israel. It will hire a British law firm to pursue an apology, and plans to explore similar actions in European and other international courts, according to Foreign Minister Riad Malki. 'The Palestinian government has made every effort to persuade the British government to abandon its decision to celebrate the centennial of the Balfour Declaration,' Malki said in an emailed statement quoted by Bloomberg. Palestinians 'will exhaust all possibilities for a partial realization of the stolen justice that was executed by Britain through its ominous promise.'").

34 *See, e.g.,* Palestinian News and Information Agency press release, "Ashrawi: 'With the Expansion of its Illegal Settlement Enterprise, Israel Seeks not only to Defy but to Defeat the Whole World'" (23 Aug. 2018), http://english.wafa.ps/page.aspx?id=55Kui6a98880474429a55Kui6 (last accessed 4 Dec. 2023); Palestine Liberation Organization website, Dr. Saeb Erakat, Secretary General of the P.L.O., "The Grinch 'Occupation' who Decided to Steal the Spirit of Christmas" (26 Sept. 2018) (describing Israeli settlement activity in the West Bank as "part of Israel's bank of violations to international law," and calling upon the International Criminal Court with the "utmost urgency and importance" to "accelerat[e] the process of investigating Israeli crimes"), http://www.plo.ps/en/article/119/DrSaeb-Erakat-Secretary-General-Of-the-P-LOThe-Grinch-%E2%80%98occupation%E2%80%99-who-decided-to-steal-the-spirt-of-Christmas (last accessed 4 Dec. 2023).

35 *Legal Consequences of the Construction of a Wall in the Occupied Palestinian Territory*, Advisory Opinion, I.C.J. Reports 2004 at 136 (International Court of Justice, 9 July 2004).

36 The BDS Website describes the purpose of the movement: "The Boycott, Divestment, Sanctions (BDS) movement works to end international support for Israel's oppression of Palestinians *and pressure Israel to comply with international law*" [emphasis added], https://bdsmovement.net/ (last accessed 4 Dec. 2023); *see also* J. Sperber, *BDS, Israel, and the World System*, Journal of Palestine Studies, 45:1 (177) at 8 (Autumn 2015) (BDS "represents a series of strategies designed *to force Israel to comply with international law*") [emphasis added].

37 U.N. Sec. Council Resolution 2334, S/Res/2334 (23 Dec. 2016).

38 *See* International Criminal Court website, "Preliminary Examination: Palestine," https://www.icc-cpi.int/palestine ("On 2 January 2015, the Government of Palestine acceded to the Rome Statute by depositing its instrument of accession with

the UN Secretary-General. The accession entered into force on 1 April 2015.") (last accessed 4 Dec. 2023).

39 *See, e.g.*, Al Jazeera, "Palestine Submits ICC Referral to Open Probe into 'Israel Crimes'" (22 May 2018), https://www.aljazeera.com/news/2018/05/palestine-submits-icc-referral-open-probe-israel-crimes-180522101121093.html (last accessed 4 Dec. 2023); Daily Sabah, "Gaza Officials Submit Proof of Israeli Crimes to International Criminal Court" (2 Aug. 2018), https://www.dailysabah.com/mideast/2018/08/02/gaza-officials-submit-proof-of-israeli-crimes-to-international-criminal-court (last accessed 4 Dec. 2023).

40 ICC-01/18, *Situation in the State of Palestine*, Pre-Trial Chamber I, *Decision on the 'Prosecution Request Pursuant to Article 19(3) for a Ruling on the Court's Territorial Jurisdiction in Palestine* (5 Feb. 2021).

41 United Nations, A/RES/77/247 (30 Dec. 2022).

42 *Legal Consequences arising from the Policies and Practices of Israel in the Occupied Palestinian Territory, including East Jerusalem (Request for advisory opinion submitted by the General Assembly of the United Nations)*, Public sitting held on Monday 19 February 2024, at 10 a.m., at the Peace Palace, President Salam presiding, p. 52.

43 *Application of the Convention on the Prevention and Punishment of the Crime of Genocide in the Gaza Strip (South Africa v. Israel)*, 28 Dec. 2023.

44 *Application of the Convention on the Prevention and Punishment of the Crime of Genocide in the Gaza Strip (South Africa v. Israel)*, Order of 26 Jan. 2024; Order of 28 Mar. 2024.

45 Shaw (2021), *op. cit.* at 50–51.

46 *See generally* M. de Blois and A. Tucker, *Israel on Trial: How International Law is Being Misused to Delegitimize the State of Israel* (The Hague Initiative for International Cooperation, 2018).

47 J.L. Brierly, *The Law of Nations: An Introduction to the International Law of Peace* (5th ed.) at 53 (Oxford Univ. Press, 1955).

48 Sadly but not surprisingly, the UN failed to condemn the 7 Oct. 2023 Hamas murders, rapes and kidnappings. Even worse, a Gaza school teacher employed by UNRWA (UN Refugee and Works Agency for Palestine Refugees in the Near East) held one of the Israeli hostage captive in the attic of his home for more than 50 days. "Released Hostage Says he was Held by UNRWA Teacher in Gaza – report," Jerusalem Post, 30 Nov. 2023. Neither UNRWA nor the UN have thus far taken any action against their employee.

2

PALESTINIAN LEGAL FRAMING AND NARRATIVE

Introductory Note

The Israeli-Palestinian conflict is fundamentally a political, non-justiciable dispute. The parties recognized this in the Oslo Accords, where they agreed to comply with an internal dispute resolution process that precluded resorting to external litigation. This approach dovetailed with the parties' overall agreement to pursue all issues exclusively through negotiation.

In light of the parties' agreement in the Oslo Accords to resolve all issues through negotiation, it is useful to remember the words of Judges Spender and Fitzmaurice in their dissenting opinion in the 1962 *Namibia* case, cautioning the international courts against taking jurisdiction over political cases:

> We are not unmindful of, nor are we insensible to, the various considerations of a non-juridical character, social, humanitarian and other, which underlie this case; but these are matters for the political rather than for the legal arena. They cannot be allowed to deflect us from our duty of reaching a conclusion strictly on the basis of what we believe to be the correct legal view.[1]

The International Court of Justice has, however, sometimes asserted jurisdiction over cases where "a legal question has political aspects."[2]

The Palestinians have therefore expended considerable efforts to frame the inherently political conflict between Palestinian nationalism and Zionism as a *legal* conflict, giving rise to an ongoing Palestinian narrative of justice, injustice, and victimization. This effort is not new, as it began a century ago. Ever since then, the Palestinians have cloaked themselves in the twin mantles

DOI: 10.4324/9781032686561-4

of *justice* and *victimhood*, attracting enormous support from most of the world community, especially since the 1970s. The United Nations has enthusiastically embraced the Palestinian framing and narrative, focusing more attention in the last five decades on the Israel-Palestine dispute than *all* other global issues combined.[3]

We begin with a review of framing theory as a way to interrogate the role of legal discourse in the fundamentally non-justiciable political conflict between Palestinian Arab nationalism and Zionism.

Modalities and Typologies of Framing

De Bruycker (2017) focused on the key role of frames as the "building blocks" in constructing policy debates.[4] Muller and Slominski (2019) similarly defined framing as a means for policy advocates, sometimes described as *frame entrepreneurs*, to "shape the debate surrounding a policy issue with the aim of influencing policy outcomes."[5] Junk and Rasmussen (2019) explain the importance of framing in social and political movements, particularly emphasizing how framing can impact policy definition and policy outcomes.[6]

I propose a new typology, *transformational legal framing*, as the appropriate analytical framework for the Palestinian Arab-Jewish conflict beginning during the British Mandate years and continuing through the modern Israeli-Palestinian conflict. Transformational Legal Framing describes how inherently socio-political movements frame themselves in a narrative of justice, injustice, and victimization to reorient their cause from the political to the legal arena, creating opportunities to seek judicially imposed remedies such as damages, restitution, rescission, and restoration.

Legal Framing

Marshall (2003) described efforts to conflate social grievances with legal claims, even where such claims are "neither approved nor acknowledged by law."[7] Leachman (2013) built on Marshall's work, explaining how "social movement actors strategically link together these legal concepts (and nonlegal ones) to convince others to support their cause."[8]

More recently, Muller and Slominski (2019) focused on law as a "master frame," noting how socio-political activists use legal arguments to achieve political objectives.[9] Muller and Slominksi applied their legal framing construct to public policy debates in the European Union, describing how "the interaction of legally savvy frame entrepreneurs with the law-thick world of EU politics has generated a distinct 'legal' discourse, which has gradually shaped political deliberations both within the EU and beyond."[10]

Other scholars have also focused on "injustice" frames, although they disagree regarding the exact characterization of such frames. More recently,

Baumgart-Ochse (2017) noted how "injustice frames appear to be fairly ubiquitous across movements advocating some form of political and/or economic change."[11]

A New Typology: Transformational Legal Framing

While the focus on generic legal framing and the subset of justice/injustice framing is somewhat useful for the Israeli-Palestinian conflict, further theoretical refinement is necessary to analyze phenomena in which frame entrepreneurs seek to frame/reframe inherently *political* disputes as *legal* disputes, characterizing the movement's grievances, goals and objectives as grounded in *legal rights* and *justice* rather than politics and policy. This suggests the need for an additional framing modality.

Pedriana (2006) notes that "because 'law may be the source of new expectations for existing relations,' aggrieved groups can also sustain successful challenges by reframing a movement's grievances and objectives around new or alternative *legal* symbols."[12] This modality of "reframing" may be regarded as a new framing typology – *transformational legal framing.*

Transformational legal framing describes how socio-economic, environmental, or in the Israel-Palestine conflict, nationalist movements employ framing to *redefine* the terms of their engagement and shift discourse from politics and policy to the law and legal rights.

Transformational legal framing aims to infuse social and political movements and causes with *legal* significance, converting inherently non-legal *causes* into *legal disputes* about *justice* and *injustice.*[13] Transformational legal frame entrepreneurs recast their constituencies as *victims* of a legal wrong or injustice, entitling them to hold the wrongdoer(s) civilly and/or criminally liable and to receive legal and equitable remedies.

Transformational Legal Framing during the British Mandate

Agne (2007) has noted that "[f]rames and conflict framing have been especially useful in the study of intractable conflicts."[14] The Jewish-Arab conflict in Palestine is perhaps the most intractable of all the world's political conflicts, pitting competing Jewish and Arab political and nationalist movements against each other for the past century.

Gamson (1992) first noted the tendency of Israelis and Palestinians to make "strong and competing claims about deep historical injustices."[15] Burgis-Kasthala (2014) has explained how Palestinian frame entrepreneurs have sought to transform the political conflict with Israel into the legal arena:

> [A]n evolving discourse and practice within Palestine does suggest that international legal ideals are being embraced, often in contrast with earlier,

> unsuccessful, politically-characterized ventures. Through their acts of stating and sometimes over-stating the centrality of international law in shaping and perhaps solving the conflict, Palestinian lawyers, activists, and intellectuals are contributing to a growing legalization of political debate within Palestine.[16]

Throughout the British Mandate years, the Palestinian Arabs engaged in transformational legal framing, casting the political dispute between competing Jewish and Arab nationalist movements in Palestine as a legal battle, in which the Palestinian Arabs were fighting for justice as the victims of Jewish colonization, immigration, and land purchases. The Palestinian Arabs and their supporters throughout the Arab world invoked transformational legal framing in their testimony and arguments at the London Conferences in 1939, before the Anglo-American Committee of Inquiry in 1946, to UNSCOP and the Ad Hoc Committee in 1947, and even after the adoption of United Nations Resolution 181(II) in late November 1947.

During the Mandate years and afterward the Palestinian Arabs also justified violence and terrorism through the lens of legal narrative. For example, the Palestinian Arabs argued before the Shaw Commission in 1929 that the August 1929 Arab massacre of Jews in Hebron resulted from British and Zionist *injustices* perpetrated against the local Arab population.

From the inception of the Jewish-Arab conflict in Palestine, all three protagonists – Arab, Jewish, and British – utilized transformational legal framing to gain leverage against each other and to influence international opinion in the conflict. The Palestinian Arabs in particular began framing the conflict this way a century ago, creating a narrative characterizing the conflict as a battle between the "justice" of Palestinian Arab nationalism and the "injustice" of Zionism. Zionism was portrayed as a powerful, oppressive form of western-style settler colonialism, and the local Palestinian Arabs as the victims of a grievous injustice.[17] Wheatley (2015) describes how the Palestinian Arabs "played law" and employed "legal hermeneutics" in the hundreds of petitions they filed with the Permanent Mandates Commission (PMC) during the Mandate years.[18]

The Jews also employed transformational legal framing from the beginning of the Zionist movement. Strawson (2010) describes how the Zionist leadership from the inception of the movement intended to place "great emphasis on a legal campaign to secure their objectives."[19] At the first Zionist Congress in Basle, Switzerland in August 1897, the delegates agreed it was necessary to characterize the desire for a Jewish homeland in Palestine as a *legal* right. A drafting committee proposed language stating, "[t]he aim of Zionism is to create for the Jewish people a home in Eretz Israel secured by law." Other delegates preferred the phrase "secured by international law." Ultimately the Basle Congress adopted Herzl's compromise formula:

"Zionism seeks to establish a home for the Jewish people in Eretz Israel secured under public law."[20]

The British also used transformational legal framing, both substantively and procedurally, throughout the Mandate period. The British Government employed transformational legal framing substantively, by characterizing the League of Nations Mandate as a *legal* document containing a variety of contradictory and conflicting *legal* obligations. By framing the Mandate that way, the British Government allowed itself room to justify its inconsistent yet politically expedient Palestine policy throughout the Mandate years as driven by the *legal* requirements of the Mandate.[21]

Britain also employed transformational legal framing in the procedural sense by sending judges to "adjudicate" disputes that more appropriately should have been the province of diplomacy and negotiation.[22] By imposing judicial process and procedure on an inherently political dispute, Britain sought to persuade international opinion, including its overseers at the PMC of the League of Nations, of the procedural fairness, objectivity and normative credibility with which it addressed disputes between the Arabs and Jews of Palestine.

Arabs and Jews alike embraced Britain's transformational procedural legal framing throughout the Mandate years. Both sides sent small armies of lawyers to argue their cases in the various trials the British authorities convened in Palestine, beginning with the Palin and Haycraft Commissions of the early 1920s and continuing through the Shaw, Lofgren, and Peel Commissions of the late 1920s–1930s, and culminating in the Anglo-American Committee of Inquiry in 1946 and the UNSCOP hearings in the summer of 1947. Both Arabs and Jews repeatedly invoked transformational legal framing, casting their claims as based on "justice" and "injustice." Both sides jockeyed for position as the true "victims," each seeking remedies for various "injustices" perpetrated against them.

Transformational Legal Framing in the Israel-Palestine Conflict Today

The Palestinian Arabs continue to the present day invoking transformational legal framing to justify violence as a lawful form of "self-defense" against Israeli "injustices."

In recent years the Palestinian Arabs, frustrated and dismayed with the lack of progress on the political front, have converted the peace process into a legal contest, intensifying their demands for legal and equitable remedies including the rescission of the Balfour Declaration, the return of Palestinian refugees and their descendants, and the prosecution of Israelis they hold responsible for "crimes" in occupied areas.[23]

The Palestinian Arabs and their supporters have continued using transformational legal framing to support their victimization, justice, and injustice narratives since the birth of the State of Israel in 1948, which they frame as the *Nakba* (catastrophe), and especially after June 1967, when Israel replaced Jordan as the occupying power in the West Bank and Israel replaced Egypt as the occupant of the Gaza Strip.[24] Palestinian advocates, including many lawyers and law professors, have joined the fray, using transformational legal framing to convert the conflict from the realm of politics to one grounded in justice, injustice, and victimhood.[25] The Palestinians and their supporters have embellished the narrative even further since the horrific Hamas attacks of 7 October 2023, justifying the attacks as a lawful response to "75 years" of alleged Israeli oppression of the Palestinians, neglecting to mention that for the first 19 of those years Jordan occupied the West Bank and Egypt occupied the Gaza Strip.

Even following Israel's complete withdrawal from the Gaza Strip in September 2005, Palestinian advocates continued employing transformational legal framing, most often by characterizing Gaza as "the world's largest open-air prison." The Hamas invasion of southern Israel on 7 October 2023 should put the lie to this narrative once and for all.

"Settler Colonialism"

Zionism was the first great 20th-century national liberation movement. Zionism reflects the centuries-long Jewish aspiration for self-determination in their ancient homeland.

The League of Nations Council unanimously proclaimed in the Preamble to the July 1922 Palestine Mandate, "Whereas recognition has thereby been given to the *historical connection* of the Jewish people with Palestine and to the grounds for *reconstituting* their national home in that country." The words "historical connection" and "reconstituting" are extremely important, as they accord recognition to Jewish indigeneity in Palestine, and treat the Jewish return to their ancient homeland as an international legal right.

The Palestinians have argued for more than a century that Zionism represents a form of European 20th century "settler colonialism." The official Palestinian line rejects Jewish indigeneity in the Land of Israel. Cattan (1981), for example, has argued:

> [T]he Jews of the twentieth century who emigrated to Palestine during the British Mandate or since the establishment of Israel are in many cases not the descendants of the biblical Israelites, but are converts to Judaism who have exploited religion for political and nationalistic purposes. Joseph Reinach, a French politician of Jewish origin, has explained that very few of today's Jews have any connection with Palestine and that the great majority of Russian and Polish Jews – who incidentally constituted the majority of immigrants to Palestine during the British Mandate – descend from the

> Khazars, a Tartar people of southern Russia who were converted in a body to Judaism at the time of Charlemagne.[26]

Cattan's argument reflects a longstanding element of the Palestinian narrative, focused on characterizing Jews as "invaders" seeking to displace the "indigenous" Arab population of Palestine. The false narrative has reemerged in recent years with newfound strength, as it has been embraced by social justice advocates and university professors around the world. The increasingly popular chant "From the River to the Sea, Palestine will be Free" represents the most recognizable manifestation of Palestinian denial of Jewish rights of self-determination in their ancient homeland.

Describing Zionism as a form of "settler colonialism" ignores key historical facts.

First, the claim ignores the continuous presence of the Jewish people in the Land of Israel for the last 3,500 years. Archaeological evidence, including the excavation of the City of David adjacent to the Old City of Jerusalem, prove Jerusalem existed as the capital of the Judean Kingdom 3,000 years ago.

Second, the claim ignores the ongoing presence of Jews in the Land of Israel, especially in Tiberias, Tzfat, Jerusalem, and Hebron for two millennia following the Roman conquest in 70 A.D.

Third, the claim ignores Ottoman Turkish census records showing Jews comprised the largest single population group in Jerusalem as early as the 1840s.

Fourth, the claim ignores the Ottoman Empire's acceptance of Jewish immigration from Europe in the late 19th and early 20th centuries.

Fifth, the claim ignores the inconvenient fact that Jewish land acquisition in Ottoman and British Palestine occurred through lawful, arms-length purchases from willing *Arab* sellers at mostly above-market prices.

Boycott, Divestment and Sanctions (BDS)

The Palestinian-founded Boycott, Divestment and Sanctions (BDS) movement of recent years justifies its effort to isolate Israel economically, culturally, and politically as a "legal" response to Israeli "illegality" in the Occupied Territories.[27] Baumgart-Orsche (2017) notes how the BDS campaign has framed itself within the "global justice" movement:

> In 2005, Palestinian activists called on civil society organizations and 'people of conscience' worldwide to impose boycotts, implement divestment initiatives and urge their respective states to impose embargoes and sanctions against Israel until it recognizes the Palestinian right to self-determination. This call for Boycott, Divestment, Sanctions (BDS) can be seen as a continuation of earlier attempts at pressuring Israel to change its

> policies toward the Palestinians ... [T]he campaign has been deliberately framed by its Palestinian initiators as being a part of the Global Justice Movement (GJM). It employs the globally shared language of justice and human rights, thus appealing to allegedly universal, uncontested norms ... By embedding itself within the GJM, the BDS campaign borrows these prognostic and motivational frames which are familiar to civil society activists across the world ...[28]

Social Justice Intersectionality

The Palestinians have also very effectively framed themselves through the prism of intersectionality as part of the same, decades-long global justice movement that once included the struggle against South African apartheid and more recently the Black Lives Matter movement and other causes in the United States.[29]

The Palestinian framing has found an enthusiastic reception on university campuses and among various social advocacy organizations, who view Jews and the Jewish State as "oppressors" and the Palestinians as "victims" on an equal footing with other "oppressed" groups.[30]

Several commentators have employed the concept of intersectionality to link police shootings of unarmed black men in the United States, such as the killing of Michael Brown in Ferguson, Missouri in August 2014, with the Israeli-Palestinian conflict:

> Since 'intersectionality' was coined, the term has been used to analyze the experiences of diverse groups ... Its overall benefit is that it shows how people who are categorized or labeled in two or more ways can experience these things together rather than separating these experiences from one another. Ferguson, like Hebron, had the attention of the world. Messages of black/Palestinian solidarity echoed in cities across the U.S. Marchers filed into the streets, including a delegation of Palestinians and Palestinian activists who gathered to express shared aims with Ferguson. Black and Palestinian solidarity matured as communities linked the points between state violence, the penal industry, and war-footing policing. What Palestine and Ferguson have in common is that they lay bare the reality of racism, the systematic subjugation of one social group by a more powerful group for the social, economic, and political benefit of the more powerful social group. Racism in Palestine and Ferguson are two interrelated, mutually supporting systems of domination. Their relationship is essential to understanding the subordination of minorities by majorities.[31]

It is, of course, utter nonsense as an empirical matter to suggest the tragic shooting of Michael Brown in Ferguson Missouri has anything to do with the Israeli-Palestinian conflict. But when framed as a shared experience of "oppressed peoples," the narrative takes on a powerful appeal to those ignorant of the facts.

Other Examples of Palestinian Framing

The late Palestinian literary scholar Edward Said (1979, 2006) employed transformational legal framing to describe the modern Israeli-Palestinian conflict as one involving justice, injustice, victimization, and the suppression of Palestinian rights.[32] "For Palestinians," Said once wrote, "*a vast collective feeling of injustice* continues to hang over our lives with undiminished weight … I do not think that anyone can honestly disagree that *since 1948 the Palestinians have been the victims*, Israelis the victors."[33]

Noura Erakat (2019), the most recent exponent of transformational legal framing from the Palestinian Arab perspective, nevertheless has reemphasized the conflict as a battle between legality and illegality. Erakat argues "the very origins of the Palestinian-Israel conflict suggest that it is characterized by outright lawlessness."[34] Erakat therefore continues the century-long Palestinian narrative, transformationally framing the *political* conflict between Israelis and Palestinians as a *legal* conflict between lawless oppressors and innocent victims.

Palestinian frame entrepreneurs invoked transformational legal framing during and following the May 2021 Gaza conflict. For example, at a rally in Paris two days following the 21 May 2021 cease fire, the president of the France Palestine Solidarity Association exclaimed, "this fight concerns all those who are attached to the values of justice, dignity and law."[35]

Palestinian frame entrepreneurs also leveraged the Covid-19 pandemic to characterize alleged Israeli actions as "war crimes," including unsubstantiated accusations that Israel deliberately infected Palestinians with the virus and then "denied the Palestinian Authority access to vaccines."[36]

More recently, Jibril Rajoub, who serves as the PLO's Central Committee Secretary in the West Bank, was quoted on the Kuwaiti news website *Al-Anba* on 26 November 2023 describing the 7 October 2023 Hamas massacres, rapes and hostage-taking as "an earthquake, an unprecedented incident, and a war of defense full of epics and acts of heroism."[37]

Notes

1 *South West Africa Cases (Ethiopia v. South Africa; Liberia v. South Africa)*, *op. cit.*, Joint Dissenting Opinion of Sir Percy Spender and Sir Gerald Fitzmaurice at 466.

2 *See, e.g.*, *Legal Consequences of the Construction of a Wall in the Occupied Palestinian Territory*, ICJ Rep 2004, 136 at para. 41 (Advisory Opinion) (9 July 2004). The *Wall* case actually presented the opposite situation – a purely political case in

which the Palestinian side successfully injected enough of a "legal" flavor to give the ICJ a colorable but questionable basis for exercising its advisory jurisdiction.

3 *See generally* D. Huber, *The International Dimension of the Israel-Palestinian Conflict: A Post-Eurocentric Approach* (State Univ. of New York Press, 2021), ch. 6 (discussing the UN's longstanding and evolving "normative framing" of the Israeli-Palestinian conflict).

4 I. De Bruycker, *Framing and Advocacy: A Research Agenda for Interest Group Studies*, Journal of European Public Policy, 24:5 at 779–80 (2017).

5 P. Muller and P. Slominski, *Legal Framing and the EU's External Relations: How NGOs Shaped the Negotiations for an Israel-Europol Cooperation Agreement*, Journal of European Public Policy, 26:6 at 908 (2019); *see also* E. McKee, *Environmental Framing and Its Limits: Campaigns in Palestine and Israel*, International Journal of Middle East Studies, 50 at 451 (2018) ("The work of framing gives meaning to advocacy and activism, and activists often strive to bend and stretch existing communicative frames to expand the reach of their messages. Sociopolitical context shapes and limits framing in all cases of activism").

6 W.M. Junk and A. Rasmussen, *Framing by the Flock: Collective Issue Definition and Advocacy Success*, Comparative Political Studies, 52:4 at 486 (2019).

7 A.M. Marshall, *Injustice Frames, Legality, and the Everyday Construction of Sexual Harassment*, Law & Social Inquiry, 28:3 at 661–62 (2003) [citations omitted].

8 G. Leachman, *Legal Framing*, Studies in Law, Politics and Society, 61:25–59 at 29 (2013).

9 Muller and Slominski, *op. cit.* at 909–10 (emphasis in original).

10 *Id.* at 907.

11 C. Baumgart-Ochse, *Claiming Justice for Israel/Palestine: The Boycott, Divestment, Sanctions (BDS) Campaign and Christian Organizations*, Globalizations, 14:7 at 1174 (2017).

12 N. Pedriana, *From Protective to Equal Treatment: Legal Framing Processes and Transformation of the Women's Movement in the 1960s*, The American Journal of Sociology, 111:6 at 1724 (2006) [citation omitted; emphasis added].

13 *Id.* at 1729.

14 R. Agne, *Reframing Practices in Moral Conflict: Interaction Problems in the Negotiation Standoff at Waco*, Discourse and Society, 18:5 at 552 (2007).

15 Gamson, *op. cit.* at 54.

16 M.L. Burgis-Kasthala, *Overstating Palestine's UN Membership Bid? An Ethnographic Study on the Narratives of Statehood*, European Journal of International Law, 25:3 at 690, 700 (2014); *see also* N. Khader, *Interview with Noura Erakat: Framing the Palestinian Narrative*, Journal of Palestine Studies, 44:1 at 106–17 (2014); *see also* J. Strawson, *Partitioning Palestine: Legal Fundamentalism in the Palestinian-Israeli Conflict* at 1 (Pluto Press, 2010) (describing how Israelis and Palestinians have used international law as a resource in the conflict for more than a century: "This use of law has engendered a festering sense of justice amongst Palestinians and Israelis that has fostered conflict rather than offering a means for its resolution. Each side has become cocooned within a legal righteousness in which its own legitimacy is unimpeachable while that of the other is compromised. This has nourished the existential character of the conflict. As a consequence war, occupation, and defiance of the international community are justified as the exercise of legal rights. A cycle of law has sustained a cycle of violence").

17 Describing Zionism as a form of "settler colonialism" ignores historical facts, including (i) the continuous presence of Jews in Palestine (especially Jerusalem, Tiberias, Tzfat and Hebron) for centuries *before and after* the Muslim conquest of 637 A.D.; (ii) the Ottoman Empire's acceptance of Jewish immigration from Europe in the late 19th and early 20th centuries; and (iii) Jewish land acquisition

in Ottoman and British Palestine occurred through lawful, arms-length purchases from willing *Arab* sellers at mostly above-market prices.

18 N. Wheatley, *Mandatory Interpretation: Legal Hermeneutics and the New International Order in Arab and Jewish Petitions to the League of Nations*, Past and Present, 227:1 at 219–20, 248 (2015). For a discussion of Sinn Fein's master framing strategy with the League of Nations, *see* W.J. Swart, *The League of Nations and the Irish Question: Master Frames, Cycles of Protest, and "Master Frame Alignment"*, The Sociological Quarterly, 36:3 at 465–81 (1995).

19 Strawson, *op. cit.* at 15.

20 *See generally* L. Epstein, *The Dream of Zion: The Story of the First Zionist Congress* (Rowman & Littlefield, 2016); C. Klein, *Zionism Revisited*, Israel Affairs, 11:1 at 240 (2005) ("It should be recalled that Herzl had obtained a law degree (from the University of Vienna). He actually signed the *Judensstaat* as Theodor Herzl, Doctor of Law. The distinction between public law and private law is one of the basics of all European legal systems. This concept was used instead of the proposed concept of (public) international law which might have antagonized the Sultan"); "Zionist Congress in Basel," *New York Times*, 31 Aug. 1897 at 7 (quoting Theodore Herzl saying, "My plan is simple enough. *We must obtain sovereignty over the whole of Palestine – our never-to-be-forgotten, historical home.*") (emphasis added).

21 For an interesting discussion of British framing of the Palestine issue for the past century, *see* R. Hollis, *Palestine and the Palestinians in British Political Elite Discourse: From 'The Palestine Problem' to 'The Two-State Solution'*, International Relations, 30:1 at 3–28 (2016).

22 *See, e.g.*, FO 371/5121, Palin Commission, *Secret (Unpublished) Report of the Court of Inquiry Convened by order of H.E. the High Commissioner and Commander-in-Chief* (1920); Cmd. 1540, Haycraft Commission. *Palestine Disturbances in May 1921, Report of the Commission of Inquiry with Correspondence Relating Thereto* (1921); Cmd. 3530, Shaw Commission, *Report of the Commission on the Palestine Disturbances of August, 1929* (1930); Lofgren Commission. *Report of the Commission Appointed by His Majesty's Government in the United Kingdom of Great Britain and Northern Ireland, with the Approval of the Council of the League of Nations, to Determine the Rights and Claims of Moslems and Jews in connection with the Western or Wailing Wall at Jerusalem*, 58-9096 (Dec. 1930); Cmd. 5479, Peel Commission, *Palestine Royal Commission Report* (July 1937).

23 *See, e.g.*, E. Alimi, *Israeli Politics and the First Palestinian Intifada: Political Opportunities, Framing Processes and Contentious Politics* (Routledge, 2007).

24 Even some Jewish organizations have employed transformational legal framing on behalf of the Palestinians. J Street, for example, has emerged as a leading pro-Palestinian frame entrepreneur. *See, e.g.*, J Street Press Release, "J Street Deeply Concerned by Ongoing Evictions of Palestinian Families in Occupied East Jerusalem" (discussing Sheikh Jarrah and Silwan residential housing disputes and proclaiming, "[i]t's therefore critical that the Biden administration urgently warn the Israeli government that these provocative and *unjust evictions are illegal under international law*") (emphasis added), https://jstreet.org/press-releases/j-street-deeply-concerned-by-ongoing-evictions-of-palestinian-families-in-occupied-east-jerusalem/#.YJrRyLVKhyw (last accessed 20 Oct. 2022).

25 *See, e.g.*, S. Akram, "Myths and Realities of the Palestinian Refugee Problem: Reframing the Right of Return," in S. Akram, et al. (ed.), *International Law and the Israeli-Palestinian Conflict: A Rights-Based Approach to Middle East Peace* at 13–44 (Routledge, 2011).

26 H. Cattan, *The Status of Jerusalem under International Law and United Nations*, Journal of Palestine Studies, 10:3, 3–15 at 10–11 (1981).

27 The BDS Website describes the purpose of the movement: "The Boycott, Divestment, Sanctions (BDS) movement works to end international support for Israel's oppression of Palestinians *and pressure Israel to comply with international law*" [emphasis added], https://bdsmovement.net/ (last accessed 20 Oct. 2022); *see also* J. Sperber, *BDS, Israel, and the World System*, Journal of Palestine Studies, 45:1 (177) at 8 (Autumn 2015) (BDS "represents a series of strategies designed *to force Israel to comply with international law*") [emphasis added].

28 C. Baumgart-Osche, *Claiming Justice for Israel/Palestine: The Boycott, Divestment, Sanctions (BDS) Campaign and Christian Organizations*, Globalizations, 14:7 at 1173, 1174–75 (2017); *see generally* E. Rettig and E. Avraham, *The Role of Intergovernmental Organizations in the "Battle over Framing:" The Case of the Israeli–West Bank Separation Barrier*, International Journal of Press/Politics, 21:1 at 111–33 (2016); N.A. Hatoum, *Framing Visual Politics: Photography of the Wall in Palestine*, Visual Anthropology Review, 33:1 at 18–27 (2017); *see also* A. Bakan and Y. Abu-Laban, *Palestinian Resistance and International Solidarity: The BDS Campaign*, Race & Class, 51:1 at 29–54 (2009). Blizzard (2017) has described how BDS frame entrepreneurs have counter-framed the Israeli response to the BDS movement: "Through framing Israel as the 'victim' of 'Muslim backwardness' and appealing to the nefarious modern drift toward Islamophobia, pro-Zionists attempt to undermine BDS and sponsor a moral assessment that BDS is illegitimate, unethical, and dangerous. By reinforcing artificial 'faux-conflict framing,' pro-Zionist media blur the 'occupier/apartheid/colonial/settler state versus nonviolent human rights movement' factual character." E. Blizzard, *Peace Journalism in Palestine's BDS Campaign*, Peace Review: A Journal of Social Justice, 29:4 at 469 (2017); *see also* O. Barghouti, *Opting for Justice: The Critical Role of Anti-Colonial Israelis in the Boycott, Divestment, And Sanctions Movement*, Settler Colonial Studies, 4:4 at 407–12 (2014); J. Peteet, *Language Matters: Talking About Palestine*, Journal of Palestine Studies, 45:2 at 25 (2016) ("Discussion of Israel-Palestine is bounded by a set of terms, phrases, and lexicons as well as strategies for argument and debate, that is, talking points readily discerned by their consistent mantra-like repetition. While these repertoires and categories shape understandings, they simultaneously work to marginalize and render a Palestinian narrative 'unthinkable.' These bundled linguistic repertoires and categories are deeply entangled with power and until recently unquestionably accompanied the colonial endeavor in Palestine").

29 A. Omer, *'It's Nothing Personal:' The Globalisation of Justice, the Transferability of Protest, and the Case of the Palestine Solidarity Movement*, Studies in Ethnicity and Nationalism, 9:3 at 499, 506 (2009).

30 *See generally* M. Fischbach, *Black Power and Palestine: Transnational Countries of Color* (Stanford Univ. Press, 2018).

31 J. Thomas, *The Intersection of Palestine with Ferguson, Missouri*, Journal of Ecumenical Studies, 55:1, 82–90 at 88–89 (2020); *see also* A. Davis, *Freedom Is a Constant Struggle: Ferguson, Palestine, and the Foundations of a Movement* (Haymarket Books, 2016). After months of investigation, local prosecutors in Missouri and federal prosecutors at the U.S. Department of Justice each declined to file criminal charges against the police officer who killed Mr. Ferguson, as the evidence did not disprove the officer's claim that he reasonably feared for his life during the incident.

32 E. Said, *The Question of Palestine* (Random House, 1979).

33 E. Said, *A Method for Thinking About Just Peace*, in P. Allena and A. Keller (eds.), *What Is a Just Peace?* at 182, 187 (Oxford Univ. Press, 2006) (emphasis added).

34 N. Erakat, *Justice for Some: Law and the Question of Palestine* at 3 (Stanford Univ. Press, 2019).

35 *Times of Israel*, 23 May 2021, https://www.timesofisrael.com/israeli-flag-dragged-through-london-street-as-thousands-rally-in-european-cities/?utm_source=The+Daily+Edition&utm_campaign=daily-edition-2021-05-23&utm_medium=email (last accessed 20 Oct. 2022) (quoting Bertrand Helibron).

36 The Israeli NGO Palestinian Media Watch (PMW) has compiled a broad range of articles from official and unofficial Palestinian Arab media making wild and unsubstantiated claims of Israeli Covid-19 "war crimes" against Palestinians. *See* PMW website, https://palwatch.org/analysis/1666 (last accessed 20 Oct. 2022).

37 N. Zilberdik, "Top Fatah Official Promises: 'The Next and More Violent Explosion will be in the West Bank,'" Palestine Media Watch, https://palwatch.org/page/34815 (last accessed 4 Dec. 2023).

3 PALESTINIAN LAWFARE

Introductory Comments

Two decades ago, the Palestinians launched a lawfare/litigation campaign against Israel, even though they previously agreed in the Oslo Accords to pursue all their claims solely through negotiation, not litigation or violence.[1] The lawfare campaign began with a two-pronged strategy of persuading the International Court of Justice (ICJ) to declare various Israeli practices in the West Bank and Jerusalem to be "illegal,"[2] and to spur and the International Criminal Court (ICC) and its Prosecutor to entertain criminal investigations of Israel and its nationals arising from Israeli activity in the Gaza Strip and the West Bank.[3]

The lawfare campaign has also spread beyond the ICJ and the ICC with the launch two decades ago of the global "Boycott, Divestment and Sanctions," or BDS campaign against Israel. As discussed in Chapter 2, the BDS campaign's website and other literature characterize BDS as a *legal* response to *illegal* Israeli settlement activity.[4] The campaign's supporters have used litigation and other forms of lawfare against Israel in various fora, especially in the European Union, to challenge the legality of Israel's presence in the West Bank and to accuse Israel (with no factual or legal basis) of the crimes of apartheid and genocide.

Kittrie (2016) defines "lawfare" as deploying the law as a weapon of war.[5] Perhaps a better definition would characterize lawfare as using the law as both a weapon of war and as a weapon to gain leverage and influence international opinion in political disputes.

Kittrie proposes two lawfare typologies: *instrumental lawfare* and *compliance-leverage disparity lawfare*. Instrumental lawfare involves the use of legal tools including international, national, and subnational laws and fora. Kittrie describes "instrumental lawfare" in the Israel-Palestinian conflict

DOI: 10.4324/9781032686561-5

as including a variety of tactics. For example, the Arab League attempted to manufacture a new international law designed to harm Israel by inserting a criminal offense into the ICC's governing Rome Statute aimed at criminalizing Israeli settlements in the West Bank.

Likewise, the Palestinians and their supporters have devoted considerable efforts for generating ICC investigations and potential prosecutions of Israel and Israeli nationals, as well as persuading various international organizations to investigate, condemn, and/or boycott Israel and companies doing business with Israel.[6]

The second lawfare typology, compliance-leverage disparity lawfare, refers to situations in which one party (e.g., Hamas) deliberately violates international law (e.g., by firing rockets from schools and hospitals and using human shields to deter counterattack) to provoke the other party (e.g., Israel) to respond in a way that draws international condemnation.[7]

Kittrie identified three key goals of the overall Palestinian lawfare campaign against Israel. The first involves the campaign to gain recognition of Palestinian statehood and Palestinian membership in various international organizations and treaties to buttress its claim to statehood. The second component involves the Palestinian decision in January 2015 to use what Kittrie describes as its "nuclear option" and join the ICC. The third component involves the Palestinian use of various international organizations and treaties to gain leverage against Israel.[8]

The Palestinian lawfare campaign has achieved considerable success. The architects of these efforts, emboldened by those successes, more recently have enlarged the campaign to delegitimize Israel and to challenge its very existence. A case currently pending at the ICJ raises the possibility of potential UN sanctions against Israel, including the possibility of suspension or revocation of Israel's UN membership. BDS supporters, meanwhile, have aggressively touted the slogan "From the River to the Sea, Palestine will be Free," meaning the elimination of the State of Israel and its replacement with a Palestinian State from the Jordan River to the Mediterranean Sea.

Palestinian lawfare has focused for the past two decades on persuading the ICJ and the ICC to treat the Israeli-Palestinian political conflict as a *legal* matter requiring *judicial* intervention and the imposition of legal/equitable remedies. The Palestinians have been very successful in weaponizing both courts in their lawfare campaign against Israel.

The International Criminal Court

The Rome Statute

The ICC was established in 1998 pursuant to the "Rome Statute of the International Criminal Court."[9] Article 1 of the Statute describes the mission of the Court:

> An International Criminal Court ("the Court") is hereby established. It shall be a permanent institution and shall have the power to exercise its jurisdiction over persons for the *most serious* crimes of international concern, as referred to in this Statute, and shall be complementary to national criminal jurisdictions.

Gravity Requirement. Article 17(1)(d) of the Rome Statute elaborated on the "most serious" requirement of Article I, requiring the Court to decline cases that lack "sufficient gravity" to justify the Court's intervention. Kontorovich (2014) explained that taken together, Articles 1 and 17 stand for the proposition that:

> Article 17 explicitly 'limits' the Court's jurisdiction over the enumerated crimes; that is, from among these already extremely serious crimes, the jurisdiction of the Court is restricted by the gravity requirement to the most serious violations of the already serious crimes within the Court's jurisdiction. As the Court itself put it, the gravity requirement is an 'additional safeguard'; a necessary consequence is that even some of the 'most serious' international crimes will not meet the test.[10]

Not surprisingly, in a recent ruling regarding the "gravity" requirement, the ICC Pre-Trial Chamber took the opposite approach and significantly diluted the requirement when applied to a potential investigation of Israel's confrontation with the Turkish ship *Mavi Marmara*:

> [T]he purpose of the gravity requirement under article 17(1)(d) of the Statute is not to oblige the Court to select the most serious cases, but to oblige it not to prosecute cases of *marginal gravity* ... the gravity requirement has an 'exclusionary nature', in that it is meant to 'exclude from the purview of the Court those rather unusual cases when conduct that technically fulfils all the elements of a crime under the Court's jurisdiction is nevertheless of marginal gravity only.' Therefore, gravity under article 17(1)(d) of the Statute is not a criterion for the *selection* of the most serious situations and cases ... but a requirement for the *exclusion* of (potential) cases of *marginal gravity* ... gravity at the situation stage (and admissibility, in general) is assessed against 'potential cases' arising from a situation. The assessment concerns the gravity of potential cases, not the gravity of the situation.[11]

Article 5 of the Rome Statute vests the ICC with jurisdiction over "genocide, crimes against humanity, war crimes, and aggression." Articles 6–8 of the statute define the scope of those offenses.

Genocide. Article 6 defines "genocide" as:

> "[A]ny of the following acts committed with intent to destroy, in whole or in part, a national, ethnical, racial or religious group, as such: (a) Killing

> members of the group; (b) Causing serious bodily or mental harm to members of the group; (c) Deliberately inflicting on the group conditions of life calculated to bring about its physical destruction in whole or in part; (d) Imposing measures intended to prevent births within the group; (e) Forcibly transferring children of the group to another group."

Crimes Against Humanity. Article 7 of the Rome Statute defines "Crimes against humanity" as including murder, extermination, enslavement, enforced disappearance of persons (meaning severe deprivation of physical liberty in violation of fundamental rules of international law), torture, rape, "the crime of apartheid," and other inhumane acts of a similar character "intentionally causing great suffering, or serious injury to body or to mental or physical health."

Article 7(2)(h) of the Rome Statute defines the "crime of apartheid" as "inhumane acts ... in the context of an institutionalized regime of systematic oppression and domination by one racial group over any other racial group or groups and committed with the intention of maintaining that regime."

Article 7(2)(i) defines "enforced disappearance of persons" as, among other things, the

> abduction of persons by, or with the authorization, support or acquiescence of, a State or a political organization, followed by a refusal to ... to give information on the fate or whereabouts of those persons ...

War crimes. Article 8(1) of the Rome Statute authorizes the ICC to exercise jurisdiction where such crimes are "committed as part of a plan or policy or as part of a large-scale commission of such crimes."

Article 8 defines international "war crimes" as, among other things, torture or inhumane treatment, willfully causing great suffering or serious injury to body or health, hostage-taking, intentionally directing attacks against civilians and non-military targets, pillaging, committing outrages upon personal dignity, rape and other forms of sexual violence, using civilians as human shields, and willfully impeding relief supplies.

Article 8(2)(b)(viii) also defines "war crimes" as including

> [t]he transfer, directly or indirectly, by the Occupying Power of parts of its own civilian population into the territory it occupies, or the deportation or transfer of all or parts of the population of the occupied territory within or outside this territory.

This provision expands the prohibition in Article 49 of the Fourth Geneva Convention that an occupying power "shall not deport or transfer parts of its own civilian population into the territory it occupies."[12]

Aggression. Article 8 *bis* of the Rome Statute defines "crime of aggression" as including invasion or attack by the armed forces of a State of the territory of another State, bombardment by a State against the territory of another State, blockading ports or coasts of a State, and the sending by or on behalf of a State of armed bands, groups, irregulars or mercenaries, which carry out grave acts of armed force against another State.

Jurisdiction. The Rome Statute contains several key provisions regarding jurisdiction. First, the Court's jurisdiction is limited to individuals, not States. Article 25 vests the Court with "jurisdiction over natural persons pursuant to this Statute. Articles 17 and 53 deprive the Court of jurisdiction under the principle of complementarity whenever the relevant state is already investigating or prosecuting the same individuals. Pursuant to Article 12, the crime must have been committed either on the territory of the national's own country (but only if such country is a party to the Rome Statute), or on the territory of another state which is a party to the Rome Statute.

Referrals. Articles 13 and 14 address referrals to the ICC. Article 13 permits referrals by a State Party to the Rome Statute, or by the UN Security Council, or the ICC Prosecutor initiates an investigation on its own, subject to the approval of the ICC's Pre-Trial Chamber. Article 14 permits a State Party to submit a referral to the ICC Prosecutor regarding a "situation" in which one or more crimes within the jurisdiction of the Court appears to have been committed, and to request the Prosecutor investigate the "situation" to determine whether any individuals should be charged.

The ICC and the Israeli-Palestinian Conflict

For the past 15 years, the Palestinians have attempted to use the ICC as a means of pressuring Israel by referring Israeli nationals for prosecution, arising primarily from the various Israel-Hamas military conflicts since 2007. The Palestinians, acting through the Palestinian Authority on behalf of Gaza, have accused Israel and Israelis of various war crimes.

Operation Cast Lead

In January 2009, the Palestinians made their first effort to invoke the ICC's jurisdiction, filing an *ad hoc* declaration asking the ICC Prosecutor to investigate Israeli actions during Operation Cast Lead, the late 2008-early 2009 military conflict in Gaza between Israel and Hamas.[13] The ICC Prosecutor determined Palestine had not proven its statehood and declined to take further action.

The Gaza Flotilla

Undaunted by their failure to persuade the ICC to investigate Israeli actions arising from Operation Cast Lead, the Palestinians and their supporters in Turkey tried again. In a classic example of lawfare, a Turkish law firm sought to invoke the ICC's jurisdiction to investigate the May 2010 Israeli clash with a Turkish vessel, the *Mavi Marmara*, the largest ship in a six-vessel Turkish flotilla attempting to circumvent the Israeli-Egyptian naval blockade of the Hamas-controlled Gaza Strip. The Israeli blockade was established on 3 January 2009 during an armed conflict between Israel and Hamas following Hamas rocket and mortar fire against Israel.

Israeli helicopter-borne commandos boarded the *Mavi Marmara* after the captain had ignored repeated Israeli warnings not to attempt to break the blockade. Those aboard the Mavi Marmara attacked the Israeli soldiers, wounding ten, one seriously. The Israelis defended themselves and killed nine of the attackers.

The flotilla's sponsors claimed their purpose was solely humanitarian.[14] The UN Secretary General convened a blue-ribbon panel to investigate the incident. The panel, co-chaired by former New Zealand Prime Minister Sir Geoffrey Palmer and former Colombia President Alvaro Uribe, perhaps shocked the General Assembly by issuing a lengthy and scathing report criticizing the flotilla's organizers for "recklessly" pursuing a purely political agenda.[15]

The Palmer-Uribe report noted that "Israeli Defense Forces personnel faced significant, organized and violent resistance from a group of passengers when they boarded the Mavi Marmara requiring them to use force for their own protection."[16]

The Palmer-Uribe report also found that Israel's naval blockade of the Gaza Strip "was imposed as a legitimate security measure in order to prevent weapons from entering Gaza by sea and its implementation complied with the requirements of international law."[17] The panel explained how it came to this conclusion:

> [W]e are satisfied that the naval blockade was based on the need to preserve Israel's security. Stopping the importation of rockets and other weapons to Gaza by sea helps alleviate Israel's situation as it finds itself the target of countless attacks, which at the time of writing have once again become more extensive and intensive. On the other hand, the specific impact of the naval blockade on the civilian population in Gaza is difficult to gauge because it is the land crossings policy that primarily determines the amount of goods permitted to reach Gaza. One important consideration is the absence of significant port facilities in Gaza. The only vessels that can be handled in Gaza appear to be small fishing vessels. This means that the prospect of delivering significant supplies to Gaza by sea is very low. Indeed, such supplies were not entering by sea prior to the blockade. So it seems unrealistic to hold the naval blockade disproportionate as its own consequences—either alone or by compounding the restrictions imposed by Israel on the entry of goods to Gaza via its border crossings—are slight in the overall humanitarian situation.[18]

The Palmer-Uribe report therefore concluded the blockade was entirely legal:

> The fundamental principle of the freedom of navigation on the high seas is subject to only certain limited exceptions under international law. Israel faces a real threat to its security from militant groups in Gaza. The naval blockade was imposed as a legitimate security measure in order to prevent weapons from entering Gaza by sea and its implementation complied with the requirements of international law.[19]

The Palmer-Uribe report next questioned the legitimacy of the flotilla's stated "humanitarian" purpose, noting the flotilla's organizers knew Gaza lacked any port facilities for offloading the ships' containers:

> No adequate port facilities exist in Gaza capable of receiving vessels of the size of the Mavi Marmara. It appears that arrangements had been made to offload the cargo onto smaller vessels at sea, which no doubt would be awkward and inefficient. Yet the flotilla rejected offers to unload any essential humanitarian supplies at other ports and have them delivered to Gaza by land. These offers were made even during the voyage. The conclusion that the primary objective of the flotilla organizers was to generate publicity by attempting to breach the blockade is further reinforced by material before the Panel that suggests that *a reception for the flotilla had been arranged by Hamas.*[20]

Turkey at that time (and still today) was not a state party to the ICC, nor was the Palestinian Authority. Prior to leaving Turkey the *Mavi Marmara* was reflagged under the Union of the Comoros, which was a State Party to the statute. Several weeks after the incident the *Mavi Marmara* was again reflagged back to its Turkish origin, raising the clear likelihood that the incident was premeditated solely for the purpose of manufacturing an international criminal case against Israeli soldiers.[21]

In any event, on 14 May 2013, the Union of the Comoros referred the *Mavi Marmara* "situation" to the ICC Prosecutor and requested her to initiate an investigation. The ICC Prosecutor had no choice but to follow the findings of the Palmer-Uribe report. Thus, on 6 November 2014, the Prosecutor determined the potential case(s) arising from the "situation" were not sufficiently "grave" to justify further action, and she therefore decided not to initiate an investigation. In declining to pursue the case, she wrote:

> Based on the available information and taking into account the foregoing, the flotilla does not appear to reasonably fall within the humanitarian assistance paradigm envisioned under Article 8(2)(b)(iii), due to its apparent lack of neutrality and impartiality as evidenced in the flotilla's explicit and

primary political objectives (as opposed to a purpose limited to delivery of humanitarian aid), failure to obtain Israeli consent, and refusal to cooperate with the Israeli authorities in their proposals for alternative methods of distributing the relief supplies.[22]

The Comoros appealed to the Pre-Trial Chamber, which issued a ruling on 16 July 2015 requesting the Prosecutor reconsider her decision not to investigate. On 29 November 2017 the Prosecutor again decided not to commence an investigation, as she continued to believe the "situation" failed the "gravity" requirement of Article 17(1)(d).

On 15 November 2018, the Pre-Trial Chamber again overruled the Prosecutor. It set aside the 2017 decision not to investigate and requested the Prosecutor reconsider her 2014 and 2017 decisions not to investigate. The Appeals Chamber upheld this ruling. But on 2 December 2019 the Prosecutor again announced she would not undertake an investigation due to the lack of gravity.

On 16 September 2020 the Pre-Trial Chamber once again harshly rebuked the prosecutor for refusing to consider the "situation" sufficiently grave to justify an investigation. This time, however, the Chamber decided against asking the Prosecutor to reconsider her original position, instead complaining that the ICC's Appeals Chamber had not sufficiently clarified the Pre-Trial Chamber's supervisory authority over the Prosecutor.[23]

Palestinian Accession to the Rome Statute

While the *Mavi Marmara* referral was pending, the Palestinians attempted in January 2015 to become a "State Party" to the Rome Statute through a procedural maneuver known as "accession."[24] Three years later, the Palestinian Authority, calling itself the "State of Palestine," submitted a referral to the ICC. The PA demanded the ICC's Chief Prosecutor investigate potential criminal charges against Israeli military and civilian officials for alleged violations of international law in the West Bank and Gaza.[25]

The ICC Prosecutor asked the Court's Pre-Trial Chamber to determine in the first instance whether the Palestinians had standing to make such a request; in other words, whether Palestine qualified as a "State" within the meaning of Article 12(3) of the Rome Statute.[26] If Palestine were deemed a "state," then it would be eligible under the Rome Statute to make referrals to the ICC.

In a highly controversial split decision, the Pre-Trial Chamber ruled in a 2-1 majority opinion in February 2021 that while Palestine is not a "state" under principles of general international law because it lacks recognized international borders and many other attributes of statehood, Palestine nevertheless would be deemed a "state" for ICC jurisdictional purposes because it had previously utilized the accession process.[27]

The ICC panel's ruling was flawed as a matter of law. The panel overlooked the basic fact that Palestine *never* should have qualified for accession to the Rome Statute in the first instance, as Palestine was not a "state" when it deposited its accession request with the Secretary General. The panel bootstrapped the improper accession as the basis for its ruling, which essentially boiled down to the illogical proposition that even though Palestine is *not* a "state" under international law, it *is* a state for purposes of the Rome Statute.

The International Court of Justice

The International Court of Justice (ICJ) functions as the judicial organ of the United Nations. The court was established pursuant to the UN Charter (Articles 92–96) as the successor to the pre-war Permanent ICJ.[28]

The ICJ and Political Disputes

The Palestinian lawfare effort has found sympathy among judges at the ICJ. The Court has waded into the Israeli-Palestinian political dispute multiple times in the last two decades, even though the conflict is fundamentally a political dispute, which should also be deemed non-justiciable and beyond the ICJ's jurisdictional purview.[29] However, the Court has justified taking jurisdiction over the political dispute between the Israelis and Palestinians as consistent with its occasional practice of asserting jurisdiction over cases where "a legal question has political aspects."[30]

The ICJ's willingness, perhaps better described as eagerness, to intervene in the Israeli-Palestinian conflict stands in contrast with the views of two of the Court's most distinguished jurists, Judges Sir Percy Spender and Sir Gerald Fitzmaurice, who cautioned the Court in their dissenting opinion in the 1962 *Namibia (South West Africa)* cases against taking jurisdiction over political cases, no matter how tempting or high-profile:

> We are not unmindful of, nor are we insensible to, the various considerations of a non-juridical character, social, humanitarian and other, which underlie this case; but these are matters for the political rather than for the legal arena. They cannot be allowed to deflect us from our duty of reaching a conclusion strictly on the basis of what we believe to be the correct legal view. They do however lead us to draw attention to another aspect of the matter. A Court called upon to consider objections to its jurisdiction must exclude from consideration all questions relating to the merits of the dispute, unless the jurisdictional issues are so intertwined with the merits that they cannot be considered separately, and must be joined to the merits. It is nevertheless legitimate for a Court, in considering the jurisdictional aspects of any case, to take into account a factor

> which is fundamental to the jurisdiction of any tribunal, namely whether the issues arising on the merits are such as to be capable of objective legal determination.[31]

Interestingly, one of the key jurisdictional questions in the *Namibia (South West Africa)* cases concerned the interpretation of Article 7 of the Mandate for South-West Africa (adopted by the League Nations 17 Dec. 1920), which provided:

> The Mandatory agrees that, if any dispute whatever should arise between the Mandatory and another Member of the League of Nations relating to the interpretation or the application of the provisions of the Mandate, such dispute, if it cannot be settled by negotiation, shall be submitted to the Permanent Court of International Justice ...'

Judges Spender and Fitzmaurice in their dissenting opinion unpacked the language of Article 7, noting the provision

> clearly conditions the obligation in three, or perhaps four, ways: there must be a 'dispute'; this dispute must arise between the Mandatory and 'another Member of the League of Nations;' it must relate to 'the interpretation or ... application of the provisions of the Mandate'; and, finally, it must be such as 'cannot be settled by negotiation.' We stress the word 'cannot.'[32]

Article 26 of the Palestine Mandate contains language identical to Article 7 of the South-West Africa Mandate. But unlike the situation involving South Africa and Namibia, Israel did not step into Britain's shoes as Mandatory after Britain unilaterally terminated the Mandate on 14 May 1948 and withdrew from Palestine. Moreover, as discussed in Chapter 14, the Palestinians and Israelis agreed in the 1993–1995 Oslo Accords to resolve *all* their disputes through negotiation. Furthermore, the Israelis and Palestinians limited themselves to a specific dispute resolution process that did *not* include giving either party the right to initiate or seek litigation at the ICJ or anywhere else.

The ICJ's Advisory Jurisdiction and the Israeli-Palestinian Conflict

The ICJ has aggressively asserted jurisdiction over the Israeli-Palestinian conflict, especially its advisory jurisdiction pursuant to Article 96 of the UN Charter.[33]

Article 65(1) of the ICJ Statute provides, "The Court may give an advisory opinion on any legal question at the request of whatever body may be authorized by or in accordance with the Charter of the United Nations to make such a request." The ICJ has described its advisory jurisdiction as existing to "offer legal advice to the organs and institutions requesting the opinion."[34]

In the *Nuclear Weapons* Advisory Opinion, the ICJ said it "is mindful that it should not, in principle, refuse to give an advisory opinion. In accordance with the consistent jurisprudence of the Court, only 'compelling reasons' could lead it to such a refusal." The Court further noted that it had never in its post-war history refused a request to render an advisory opinion.[35]

The ICJ's website declares that while its advisory opinions are not binding,

> the Court's advisory opinions nevertheless carry great legal weight and moral authority. They are often an instrument of preventive diplomacy and help to keep the peace. In their own way, advisory opinions also contribute to the clarification and development of international law and thereby to the strengthening of peaceful relations between States.[36]

Hirsch (2005) noted the importance of the ICJ's advisory jurisdiction:

> Advisory Opinions of the ICJ are judicial statements on the legal questions submitted to the Court by the UN organs and some other international organizations; these Opinions aim to assist these organs to fulfill their functions and furnish them guidance regarding legal issues involved in their operations. Thus, advisory opinions are of consultative character and they do not bind neither the requesting organ nor the involved states. Still, these opinions are often considered as authoritative statements of the law and past experience shows that they had considerable impact on the evolution of international law. ICJ advisory opinions also carry moral and political weight and they often affect international public opinion. The influence of these Opinions derives from the authoritative role of the Court as the principal judicial organ of the UN, the fact that they are rendered at the end of judicial proceedings, and that the Court is bound in these proceedings by the rules of international law.[37]

In determining whether to exercise its advisory jurisdiction, the ICJ engages in a two-step process. The first step is to determine whether it indeed has jurisdiction. The second step is to determine whether, even if the Court does have jurisdiction, it should nevertheless exercise its discretion not to take the case.[38]

The ICJ's predecessor Court, the Permanent Court of International Justice, decided a century ago in the *Eastern Carelia* dispute between Finland and Russia to decline to render an advisory opinion. Russia, as a non-member of the League of Nations, had not consented to the Court's jurisdiction. Moreover, the Court expressed concern that it lacked sufficient information to resolve the factual disputes between the parties, and therefore it would have been inappropriate to render an advisory opinion:

> The question whether Finland and Russia contracted on the terms of the Declaration as to the nature of the autonomy of Eastern Carelia is really one of fact ... It appears now to be very doubtful whether there would be available to the Court materials sufficient to enable it to arrive at any judicial conclusion upon the question of fact: What did the parties agree to? The Court does not say that there is an absolute rule that the request for an advisory opinion may not involve some enquiry as to facts, but, *under ordinary circumstances, it is certainly expedient that the facts upon which the opinion of the Court is desired should not be in controversy, and it should not be left to the Court itself to ascertain what they are*. The Court is aware of the fact that it is not requested to decide a dispute, but to give an advisory opinion ... The question put to the Court is not one of abstract law, but concerns directly the main point of the controversy between Finland and Russia, and can only be decided by an investigation into the facts underlying the case. Answering the question would be substantially equivalent to deciding the dispute between the parties. The Court, being a Court of Justice, cannot, even in giving advisory opinions, depart from the essential rules guiding their activity as a Court.[39]

In 2003 the Palestinians persuaded the ICJ to take advisory jurisdiction over the dispute involving the Israeli security barrier or "wall of separation." Even though the *Eastern Carelia* limitation on exercising advisory jurisdiction should apply with even greater force to the Israeli-Palestinian conflict, the ICJ insisted it had "sufficient information and evidence to enable it to give the advisory opinion requested by the General Assembly" and could resolve disputed factual issues despite the overwhelmingly one-sided nature of the pro-Palestinian information submitted to the Court.[40]

The ICJ ultimately issued a nearly unanimous Advisory Opinion in July 2004 finding portions of the separation barrier traversing the West Bank to be illegal.[41]

Palestinian Litigation Against the United States Regarding the Embassy Relocation

The Palestinians commenced litigation in 2018 at the ICJ challenging the legality under the Vienna Convention on Diplomatic Relations of the Trump Administration's decision to relocate the United States Embassy from Tel Aviv to West Jerusalem.[42]

The case raises the issue whether the ICJ has jurisdiction to decide the legal status of Jerusalem. The case also raises the possibility that the ICJ, like the ICC will declare Palestine a "state" for purposes of invoking its rights under the Vienna Convention.

The Court has not yet indicated whether it will take jurisdiction.

December 2022 General Assembly Referral Regarding the Occupation and Jerusalem

Most recently, on 30 December 2022 the UN General Assembly adopted Resolution 77/247.[43] Running nearly nine single-spaced pages, the Resolution reads more like an indictment of Israel than a sincere request for legal advice. The Resolution culminated in a request to the ICJ to render an advisory opinion on the following two questions:

a) What are the legal consequences arising from the ongoing violation by Israel of the right of the Palestinian people to self-determination, from its prolonged occupation, settlement, and annexation of the Palestinian territory occupied since 1967, including measures aimed at altering the demographic composition, character and status of the Holy City of Jerusalem, and from its adoption of related discriminatory legislation and measures?
b) How do the policies and practices of Israel referred to ... above affect the legal status of the occupation, and what are the legal consequences that arise for all States and the United Nations from this status?

The language of the resolution – "ongoing violation," "right of the Palestinian people to self-determination," "prolonged occupation," "discriminatory legislation," – seems intended to predetermine the outcome. Moreover, the language runs afoul of the ICJ's prior warning that questions raised in a request for an advisory opinion should be asked "in neutral terms rather than assuming conclusions of law that are in dispute" and "should not include reasoning or argument."[44]

One wonders how an Advisory Opinion would be of any use to the General Assembly, given that it has already made up its mind regarding the matters for which it ostensibly needs advice.

And one wonders how the ICJ can possibly issue an Advisory Opinion, where, as in the *Eastern Carelia* case, the Court is incapable of obtaining sufficient reliable information to resolve factual disputes and upon which to base any factual determinations. The ICJ has access to voluminous information submitted in support of Palestinian claims, but it has no ability to weigh that information against Israeli objections or to make any meaningful factual determinations.

The ICJ nonetheless ordered parties to file opening briefs by 25 July 2023, and responsive briefs by 25 October 2023. The ICJ conducted public hearings in February 2024 in The Hague.

As discussed in Chapter 14, the Oslo Accords deprive the ICJ of jurisdiction to issue the Advisory Opinion. But if the ICJ asserts jurisdiction anyway (which it will certainly do), then it should nevertheless exercise its discretion to decline the case and defer to the political process the parties agreed upon in the Oslo Accords. At Oslo the parties agreed to resolve all disputed issues through negotiation. They further agreed to abide by a narrowly defined dispute resolution process that precludes either party from initiating litigation or asking other to initiate litigation on their behalf.

The Court should also decline to render an opinion on the General Assembly's questions. Those questions focus entirely on issues the Palestinians and Israelis previously resolved in the Oslo Accords, including the Palestinian agreement that the Israeli occupation and Israeli settlements could remain in place pending the completion of permanent status negotiations, and the Palestinian agreement that issues involving Jerusalem would be deferred to the permanent status negotiations.

Other Examples of Palestinian Lawfare

The Palestinians in recent years have ramped up their lawfare campaign by making extremely controversial and unsupported allegations of "apartheid" and "genocide." The Palestinians have also threatened litigation against Britain for having issued the Balfour Declaration.

"Apartheid"

As noted above, article 7(2)(h) of the Rome Statute defines the "crime of apartheid" as "inhumane acts ... in the context of an institutionalized regime of systematic oppression and domination by one racial group over any other racial group or groups and committed with the intention of maintaining that regime."

Palestinian advocates and their supporters in recent years have repeatedly accused Israel of practicing "apartheid" in an effort to equate Israel with pre-1994 South Africa.[45] They argue Israeli practices both inside Israel itself and in the West Bank and Gaza Strip reflect an intent by the Jews to "maintain domination" and "systematic oppression" of the Palestinians. They also allege Israel practices "inhumane acts" against the Palestinians.[46]

The apartheid claim as applied to Israel cannot be sustained either factually or legally. The claim fails as to both Arab citizens of Israel and Palestinian residents of the West Bank.

No one can seriously contend that the millions of Arab citizens of Israel live under apartheid. Arab-Israelis enjoy full civil rights. They vote. They serve in the Knesset. They serve on the Israeli Supreme Court, and as lawyers, law school Deans, doctors, pharmacists, police officers, engineers, and in many other professions at all levels of Israel society. The 2021–2022 government included an Arab Cabinet Minister. The contrast with apartheid-era South Africa could not be any starker.

Nor can the apartheid allegation be sustained regarding West Bank Palestinians. The separation of Jews and Arabs in the West Bank is the result of the Palestinian-Israeli agreement in the Oslo Accords (specifically the 1995 Interim Agreement, as discussed in Chapter 14) to divide the West Bank into three separate areas until a permanent status agreement would be negotiated. Two of those areas (Areas A and B), comprising the large Arab towns and smaller Arab villages, have been under Palestinian civil control for the last 30 years.

The third (Area C), comprising the Israeli settlements and military installations, remains under Israeli control, exactly as the Palestinians agreed in the Oslo Accords.

The Palestinians further agreed at Oslo that the Israeli occupation and Israeli settlements could remain until the completion of permanent status negotiations. The political situation and separation of Jews and Arabs in the West Bank thus reflects exactly what the Palestinians bargained for at Oslo. Therefore, the ongoing dynamic in the West Bank does not come anywhere close to constituting an "institutionalized regime of systematic oppression and domination by one racial group over any other racial group or groups and committed with the intention of maintaining that regime."[47]

There is no indication of any form of unilateral, Israeli-imposed apartheid anywhere in Areas A and B. If apartheid exists at all, it is because the Palestinians do not allow any Jews to live among them in Areas A and B.

"Genocide"

The genocide allegation against Israel is the most offensive and baseless component of the Palestinian lawfare campaign.

Article II of the 1948 Convention on the Prevention and Punishment of Genocide defines the crime of genocide as follows:

> Genocide means any of the following acts committed with intent to destroy, in whole or in part, a national, ethnical, racial or religious group, as such: (a) Killing members of the group; (b) Causing serious bodily or mental harm to members of the group; (c) Deliberately inflicting on the group conditions of life calculated to bring about its physical destruction in whole or in part; (d) Imposing measures intended to prevent births within the group; (e) Forcibly transferring children of the group to another group.[48]

Article 6 of the Rome Statute defines "genocide" as:

> "[A]ny of the following acts committed with intent to destroy, in whole or in part, a national, ethnical, racial or religious group, as such: (a) Killing

> members of the group; (b) Causing serious bodily or mental harm to members of the group; (c) Deliberately inflicting on the group conditions of life calculated to bring about its physical destruction in whole or in part; (d) Imposing measures intended to prevent births within the group; (e) Forcibly transferring children of the group to another group."

In late December 2023 the Republic of South Africa, acting on behalf of Hamas (which obviously is not a signatory to the Genocide Convention or the Rome Statute) initiated proceedings at the ICJ and requested the Court "indicate provisional measures" against Israel for alleged violations of the Genocide Convention during the course of its defensive war in Gaza following the 7 October 2023 Hamas massacres in southern Israel.[49] The South African application represents a classic and particularly insidious example of lawfare by weaponizing the post-World War II Genocide convention against the Jewish state born from the ashes of the Holocaust.

If the definition of genocide applies to anyone in the region, it fits exactly the Hamas charter's call for the destruction of Israel and the murder of all Jews worldwide. But no aspect of the above definition applies to Israel's conduct – not in the West Bank, nor in the Gaza Strip, nor anywhere else.

First, the demographic data contradict the "genocide" claim. The Arab population inside Israel's borders rose from 167,000 in 1950 to 2.1 million in 2023.[50] The Palestinian population in the West Bank stood at 598,637 as of June 1967, when Israel replaced Jordan as the occupant.[51] The population of the Gaza Strip as of June 1967 was 356,261. By 2023, according to the Palestinian Central Bureau of Statistics, the population of the West Bank had swelled to 3,256,906, while the population of the Gaza Strip had grown to 2,226,544.[52] The dramatic population growth in the West Bank and the Gaza Strip belies any claim of an alleged Israeli "intent to destroy" the Palestinian people.

Moreover, the above figures negate the related Palestinian claim that Israel has engaged in "ethnic cleansing" of the Palestinian population. The only population in the Middle East who experienced ethnic cleansing during the past century were the more than one million Jewish inhabitants of Arab countries, nearly all of whom were expelled between 1948 and 1950 following Israel's declaration of independence.[53] None of those Jewish refugees have received any form of compensation. Nor have they received any support from the United Nations, which instead focuses solely through the United Nations Relief and Works Agency (UNRWA) on the far smaller number of approximately 400,000 Palestinian refugees who fled the area during the war the Mufti and the surrounding Arab countries launched against the nascent Jewish State in 1948.

Second, the "genocide" accusation is especially offensive given the Nazi genocide of the Jewish people during World War II. The Nazis slaughtered *more than one-third of the entire worldwide Jewish population* during the war. Most were transported hundreds of miles to death camps designed and constructed for one purpose: to murder thousands of Jews per day on an industrial scale. Nothing even remotely as horrific has ever befallen any other group of people in human history.

It is especially shameful for the Palestinians and their supporters to claim the Jews are doing the same to them. Yet time and again the Palestinians and their supporters insist on characterizing Israeli military responses to Hamas rocket attacks as a "genocide." The most recent such claims began a mere three days after Israel's military response to the Hamas rampage through southern Israel on 7 October 2023, when Hamas massacred 1,400 children, women and elderly and kidnapped nearly 250 hostages.[54] The death of Palestinian civilians during the war is a tragedy, but it does not come anywhere close to an "intent to destroy, in whole or in part, a national, ethnical, racial or religious group, *as such*."

Palestinian advocates have also repeatedly characterized Israelis as "Nazis," in a cynical and deplorable attempt to equate Jews as morally equivalent with the regime that perpetrated the Holocaust against them.

The modern-day Palestinian "genocide" claim has its origins in the January 1937 testimony of one of its most famous lawyers, Auni Bey Abdul Hadi to the Palestine Royal Commission. Auni Bey claimed the "plight" of the Palestinian Arabs as of early 1937 was "worse" than the plight of German Jews on the eve of the Holocaust

Commissioner Horace Rumbold seemed taken aback by Auni Bey's testimony:

Q: Are you taking a leaf out of Germany's book?
A: It is different here. The case here is the contrary. Here we are in the same position as the Jews in Germany.
Q: How do you make that out?
A: The Jews are being driven out of the land upon which they lived for centuries and they are losing their existence, but the policy which is being adopted here will culminate in destroying our national existence here.
Q: You compare yourselves, in fact, to the Jews in Germany?
A: We are in an even worse position. There their personal rights are affected, but here the national rights of a people are affected.[55]

Threats to Sue the United Kingdom

Other examples of the Palestine lawfare campaign abound. In October 2016 the official Palestinian news agency announced a year-long campaign marking the 100th anniversary of the Balfour Declaration, demanding the United Kingdom "atone for the big crime Britain had committed against the Palestinian people."[56] In 2017, as part of that campaign, the Palestinians increased the pressure, insisting Britain either voluntarily apologize for and rescind the Balfour Declaration, *or face litigation* forcing it to do so.[57]

Concluding Comment

The Palestinian lawfare campaign has chalked up many successes during the past two decades. Other than the failed attempt to seek ICC prosecutions arising from the *Mavi Marmara* episode, the Palestinians have won every key lawfare engagement thus far, and all signs point to continued success in the future. Both the ICC and the ICJ are demonstrably biased in favor of the Palestinian side. Both Courts will remain eager to intervene in the Israeli-Palestinian dispute, despite the many compelling reasons for them to avoid doing so.

Notes

1 *See* Ch. 13, *infra.*
2 *See, e.g.*, Palestinian News and Information Agency press release, "Ashrawi: 'With the Expansion of Its Illegal Settlement Enterprise, Israel Seeks Not Only to Defy but to Defeat the Whole World'" (23 Aug. 2018), http://english.wafa.ps/page.aspx?id=55Kui6a98880474429a55Kui6 (last accessed 20 Oct. 2022).
3 *See, e.g.*, E. Alimi, *Israeli Politics and the First Palestinian Intifada: Political Opportunities, Framing Processes and Contentious Politics* (Routledge, 2007).
4 The BDS Website describes the purpose of the movement: "The Boycott, Divestment, Sanctions (BDS) movement works to end international support for Israel's oppression of Palestinians *and pressure Israel to comply with international law*" [emphasis added], https://bdsmovement.net (last accessed 4 Dec. 2023); *see also* O. Barghouti, *BDS: The Global Struggle for Palestinian Rights* (Haymarket Press, 2011); J. Sperber, *BDS, Israel, and the World System*, Journal of Palestine Studies, 45:1 (177) at 8 (Autumn 2015) (BDS "represents a series of strategies designed *to force Israel to comply with international law*") [emphasis added].
5 O. Kittrie, *Lawfare: Law as a Weapon of War* at 8 (Oxford Univ. Press, 2016).
6 *Id.* at 12–13.
7 *Id.* at 20–21.
8 *Id.* at 200–01.
9 United Nations Treaty Series, vol. 2187, No. 38544, Done at Rome on 17 July 1998, in force on 1 July 2002, Depositary: Secretary-General of the United Nations, http://treaties.un.org.
10 E. Kontorovich, *When Gravity Fails: Israeli Settlements and Admissibility at the ICC*, Israel Law Review, 47:3 at 379, 381 (2014).
11 ICC 01-13, *Situation on the Registered Vessels of the Union of the Comoros, The Hellenic Republic and The Kingdom of Cambodia*, Public Decision on the 'Application for Judicial Review by the Government of the Comoros' at 43–44, paras. 96–97 (16 Sept. 2020).
12 Convention (No. IV) Relative to the Protection of Civilian Persons in Time of War, 12 Aug. 1949, 75 U.N.T.S. 87.
13 S. Adem, *Palestine and the International Criminal Court* at 50–55 (Springer, 2019).

14 G.-J.A. Knoops and T. Zwart, *The Flotilla Case before the ICC: The Need to Do Justice While Keeping Heaven Intact*, International Criminal Law Review, 15:6 at 1069, 1070 (2015) (citing G. Palmer, A. Uribe, J.C. Itzhar and S.O. Sanberk, Report of the Secretary-General's Panel of Inquiry on 31 May 2010 Flotilla Incident, Sept. 2011, para. 95, and Carol Migdalovitz, 'Israel's Bockade of Gaza, the Mavi Marmara Incident, and Its Aftermath', Congressional Research Service, 23 June 2010).

15 *Report of the Secretary-General's Panel of Inquiry on the 31 May 2010 Flotilla Incident* at 4, para. iv (Sept. 2011).

16 *Id.* at 4, para. vii.

17 *Id.* at 4, para. ii.

18 *Id.* at 43, para. 78.

19 *Id.* at 45, para. 82.

20 *Id.* at 47, para. 90 (emphasis added).

21 Knoops and Zwart, *op. cit.* at 1071 ("The Mavi Marmara, originally a Turkish vessel, was reflagged to the Union of the Comoros just over a week before it headed towards the naval blockade. Most of the victims of the Mavi Marmara incident were Turkish nationals. These observations might lead to the appearance that the vessel was reflagged in order to initiate an ICC Prosecution (Turkey is not a signatory to the ICC), while the referral was de facto not a 'State referral.'").

22 *Situation on Registered Vessels of Comoros, Greece and Cambodia*, Article 53(1) Report, Office of the Prosecutor, 6 Nov. 2014 at 52–53, para. 125.

23 The lengthy procedural history of the *Mavi Marmara* case is discussed in *Situation on the Registered Vessels of the Union of the Comoros, The Hellenic Republic and The Kingdom of Cambodia*, Public Decision on the 'Application for Judicial Review by the Government of the Comoros' ICC 01-13 at 4–6, paras. 1–7 (16 Sept. 2020).

24 *See* International Criminal Court website, Preliminary Examination: Palestine, https://www.icc-cpi.int/palestine ("On 2 January 2015, the Government of Palestine acceded to the Rome Statute by depositing its instrument of accession with the UN Secretary-General. The accession entered into force on 1 April 2015") (last accessed 20 Oct. 2022); Al Jazeera, Palestine Submits ICC Referral to Open Probe into 'Israel Crimes' (22 May 2018), https://www.aljazeera.com/news/2018/05/palestine-submits-icc-referral-open-probe-israel-crimes-180522101121093.html (last accessed 20 Oct. 2022); Daily Sabah, Gaza Officials Submit Proof of Israeli Crimes to International Criminal Court (2 Aug. 2018), https://www.dailysabah.com/mideast/2018/08/02/gaza-officials-submit-proof-of-israeli-crimes-to-international-criminal-court (last accessed 20 Oct. 2022).

25 International Criminal Court, *Situation in Palestine*, PAL-180515-Ref, *State of Palestine, Referral by the State of Palestine Pursuant to Articles l3(a) and 14 of the Rome Statute* (15 May 2018). Israel has raised a variety of jurisdictional objections to the referral, including that Palestine is not a "state" and therefore lacks the legal standing to delegate jurisdiction to the ICC; but even if it were deemed to be a "state," pursuant to the Oslo Accords it has waived jurisdiction "either in law or in fact over Area C, Jerusalem and Israeli nationals – and thus cannot validly delegate such jurisdiction to the Court." International Criminal Court, *Situation in Palestine*, PAL-180515-Ref, *State of Israel, Office of the Attorney General, The International Criminal Court's Lack of Jurisdiction over the So-Called "Situation in Palestine"* (20 Dec. 2019), https://www.gov.il/BlobFolder/reports/20-12-2019/en/Memorandum-Attorney-General.pdf. The Israeli submission to the ICC also preserved Israel's own claims to the West Bank, the Gaza Strip and East Jerusalem, arguing sovereignty over those areas has been in "abeyance" since the termination of the Palestine Mandate on 14 May 1948. *Id.* paras. 29–30.

26 *Rome Statute of the International Criminal Court*, 2187, U.N.T.S., 38544. (17 July 1998), https://www.icc-cpi.int/NR/rdonlyres/ADD16852-AEE9-4757-ABE7-9CDC7CF02886/283503/RomeStatutEng1.pdf. Article 12 is entitled "Preconditions to the Exercise of Jurisdiction." Article 12(3) provides as follows: "If the acceptance of a State which is not a Party to this Statute is required under paragraph 2, that State may, by declaration lodged with the Registrar, accept the exercise of jurisdiction by the Court with respect to the crime in question. The accepting State shall cooperate with the Court without any delay or exception in accordance with Part 9." Legal commentators have disagreed as to whether Palestine qualifies as a "state" within the plain meaning of Article 12(3). Some have argued it does not, based on traditional norms of international law such as the *Montevideo* criteria for statehood. Others have urged a more liberal, "functional" reading of Article 12(3), urging Palestine be deemed a state "for purposes of" effectuating the purpose of Article 12(3). *See, e.g.*, H. Lee, *Defining State for the Purpose of the International Criminal Court: The Problem Ahead After the Palestine Decision*, University of Pittsburg Law Review, 77 at 345, 384 (2016) ("The term 'state' in the [Rome Statute] should be defined broadly to include self-proclaimed entities that exercise *de facto* governmental function, regardless of whether the entity received any formal recognition"); W. Worster, *The Exercise of Jurisdiction by the International Criminal Court Over Palestine*, American University International Law Rev, 26:5 at 1208 (2011) ("Although the text of the Rome Statute appears to limit membership to 'states,' the practice of international organizations is that that term 'state' may be used liberally to include quasi-states with some degree of statehood, notwithstanding the clear language of the text. There is no requirement of international law that the term be interpreted restrictively ... Thus, there is no barrier under international law to Palestinian accession to the Rome Statute or acceptance of the ICC's jurisdiction"); A. Zimmermann, *Palestine and the International Criminal Court Quo Vadis: Reach and Limits of Declarations under Article 12(3)*, Journal of International Criminal Justice, 11:2 at 303–30 (2013) (arguing Palestine satisfies the requirements of Article 12(3) as of the 2012 UN resolution upgrading Palestine's status to "non-member observer state"); J. Quigley, *Palestine Is a State: A Horse with Black and White Stripes Is a Zebra*, Michigan Journal of International Law, 32:4 at 749 (2011) (arguing Palestine is a state, consistent with Quigley's previous writings); *but see* R. Barnidge, *Palestinian Engagement with The International Criminal Court: From Preliminary Examination To Investigation?*, The Journal of the Middle East and Africa, 7:2 at 122 (2016) ("When the Palestinians engage with international institutions such as the ICC as a state in the absence of a final settlement that enshrines Palestinian statehood, there is a strong argument to be made that they are acting contrary to international law, since this *prima facie* would seem to prejudice the final (negotiated) status of the territories"); R.W. Ash, *Is Palestine a State: A Response to Professor John Quigley's Article, the Palestine Declaration to the International Criminal Court*, Rutgers Law Record, 36 at 200 (2009) ("[I]t is difficult to fathom how anyone could argue that there is a state of Palestine currently in existence. Even the Palestinian leaders themselves, through both their frequent statements and their voluntary participation in a process whose goal is to establish a Palestinian 'State,' testify that what they hope to achieve in the future is the creation of a viable Palestinian state. If creation of a viable Palestinian state is the goal Palestinian leaders continue to pursue, that is proof positive that no such 'State' currently exists"); J. Vidmar, *Palestine and the Conceptual Problem of Implicit Statehood*, Chinese Journal of International Law, 12 at 19–41 (2013) ("Setting Palestine next to States and giving it the competencies to do certain things that States tend to do does not automatically

and implicitly make it a State … Palestine, in many respects, has the capacity to act like a State internationally, yet such a capacity does not create Palestinian statehood"); E. Kontorovich, *Israel/Palestine – The ICC's Uncharted Territory*, Journal of International Criminal Justice, 11 at 979 (2013) (noting potential ICC recognition of Palestinian "statehood" would lead to many similarly questionable claims around the world).

27 International Criminal Court, No. ICC-01/18, *Situation in The State of Palestine* at paras. 106–07 (5 Feb. 2021) ("Therefore, the reference to '[t]he State on the territory of which the conduct in question occurred' in article 12(2)(a) of the Statute cannot be taken to mean a State fulfilling the criteria for statehood under general international law … the Rome Statute insulates the Court from making such a determination, relying instead on the accession procedure and the determination made by the United Nations General Assembly. The Court is not constitutionally competent to determine matters of statehood that would bind the international community. In addition, such a determination is not required for the specific purposes of the present proceedings or the general exercise of the Court's mandate.") The Court further noted, "in accordance with the ordinary meaning given to its terms in their context and in the light of the object and purpose of the Statute, the reference to '[t]he State on the territory of which the conduct in question occurred' in article 12(2)(a) of the Statute must be interpreted as a reference to a State Party to the Statute." *Id.* para. 109. Judge Kovacs issued a lengthy, partial dissent from the majority opinion, noting "I agree neither with the conclusion, nor with the Majority's reasoning and analysis in reaching such a conclusion" regarding the issue of Palestine's "statehood" for purposes of the Rome Statute. *Judge Péter Kovács' Partly Dissenting Opinion*, para. 2.

28 UN Charter, 26 June 1945, T.S. No. 993.

29 *South West Africa Cases (Ethiopia v. South Africa; Liberia v. South Africa)*, *op. cit.*, Joint Dissenting Opinion of Sir Percy Spender and Sir Gerald Fitzmaurice at 466; *see also* J. Odermatt, *Patterns of Avoidance: Political Questions Before International Courts*, International Journal of Law in Context, 14 at 221–36 (2018).

30 *See, e.g.*, *Legal Consequences of the Construction of a Wall in the Occupied Palestinian Territory*, ICJ Rep 2004, 136 at para. 41 (Advisory Opinion) (9 July 2004).

31 *South West Africa Cases (Ethiopia v. South Africa; Liberia v. South Africa)*, Preliminary Objections, Judgment of 21 Dec. 1962, I.C. J. Reports, 1962, p. 319, Joint Dissenting Opinion of Sir Percy Spender and Sir Gerald Fitzmaurice at 466.

32 *Id.* Joint Dissenting Opinion of Sir Percy Spender and Sir Gerald Fitzmaurice at 470.

33 Statute of the International Court of Justice, Arts. 65–68, https://www.icj-cij.org/statute (last accessed 6 Nov. 2023).

34 *Legality of the Threat or Use of Nuclear Weapons*, ICJ Reports, 1996, pp. 226, 236 para. 15 (8 July 1996).

35 *Id.* at 235, para. 14.

36 ICJ Website, Advisory Jurisdiction, https://www.icj-cij.org/advisory-jurisdiction#:~:text=Since%20States%20alone%20are%20entitled,organizations%20and%20to%20them%20alone (last accessed 6 Nov. 2023).

37 M. Hirsch, *The Legal Status of Jerusalem following the ICJ Advisory Opinion on the Separation Barrier*, Israel Law Review, 38 at 298, 306 (2005).

38 M. Shaw, *International Law* (9th ed.) at 974 (Cambridge Univ. Press, 2021).

39 Permanent Court of International Justice, Third Ordinary Session, File F, c.VII, Docket III.3 (23 July 1923) (emphasis added).

40 *Legal Consequences of the Construction of a Wall in the Occupied Palestinian Territory*, Advisory Opinion, I.C J. Reports 136, 161–62 (2004).

41 *Legal Consequences of the Construction of a Wall in the Occupied Palestinian Territory*, Advisory Opinion, I.C J. Reports 136 (2004). For an interesting discussion of the Court's decision from an Israel perspective, *see* R. Sabel, *The Status of the Territories: The International Court of Justice Decision on The Separation Barrier and the Green Line*, Israel Law Review, 38 at 316–78 (2005). For a favorable reaction to the Court's decision, see P.J.I.M. de Waart, *International Court of Justice Firmly Walled in the Law of Power in the Israeli-Palestinian Peace Process*, Leiden Journal of International Law, 18 at 467 (2005).

42 *Palestine v. United States of America, Relocation of the United States Embassy to Jerusalem*, Application Instituting Proceedings (28 Sept. 2018).

43 United Nations, A/RES/77/247 (30 Dec. 2022).

44 *Judgment No. 2867 of the Administrative Tribunal of the ILO upon a Complaint Filed Against the International Fund for Agricultural Development*, Advisory Opinion, ICJ Reports, 2012, pp. 10, 36, para. 62.

45 *See, e.g.*, Barghouti (2011), *op. cit.* ch. 3 ("The South Africa Strategy for Palestine"); S. Power, The Legal Architecture of Apartheid, Al Haq (2 Apr. 2021), https://aardi.org/2021/04/02/the-legal-architecture-of-apartheid-by-dr-susan-powers-al-haq/.

46 *See, e.g.*, Human Rights Watch, A Threshold Crossed: Israeli Authorities and the Crimes of Apartheid and Persecution (27 Apr. 2021), https://www.hrw.org/report/2021/04/27/threshold-crossed/israeli-authorities-and-crimes-apartheid-and-persecution.

47 For an excellent refutation of the "apartheid" claim, *see* J. Kern and A. Hertzberg, *Neo-Orientalism: Deconstructing Claims of Apartheid in the Palestinian Israeli Conflict*, NGO Monitor (Mar. 2022), https://ngo-monitor.org/pdf/NGOMonitor_ApartheidReport_2022.pdf (last accessed 8 Nov. 2023).

48 UN General Assembly, *Convention on the Prevention and Punishment of the Crime of Genocide*, 9 Dec. 1948, United Nations, Treaty Series, vol. 78, p. 277.

49 *Application of the Convention on the Prevention and Punishment of the Crime of Genocide in the Gaza Strip* (South Africa v. Israel) ICJ, CR 2024/2 (28 Dec. 2023). South Africa also asked the ICJ in March and May 2024 asking the court to order Israel not to engage in certain military activities, including not entering Rafah in the southern Gaza Strip. The ICJ's willingness to consider such requests represent another example of how parties are bypassing the UN Security Council on matters of international peace and security, and asking the ICJ to fill that role instead, in derogation of the ICJ's purely judicial function.

50 Government of Israel, Central Bureau of Statistics.

51 State of Israel, Central Bureau of Statistics, *West Bank of the Jordan, Gaza Strip and Northern Sinai, Golan Heights, Data from Full Enumeration* (Jerusalem, 1967), https://www.levyinstitute.org/pubs/1967_census/vol_1_intro.pdf (last accessed 7 Nov. 2023).

52 Palestine Central Bureau of Statistics, 2023 mid-year population report, https://www.pcbs.gov.ps/statisticsIndicatorsTables.aspx?lang=en&table_id=676 (last accessed 7 Nov. 2023).

53 See D. Littman, "The Forgotten Refugees: An Exchange of Population," The National Review (3 Dec. 2002).

54 "Palestinian UN Envoy Accuses Israel of 'Genocidal' Campaign Against Gaza," Reuters (10 Oct. 2023), https://www.reuters.com/world/middle-east/palestinian-un-envoy-accuses-israel-genocidal-campaign-against-gaza-2023-10-10/ (last accessed 7 Nov. 2023).

55 Palestine Royal Commission, Minutes of Evidence Heard at Public Sessions, Colonial Paper 134 (1937) at 312–13, paras. 4906-08 (Auni Bey Abdul Hadi Testimony, 13 Jan. 1937).

56 Palestinian News and Information Agency (WAFA), "Palestinians Prepare to Mark One Hundred Years of Balfour Declaration" (24 Oct. 2016), http://english.wafa.ps/page.aspx?id=G8NFN5a50719869123aG8NFN5 (last accessed 20 Oct. 2022).

57 "Palestinian Authority Plans to Sue UK over Balfour Declaration," Arab News (4 Nov. 2017), http://www.arabnews.com/node/1187831/middle-east (last accessed 20 Oct. 2022) ("The Palestinian Authority plans to sue the UK over the 100-year-old Balfour Declaration, which paved the way for the creation of Israel. It will hire a British law firm to pursue an apology, and plans to explore similar actions in European and other international courts, according to Foreign Minister Riad Malki. 'The Palestinian government has made every effort to persuade the British government to abandon its decision to celebrate the centennial of the Balfour Declaration,' Malki said in an emailed statement quoted by Bloomberg. Palestinians 'will exhaust all possibilities for a partial realization of the stolen justice that was executed by Britain through its ominous promise.'").

PART II

Relevant Legal History

4

THE McMAHON-HUSSEIN CORRESPONDENCE, 1915–1916

Background

In September 1914, shortly after the outbreak of World War I, Lord Kitchener, the newly-appointed British Secretary of State for War, directed British officials in Cairo to make a secret overture to the Sherif Hussein of Mecca, later King of the Hejaz and father of the future Jordanian King Abdullah I and the future Iraqi King Feisal.

The British first approached Abdullah to ascertain whether the Arabs would side with Britain in the event Turkey were to join an alliance with Germany.[1] Abdullah responded favorably, writing the Arabs would be

> well satisfied with a more close union with Great Britain ... so long as she protects the rights of our country and the rights of the person his Highness our present Emir and Lord and the rights of his Emirate and its independence in all respects without any exceptions or restrictions.[2]

The British Government replied "[i]f the Emir of Mecca is willing to assist Great Britain with this conflict, Great Britain is willing ... to guarantee the independence, rights and privileges of the Sherifate."[3]

In April 1915 the Foreign Office authorized British officials in the region to

> let it be known ... that His Majesty's Government will make it an essential condition in the terms of peace that the Arabian peninsula and its Mohammedan Holy Places should remain in the hands of an independent sovereign state. It is not possible to define at this stage exactly how much territory should be included in this State.[4]

DOI: 10.4324/9781032686561-7

By the end of June 1915 the British were distributing proclamations announcing this policy in Egypt and Sudan, and air-dropping the same proclamations over Arabia.[5]

The 24 October 1915 Letter

Against this background, Hussein wrote directly to Sir Henry McMahon, the British High Commissioner in Cairo in mid-July 1915, initiating what was to become known as the "McMahon-Hussein Correspondence." McMahon and Hussein wrote a total of ten letters to each other between July 1915 and March 1916.[6] The correspondence was conducted completely in Arabic, with McMahon's English originals translated into Arabic for transmission to Hussein.[7]

The letters reveal Hussein's willingness to lead a British-funded Arab revolt against the Turks in exchange for Britain promising independence and self-determination for the Arabs.[8] Hussein wanted Britain to agree on the outer boundaries of the territory encompassing the future Arab states. Hussein also insisted Britain not sell out the Arabs in any future peace negotiations with Turkey.

McMahon, acting on instructions from London, first tried to delay any discussion of borders. Eventually, however, McMahon agreed to Hussein's terms in a letter dated 24 October 1915,[9] but subject to two crucial exceptions. First, McMahon excluded areas where French interests were implicated, but without saying exactly which areas that meant.[10] Second, McMahon excluded "certain areas" lying to the west of four Syrian towns as not "purely Arab," but again he did not say precisely which areas that meant.[11]

Translated from the original Arabic, the key language in the 24 October 1915 letter read as follows:

> The two districts west of Mersina and Alexandretta and *portions of Syria lying to the west of the Districts of Damascus, Homs, Hama and Aleppo cannot be said to be purely Arab*, and should be excluded from the limits demanded. With the above modifications, and without prejudice to our existing treaties with Arab chiefs, we accept those limits. As for those regions lying within those frontiers wherein Great Britain is free to act *without detriment to the interests of her ally France*, I am empowered to give the following assurances ... (2) Great Britain will guarantee the Holy Places against all external aggression and will recognize their inviolability.[12]

The key question raised by McMahon's two exceptions is whether Palestine would be *included* in or *excluded* from the post-war Arab state promised to Hussein.[13] The precise meaning of those two exceptions has dominated legal debate ever since, including the impact of McMahon's language on the legality of (i) the November 1917 Balfour Declaration; (ii) the portions of the Mandate for Palestine implementing the Balfour Declaration; (iii) the United Nations November 1947 partition resolution; and (iv) the State of Israel itself.

Some Palestinian advocates and their supporters argue to the present day that McMahon unconditionally promised *all* of Palestine to the Arabs in the 24 October 1915 letter. Therefore, any subsequent efforts to claw back those promises should be deemed null and void. But the two exceptions in the 24 October 1915 letter undermine that interpretation.

First Exception: French Interests

French involvement in the Middle East and the Levant began centuries ago. France had long regarded itself as the protector of the Maronite Catholics in Lebanon, and had always claimed an interest in the Holy Land.[14] Those interests remained as strong as ever at the beginning of the 20th century.

In late 1912 tensions flared between Britain and France after French agents noted the presence of a number of Cairo-based British personnel in Syria. France suspected the British were engaged in efforts to undermine French interests in the Middle East, including plotting a British occupation of Syria. French Foreign Minister Paul Cambon sought and received assurances from his British counterpart, Foreign Secretary Edward Grey, that such was not the case.

A few days later (21 December 1912) the French Prime Minister, Raymond Poincare, gave a speech to the French Senate reiterating French aspirations in Syria and Lebanon, and disclosing Britain's concession to those interests:

> I have no need to tell the Senate that in Syria and Lebanon we have traditional interests and that we intend to see they are respected. I am happy to be able to add that the rumours about the existence of some disaffection between the English Government and us on this point are completely baseless. The English Government has declared to us in a very friendly manner that in these regions it has neither intentions nor designs, nor political aspirations of any sort. We ourselves are resolved to maintain, in Asia, the integrity of the Ottoman Empire, but we shall not abandon any of our traditions there, nor repudiate any of the sympathies we have acquired.[15]

In mid-March 1915 the French government informed the British government it claimed all of Syria, which at that time included Palestine.[16] A British Government Committee (the de Bunsen Committee) noted the claim in its report of June 1915, just one month before Hussein's first letter to McMahon, and four months before McMahon's 24 October 1915 letter.[17] French interests in the Middle East were, therefore, high on the radar of British wartime diplomacy in the summer and fall of 1915.

The English version of McMahon's 24 October 1915 letter indicated Britain was willing to promise Arab independence in those areas of the Middle East where Britain was "free to act *without* detriment to the interests of her ally France." That seemingly unambiguous reservation on behalf of French interests, however, came out less clearly when the letter was translated into Arabic for transmission to Hussein: "We accept those limits and boundaries, and in regard to the areas (or provinces) which those boundaries enclose, where (or whereas) Great Britain is free to act without affecting the interests (or policy) of her ally France..."[18]

McMahon reported to London, however, that

> the Arab representatives admitted and fully understood that the ... provision holds good only so far as concerns those parts of Arab territory where the British can act freely and without prejudice to their French allies: this limitation being due to the fact that our obligations toward the latter do not give us a free hand as regards the whole of Arabia.[19]

Nevertheless, one could argue, as did a Foreign Office lawyer nearly 25 years later, that this

> careless translation completely changes the meaning, or at least makes the meaning exceedingly ambiguous, entitling the Sherif to think the reservation merely meant the British were free to act in the area covered by the specific reservation without regard to French interests.[20]

But the Arab side never pursued this line of argument, preferring instead to claim the general reservation in favor of France had simply lapsed once France declared its support for the Balfour Declaration in 1918 and voted for the British Mandate in 1922, thereby abandoning its claims to Palestine.[21]

Second Exception: Areas West of Damascus, Homs, Hama, and Aleppo

The Ottomans governed their empire through a system of administrative/geographic divisions. In 1864, the Sublime Porte promulgated an edict establishing the *Vilayet* system, in which the Empire was divided into *Vilayets* (Provinces) comprised of subdivisions known as *Sanjaks*.[22] Several *Sanjaks*, including the *Sanjak* of Jerusalem, were "independent," meaning they were not part of a larger *Vilayet* and instead reported directly to Constantinople for strategic reasons or, in the case of Jerusalem, for religious and political reasons.[23] By 1905 the Empire outside Constantinople contained 29 *Vilayets* encompassing a total of 120 subordinate *Sanjaks*, plus six independent *Sanjaks*.[24]

The independent *Sanjak* of Jerusalem comprised portions of ancient Judea and the northern Negev Desert. Palestine itself, however, was not a *Vilayet* and had no recognized political or geographic status in the Ottoman Empire. The remainder of Palestine outside the independent *Sanjak* of Jerusalem was subsumed within the *Vilayet* of Beirut.

Damascus, Homs, and Hama were part of the *Vilayet* of Syria. Aleppo was considered both a *Vilayet* and a *Sanjak*. Damascus was the capital of the *Vilayet* of Syria, and the City of Aleppo was also the capital of the *Vilayet* of Aleppo.

A traditional legal analysis of the meaning of McMahon's 24 October 1915 letter would focus on the plain, ordinary meaning of McMahon's words. However, this traditional mode of legal analysis does not serve well in ascertaining the meaning of McMahon's letter.

First, McMahon's use of the word "District" has caused great interpretational difficulty, as there was no such thing as a "District" in the Ottoman governance system. Neither the Turkish words *Vilayet* or *Sanjak* translate into English as "District." Moreover, when McMahon's letters were translated into Arabic, the word "District" was translated as *Wilaya*. The word *Wilaya* could have been read as *Vilayet*, but that would not necessarily have made sense given Damascus, Homs, and Hama were *towns*, not *Vilayets*.

Wilaya could also have meant a "region or district," implying a smaller geographic area than a *Vilayet*. In 1920 a British official who had served in the Arab Bureau in Cairo during the war studied the Arabic version of the correspondence and determined the Arabic for "District of Damascus" meant "*Vilayet* of Damascus." Thus, he argued, it would not be unreasonable to read the incorrectly rendered term *Vilayet of Damascus* to mean the actual *Vilayet of Syria*, of which Damascus was the capital.[25] Moreover, "Turkish usage frequently employed 'Sham' (Damascus) as a general appellation for Syria," further supporting the interpretation of *Vilayet of Damascus* as equivalent to *Vilayet of Syria*.[26]

The issue, therefore, depends on whether the words "District of Damascus" should be read broadly, as equivalent to "*Vilayet* of Syria," or narrowly, as equivalent to "vicinity of Damascus" or "Damascus and environs" or "regions of Damascus."[27]

If read broadly, then *all* of Palestine would have been *excluded* from McMahon's pledge to the Arabs, because Palestine lies to the west of the *Vilayet* of Syria. However, reading "District" as synonymous with *Vilayet* ignores the geographic fact that there is nothing "lying to the west" of the *Vilayet* of Aleppo except water – the Mediterranean Sea. So the broad reading of "District" is somewhat problematic from that perspective.

On the other hand, a narrow reading of the word "District" would have meant Palestine was *included* in McMahon's pledge, as the area lying to the west of the immediate vicinity of Damascus, Homs, Hama, and Aleppo was

Lebanon and northern Syria, but *not* Palestine. The Arab side pursued this line of argument throughout the 1920s–1930s and beyond.

However, this narrow reading of the word "District" also creates a difficult legal problem for the Arab side. If we accept the Arab interpretation that McMahon meant to exclude all areas lying to the west of the immediate environs of the four towns, then the Lebanese-Syrian border would have ended up along the north-south line connecting Aleppo to Damascus, much further east than Syria's eventual border with Lebanon. Syria thus would have lost a large amount of its future territory; namely, all of modern Syria falling between the Aleppo to Damascus line on the east and the Lebanese border on the west. This would have created a true conundrum for the Arab side: either accept a much smaller Syria that included Palestine, or a much larger Syria that did not include Palestine.

Lord Frederic Maugham, the Lord Chancellor of England, highlighted this dilemma after reviewing the McMahon-Hussein correspondence more than two decades later:

> [T]he phrase 'districts of Damascus, etc.' would hardly have been desired by the Sharif to mean small areas immediately surrounding the towns in question ... since if this had been the case the territory in which the Arabs would have been denied independence would have been brought much further east than on a more liberal interpretation of the phrase. The non-Arab territory would in fact have reached eastwards almost to the outskirts of Damascus and the other towns, and have covered substantial portions of Transjordan and considerable sections of the Hejaz Railway.[28]

Second, neither McMahon's 24 October 1915 letter nor any of the other letters McMahon and Hussein wrote to each other, ever mention the words "Palestine" or "Jerusalem," thereby making it extremely difficult to ascribe a particular meaning to the letter based solely on the language contained in the letter itself.

Given the ambiguities in the 24 October 1915 letter, including the problems with both the broad and narrow readings of the word *Vilayet*, as well as the absence one way or the other of any specific reference to Palestine, the next step in the legal inquiry would be to ascertain the understanding and intent of both parties to the correspondence based on their contemporaneous and subsequent conduct.

Initial Arab Position: Palestine Excluded

Prior to 1921, the Arabs did not claim the McMahon pledge included Palestine. In fact, some historians argue the Arabs' statements and conduct showed they understood and *accepted* the exclusion of Palestine from the pledge.

For example, Hussein refused to condemn the Balfour Declaration for more than two years after it was issued, ignoring calls from Syrian notables to do so. Hussein even ordered his sons Abdullah and Feisal to calm their followers and allay their fears about the Balfour Declaration.[29] This conduct, argue the British and Jewish sides, demonstrates Hussein knew and understood Palestine was *not* included in McMahon's pledges.

In January 1918 Commander David Hogarth, Head of the Arab Bureau in Cairo, met with Hussein in Cairo, delivering what became known as the "Hogarth Message," stating in part:

> So far as Palestine is concerned we are determined that no people shall be subject to another, but ... In view of the fact that there are in Palestine shrines, Wakfs and Holy places, sacred in some cases to Moslems alone, to Jews alone, to Christians alone, and in others to two or all three, and inasmuch as these places are of interest to vast masses of people outside Palestine and Arabia, there must be a special regime to deal with these places approved of by the world ... As regards the Mosque of Omar it shall be considered as a Moslem concern alone and shall not be subjected directly or indirectly to any non-Moslem authority ... Since the Jewish opinion of the world is in favour of a return of Jews to Palestine and inasmuch as this opinion must remain a constant factor, and further as His Majesty's Government view with favour the realisation of this aspiration, His Majesty's Government are determined that in so far as is compatible with the freedom of the existing population both economic and political, no obstacle should be put in the way of the realisation of this ideal.[30]

Gilbert Clayton, a Cairo-based British General, cabled the Foreign Office to report on Hogarth's meeting with Hussein, reporting "Commander Hogarth has interviewed King of Hejaz and sounded him on the subject of the Zionist movement. King Hussein was evidently prepared for the development of Zionism and declared himself ready to welcome Jews to any Arab country."[31]

In March 1918, Hussein published an article in his official newspaper welcoming the Jewish return to Palestine. Clayton, however, reported to London that same month the Arabs were "nervous" about the Zionist movement, fearing "British authorities intend to set up a Jewish Government."[32] Those fears seemed to diminish by the end of the month, as William Ormsby-Gore[33] sent a report to Sykes on 31 March regarding Weizmann's visit to the region, noting Weizmann had met with local Arab leaders and "with great skill" had "said just what they wanted to hear," namely that Palestine would remain British.[34]

By the summer of 1918, the Arabs again raised concerns about Jewish land purchases in Palestine, reprising for the new British rulers many of the same arguments they had made in petitions to the Ottoman Sultan prior to the War. Some Arab landowners, however, only paid lip service to these concerns while secretly hoping to sell their own land to the Jewish newcomers and their financial supporters. As Ormsby-Gore related in a confidential report to London:

> There is of course a pretty wide-spread fear among the Moslem landowners that the progress of Zionism is inimical to their interests. Societies have been formed to organize resistance to the sale of land to the Jews, but it is a significant fact that one of the principal movers in this association paid a visit to the head office of the Zionist Bank in Jaffa in order to intimate that while he was openly advocating a policy of resistance to land sales, he was anxious to sell his land either to Baron Edmund de Rothschild or the Zionists as soon as transfers of land are permitted by the [British] Administration.[35]

More evidence supporting the claim that Feisal understood McMahon had excluded Palestine arose from an October 1918 discussion between Feisal and General Edmund Allenby. Feisal said he understood from Colonel Lawrence the Arabs were to have the whole of Syria, *including Lebanon but excluding Palestine.*[36]

In January 1919 Feisal seemed to confirm this understanding by signing an agreement with Chaim Weizmann, in which Feisal largely acceded to Zionist aims in Palestine on condition the Arabs obtained independence in Syria.[37] The Palestine Royal Commission many years later reflected on the Weizmann-Feisal Agreement as marking "the one brief moment in the whole story at which a genuine harmony was established between Arab and Jewish statesmanship."[38] In one of the many ironies characterizing the history of the period, Weizmann and the Jewish Agency later characterized the agreement with Feisal as a "treaty," just as Hussein and other Arab leaders would later describe McMahon's 24 October 1915 letter as a legally binding "treaty."[39]

Soon thereafter, Feisal told the Supreme Council at the Versailles Conference he was willing to leave out Palestine from the Arabs' request for independence, "for its universal character" and for the "mutual consideration of all parties concerned."[40] Feisal also expressed a willingness to accept a solution under which the Zionists would be allowed to pursue the establishment of a National Home in Palestine so long as Feisal achieved his aims in Syria.[41]

Furthermore, on 3 March 1919, while still at Versailles, Hussein (with help from Colonel Lawrence) signed a very conciliatory letter to Felix Frankfurter, proclaiming

> [w]e Arabs, especially the educated among us, look with deepest sympathy on the Zionist movement ... We will wish the Jews a hearty welcome home ... We are working together for a reformed and revised Near East, and our two movements complement one another.[42]

The authenticity of this letter became an important issue during the Grand Mufti's testimony before the Shaw Commission in 1929.

Kedourie (1976) identifies further evidence demonstrating Hussein understood Palestine was not included in the McMahon pledge. Hussein in 1918–1919 showed "lack of interest in Palestine ... lack of concern over the Balfour Declaration and Zionist aims;" instead, Hussein's top priority was to be recognized as the leader of the Arab race over his rival Ibn Saud.[43] Feisal wrote a letter to his father Hussein on 19 January 1918 describing the correspondence with McMahon as nothing more than a "preliminary and limited contract."[44]

Kedourie also cites Feisal's 27 December 1918 meeting with Edwin Montagu, then Secretary of State for India, as evidence the Arabs understood Palestine was not included in the McMahon Pledge. According to John Shuckburgh, a Colonial Office representative who prepared a memorandum of the meeting three days later, Feisal said "the Arabs recognize that many conflicting interests are centered in Palestine. They admit the moral claims of the Zionists. They regard the Jews as kinsmen whose just claims they will be glad to see satisfied."[45]

Less well known was a letter written in French from Feisal to Sir Herbert Samuel dated 1 December 1919 on the letterhead of the Hejaz Delegation to the Versailles Peace Conference. Feisal expressed solidarity with both Weizmann and Samuel in pursuit of the common Arab-Jewish cause:

> ... J'ai la ferme conviction que la confiance reciproque etablie entre nous et le parfait accord de notre point de vue qui a permis une parfait comprehension entre Dr. Weizman [sic] et moi, empecheront a l'avenir de areils malentendus et maintiendront entre nous cette harmonie si necessaire pour le success de notre cause commune.[46]

Finally, according to another historian, as late as Versailles, Hussein was "probably ... aware that the McMahon letters did not constitute a binding obligation on the part of the British."[47]

The weight of the evidence, therefore, suggests Hussein well understood McMahon's 24 October 1915 letter did not include Palestine within the pledged areas for future Arab independence.

Subsequent Arab Position: Palestine Included

Feisal's attitude, however, changed dramatically in mid-1920, soon after the French expelled him from Syria. Almost immediately Feisal turned his attention to Palestine, seizing on McMahon's correspondence with his father as having formed a legally binding "treaty," creating a legal basis for the Arabs to claim McMahon had promised them independence in Palestine.[48]

Moreover, the Arabs argued, because the McMahon-Hussein correspondence should be regarded as forming a binding treaty, Britain had a legal obligation to comply by ensuring Palestine became part of the areas designated for Arab independence.

But, according to the Arab argument, Britain violated the McMahon-Hussein "treaty" by promising Palestine to the Jews when it issued the Balfour Declaration two years later. Therefore, the Arabs argued that the Balfour Declaration was null and void as a matter of law:

> [T]he McMahon promises included Palestine and had the force of a treaty, [and] they inevitably utilized the argument that the Balfour Declaration was contrary to this treaty. And inasmuch as the "treaty" preceded the "Declaration" and since the "treaty" was made with a recognized monarch while the Declaration was given to an amorphous body lacking political form and juridical definition, the "treaty" was obviously to be preferred and the Declaration was void *ab initio*.[49]

The first time Feisal formally suggested Palestine was included in the McMahon pledge occurred during a meeting with R.C. Lindsay of the Foreign Office on 20 January 1921. Feisal claimed Palestine had been promised to the Arabs, because the language of the McMahon-Hussein correspondence never specifically mentioned or excluded Palestine. The relevant portions from McMahon's 24 October 1915 letter were read aloud in Arabic to Feisal. Lindsay noted Palestine *was* excluded because it lay to the west of the *Vilayet* of Damascus.[50]

Feisal responded by noting "if the word 'vilayet' was to be interpreted strictly as applicable to Damascus, the word must also be interpreted to mean 'vilayet' with regard to Homs and Hama, neither of which was or ever had been a vilayet."[51] Feisal demanded "these pledges now be fulfilled."[52] Lindsay replied with a veiled threat, noting Hussein's refusal to sign the Treaty of Versailles meant the British Government "could not possibly" recognize Hussein's "right to discuss the disposal of the areas liberated from the Turks."[53]

Feisal's assertion regarding the interplay between "District" and "*Vilayet*" represented the first in a long series of arguments underpinning the Arab legal interpretation of McMahon's 24 October 1915 letter as including Palestine in the pledge. The arguments formed the core of the Arab legal strategy to attack the subsequently issued Balfour Declaration as unlawful because it conflicted with McMahon's pre-existing, legally enforceable promise of Palestine to the Arabs. If the Balfour Declaration were rendered null and void, then all subsequent instruments incorporating the Balfour Declaration, including the relevant provisions of the San Remo Resolution, the Palestine Mandate, and even the 29 November 1947 United Nations Resolution 181 approving the partition of Palestine into Jewish and Arab states would also be null and void.

After Lindsay's threat, Feisal seemed to back away, saying

> he was quite prepared to accept that it had been the original intention of H.M.G. to exclude Palestine. He was merely acting in this respect in strict accordance with instructions received from his father [Hussein], the King of the Hejaz. The matter was then dropped.[54]

But the matter was not dropped for long, as the Arabs continued to press their new interpretation of the correspondence as promising Palestine to them. For example, at a high-level 28 March 1921 meeting at Government House in Jerusalem, then-Colonial Secretary Winston Churchill explained Britain's support for Arab nationalism to Feisal's brother Abdullah by "using the Sherifian family as a medium."[55] Churchill, however, noted there were "parts of the Arab world in which His Majesty's Government were not able to carry out this policy, owing to the decisions of the Allies and to promises made to third parties. These parts were Syria and Palestine."[56]

Abdullah acknowledged Britain was not free to act in Syria and "Western Palestine." But he demanded Churchill and High Commissioner Herbert Samuel disclose Britain's "true intentions" in Palestine, including whether Britain intended to establish a "Jewish Kingdom."[57] Abdullah wanted Palestine and Transjordan combined under the sovereignty of a single Emir, namely himself. At this point a clearly exasperated Churchill threatened Abdullah that Britain could "go in a different direction" and divide the Arab world into smaller pieces if Abdullah were uncooperative.[58]

Undaunted, the Arab side continued insisting Palestine was rightfully theirs. In a March 1922 letter from the Palestine Arab delegation to Churchill discussing the ongoing consultations between the British Government, the Zionist Organization, and the Palestinian Arabs regarding the governance system for the future British Mandate, the Arab delegation said they could not accept the creation of a Jewish National Home in Palestine:

> In 1915, before the Balfour Declaration was published, His Majesty's Government made a pledge to the Arabs in which it undertook to recognise the independence of those Arab States which had formerly belonged to Turkey. Palestine is one of those States as is clearly seen by reference to King Hussein's letter dated 14th July, 1915, in which the western boundary is denoted by the "Red Sea and Mediterranean." There can be no question that Palestine comes within these boundaries.[59]

Churchill responded to this argument in a 3 June 1922 official statement of British policy in Palestine, which became known as the "Churchill White Paper."[60] Commenting on the apparent ambiguity in McMahon's 24 October 1915 letter, Churchill insisted McMahon's 24 October 1915 letter excluded the Vilayet of Beirut, which encompassed the entire area of Palestine north of Jerusalem:

> [I]t is not the case, as has been represented by the Arab Delegation, that during the war His Majesty's Government gave an undertaking that an independent national government should at once be established in Palestine. This representation mainly rests upon a letter dated 24th October, 1915 from Sir Henry McMahon, then His Majesty's High Commissioner in Egypt, to the Sherif of Mecca, now King Hussein of the Kingdom of the Hejaz. That letter is quoted as conveying the promise to the Sherif of Mecca to recognize and support the independence of the Arabs within the territories proposed by him. But this promise was given subject to a reservation made in the same letter, which excluded from its scope, among other territories, the portions of Syria lying to the West of Damascus. This reservation has always been regarded by His Majesty's Government as covering the Vilayet of Beirut and the independent Sanjak of Jerusalem. The whole of Palestine west of Jordan was thus excluded from Sir H. McMahon's pledge.[61]

The Arab Delegation had previously replied to a draft of the Churchill White Paper with a more detailed legal argument about McMahon's 24 October 1915 letter. They noted the use of the word "District" in the English version of the letter, arguing McMahon must have intended the narrower geographic meaning of "district" rather than the broader meaning of *vilayet*, because it would have been superfluous to mention Homs and Hama in the same category as Aleppo and Damascus. Moreover, if McMahon meant to refer to the actual *Vilayet of Syria*, then he could have said so, as there was no such thing as a *Vilayet of Damascus*. Thus, the only logical reading of McMahon's letter was that Palestine was *included* in the pledge. The only area *excluded* was Lebanon, which lies directly to the west of the line running from Aleppo southward through Hama and Homs to Damascus.[62]

The Arabs continued to press this and other arguments of a more legal nature over the next few decades.[63] Those arguments have continued to this day, including:

First, the McMahon-Hussein correspondence had the legal status of a binding treaty, imposing a solemn legal obligation on Britain to comply.[64]

Second, Hussein had claimed all Arab lands, including by implication Palestine in his first letter to McMahon of 14 July 1915, and despite multiple opportunities to do so, McMahon never explicitly excluded Palestine (much less mentioned the word "Palestine") in *any* of the subsequent exchanges with Hussein.

Third, British legal precedents require the correspondence (especially the 24 October 1915 letter) to be construed based on the ordinary and plain meaning of the words used, thereby rendering irrelevant any consideration of intent, but if anyone's intent were deemed relevant it would be the British Government's and not McMahon's personal intent.

Fourth, the plain meaning and ordinary usage of the phrase "portions of Syria lying to the west of the Districts of Damascus, Homs, Hama, and Aleppo cannot be said to be purely Arab" could not reasonably be read as referring to or including Palestine.

Fifth, any construction of the correspondence that would lead to an absurd result would violate principles of British and International law. As the former Chief Justice of Palestine, Sir Michael McDonnell, would later say when the Arab side retained him in 1939 to review the McMahon-Hussein correspondence,

> [t]o say that when Sir Henry McMahon wrote of the 'district of Damascus' he meant the Ottoman Vilayet of Syria is exactly as though one should be asked to believe that a reference to the district of Maidstone meant the County of Kent.[65]

Sixth, the ordinary and plain meaning of "district" or *wilaya* was the "environs," "vicinity" or "regions" of each of the four named towns in McMahon's October 24, 1915 letter, and thus could not have compassed the larger geographic area of Palestine.

Seventh, excluding certain areas west of the four named towns "as not purely Arab" cannot logically have meant Palestine, which (except for Jerusalem) was predominantly Arab at the time.

Eighth, applying the general exception in favor of French interests may have made sense as to Lebanon but *not* as to Palestine. This was especially so because in June 1915, prior to the McMahon-Hussein correspondence, Lord Kitchener had recommended southern Syria (including Palestine) be *separated* from the area of French influence. Thus, by October 1915 Britain could *not* have intended the exception in favor of French interests be applied to Palestine.

Ninth, in any event, France subsequently renounced whatever interests it may have had in Palestine when it endorsed the Balfour Declaration and subsequently voted in favor of awarding the Mandate for Palestine to Great Britain.[66]

British Position: Ambiguous, but Palestine Excluded

The British government, initially adamant in its interpretation of McMahon's 24 October 1915 letter as excluding Palestine, eventually began to harbor certain doubts about the validity of that interpretation. One early skeptic was the Palin Commission, set up as a Military Court of Inquiry to examine the causes of the 1920 *Nebi Musa* riots in Jerusalem. According to the Commission:

> The tendency of the evidence is to show that in spite of the fact that nothing had been said about Palestine being included in the Hejaz Empire and the fact that the Balfour Declaration had been published in 1917, the early impression left upon the Arabs generally was that the British were going to set up an independent Arab State which would include Palestine.[67]

Another early skeptical British official was the famous historian Arnold Toynbee, then serving as a temporary office clerk in the Political Intelligence Department of the Foreign Office. Toynbee wrote two memoranda in the fall of 1918, arguing McMahon's 24 October 1915 letter did not exclude Palestine.[68]

Toynbee's early interpretation of the correspondence, however, represented a minority viewpoint within the British Government at that time. As noted, the Churchill White Paper, issued in July 1922, declared Britain's official position that McMahon's 24 October 1915 letter "excluded from its scope, among other territories, the portions of Syria lying to the West of Damascus. This reservation has always been regarded by His Majesty's Government as covering the Vilayet of Beirut and the independent Sanjak of Jerusalem."[69] Thus, according to Churchill and the British Government, *all* of Palestine was *excluded* from the McMahon pledge.[70]

The Churchill White Paper's reading of McMahon's 24 October 1915 letter was based on an examination of the Arabic version of the correspondence in 1920 by Major Hubert Young of the Foreign Office, who had previously served in the Arab Bureau in Cairo. According to Major Young, the Arabic word *Wilaya* meant the same thing as the Turkish word *Vilayet*. Although there was no such thing as the *Vilayet of Damascus*, Major Young, in a bit of linguistic gymnastics, argued that because Damascus was the capital of the *Vilayet of Syria*, and because Palestine lay to the west of the *Vilayet of Syria*, Palestine had been excluded from the McMahon pledge.[71]

Interestingly, the drafters of the Churchill White Paper chose not to rely on Major Young's stretched formulation, instead positioning the argument from another angle by focusing on the location of the *Vilayet* of Beirut as "a portion of Syria lying to the west of the district of Damascus." Because the *Vilayet* of Beirut encompassed a large portion of Palestine, McMahon's pledge therefore must be read as excluding *all* of Palestine, including the independent *Sanjak* of Jerusalem (which lay *southwest*, but not *due west* of the "District of Damascus"). Although this formulation was somewhat more plausible than Major Young's, it still failed to satisfy the Arab side, as they claimed it ignored the plain language of McMahon's 24 October 1915 letter.

The behind-the-scenes activity during the months preceding the issuance of the 1 July 1922 Churchill White Paper helps explain why the British

Government was so confident McMahon's 24 October 1915 letter excluded Palestine. The written exchanges between the Palestine Arab Delegation and the Colonial Office began on 21 February 1922 with a letter from the Arab Delegation to the Colonial Secretary, in which the Arabs claimed Palestine had been promised to them.[72] John Shuckburgh of the Colonial Office replied to the Arab Delegation on 1 March 1922, rejecting their claim.[73]

Nine days later, however, Shuckburgh met with McMahon to make sure the British Government stood on solid ground. Shuckburgh asked McMahon point-blank whether or not he had intended to include or exclude Palestine from his 24 October 1915 letter to Hussein. McMahon said his and the British Government's intent was to *exclude* Palestine from the areas pledged to the Arabs. Shuckburgh asked McMahon to write a private letter so confirming. McMahon obliged and sent the following letter to Shuckburgh on 12 March 1922:

> My dear Shuckburgh;
>
> With reference to our conversation on Friday (10th), I write you these few lines to place on record the fact that in my letter of the 24th October 1915 to the Sherif of Mecca, it was my intention to exclude Palestine from independent Arabia, and I hoped that I had so worded the letter as to make this sufficiently clear for all practical purposes.
>
> My reasons for restricting myself to specific mention of Damascus, Hama, Homs and Aleppo is that connection in my letter were (1) that these were places to which the Arabs attached vital importance and (2) that there was no place I could think of at the time of sufficient importance for purposes of definition further South of the above.
>
> It was as fully my intention to exclude Palestine as it was to exclude the more Northern coastal tract of Syria.
>
> I did not make use of the Jordan to define the limits of the Southern area, because I thought it might possible [sic] be considered desirable at some later stage of negotiations to endeavor to find some more suitable frontier line east of the Jordan and between that river and the Hejaz Railway. At that moment moreover very detailed definitions did not seem called for.
>
> I may mention that I have no recollection of ever having anything from the Sherif of Mecca, by letter or message, to make me suppose that he did not also understand Palestine to be excluded from independent Arabia.
>
> I trust that I have made my intention clear.
>
> Yours sincerely,
>
> (Signed) A. Henry McMahon[74]

Shuckburgh forwarded McMahon's letter the following day to Eric Forbes Adam, First Secretary at the Foreign Office. Shuckburgh mentioned in his cover note "the vexed question whether Palestine was or was not excluded from the scope of the McMahon pledge." Noting McMahon was "quite clear on the point that the intention was to exclude Palestine," Shuckburgh expressed hope the issue would not be raised, "but it is just as well that we should have all the evidence at our disposal in case we are definitely challenged on the subject."[75]

As it happened, the Arab Delegation raised the McMahon-Hussein correspondence in their very next letter to the Colonial Office only three days later, on 16 March 1922,[76] leading to the Government's response in the 1 July 1922 Churchill White Paper. The White Paper, however, made no mention of McMahon's 12 March 1922 letter to Shuckburgh, which remained confidential until McMahon himself went public 15 years later.

But the White Paper was not the end of the McMahon-Hussein story from the British perspective. On 27 March 1923, former Foreign Secretary Grey (now Lord Falladon) commented in the House of Lords that Britain had made inconsistent promises to the Jews and Arabs during the War.[77] Sir Herbert Samuel, then serving as the High Commissioner in Palestine, asked General Gilbert Clayton, who had served alongside McMahon in Cairo during the McMahon-Hussein correspondence, whether he could "throw any light" on the issue. Clayton responded with a memorandum to Samuel dated 12 April 1923.

The Clayton Memorandum to Samuel provides additional evidence supporting the British legal interpretation that McMahon's 24 October 1915 letter excluded Palestine from the areas pledged to the Arabs. Clayton said he was in daily contact with McMahon during their service together in Cairo. Clayton said he wrote the preliminary drafts of McMahon's letters to Hussein. "I can bear out the statement," said Clayton in his Memorandum to Samuel,

> that it was never the intention that Palestine should be included in the general pledge given to the Sherif; the introductory words of Sir Henry's letter were thought at the time – perhaps erroneously – clearly to cover that point. It was, I think, obvious that the peculiar interests involved in Palestine precluded any definite pledges in regard to its future at so early a stage.[78]

Several years later, on 24 October 1930, W.J. Childs, a temporary clerk at the Foreign Office, wrote a lengthy analysis described as "the best and most comprehensive historical survey of the McMahon-Hussein correspondence to be produced by a British official."[79] Childs concluded that McMahon's 24 October 1915 letter had excluded Palestine.

First, Childs noted the reason why McMahon used the word "districts" in his letter to the Sherif was because Farouki himself had used the *same* word during his meeting with McMahon. Second, the word "district" should properly have been understood as referring to a broad "administrative area," also based on language Farouki used with McMahon in their Cairo meeting. Thus, Childs argued, it was "beyond question" and "perfectly clear" Farouki intended the word "districts" to convey the broader geographic equivalent of Vilayets.[80] Third, Childs concluded Palestine had been excluded from the pledge based on both the specific geographic reservation and especially the general reservation in favor of France.[81]

Nearly three months before Childs wrote his memo, Dr. Drummond Shiels, the Undersecretary of State for the Colonies, reiterated the Government's position in a speech to the House of Commons that Palestine was excluded from Britain's wartime promise to Hussein:

> There are not sufficient grounds for holding that by this correspondence His Majesty's Government intended to pledge themselves, or did, in fact, pledge themselves, to the inclusion of Palestine in the projected Arab State. Sir H. McMahon has himself denied that this was his intention. The ambiguous and inconclusive nature of the correspondence may well, however, have left an impression among those who were aware of the correspondence that His Majesty's Government had such an intention.[82]

The Peel Commission and the McMahon-Hussein Correspondence

Former Palestine High Commissioner Sir Herbert Samuel (now Viscount Samuel), took an active behind-the-scenes role regarding the McMahon-Hussein correspondence during the work of the Palestine Royal Commission in 1936-1937. On 3 August 1936, less than one week after the members of the Peel Commission had been named, Samuel wrote to Lord Peel regarding the McMahon-Hussein correspondence, urging "it is of the first importance that this issue should be finally cleared up."

Samuel enclosed a copy of the April 1923 Clayton Memorandum (see above), in which Clayton confirmed he had drafted McMahon's letters to Sherif Hussein, and therefore he could say with confidence those letters were never intended to include Palestine in the areas pledged for future Arab independence.[83]

Samuel also enclosed a copy of Feisal's 10 December 1919 letter to Samuel, in which Feisal had expressed sympathy for the Zionist cause.[84] Samuel sent the originals of both documents to the Peel Commission's Secretary, John M. Martin, on 7 September 1936.[85]

Samuel eventually testified in secret before the Commission on 5 March 1937. Samuel made the following comments in response to a question about the McMahon-Hussein correspondence:

> The Arabs feel that they have a grievance because they took part in the War, not particularly the Palestinian Arabs, but the Arab World generally, on the side of the Allies, and now they have been let down, because

> the Balfour Declaration cut across the McMahon promise. Well, I do not think that is true and if the Commission did feel it right to clear up this matter it would be, in my judgement, a useful service.[86]

Samuel then discussed his 3 August 1936 letter to Lord Peel, and read aloud the entire text of Clayton's 12 April 1923 memorandum. Samuel described Clayton's memorandum as "a document of importance."[87] Samuel said the reason for the "rather indirect terms" in McMahon's 24 October 1915 letter was "on account of the feelings of the French and the fact that the situation was not cleared up *vis a vis* the French, that it was not desirable in so many words to say 'Palestine west of the Jordan' and, therefore, they put it 'Districts west of the Damascus Jerusalem line.'"[88]

This explanation did not seem to satisfy the Commission. Samuel tried to convince them the McMahon letter made sense in the context of how Palestine was eventually divided along the Jordan River into two separate halves:

> Now Palestine east of the Jordan was clearly within the McMahon pledge and when the Jews complain, as they do complain, that I was a party to excluding Trans-Jordan form the scope of the Balfour Declaration, my reason was solely that there was a pledge and it seemed to me as definite a pledge on one side as the Balfour Declaration was on the other side; and if the Jews claim that Britain is bound, as I think she is bound, to carry out the Balfour Declaration, they must admit that she is equally bound to carry out the McMahon pledge which applies to Trans-Jordan.[89]

But this still did not satisfy the Commission:

Sir Laurie Hammond: In your opinion, it was impossible for McMahon to have put it down in black and white that Palestine was excluded? It strikes the average man as being unfortunate?

A: I do not know whether it was impossible or not, but he did not put it and apparently for those reasons, that the situation was so very delicate. It was previous to the Sykes-Picot Agreement, which itself was afterwards disallowed and never ratified, and I imagine that must have been the reason, but you see what Sir Gilbert Clayton says in his note.

Sir Harold Morris: From the lawyer's point of view, it is not the intention of the writer; it is what the words actually mean; and you have always to look at it from the point of view of the recipient, and the recipients might well have been misled?

A: I do not think so, because I think King Hussein and his sons quite clearly understood the position ...

Q: The difficulty in that is this. What was the position they understood? What did they think was going to happen in Palestine?

A: They knew perfectly well that it was not to be included in the Arab domain. ...

Chairman: I can only say it is unfortunate, is it not, that in the McMahon statement [July 1922 letter to Shuckburgh] he says it was never the intention; he does not argue that the words mean what he says; he merely argues the intention, and exactly the same thing is said by Sir Gilbert Clayton ...

A: If I may say so, Sir Gilbert Clayton does not say that it was merely regarded, he says the introductory words of Sir Henry's letter 'were thought at the time, perhaps erroneously, clearly to cover that point.'

Q: If you read the statement itself, there is ambiguity. There is no doubt about that?

A: Not if you take map, a Turkish map, and look at the districts as they were then ...[90]

Samuel seemed determined, from the moment the Royal Commission was formed, to advocate against the Arab interpretation of the McMahon-Hussein correspondence. Whether he was motivated as a member of the House of Lords by the desire to uphold British honor, or as a Jew to help the Zionist cause is unclear. He remains something of an enigma.

On 21 July 1937 the Colonial Secretary, William Ormsby-Gore, who had served with McMahon in Cairo during World War I, made the following statement in the House of Commons:

> I served in 1916 in the Arab Bureau in Cairo on Sir Henry McMahon's staff, and I wish myself to testify to the fact that it never was in the mind of anyone on that staff that Palestine west of the Jordan was in the area within which the British Government then undertook to further the cause of Arab independence.[91]

Two days later, on 23 July 1937, the *Times of London* published a letter to the editor from McMahon himself.[92] McMahon's letter to the *Times* reiterated the statements he made in his 12 March 1922 letter to Shuckburgh:

> Sir,
>
> Many references have been made in the Palestine Royal Commission [Peel Commission] Report and in the course of the recent debates in both Houses of Parliament to the 'McMahon Pledge,' especially to that portion of the pledge which concerns Palestine and of which one interpretation has been claimed by the Jews and another by the Arabs.
>
> It has been suggested to me that continued silence on the part of the giver of the pledge may itself be misunderstood.
>
> I feel, therefore, called upon to make some statement on the subject, but I will confine myself in doing so to the point now at issue – i.e., whether that portion of Syria now known as Palestine was or was not intended to be included in the territories in which the independence of the Arabs was guaranteed by my pledge.
>
> I feel it is my duty to state, and I do so definitely and emphatically, that it was not intended by me in giving this pledge to King Hussein to include Palestine in the area in which Arab independence was promised.
>
> I also had every reason to believe at the time that the fact that Palestine was not included in my pledge was well understood by King Hussein.
>
> Yours faithfully,
>
> A. Henry McMahon

Ormsby-Gore sent a private letter to McMahon that same day, expressing "cordial thanks" for McMahon's letter to the *Times*. "This authoritative statement by the giver of the famous 'Pledge' to King Hussein," wrote Ormsby-Gore,

> is of great value to the Government, and particularly to myself, corroborating as it does all I said in the House on Wednesday, as to the intention to exclude the country now known as Palestine from the area in which Arab independance [sic] was to be guaranteed.[93]

At least one British official, however, disapproved of McMahon's letter to the *Times*. George W. Rendell, the Head of the Eastern Department of the Foreign Office, minuted his reaction three days later:

> This is rather a remarkable letter, and has already been freely quoted. My own impression from reading the [McMahon-Hussein] correspondence has always been that it is stretching the interpretation of our *caveat* to the breaking point to say that we definitely did not include Palestine, and the short answer is that if we did not want to include Palestine we might have said so in terms, instead of referring vaguely to areas west of Damascus and to extremely shadowy arrangements with the French, which in any case ceased to be operative shortly afterwards.[94]

The London Conferences and the McMahon-Hussein Correspondence

In January 1939, the Foreign Office prepared a Secret Memorandum for the Secretary of State for Foreign Affairs, who circulated it among the British Cabinet, entitled "The Juridical Basis of the Arab Claim to Palestine." The Memorandum was prepared to assist the British side in the upcoming parallel conferences at St. James's Palace with Arab and Jewish representatives over Palestine, as it was anticipated the Arabs would again raise the McMahon-Hussein correspondence.[95]

The Memorandum describes certain "weak points" in the British legal case for defending its interpretation of the word "District" in McMahon's October 24, 1915. The Memorandum noted "[i]t may be possible to produce arguments designed to explain away some of these difficulties individually ... but it is hardly possible to explain them away collectively."[96]

The Memorandum also criticized the general reservation in favor of French interests as having "little, if any validity," given Britain felt unconstrained regarding French interests when it issued the Balfour Declaration.[97] The Memorandum summed up by noting "there are points of serious weakness in the government's case ... the correspondence lacks that self-evident and decisive clarity which ought to form the basis of international acts."[98]

"The best that can be done," according to the Memorandum, would be for the government to argue the ambiguous language in McMahon's 24 October 1915 letter entitled the government to rely on its *own* intentions at the time, while acknowledging McMahon's own statements in his letters to Shuckburgh and to the *Times* are "not evidence."[99]

Lacy Baggallay of the Foreign Office sent the Memorandum to H.F. Downie at the Colonial Office for his review before the upcoming conference with the Arabs to discuss the McMahon-Hussein correspondence. Baggallay commented in his cover letter, "I must say that, after going into the whole question of the McMahon-Hussein correspondence again, our position in regard to this correspondence seems to me even weaker than it did before!"[100]

Downie, however, felt no need to reconsider the Government's position:

> The idea that the fundamental issue whether or not Palestine is to be turned into an Arab state can be decided (or even seriously affected by) a legal interpretation of the McMahon correspondence is too ridiculous to need refutation ... Surely we need only concern ourselves with refuting the offensive insinuation (which constitutes the sting of the Arab case) that HMG has been guilty of bad faith in the matter. On this point there is no reason why we should condescend to argument with the Arabs. We have always maintained that our intention was to exclude Palestine from the pledges given to the Sharif.[101]

Several days later, Baggallay and Beckett from the Foreign Office met with the Lord Chancellor (Lord Frederic Maugham) to discuss the Memorandum. The Lord Chancellor had seen the Memorandum and requested the meeting to express his view that "the memorandum did not state the [legal] case for His Majesty's government as well as it could be stated."[102] Regarding the specific reservation in McMahon's 24 October 1915 letter, the Lord Chancellor noted that while McMahon's intent might not be "strictly relevant to any construction of the letter, ... it was permissible to take into account the whole of the surrounding circumstances when attempting to get at the true meaning of the words used."[103]

According to the Lord Chancellor, those circumstances included the importance to Britain and France of the strategically vital ports of Acre, Haifa, and Jaffa and the unlikelihood that McMahon would have promised those ports to Hussein. The Lord Chancellor also viewed as relevant the even greater unlikelihood that McMahon would have ceded the Holy Sites throughout Palestine to solely Muslim control.

The Lord Chancellor further argued the general reservation in favor of French interests supported the Government's position that Palestine had been excluded from the pledge, and "if the Sherif of Mecca was unaware of the fact that the claims of France extended to Palestine at that time, the onus lay on him, to make sure of the extent of those claims."[104]

As noted above, in early February 1939 the British Government convened parallel conferences at St. James's Palace in London with separate Arab and Jewish delegations to discuss the future of Palestine.

The British delegation met jointly with the Palestinian Arabs and the representatives of the Arab States in plenary sessions from early February through mid-March. The British and Palestinian Arab delegations also formed a smaller, joint committee to meet separately to discuss their differing interpretations of the McMahon-Hussein correspondence.

The British and Arab delegations commenced their separate meetings on 9 February 1939. Jamal Husseini, the lead delegate for the Palestinian Arabs, read an opening statement.[105] The statement had been typewritten on the letterhead of the Egyptian Embassy in London and signed by both Husseini and George Antonius.[106]

Husseini's opening statement was laced with the longstanding Palestinian Arab legal framing and legal narrative. He began by arguing the Palestinian Arab case was based on "self-evident justice." He then took aim at the Balfour Declaration and the Mandate, arguing both were invalid because they conflicted with Britain's prior pledge of Palestine to the Arabs in the McMahon-Hussein correspondence. Husseini based his argument on legal concepts, in what the *Times* would characterize as "an appeal for justice"[107]:

> The Arabs have never recognised and never will recognise the Balfour Declaration or the Mandate. The first contained a promise which Great

> Britain was not entitled to make without Arab consent and which was, in any case, invalid, *since it conflicted with a previous and binding British pledge*. The second is an illegal document. The terms of the Mandate which could only have derived their sanction from the Covenant of the League of Nations are demonstrably in conflict with the letter and spirit of the relevant article (namely Article XXII) of the Covenant. The Palestine Arab delegation are prepared to present an argument to prove conclusively the invalidity of the Balfour Declaration and the basic illegality of the Mandate. They consider that the measures taken in virtue of the provisions of the Mandate, such as facilities given Jews to enter Palestine, acquire land, and enjoy other exceptional privileges ... must be regarded as null and void and deserving, on legal as well as on moral and political grounds, to be abrogated.[108]

At the next meeting, on 11 February 1939, Husseini again addressed the McMahon-Hussein correspondence in legal terms, noting "a question of contract was at issue, and ... such a question could not be discussed on the basis of the intention of the parties, but the text of the documents."[109]

On 13 February Iraqi Prime Minister Nuri al-Said discussed the McMahon-Hussein correspondence, invoking many of the legal arguments the Arabs had been making for the past nearly 20 years. For example, Nuri argued, in decidedly legal terms, that McMahon had been communicating on behalf of the British Government, and therefore his explanation years later regarding his personal intent was irrelevant:

> Sir Henry McMahon was therefore only an instrument in the matter and his personal opinion at a later date was not relevant to the argument. When a dispute between parties over the interpretation of documents arose in an English court, it was the custom to take the grammatical and literal sense of the words as binding, and intentions were not taken into account unless it was evident that at the time both parties had been using certain words in a special sense.[110]

Nuri further argued the Balfour Declaration had caught the Arabs by surprise, coming as it did while the war against Turkey was still underway. The Arabs sought reassurances from the British Government, which they received from Commander Hogarth in his January 1918 message to the Sherif Hussein. The Hogarth Message, according to Nuri, had clarified the "National Home" Britain promised the Jews in the Balfour Declaration would amount to nothing more than a Jewish "spiritual or cultural center" in Palestine, without prejudice to Palestinian Arab political and economic rights in Palestine.[111] Thus, Nuri argued, Britain undertook legal obligations regarding future sovereignty in Palestine solely to the Arabs, and not the Jews.

On 14 February Prince (and future King) Faisal of Saudi Arabia made a lengthy legal argument on behalf of the Palestinian Arab cause. Faisal began by asserting the familiar Arab legal argument that the McMahon-Hussein correspondence had promised independence to the Arabs of Palestine. Faisal argued the international community had supported that view when it enacted Article 22 of the Covenant of the League of Nations, promising independence for *all* former Ottoman-ruled Arab lands.[112]

Faisal then attacked the legality of the Balfour Declaration:

> The Balfour Declaration was illegal on four grounds; first, because it was subsequent to the undertaking given to the Arabs which, therefore, had the prior right in the event of conflict; secondly, because it was made without consultation with the Arabs; thirdly, because it was inconsistent with Article 22 of the Covenant; ... and fourthly, because it was inconsistent with international law and morality.[113]

On 15 February the British and Arab delegations convened for their sixth formal meeting. The meeting was dominated by the discussion of the McMahon-Hussein correspondence, including the Arab view that the dispute regarding the proper interpretation of the correspondence required "a careful legal examination."[114] The Prince of Yemen, for example, emphasized the legal nature of the dispute regarding the correspondence:

> His Royal Highness said there should be no difference of opinion among those who wanted to take a fair view, and certainly among scholars, that the only method of interpreting legal documents was to bring out the clarity of the meaning of the words in their ordinary and every day sense.[115]

The Prince suggested the matter of the McMahon-Hussein correspondence be referred to a sub-committee comprised of British and Palestinian Arab representatives and legal experts, as well as representatives from the surrounding Arab States. The subcommittee, later renamed the Joint Committee, would submit its report to the entire British-Arab conference for approval. MacDonald agreed with the suggestion, and the formation of the Joint Committee was approved.[116]

The Joint Committee met four times in London between 23 February and 16 March 1939. The Joint Committee considered the longstanding Arab legal arguments regarding the McMahon-Hussein correspondence and the British responses to those arguments.[117]

The Arab members of the Joint Committee included the famed Palestinian lawyer, Auni Bey Abdul Hadi, who had represented the Arab side before the Shaw, Lofgren, and Peel Commissions. Sir Michael McDonnell, the former Chief Justice of Palestine, served as legal adviser to the Arab members of the Joint Committee and participated actively as their advocate during the Committee's discussions.

The British members were the Lord Chancellor (who acted as overall Chair of the Joint Committee), Sir Grattan Bushe, the Legal Adviser to the Colonial Office, and Lacy Baggallay of the Foreign Office. The Lord Chancellor announced at the Joint Committee's first meeting that

> [H]e was not present in any judicial capacity and that he made no claim to decide, as a judge, whether the views of His Majesty's Government in the United Kingdom upon the questions at issue, or the views of the Arabs, were right: he was present as the representative of His Majesty's Government only, with the sole function of expounding and advocating their views upon these questions.[118]

The Joint Committee considered various new legal arguments the Arab side had not previously offered during the various legal proceedings and commissions of inquiry that had convened during the Mandate years. The most important of those arguments involved the meaning of the so-called "Hogarth Message" of 4 January 1918, delivered to the Sherif Hussein two months after the Balfour Declaration. George Antonius, one of the Arab members of the Joint Committee, disclosed the existence of the Hogarth Message in his book *The Arab Awakening*, published only a few months prior to the start of the London Conferences.[119]

According to Antonius, the Sherif Hussein was "greatly disturbed" by the 2 November 1917 Balfour Declaration, and requested an explanation, lest he change his mind about continuing to support the British against Turkey during World War I. The British Government dispatched Commander David George Hogarth to Jeddah to meet with Hussein during the first week of January, 1918. Hogarth did not deliver anything in writing to Hussein. But according to Antonius, Hussein's contemporaneous notes reveal Hogarth, acting on instructions from London, gave Hussein an "explicit assurance that 'Jewish settlement in Palestine would only be allowed in so far as would be consistent with the *political* and economic freedom of the Arab population.'"[120]

Antonius argued the wording of the Hogarth Message, especially the phrase "*political* and economic freedom," should be viewed as a "fundamental departure from the text of the Balfour Declaration."[121] According the Antonius, the Hogarth Message *expanded* the Balfour Declaration's promise to the Arabs to protect the *civil* and religious rights of existing non-Jewish communities in Palestine, and simultaneously *narrowed* the scope of the Declaration's promise to the Jewish people of a National Home in Palestine. Hogarth's use of the broader term "political," according to Antonius, meant Britain *never* intended the Balfour Declaration to permit the Jews to become the majority population in Palestine or to achieve Jewish statehood in *any* portion of Palestine.[122]

In the eyes of the Arab advocates, the Hogarth Message represented the smoking gun the Palestinian Arabs had long sought. For them, it meant game, set, and match.

Subsequent commentators, however, have vigorously disputed Antonius' reliance on the Hogarth Message as reliable evidence of British intent regarding the Balfour Declaration. One historian has assailed Antonius' account as having "no basis in fact" and "worthless," noting the drafters of the Hogarth Message intended it to serve as "nothing more than a reiteration of the Balfour Declaration."[123]

Another commentator, relying on Hogarth's own contemporaneous notes and correspondence, argued the phrase "in so far as is compatible with the political and economic freedom of the Arab population" was *not* intended to concede *any* claims of Arab sovereignty over Palestine, and at most should be understood as referring *only* to local self-government.[124] Even more significantly, Hogarth reported to London that Hussein raised *no* objections to the Balfour Declaration.[125]

But one passage from Hogarth's subsequent notes of his meeting with the Sherif tends to support the Palestinian Arab interpretation of the Hogarth message:

> The King would not accept an independent Jew State in Palestine, *nor was I instructed to warn him that such a state was contemplated by Great Britain.* He probably knows little or nothing of the actual or possible economy of Palestine and his ready assent to Jewish settlement there is not worth very much. But I think he appreciates the financial advantage of Arab co-operation with the Jews.[126]

The British Government was aware of the significance of this phrase in Hogarth's note, and decided not to publish it when it released the text of the Hogarth message as an Appendix to the Joint Committee's report. Baggallay minuted the phrase would be "rather damaging" if made public.[127] Both Baxter and Butler of the Foreign Office agreed with Baggallay, and the decision was made to keep Hogarth's notes concealed from public view.[128]

The Hogarth Message made a big impact on Lord Maugham, who told the Cabinet in early March:

> [H]aving made a careful study of the pledges and undertakings given at various dates, in particular the statement made by Commander Hogarth to the Sherif of Mecca as to the meaning of the Balfour Declaration, he [the Lord

> Chancellor] felt satisfied that the honour of this country demanded some such limitation of Jewish immigration as the Colonial Secretary now proposed.[129]

The Hogarth Message was not the only piece of evidence brought before the Joint Committee. Other evidence tended to support the British claim that the Sherif understood that McMahon had not included Palestine in his pledge.

For example, another first-hand recollection, made public only four days before the Joint Committee's first meeting, came from Colonel C.E. Vickery, who served as the British Agent at Jeddah to the Sherif Hussein (by this time King of the Hedjaz) from 1919 to 1920. Vickery described a meeting with King Hussein in 1920, during which they discussed McMahon's 24 October 1915 letter. According to Vickery:

> I read the letter through very slowly; it was not written in very scholarly Arabic and had no English translation in the margin, and it was quite evident that Palestine was not included in the proposals to the King. I can say most definitely that the whole of the King's demands were centered round Syria, and only round Syria. Time after time he referred to that vineyard, to the exclusion of any other claim of interest. He stated most emphatically that he did not concern himself at all with Palestine, and had no desire to have suzerainty over it for himself or for his successors.[130]

The most important piece of first-hand evidence came from McMahon himself, who went public with his version of the events in a July 1937 letter to the *Times*, published several days after the release of the Palestine Royal Commission (Peel Commission) Report. As noted earlier, Iraqi Prime Minister Nuri al-Said had already argued prior to the formation of the Joint Committee that McMahon's intent carried no legal weight in construing the meaning of his letters to the Sherif.[131] But McMahon's letter to the *Times* addresses not just his own intent, but also the Sherif's understanding of McMahon's intent:

> Sir,
>
> Many references have been made in the Palestine Royal Commission [Peel Commission] Report and in the course of the recent debates in both Houses of Parliament to the 'McMahon Pledge,' especially to that portion of the pledge which concerns Palestine and of which one interpretation has been claimed by the Jews and another by the Arabs.
>
> It has been suggested to me that continued silence on the part of the giver of the pledge may itself be misunderstood.
>
> I feel, therefore, called upon to make some statement on the subject, but I will confine myself in doing so to the point now at issue – i.e., whether

> that portion of Syria now known as Palestine was or was not intended to be included in the territories in which the independence of the Arabs was guaranteed by my pledge.
>
> I feel it is my duty to state, and I do so definitely and emphatically, that it was not intended by me in giving this pledge to King Hussein to include Palestine in the area in which Arab independence was promised.
>
> I also had every reason to believe at the time that the fact that Palestine was not included in my pledge was well understood by King Hussein.
>
> Yours faithfully,
>
> A. Henry McMahon[132]

Faced with conflicting evidence, the British side decided to agree with the Arab members of the Joint Committee that the Sherif intended to *include* Palestine in his original letter to McMahon. However, the British side stood behind McMahon and his July 1937 explanation of *his* intent to *exclude* Palestine from the areas earmarked for Arab independence:

> The United Kingdom representatives ... maintain that on a proper construction of the Correspondence Palestine was in fact excluded. But they agree that the language in which its exclusion was expressed was not so specific and unmistakable as it was thought to be at the time.[133]

Despite the British-Arab disagreement regarding the meaning of McMahon's October 24, 1915 letter to the Sherif, the British side agreed to the following language in the Joint Committee's final report, aligning with the Arab side in declaring:

> In the opinion of the Committee it is, however, evident ... that His Majesty's Government were not free to dispose of Palestine without regard to the wishes and interests of the inhabitants of Palestine, and that these statements must all be taken into account in any attempt to estimate the responsibilities which – upon any interpretation of the Correspondence – His Majesty's Government have incurred towards those inhabitants as a result of the Correspondence.[134]

The Palestinian Arabs, thanks to Antonius' work in unearthing the Hogarth Message, had achieved a huge victory. The British, who for the past two decades had rejected *all* Arab claims regarding the McMahon-Hussein correspondence, now agreed the Arab claims had "greater force than has appeared hitherto,"[135] requiring Britain to take those claims into consideration as it formulated a new policy for Palestine. Given the British had already decided to take a new direction in Palestine even before the London Conferences convened, the Joint Committee's work provided additional cover for Britain's dramatic policy change and abandonment of its support for Zionism.

The Jewish Agency, excluded from the Joint Committee and suspicious of its activity, wrote to MacDonald on 28 March, offering its own interpretation of the McMahon-Hussein correspondence. The Jewish Agency argued the correspondence did not promise Palestine to the Arabs, and complained the Jews had not been included on the Joint Committee. The letter concluded with a largely legal point; namely, that the Jewish people held an "inalienable right" to reconstitute their home in Palestine, based on the terms of the Balfour Declaration and the Mandate.[136]

The Colonial Office rejected the Jewish Agency's letter in an internal memorandum explaining the Jewish side lacked standing to intervene in the debate regarding the McMahon-Hussein controversy, which involved purely British and Arab interests.[137]

The British Government reiterated the Joint Committee's findings in the White Paper, published two months later:

> In the recent discussions the Arab delegations have repeated the contention that Palestine was included within the area in which Sir Henry McMahon, on behalf of the British Government, in October, 1915, undertook to recognise and support Arab independence. The validity of this claim, based on the terms of the correspondence which passed between Sir Henry McMahon and the Sharif of Mecca, was thoroughly and carefully investigated by the British and Arab representatives during the recent conferences in London. Their report, which has been published, states that both the Arab and the British representatives endeavoured to understand the point of view of the other party but that they were unable to reach agreement upon an interpretation of the correspondence ... His Majesty's Government regret the misunderstandings which have arisen as regards some of the phrases used. For their part they can only adhere, for the reasons given by their representatives in the Report, to the view that the whole of Palestine west of Jordan was excluded from Sir Henry McMahon's pledge, and they therefore cannot agree that the McMahon correspondence forms a just basis for the claim that Palestine should be converted into an Arab State.[138]

Implications for the Palestinian Legal Case Today

The weight of the evidence demonstrates the McMahon-Hussein correspondence excluded Palestine from the boundaries of the post-war Arab state. While the 24 October 1915 letter could and should have been drafted with more precision, there is no question the British Government (and McMahon) intended, and Hussein understood, that Palestine had been excluded.

Accordingly, modern Palestinian claims to the West Bank, Gaza Strip, or any other portion of Palestine find no support in the McMahon-Hussein correspondence. Nor are Palestinian Arab attempts to characterize the correspondence as forming a "treaty" persuasive. Treaties at that time could only be formed between *states*. As of October 1915 the Arabs had no state in the areas still under Turkish rule. The correspondence itself discussed the formation of an Arab state in the future. But at that time Hussein was not the ruler of a sovereign state capable of entering into treaty relations.[139] Thus, the correspondence cannot be characterized as a "treaty" under international law.

But if one accepts the Arab view that a treaty nonetheless was formed, then it still becomes necessary to interpret the treaty's meaning. Given the ambiguous language of the McMahon-Hussein correspondence, the international law of treaty interpretation provides a useful framework for assessing the validity of the Arab and British positions regarding whether McMahon's and the British Government's intent was relevant.

Article 31 of the Vienna Convention on the Law of Treaties provides, "A treaty shall be interpreted in good faith in accordance with the *ordinary meaning to be given to the terms* of the treaty in their context and *in the light of its object and purpose*." Article 31 further states, "A special meaning shall be given to a term if it is established that the parties so intended."[140]

Article 32 of the Vienna Convention permits resort to "supplementary means of interpretation" to determine the meaning of a treaty, including the circumstances of the Treaty's conclusion, to avoid a result which is "ambiguous or obscure" or "manifestly absurd or unreasonable."[141]

The Vienna Convention is based on customary international law, requiring treaties to be interpreted "according to their reasonable, in contradistinction to their literal, sense." In the event of ambiguity,

> [i]f two meanings of a provision are admissible according to the text of a treaty, such meaning is to prevail as the party imposing the stipulation knew at the time to be the meaning preferred by the party accepting it,

and "if two meanings of a provision are admissible, that which is least to the advantage of the party for whose benefit the provision was intended in the treaty should be preferred."[142]

In his advocacy on behalf of the Arab side to the Joint Arab-British Committee in 1939, Sir Michael McDonnell, the former Chief Justice of Palestine, argued British legal precedents and British law required the McMahon-Hussein correspondence be interpreted by reference to what he described as the clear and unambiguous language of the correspondence, without regard to McMahon's or the British Government's intent.[143] But customary international law and the Vienna Convention take a somewhat broader view, emphasizing both the ordinary meaning of the language as well as the object and purpose of the document, which may need to be interpreted in light of what the parties intended.

The Permanent Court of Arbitration, adjudicating a dispute between France and the Netherlands, noted that recourse to external evidence may be necessary in cases where the text of an international instrument may be unclear:

> In so far as the text is not sufficiently clear, it is allowable to have recourse to the intention of the parties concerned. If, in this case, the intentions are clear and unanimous, they must prevail over every other possible interpretation. If, on the contrary, they diverge or are not clear, that meaning must be sought which, within the context … best gives either a reasonable solution of the controversy, or the impression which the offer of the party which took the initiative must reasonably and in good faith have made on the mind of the other party.[144]

Palestinian advocates have argued for the last century that based on the above legal principles, and whether British or international law were applied, the phrase "lying to the west of the Districts of Damascus, Homs, Hama, and Aleppo" was *not* ambiguous and should be interpreted literally to mean *only* Lebanon, but *not* Palestine was excluded from the pledge. But even if the phrase were deemed ambiguous, the Arab side would argue the ambiguity should be construed *against* the British drafters of the 24 October 1915 letter and resolved in favor of Hussein.

The British, on the other hand, argued that even if the phrasing were ambiguous, both McMahon and Hussein knew and intended that the *sole* purpose of the 24 October 1915 letter was to assure him the four Syrian towns would be included in the future Arab state. The correspondence, therefore, had *nothing* to do with Palestine.

The McMahon-Hussein correspondence continues to provoke controversy to this day and continues to form the foundation of Arab legal arguments against the legitimacy of the Balfour Declaration, the Mandate, and even the State of Israel. However, the weight of the evidence supports Britain's longstanding position that Palestine was *excluded* from McMahon's wartime promises to Hussein.

Notes

1 FO 371/6247, Telegram No. 219, 24 Sept. 1914, reproduced and discussed in Foreign Office, Arab Bureau, *Summary (Secret) of Historical Documents from the Outbreak of War between Great Britain and Turkey, 1914, to the Outbreak of the Revolt of the Sherif of Mecca in June 1916* (Jan. 1921, hereafter "*Foreign Office Historical Summary*") at 8.

2 *Id.* (Telegram No. 233, 30 Oct. 1914, reporting on reply letter from Abdullah).

3 *Id.* at 9 (Telegram No. 303, 31 Oct. 2014, sent the same day Great Britain and Turkey formally declared war on each other).
4 *Id.* at 11 (Telegram No. 173, 14 Apr. 1915).
5 *Id.* at 13. The full text of the air-dropped proclamation can be found in Cmd. 3530, Report of the Commission on the Palestine Disturbances of August, 1929 at 126 (1930).
6 Cmd. 5957, *Correspondence between Sir Henry McMahon, His Majesty's High Commissioner at Cairo and the Sherif Hussein of Mecca, July 1915–March 1916* (1939).
7 *Id.* at 1 (Explanatory note).
8 One historian argues the Sherif did not uphold his end of the bargain, as the promised Arab Revolt never truly materialized to the extent promised: "the deal was not a unilateral one. Its permanence and strength depended on how the Arabs fulfilled their part ... when the general Arab uprising in the regions of the Fertile Crescent failed to materialize, the corresponding part of the understanding, pledging the recognition of Arab independence east of the Jordan and in the Syrian hinterland, lapsed." I. Friedman, *The McMahon-Hussein Correspondence and the Question of Palestine*, Journal of Contemporary History, 5:2 at 96–103, 121 (1970).
9 Cmd. 5957, *op. cit.* at 7–9. In early Oct. 1915, an Arab (or possibly Kurdish) Officer in the Turkish Army named Mohammed al Farouki deserted and crossed over to the British lines in the Dardanelles. The British brought Farouki to Cairo for interrogation. Farouki, who belonged to a secret society within the Young Arab Party known as "Fatat al Arab," eventually met with McMahon. During the meeting Farouki told McMahon the Germans had made an overture to the Arabs, offering to meet all their demands, including independence, in exchange for helping Germany and Turkey against the British.

McMahon sent a report of the Farouki conversation to Foreign Secretary Sir Edward Grey (later Lord Falladon). According to McMahon, Farouki said the Arabs would be willing to reject the German offer and align with Britain if:

> In so far as she is free to without detriment to the interest of her present Allies, Great Britain accepts the principle of the independence of Arabia within limits propounded by the Sherif of Mecca ... England to guarantee the Holy Places against external aggression and recognize their inviolability. The occupation by France of purely Arab districts of Aleppo, Hama, Homs and Damascus would be opposed by Arabs with force of arms, but with this exception Faroki thinks they would accept some modification of the north-western boundaries proposed by the Sherif of Mecca.

FO 371/6247, *Foreign Office Historical Summary*, *op. cit.* at 17–18, unnumbered telegram dated 18 Oct. 1915 from McMahon to Grey [emphasis added]; *see also Id.* at 30 (quoting extensively from memorandum by General Gilbert Clayton reporting on meeting with Farouki, 11 Oct. 1915); Cmd. 5479, Palestine Royal Commission (Peel Commission) Report at 18, para. 5 (July 1937); *see also* FO 371/14495, W.J. Childs, Memorandum (Confidential) No. 13778, *Memorandum on the Exclusion of Palestine from the Area Assigned for Arab Independence by McMahon-Hussein Correspondence of 1915–16* (24 Oct. 1930).

McMahon incorporated Farouki's use of the word "districts" in his next letter to Hussein, the crucial letter of 24 Oct. 1915. General Gilbert Clayton, who worked with McMahon in Cairo, wrote a longer summary of the meeting with Farouki, noting:

> [Farouki said a] guarantee of the independence of the Arabian peninsula would not satisfy them, but this, together with the institution of an increasing measure

> of autonomous government, under British guidance and control, in Palestine and Mesopotamia, would probably secure their friendship ... In El Faroki's own words, 'our scheme embraces all the Arab countries, including Syria and Mesopotamia, but, if we cannot have all, we want as much as we can get.' ... A favourable reply to the Arab proposals, even though it did not satisfy their aspirations entirely, would probably put the seal on their friendship. The [Arab Party] would at once begin to work actively, and their operations, begun in the Hejaz where the Sherif is a great power, would soon extend to Syria and Palestine ...

FO 371/6247, *Foreign Office Historical Summary*, *op. cit.* at 30–31. Many historians regard Farouki as a huckster who duped Clayton, McMahon and Sykes into making promises to the Arabs by exaggerating, if not inventing out of whole cloth, both the Young Arab Party's interactions with the Germans as well as their ability to galvanize a meaningful Arab revolt against the Turks. *See, e.g.*, D. Fromkin, *A Peace to End All Peace: The Fall of the Empire and the Creation of the Modern Middle East* at 199 (Henry Holt & Co., 1989) (describing British officials in Cairo as having been "taken in by al-Faruqi's hoax"); Friedman, *op. cit.* at 90–92 ("al-Faruqi's report about Turco-German overtures to [the Young Arab Party], and the latter's ability to foment a revolt against the Ottoman government merit[ed], little credence").

Against this backdrop, the Foreign Office cabled McMahon on 20 Oct. 1915, authorizing him to convey to Hussein "your suggested reserve about our allies," and "unless something more precise is required, and in that case you may give it, the simplest plan would be to give assurance of Arab independence, adding that, if they will send their representatives, we will proceed at once to discussion of boundaries." The Foreign Office emphasized giving "an assurance that will prevent the alienation of the Arabs is the most important thing." FO 371/6247, *Foreign Office Historical Summary*, *op. cit.* at 18, Telegram No. 796 (20 Oct. 1915). According to Kedourie, McMahon had also received instructions from Maxwell and General Clayton at the Foreign Office on 18 Oct., two days earlier, notifying him "[i]n regard to non-western boundaries proposed by Sherif of Mecca, Faroki thinks Arabs would accept modification leaving in Arabia purely Arab *districts* of Aleppo, Damascus, Hama and Homs ..." E. Kedourie, *In the Anglo-Arab Labyrinth: The McMahon-Husayn Correspondence and Its Interpretations 1914–1939* at 102 (Frank Cass, 1976) [emphasis added]. Kedourie, therefore, argues McMahon's instructions were simply to convey to the Sherif that Britain would be willing to agree the area of independence to be granted to the Arabs would comprise *only*, using Farouki's terminology, the "purely Arab districts" of Aleppo, Hama, Homs and Damascus. Kedourie argues McMahon, "without authority and for reasons which must remain unknown owing to the disappearance of the relevant residency file, significantly modified the formula. Instead of telling the Sherif that the four towns would form the territory of the Arab state in Syria – which is what he, himself, Maxwell and Clayton unanimously declared to be the Arab demand – McMahon chose to tell the Sherif that 'portions of Syria lying to the west of the Districts of Damascus, Homs, Hama and Aleppo cannot be said to be purely Arab, and should be excluded from the limits demanded.'" Kedourie attributes McMahon's error to carelessness, quoting McMahon's contemporaries in the British Government describing him as "slow[] of mind," (Hardinge to Nicolson), "the laziest man I have ever met" (Graham to Hardinge), "frightfully slow at the uptake and difficult to coach," (Chirol to Hardinge), and "slow[] of mind and lack[ing] interest in his duties ... astonishing ignorance" (Herbert, Secretary of the Residency in Cairo). Kedourie, apparently unaware it was Clayton who had actually drafted the letters for McMahon (*see* n.107 *infra* and accompanying text), also condemned McMahon's carelessness in drafting language that "could, in logic, equally include and exclude Palestine." Kedourie, *op. cit.* at 35, 102, 242. Friedman, on the other hand, defends McMahon's use of the formulation in the 24 Oct. 1915 letter: "the fault was not McMahon's. As Childs has shown, this phrase ["purely Arab districts"] originated with al-Faruqi." A. Toynbee and I. Friedman, *The McMahon Hussein Correspondence: Comments and a Reply*, Journal of Contemporary History, 5:4 at 190, 198 (1970).

10 French interests were particularly acute in Syria, which at that time included all of modern-day Palestine. *See* Introduction at nn. 24–25 and accompanying text, noting Palestine was not a recognized geographic or political entity as of the early post-World War I period.

11 Command (Cmd.) Paper 5957 (1939) is the official British publication containing the entire McMahon-Hussein correspondence.

12 *Id.* at 8 [emphasis added].

13 *See, e.g.*, Cmd. 5974, *Report of a Committee Set up to Consider Certain Correspondence between Sir Henry McMahon and the Sharif of Mecca in 1915 and 1916*, (Mar. 1939, hereafter "*Report of a Committee*"); CAB/24/282/19, Memorandum (Secret) by Lord Halifax, Secretary of State for Foreign Affairs, *Palestine: Legal Arguments Likely to be Advanced by Arab Representatives* (23 Jan. 1939, hereafter "*Halifax Memorandum*"); Kedourie, *op. cit.*; Friedman, *op. cit.* at 83–120; A. Toynbee, *The McMahon-Hussein Correspondence: Comments and a Reply*, Journal of Contemporary History, 5:4 at 185–201 (1970).

14 *But see* J. Quigley, *The Statehood of Palestine: International Law in the Middle East Conflict* at 11 (Cambridge Univ. Press, 2010) (suggesting French interests were limited to Lebanon and did not include Palestine).

15 W. Shorrock, *French Suspicion of British Policy in Syria, 1900–1914*, Journal of European Studies 6:23, 190–208, at 197–98 (1976).

16 Cmd. 5479, Peel Commission Report, *op. cit.* at 17, para. 3; *see also* H. Sidebotham, *Great Britain and Palestine* at 236 (MacMillan & Co., 1937) ("Now France had previously informed us that she claimed the whole of Syria including Palestine, which had no separate political existence under Turkey; and the interests of France which were excepted from our promise to Hussein must therefore have included Palestine at that time. The contention of the British Government, confirmed by Sir Henry McMahon's explicit statement recently [in a letter to the *Times of London*, 23 July 1936], that Palestine was never promised to the Arabs, is sound beyond any question.").

17 CAB/24/282/19, *Halifax Memorandum*, *op. cit.* at 4, para. 19.

18 *Id.* at 6, paras. 27–28.

19 FO 371/6247, *Foreign Office Historical Summary*, *op. cit.* at 21, Telegram No. 677 (7 Nov. 1915).

20 *Id.* On closer inspection, the Arabic translation appears entirely consistent with the English version. The English version indicated Britain could promise independence only in those areas where France had no interests, meaning Britain could not promise independence anywhere else. The Arabic translation says the same thing—Britain could promise independence for the specific areas within the boundaries of the contemplated Arab state, a state extending eastward from Damascus, Homs, Hama and Aleppo, simply because France had claimed no interest in those areas.

21 *Report of a Committee, op. cit.*, Annex A at 15–16, para. 15.

22 A. Heidborn, *Manuel de Droit Public et Administratif de l'Empire Ottoman*, Vol. I at 7 (1908), https://archive.org/details/manueldedroitpu00heidgoog/page/n18.

23 *Id.*

24 *Id.* at 7–8.

25 CAB/24/282/19, *Halifax Memorandum, op. cit.* at 2, para. 7 (23 Jan. 1939).
26 *Id.* at 3, para. 12.
27 The Israeli historian Yehoshua Porath argued the word "*Vilayets*" in McMahon's 24 Oct. 1915 letter should logically have been understood to mean "regions," and thus "the area west of the Damascus region lies north of Palestine and does not include it." Porath, *op. cit.* at 45.
28 *Report of a Committee, op. cit.*, Annex B at 25, para. 21.
29 Friedman, *op. cit.* at 117.
30 *Report of a Committee, op. cit.* at 10–11, paras. 19–20 and Annex F at 48–49.
31 Telegram No. 93 from Clayton via Wingate (Cairo) to Foreign Office (14 Jan. 1918), *reproduced in* J. Priestland, *Records of Jerusalem 1917–1971* Vol. I at 101–02 (Cambridge Univ. Press, Archive Editions 2002).
32 Telegram no. IAT 0838/4.9 from Clayton (Jerusalem) to Foreign Office, para. B (9 Mar. 1918), *reproduced in* Priestland, *op. cit.* Vol. I at 105–06.
33 Ormsby-Gore was an intelligence officer attached to the Arab Bureau in Cairo during the War, and would later serve as Colonial Secretary.
34 Letter from William Ormsby-Gore to Mark Sykes, 31 Mar. 1918, *reproduced in* Priestland, *op. cit.* Vol. I at 107–12.
35 *Report (Confidential) on the Existing Political Situation in Palestine and Contiguous Areas by the Political Officer in charge of the Zionists* Commission, No. 147225 at 5, para. 16 (Aug. 1918), *reproduced in* Priestland, *op. cit.* Vol. I at 127, 131; *see also* CO 967/91, *Commission of Enquiry on Palestine Disturbances of August, 1929, Chairman's Copy of Evidence Taken in Camera* (hereafter "Shaw Commission *In Camera* Transcript"), testimony of Pinchas Rutenberg at 9–10, 16 (1 Nov. 1929) (Rutenberg claimed Arab owners were happy to sell their land at double or triple the market value to Jews without compensating their long-standing tenant farmers, and "Kasim Pasha, the President of the Arab Executive, recently offered, after the [August 1929] riots, to the Jews to buy his land").
36 Friedman, *op. cit.* at 118–19.
37 J.N. Moore, *The Arab-Israeli Conflict, Vol. III (Documents)* at 40–41 (Princeton Univ. Press, 1974). Some British officials were not impressed with the Weizmann-Feisal agreement. *See, e.g.*, Report (Secret) M/56 from Major J.N. Camp, Asst. Political Officer, Intelligence Office, Jerusalem to Chief Political Officer, Cairo entitled "Arab Movement and Zionism" at 4 (12 Aug. 1919), *reproduced in* Priestland, *op. cit.* Vol. I at 423:

> In my opinion, Dr. Weizmann's agreement with Emir Feisal is not worth the paper it is written on or the energy wasted in the conversation to make it. On the other hand, if it becomes sufficiently known among the Arabs, it will be somewhat in the nature of a noose around Feisal's neck, for he will be regarded by the Arab population as a traitor ... it seems that he is capable of making contradictory agreements with the French, the Zionists and ourselves, of receiving money from all three, and then endeavouring to do as he pleases. This is an additional reason why his agreement with Weizmann is of little or no value.

38 Cmd. 5479, Peel Commission Report, *op. cit.* at 27, para. 26. At least one historian has described the standard characterizations of Feisal's seemingly positive attitude toward Zionism as misplaced. Feisal's personal secretary and confidant, the Palestinian lawyer Auni Bey Abdul Hadi (about whom we will hear much more in this study), told various Jewish delegates at the conference that it was "obvious" why Feisal had "said these nice things:" Feisal believed Palestine belonged to him, and he was merely expressing a willingness to allowing some Jews to live there among the Arab majority. N. Caplan, *Palestine Jewry and the Arab Question, 1917–1925* at 31–32 (Frank Cass, 1973).

39 The text of the agreement appears at Priestland, *op. cit.* Vol. I at 341–44. Weizmann described the agreement with Feisal in his testimony before the Peel Commission as a treaty, claiming "I actually signed a treaty." Peel Public Testimony, *op. cit.* at 37 paras. 702–03 (25 Nov. 1936); the reference to the Weizmann-Feisal Agreement as a "treaty" can also be found at Jewish Agency for Palestine, *Memorandum Submitted to the Palestine Royal Commission on behalf of the Jewish Agency for Palestine* (hereafter "*Jewish Agency Memorandum*") Nov. 1936 at 68 para. 118, reproduced in A. Klieman (ed.), *The Rise of Israel: A Documentary Record from the Nineteenth Century to 1948*, Vol. 23 at 68 (Garland Pub., 1987) ("On January 3rd, 1919, The Emir Feisal and Dr. Weizmann met in London and signed a formal agreement, *sometimes referred to as the Faisal-Weizmann treaty.*") [emphasis added].

40 Friedman, *op. cit.* at 119.

41 *Id.*

42 *See* https://www.jewishvirtuallibrary.org/feisal-frankfurter-correspondence-march-1919 (last accessed 4 Dec. 2023).

43 Kedourie, *op. cit.* at 191, 192, 197–99.

44 *Id.* at 223 (Kedourie provides an incomplete citation to "Sulayman Musa, ed., *The Great Arab Revolt: Documents and Records*, document no. 40").

45 *Id.* at 221–22.

46 CO 733/320/3, Letter from Sir Herbert Samuel to Lord Peel dated 3 Aug. 1936, enclosing copy of Clayton Memorandum (*see* nn.107 and 114 and accompanying text, *infra*) and Letter from King Feisal to Samuel dated 1 Dec. 1923 ("I firmly believe the reciprocal trust established between us and the perfect agreement from our point of view which allowed a perfect understanding between Dr. Weizman [sic] and me, will prevent future misunderstandings and will maintain between us this harmony so necessary for the success of our common cause.").

47 Porath, *op. cit.* at 47–48.

48 Friedman, *op. cit.* at 119–20 (quoting H.M.V. Temperley, *History of the Peace Conference* (London 1920–1924), VI, 175).

49 Porath, *op. cit.* at 52.

50 FO 371/6237, *Conversation with Emir Feisal*, File No. 1-5311-u-1, at 1-3 (Foreign Office, 20 Jan. 1921) (draft minutes, with handwritten notations and corrections, of the meeting between Lindsay and the Emir Feisal.)

51 *Id.* at 1–3; CAB/24/28219, *Halifax Memorandum*, *op. cit.* at 3, para. 9 (discussing the Lindsay-Feisal meeting); FO 371/7797, Foreign Office, *Draft Reply to Parliamentary Inquiry of 11 July 1922*; Friedman, *op. cit.* at 120 (noting W.C. Childs of the Foreign Office regarded Feisal's argument about the word "district" as "deliberately disingenuous.") Although a group of Palestinian Arabs had urged (prior to Feisal's Jan. 1921 meeting at the Foreign Office) the Versailles Peace Conference to treat Palestine as part of the area of Arab independence by merging it into Syria (*see* Introduction at n.6 and accompanying text), the Palestinians did not base that position on any of the language from the McMahon-Hussein correspondence.

52 FO 371/6237, *Conversation with Emir Feisal*, *op. cit.* at 3.

53 *Id.* at 4.

54 FO 371/7797.

55 P. Toye, *Palestine Boundaries 1833–1947* Vol. III at 702 (Cambridge Univ. Press, Archive Editions, 1989).

56 *Id.*

57 *Id.* at 704.

58 *Id.* at 705.

59 Cmd. 1700, *Palestine: Correspondence with the Palestine Arab Delegation and the Zionist Organisation* (hereafter "*Churchill White Paper*") at 11 (16 Mar. 1922).
60 *Id.* at 17–21.
61 *Id.* at 20 (letter from J.E. Shuckburgh, Colonial Office, to the Zionist Organsation dated 3 June 1922 (enclosing at Churchill's request an official statement dealing with British policy in Palestine to be published 1 July 1922).
62 *Id.* at 26.
63 *See, e.g.*, H. Cattan, *Palestine and International Law: The Legal Aspects of the Arab-Israeli Conflict* (2d ed.) (Longmans, 1973); A. Abdul Hadi, *The Balfour Declaration*, Annals of the American Academy of Political and Social Science, 164:1 at 12–21 (1932).
64 Porath, *op. cit.* at 46. Although the McMahon-Hussein correspondence was not a treaty between states, references to the international law of treaty interpretation can be useful in assessing the validity of the Arab and British positions regarding whether McMahon's intent was relevant.
65 *Report of a Committee, op. cit.*, Annex C at 33 (Statement by Sir Michael McDonnell [former Chief Justice of Palestine] on Certain Legal Points Arising out of the Lord Chancellor's Statement at the Second Meeting of the Committee on the 24 Feb.).
66 *See generally id.*, Annexes A and C, where the opposing Arab legal arguments regarding the proper interpretation of the McMahon-Hussein correspondence were made with great force by George Antonious and Michael McDonnell; Kedourie, *op. cit.* at 246, 255, 266–67 (the Arab delegations to the 1939 Palestine Conference "were bent on treating the McMahon-Hussein correspondence as a legal contract to be interpreted as strictly as the courts would interpret a contract drawn up in due form." One of the Palestinian Arab delegates, Jemal al-Husseini, argued "a question of contract was at issue and ... such a question could not be discussed on the basis of the intentions of the parties, but the text of the documents.").
67 FO 371/5121, Palin Commission Report, *op. cit.* at para. 5.
68 Friedman, *op. cit.* at 112–14; Toynbee and Friedman, *op. cit.* at 185–91; *see also* I. Friedman, *Palestine, A Twice Promised Land? The British, the Arabs and Zionism 1915–1920* Vol. I at 61–100 (Transaction, 2000); I. Friedman, *The Question of Palestine, 1914–1918: British-Arab-Jewish Relations*, at 88–89 (Schocken, 1973).
69 Cmd. 1700, *op. cit.* at 20.
70 *Id.*
71 CAB/24/282/19, *Halifax Memorandum*, *op. cit.* at 2, para. 7 (23 Jan. 1939).
72 Cmd. 1700, *op. cit.* at 2–4.
73 *Id.* at 5–11.
74 FO 371/7797.
75 *Id.* Shuckburgh admitted, several years later in a letter to the British High Commissioner for Palestine, Sir John Chancellor, "I have always felt that, on a strict and literal interpretation of McMahon's famous letter of October, 1915, our case is a weak one, though I do not believe that the intention – so far as His Majesty's Government had any considered intentions in those hectic days – is open to serious doubt." Chancellor Papers, *op. cit.* Box 16/4, Letter from Shuckburgh to Chancellor (2 Jan. 1930).
76 Cmd. 1700, *op. cit.* at 11–15.
77 Hansard, HL Deb. 27 Mar. 1923 vol. 53 at 653–57 (27 Mar. 1923).
78 CO 733/320/3, Letter from Sir Herbert Samuel to Lord Peel dated 3 Aug. 1936, enclosing copy of Memorandum from Clayton to Samuel dated 12 Apr. 1923. Samuels also read the text of the Clayton Memorandum to the House of Lords on 20 July 1937, Hansard, HL Deb. 20 July 1937 vol. 106 at 630–31.

79 Kedourie, *op. cit.* at 253; FO 371/14495, E-6491, W.J. Childs, Memorandum (Confidential) No. 13778, *Memorandum on the Exclusion of Palestine from the Area assigned for Arab Independence by McMahon-Hussein Correspondence of 1915–16* (24 Oct. 1930, hereafter "*Childs Memorandum.*").

80 *Childs Memorandum*, *op. cit.* at 49. Childs added "we can have no view of the elastic sense in which El Faroki spoke of the word 'districts' of the four towns ... it is inconceivable that by the 'district of Damascus' Faroki could have intended the 'immediate neighbourhood,' for that would have admitted the possibility of Northern Syria being separated from the Hejaz by French occupation south of Damascus."

81 FO 371/14495 at 67–68.

82 Hansard, HC Deb 1 Aug. 1930 vol. 242 at 902–03. The Peel Commission Report adopted Dr. Shiels' position, noting "[i]t was in the highest degree unfortunate that, in the exigencies of war, the British Government was unable to make their intention clear to the Sherif." Cmd. 5479, Peel Commission Report, *op. cit.* at 20.

83 *See* n. 46, supra and accompanying text.

84 *See* n. 46, supra and accompanying text.

85 CO 733/320/3, Letter from Samuel to Martin (7 Sept. 1936).

86 Peel Secret Testimony, *op. cit.* at 481, para. 8413 (Samuel testimony).

87 *Id.* at 481, para. 8415. Samuel would later read an excerpt from the Clayton Memorandum to the House of Lords after the Peel Commission released its Report and made no mention of the Memorandum.

88 *Id.*

89 *Id.* at 482, para. 8416.

90 *Id.* at 482, paras. 8418–20, 8423–24.

91 Hansard, HC Deb., 21 July 1937, vol. 326 at 2236. Another first-hand recollection, made public in July 1939, came from Colonel C.E. Vickery, who served as the British Agent at Jeddah to Hussein (now King of the Hejaz) from 1919 to 1920. Vickery described a meeting with King Hussein in 1920, during which they discussed McMahon's 24 Oct. 1915 letter. According to Vickery: "I read the letter through very slowly; it was not written in very scholarly Arabic and had no English translation in the margin, and it was quite evident that Palestine was not included in the proposals to the King. I can say most definitely that the whole of the King's demands were centred round Syria, and only round Syria. Time after time he referred to that vineyard, to the exclusion of any other claim of interest. He stated most emphatically that he did not concern himself at all with Palestine, and had no desire to have suzerainty over it for himself or for his successors." C.E. Vickery, Letter to the Editor, *Times of London*, 23 July 1937.

92 *Times of London*, Letter to the Editor, "Independence of the Arabs, The 'McMahon Pledge,' A Definite Statement" (23 July 1937).

93 CO 733/353/2, Ormsby-Gore to McMahon, 23 July 1937. Ormsby-Gore's letter has not previously been published.

94 FO 371/20810, Rendell minute (26 July 1937); *see also* Rendell's even more harshly critical 11 Oct. 1937 minute, written after he examined a copy of McMahon's 26 Oct. 1915 telegram describing the 24 Oct. 1915 letter to Hussein.

95 CAB/24/282/19, *Halifax Memorandum*, *op. cit.* According to Kedourie, J. Z. Mackenzie of the Foreign Office wrote the memorandum, which later was endorsed by W.E. Beckett, the legal advisor to the Foreign Office. Kedourie, *op. cit.* at 267–70.

96 *Halifax Memorandum*, *op. cit.* at 3, para. 14.

97 The author of the Memorandum failed to mention, and was presumably unaware of the so-called "Cambon Letter" of 4 June 2017, in which Jules Cambon,

the head of the political section of the French Foreign Ministry, wrote to the Zionist diplomat Nahum Sokolov that the French Government supported the development of Jewish colonization in Palestine ("Vous avez bien voulu m'exposer le projet auquel vous consacrez vos efforts et qui a pour objet de developer la colonisation israelite en Palestine ... Je suis heureux de vous en donner ici l'assurance.") ("You have kindly explained to me the project to which you are devoting your efforts and whose object is to develop Jewish colonization in Palestine... I am happy to give our assurance."), http://www.balfourproject.org/french-support-for-the-zionist-cause/ (last accessed 4 Dec. 2023).

98 CAB/24/282/19, *Halifax Memorandum, op. cit.* at 6, para. 29.

99 Id. at 3–4, paras. 14–15; at 5–6, paras. 26–30; at 9, para. 46. MacKenzie argued, among other things, that an additional weakness in the British legal position arose from Britain's issuance of the Balfour Declaration, thus undermining the validity of the argument that Britain was not free to act in Palestine without detriment to French interests, thereby questioning the basis for reading McMahon's 24 Oct. 1915 letter as excluding Palestine based on the "general reservation" in favor of French interests. The original file, FO 371/23219, shows that Beckett did not exactly "endorse" MacKenzie's memorandum, but instead took issue with various portions of the draft memo and asked MacKenzie to revise it accordingly.

100 FO 371/23219, Letter from Baggally to Downie (19 Jan. 1939).

101 Kedourie, *op. cit.* at 272, quoting undated minute written by H.F. Downie of the Colonial Office.

102 E 891/6/31, Baggallay minute (30 Jan. 1939) enclosing memorandum by Baggallay, *The Juridical Basis of the Arab Claim to Palestine: Views of the Lord Chancellor* (30 Jan. 1939), *reprinted in* Priestland, *op. cit.* Vol. IV at 201–09.

103 *Id.*

104 *Id.* The Lord Chancellor reiterated these and other arguments in support of the British position at a 24 Feb. 1939 meeting of the British and Arab delegations regarding the McMahon-Hussein correspondence. *See* n.52 and accompanying text, *supra*.

105 George Antonius Papers, Middle East Centre Archive, St. Antony's College, Oxford, GB 165-0011, Box 2/5/1, Conferences on Palestine, United Kingdom-Arab Delegation, Draft Notes of the Second Meeting held at St. James's Palace, London, at 1 (9 Feb. 1939).

106 George Antonius Papers, Middle East Centre Archive, St. Antony's College, Oxford, GB 165-0011, Box 2/5/1, Statement by the Palestine Arab Delegation (9 Feb. 1939).

107 *The Times*, "The Arab Case: An Appeal for Justice" (11 Feb. 1939).

108 George Antonius Papers, Middle East Centre Archive, St. Antony's College, Oxford, GB 165-0011, Box 2/5/1, Statement by the Palestine Arab Delegation, at 4 (9 Feb. 1939).

109 George Antonius Papers, Middle East Centre Archive, St. Antony's College, Oxford, GB 165-0011, Box 2/5/1, Conferences on Palestine, United Kingdom-Arab Delegation, Draft Notes of the Third Meeting held at St. James's Palace, London, at C1 (11 Feb. 1939).

110 *Id.* at B2.

111 *Id.* at B3–B4.

112 George Antonius Papers, Middle East Centre Archive, St. Antony's College, Oxford, GB 165-0011, Box 2/5/1, Conferences on Palestine, United Kingdom-Arab Delegation, Draft Notes of the Fifth Meeting held at St. James's Palace, London, at A1–A3 (14 Feb. 1939).

113 *Id.* at B1.
114 George Antonius Papers, Middle East Centre Archive, St. Antony's College, Oxford, GB 165-0011, Box 2/5/1, Conferences on Palestine, United Kingdom-Arab Delegation, Draft Notes of the Sixth Meeting held at St. James's Palace, London, at C3 (15 Feb. 1939) (statement of Prince Said ul-Islam of Yemen).
115 *Id.* at D1.
116 *Id.* at E5, F2; *see also* CO 733/415/17, Conferences on Palestine, 1939: Notes on General Arrangements at 8–9.
117 For further background regarding those legal arguments, *see* S. Zipperstein, *op. cit.* ch. 1.
118 Cmd. 5974, *Report of a Committee Set Up to Consider Certain Correspondence between Sir Henry McMahon [His Majesty's High Commissioner in Egypt] and the Sharif of Mecca in 1915 and 1916* at 4 (16 Mar. 1939).
119 G. Antonius, *The Arab Awakening* at 267–68 (Allegro 1938). Jamal Husseini years later described Antonius as one of the two "main Arab strategists" during the 1939 London Conferences. W. Khalidi, *On Albert Hourani, the Arab Office, and the Anglo-American Committee of 1946*, Journal of Palestine Studies, 35:1, 60–79 at 64 (2005).
120 Cmd. 5964, *Statements Made on Behalf of His Majesty's Government during the Year 1918 in Regard to the Future Status of Certain Part of the Ottoman Empire (1939) (including the Hogarth Message)*; G. Antonius, *The Arab Awakening: The Story of the Arab National Movement* at 269 (Allegro, 1939). Antonius' book is widely regarded as a classic text of the history of Arab nationalism in the early 20th century. Unfortunately, however, Antonius dedicated his book to the notorious anti-Semite Charles R. Crane, who had served as co-Chair of the King-Crane Commission. President Woodrow Wilson sent the Commission to Palestine and Syria in 1919 to study the proposed post-War mandates and the Arab desire for self-determination. Crane told William E. Dodd, the incoming United States Ambassador to Germany in 1934, that Hitler should be allowed to "have his way" with the Jews. W. E. Dodd and M. Dodd, *Ambassador Dodd's Diary* at 24–25 (diary entry, 4 July 1933) (Victor Gollancz, 1945). Crane also complained to Sir John Chancellor, the former British High Commissioner in Palestine, that "I do not like the idea of attributing everything that goes wrong in the Jewish world to Hitler. The minute they are caught in one of their tricks they immediately cry Hitler! Hitler!!" Chancellor Papers, MSS. Brit. Emp. S.284, Bodleian Libraries, Oxford, Box 20/MF16 (Letter from Crane to Chancellor, 11 Feb. 1934).
121 Antonius, *op. cit.* at 268.
122 *Id.* at 267–69.
123 Kedourie, *op. cit.* at 282–84. According to Kedourie, Sir Mark Sykes, who drafted the Hogarth Message, "could not have had in mind any substantive, let alone fundamental, change in the Balfour declaration; for this reason if no other: such a change would have required ministerial authority." *Id.* at 283.
124 Esco Foundation for Palestine, *Palestine, A Study of Jewish, Arab and British Policies* Vol. I at 191–93 (Yale Univ. Press, 1947).
125 C. Sykes, *Crossroads to Israel: 1917–1948* at 30 (Indiana Univ. Press, 1965).
126 FO 371/23229, Hogarth note to High Commissioner, Cairo (extract) (15 Jan. 1918) (emphasis added).
127 FO 371/23229, Baggallay Minute (10 Mar. 1939); *see also* FO 371/23229, Letter from Baggallay to MacDonald (9 Mar. 1939) ("we should give the Arabs enough to show that the message was in fact delivered in the form intended, but need not go into the matter of King Hussein having given the impression that he would refuse to have a Jewish State").

128 FO 371/23229, Baxter and Butler Minutes (both 11 Mar. 1939).

129 CAB 23/97/10, Minutes (Secret) of Cabinet Meeting at 16 (8 Mar. 1939); CO 733/406/11, C.P. 10 (39), Extract (Secret) from Conclusions of a Meeting of the Cabinet (8 Mar. 1939) (same). The Lord Chancellor, who in January felt the legal arguments in support of Britain's position had not been articulated strongly enough in the MacKenzie memorandum, by early March came to harbor serious doubts about the strength of the British argument, telling the Cabinet "the correspondence in question was extremely unsatisfactory ... it was very difficult to contend that the letter of the 24th October, 1915, contained any specific exclusion of Palestine." CAB 23/97/9, Minutes (Secret) of Cabinet Meeting at 5 (2 Mar. 1939); CO 733/406/11, C.P. 9 (39), Extract (Secret) from Conclusions of a Meeting of the Cabinet (2 Mar. 1939) (same).

130 The *Times*, 21 Feb. 1939 at 10.

131 *See supra* n.110 and accompanying text.

132 H. McMahon, Letter to the Editor, "Independence of the Arabs, The 'McMahon Pledge,' A Definite Statement," The *Times*, 23 July 1937.

133 Cmd. 5974, *Report of a Committee Set up to Consider Certain Correspondence between Sir Henry McMahon and the Sharif of Mecca in 1915 and 1916*, para. 18 (16 Mar. 1939); *see also* CO 733/406/11, Code telegram from Foreign Office to British Ambassadors to Egypt, Iraq and Saudi Arabia (19 Mar. 1939) (summarizing the Joint Committee's report and Britain's position that the McMahon pledge had excluded Palestine).

134 Cmd. 5974, *op. cit.* para. 22. The British and Arab delegations unanimously adopted the Committee's report at their last formal session on 17 Mar. 1939. George Antonius Papers, Middle East Centre Archive, St. Antony's College, Oxford, GB 165-0011, Box 2/5/2, Conferences on Palestine, United Kingdom-Arab Delegation, Draft Notes of the 14th Meeting held at St. James's Palace, London at A6 (17 Mar. 1939).

135 CO 733/406/11, Code telegram from Foreign Office to British Ambassadors to Egypt, Iraq and Saudi Arabia (19 Mar. 1939).

136 CO 733/411/16, Letter from Selig Brodetsky on behalf of the Jewish Agency to MacDonald (28 Mar. 1939).

137 CO 733/411/16, J.S. Bennett, Colonial Office, Note on Jewish Criticisms of the Report of the "McMahon-Hussein Committee" (3 Apr. 1939).

138 Cmd. 6019, *Palestine: Statement of Policy* (hereafter "MacDonald White Paper") para. 7 (May 1939).

139 Porath, *op. cit.* at 46 ("Not only did the McMahon-Husayn correspondence by itself not constitute a treaty, but the correspondence was never completed and left both sides in their original positions. At most we are dealing with a promise or moral obligation on the part of Britain, but between this and a treaty there is a considerable gap."); *see also* P. Graves, *Palestine, the Land of Three Faiths* at 50 (J. Cape, 1923) ("there was no 'agreement' with Hussein of Mecca in the sense of a Treaty, and there were no negotiations then or subsequently on the basis of any draft instrument.").

140 Vienna Convention on the Law of Treaties, *op. cit.*, art. 31 [emphasis added].

141 *Id.*, art. 32.

142 B. Oppenheim and H. Lauterpacht, *International Law: A Treatise* (8th ed.) at 952, 954 (Longman, Green, 1955).

143 Cmd. 5974, *op. cit.* at 31, 38. While serving as the Chief Justice of Palestine, McDonnell had urged High Commissioner John Chancellor to fire the "ardent partisan of Zionism," the Jewish Attorney General of Palestine, Norman Bentwich, "in view of the importance of maintaining the reputation of the British Government for strict impartiality in the administration of justice."

CO733/175/3, Despatch (Secret) from High Commissioner for Palestine to Secretary of State for the Colonies at 2–3 (20 Sept. 1929).

144 *Rhine Chlorides*, 144 ILR 259 at 298, para. 74 (2004), quoting the award in *Georges Pinson (France) v. United Mexican States*, Franco-Mexican Claims Commission, as translated in Annual Digest of Public International Law Cases 1927–1928 para. 50 at 426 (19 Oct. 1928), cited in R. Gardiner, *Treaty Interpretation* (2nd ed.) at 174 (Oxford Univ. Press, 2015).

5
THE PALESTINE MANDATE, 1922

The Balfour Declaration

On 2 November 1917, as British troops were readying their advance northward toward Beersheva, Jerusalem, and Damascus, the British War Cabinet authorized Foreign Secretary Lord Arthur Balfour to send the following letter to Lord Lionel Rothschild, a leading member of Britain's Jewish community:

> His Majesty's Government view with favour the establishment in Palestine of a national home for the Jewish people, and will use their best endeavors to facilitate the achievement of this object, it being clearly understood that nothing shall be done which may prejudice the civil and religious rights of existing non-Jewish communities in Palestine, or the rights and political status enjoyed by Jews in any other country.[1]

The wording of the Balfour Declaration was a model of ambiguity and compromise, much like McMahon's 24 October 1915 letter to Hussein. As one historian has noted, "[t]he precise meaning of the Balfour Declaration was not known to anyone and it is doubtful if its formulators knew themselves exactly what they had declared. This lack of clarity left much room for interpretation."[2]

At least six issues emerge from the text of the Declaration:

First, what was meant by the word "Palestine?" Palestine, as we have seen, was not a recognized political entity at that time and had no recognized borders. As of 2 November 1917, it was still part of the Ottoman Empire.

Second, what did Balfour mean by "*in* Palestine?" In *all* of Palestine? Or only *part* of Palestine?[3] If so, *which* part or parts?

DOI: 10.4324/9781032686561-8

Third, what did the term "National Home" mean? A state? A canton or province of a larger Arab or British state? Or something else?

Fourth, what was meant by the word "establishment'? Weizmann had pushed for the word "re-establishment," to indicate Palestine *already* belonged to the Jews, and they were simply returning to reclaim what was rightfully theirs.[4] But the British chose "establishment" over "re-establishment," preferring diplomatic vagueness to the more far-reaching and definitive formulation Weizmann and the Zionists wanted.

Fifth, what was meant by the phrase "existing non-Jewish communities in Palestine?" Why was the word "Arabs" omitted? Why was there no mention about Arab *political* rights, such as the right to a separate homeland, perhaps somewhere else "in Palestine?" Did the drafters intend the Jews eventually would become the majority in Palestine, leaving the non-Jewish communities as a protected but relatively powerless minority? Moreover, unlike the affirmative obligation the British undertook, to "use their best endeavors to facilitate the achievement" of a Jewish National Home in Palestine, why did the Declaration not include any parallel, affirmative obligation on behalf of the non-Jewish communities, other than the passive obligation *not* to prejudice the Arabs' civil and religious rights?

Sixth, on what legal basis did Britain issue the Balfour Declaration, given Palestine belonged to the Ottoman Empire as of November 1917, and Britain arguably had already committed Palestine to the Arabs in the McMahon-Hussein correspondence?

The French and Italian Governments both endorsed the Balfour Declaration publicly during the first half of 1918.[5] Japan offered its endorsement in January 1919.[6]

Treaty of Versailles and Covenant of the League of Nations

Following the end of World War I, the Treaty of Versailles, including the Covenant of the League of Nations (Part I of the Treaty itself) was on signed 28 June 1919, and the League of Nations was established on 10 January 1920. Article 20 of the Covenant provided:

> The Members of the League severally agree that this Covenant is accepted as abrogating all obligations or understandings *inter se* which are inconsistent with the terms thereof, and solemnly undertake that they will not hereafter enter into any engagements inconsistent with the terms thereof.[7]

Article 22 of the Covenant provided for creating various Mandates around the world to administer former Ottoman and German territories and colonies "as a sacred trust of civilization" which had ceased to be under the sovereignty of the nations who had governed them before World War I.[8]

Article 22 codified this new approach:

> To those colonies and territories which as a consequence of the late war have ceased to be under the sovereignty of the States which formerly governed them and which are inhabited by peoples not yet able to stand by themselves under the strenuous conditions of the modern world, there should be applied the principle that the well-being and development of such peoples form a sacred trust of civilisation and that securities for the performance of this trust should be embodied in this Covenant. The best method of giving practical effect to this principle is that the tutelage of such peoples should be entrusted to advanced nations who by reason of their resources, their experience or their geographical position can best undertake this responsibility, and who are willing to accept it, and that this tutelage should be exercised by them as Mandatories on behalf of the League.[9]

Paragraph Four of Article 22 specifically addressed the Middle East:

> Certain communities formerly belonging to the Turkish Empire have reached a stage of development where their existence as independent nations can be provisionally recognized subject to the rendering of administrative advice and assistance by a Mandatory until such time as they are able to stand alone.

Article 22 divided the mandates into three categories, based on the local population's readiness for self-rule. The Class A mandates included former Ottoman Empire territories (including Palestine) that had "reached a stage of development where their existence as independent nations can be provisionally recognized subject to the rendering of administrative advice and assistance by a Mandatory until such time as they are able to stand alone."[10] The Class B and Class C mandates consisted of territories in Africa and the South Pacific where self-rule would be deferred for a longer time.

One of the principal Arab legal arguments against the Balfour Declaration concerned the alleged conflict between the Balfour Declaration and Article 22. The global Jewish People, to whom the Balfour Declaration had promised a National Home in Palestine, were not a "communit[y] formerly belonging to the Turkish Empire," and thus had no rights under Article 22 to eventual self-determination in any former Turkish areas, including Palestine. Thus, according to the Arab legal argument, because Article 20 abrogated all existing obligations or undertakings inconsistent with the Covenant, the Balfour Declaration was nullified because it conflicted with Article 22.[11]

The Palestinian Arab lawyer Auni Bey Abdul Hadi summarized the Arab legal argument on this point in a 1932 article:

> The truth is that European diplomacy deceived the Arabs on three different occasions. In the first instance the Arabs were promised independence if they would join the Allies in their attack on the Turks. And when the Turks were defeated through the cooperation of the Arabs their reward was Article 22 of the Covenant of the League of Nations, placing portions of former Turkish Territory under a Mandate, which was anything but the promised liberty and independence. Not content with this blow, the Allied inflicted a foreign government [Britain] which has shattered all Arab hopes of independence. As a *coup de grace*, the Allies devised the obnoxious 'Balfour Declaration' which is in utter disregard of Article 22 and, if continued to be carried out, will wipe out the Arab nationality in Palestine and replace it by the national home for the Jews.[12]

San Remo Conference and Treaty of Sèvres

Three months following the establishment of the League of Nations, the Principal Allied Powers (Britain, France, Italy, and Japan) issued the following Resolution in favor of the Balfour Declaration at the San Remo Conference on 25 April 1920:

> The High Contracting Parties agree to entrust, by application of the provisions of Article 22, the administration of Palestine, within such boundaries as may be determined by the Principal Allied Powers, to a Mandatory, to be selected by the said Powers. The Mandatory *will be responsible for putting into effect* the [Balfour] declaration originally made on November 2, 1917, by the British Government, and adopted by the other Allied Powers, in favour of the establishment in Palestine of a national home for the Jewish people, it being clearly understood that nothing shall be done which may prejudice the civil and religious rights of existing non-Jewish communities in Palestine, or the rights and political status enjoyed by Jews in any other country.[13]

This international endorsement of the Balfour Declaration at San Remo represented the first step in rendering the Declaration part of international law.[14]

Less than four months later, on 10 August 1920, the Treaty of Sèvres (annulled three years later after Turkey refused to sign) converted the San Remo Resolution into an international legal instrument. Article 95 of the Treaty provided:

> The High Contracting Parties agree to entrust, by application of the provisions of Article 22, the administration of Palestine, within such boundaries as may be determined by the Principal Allied Powers, to a Mandatory to be selected by the said Powers. The Mandatory *will be responsible for*

> *putting into effect the declaration originally made on November 2, 1917, by the British Government, and adopted by the other Allied Powers, in favour of the establishment in Palestine of a national home for the Jewish people*, it being clearly understood that nothing shall be done which may prejudice the civil and religious rights of existing non-Jewish communities in Palestine, or the rights and political status enjoyed by Jews in any other country.[15]

Article 129 of the Treaty provided that

> Jews of other than Turkish nationality who are habitually resident, on the coming into force of the present Treaty, within the boundaries of Palestine, as determined in accordance with Article 95 will ipso facto become citizens of Palestine to the exclusion of any other nationality.[16]

The Palestine Mandate

Introduction

The post-World War I Mandate system represented a new creation of international law.[17] The League appointed Britain and France as "Mandatories" over the former Ottoman and German territories conquered during the war.[18] The League asked Britain and France to provide tutelage to the local populations until such time as they could govern themselves as independent states.

The League's decision to adopt the Mandate system to oversee the transition from conquered territory to self-rule reflected a new notion in international law, later codified in the 1928 Kellogg-Briand Pact of Nations, rejecting war as an instrument of national policy and the acquisition of territory through offensive conquest.[19] Article 1 of the Kellogg-Briand Pact provides:

> The High Contracting Parties solemnly declare in the names of their respective peoples that they condemn recourse to war for the solution of international controversies, and renounce it, as an instrument of national policy in their relations with one another.

Significantly, however, the Kellogg-Briand Pact does not preclude the acquisition of territory resulting from a lawful war of self-defense against an aggressor.

Britain maintained military rule in Palestine from December 1917 through 1 July 1920, when a civilian government was established in its place.[20] On 24 July 1922, the Council of the League of Nations voted to designate Palestine as a Mandate and to appoint Britain as the Mandatory.[21] Turkey signed the Treaty of Lausanne on 24 July 1923, officially ending World War I and formally renouncing its territorial claims to Palestine.[22] The British Mandate officially took effect two months later, on 29 September 1923.

The Preamble to the Mandate incorporated and adopted the Balfour Declaration:

> Whereas the Principal Allied Powers have also agreed that the Mandatory *should be responsible for putting into effect* the [Balfour] declaration originally made on November 2, 1917, by the Government of His Britannic Majesty, and adopted by the said Powers, in favour of the establishment in Palestine of a national home for the Jewish people, it being clearly understood that nothing should be done which might prejudice the civil and religious rights of existing non-Jewish communities in Palestine, or the rights and political status enjoyed by Jews in any other country ...[23]

Most importantly, the Preamble granted recognition "to the historical connection of the Jewish people with Palestine and to the grounds for reconstituting their national home in that country." As discussed in Chapter 2, the word "reconstitute," and the League Council's unanimous recognition of the "historical connection" of the Jewish people to Palestine belie modern-day claims of Jewish settler colonialism. On the contrary, the League Council accorded legal recognition to Zionism as the national liberation and self-determination movement of the Jewish People.

The incorporation of the Balfour Declaration in the Mandate, following the codifications of the Balfour Declaration at San Remo and Sèvres, established the Balfour Declaration as part of international law.[24] One of the Members of the Permanent Mandates Commission of the League of Nations, D.F.W. Van Rees of the Netherlands, noted several years later, "the Balfour Declaration, especially confirmed by the [M]andate for Palestine ... accorded to the Jews a special legal position and special legal conditions."[25]

The League of Nations Council unanimously approved the Mandate for Palestine in July 1922.[26] The Minutes of the League Council's 22 July 1922 meeting state "The Council decided that the mandate for Palestine was approved." The Council met again two days later, on 24 July 1922. The minutes of that meeting confirmed that "France had considered and Great Britain agreed that the mandate for Syria and Palestine should be taken together. The Council had confirmed this agreement by a *unanimous* vote."[27]

The Palestine Mandate, like all the other Mandates, acquired the force of international law upon the League Council's ratification. As the International Court of Justice noted in the 1962 *Namibia* opinion, Mandates have "the character of a treaty or convention and embodying international engagements for the Mandatory as defined by the Council and accepted by the Mandatory."[28]

Political Rights Granted to the Jewish People, but Not the Palestinian Arabs

The League of Nations treated Palestine differently from the other Class A Mandates (Iraq, Syria, Lebanon, and Transjordan) mandates, excluding it from the areas reserved for future Arab independence.[29]

Instead, the Palestine Mandate contained several provisions granting political rights exclusively to the Palestinian Jews and the Jewish people worldwide. For example, and as noted above, the Preamble to the Mandate established as a matter of international law "the historical connection of the Jewish people with Palestine" and the grounds for "reconstituting their national home in that country."

Moreover, Article 2 of the Mandate made Britain "responsible for placing the country under such political, administrative, and economic conditions as will secure the establishment of the Jewish national home." Article 4 recognized the Zionist Organization as responsible for working with the British authorities to establish the Jewish National Home in Palestine. Article 6 required Britain to facilitate Jewish immigration and "close settlement" of the land of Palestine, with no geographic restrictions. The West Bank was as open for Jewish immigration and land acquisition as the coastal plain and the remaining regions of the Mandatory area.

The Mandate, as noted, conferred no political rights on the Palestinian Arabs, other than Article 25, which provided the area of Palestine situated east of the Jordan River (Transjordan) would be severed and eventually become an Arab state (Jordan), consistent with the British pledge to the Sheriff Hussein of Mecca in October 1915.[30]

The Mandate, however, said nothing about a "national home" or statehood for the Arabs in the remaining portion of Palestine west of the Jordan River. Nor did it recognize any Arab counterpart to the Zionist Organization. Based on the plain meaning of the text of the Palestine Mandate, the global Jewish people were the *exclusive* recipients of political rights, including rights of self-determination, in the Cisjordanian portion of Palestine.

As the following table shows, the Mandate granted to the Palestinian Arabs only civil and religious protections. The Mandate granted no political or self-determination rights to the Palestinian Arabs residing west of the Jordan River. Articles 2 and 15 provided for the rights of non-discrimination and freedom of worship to all Palestinians, including all Palestinian Jews, Muslims, and Christians. Article 13 prevented Britain from interfering "with the fabric or the management of purely Moslem sacred shrines."

Stoyanovsky (1928) argued the Mandate created an international legal obligation for Britain, as mandatory, to administer Palestine as a trustee, charged with safeguarding and implementing the legal promise made to the Jewish people for a National Home in Palestine.[31] Stoyanovsky also characterized the Mandate's recognition of the Jewish people's historical connection to Palestine

TABLE 5.1 Palestine Mandate – Allocation of Rights

Rights Conferred by the Palestine Mandate	*Jews*	*Arabs*
Right to a National Home in Palestine (Art. 2)	Yes (all Jews worldwide)	No
Civil and Religious Rights (Art. 2)	Yes	Yes
Political Representation (Art. 4)	Yes (Jewish Agency)	No
Immigration (Art. 6)	Yes (all Jews worldwide)	No
Land Settlement (Art. 6)	Yes (all Jews worldwide)	No
"Rights and Position" of Non-Jews (Art. 6)	N/A	Yes
Purely Muslim Sacred Shrines (Art. 13)	No	Yes (sole control; no interference by Britain)
Free Exercise of Worship (Arts. 2 and 15)	Yes	Yes
Non-Discrimination (Art. 15)	Yes	Yes

as grounded in *legal* rights. Because the Jewish people never expressly or implicitly renounced their claims to Palestine, "no exclusive rights could either morally or legally have been acquired over that territory by any other people."[32]

Stoyanovsky's view finds support in the legal principle that when a treaty or other international instrument denotes specific rights or obligations, it cannot be interpreted to extend additional unspecified rights or obligations.[33] The principle presumes that when the drafters of international instruments want to include particular rights and obligations, they do so expressly. Likewise, the absence of specified rights and obligations indicates the drafters intended to omit them. Hence, the Mandate's express mention of Arab "civil and religious rights," but *not* Arab "political" rights, means the drafters did not intend the Mandate to confer political or self-determination rights on the Palestinian Arabs, as the League had done separately for the Arabs in the Mandates for Syria, Lebanon, and Iraq (and eventually Transjordan).

The Grand Mufti of Jerusalem, Haj Amin al-Husseini, conceded this point in his testimony to the Palestine Commission on the Disturbances of August 1929, otherwise known as the Shaw Commission. The Mufti, testifying in early December 1929, admitted the Palestine Mandate

> did not refer to the protection of the political rights of the Arabs but refers only to the political rights of the Jews. If there is any mention of political rights in the Mandate it is only in connection with the rights of the Jews.[34]

The Mufti's reading of the Mandate reflected the common understanding at the time. For example, King George V issued a proclamation in July 1920 in

English, Hebrew, and Arabic upon the arrival of Britain's first High Commissioner to Palestine, Sir Herbert Samuel. The King declared the purpose of the Mandate was to ensure the

> gradual establishment in Palestine of a National Home for the Jewish People ... I shall watch with deep interest and warm sympathy the future progress and development of a State whose history has been of such tremendous import to the world.[35]

Arab Legal Arguments Against the Palestine Mandate

The Palestinian Arabs raised a variety of legal arguments against the Mandate both before and after its formal adoption. One of the earliest examples can be found in a letter from the Palestinian Arabs to British Prime Minister David Lloyd George on 22 January 1922, in which the Palestinian Arabs protested the provisions of the draft Mandate prior to its promulgation. The letter requested a plebiscite, an elected national government based on majority rule, renunciation of the principle of creating a National Home for the Jewish people in Palestine, and an assurance that Palestine would "not be separated from her Arab neighbouring sister states."[36]

In later years and up to the present day, the Palestinian Arabs lodged additional legal arguments against the Mandate, as follows:

First, the Palestinians argued the Balfour Declaration of 2 November 1917, and its statement that the British Government "viewed with favour the establishment of a National Home in Palestine for the Jewish People," was void from the outset, because Britain had no legal right or standing to demise Palestine to anyone as of November 1917. Britain had not yet conquered Palestine. World War I had not yet ended. No treaties had yet been signed giving Britain *any* legal standing to assign Palestine or any portion of it to anyone other than the pre-existing indigenous Arab majority.

Second, the Palestinians argued that even if Britain possessed any legal right or authority to give or promise Palestine (or any portion of it) to anyone while the war was still raging, it had *already* exercised those rights in favor of the local Palestinian Arabs when it allocated Palestine *to them* in McMahon's 24 October 1915 letter to the Sherif, a full two years and 18 days prior to the Balfour Declaration.

Third, the Palestinians argued that McMahon's 24 October 1915 letter and the Sherif's response to the letter formed a treaty between current and future sovereigns, binding Britain thereafter to uphold McMahon's pledges to Hussein.

Fourth, Palestinians argued the Covenant of the League of Nations, in paragraph four of Article 22, *ratified* McMahon's pledge of Palestine to the Sherif by declaring:

> *Certain communities formerly belonging to the Turkish Empire* have reached a stage of development where their existence as independent nations can be provisionally recognised subject to the rendering of administrative advice and assistance by a Mandatory until such time as they are able to stand alone. The wishes of these communities must be a principal consideration in the selection of the Mandatory.

The explicit reference to "certain communities formerly belonging to the Turkish Empire" can only be read to mean the population of Palestine as it existed as of the end of the War, a population consisting of more than 90% Arabs and less than 10% Jews. Thus, the text of the Covenant is consistent with McMahon's correspondence with Hussein, promising Palestine as one of the future territories for Arab independence.

The League, moreover, viewed this as a hallowed obligation, as a *sacred trust* of civilization, codifying President Wilson's commitment to self-determination for the former Ottoman imperial territories.

Fifth, the Palestinians argued the McMahon-Hussein correspondence neither explicitly nor implicitly excluded Palestine or reserved *any* portion of Palestine for additional Jewish immigration and settlement. The word "Palestine" appears nowhere in any of McMahon's letters. The specific reservation in McMahon's 24 October 1915 letter of "portions of Syria lying to the west of the Districts of Damascus, Homs, Hama and Aleppo" can only logically be understood as referring to modern-day Lebanon, which lies directly to the *west* of those four cities, and not Palestine, which lies to the *southwest*. The ordinary canons of construction under English and International law require the 24 October 1915 letter to be interpreted based on the unambiguous wording of the letter. Any attempt to alter the meaning by reading McMahon's supposed intent into the letter fails as a matter of law.

Sixth, the Palestinians argued the general reservation in favor of French interests does not support the argument that Palestine was excluded. After all, France voted for the Covenant of the League of Nations (it even hosted the Peace Conference that produced the Covenant). The Covenant says *nothing* about Palestine or any supposed exclusion of Palestine from the areas set aside for future Arab independence, nor does it say *anything* about the Balfour Declaration or the Jewish People. Certainly, France, if indeed it claimed any interests in Palestine, would have taken steps to protect those interests by demanding language be included in the Covenant, rather than voting for it without such language.

Seventh, the Palestinians argued that even if the Balfour Declaration was somehow valid from the outset, its promise of a national home in Palestine to the "Jewish people," wherever they may have been located, cannot be reconciled with the very specific reference to "certain communities *formerly belonging to the Turkish Empire*" in Article 22 of the Covenant of the League of Nations. The irreconcilable conflict between the Balfour Declaration and Article 22 thus rendered the Balfour Declaration legally null and void the moment the Covenant was ratified, based on the language of Article 20:

> The Members of the League severally agree that this Covenant is accepted as *abrogating all obligations or understandings inter se which are inconsistent with the terms thereof*, and solemnly undertake that they will not hereafter enter into any engagements inconsistent with the terms thereof.

The Balfour Declaration constituted an official British Government promise of a national home in Palestine to the entire "Jewish people," wherever they lived throughout the world. But the language of Article 22 of the Covenant would, at most, *only* have applied to the Jewish community *already* residing in Palestine as of the end of the War, "a community formerly belonging to the Turkish Empire." The Balfour Declaration's far broader promise to the non-Palestinian Jews living in Europe and elsewhere conflicted directly with Article 22 and therefore became void upon the ratification of the Covenant.

Eighth, the Palestinians argued the Balfour Declaration, even if it were somehow legally valid initially, was abrogated by operation of law the moment 42 nations ratified the Covenant of the League of Nations on 10 January 1920. Thus, the subsequent incorporation of the legally abrogated Balfour Declaration into the San Remo resolutions on 25 April 1920 was itself legally null and void, as was the incorporation of the San Remo resolutions into the never-ratified Treaty of Sèvres on 10 August 1920.

Ninth, the Palestinians argued the incorporation of the Balfour Declaration into the 24 July 1922 Mandate for Palestine likewise was legally null and void, regardless of whether the Declaration was void initially or subsequently voided as a result of the ratification of the Covenant of the League of Nations. Therefore, all the provisions of the Mandate referencing the Balfour Declaration, the establishment of a National Home for the Jewish people in Palestine, the role of the Jewish Agency, and the close settlement of the Jews on the land of Palestine, had no legal validity and must be struck from the Mandate. Palestine, therefore, should have been treated the same way as the other former Ottoman Class A mandates such as Iraq, Transjordan, Syria, and Lebanon.

Tenth, the Palestinians argued the Mandate was also null and void for the separate reason that Britain was selected as the Mandatory Power in violation of Article 22 of the Covenant of the League of Nations, which required "the wishes of those communities [formerly under Turkish rule] must be a principal consideration in the selection of the Mandatory." Because the Palestinian Arabs had not been consulted regarding the selection of Britain as the Mandatory Power, Britain's appointment should have been rescinded until a new Mandatory Power could be chosen after consultation with the

Palestinian Arabs. The Mandate should not have taken effect until that selection process could be completed.[37]

Eleventh, the Palestinians argued the only legally valid document bearing on Palestine subsequent to the ratification of the Covenant of the League of Nations was the Treaty of Lausanne, ratified on 24 July 1923. The Treaty formally ended World War I, with Turkey surrendering all claims to its former Arab territories, including Palestine. As with the Covenant of the League of Nations, but unlike the ill-fated Treaty of Sèvres, the Treaty of Lausanne said *nothing* about the Balfour Declaration and said *nothing* about a national home for the Jewish People in Palestine.

Twelfth, the Palestinians argued that pursuant to the Covenant of the League of Nations, Palestine, like the other Arab Mandates (Syria/Lebanon, Iraq, and Transjordan) was supposed to have been treated as a "Class A" mandate. "Class A" status applied to those formerly Ottoman-controlled territories that, pursuant to Article 22 of the Covenant, had "reached a stage of development where their existence as independent nations can be provisionally recognized subject to the rendering of administrative advice and assistance by a Mandatory until such time as they can stand alone."[38]

Instead, however, because of the Balfour Declaration and the reference to it in Article 2 of the Covenant of the League of Nations, Britain had ended up treating Palestine as a "Class B" mandate (like the territories in West and Central Africa), where "the Mandatory must be responsible for the administration of the territory under conditions which will guarantee freedom of conscience and religion."[39] This inconsistency between treating Palestine as a *de facto* Class B mandate instead of a *de jure* Class A mandate should have been resolved, according to the Arab argument, by treating Article 22 of the Covenant as equivalent to a "charter," and the Mandate as merely the "by-laws" implementing the charter. In this case, the "by-laws" conflicted with the "charter" and thus should be invalidated.[40]

Responses to Arab Legal Arguments Regarding the Mandate

The Arab legal arguments against the Mandate ignore the legal force and the plain meaning of the Mandate. They also ignore the Mandate's political commitments to the Jewish people and the corresponding absence of any political commitments to the Palestinian Arabs.

First, many of the same nations who had ratified the Covenant of the League of Nations in January 1920 also approved the incorporation of the Balfour Declaration into the San Remo Resolutions only three months later. By doing so, those nations elevated the Balfour Declaration to the status of an enforceable international legal instrument, thereby undermining the Arab claim that the Balfour Declaration lacked the support of the international community because of the absence of any mention of it in the Covenant of the League.

Second, the Council of the League of Nations, acting on behalf of *all* member states, approved the Mandate for Palestine in 1922. The Preamble not only repeated the wording of the Balfour Declaration but took it a step further, declaring "recognition has thereby been given to the *historical connection of the Jewish people with Palestine and to the grounds for reconstituting their national home in that country*."

Third, the implementing provisions of the Mandate also made clear that establishing a National Home for the Jewish people was the top priority and main focus of the Mandate. Hence, Article 2 required the Mandatory to place the country under such political, administrative, and economic conditions as would secure the establishment of the Jewish national home. Article 4 recognized the Zionist Organization as a public body for the purpose of advising and cooperating with the Administration of Palestine in such economic, social, and other matters as may affect the establishment of the Jewish national home and the interests of the Jewish population in Palestine. Article 6 required the Mandatory to facilitate Jewish immigration and encourage "close settlement by Jews." Article 22 recognized the recently reborn Hebrew language as one of the official languages of the country, and required Hebrew to appear on all postage stamps and currency. Significantly, *no* similar provisos were included on behalf of the Palestinian Arabs.

Fourth, the McMahon-Hussein correspondence lacked legal force. It was not a treaty between states. No international bodies ever recognized it as having the force of law. Moreover, the British Government reaffirmed on multiple occasions McMahon's intent to exclude Palestine from his 24 October 1915 letter to Sherif Hussein. Moreover, McMahon's letter did not expressly promise Palestine to the Arabs, based on both the specific geographic reservation of areas lying to the west of the Districts of Damascus, Homs, Hama, and Aleppo, and the general reservation in favor of French interests. Thus, the correspondence did not create any legally binding promise of Palestine to the Arabs. Therefore, neither the Balfour Declaration nor the Mandate were in conflict with the McMahon-Hussein correspondence.

Fifth, regarding the alleged conflict between the Balfour Declaration and the Mandate with Articles 20 and 22 of the Covenant of the League of Nations, the words "*certain* communities" meant *some*, but not *all* the communities formerly belonging to the Turkish Empire. Therefore, absent any clear language referencing the indigenous Arab community of Palestine, there was no basis for finding a conflict between Article 22 and the Mandate. Furthermore, even if the Palestine Arabs were included in the term "certain communities," at most their independence was treated merely as a future possibility, "*provisionally* recognised subject to the rendering of administrative advice and assistance by a Mandatory until such time as they are able to stand alone."

Moreover, the words "*inter se*" in Article 20 limited the abrogation of prior inconsistent agreements *only* to those agreements *between* members of the League of Nations. The Balfour Declaration was *not* such an agreement, as neither Lord Rothschild nor the "Jewish People" were members of the League, which did not even exist at the time the Declaration was issued in November 1917. Thus, the abrogation requirement of Article 20 had no legal impact on either the Balfour Declaration or the related provisions of the Palestine Mandate.

Sixth, regarding the Arab claim that the Mandate was void because the Palestinian Arabs had not been consulted regarding the selection of Britain as the Mandatory Power, the language merely indicated the wishes of the local community were *a* principal consideration, but not *the* principal consideration in determining who to select as the Mandatory.

Whither Sovereignty under the Palestine Mandate?

Although the League of Nations appointed Britain as Mandatory, most commentators agree sovereignty did not pass to Britain. Sovereignty instead lapsed into abeyance or suspension during the entire period of the Mandate. The early commentator Wright (1923) argued Article 22 of the Covenant of the League of Nations did not expressly confer sovereignty over the mandated areas.[41] Under international law, sovereignty over mandated former Ottoman territories resided in no particular nation following Turkey's ouster, and remained *suspended* or in *abeyance* pending the final disposition of such areas.[42]

Subsequent court rulings agreed with Wright's analysis regarding the unresolved status of sovereignty over mandated territories.

For example, the Australian High Court in 1937 considered whether the New South Wales *Fugitive Offenders Act* applied to a defendant alleged to have committed a murder in New Guinea, over which Australia was serving as Mandatory. The High Court rejected the extraterritorial application of Australian law to New Guinea, noting "every recognized authority on international law accepts the view that the Mandated Territory of New Guinea is not part of the King's dominions."[43] Interestingly, the High Court cited a prior ruling from the United Kingdom Privy Council that "[Palestine] is not within the King's dominions."[44]

Several years later, Judge McNair of the International Court of Justice also agreed with Wright, noting in his separate statement supporting the *Advisory Opinion on the International Status of South West Africa*:

> Upon sovereignty a very few words will suffice. The Mandates System ... is a new institution – a new relationship between a territory and its inhabitants on the one hand and the government which represents them internationally on the other – a new species of international government, which does not fit into the old conception of sovereignty and which is alien to it. The doctrine of sovereignty has no application to this new System.

> *Sovereignty over a Mandated Territory is in abeyance*; if and when the inhabitants of the territory obtain recognition as an independent State, as has already happened in the case of some Mandates, sovereignty will revive and vest in the new State.[45]

Some pro-Palestinian commentators disagree and believe the Mandate created a "state" in Palestine, and that the modern-day Palestinian Arabs are the successors to that state. This argument will be addressed further in Chapter 19.

Implications for the Palestinian Legal Case Today

Contrary to the arguments of some advocates of the Palestinian legal case, the League of Nations lawfully adopted the Palestine Mandate pursuant to its authority under the Treaty of Versailles and the Covenant of the League. Sovereignty did not pass from the ousted Ottoman Empire to the League of Nations, or to Britain, or to anyone else after Turkey renounced sovereignty in the 1923 Treaty of Lausanne. Nor did the Mandate purport to confer sovereignty on Britain or anyone else.

Moreover, the Mandate did not create a Palestinian state. The overarching purpose of the Mandate, as its Preamble and its various provisions make clear, was to pave the way for a National Home in Palestine for the Jewish people through immigration, land settlement, and institution-building, without prejudice to the civil and religious rights of the local non-Jewish population. If the Mandate contemplated an eventual state in Palestine, it would have been a Jewish state, not an Arab state. Britain, France, and the League delivered on the wartime promise of statehood for the Arab peoples liberated from Ottoman rule. Jordan, Saudi Arabia, Iraq, Syria, and Lebanon are the living embodiments of those kept promises.

Notes

1 Letter from Balfour to Lord Rothschild (2 Nov. 1917), http://gpophotoeng.gov.il/fotoweb/Grid.fwx?search=balfour%20declaration#Preview7 (last accessed 3 Feb. 2023).

2 Y. Porath, *The Emergence of the Palestinian-Arab National Movement, 1918–1929* (Frank Cass, 1974) at 35.

3 For a legalistic argument that the Balfour Declaration promised *all* of Palestine to the Jewish people, *see* L. Gribetz, *The Case for the Jews: An Interpretation of their Rights Under the Balfour Declaration and the Mandate for Palestine* at 44–46 (Bloch Publishing Co., 1930).

4 *See* War Cabinet Memorandum (Secret), G-164, CAB 24, pp. 169–186 (Oct. 1917). Appendix One, Item 5 at 4 (written statement of Dr. [Chaim] Weizmann, President of the English Zionist Federation, responding to the draft of Balfour Declaration: "Instead of 'establishment' would it not be more desirable to use the word 're-establishment'? By this small alteration, the historical connection with the ancient tradition would be indicated and the whole matter put in its true

light."), *reproduced in* J. Priestland, *Records of Jerusalem 1917–1971* Vol. I at 52 (Cambridge Univ. Press, Archive Editions, 2002).

5 Cmd. 5479, Palestine Royal Commission Report at 22, para. 14 (July 1937).

6 Israel Ministry of Foreign Affairs, The Balfour Declaration: 100 Years of International Recognition of the Jewish People's Tight to Self-Determination in their Historic Homeland, the Land of Israel (29 Oct. 2017), https://mfa.gov.il/MFA/ForeignPolicy/Issues/Pages/The-Balfour-Declaration.aspx (last accessed 3 Feb. 2023).

7 Covenant of the League of Nations, art. 20, http://iilj.org/wp-content/uploads/2016/08/The-Covenant-of-the-League-of-Nations.pdf (last accessed 3 Feb. 2023).

8 According to a League of Nations pamphlet published in 1927, the Mandate system was "an attempt to apply to the territories which were at the disposal of the Allied Powers a new device ensuring that the government of the backward peoples concerned shall not be the cause of the evils which have resulted in the past." League of Nations Information Section (League of Nations Secretariat, Geneva), *The Mandate System* at 5–6 (Feb. 1927).

9 Covenant of the League of Nations, Art. 22 (1920).

10 *Id.*

11 *See, e.g.,* Letter from Jamal Husseini, General Secretary, Executive Committee, Palestine Arab Congress to the President of the Council, League of Nations, 12 Apr. 1925 (arguing the League of Nations "should have asked Great Britain to abolish the Balfour Declaration which conflicts with the principles of its Covenant in accordance with article 20.")

12 A. Abdul Hadi, *The Balfour Declaration*, Annals of the American Academy of Political and Social Science, 164:1 at 20 (1932).

13 San Remo Resolution (25 Apr. 1920), https://ecf.org.il/media_items/299 (last accessed 4 Dec. 2023) [emphasis added].

14 See H. Grief, *The Legal Foundation and Borders of Israel Under International Law* at 18–44 (Mazo Pub., 2008); but see P. Terry, *Britain in Palestine (1917–1948) - Occupation, the Palestine Mandate, and International Law*, University of Bologna Law Review, 2:2 at 202–03 (2018) ("there can be no doubt that the [Balfour] Declaration did not have any status in international law.").

15 Treaty of Sèvres (10 Aug. 1920), https://treaties.fcdo.gov.uk/awweb/pdfopener?md=1&did=63986 (last accessed 12 Apr. 2024) [emphasis added].

16 *Id.*

17 *South West Africa Cases (Ethiopia v. South Africa; Liberia v. South Africa)*, Judgment of 29 Dec. 1962, I.C.J. Reports 319 at 329 (1962) ("[E]ach Mandate under the Mandates System constitutes a new international institution.").

18 The Mandates from the Ottoman Empire were Syria and the Lebanon, Mesopotamia (Iraq), and Palestine. The Mandates from Germany were British Cameroons, British Togoland, French Cameroons, French Togoland, Nauru, Ruanda-Urundi, South Pacific Mandate, South-West Africa, Tanganyika, the Territory of New Guinea, and Western Samoa.

19 League of Nations Treaty Series, Vol. XCIV, No. 2137, 27 Aug. 1928 at 57 (1929).

20 See generally J. McTague, *The British Military Administration in Palestine 1917–1920*, Journal of Palestine Studies, 7:3 at 55–76 (1978).

21 The Mandate for Palestine originally encompassed both Trans Jordan (the modern-day Hashemite Kingdom of Jordan) and Cis Jordan (the modern day State of Israel and the West Bank). In 1923 Britain, keeping McMahon's pledge to the Sherif Hussein, separated Trans Jordan from the Palestine Mandate and administered the territory separately until it gained independence in 1946. One historian has argued the Mandate should not be viewed as having legally taken effect until peace with Turkey was finalized on 6 Aug. 1924, calling into question the legality of certain local ordinances adopted in Palestine between Dec. 1917 and 1924. S.

Huneidi, *A Broken Trust: Herbert Samuel, Zionism and the Palestinians* at 21–22 (I.B. Tauris, 2001).

22 *See* Treaty of Peace with Turkey, signed at Lausanne (24 July 1923), http://sam.baskent.edu.tr/belge/Lausanne_ENG.pdf.

23 Cmd. 1785, *Mandate for Palestine, Together with a Note by the League of Nations Secretary General Relating to its Application to the Territory Known as Transjordan, Under the Provisions of Article 25* at 2 (1922) [emphasis added].

24 *See* B. Oppenheim and H. Lauterpacht (eds.), International Law: A Treatise (8th ed.) at 217–18 (1955); T.W. Mallison and S. Mallison, *The Palestine Problem: International Law and World Order* at 71 (Longmans, 1986) ("The [Balfour] Declaration is thereby established as international law through the recognized customary law-making processes of the implicit agreement of states expressed by toleration, acquiescence and silence."); K. Loevy, *Reinventing a Region (1915–22): Visions of the Middle East in Legal and Diplomatic Texts Leading to the Palestine Mandate*, Israel Law Review, 49:3 at 310 (2016) ("the Palestine Mandate legalised" the Balfour Declaration); S. Huneidi, *Was Balfour Reversible, The Colonial Office and Palestine, 1921–23*, *Journal of Palestine Studies*, 27:2 at 37–38 (1998) ("When the Mandate came into force ... the Balfour Declaration, which had been a political document, acquired a legal status."); *but see* G. Watson, *The Balfour Declaration in International Law*, Journal of Levantine Studies, 8:1, 101–20 at 107 (2018) ("In a sense, then, it is a category error to ask whether the Mandate transformed the Balfour Declaration into a legally-binding document, because the Mandate did not incorporate the Declaration word-for-word. Rather, the Mandate was a treaty-like instrument unto itself, as it was founded on a series of agreements, including the League Covenant, the San Remo Conference, the Treaty of Sèvres, and the actions of the League Council confirming the Mandate. There is little doubt that the Mandate had a binding character.").

25 Permanent Mandates Commission, *Minutes of the Fourteenth Session held at Geneva* (26 Oct.–13 Nov. 1928).

26 Cmd. 1785, Mandate for Palestine, Together with a Note by the League of Nations Secretary General Relating to its Application to the Territory Known as Transjordan, Under the Provisions of Article 25 (1922). The Minutes of the League Council's 22 July 1922 meeting state "The Council decided that the mandate for Palestine was approved." The Minutes of the Council 24 July 1922 meeting say "France had considered and Great Britain agreed that the mandate for Syria and Palestine should betaken together. The Council had confirmed this agreement by a unanimous vote."

27 League of Nations Official Journal, Aug. 1922 at 823 (emphasis added).

28 South West Africa Cases (Ethiopia v. South Africa; Liberia v. South Africa), *op. cit.* at 331.

29 E. Kedourie, *In the Anglo-Arab Labyrinth: The McMahon-Husayn Correspondence and Its Interpretations 1914–1939* (Frank Cass, 1976).

30 Cmd. 5957, Correspondence between Sir Henry McMahon, His Majesty's High Commissioner at Cairo and the Sherif Hussein of Mecca, July 1915–March 1916 (1939), containing letter from Sir Henry McMahon to the Sherif Hussein of Mecca, 24 Oct. 1915 (promising post-war independence to the Arabs on condition they ally with Britain against Turkey, but excluding "portions of Syria lying to the west of the districts of Damascus, Homs, Hama and Aleppo" and additional areas where French interests were implicated). Sir Herbert Samuel, the former British High Commissioner in Palestine, testifyied in secret before the Palestine Royal Commission in 1937 that Article 25 of the Mandate and the separation of Transjordan from Cisjordan reflected Britain's compliance with McMahon's pledge to Hussein. FO 492/19, Palestine Royal Commission, Minutes of Evidence Heard at Secret Sessions at 482, para. 8416 (1937).

31 J. Stoyanovksy, *The Mandate for Palestine: A Contribution to The Theory and Practice of International Mandates* at 55 (Longmans Green, 1928).
32 *Id.* at 66.
33 C. Williams, *Expressio Unius Est Exclusio Alterius*, Marquette Law Review, 15 at 191 (1931).
34 Palestine Commission on the Disturbances of Aug. 1929, *Evidence Heard by the Commission in Open Sittings and a Selection from the Exhibits Put in During those Sittings*, Colonial Paper No. 48 ("Shaw Commission Transcript"), para. 12,872 (1930) (testimony of Haj Amin al Husseini, 3 Dec. 1929).
35 King George V, "To the People of Palestine" (1 July 1920).
36 Letter from Palestine Arab Delegation to Lloyd George (5 Jan. 1922), *reproduced in* Priestland, *op. cit.*, Vol. I at 87–93.
37 For a contemporary version of this particular argument, *see* J. Quigley, *The Legality of a Jewish State: A Century of Debate over Rights in Palestine* at 93–97 (Cambridge Univ. Press, 2021).
38 Covenant of the League of Nations, *op. cit.* Art. 22.
39 *Id.*
40 Huneidi (2001), *op. cit.* at 24–25.
41 Q. Wright, *Sovereignty of the Mandates*, The American Journal of International Law, 17:4 at 694 (1923); Q. Wright, *Mandates Under the League of Nations* at 445–47 (Univ. of Chicago Press, 1930).
42 Wright (1923), *op. cit.* at 695, 697–98.
43 *Ffrost v. Stevenson* (1937) 58 C.L.R. 528, 581–82 (Evatt, J., who served ten years later as Chair of the United Nations Ad Hoc Committee for Palestine); *see also* J.L. Brierly, *The Law of Nations: An Introduction to the International Law of Peace* (5th ed.) at 165–67 (Oxford Univ. Press, 1956).
44 Ffrost v. Stevenson, *op. cit.* at 581.
45 *International Status of South-West Africa*, Advisory Opinion, 010-19500711-ADV-01-01, I.C.J. Reports at 150 (11 July 1950) [emphasis added]. As discussed in Chapter 4, Britain acted in derogation of these principles when it offered sovereignty without League of Nations approval to the Palestinian Arabs in the 1939 White Paper.

6

PALESTINIANS DENY THE EXISTENCE OF PALESTINE, 1920s–1930s

Pan-Arabism and Greater Syria

Immediately following World War I and continuing throughout the British Mandate period (1922–1948), Palestinian lawyers responded to the issuance of the Mandate with a variety of legal arguments, in much the same way the modern Palestinian movement has deployed legal arguments in its ongoing conflict with the State of Israel.

But unlike today's Palestinian legal goal of obtaining statehood in the West Bank, Gaza, and East Jerusalem, the Palestinian legal strategy following World War I and during the Mandate years was to *deny* the existence of Palestine as a separate political entity. Indeed, the concept of a separate "Palestinian people" or Palestinian nationalism *never* existed prior to the 1920s. Palestinian Arab lawyers and witnesses in the 1920s and 1930s repeatedly claimed the area known colloquially as "Palestine" was in fact part of Syria, or "southern Syria" to be precise.

Palestinian lawyers and witnesses thus urged that "Palestine" be merged into the rest of Syria. Doing so would thereby eliminate the legal basis for a stand-alone Palestine Mandate and the accompanying promise of a National Home in Palestine for the Jewish people, as well as the commitments regarding Jewish immigration and land settlement.

While it would be inconceivable today for any Palestinian lawyer or leader to urge the absorption of the West Bank and Gaza into Syria, that was exactly the Palestinian legal position for most of the post-World War I years through the mid-1930s.

The Arab denial of "Palestine" as a separate entity can be understood in a historical context. During the four centuries of Ottoman Turkish rule in the

DOI: 10.4324/9781032686561-9

Middle East (1517–1917), there was no geographic entity known as "Palestine." As discussed in Chapter 4, most of central and northern modern-day Israel and the West Bank were part of the Ottoman administrative district known as the *Vilayet* of Beirut. The southern part of Israel and the West Bank comprised the independent *Sanjak* of Jerusalem, reporting directly to Constantinople.

Ben-Bassat (2013) notes that "[a]t the end of the nineteenth century, Palestine did not constitute a separate geo-political entity or a recognized well-defined national state, as is often erroneously implied or assumed in research."[1]

Against this background, the Palestinian Arab post-mandate rejection of the existence of "Palestine" can be understood in three ways. First, to the extent the Balfour Declaration and the Mandate promised the establishment of a national home for the Jewish people "in Palestine," the Arabs countered by arguing there was no such place as "Palestine." Therefore, the League of Nations had acted outside its authority by granting Jewish rights in a non-existent, fictitious geopolitical entity.

As Porath (1974) noted:

> From the time the inhabitants of Syria were promised the right to choose their government, while the inhabitants of Palestine were excluded from this promise, it was reasonable to expect that the Palestinians would attribute their exclusion to the Balfour Declaration—and this fact then reinforced their desire to be considered a part of the population of Syria.[2]

Second, Palestinian Nationalism as such did not exist during the four centuries of Ottoman rule. The Arabs living in the areas known today as Israel, the West Bank, and Gaza never sought independence from Turkey prior to World War I. It was only at the behest of Britain during 1915–1916 that Hussein agreed to switch sides and fight Turkey in exchange for British pledges of post-war independence.[3] Pan-Arabism and anti-Zionism represented far more powerful galvanizing and motivating forces at that time than Palestinian nationalism.

Third, the French-British rivalry for influence in the Middle East during and after World War I played a role in rallying Arab support for the idea of a "Greater Syria" that would also include the area known as Palestine. As Porath (1974) explained:

> Thus it happened that two mutually antagonistic sides found themselves united on this point, although for different reasons: the French strove towards a 'Greater Syria' under their rule, while Arab nationalists strove for an independent 'Greater Syria,' with the Palestinians joining them primarily because of their fear of Zionism. The term 'Southern Syria,' which was common in French, passed into Palestinian usage and was adopted by the Arab nationalist movement.[4]

Palestine's Existence Denied

This background explains the multiple Palestinian Arab efforts after World War I to deny Palestine's separate political existence. In late November 1918, for example, a Palestinian Arab group filed a petition with the French Commissariat in Jerusalem "begging that Palestine might be formally included in Syria."[5]

Beginning in 1918, two Palestinian Arab organizations—*Al-Muntada al-Adabi* and *Al-Nadi al-Arabi*—issued calls for the absorption of Palestine into Syria. These groups were comprised of members from the two most prominent Palestinian Arab families, the Nashashibis (*Al-Muntada al-Adabi*) and the Husseinis (*Al-Nadi al-Arabi*). Despite a long history of rivalry between the two families, they were unified between 1918 and 1921 in pursuit of the elimination of a separate Palestine and its absorption into Syria.[6]

In February 1919, the Arab Delegation from Palestine to the Versailles Peace Conference submitted a formal petition (labeled as a "Decision"), urging that rather than be recognized as an independent Arab state, Palestine be deemed part of and merged into Syria:

> We consider Palestine as part of Arabic Syria as it has never been separated from it at any time. We are connected with it by national, religious, linguistic, natural, economical and geographic bonds ... In view of the above we desire that our distinct Southern Syria or Palestine should not be separated from the Independent Arabic Syrian Government.[7]

The "Decision" submitted to the Versailles Peace Conference stemmed from resolutions passed at the First Congress of the Muslim-Christian Associations in Jerusalem in January 1919. The delegates to the Congress also approved a resolution stating "we desire that our distinct Southern Syria not be separated from the Independent Arab Syrian Government."[8]

The Arab legal argument that there was no such political entity as "Palestine" continued after the League of Nations awarded the Palestine Mandate to Britain. In 1925, Jamal Husseini, a prominent Palestinian Arab and cousin of the Grand Mufti of Jerusalem, Haj Amin al-Husseini, filed a lawsuit challenging a decision of British High Commissioner Sir Herbert Samuel allowing local postage stamps to bear an inscription in Hebrew identifying the country as "Palestine E.I." (Palestine Eretz Israel).

Husseini's lawyer was the famed Auni Bey Abdul Hadi, who had attended the Versailles Conference as one of Sherif Hussein's two representatives, alongside Hussein's son and future King of Iraq, Prince Feisal. Abdul Hadi argued to the British court in Jerusalem that the correct name for the country should have been "Southern Syria." According to Abdul Hadi, "Palestine" was "not an Arab word." Palestine, he insisted to the court, was, in fact, part of Syria.[9]

Following the Hebron massacre and other violent outbreaks in Jerusalem, Tzfat, Haifa, and elsewhere in Palestine in late August 1929, the British Government convened an inquiry commission under the leadership of Sir Walter Shaw to conduct a trial in Jerusalem to determine the causes of the violence. At the Shaw Commission trial on 27 November 1929, the Arab side called as a witness Saleem Farah, a Cornell-trained agricultural expert. Under direct examination from the Arab lawyer M.E. Moghannam, Farah testified under oath as follows:

Q: Before the War, when we mention the word 'Syria,' can you tell us what that included?
A: That included the land from the Tarsus Mountains to the Sinai Peninsula and from the Mediterranean Sea to the Syrian Desert on the East.
Q: Do you mean by that that you never knew a separate Palestine, it did not have a separate entity at all?
A: No, I did not know ... that Palestine was a separate independent country.[10]

The Chief Secretary of the British Government of Palestine, Sir Harry Luke, also testified before the Shaw Commission in November 1929 in secret. Luke explained "Palestine is a purely artificial conception. There has never been until 1920 a political unit of Palestine. Palestine, Syria and Transjordan are from every point of view except the political one at the moment one country."[11]

Many other prominent Arabs also argued Palestine should have been regarded as part of Syria. George Antonius, author of the acclaimed book "The Arab Awakening," wrote a Memorandum dated 23 February 1939 explaining "[t]he term Syria in those days [pre-World War I] ... included that part of the country which was afterwards detached from it to form the mandated territory of Palestine."[12]

Antonius repeated this view when he appeared before the Palestine Royal Commission (the Peel Commission) on 18 January 1937 in Jerusalem. Antonius spent a considerable portion of his testimony arguing Palestine had always been part of Syria. He argued that detaching Palestine (or a portion of it) for a Jewish National Home ignored the reality that "Palestine has always been an integral part of Syria and that what was common to Syria was common to Palestine."[13]

Implications for the Palestinian Legal Case Today

The early denial of Palestine's separate geopolitical existence soon gave way to Palestinian national aspirations for the entirety of the area encompassed by the British Mandate. The Grand Mufti of Jerusalem, Haj Amin al-Husseini, emerged in the late 1920s as the driving force of Palestinian nationalism through a powerful combination of anti-Zionism, religio-nationalism, and violence.

The early Palestinian legal arguments and witness testimony denying Palestine's existence stand in stark contrast to the Palestinian political and legal positions today. While those arguments and testimonies may not be legally binding on the Palestinians today, they demonstrate an early example of Palestinian legal argumentation that miscalculated the political environment. The Palestinians hoped at the time that by denying Palestine's existence, they would be able to convince the international community not to create a separate Mandate for Palestine, and thereby not to pursue the reconstitution there of the Jewish national home. If the area of Palestine were instead absorbed into Syria, then there would have been no basis for pursuing the Jewish national home, at least according to Palestinian thinking at the time.

The League of Nations Council nevertheless unanimously approved the Palestine Mandate in July 1922. No amount of subsequent Palestinian legal argumentation against the existence of "Palestine" caused the League to rescind the Mandate, or to merge Palestine into the Mandate for Syria.

The Palestinian argument denying the existence of Palestine during the 1920s and 1930s also undermines the Palestinian narrative that Palestinian nationhood has existed for hundreds of years and was disrupted by Zionist "invasion" and "settler colonialism." In fact, the concept of Palestine as a separate Arab nation did not arise fully until after the Palestine Mandate had ended in May 1948. As will be discussed in succeeding chapters, Palestinian nationhood took a brief and quixotic form in the fall of 1948 with the formation of the short-lived "All-Palestine Government," which existed on paper only. Thereafter, the Palestinians abandoned the concept of an Arab Palestinian entity until the late 1950s. The Palestine Liberation Organization promulgated its original charter in 1964, but even at that time still disclaimed sovereignty over the West Bank and the Gaza Strip.

Notes

1 Y. Ben-Bassat, *Petitioning the Sultan: Protests and Justice in Late Ottoman Palestine 1865–1908* at 6 (I.B. Tauris, 2013).
2 Y. Porath, *The Emergence of the Palestinian-Arab National Movement, 1918–1929* at 72 (Frank Cass, 1974).
3 Winston Churchill testified many years later (12 Mar. 1937) before the Palestine Royal Commission that the Palestinian Arabs continued fighting alongside Turkey and attacking British troops until the end of the War. FO 492/19, *Palestine Royal Commission, Minutes of Evidence Heard at Secret Sessions* (Churchill *in camera* testimony).
4 Y. Porath, *The Emergence of the Palestinian-Arab National Movement, 1918–1929* at 74 (Frank Cass, 1974).
5 J. Priestland (ed.), *Records of Jerusalem 1917–1971*, Vol. I (1917–1920) at 152 (Cambridge Univ. Press, Archive Editions, 2002); *see also* Y. Porath, *The Emergence of the Palestinian-Arab National Movement, 1918–1929* at 79–82 (Frank Cass, 1974).
6 Porath (1974), *op. cit.* at 74–79.

7 Priestland, *op. cit.*, Vol. I at 324. Non-Arab observers, such as the American Section of the International Commission on Mandates in Turkey (otherwise known as the "King-Crane Commission") agreed "there should be no separation of the southern part of Syria, known as Palestine or the littoral western zone which includes Lebanon from the Syrian country." *Report of the American Section of the International Commission on Mandates in Turkey*, (28 Aug. 1919) Recommendation 8, https://ecf.org.il/media_items/951 (last accessed 20 Oct. 2022).
8 Porath (1974), *op. cit.* at 81–82.
9 *Husseini v. Government of Palestine*, High Court No. 55 (1925).
10 Colonial Paper 48, *Palestine Commission on the Disturbances of August, 1929, Evidence Heard by the Commission in Open Sittings and a Selection from the Exhibits Put in During those Sittings*, paras. 11, 257–58 (27 Nov. 1929).
11 *Palestine Commission of Enquiry on Disturbances of August, 1929, Chairman (Sir Walter Shaw's) Copy of Evidence Taken in Camera*, Colonial Office file CO 967/91 (1929) (Luke secret testimony).
12 *Correspondence between Sir Henry McMahon, His Majesty's High Commissioner at Cairo and the Sherif Hussein of Mecca, July 1915–March 1916*, Cmd. 5957, Annex A (Memorandum from George Antonius, 23 Feb. 1939).
13 Palestine Royal Commission, *Minutes of Evidence Heard at Public Sessions*, Colonial Paper 134, para. 5626 (18 Jan. 1937).

7

PALESTINIANS REJECT THE TWO-STATE SOLUTION, 1937

The Peel Commission Report

In 1936 the Mufti launched an all-out uprising against British rule, prompting the British Government to appoint a Royal Commission under the leadership of Lord Peel to conduct a thorough investigation and make recommendations for Palestine's future.

The Commission heard live testimony in the fall of 1936 and early 1937 from 60 witnesses at 30 public sessions in Jerusalem, and from 53 witnesses at 40 non-public sessions. The Commission also received public testimony from two witnesses and non-public testimony from eight additional witnesses when it returned to London in early 1937.[1]

The Royal Commission's Report was dated 22 June 1937, and made public on 7 July 1937.[2] The Report recommended the original version of the two-state solution for Palestine, allocating a tiny portion of northwest Palestine to the Jews, and the remainder to the Arabs for a separate state in confederation with Transjordan.

The Report addressed comprehensively the Balfour Declaration, the Mandate, land and immigration, education and public health, and a broad range of other issues. Regarding the Balfour Declaration, the Report noted, quoting former Prime Minister David Lloyd George's non-public testimony, the strategic importance of the Declaration to the Allied war victory, and the benefits that victory brought to the Arabs:

> The Arabs do not appear to realize in the first place that the general position of the Arab world as a whole is mainly due to the great sacrifices made by the Allied and Associated Powers in the War and secondly, that,

DOI: 10.4324/9781032686561-10

> in so far as the Balfour Declaration helped to bring about the Allies' victory, it helped to bring about the emancipation of all the Arab countries from Turkish rule. If the Turks and Germans had won the War, it is improbable that all the Arab countries, except Palestine, would now have become or about to become independent States.[3]

The Report also explained, however, how the Arabs perceived the Balfour Declaration as a breach of Britain's wartime promises to the Sherif Hussein of Mecca, and therefore the Arabs considered the Balfour Declaration and those portions of the Mandate implementing the Balfour Declaration null and void.

The Report further addressed the Arab legal claims regarding the conflict between the Balfour Declaration and Article 22 of the Covenant of the League of Nations. The Report noted the language of the fourth paragraph of Article 22, provisionally recognizing "certain communities formerly belonging to the Turkish Empire" as prime candidates for early independence should be read merely as permitting, but not *requiring* independence for all such communities. Moreover, the Report pointed to other language in Article 22 vesting broad power in the League of Nations to define the degree of authority to be vested in the Mandatory Power.

Finally, the Report noted the fundamental differences between the Palestine Mandate and the mandates for Iraq and Syria. The Report described the Palestine Mandate as imposing a "double-duty" and "equally binding" obligations on Britain, but "[u]nquestionably, however, the primary purpose of the Mandate, as expressed in its preamble and its articles, is to promote the establishment of the Jewish National Home."[4]

The Two-State Solution

The Peel Commission Report noted that all attempts to reconcile the Arab and Jewish sides had failed, and therefore "[t]he situation in Palestine has reached a deadlock."[5] Therefore, a "drastic" new approach was needed, namely, the two-state solution:

> Manifestly the problem cannot be solved by giving either the Arabs or the Jews all they want. The answer to the question 'Which of them in the end will govern Palestine?' must surely be 'Neither' ... Partition seems to offer at least a chance of ultimate peace. We can see none in any other plan.[6]

The Commission proposed the tripartite division of Palestine into Jewish and Arab states, with an "exchange of populations" resulting in the resettlement of Galilee Arabs, and the payment of British and Jewish subventions to the Arab State.[7] The Arab state would be confederated with Transjordan.

A small area in the middle of the country from Jaffa to Jerusalem and Bethlehem would remain under permanent British Mandatory rule.[8]

Two months before the Peel Commission issued its report, Commissioner Sir Laurie Hammond wrote a note for the file regarding the "Clean Cut," the Commissioners' confidential short-hand description for partition:

> I am as fully convinced as any of my colleagues that the present system of Mandatory Government is hopeless and can only lead to great trouble and expense in the future. Our report proves this in my opinion most convincingly. Further, I believe the only remedy lies in giving the Arabs and the Jews separate States with full sovereign powers except to such extent as they may be curtailed by reluctant acquiescence in an imposed treaty ... I dislike signing in the dark.[9]

The Peel Commission Report concluded with these famous words:

> 'Half a loaf is better than no bread' is a peculiarly English proverb; and, considering the attitude which both Arab and the Jewish representatives adopted in giving evidence before us, we think it improbable that either Party will be satisfied at first sight with the proposals we have submitted for the adjustment of their rival claims. For Partition means that neither will get all it wants. It means that the Arabs must acquiesce in the exclusion from their sovereignty of a piece of territory, long occupied and once ruled by them. It means that the Jews must be content with less than the Land of Israel they once ruled and have hoped to rule again. But it seems to us possible on reflection both parties will come to realize that the drawbacks of Partition are outweighed by its advantages. For, if it offers neither party all it wants, it offers each what it wants most, namely freedom and security ... To both Arabs and Jews Partition offers a prospect – and we see no such prospect in any other policy – of obtaining the inestimable boon of peace.[10]

Palestinian Arab Rejection of the Two-State Solution

Palestinian Arab reaction to the Peel Commission Report was highly negative, despite the Report's recommendation that the vast majority of Palestine's territory be allocated to them for statehood in confederation with Transjordan. The Arab Higher Committee (AHC) sent a lengthy letter, dated 23 July 1937, to the High Commissioner in Palestine and the Permanent Mandates Commission in Geneva, expressing its "extreme disappointment" in the Report and "repugnance to the whole of the partition scheme."[11] The letter outlined many arguments that continue resonating in the conflict today.

The AHC letter began with a general objection to the Report's treatment of the Jews as equal to the Arabs of Palestine:

> We regard as a profound error the point of view adopted by His Majesty's Government that in their mutual relations the Arabs and the Jews of Palestine stand as opposed litigants with equal rights ... For the Arabs of Palestine are the owners of the country and lived in it prior to the British occupation for hundreds of years and in it they still constitute the overwhelming majority. The Jews on the other hand are a minority of intruders ...[12]

The letter reiterated the Arabs' repudiation of the Balfour Declaration and their demand that it be rescinded. The letter criticized the partition proposal as "strange." It noted the presence of "hundreds" of mosques, churches, religious shrines, and cemeteries in the area designated as the future Jewish State, and argued placing such sites under Jewish control would be "illogical, humiliating, impracticable, and fraught with danger."[13]

The letter also objected to the creation of a permanent British-controlled area in the center of the country, noting "this corridor effectively cuts off the Southern from the Eastern and Northern sections of the proposed Arab State."[14] The letter expressed additional concerns, on behalf of the Muslim and Christian Arabs of Palestine, that "[t]he security of the Holy Places ... can only be prejudiced by the establishment of a mandatory regime in which the Jews will undoubtedly be predominant."[15]

The letter then noted the "Arabs of Palestine, of whatever party or class, forcibly repudiate the partition scheme in its entirety."[16] The letter bluntly threatened further violence, noting prior disturbances in Palestine had been caused by Jewish encroachment, and therefore:

> [I]t is only natural to expect that the struggle will be intensified if the Jews receive immediately many times the extent of the territory which they have been able to acquire in the 15 years during which the mandate has been fully implemented ... We therefore assert without hesitation or doubt that the peace for which the Royal Commission declares it is working and which it calls an 'indispensable [sic] boon' cannot be established in this country by continuation of these arbitrary experiments.[17]

The letter concluded with the familiar Arab legal argument that Palestine belonged solely to the Arabs, based on Britain's wartime pledge of independence to the Middle East Arabs, and Articles 20 and 22 of the Covenant of the League of Nations.[18]

In January 1938 the British Government announced it would send a technical commission to Palestine to prepare a detailed report regarding the mechanics of partition. The Technical Commission (which the Arabs boycotted),[19] was chaired by Sir John Woodhead. The Government indicated it would withhold final judgment on whether to seek approval from the League of Nations to implement the two-state solution pending receipt of the Woodhead Commission's report.[20]

The Woodhead Commission released its report on 8 November 1938, ironically only one day before the *Kristallnacht* pogrom in Germany. The Woodhead Commission concluded the Peel Commission's partition recommendation was unworkable, and recommended it not be implemented:

> We conclude that, apart from the question whether plan C, which is the best plan that the majority of us have been able to devise, will be accepted by those concerned, the financial and economic objections to that plan without a customs union between the three areas, are so serious that we could not recommend it. If, therefore, we were to confine ourselves strictly to our terms of reference, we should have no choice but to report that we have been unable to recommend boundaries which will afford a reasonable prospect of the eventual establishment of self-supporting Arab and Jewish States.[21]

The British Government accepted the recommendation and shelved the two-state solution.

Implications for the Palestinian Legal Case Today

The Palestine Royal Commission's two-state solution would have given the Palestinian Arabs statehood over the vast majority of Mandate Palestine, yet the Mufti adamantly rejected the offer.

The Mufti's unwillingness to compromise cost the Palestinian Arabs their independence in 1937 (albeit under Transjordanian sovereignty). The British Government, as will be discussed in the next chapter, made an even better offer to the Mufti in May 1939 for a single, majority-ruled Palestinian Arab state to replace British rule after ten years. But the Mufti inexplicably rejected that offer too. The Palestinian Arabs have never recovered from the Mufti's strategic blunders.

Following World War II, the United Nations General Assembly reinvigorated the two-state solution, approving Resolution 181 on 29 November 1947. The Resolution adopted a variant of the original Peel Commission partition proposal, and ordered the British Mandate terminated no later than 1 August 1948.[22] The Jewish side accepted the Resolution and the partition plan, even though once again the amount of land allocated for the Jewish state was far less than the available land in Palestine. The Arab side, consistent as always, rejected Resolution 181, rejected partition, rejected the two-state solution, and instead declared war on the nascent Jewish State. When the war ended, Jordan wound up with control of most of the area that Resolution 181 had designated for Palestinian Arab statehood.

For the next 19 years (1948–1967), Arab policy continued the all-or-nothing demand for Arab sovereignty over *all* of pre-1948 Palestine. During those two decades, the Arab world and the international community did *nothing* to promote the creation of a Palestinian State in the West Bank and the Gaza Strip, the former areas of Palestine now under Jordanian and Egyptian control. The Arabs argued instead after 1948, using the same arguments the Mufti and Auni Bey had been making since the 1920s, that Israel (the "Zionist Entity") should be declared legally null and void, as it was based on the "illegal" Balfour Declaration and the "illegal" implementing provisions of the Mandate. It was only *after* Israel occupied the West Bank and Gaza Strip during and after the June 1967 Six-Day War that the international community and the Palestinians themselves asserted Palestinian self-determination rights in the West Bank.

More than 80 years after the Peel Commission issued its Report, most observers continue to believe the two-state solution provides the only viable option for a peaceful resolution of the conflict. Ironically, the Mufti (followed by the entire Arab world, who voted unanimously against Resolution 181) rejected the very outcome that the Palestinians and their supporters demand today.

Notes

1 Cmd. 5479, Peel Commission Report, *Palestine Royal Commission Report* at x. (July 1937).
2 *Id.*
3 *Id.* at 24, para. 19.
4 *Id.* at 39, para. 42.
5 *Id.* at 363.
6 *Id.* at 375–76.
7 Commissioner Coupland wrote a lengthy memorandum to the other Commissioners regarding the partition proposal, indicating it represented his and Commissioner Hammond's "joint suggestions on the main points." The note characterized the swaps of land and populations as "far the most difficult part of the whole scheme." CO 733/346/9, R. Coupland, "Note for Discussion of Partition" (the note is undated, but the file indicates a date of 7 Dec. 1936, which is remarkable given the Commission was still several months away from completing the hearings).
8 *Id.* at 381–91. A note by Commissioner (Professor) Coupland, written prior to the completion of the final Report, sheds interesting light on the Commission's deliberations regarding partition. Coupland described the partition proposal as the "Clean Cut" idea, saying "[i]n broad outline it amounts to an effort to buy out the Arabs from a part of Palestine in which the Jews would be left, we hope, undisturbed. We have no idea of what it may cost, or whether it is really

practicable ... I own to a fear that the 'clean cut' may result in a constused festering wound, and the blame for hasty clumsy surgery may be laid at our door." CO 733/346/9, R. Coupland, "Note on 'Clean Cut'" (23 May 1937).

9 CO 733/346/9, Sir L. Hammond, "Note on 'Clean Cut'" (21 May 1937).

10 *Id.* at 394–95.

11 FO 371/20810, Letter from Arab Higher Committee to High Commissioner of Palestine (23 July 1937). The letter was also published in pamphlet form, and can be viewed at https://www.loc.gov/rr/amed/pdf/palestine1/Memorandum-submitted-by-Arab%20higher-committe.pdf (last accessed 4 Dec. 2023).

12 *Id.* at 2.

13 *Id.* at 6, 8–9.

14 *Id.* at 11.

15 *Id.* at 13.

16 *Id.* at 19.

17 *Id.*

18 *Id.* at 19–20. Arab reaction outside Palestine was also harsh. The British High Commissioner in Egypt, Sir Miles Lampson, cabled the Foreign Office on 27 July 1937 to report his conversation the previous evening with the Prime Minister of Egypt, Mostafa el-Nahas:

> Nahas said he could not too strongly deplore the suggestion of partition. To start with Egypt could not regard with equanimity prospect of an independent Jewish State as her neighbor. Apart from questions of defence, etc., who could say the voracious Jews would not claim Sinai next? Or provoke trouble with the Jewish community in Egypt itself? He urged only solution was creation of an independent Arab State allied with Great Britain and with fullest guarantees of religious and racial toleration for the Jews, Arabs, Moslems and Christians alike.

FO 371/20810, Telegram No. 427 from Sir Miles Lampson to Foreign Office (27 July 1937).

19 Cmd. 5854, *Palestine Partition Commission Report* at 8 (Nov. 1938).

20 *Id.* at 4.

21 *Id.* at 13–14.

22 United Nations General Assembly, Resolution 181 (II), A/RES/181(II) (29 Nov. 1947).

8

PALESTINIANS REJECT THE ONE-STATE SOLUTION, 1939

The White Paper

As discussed in Chapter 4, in early February 1939 the British Government convened representatives of the Jews, the Palestinian Arabs, and the surrounding Arab States in parallel conferences at St. James' Palace in London under the auspices of Colonial Secretary Malcolm MacDonald to negotiate the future of Palestine. The conferences collapsed without agreement in mid-March 1939.

The failure of the London Conferences led the British Government to act unilaterally, issuing the so-called MacDonald White Paper on 17 May 1939.[1]

The White Paper eliminated Jewish immigration to Palestine and land purchases on the eve of the Holocaust. The White Paper also rejected Jewish statehood in Palestine. Instead, Palestine would become a majority-ruled, Palestinian Arab state ten years later, meaning May 1949. The Arabs received an absolute veto over future Jewish immigration after an initial five-year period during which a maximum total of 75,000 Jews would be permitted to immigrate, thereby locking in a two-to-one Arab majority in Palestine. The White Paper contemplated Palestine would become independent by 1949 under majority/Arab rule.

The Palestinian Arab strategy, combining violence on the ground with legal framing and a keen sense of Britain's desire to appease and neutralize the Arabs as potential Nazi allies, had succeeded in achieving an enormous change in British policy toward Zionism. Ironically, despite Britain's overarching effort to placate Arab demands, the Mufti nevertheless chose to spend most of the coming war in Berlin collaborating with the Nazi regime, helping recruit Bosnian Muslims to the Wehrmacht and urging Hitler

DOI: 10.4324/9781032686561-11

to bomb Tel Aviv, rather than leveraging the White Paper to build a state for his people in Palestine.

MacDonald sent the draft White Paper to the entire Cabinet on 13 April 1939.[2] The Cabinet convened several times during April and May 1939 to consider various additional drafts of the White Paper.[3] The Cabinet met again on 17 May 1939 and authorized MacDonald to release the White Paper later that same day.[4]

MacDonald said the Government should be prepared for the possibility the League of Nations Council might ask the Permanent Court of International Justice in the Hague to determine whether the White Paper unlawfully breached the Mandate. British Foreign Secretary Lord Halifax, in a remark that would be inconceivable for anyone to make about today's United Nations, expressed "anxiety" about the prospect of the Council of the League, which was "much under the influence of Zionist opinion," referring the White Paper to the Permanent International Court for judicial review.[5]

Within one month of issuing the White Paper, the British Government vested the High Commissioner in Palestine with the authority to promulgate regulations governing land transfers, retroactively to the 17 May 1939 publication date of the White Paper. The new regulations, almost entirely banning Jewish land acquisition in Palestine in violation of the anti-discrimination provision of the Mandate, were published in early 1940.[6]

The most important elements of the White Paper included:

First, the British Government declared "unequivocally that it is not part of their policy that Palestine should become a Jewish State."[7]

Second, instead of a wholly Jewish or Arab State, the British Government declared its support for the establishment within ten years (unless circumstances at the time would warrant postponement) of an "independent Palestine State" with treaty relations with Britain, "in which the two peoples in Palestine, Arabs and Jews, share authority in government in such a way that the essential interests of each are secured."[8] This language masked the true intent of the White Paper, which was the creation of a single, majority-ruled Arab State in Palestine, as evidenced most clearly by the White Paper's severe limits on Jewish immigration and land acquisition.

Third, during the ten-year transitional period, local Arabs and Jews would have "an opportunity to participate in the machinery of government."[9] Palestinian Arabs and Jews would eventually assume control of certain government departments (assisted by British advisers), and Arabs and Jews would be offered seats on the Executive Council, the body advising the High Commissioner.

Fourth, Jewish immigration would be capped at a *maximum* of 75,000 (10,000 per year plus 25,000 refugees) over the next five years (May 1939 through May 1944), subject to the country's economic absorptive capacity.[10]

Fifth, at the end of five years, "no further Jewish immigration will be permitted unless the Arabs of Palestine are prepared to acquiesce in it."[11]

Sixth, the High Commissioner of Palestine would be vested with the authority to prohibit or restrict land sales to Jews.[12]

The White Paper represented an overwhelming victory for the Palestinian Arabs. It spelled the end of Zionist political aspirations in Palestine. It condemned millions of trapped European Jews to slaughter at the hands of the Nazis. Yet in another terrible miscalculation, the Mufti rejected the British offer of the one-state solution.

The Mufti-led Arab Higher Committee (AHC) for Palestine issued a formal response to the White Paper on 30 May 1939. Teeming with repeated reference to Palestinian "natural rights" and "justice," the AHC response faulted nearly every aspect of the White Paper.[13] The AHC slammed the British Government for not imposing an *immediate* ban on Jewish immigration. The land transfer restrictions were also unacceptable, because the Jews should have been banned *immediately* from buying even a single additional dunam of land anywhere in the country. The AHC also objected to any form of Jewish "participation" in the future Palestinian state, presumably including the right to citizenship and voting.

Any Arabs willing to say anything even remotely favorable about the White Paper were threatened. The Mufti's followers assassinated one member of the Arab National Defense Party who dared to signal the White Paper might be acceptable.

Appeal to the Permanent Mandates Commission

The Permanent Mandates Commission (PMC) of the League of Nations took up the White Paper at its regularly scheduled meetings in Geneva in June 1939.[14]

The PMC had, almost since its inception, functioned as a sort of appellate court where aggrieved Jewish and Arab parties, continuing a custom and practice they had pursued since the onset of the Mandate, would seek relief via highly legalistic petitions challenging various British actions and policies in Palestine as impermissible under the Covenant and the Mandate.

Natasha Wheatley (2015) described how Arabs and Jews employed "legal hermeneutics" in their petitions to the PMC during the Mandate years:

> Jews and Arabs in the former Ottoman territory turned this new legal architecture into a mode of politics. They wrote hundreds of petitions to the League and its Permanent Mandates Commission (PMC) that engaged closely with the structure of the system and its laws ... Both Jews and Arabs devoted extraordinary attention to composing their petitions [to the Permanent Mandates Commission] in an emphatically legal style. They combed the League's Covenant and the Mandate for Palestine with interpretative zeal, dissecting sentence structures, comparing and counting

articles, and arguing for the priority of one subsection over another. No comma or clause was left unexamined as both communities looked to unearth guarantees of their rights in the League's laws.[15]

The PMC and the League of Nations were far more sympathetic to Zionism than today's United Nations. The PMC had frequently expressed disagreement with those British policies it viewed as less than faithful to the letter of the Mandate and the Balfour Declaration. The Zionist leader Chaim Weizmann frequently lobbied various members of the PMC behind the scenes, and he did on this occasion as well.[16]

MacDonald's Reliance on the Hogarth Message

Colonial Secretary Malcolm MacDonald personally appeared before the PMC on behalf of the British Government, accompanied by his Legal Advisor, Sir Grattan Bushe. MacDonald made a lengthy, detailed and highly legalistic opening statement to the PMC at its 15 June 1939 session. Among other arguments, MacDonald relied heavily on the 4 January 1918 "Hogarth Message" (see Chapter 1) to support the British Government's position that the phrase "without prejudice to the civil and religious rights" in the Balfour Declaration was also intended to include the *political* rights of the indigenous Palestinian Arab population.

George Antonius, one of the Arab delegates to the London Conferences, had disclosed the existence of the Hogarth Message in his book *The Arab Awakening*, published only a few months prior to the start of the conferences.[17] According to Antonius, the Sherif Hussein was "greatly disturbed" by the 2 November 1917 Balfour Declaration, and requested an explanation, lest he change his mind about continuing to support the British against Turkey during World War I. The British Government dispatched Commander David George Hogarth to Jeddah to meet with Hussein during the first week of January 1918. Hogarth did not deliver anything in writing to Hussein. But according to Antonius, Hussein's contemporaneous notes reveal Hogarth, acting on instructions from London, gave Hussein an "explicit assurance that 'Jewish settlement in Palestine would only be allowed in so far as would be consistent with the *political* and economic freedom of the Arab population.'"[18]

Antonius argued the wording of the Hogarth Message, especially the phrase "*political* and economic freedom," should be viewed as a "fundamental departure from the text of the Balfour Declaration."[19] According to Antonius, the Hogarth Message *expanded* the Balfour Declaration's promise to the Arabs to protect the *civil* and religious rights of existing non-Jewish communities in Palestine and simultaneously *narrowed* the scope of the Declaration's promise to the Jewish people of a National Home in Palestine.

Hogarth's use of the broader term "political," according to Antonius, meant Britain *never* intended the Balfour Declaration to permit the Jews to become the majority population in Palestine or to achieve Jewish statehood in *any* portion of Palestine.[20]

Subsequent commentators, however, have vigorously disputed Antonius' reliance on the Hogarth Message as reliable evidence of British intent regarding the Balfour Declaration. One historian has assailed Antonius' account as having "no basis in fact" and "worthless," noting the drafters of the Hogarth Message intended it to serve as "nothing more than a reiteration of the Balfour Declaration."[21]

Another commentator, relying on Hogarth's own contemporaneous notes and correspondence, argued the phrase "in so far as is compatible with the political and economic freedom of the Arab population" was *not* intended to concede *any* claims of Arab sovereignty over Palestine, and at most should be understood as referring *only* to local self-government.[22] Even more significantly, Hogarth reported to London that Hussein raised *no* objections to the Balfour Declaration.[23]

But one passage from Hogarth's subsequent notes of his meeting with the Sherif tends to support the Palestinian Arab interpretation of the Hogarth message:

> The King would not accept an independent Jew State in Palestine, *nor was I instructed to warn him that such a state was contemplated by Great Britain.* He probably knows little or nothing of the actual or possible economy of Palestine and his ready assent to Jewish settlement there is not worth very much. But I think he appreciates the financial advantage of Arab co-operation with the Jews.[24]

The British Government was aware of the significance of this phrase in Hogarth's note and decided not to publish it when it released the text of the Hogarth message in the spring of 1939. Foreign Office official Lacy Baggallay minuted the phrase would be "rather damaging" if made public.[25] Others in the Foreign Office agreed with Baggallay, and the decision was made to keep Hogarth's notes concealed from public view.[26]

The Hogarth Message made a big impact on the Lord Chancellor, Lord Maugham, who told the Cabinet in early March 1939:

> [H]aving made a careful study of the pledges and undertakings given at various dates, in particular the statement made by Commander Hogarth to the Sherif of Mecca as to the meaning of the Balfour Declaration, he [the Lord Chancellor] felt satisfied that the honour of this country demanded some such limitation of Jewish immigration as the Colonial Secretary now proposed.[27]

During his June 1939 presentation to the PMC, Colonial Secretary Malcolm MacDonald characterized the Hogarth Message as "important evidence" of the intent of the drafters of the Balfour Declaration. Therefore, the British Government believed it had the authority to issue the May 1939 White Paper. Accordingly, MacDonald argued, the White Paper "did not require any alteration of the Mandate; and, in coming to that conclusion, it had naturally consulted its own legal advisors on the matter."[28]

The PMC Rejects the White Paper's Legality

Nevertheless, several members of the PMC were highly skeptical of the White Paper's legality, believing it conflicted with Britain's obligations under the Mandate. For example, Commissioner Frederick Mari Asbeck (the Baron van Asbeck) said the Mandate imposed *one* overriding international legal obligation on Britain – to establish the Jewish National Home in Palestine. Van Asbeck criticized MacDonald and the British Government for shirking that obligation.

Britain's obligation to protect the civil and religious rights of the existing non-Jewish population of Palestine was *subordinate* to that obligation, according to van Asbeck. The phrase "civil and religious rights" meant exactly what it said, and could not be stretched to include "political" rights for the Palestinian Arabs. If the League had intended to include political rights for the Arabs, it would have added that language to the Mandate. Moreover, if Britain had intended for the Mandate to include such rights, it should have so requested when the wording of the Mandate was negotiated.[29]

Commissioner van Asbeck also discounted MacDonald's newfound reliance on the Hogarth message, especially because the British Government had *never* previously relied on it or brought it to the PMC's attention:

> The basis for that change of emphasis was the Hogarth message ... But it could not have been known to the British and Allied statesmen, otherwise they would have been much more careful when referring to a Jewish State or Commonwealth; and it was unknown in 1922, or it would naturally have been referred to in the Churchill White Paper. It was unknown in 1930 when, at the seventeenth (extraordinary) session [of the PMC], the whole question of Palestine came up before the Mandates Commission. It was unknown to the Royal Commission which did not mention that important message in its report, although it was accustomed to examine thoroughly the material available; and it was not mentioned by the accredited representative of the mandatory Power in his explanations to the Commission at its thirty-second (extraordinary) session [of the PMC] in 1937, although there had then been ample occasion and necessity for bringing the message fully to light ... If, under the terms of the Hogarth

> message, the Arabs had the right to oppose immigration, and, in that respect, retained their previous freedom, that was the very antithesis of the Balfour Declaration and of the mandate which contained a very important obligation to facilitate immigration.[30]

Commissioner William Rappard, a Swiss lawyer and law professor who had been a frequent critic of British policy in Palestine, also asked why no British official had ever previously mentioned the Hogarth Message to the PMC or the League of Nations during the negotiations leading to the Mandate in 1922 or anytime thereafter. Rappard expressed great skepticism regarding the evidentiary value of the Hogarth Message, noting "a great deal was now being made after some seventeen years of silence."[31]

Commissioner van Asbeck also attacked the White Paper's conferral of an Arab veto on future Jewish immigration after the initial five-year period had expired. Van Asbeck challenged this "new interpretation [of the Mandate], and one based on data unknown to the Mandates Commission and the Council of the League."[32]

MacDonald tried to defend the White Paper in response to these arguments, relying on Article 22 of the Covenant of the League of Nations as a legal basis for justifying the new restrictions on Jewish immigration.

However, the majority of the PMC members remained unconvinced. PMC Chairman Pierre Orts of France summarized his view:

> The Mandate, in which the Balfour Declaration had been enshrined, placed Palestine under an international lien. It was only natural that the lien should seem a heavy one to the Arab inhabitants of the country. The Balfour Declaration was, however, an historic fact ... was not consent to the establishment of a Jewish National Home in Palestine the price – and a relatively small one – which the Arabs had paid for the liberation of lands from the Red Sea to the border of Cilicia on the one hand, Iran and the Mediterranean on the other, for the independence they were now winning or had already won, none of which they would ever have gained by their own efforts, and for all of which they had to thank the Allied Powers and particularly the British force in the Near East?[33]

Following several days of debate with MacDonald, the PMC members met privately in July 1939 to discuss the legality of the White Paper. The PMC unanimously agreed, and so reported to the Council of the League, that "the policy set out in the White Paper was not in accordance with the interpretation which, in agreement with the mandatory Power and the Council [of the League of Nations], the Commission had always placed upon the Mandate."[34]

Four of the seven members of the PMC went further, saying they

> did not feel able to state that the policy of the White Paper was in conformity with the Mandate, any contrary conclusion appearing to them to be ruled out by the very terms of the Mandate and by the fundamental intentions of its authors.[35]

The remaining three members believed "existing circumstances would justify the policy of the White Paper, provided the Council did not oppose it."[36]

The League Council never had the opportunity to consider the PMC's findings regarding the White Paper, as the outbreak of war in September 1939 left the League in limbo until it met in April 1946 to dissolve itself in favor of its successor, the newly-established United Nations.

Implications for the Palestinian Legal Case Today

The British Government offered the one-state solution to the Palestinian Arabs in May 1939. But the Palestinians, in yet another miscalculation, refused to embrace the stunning victory they achieved in London, in which they won almost everything they had demanded.

By maintaining their absolutist, uncompromising demands for "justice" and insisting the British Government give them *everything* they demanded, the Palestinians missed their best chance ever for statehood.[37] The Mufti's all-or-nothing approach set the stage for decades of subsequent Palestinian rejectionism, especially their rejection of the United Nations' November 1947 two-state solution and later variations on that solution.

The Palestinian rejection of the May 1939 White Paper also carried legal consequences. Britain offered statehood and sovereignty to the Palestinian Arabs. The Mufti and the Arab Higher Committee, acting on behalf of the Palestinian Arabs, flatly rejected the offer. That rejection arguably amounted to a *waiver* of statehood and sovereignty, as will be discussed in Chapter 18.

The Mufti's irredentism and extremism proved catastrophic to Palestinian Arab nationalism, dooming his people to a state of statelessness lasting well into the 21st century.

Notes

1 *Palestine: Statement of Policy*, Cmd. 6019 (1939) (hereafter "MacDonald White Paper"); *see also* CO 733/406/11, Code telegram from Foreign Office to British Ambassadors in Egypt, Iraq, Saudi Arabia and the United States (19 Mar. 1939) (describing key principles to be included in the White Paper).

2 CAB 24/285/1, Memorandum by the Secretary of State for the Colonies (13 Apr. 1939).

3 CO 733/410/9, Cabinet 21(39), Extract (Secret) from Conclusions of a Meeting (19 Apr. 1939); Cabinet 24(39), Extract (Secret) from Conclusions of a Meeting (26 Apr. 1939); Cabinet 25(39), Extract (Secret) from Conclusions of a Meeting (1 May 1939); Cabinet 26(39), Extract (Secret) from Conclusions of a Meeting (3 May 1939).
4 CAB 23/99/7, Minutes (Secret) of a Meeting of the Cabinet at 16 (17 May 1939).
5 *Id.* at 12–13; *see also* FO 371/23235, CP 28(39), Extract from Cabinet Conclusions at 2, 3 (17 May 1939); *see also* CO 733/410/9 (same).
6 *See* CO 733/418/13, Palestine Land Transfer Regulations: Notes on League of Nations Aspect (4 Mar. 1940).
7 MacDonald White Paper, para. 4. MacDonald prepared an undated handwritten draft of the White Paper on the stationery of his country home, Hyde Hall in Essex. MacDonald's original handwritten draft stated this somewhat differently: "They therefore declare that, after twenty years' experience, the Balfour Declaration should no longer be read as envisaging the possibility of Palestine becoming a Jewish State, and that is no part of their policy to promote such a change." CO 733/410/9, MacDonald draft at 2–3.
8 MacDonald White Paper, paras. 8, 10(1) and 10(7). MacDonald's original handwritten draft made no mention of a fixed period for the transition, indicating instead the Mandate would continue until the Jews and Arabs had demonstrated the ability to cooperate and work together (effectively giving the Jews a veto over the future creation of an independent Palestine State). CO 733/410/9, MacDonald draft at 4–8.
9 MacDonald White Paper, para. 10(3).
10 *Id.* para. 14(1). MacDonald's original handwritten draft set the limit at 100,000 immigrants over the next five years, which would have brought the Jewish population of Palestine to 35% of the total. CO 733/410/9, MacDonald draft at 12.
11 MacDonald White Paper, para. 14(3).
12 *Id.* para. 17. MacDonald's original handwritten draft said the land transfer prohibitions and restrictions "will not necessarily be permanent." CO 733/410/9, MacDonald draft at 14. That language was not included in the published version of the White Paper. In Feb. 1940 the High Commissioner for Palestine issued the Land Transfer Regulations contemplated by the White Paper. The regulations divided the country into three zones. Land sales to Jews were prohibited in Zone A (6/615 sq. miles), largely corresponding to the modern day West Bank, Galilee, upper Negev and Gaza. Land sales to Jews were permissible but highly restricted in Zone B (3,295 sq. miles), consisting mostly of the lower Negev desert, portions of the Huleh Valley and the area around Ashkelon. Land sales were not restricted in Zone C (only 519 sq. miles), corresponding roughly to the modern day Tel Aviv metropolitan area, from Bat Yam to Netanya as well as other municipal areas, plus a small industrial area south of Haifa. Cmd. 6180, *Palestine Land Transfers Regulations* (28 Feb. 1940).
13 League of Nations Archives, Geneva, R4076/6A/30296/668, *Reply of the Arab Higher Committee for Palestine to the White Paper Issued by the British Government on May 17, 1939* (30 May 1939).
14 League of Nations, Permanent Mandates Commission, Minutes of the 36th Session, Held at Geneva from June 8 to June 29, 1939, Official No. C.170.M.100.1939.VI (June 1939).
15 N. Wheatley, *Mandatory Interpretation: Legal Hermeneutics and the New International Order in Arab and Jewish Petitions to the League of Nations*, Past and Present, 227:1 at 206–07 (2015).
16 CO 733/390/5, Letter from Lord Hankey (British member of the PMC) to MacDonald at 1 (30 June 1939) ("the Jews ... have carried out an active propaganda [campaign] with the members of the P.M.C").

17 G. Antonius, *The Arab Awakening* at 267–68 (Allegro, 1938). Jamal Husseini years later described Antonius as one of the two "main Arab strategists" during the 1939 London Conferences. W. Khalidi, *On Albert Hourani, the Arab Office, and the Anglo-American Committee of 1946*, Journal of Palestine Studies, 35:1, 60–79 at 64 (2005).

18 Cmd. 5964, *Statements Made on Behalf of His Majesty's Government during the Year 1918 in regard to the Future Status of Certain Part of the Ottoman Empire (1939) (including the Hogarth Message)*; Antonius, *op. cit.* at 269. Antonius' book is widely regarded as a classic text of the history of Arab nationalism in the early 20th century. Unfortunately, however, Antonius dedicated his book to the notorious anti-Semite Charles R. Crane, who had served as co-Chair of the King-Crane Commission. President Woodrow Wilson sent the Commission to Palestine and Syria in 1919 to study the proposed post-War mandates and the Arab desire for self-determination. Crane told William E. Dodd, the incoming United States Ambassador to Germany in 1934, that Hitler should be allowed to "have his way" with the Jews. W.E. Dodd and M. Dodd, *Ambassador Dodd's Diary* at 24–25 (diary entry, 4 July 1933) (Victor Gollancz, 1945). Crane also complained to Sir John Chancellor, the former British High Commissioner in Palestine, that "I do not like the idea of attributing everything that goes wrong in the Jewish world to Hitler. The minute they are caught in one of their tricks they immediately cry Hitler! Hitler!!" Chancellor Papers, MSS. Brit. Emp. S.284, Bodleian Libraries, Oxford, Box 20/MF16 (Letter from Crane to Chancellor, 11 Feb. 1934).

19 Antonius, *op. cit.* at 268.

20 *Id.* at 267–69.

21 E. Kedourie, *In the Anglo-Arab Labyrinth: The McMahon-Husayn Correspondence and Its Interpretations 1914–1939* at 282–84 (Frank Cass, 1976). According to Kedourie, Sir Mark Sykes, who drafted the Hogarth Message, "could not have had in mind any substantive, let alone fundamental, change in the Balfour declaration; for this reason if no other: such a change would have required ministerial authority." *Id.* at 283.

22 Esco Foundation for Palestine, *Palestine, A Study of Jewish, Arab and British Policies* Vol. I at 191–93 (Yale Univ. Press, 1947).

23 C. Sykes, *Crossroads to Israel: 1917–1948* at 30 (Indiana Univ. Press, 1965).

24 FO 371/23229, Hogarth note to High Commissioner, Cairo (extract) (15 Jan. 1918) (emphasis added).

25 FO 371/23229, Baggallay Minute (10 Mar. 1939); *see also* FO 371/23229, Letter from Baggallay to MacDonald (9 Mar. 1939) ("we should give the Arabs enough to show that the message was in fact delivered in the form intended, but need not go into the matter of King Hussein having given the impression that he would refuse to have a Jewish State").

26 FO 371/23229, Baxter and Butler Minutes (both 11 Mar. 1939).

27 CAB 23/97/10, Minutes (Secret) of Cabinet Meeting at 16 (8 Mar. 1939); CO 733/406/11, C.P. 10 (39), Extract (Secret) from Conclusions of a Meeting of the Cabinet (8 Mar. 1939) (same). The Lord Chancellor, who in January felt the legal arguments in support of Britain's position had not been articulated strongly enough in the MacKenzie memorandum, by early March came to harbor serious doubts about the strength of the British argument, telling the Cabinet "the correspondence in question was extremely unsatisfactory ... it was very difficult to contend that the letter of the 24th October, 1915, contained any specific exclusion of Palestine." CAB 23/97/9, Minutes (Secret) of Cabinet Meeting at 5 (2 Mar. 1939); CO 733/406/11, C.P. 9 (39), Extract (Secret) from Conclusions of a Meeting of the Cabinet (2 Mar. 1939) (same).

28 League of Nations, Permanent Mandates Commission, Minutes of the 36th Session, Held at Geneva from June 8 to June 29, 1939, Official No. C.170.M.100.1939.

VI at 95–102, 110. (June 1939). Downie also prepared a lengthy set of questions and answers for MacDonald to use in preparation for his appearance before the PMC. CO 733/410/9, H.F. Downie, Palestine: Points for Geneva (10 June 1939).

29 League of Nations, Permanent Mandates Commission, Minutes of the 36th Session, Held at Geneva from June 8 to June 29, 1939, Official No. C.170.M.100.1939.VI at 115 (June 1939). The original PMC verdict is located in the League of Nations Archives, R4079/6A/38140/668, Folios 85–96 ("Observations of the Permanent Mandates Commission on the policy laid down in the document entitled 'Palestine: Statement of Policy of May 1939'").

30 *Id.* at 116.

31 *Id.* at 105.

32 *Id.* at 116.

33 *Id.* at 183–84.

34 *Id.*, Annex 14, *Report to the Council on the Work of the Commission* at 275, para. 9.

35 *Id.*, para. 14.

36 *Id.*, para. 15. Lord Hankey, the British member of the PMC, attempted unsuccessfully to obtain even stronger language from the minority members of the PMC expressing support for the White Paper based on the British Government's *legal* argument that the White Paper did not violate the Mandate. League of Nations Archive, R4079/6A/38689/668, Folio 78, *Variante su dernier paragraphs de la conclusion* (with handwritten note indicating "*Prepare por Lord Hankey*") (28 June 1939) ("Finally, other members of the Commission … . believe also that present circumstances justify the policy of the White Paper, and they see not sufficient reasons for adding to the difficulties of the responsible Mandatory Power by dissenting from the view expressed by the Accredited [British Government] Representative [Malcolm MacDonald] *on the highest legal advice available to it that its policy is consistent with the Mandate*") (emphasis added).

37 The Arab Higher Committee's reply to the White Paper ended by proclaiming, in all capital letters, "PALESTINE SHALL BE INDEPENDENT WITHIN AN ARAB FEDERATION AND SHALL REMAIN FOREVER ARAB." *Id.* at 14. Nevertheless, several Arab and Palestinian leaders expressed support for the White Paper privately, but were afraid to oppose the Mufti publicly. Y. Porath, *The Emergence of the Palestinian-Arab National Movement, 1918–1929* at 290–91 (Frank Cass, 1974). Only Auni Bey Abdul Hadi seemed to understand the Palestinian Arabs had blown a tremendous opportunity, confiding to Kingsley Heath his wish the Palestinian Arabs would stop fighting over "details" since the White Paper "had, to a great extent, conceded Arab demands." CO 733/408/15, Letter from Kingsley Heath to High Commissioner MacMichael (14 July 1939).

9

PALESTINIANS AGAIN REJECT THE TWO-STATE SOLUTION, 1947

Britain Enlists the United Nations

World War II began less than four months after Britain issued the May 1939 White Paper. After the War ended, the League of Nations met for the last time on 18 April 1946 to dissolve itself in favor of the newly created United Nations.[1] The League adopted a Resolution, supported by Great Britain and others, noting the declared intention of the Mandatory Powers to continue administering their existing mandates "until other arrangements have been agreed upon between the United Nations and the respective Mandatory Powers."[2] The Mandate for Palestine continued in full force and effect pursuant to Article 80 of the United Nations Charter.[3]

Britain, however, had run out of patience with Palestine by early 1947. Following the failure of various last-ditch efforts in late 1946 and early 1947 to resolve the Palestine issue, a frustrated and depleted Britain turned the matter over to the newly-created United Nations. Britain asked the United Nations to make recommendations for Palestine's future, but said it would not enforce any such recommendations against the will of either the Palestinian Jewish or Arab communities.[4]

Accordingly, on 2 April 1947, the British Government submitted a formal written notice to the United Nations, requesting the Secretary-General place the question of Palestine on the Agenda of the General Assembly at its next regular Annual Session. The notice requested the appointment of a Special Committee under the auspices of the United Nations to undertake a study of the Palestine problem. The notice said Britain would ask the General Assembly to make recommendations, under Article 10 of the Charter of the United Nations, concerning the future government of Palestine.[5]

DOI: 10.4324/9781032686561-12

The General Assembly Offers the Two-State Solution

The British Government's notice set in motion a chain of events leading to the formation of the United Nations Special Committee on Palestine (UNSCOP) and its successor, the General Assembly Ad Hoc Committee on Palestine. Both committees, following months of public hearings, recommended in the fall of 1947 by majority votes that Palestine be partitioned into two states, one Jewish and one Arab.[6] The two-state solution, which the Palestine Royal Commission had first proposed a decade earlier, had come full circle.

The matter came to a vote before the United Nations General Assembly on 29 November 1947. Following a lengthy and tense debate featuring a variety of Arab appeals for "justice" on behalf of the Palestinians[7] the General Assembly approved, by the required two-thirds majority, the two-state solution for Palestine embodied in the "Plan of Partition with Economic Union" set forth in General Assembly Resolution 181(II).[8] Thirty-three nations (including both the United States and the Soviet Union) voted in favor, 13 voted against, and 11 (including Great Britain) abstained.[9]

The Partition Plan recommended Palestine be divided into separate Jewish and Arab countries with some form of economic union. Jerusalem, broadly defined as the entire metropolitan area including Bethlehem, would remain a separate entity under international control.

The United Nations recommended in Resolution 181(II) that the Mandate for Palestine be terminated no later than 1 August 1948. On 30 January 1948 Britain announced it would terminate the Palestine Mandate on 15 May 1948, three months earlier than the initial planned termination date of August 1948.[10]

We turn now to a closer look at the events leading to the United Nations' November 1947 two-state solution.

Resolution 181(II)

UNSCOP Report

The UNSCOP began its work in the spring of 1947, after Britain's decision in early 1947 to hand the Palestine matter over to the United Nations. The Committee conducted several weeks of evidentiary hearings in Jerusalem in the summer of 1947. The Palestinian Arabs boycotted the Committee, refusing to offer witnesses or otherwise cooperate in any manner.

Ultimately, the Special Committee could not agree unanimously on a solution for Palestine to recommend to the General Assembly. A majority (seven out of eleven) of the Special Committee members (Canada, Czechoslovakia, Guatemala, the Netherlands, Peru, Sweden, and Uruguay) supported the two-state solution. A minority of four countries (Iran, India, Australia, and Yugoslavia) favored the one-state solution under Palestinian Arab rule.

The Committee submitted its full Report to the Secretary General on 1 September 1947.

The Report began with a recitation of 11 unanimous recommendations, and then described the separate majority and minority recommendations.[11] The 11 unanimous recommendations included terminating the Mandate and granting independence to Palestine at the earliest possible date, following a short transition period. The unanimous recommendations also addressed the need to preserve access to the Holy Places in Palestine, to protect the human rights and religious freedom of minority groups in Palestine, and to preserve the economic unity of the country. The Special Committee also recommended unanimously that the international community take steps to deal urgently with the problem of European Jewish displaced persons, including admitting 150,000 Jewish Holocaust survivors into Palestine.

The Majority Report endorsed the two-state solution. It recommended partitioning Palestine into three separate entities – a Jewish state, an Arab state, and Jerusalem under international control as a separate entity at least for the first ten years. The Majority also recommended some sort of "economic union" between the Jewish and Arab states.[12]

The Majority Report began by assessing the competing nationalist claims of the Jews and Palestinian Arabs. The Majority Report first addressed the Jewish claim, examining whether the term "National Home for the Jewish People," as used in the Balfour Declaration and the Mandate, could be deemed as a matter of law to mean a Jewish State in all or part of Palestine:

> [N]either the Balfour Declaration nor the Mandate precluded the eventual creation of a Jewish State. The Mandate in its Preamble recognized, with regard to the Jewish people, the 'grounds for reconstituting their National Home.' By providing, as one of the main obligations of the mandatory Power the facilitation of Jewish immigration, it conferred upon the Jews an opportunity, through large-scale immigration, to create eventually a Jewish State with a Jewish majority. Both the Balfour Declaration and the Mandate involved international commitments to the Jewish people as a whole.[13]

The Majority Report acknowledged the provisions of both the Balfour Declaration and the Mandate regarding the civil and religious rights of the indigenous Arab population. But the Report, in language impossible to find in any modern-day United Nations publication, rejected any notion that the Palestinian Arabs enjoyed a superior claim to Palestine than the Jews:

> The Jewish assurance that no political injustice would be done to the Arabs by the creation of a Jewish State in Palestine, since the Arabs have never established a government there, gains some support from the fact

> that not since 63 B.C., when Pompey stormed Jerusalem, has Palestine been an independent State.[14]

The Majority Report then turned to an assessment of the Palestinian Arab case. Significantly, again in language one would never see from the modern-day United Nations, the Report cast doubt on the strength of Palestinian Arab nationalism:

> The Arabs consider that all of the territory of Palestine is by right Arab patrimony. Although in an Arab State they would recognize the right of Jews to continue in possession of land legally acquired by them during the Mandate, they would regard as a violation of their 'natural' right any effort, such as partition, to reduce the territory of Palestine. The desire of the Arab people of Palestine to safeguard their national existence is a very natural desire. However, Palestinian nationalism, as distinct from Arab nationalism, is itself a relatively new phenomenon, which appeared only after the division of the 'Arab rectangle' by the settlement of the First World War. The National Home policy and the vigorous policy of immigration pursued by the Jewish leadership has sharpened the Arab fear of danger from the intruding Jewish population.[15]

The Majority Report, in a further blow to Palestinian Arab nationalists, decisively rejected Palestinian Arab rights of self-determination in all of Palestine:

> With regard to the principle of self-determination, although international recognition was extended to this principle at the end of the First World War and it was adhered to with regard to the other Arab territories, at the time of the creation of the 'A' Mandates, it was not applied to Palestine, obviously because of the intention to make possible the creation of the Jewish National Home there. Actually, it may well be said that the Jewish National Home and the *sui generis* Mandate for Palestine run counter to that principle.[16]

The Majority Report likewise flatly rejected the longstanding Palestinian Arab legal argument (still made today in some quarters) that the Mandate was void because it conflicted with Article 22 of the Covenant of the League of Nations:

> There would seem to be no grounds for questioning the validity of the Mandate for the reason advanced by the Arab States. The terms of the Mandate for Palestine, formulated by the Supreme Council of the Principal Allied Powers as a part of the settlement of the First World War, were subsequently approved and confirmed by the Council of the League of Nations.[17]

The Majority Report then offered various reasons in support of the majority recommendation of the two-state solution:

> The basic premise underlying the partition proposal is that the claims to Palestine of the Arabs and Jews, both possessing validity, are irreconcilable, and that among all of the solutions advanced, partition will provide the most realistic and practicable settlement, and is the most likely to afford a workable basis for meeting in part the claims and national aspirations of both parties. It is a fact that both of these peoples have their historic roots in Palestine, and that both make vital contributions to the economic and cultural life of the country. The partition solution takes these considerations fully into account. The basic conflict in Palestine is a clash of two intense nationalisms ... Only by means of partition can these conflicting national aspirations find substantial expression and qualify both peoples to take their places as independent nations in the international community and in the United Nations. The partition solution provides that finality which is a most urgent need in the solution.[18]

The Majority Report is a remarkable document. Largely drafted by the American diplomat Ralph Bunche, who personally disfavored Jewish statehood in Palestine, it nevertheless stands as a powerful endorsement of Jewish national aspirations in Palestine. Moreover, in today's world, it would be unimaginable for any Committee of the United Nations to make such a powerful endorsement of Zionism. Indeed, less than three decades later the General Assembly had drifted so far away from UNSCOP and Resolution 181(II) that it voted to condemn Zionism as a form of "racism and racial discrimination."[19]

General Assembly Ad Hoc Committee and the International Court of Justice

On 22 November 1947 the General Assembly's Ad Hoc Committee on Palestine, formed to continue the work of UNSCOP and further refine the contours of the two-state solution, met in an atmosphere of high drama to consider a proposal from some of its members to seek an advisory opinion from the International Court of Justice on the legal issues regarding the two-state solution. The proposal lost by one vote, with the Chair of the Ad Hoc Committee, Australian Foreign Minister Herbert Evatt, casting the deciding vote against it.[20]

It was no surprise that Evatt, who had also served as a High Court Judge in Australia, preferred to protect the "court" over which he presided – the Ad Hoc Committee – and therefore objected to referring the matter to the International Court of Justice:

> "In exercising his casting vote against a proposal for judicial review, Evatt's conduct seems uncharacteristic. In fact, he knew a decision would

have been derailed by this unpromising reference to the Hague ... Evatt's instinct to avoid a reference to the Court ... had been correct: too much energy had been invested in grappling with the conundrum to make the prospect attractive to over-strained delegates. The law, as Evatt knew, was on his side: the United Nations Charter specifically empowered the Assembly to determine such matters referred by mandatory powers under Article 14. Advising the Security Council on matters of international peace and security was authorised under Article 11."[21]

Evatt's view echoed his prior rulings as a Judge of Australia's High Court regarding the legal status of mandated territories. The League of Nations had appointed Australia as the mandatory for New Guinea after World War I. In 1937 the Australian High Court considered whether the New South Wales Fugitive Offenders Act applied to a defendant alleged to have committed murder in New Guinea.

Evatt, writing for the Australian High Court, rejected the claim, noting "every recognized authority on international law accepts the view that the Mandated Territory of New Guinea is not part of the King's dominions."[22] Interestingly, Evatt supported his decision by citing a prior ruling from the United Kingdom Privy Council that "[Palestine] is not within the King's dominions."[23]

Evatt therefore dismissed the Arab push to "refer almost every aspect of the problem to the International Court of Justice" as "patently absurd ... for instance the question whether or not the Balfour Declaration is a legally binding declaration."[24] Evatt also argued the United Nations had sufficient legal authority to decide Palestine's future:

> As to the validity of the action proposed to be taken by the U.N. Assembly, I never had any doubt. The Palestine situation was obviously one likely to impair friendly relations among nations, and accordingly the Assembly was competent under Article 14 of the Charter to recommend measures for its peaceful adjustment, regardless of the origins of the situation. In addition the question also concerned the maintenance of international peace and security and accordingly the General Assembly could act under Article 11 of the Charter to call the attention to the Security Council to the position and make the appropriate recommendations to all States concerned.[25]

Legality of Resolution 181(II)

The United Nations General Assembly debated the two-state solution on 26 November 1947, three days prior to the 29 November vote. The Arab delegates raised a long list of legal objections to the two-state solution, including (i) the United Nations lacked jurisdiction over Palestine; (ii) the General Assembly could only make "recommendations," and lacked the legal authority to "impose" the two-state solution; (iii) partition constituted an act of "aggression" against the Palestinian Arabs, in violation of the United Nations Charter; (iv) the two-state solution violated Palestinian Arab rights of self-determination and Palestinian Arab "natural" and "historic" rights to sovereignty over all of Palestine; and (v) the two-state solution violated principles of democratic rule, as the Palestinian Arabs comprised two-thirds of the country's population.[26]

The Arab delegates also asserted the Palestinian Arabs had the right under the United Nations Charter's self-defense principles to resist the partition plan with violence, leading to the absurd proposition that the United Nations Charter allows member states and other objecting parties to resist United Nations resolutions with armed conflict and bloodshed.

The United Nations rejected every one of the Arab legal arguments.

The "Jewish State and the Arab State," wrote UNSCOP member Jorge Garcia Granados of Guatemala, "had been legally created by the supreme authority of civilized mankind."[27] As Gerson (1973) later explained:

> The United Nations was thus the most competent international body to determine the future of the Mandate on its termination in light of the fact that (a) the rights of the parties under the Mandate required preservation under article 80, and (b) the supervisory powers of the League of Nations, which included the interpretation of sovereign rights under the terms of the Mandate, had passed to the United Nations. The General Assembly's Partition Resolution was, moreover, a product of maximum international consideration and analysis of both Arab and Jewish positions. In this light, the United Nations Resolution must, as the Jewish Agency maintained at the time, be termed sui generis and to have been legally binding upon the parties.[28]

Other authorities agreed with Garcia Granados and Evatt that the United Nations, acting through the General Assembly, had the full legal authority to adopt the two-state solution for Palestine. The U.S. State Department's legal advisor, for example, noted in a May 1948 memorandum that "by virtue of the Assembly's passage of the resolution and Great Britain's 'acceptance' of the plan, these authorities appear to have made a legal disposition for the future of Palestine."[29] The Legal Adviser further noted the legitimacy of Resolution 181(II) stemmed from the international community's elevation of the Balfour Declaration to the status of an internationally binding legal instrument when it was incorporated into the Mandate for Palestine.[30]

Cassese (1981) argued that Resolution 181 was entitled to more legal weight than an ordinary General Assembly resolution:

> "What was the legal value of the Resolution? I submit that, since the General Assembly had special powers on mandated territories, its

> recommendations bore more weight than any ordinary Assembly resolution. If accepted by the parties concerned, they would have given rise to an *international agreement* binding on the parties. Under the system envisaged in 1946, actual acquisition of sovereignty should result from the above agreement, coupled with the actual display of control over the territory by the State on which the agreement had conferred sovereign rights. By contrast, as long as a State showed that it controlled the territory without the consent of the United Nations, it could not claim to be sovereign there; for the United Nations authorization or approval was necessary prerequisite for the conveyance of the legal title over the territory."[31]

However, Cassese also conceded the Arab rejection of Resolution 181 "led to the Resolution remaining a dead letter."[32]

Crawford (2005) agreed the United Nations acted lawfully in adopting Resolution 181(II):

> Three views of the validity and legal effects of GA resolution 181(II) are possible. It might have been ultra vires; it might have been only a recommendation, or it might have constituted a valid and effective disposition of Palestine, at least to the extent of authorizing those concerned to implement it. The view that the resolution was ultra vires derives from a general implication as to the dispositive powers of the General Assembly. However, even earlier practice suggested that United Nations organs can make binding dispositions of territory in appropriate circumstances, pursuant to a delegation of power from States concerned or otherwise.[33]

The International Court of Justice's *Namibia* opinion provides further support for this position. There, the Court said the General Assembly possesses more than mere recommendatory powers when it acts as a successor to the League of Nations regarding the disposition of mandated territories:

> In a further objection to General Assembly resolution 2145 (XXI) it is contended that it made pronouncements which the Assembly, not being a judicial organ, and not having previously referred the matter to any such organ, was not competent to make ... To deny to a political organ of the United Nations which is a successor of the League in this respect the right to act, on the argument that it lacks competence to render what is described as a judicial decision, would not only be inconsistent but would amount to a complete denial of the remedies available against fundamental breaches of an international undertaking ... For it would not be correct to assume that, because the General Assembly is in principle vested with recommendatory powers, it is debarred from adopting, in specific cases

within the framework of its competence, resolutions which make determinations or have operative design.[34]

Therefore, Britain lawfully continued as mandatory for Palestine following the termination of the League's existence; Britain lawfully referred the Palestine matter to the United Nations in February 1947; and the General Assembly lawfully adopted Resolution 181(II).

The United Nations recognized it would have made no sense to interpret the United Nations Charter as depriving the United Nations of at least recommendatory jurisdiction over former League of Nations-mandated territories. The United Nations also possessed authority under Articles 77 and 80 of the Charter to decide whether and how to convert a League of Nations mandate into a trusteeship.[35] But the United Nations failed to exercise that authority over Palestine. As a matter of law, therefore, the United Nations lost legal jurisdiction over Palestine and Jerusalem when the Mandate ended on 14/15 May 1948 with the United Nations having taken no steps pursuant to the requirements of Articles 77, 79, and 85 of the Charter to fill the void created by Britain's departure.[36]

At least one Arab commentator has explicitly acknowledged the legality of Resolution 181(II), noting "the Partition Plan was viewed as a legally binding decision," and the United Nations had the legal authority to modify and terminate the Mandate when it adopted Resolution 181(II).[37] Some Arab commentators argue Resolution 181(II) and the partition boundaries it proposed carry the force of law, and therefore Israel should be divested of sovereignty over the Arab-designated additional areas it captured during the 1948–1949 war.[38]

But other Arab legal commentators disagree. They contend Resolution 181(II) was either legally invalid or, even if it were legally valid, as a General Assembly resolution it merely set forth a recommendation and carried no legal weight:

> The Assembly's powers according to Articles 10, 11, 12, and 14 of the Charter are only recommendatory and without binding force on Member States. Hence, the Arab states did not contravene their Charter obligations when they, responding to the will of the Palestine Arab majority, rejected the Partition Plan ... the General Assembly could do no more than recommend a solution and ... its recommendation was not accepted by an Arab majority in Palestine.[39]

Dugard (2014) and others have taken this argument even further, insisting the Mandate for Palestine was never legally terminated, primarily because General Assembly resolutions (unlike Security Council resolutions) are non-binding.[40] General Assembly Resolution 181(II), they argue, was recommendatory only and carried no legal force. Consequently, the Mandate remains in effect today, and the international community continues to be bound by the "sacred trust" language in Article 22 of the Covenant of the League of Nations to deliver statehood to the Palestinian Arabs.

As discussed in Chapter 15, Dugard's argument, even if it possessed any validity, would be a double-edged sword for the Palestinians. For example, if the Mandate were still in effect today, then all Israeli settlements and land acquisition in the West Bank would be deemed lawful under Article Six of the Mandate, which required the Mandatory to facilitate Jewish land acquisition and settlement *everywhere* in Palestine west of the Jordan River.

In any event, Dugard and others argue the unilateral Israeli declaration of statehood on 14 May 1948 was invalid, as the Mandate says nothing about Jewish "statehood" in Palestine. Instead, when read together with Articles 22 and 20 of the Covenant of the League of Nations, the Mandate should have been construed as contemplating solely an eventual Arab State in Palestine. Thus, Dugard and others argue, the only permissible outcome today under international law today would be to terminate the State of Israel and establish a Palestinian Arab state over the entirety of mandatory Palestine.

In response to those arguments, some legal scholars characterize Resolution 181(II) as possessing "special status" in international law, for three reasons.[41] First, in addressing the Palestine issue, the General Assembly stepped into the shoes of the League of Nations, and "assumed the [League's] functions relative to the supervision of mandated territories."[42] This meant, according to Gerson (1978), that "the General Assembly's action in voting for partition may have been legally binding and not merely recommendatory, as General Assembly resolutions normally are."[43] Even Palestinian advocates such as Imseis (2021), who argue Resolution 181(II) lacked legal validity at the time of its adoption, concede that with the passage of time and acceptance of both the Palestinian Authority and the international community of the two-state solution, Resolution 181(II) eventually acquired the status of international law.[44]

Second, as Gavison (2013) noted, when Britain handed the Palestine question to the United Nations in early 1947,

> [This] amounted to the return of the Mandate to a sovereign or responsible party representing the international community. General Assembly Resolution 181 possessed, therefore, a special status and was not merely a recommendation. Accordingly, the General Assembly resolution to regulate sovereignty in the mandate territory did not involve a change in international law, but rather was an authoritative decision regarding the fate of territory under its control and thus entitled to recognition as an expression of international law.[45]

Third, all the permanent members of the Security Council (except the United Kingdom) voted in favor of Resolution 181(II), further vesting the Resolution with "special status" under international law. Significantly, the General Assembly added language to the resolution requesting the Security Council take steps to enforce the resolution, including "the necessary measures as provided for in the plan for its implementation."[46] This request gave the Security Council the option to take jurisdiction over the Palestine matter.[47]

Finally, and most significantly, the General Assembly requested the Security Council "determine as a threat to the peace, breach of the peace or act of aggression, in accordance with Article 39 of the Charter, any attempt to alter by force the settlement envisaged by this resolution." This language, of course, anticipated the Arabs would make good on their repeated threats to resist the two-state solution by force of arms. The language, therefore, provided further evidence of the General Assembly's intent not just to make mere "recommendations" for future options for Palestine, but instead to impose binding and enforceable legal obligations on Arabs and Jews alike.

The Jewish side argued the General Assembly had the legal authority to adopt the two-state solution. Future Israel Prime Minister Moshe Shertok, serving then as the Jewish Agency's delegate to the United Nations, argued in late April 1948 that General Assembly resolutions touching the national sovereignty of member states were recommendatory only, but

> the Palestine resolution was essentially different for it concerned the future of a territory subject to an international trust. Only the United Nations as a whole was competent to determine the future of the territory and its decision, therefore, had a binding force.[48]

This view finds some support from the International Court of Justice in the 1971 *Namibia* opinion, where the court said,

> it would not be correct to assume that, because the General Assembly is in principle vested with recommendatory powers, it is debarred from adopting, in specific cases within the framework of its competence, resolutions which make determinations or have operative design.[49]

The Court added to this view 25 years later in the *Legality of the Threat or Use of Nuclear Weapons* Advisory Opinion:

> General Assembly resolutions, even if they are not binding, may sometimes have normative value. They can, in certain circumstances, provide evidence important for establishing the existence of a rule or the emergence of an opinio juris. To establish whether this is true of a given General Assembly

> resolution, it is necessary to look at its content and the conditions of its adoption; it is also necessary to see whether an opinio juris exists as to its normative character. Or a series of resolutions may show the gradua1 evolution of the opinio juris required for the establishment of a new rule.[50]

E. Lauterpacht (1968) offers a somewhat different view regarding the legality of Resolution 181:

> While, of course, it is unfortunate that the Arabs rejected the resolution, they were to some extent correct in their incidental assertion that the General Assembly was not able by resolution to dispose in a binding manner of the whole or any part of the territory of Palestine. Palestine was not the property of the U.N. to give or withhold as it pleased. The role of the U.N. was a restricted one. Its acquiescence in the termination by Britain of its obligations was ... a legal necessity. Moreover, the Assembly could, by putting forward a plan which the interested parties might accept, provide the legal basis for the settlement of the future government of the country. But resolutions of the General Assembly do not normally create legal obligations for the members of the U.N. (even if Israel and the proposed Arab state had been members at the time, which they were not); and the Partition Resolution did not have a legislative character. The Assembly could not by its resolution give the Jews and Arabs of Palestine any rights which either did not otherwise possess; nor, correspondingly, could it take away such rights as they did possess.[51]

Imseis (2021) offered the most recent view from the Palestinian perspective, arguing Resolution 181 (II) was unlawful at the time it was adopted because it failed to give due regard to the local Palestinian Arab population's opposition to the two-state solution:

> [T[he fundamental importance of assessing the legality of Resolution 181(II) through the prism of the primacy of the consent of the governed, a crucial frame of reference if subaltern interests are to be given their due. This primacy arises from the substantive limits on the exercise of the procedural right of the General Assembly to make recommendations under Article 10 of the Charter. By the very terms of that article, these limits are in turn defined by the scope of the Charter, which, because of the continuation of the principles and regime of the mandate system, necessarily includes the sacred trust principles embodied in Article 22 of the League of Nations Covenant and self-determination of peoples living within class A mandated territories. In the end, therefore, Resolution 181(II) was illegal under international law, not because it purported to impose a decision that went beyond its powers of recommendation, but because its substantive

content-namely, partition against the will of the indigenous majority of Palestine-was ipso facto in violation of the Charter and the international rule of law ... At bottom, the resolution represented the clash between the hegemonic and European-dominated General Assembly's interest in the juridical establishment of a Jewish State in Palestine, and the obstacle to doing so in the form of the very presence of a majority indigenous Muslim and Christian Arab population who persistently objected to it.[52]

Response to Imseis

Imseis' allegation that the United Nations' two-state solution of November 1947 represented a European effort to subjugate the indigenous Palestinian Arab population to the dominance of European Jews lacks support in the historical record. Imseis' position reflects an increasingly prominent aspect of the Palestinian legal case today, aimed at challenging the underlying legitimacy of Israel's creation. Imseis' argument is flawed for a variety of reasons:

First, Imseis fails to address the Palestinian Arab decision to boycott UNSCOP during its work in Palestine during the summer and early fall of 1947.

On 13 June 1947 Jamal Husseini, Vice Chairman of the Palestine Arab Higher Committee (AHC) and cousin of the exiled former Grand Mufti of Jerusalem, Haj Amin al Husseini, formally notified the United Nations Secretary General that the Palestinian Arabs would refuse all cooperation with the Special Committee.[53] Husseini's cousin, the Mufti Haj Amin al Husseini, threatened the lives of any Palestinian who dared cooperate with UNSCOP in violation of the boycott.[54]

On 30 June 1947 the United States Consul General in Jerusalem cabled the Secretary of State, noting the Special Committee had made "no headway whatever toward changing the rigid line of non-cooperation adopted by the Arab Higher Committee."[55]

UNSCOP Chairman Justice Emil Sandstrom of Sweden wrote to Jamal Husseini on 8 July 1947 asking him to reconsider. Husseini responded on 10 July, again rejecting any Palestinian Arab cooperation with the Special Committee.[56]

The Special Committee members viewed the Palestinian Arab boycott as self-defeating. UNSCOP member Jorge Garcia Granados of Guatemala, for example, recalled how "the Arab Higher Committee's uncompromising attitude, its refusal to consider the possibility of any conciliatory course, was to prove a convincing argument for partition."[57]

Jamal Husseini eventually backtracked and testified three times before UNSCOP's successor, the United Nations Ad Hoc Committee on Palestine. In his appearances before the Ad Hoc Committee on 29 September 1947, 18 October 1947, and 24 November 1947, Husseini took full advantage of the opportunity to make the Palestinian Arab case.

In his final appearance before the Committee on 24 November 1947, only three days before the partition vote, Husseini, in language remarkably similar to Imseis, argued the United Nations was powerless to make any recommendations for Palestine without the approval of the Palestinian Arabs themselves:

> Palestine was Arab by virtue of centuries of permanent occupation and possession and that the Arabs were entitled to the right of shaping the government and forming the constitution of their own country. There was no provision in the Covenant of the League of Nations or the Charter of the United Nations that enabled the minority of the population to impose its will on the majority by constituting itself a distinct political entity and forming an independent State in Palestine. The Zionists claimed that the Balfour Declaration gave them the right, but both the Declaration and the Mandate had been drawn up without the knowledge of the indigenous population of Palestine.[58]

Husseini continued his argument with the familiar Palestinian Arab legal claims regarding Britain's obligations under Article 22 of the Covenant of the League of Nations. He sharply criticized Britain's failure to grant independence to the Palestinian Arabs, arguing Britain "was morally and legally bound to surrender the whole territory and the administration of the territory to a Palestinian government." Husseini added that the AHC stood ready to take over the administration of the country. Britain's refusal to transfer power to the Palestinian Arabs, therefore, was "neither morally nor legally justifiable."[59]

Husseini concluded by threatening violence and bloodshed – including against Jewish citizens of Arab countries – if the United Nations were to adopt the two-state solution for Palestine:

> [I]t was idle to think. that the creation, of a Jewish State would not arouse a general uprising in the Arab world, and it should be remembered that there were as many Jews in the Arab world as there were in Palestine, whose positions might become very precarious, even though the Arab States did their best to protect them. If partition were forced upon Palestine, it would have little chance of permanence in the midst of a strongly aroused and genuinely apprehensive Middle East. The fight would continue, as it had in the Crusades, *until the injustice was completely removed*. By imposing partition, the United Nations would virtually precipitate Palestine into a blood bath ... One delegation defending partition had referred to the boundary line as final and a boundary line of peace. As the representative of the Arabs of Palestine, Mr. Husseini wished to place on record the serious conviction that it would be nothing but a line of fire and blood.[60]

Second, Imseis ignores that Britain, the primary Western power responsible for Palestine, had opposed statehood for the Jews throughout the Mandate, especially since issuing the May 1939 White Paper. Britain's pre-war opposition to Jewish statehood rested on the desire to prevent Hitler from luring the Arab Muslims in the Middle East and North Africa into an alliance, and to avoid alienating the large Muslim population of India. By the time the war had ended, Britain developed a new concern, fearing a potential Jewish State would ally itself with the Soviet Union.

Thus, Britain abstained from the vote on Resolution 181 and thereafter did everything it could to thwart Jewish statehood in Palestine through its close alliance with King Abdullah's Jordan. A British General, Sir John Bagot Glubb, even served as the commander of Jordan's armed forces in the 1948–1949 war against the fledging State of Israel.

Third, Imseis ignores the crucial support in the General Assembly for partition from Latin American states, and opposition from some European/Anglo countries. The same was true for UNSCOP, where three of the seven countries endorsing the two-state solution were from Central and South America (Guatemala, Peru, and Uruguay). Indeed, Jorge Garcia Granados of Guatemala and Enrique Fabregat of Uruguay were far more supportive of Zionism than UNSCOP's Swedish Chairperson, Emil Sandstrom. Moreover, two European/Anglo countries, Australia and Yugoslavia, joined Iran and India in supporting the UNSCOP minority report, which rejected the two-state solution in favor of a single binational federal-state proposal.

Fourth, the United States itself in March 1948 briefly abandoned the two-state solution, proposing ongoing Trusteeship for Palestine instead. Indeed, "[a]lmost from the first day, the U.S. State and Defense establishment waged a relentless campaign to undermine partition and President Truman's support for it."[61] The campaign almost succeeded.

Given their institutional preference for strong United States relations with the Arab states, and their concerns about the impact of the Truman Administration's support for partition on American political and economic interests in the Arab world, those officials (especially Undersecretary of State Robert Lovett, Near East Division Chief Loy Henderson, and Policy Planning Staff Chief George Kennan and their staffs) worked behind the scenes to sabotage the President's Palestine policy. The anti-partitionists urged an alternative to the two-state solution, in which Palestine would be placed under Trusteeship rather than be divided into two sovereign states.[62]

The Policy Planning Staff (under the leadership of George Kennan) at the State Department, for example, prepared a lengthy memorandum in mid-January 1948, less than two months after the United States had voted in favor of the partition resolution, recommending the United States "take no further initiative in implementing or aiding partition." The memorandum urged the United States to consider advocating the Palestine issue be returned to the United Nations for further study, including "investigat[ing] the possibilities of any other suggested solution such as a federal state or trusteeship."[63]

The State Department drumbeat against partition intensified further in a 27 January 1948 top secret memorandum from Samuel Kopper, a young lawyer and Arabist in the Near Eastern Affairs Division, who would later serve as Assistant to the Chairman of the Arabian American Oil Company (Aramco).[64] Kopper, advocating for trusteeship instead of partition, framed his argument in legal terms:

> The growing tendency to refer to the recommendation of the General Assembly as a decision which must be carried out must not be allowed to divert our attention from the fact that the action of the General Assembly was only a recommendation. The United Nations has above all an obligation to preserve peace by peaceful methods so long as this is possible. The United Nations should retain a degree of flexibility and be able to alter its suggested solution of a matter when such is necessary in the light of changing conditions. There are serious doubts as to whether the Arabs of Palestine are under any obligations whatsoever, legal or moral, to be bound by the General Assembly recommendation.[65]

Fifth, Imseis' argument proves too much – of course the local Arabs were violently opposed to Jewish statehood in any portion of Palestine, even the tiny portion the Peel Commission had suggested in July 1937, but that opposition did not create a veto right against the United Nations two-state solution.

Finally, the Arab states themselves did not assert the existence of such a veto when they tried unsuccessfully to persuade the United Nations Ad Hoc Committee on Palestine to seek an Advisory Opinion from the International Court of Justice regarding the legality of Resolution 181.

The historical record, therefore, does not support Imseis' claim that Israel's creation resulted from a white European colonial project imposed on Arab Palestine. It is ironic that Imseis would employ such a characterization of the two-state solution, when that is the very solution the Palestinians now demand.

The Security Council and Resolution 181(II)

United Nations Secretary General Trygve Lie formally transmitted Resolution 181(II) to the President of the Security Council on 2 December 1947. Lie asked the President to advise the Security Council of the various requests from the General Assembly regarding the enforcement of the resolution.[66]

The Security Council met on 9 December 1947 to determine whether to take jurisdiction over Resolution 181(II). After much discussion, the Security Council agreed it had legally been "seized of the question."[67]

The term "seized of" indicates the Security Council's determination under Article 12 of the United Nations Charter to take jurisdiction of an issue from the General Assembly. The Soviet delegate, future Foreign Minister Andrei Gromyko, insisted on the term "seized of" to emphasize the Security Council would now be responsible for implementing the two-state solution.[68]

As a matter of international law, therefore, the Security Council's decision not merely to "take note" of Resolution 181(II), but to assert jurisdiction over the implementation and enforcement of the Resolution, elevated the resolution and its offer of the two-state solution to the status of international law.[69]

Some of the same Arab legal commentators who reject the binding legal nature of Resolution 181(II) have also argued that once the Security Council deems a matter to fall within its "threat to peace" jurisdiction, "the Council establishe[s] for itself the exclusive right of complete supervision" of the matter.[70] By the same reasoning, therefore, even if Resolution 181(II) lacked legally binding force when the General Assembly adopted it, it subsequently rose to the level of a legally binding instrument when the Security Council became "seized of" the issue and took jurisdiction over Palestine.

Although the Security Council never took any steps to enforce Resolution 181(II), that does not mean Resolution 181(II) lacked legal force. Moreover, it would make no sense to argue the Security Council's reluctance to enforce Resolution 181(II) deprived the resolution of any legal weight, especially since the Security Council's reluctance stemmed from fears of exacerbating the violence the Mufti had precipitated in response to Resolution 181(II).

In any event, once Britain terminated the Mandate, the Palestinian Arabs frustrated the purpose of Resolution 181(II) by snubbing the United Nations' two-state solution and fighting alongside the invading Arab armies in an ill-fated attempt to destroy the other half of the two-state solution, the new State of Israel.

The General Assembly delegated the transfer of administrative control over Palestine to a newly appointed United Nations "Palestine Commission."[71] But the Mufti-inspired civil war rendered conditions on the ground impossible for the Palestine Commission to achieve any of its objectives or to assume any governmental functions from the departing British.[72]

On 16 February 1948 the Palestine Commission reported to the Security Council, in language impossible to imagine any United Nations organ would use today that "powerful Arab interests, both inside and outside Palestine, are defying the will of the General Assembly and are engaged in a deliberate effort to alter by force the settlement envisaged therein."[73] On 5 March 1948 the Security Council responded by adopting a resolution urging the implementation of Resolution 181(II).[74]

Palestinian Arab Opposition to the Two-State Solution

The Palestinian Arabs were "incensed" at the General Assembly's approval of the two-state solution.[75] From his new base in Beirut, the by-then ex-Mufti (who will continue to be identified as the "Mufti" for ease of reference) declared the partition resolution and offer of the two-state solution "null and void."[76] The Mufti-controlled AHC insisted the United Nations lacked authority to do anything other than adopt the one-state solution for Palestine in favor of the Arabs, even though the AHC had previously rejected Britain's May 1939 offer of the one-state solution.

The CIA, in a contemporaneous report, described Arab reaction to the General Assembly's proposed two-state solution as "prompt and violent."[77] The Mufti called a three-day general strike, and sporadic rioting ensued. The Mufti also formed an "Arab Liberation Army" to launch civil war in Palestine and thwart the implementation of the two-state solution.[78] The Mufti's goal was to gain the upper hand militarily in Palestine, which he hoped would enable him by mid-1948 to replace the outgoing British administration with a Palestinian Arab government in control of the entire country.[79]

The Mufti had long been preparing for violence. According to a CIA report from November 1946, the Mufti told a Lebanese newspaper owner that if the United Nations were to partition Palestine, the "Arabs of Palestine will resort to arms and will attack the Jews."[80] Moreover, British intelligence reported in July 1947 the Mufti was "rapidly" readying armed and violent resistance to any potential United Nations two-state solution.[81] In late July 1947, MI-6 reported the Mufti's envoys alerted the attendees at a meeting of the AHC in Haifa that the rebellion against the possible two-state solution would begin "shortly," and warned that any Arabs opposing the Mufti would be "finished."[82]

The British Government sent two police officials from Palestine to Cairo in September 1947 to contact the Mufti to ascertain whether he was "irrevocably opposed to any form of partition." The police reported the Mufti's reply was "emphatically yes."[83] Days earlier AHC spokesperson Emile Ghory condemned the General Assembly's two-state solution as "an excess of injustice to Palestine, a flagrant violation of the natural rights of the Arabs in their own country, and an echo of the influence of Zionism and world Jewry."[84]

In early October 1947, the AHC formally notified the United States Government that the "Arabs of Palestine refuse definitely to acquiesce in any solution entailing the partitioning of Palestine."[85] On 12 October 1947, the

Mufti told a British newspaper the Palestinian Arabs would "resist [the two-state solution] with all their means."[86] On 26 October 1947, Jamal Husseini categorically rejected partition, declaring, "[i]f partition is approved, the UN will add another grave resolution to the list of prejudicial and unjust resolutions hitherto taken against the Arabs."[87]

In early November 1947, MI-6 reported the Mufti was "encourage[ing] preparations for eventual clandestine and guerilla warfare" against the two-state solution.[88]

On 19 January 1948, the AHC formally notified the United Nations it had declined an invitation to appoint representatives to the United Nations Palestine Commission. The AHC said it would "persist in the rejection of partition" and that it "refus[ed] to recognize the United Nations Resolution [181(II)] or anything deriving therefrom."[89] The Guatemalan diplomat and UNSCOP member Jorge Garcia Granados characterized the Palestinian Arab refusal to cooperate with the Palestine Commission as "an attack on the United Nations."[90]

In early February 1948, less than three months following the adoption of Resolution 181(II), the AHC sent a letter to the United Nations Secretary General reiterating the Palestinian Arab rejection of the two-state solution. The letter said the Palestinian Arabs considered the two-state solution "null and void and of no legal or moral force."[91] The letter concluded ominously, threatening the "only way to establish partition is first to wipe them out – man, woman and child."[92]

The CIA reported noted in the spring of 1948 the violent Palestinian opposition to the General Assembly's two-state solution:

> It is apparent that the partition of Palestine into separate Arab and Jewish states and an international zone (with an economic union between the two states), as recommended by the United Nations General Assembly (UNGA) on 29 November 1947, cannot be implemented. The Arab reaction to the recommendation has been violent, and the Arab refusal to cooperate in any way with the five-nation United Nations Commission will prevent the formation of an Arab state and the organization of economic union. The Arabs will use force to oppose the establishment of a Jewish state and to this end are training troops in Palestine and other Arab states.[93]

Palestinian Arabs Make No Preparations for Statehood

The AHC, the Arab League, and the Government of Transjordan each wanted to serve as the lead voice for the Palestinian Arabs and began jockeying for position in late 1947. No one, however, took any steps to lay the groundwork for Palestinian Arab self-rule in the areas of Palestine the General Assembly had allocated to the Arabs in the partition plan.[94] Nevo (1996) notes the Palestinian Arabs in the spring and summer of 1948 "not only ... lack[ed] an overall political organization, but the leadership they did have was remote and inefficient."[95]

Having completely renounced the two-state solution, the Palestinian Arabs focused on fomenting violence and bloodshed instead of state-building during the crucial period between November 1947 and May 1948. During those months the Mufti's forces suffered significant military defeats, most notably the death of the senior Palestinian commander Abd al-Qadir al-Husseini at the battle of Mount Kastel near Jerusalem in April 1948. But the Mufti refused to halt the fighting and accept the General Assembly's two-state solution.

On 26 April 1948, less than three weeks before the 14 May 1948 termination of the Mandate, the Mufti's cousin Jamal Husseini, in his new capacity as the AHC's representative to the United Nations, notified the General Assembly that the Palestinian Arabs intended to establish an Arab State throughout *all* of Palestine once the Mandate ended, in violation of Resolution 181(II). But as of that time, the Palestinian Arabs had not even "attempt[ed] to work out any kind of civil administration for their part of Palestine."[96] Neither the Mufti nor any other Palestinian leaders had done anything to build the necessary political, administrative, or economic infrastructure for statehood in the area of Palestine the United Nations had designated for the Arab State.

On 18 May 1948, the Assistant Secretary General for Security Council Affairs wrote to the AHC seeking information, in light of the Arab invasion of Israel immediately following Israel's 14 May 1948 declaration of independence, about whether and how the Palestinian Arabs were governing themselves in the portion of Palestine the United Nations had allocated to them in Resolution 181(II). Jamal Husseini replied to the letter on 24 May 1948. Husseini said the AHC rejected the two-state solution and considered itself the governing body for *all* of pre-May 1948 Palestine, other than for military matters which it had ceded to the invading forces of the Arab League.[97]

The Mufti continued opposing the two-state solution even after the State of Israel had declared its independence and the armies of Egypt, Jordan, Syria, Lebanon, Iraq, and Saudi Arabia invaded the nascent state. Following a cease-fire declaration in July 1948, British intelligence reported the Mufti was "indignant" and committed to continuing the war against the two-state solution.[98]

Indeed, nearly a full year after the General Assembly had offered the Palestinians statehood pursuant to the partition plan's two-state solution, the AHC continued arguing against the two-state solution. The Palestinian lawyer Henry Cattan appeared on behalf of the AHC at a United Nations meeting in Paris on 22 November 1948. Cattan insisted the two-state solution was "the greatest injustice, the greatest treachery in the history of the world; a violation of the very principles proclaimed in the Covenant and in the Mandate."[99]

Some Arab historians take a dim view of the AHC's performance during the winter and spring of 1948:

> In Israel it is quite common to say that the Arabs fought against the partition plan and refused to accept it. It is standard to claim that this is what the Arab leadership chose, and that that decision led to the war. These statements are correct. That decision was an error and a foolish one ... There was no Palestinian leadership. The Arab Higher Committee was composed of a group of *Mukhtars*, who were the representatives of a few large families. They were never elected to office in any way, shape or form, and were not representatives of the law ... The Arab Higher Committee, contrary to what is usually thought today, did not take upon itself the role of leadership with sufficient seriousness. It did not invest any effort in the study of the Palestinian economy or its planning. It never examined the territorial question or similar issues. It did not function as the leadership of a country or even like a neighborhood committee. The members of the committee were decorative leadership (*zaamah*) and not a representative one.[100]

May 1948: The Mandate Ends; Israel Declares Statehood

The United Nations took no action on the ground to implement Resolution 181 subsequent to its adoption, largely abandoning Palestine due to the violent civil war the Mufti had fomented following the passage of Resolution 181(II).

Britain formally terminated the Mandate at the midnight of 14/15 May 1948.[101] Accordingly, the Mandate ceased to exist as a matter of law at that moment. Some scholars argue Britain merely "relinquished" responsibility for the Mandate, and that the Mandate somehow remains in effect to this day.[102] But that argument cannot be reconciled with the express command of Resolution 181(II) that "[t]he Mandate for Palestine shall *terminate* as soon as possible but in any case not later than 1 August 1948."[103]

On 14 May the Jewish Agency formally notified President Truman of the decision to declare statehood for the Jewish people within the territory authorized by Resolution 181(II):

> My Dear Mr. President: I have the honor to notify you that the state of Israel has been proclaimed as an independent republic within frontiers approved by the General Assembly of the United Nations in its Resolution of November 29, 1947, and that a provisional government has been charged to assume the rights and duties of government for preserving law and order within the boundaries of Israel, for defending the state against external aggression, and for discharging the obligations of Israel to the other nations of the world in accordance with international law. The Act of Independence will become effective at one minute after six o'clock on the evening of 14 May 1948, Washington time.[104]

Significantly, neither the United Nations nor the International Court of Justice have ever taken the position that the Mandate continued beyond Britain's exit from the country. The better view, therefore, is that the Mandate ceased to exist as of the moment Britain withdrew from Palestine on 14/15 May 1948.[105]

Legal Basis for Israeli Statehood

As discussed in Chapter 5, the League of Nations Council unanimously approved the Palestine Mandate in July 1922, thereby vesting the Mandate with the force of international law. The Mandate conferred political rights exclusively on the Jewish people in Palestine, without prejudice to the civil and religious rights of the local Arab population. King George V, Winston Churchill, and other individuals in the British Government viewed the political rights conferred on the Jewish people to include Jewish statehood in Palestine, even though the British Government officially had opposed Jewish statehood in Palestine throughout the Mandate years.

The United Nations General Assembly in Resolution 181(II) reiterated the League's legal commitments to the Jewish people, explicitly embracing the notion of Jewish statehood as part of the two-state solution. The Israeli Declaration of Independence cited Resolution 181(II) as the legal basis for the new state.[106]

Israel's letter to the UN Secretary General (sent on the first anniversary of the adoption of Resolution 181) requesting the UN to admit Israel as a member state also cited Resolution 181 (II):

> On May 14, 1948, the independence of the State of Israel was proclaimed by the National Council of the Jewish people in Palestine by virtue of the natural and historic right of the Jewish people to independence in its own sovereign State and in pursuance of the General Assembly Resolution of November 29, 1947.[107]

Crawford (2006), however, argues the legal basis for Israel's statehood was not Resolution 181(II), but *secession*, noting "Israel was effectively and lawfully established as a State by secession from Palestine in the period 1948 to 1949. Its original territory was its armistice territory [as of the end of the 1948–1949 war], not the partition territory."[108]

Stone (1981) agrees with Crawford, but for a different reason. Stone argues the Palestinian Arab rejection of Resolution 181(II) rendered the resolution legally null and void. Israel's statehood derived, therefore, not from the partition resolution, but instead from the "assertion of independence by its people and government, on the vindication of that independence by arms against assault by other states, and on the establishment of orderly government within territory under its stable control."[109]

Shany (2016) argues

> [t]he establishment of Israel in 1948 probably did not constitute an act of secession from Mandatory Palestine, as suggested by Crawford, but rather an implementation of the right to self-determination of the Jewish people in parts of Mandatory Palestine pursuant to the 1922 Palestine Mandate.[110]

Israel's Borders as of 14 May 1948: The Doctrine of Uti Possidetis Juris

The Israeli Declaration of Independence proclaimed the new state as established "in Palestine," but without specifying precise boundaries. The ambiguity in the Israeli declaration maintained the same "in Palestine" formulation as the Balfour Declaration and the Preamble to the Mandate, both of which spoke of establishing/reconstituting the Jewish National Home "*in Palestine*."

By importing the ambiguous "in Palestine" language into the Israeli Declaration of Independence, the drafters left open the possibility that the borders of the Jewish State would encompass solely the specific portions of Palestine the United Nations had allocated for the Jewish state. However, the ambiguity also left open the possibility that Israel could claim sovereignty over some or all of the remaining portions of Palestine, especially because the Palestinian Arabs had been offered but rejected statehood in the areas allocated to them, thereby leaving a sovereignty vacuum.

Indeed, the Palestinian renunciation of the General Assembly's two-state solution left Israel as the only state to emerge from the Mandate as of the moment Britain terminated the Mandate on 14/15 May 1948. Bell and Kontorovich (2015) have argued that pursuant to the international legal doctrine of *uti possidetis juris*, Israel lawfully stepped into Britain's shoes at the moment the Mandate ended and acquired sovereignty over the *entire* area of Mandate Palestine (including the West Bank, the Gaza Strip and all of Jerusalem):

> Israel's independence would thus appear to fall squarely within the bounds of circumstances that trigger the rule of uti possidetis juris. Applying the rule would appear to dictate that Israel's borders are those of the Palestine Mandate that preceded it ... Given the location of the borders of the Mandate of Palestine, applying the doctrine of uti possidetis juris to Israel would mean that Israel has territorial sovereignty over all the disputed areas of Jerusalem, the West Bank, and Gaza, except to the degree that Israel has voluntarily yielded sovereignty since its independence. This conclusion stands in opposition to the widely espoused position that international law gives Israel little or no sovereign claim to these areas ... Israel was the only state that emerged from Mandatory Palestine, and it was a state whose identity

> matched the contemplated Jewish homeland required of the Mandate and that fulfilled a legal Jewish claim to self-determination in the Mandatory territories. There was therefore no rival state that could lay claim to using internal Palestinian district lines as the basis of borders ... Thus, it would appear that uti possidetis juris dictates recognition of the borders of Israel as coinciding with the borders of the Mandate as of 1948.[111]

The concept of *uti possidetis* "provides that states emerging from the dissolution of a larger entity inherit as their borders those administrative boundaries which were in place at the time of independence."[112]

According to Crawford (2019), the notion that pre-independence boundaries remain the same post-independence reflects sound policy. Crawford argues the principle provides predictability and certainty, rendering the division of a state susceptible to only one outcome, thereby helping to avoid boundary disputes and armed conflict. Moreover, determining post-independence boundaries based on pre-independence administrative boundaries "is as valid as any other approach in principle, and far simpler in execution." Finally, Crawford argues that because the ICJ has applied *uti possidetis juris* in various cases, most prominently in the *Burkina Faso/Mali* border dispute, the doctrine "has achieved the status of a general principle or default rule of international law." [113]

In *Burkina Faso/Mali*, the ICJ described *uti possidetis* as part of general or customary international law. The court traced the doctrine's origins to 19th-century Latin America, where states emerging from Spanish rule maintained their preexisting colonial borders. The court described how the doctrine was later applied to maintain the preexisting borders of African states emerging from European colonial rule in the 20th century.[114]

The *Burkina Faso/Mali* court described the *uti possidetis juris* doctrine as grounded in the "maintenance of the territorial status quo at the time of independence," and "the principle of respect both for the frontiers deriving from international agreements and for those resulting from mere internal administrative divisions."[115] The "essence" of the doctrine, wrote the court, "lies in its primary aim of securing respect for the territorial boundaries at the moment when independence is achieved."[116] As the court explained:

> By becoming independent, a new State acquires sovereignty with the territorial base and boundaries left to it by the colonial power. This is part of the ordinary operation of the machinery of State succession. International law – and consequently the principle *of uti possidetis* – applies to the new State (as a State) not with retroactive effect, but immediately and from that moment onwards. It applies to the State as it is, *i.e.*, to the "photograph" of the territorial situation then existing. The principle of *uti possidetis* freezes the territorial title; it stops the clock, but does riot put back the hands.[117]

The *Burkina Faso/Mali* court further noted the "obvious" purpose of the doctrine was "to prevent the independence and stability of new States being endangered by fratricidal struggles provoked by the challenging of frontiers following the withdrawal of the administering power."[118]

In *El Salvador/Honduras*, the ICJ identified an additional purpose for the doctrine, noting "the principle of *uti possidetis juris* is concerned as much with title to the territory as with the location of boundaries; certainly a key aspect of the principle is the denial of the possibility of *terra nullius*."[119]

The *Burkina Faso/Mali* court also discussed the potential for the doctrine to conflict with the principle of self-determination in situations where an indigenous group might lay claim to a portion of the former colonial area. In such instances, the court wrote, *uti possidetis juris* would prevail over self-determination:

> [I]t may be wondered how the time-hallowed principle has been able to withstand the new approaches to international law as expressed in Africa, where the successive attainment of independence and the emergence of new States have been accompanied by a certain questioning of traditional international law. At first sight this principle conflicts outright with another one, the right of peoples to self-determination. In fact, however, the maintenance of the territorial status quo in Africa is often seen as the wisest course, to preserve what has been achieved by peoples who have struggled for their independence, and to avoid a disruption which would deprive the continent of the gains achieved by much sacrifice. The essential requirement of stability in order to survive, to develop and gradually to consolidate their independence in al1 fields, has induced African States judiciously to consent to the respecting of colonial frontiers, and to take account of it in the interpretation of the principle of self-determination of peoples. Thus the principle of uti possidetis has kept its place among the most important legal principles, despite the apparent contradiction ...[120]

Bell and Kontorovich offer a powerful argument for applying the *uti possidetis juris* doctrine to deem Israel's lawful borders the same as those of Mandate Palestine as of the moment the Mandate ended. If Bell and Kontorovich are correct, then Israel's lawful borders today would include the entirety of modern-day Israel, plus the West Bank and the Gaza Strip. This outcome presents an interesting variant of the Palestinian "River to the Sea" narrative.

The ICJ, however, has yet to consider *uti possidetis juris* in the context of the Israeli-Palestinian dispute. The argument was not raised before the ICJ in the *Wall* litigation, nor did the court discuss the issue in its 2004 *Wall* Advisory Opinion. But it seems highly unlikely the court would apply *uti possidetis juris* in the manner Bell and Kontorovich suggest in any future opinion regarding the Israeli-Palestinian dispute. In the *Wall* Advisory Opinion the court embraced an expansive interpretation of international law to accept every Palestinian legal argument, and a cramped interpretation of international law to reject every argument supporting Israel.[121]

Thus, there is little basis to believe, given the current composition of the court and the outlook it manifested in the *Wall* opinion, that it would take a different approach to the doctrine of *uti possidetis juris*, or for that matter to *any* of the issues the United Nations referred to the court in late December 2022 for yet another advisory opinion.

Implications for the Palestinian Legal Case Today

The United Nations offered the Palestinian Arabs statehood in approximately half the Cisjordanian portion of Palestine, after the League of Nations had previously partitioned the country in 1923 by granting statehood exclusively to the Arabs in the Transjordanian portion of Palestine. This meant that by 1948 the original Palestine Mandate territory would have been partitioned into *three* states, two for the Arabs on either side of the Jordan River, and one small Jewish State. But that outcome was unacceptable to the Palestinian Arabs, who demanded all of Cisjordanian Palestine, or nothing.

The Palestinians and the surrounding Arab nations responded to Israel's 14 May 1948 Declaration of Independence with declarations of war against the fledgling Jewish State, in violation of Resolution 181(II), the United Nations Charter, and international law.[122]

By the time the first Arab-Israeli War ended with a series of armistice agreements in 1949, Jordan had emerged as the occupying power in the West Bank and East Jerusalem, and Egypt as the occupying power in the Gaza Strip. The situation remained unchanged until the Six Day War in June 1967, when Israel replaced both Egypt and Jordan as the occupying power in the territories.

We turn next to the Mufti's short-lived effort in the fall of 1948 to establish a Gaza-based Palestinian Arab government to rule the entirety of what had been Mandate Palestine, including the new State of Israel.

Notes

1 League of Nations Archives, R4090/6A/43880/761, Letter from S. Lester, Secretary-General of the League of Nations, to Lord Hailey (2 May 1946).

2 FO 371/52563, Letter from J. Martin, Colonial Office to C.W. Baxter, Foreign Office (4 Nov. 1946).

3 United Nations, Charter of the United Nations, 1945, 1 UNTS XVI, Article 80, para. 1 ("Except as may be agreed upon in individual trusteeship agreements, made under Articles 77, 79, and 81, placing each territory under the trusteeship system, and until such agreements have been concluded, nothing in this Chapter shall be construed in or of itself to alter in any manner the rights whatsoever of any states or any peoples or the terms of existing international instruments to

which Members of the United Nations may respectively be parties"); *see also id.*, para. Article 77, para. 1(a) ("The trusteeship system shall apply to such territories in the following categories as may be placed thereunder by means of trusteeship agreements: a. territories now held under mandate"); CO 537/2362, Letter (Top Secret) from T. Smith, Colonial Office to H. Beeley, Foreign Office, enclosing notes of 18 July 1947 meeting of Colonial Office Legal Advisers (7 Aug. 1947) (noting both Colonial Office and Foreign Office legal advisers agreed that "with the demise of the League, we could in theory disregard the Mandate, but we had informed the United Nations that we would continue to administer Palestine under the terms of the Mandate until other arrangements were made ... [t]he Charter does not say that Mandates must now be placed under trusteeship ... [i]t may be argued therefore that for the time being at least H.M.G. can continue to govern Palestine by virtue of the Mandate ... "); *see also South West Africa Cases (Ethiopia v. South Africa; Liberia v. South Africa), Preliminary Objections, Judgment of 21 December 1962: I.C.J. Reports, 1962, p. 319, at 334* ("the League of Nations in ending its own existence did not terminate the Mandates but ... definitely intended to continue them by its resolution of 18 April 1946").

4 United Nations A/364, Official Records of the Second Session of the General Assembly, Supplement No. 11, *United Nations Special Committee on Palestine, Report to The General Assembly*, Vol. 1 at Ch. I, para. 12 (3 Sept. 1947) (hereafter "UNSCOP Report"). The British Cabinet decided at a 14 February 1947 meeting to hand the Palestine matter to the United Nations. CAB 128/9/22, C.M. 22 (47), Conclusions (Secret) of a Meeting of the Cabinet (14 Feb. 1947) at 146. Foreign Secretary Ernest Bevin announced the decision publicly in the House of Commons four days later. Hansard, HC Deb, Vol. 433, cols. 988–89 (18 Feb. 1947).

5 United Nations A/286, Letter from Alexander Cadogan to Dr. Victor Chi Tsai Hoo, Assistant Secretary-General (2 Apr. 1947); *see also* UNSCOP Report, Vol. 1 at Ch. I, para. 1; J. Robinson, *Palestine and the United Nations* at 50–53 (Public Affairs Press, 1947).

6 *Id.*; United Nations, GA/PAL/85, Press Release (24 Nov. 1947).

7 *See, e.g.*, FO 371/61890, Telegram No. 3554 (Immediate) from United Kingdom delegation to United Nations to Foreign Office (27 Nov. 1947) ("Feisal appealed for justice saying that if it were not granted by the United Nations the states concerned must defend it by themselves"); *see also* J. Strawson, *Partitioning Palestine: Legal Fundamentalism in the Palestinian-Israeli Conflict* at 108–17 (Pluto Press).

8 United Nations General Assembly, Resolution 181(II), A/RES/181(II) (29 Nov. 1947). The vote followed a successful French effort to obtain a one-day delay, from Friday 28 Nov. to Saturday 29 Nov. D. Mandel, *H.G. Evatt and the Establishment of Israel: The Undercover Zionist* at 153–54 (Frank Cass, 2004).

9 Prior straw votes on 22 and 26 Nov. failed to produce the required two-thirds majority necessary to adopt the Resolution. K. Roosevelt, *The Partition of Palestine: A Lesson in Pressure Politics*, The Middle East Journal, 2:1 1, 13–14 (1948).

10 CAB 129/24/10, Palestine: Withdrawal of British Civil Administration, Memorandum (Secret) by the Secretary of State for the Colonies (4 Feb. 1948).

11 One of Bunche's biographers claims he drafted the entire report, including both the majority and minority recommendations. P. Mann, *Ralph Bunche: UN Peacemaker* at 200 (Coward, McCann & Geoghegan, 1975). The Israeli historian Elad Ben-Dror, however, noted Bunche had help with the drafting from UN officials Henri Vigier and John Reedman, who flew from New York to Geneva to assist Bunche. Ben-Dror also notes, contrary to the typical narrative regarding Bunche's pro-Zionism, that Bunche in fact "opposed the establishment of an independent Jewish state," and "made strenuous attempts to torpedo its establishment." E. Ben-Dror, *Ralph Bunche and the Establishment of Israel*, Israel Affairs, 14:3 at

520, 522 (July 2008). Another historian credits Bunche with drafting the entire report. M.N. Penkower, *Palestine to Israel, Mandate to State, 1945–1948, Volume II: Into the International Arena* at 459–60 (Touro Univ. Press, 2019).

12 E. Ben-Dror, *The Success of the Zionist Strategy vis-a-vis UNSCOP*, Israel Affairs, 20:1 at 32 (2014).

13 *Id.* paras. 145–46.

14 *Id.* para. 154.

15 *Id.* paras. 165–66.

16 *Id.* para. 176.

17 *Id.* para. 179.

18 *Id.* Ch. VI, paras. 1–5. The *New York Times* editorial board reacted negatively to the UNSCOP majority report, noting how "[s]ome of us have long had doubts as to the wisdom of erecting a political state on a basis of religious faith." *New York Times*, 1 Sept. 1947 at 18.

19 United Nations, A/RES/3379 (10 Nov. 1975). The General Assembly eventually repealed the resolution in December 1991 without explanation or apology.

20 United Nations, A/AC.14/SR.32, Palestine Question, Ad Hoc Committee Debate on Reports of Subcommittee I and II (24 Nov. 1947); D. Mandel, *H.G. Evatt and the Establishment of Israel: The Undercover Zionist* at 147 (Frank Cass, 2004). The United States also announced at the 22 Nov. meeting (after Weizmann had appealed directly to Truman at an Oval Office meeting on 19 Nov.) its support for including the Negev region in the area to be allocated to the Jews. A. Radosh and R. Radosh, *A Safe Haven, Harry S. Truman and the Founding of Israel* at 261–65 (Harper Collins, 2009).

21 Mandel, *op. cit.* at 147; *see also* B. Oppenheim and H. Lauterpacht, *International Law, a Treatise* (6th ed.) at 208 (Longman, Green, 1940) ("Although, according to its wording, the [United Nations] Charter imposes no clear obligation upon states which were mandatories by virtue of Article 22 of the Covenant [of the League of Nations] to place the territories in question under the system of trusteeship, it is clear that an obligation to this effect closely approaching a legal duty follows from the principles of the Charter"); *see also* Robinson, *op. cit.* at 56 ("[T]he United Nations has clear jurisdiction with regard to former mandated territories. This jurisdiction is outlined in detail with regard to procedures and powers in so far as they concern the conversion of a mandate into a trusteeship agreement. The way is left open for any other solution of the problem of an existing mandate").

22 *Ffrost v. Stevenson* (1937) 58 C.L.R. 528, 581–82 (Evatt, J.); *see also* J.L. Brierly, *The Law of Nations: An Introduction to the International Law of Peace* (5th ed.) at 165–67 (Oxford Univ. Press, 1956).

23 *Ffrost v. Stevenson* (1937) 58 C.L.R. 528, 581 (Evatt, J.).

24 Evatt, *op. cit.* at 155.

25 *Id.* at 156.

26 United Nations, A/PV.125 at 1337–39 (26 Nov. 1947).

27 J.G. Granados, *The Birth of Israel: The Drama as I Saw It* at 268 (Alfred A. Knopf, 1948).

28 A. Gerson, Trustee-Occupant: The Legal Status of Israel's Presence in the West Bank, *Harvard International Law Journal*, 14 at 35 (1973); *see also* G. Watson, *The Oslo Accords: International Law and the Israeli-Palestinian Peace Agreements* at 26 (Oxford, 2000). ("Britain's abdication in favour of UN disposition of the Mandate for Palestine plainly gave the United Nations authority to act").

29 FRUS, 867N.01/5–1048, Memorandum by the Legal Adviser to the Under Secretary of State, "Recognition of New States and Governments in Palestine" (11 May 1948).

30 *Id.*

31 A. Cassese, *Legal Considerations on the International Status of Jerusalem*, in H. Kochler (ed.), *The Legal Aspects of the Palestine Problem with Special Regard to the Question of Jerusalem* at 145 (William Braumuller, 1981).

32 *Id.* at 146.

33 J. Crawford, *The Creation of States in International Law* (2nd ed.) at 430–32 (Oxford, 2006).

34 *Legal Consequences for States of the Continued Presence of South Africa in Namibia (South West Africa) notwithstanding Security Council Resolution 276 (1970)*, Advisory Opinion, I.C.J. Reports 1971, p. 16. at 49–50, paras. 101, 105.

35 Robinson, *op. cit.* at 56. For a contrary view *see* H. Kelsen, *The Law of the United Nations: A Critical Analysis of Its Fundamental Problems* at 195–97 n.7 (Stevens & Sons, 1951) (agreeing with Arab objections that the General Assembly had exceeded its "recommendation" authority by adopting the Plan of Partition for Palestine in Resolution 181(II)).

36 E13573, Foreign Office Minute discussing undated Legal Opinion transmitted by Government of Israel to United Kingdom delegation to United Nations, and copy of the Legal Opinion at paras. 10–18, *reprinted in* J. Priestland (ed.), *Records of Jerusalem, Vol. 5: 1946–1949* at 791–99 (Archive Editions, 2002). The Trusteeship provisions of the United Nations Charter appear in Articles 75–85, as follows:

Article 75

The United Nations shall establish under its authority an international trusteeship system for the administration and supervision of such territories as may be placed thereunder by subsequent individual agreements. These territories are hereinafter referred to as trust territories.

Article 76

The basic objectives of the trusteeship system, in accordance with the Purposes of the United Nations, laid down in Article 1 of the present Charter, shall be:

to further international peace and security; to promote the political, economic, social, and educational advancement of the inhabitants of the trust territories, and their progressive development towards self-government or independence as may be appropriate to the particular circumstances of each territory and its peoples and the freely expressed wishes of the people concerned, and as may be provided by the terms of each trusteeship agreement; to encourage respect for human rights and for fundamental freedoms for all without distinction as to race, sex, language, or religion, and to encourage recognition of the interdependence of the peoples of the world; and to ensure equal treatment in social, economic, and commercial matters for all Members of the United Nations and their nationals, and also equal treatment for the latter in the administration of justice, without prejudice to the attainment of the foregoing objectives and subject to the provisions of Article 80.

Article 77

The trusteeship system shall apply to such territories in the following categories as may be placed thereunder by means of trusteeship agreements: territories now held under mandate; territories which may be detached from enemy states as a result of the Second World War; and territories voluntarily placed under the system by states responsible for their administration. It will be a matter for subsequent agreement as to which territories in the foregoing categories will be brought under the trusteeship system and upon what terms.

Article 78

The trusteeship system shall not apply to territories that have become Members of the United Nations, the relationship among which shall be based on respect for the principle of sovereign equality.

Article 79

The terms of trusteeship for each territory to be placed under the trusteeship system, including any alteration or amendment, shall be agreed upon by the states directly concerned, including the mandatory power in the case of territories held under mandate by a Member of the United Nations, and shall be approved as provided for in Articles 83 and 85.

Article 80

Except as may be agreed upon in individual trusteeship agreements, made under Articles 77, 79, and 81, placing each territory under the trusteeship system, and until such agreements have been concluded, nothing in this Chapter shall be construed in or of itself to alter in any manner the rights whatsoever of any states or any peoples or the terms of existing international instruments to which Members of the United Nations may respectively be parties.

Paragraph 1 of this Article shall not be interpreted as giving grounds for delay or postponement of the negotiation and conclusion of agreements for placing mandated and other territories under the trusteeship system as provided for in Article 77.

Article 81

The trusteeship agreement shall in each case include the terms under which the trust territory will be administered and designate the authority which will exercise the administration of the trust territory. Such authority, hereinafter called the administering authority, maybe one or more states or the Organization itself.

Article 82

There may be designated, in any trusteeship agreement, a strategic area or areas that may include part or all of the trust territory to which the agreement applies, without prejudice to any special agreement or agreements made under Article 43.

Article 83

All functions of the United Nations relating to strategic areas, including the approval of the terms of the trusteeship agreements and of their alteration or amendment shall be exercised by the Security Council.

The basic objectives set forth in Article 76 shall be applicable to the people of each strategic area.

The Security Council shall, subject to the provisions of the trusteeship agreements and without prejudice to security considerations, avail itself of the assistance of the Trusteeship Council to perform those functions of the United Nations under the trusteeship system relating to political, economic, social, and educational matters in the strategic areas.

Article 84

It shall be the duty of the administering authority to ensure that the trust territory shall play its part in the maintenance of international peace and security. To this end, the administering authority may make use of volunteer forces, facilities, and assistance from the trust territory in carrying out the obligations towards the Security Council undertaken in this regard by the administering authority, as well as for local defense and the maintenance of law and order within the trust territory.

Article 85

The functions of the United Nations with regard to trusteeship agreements for all areas not designated as strategic, including the approval of the terms of the trusteeship agreements and of their alteration or amendment, shall be exercised by the General Assembly.

The Trusteeship Council, operating under the authority of the General Assembly shall assist the General Assembly in carrying out these functions.

37 V. Kattan, "A Critical Assessment of the Government of Israel's Memorandum to the ICC – Part I," Blog (30 Jan. 2020), https://www.ejiltalk.org/a-critical-assessment-of-the-government-of-israels-memorandum-to-the-icc-part-i/ (last accessed 18 June 2024).

38 *Id.* at 103.

39 N. Elaraby, *Some Legal Implications of the 1947 Partition Resolution and the 1949 Armistice Agreements*, Law and Contemporary Problems, 33:1, 97–109 at 102–03 (1968).

40 *See* J. Dugard, *A Tale of Two Sacred Trusts: Namibia and Palestine*, in T. Maluwa (ed.), *Law, Politics and Rights: Essays in Memory of Kader Asmal* at 287 (Martinus Nijhoff, 2014).

41 *See, e.g.*, R. Gavison (ed.), *The Two-State Solution: The UN Partition Resolution of Mandatory Palestine* at xx–xxi (Bloomsbury Academic Press, 2013).

42 A. Gerson, *Israel, The West Bank and International Law* at 47–48 (Frank Kass, 1978).

43 *Id.* at 48; *see also* Watson, *op. cit.* at 22–23 (Resolution 181(II) had "some legal effect" at the time of its adoption, although it most likely lapsed as of 14 May 1948 when Israel declared its independence).

44 A. Imseis, *The United Nations Plan of Partition for Palestine Revisited: On the Origins of Palestine's International Legal Subalternity*, Stanford Journal of International Law, 57:1, 1–54 at 23 (2021).

45 Gavison, *op. cit.*, at xxi.

46 United Nations General Assembly, Resolution 181 (II), A/RES/181(II) (29 Nov. 1947); *see also* Kelsen, *op. cit.* at 210 n.7 (General Assembly had the legal authority under Article 10 of the United Nations Charter to recommend to the Security Council that it take steps to enforce the partition resolution). Article 10 states, "The General Assembly may discuss any questions or any matters within the scope of the present Charter or relating to the powers and functions of any organs provided for in the present Charter, and, except as provided in Article 12, may make recommendations to the Members of the United Nations or to the Security Council or to both on any such questions or matters." United Nations, Charter of the United Nations, Art. 10, 1945, 1 UNTS XVI; *see also* FO 371/61889, Telegram No. 3453 from British Delegation, United Nations to Foreign Office, paras. 4, 5 (19 Nov. 1947) (reporting on Ad Hoc Committee discussions regarding the legality of the partition proposal under the United Nations Charter, and noting the Ad Hoc Committee agreed the proposals were legal, and the request to the Security Council to take the necessary measures to implement the partition plan was also intended to convey the partition proposal carried legal weight beyond serving as a mere "recommendation" by the General Assembly), *reprinted in* P. Toye and A. Seay, *Israel: Boundary Disputes with Arab Neighbours, 1946–1964*, Vol. 2 at 39–40 (Archive Editions, 1995).

47 The General Assembly also requested the Security Council "consider, if circumstances during the transitional period require such consideration, whether the situation in Palestine constitutes a threat to the peace. If it decides that such a threat exists, and in order to maintain international peace and security, the Security Council should supplement the authorization of the General Assembly by taking measures, under Articles 39 and 41 of the Charter, to empower the United Nations Commission, as provided in this resolution, to exercise in Palestine the functions which are assigned to it by this resolution." United Nations General Assembly, Resolution 181(II), *op. cit.*

48 U.N. Doc. A/c.1/SR 127 at 7 (27 Apr. 1948).

49 *Legal Consequences for States of the Continued Presence of South Africa in Namibia (South West Africa) notwithstanding Security Council Resolution 276*, Advisory Opinion, I.C.J. Reports at 50, para. 105 (1971).

50 *Legality of the Threat or Use of Nuclear Weapons*, Advisory Opinion, 1996 I.C.J. 226, 254–55, para. 70 (8 July 1996).

51 E. Lautepacht, *Jerusalem and the Holy Places* at 16 (Anglo-Israel Association, 1968).

52 A. Imseis, *The United Nations Plan of Partition for Palestine Revisited: On the Origins of Palestine's International Legal Subalternity*, Stanford Journal of International Law, 57:1, 1–54 at 19, 23 (2021). Imesis raises a series of questions attacking the legitimacy of Resolution 181, noting "the key problem with Resolution 181(11) was that it recommended a purported solution to the question of Palestine on terms that manifestly ran counter to prevailing international law. If the Assembly viewed its goal of establishing a Jewish state in Palestine as a politically legitimate end, that end was arrived at the expense of the international rule of law as it existed at the time and the rights of the indigenous people of Palestine thereunder. How could partition be legal if the only possibility envisioned under the U.N. Charter was independence of the country, either immediately as with other Class A mandates, or at some point in the immediate future following temporary administration as a U.N. Trusteeship? What of the principle of self-determination of such mandated territories, rooted in the precepts of consent of the governed and majority rule? Even if the Jewish people possessed an internationally recognized right to a Jewish national home in Palestine by virtue of the Mandate, how did that legally justify the General Assembly's recommendation to establish a Jewish state in Palestine? At any rate, how would the "Jewishness" of that state be secured, if the ratio of Arabs to Jews in it was virtually on par or the Jews were a minority in it from the start, and the plan required it to adopt a democratic constitution guaranteeing universal suffrage and equality before the law?" *Id.* at 20.

53 United Nations Archives, S-0472-0086-0011-00001, Cablegram from Arab Higher Committee to United Nations Secretary-General (13 June 1947); *see also* E. Ben-Dror, *The Success of the Zionist Strategy vis-à-vis UNSCOP*, Israel Affairs, 20:1 at 23 (2014).

54 Ben-Dror (2007), *op. cit.* at 269.

55 FRUS, 501.BB Palestine/6–3047, Telegram (Secret) No. 113 from the United States Consul General, Jerusalem, to the Secretary of State (30 June 1947).

56 UNSCOP, A/AC.13/42, Letter from Chairman Sandstrom to Arab Higher Committee (8 July 1947) (repeating invitation to cooperate with the Special Committee); United Nations A/AC.13/NC/52, Letter from Jamal Husseini, Arab Higher Committee to Chairman Sandstrom (10 July 1947) (rejecting Special Committee's request for cooperation); *see also* UNSCOP Report, Ch. I, paras. 32–34; E. Ben-Dror, *The Success of the Zionist Strategy vis-a-vis UNSCOP*, Israel Affairs, 20:1 at 23 (2014) ("Despite all the efforts to persuade it to recant, the AHC (Arab Higher Committee) continued to shun UNSCOP to the end and managed to impose the boycott on the entire Palestinian public").

57 Granados, *op. cit.* at 39.

58 United Nations, A/AC.14/SR.31, Ad Hoc Committee Debate on Reports of Subcommittee I and II (24 Nov. 1947).

59 *Id.*

60 *Id.* (Emphasis added).

61 Radosh and Radosh, *op. cit.* at 277.

62 Truman was aware the State Department was actively working to undermine his Palestine policy. In his memoirs, Truman expressed frustration about this, in words presaging former President Donald Trump's more contemporary accusations of a "deep state" actively opposed to his policies: "The difficulty with many career officials in the government is that they regard themselves as the men who really make policy and run the government. They look upon the elected officials

as just temporary occupants. Every President in our history has been faced with this problem: how to prevent career men from circumventing presidential policy. Too often career men seek to impose their own views instead of carrying out the established policy of the Administration." Truman, *op. cit.* at H. Truman, *Memoirs, Volume Two: Years of Trial and Hope* at 165 (Doubleday, 1956).

63 FRUS, N.A. PPs/19, Lot 64, D563, Memorandum (Secret) by Policy Planning Staff, U.S. Department of State, "To Assess and Appraise the Position of the U.S. with respect to Palestine, Taking into Consideration the Security Interests of the U.S. in the Mediterranean and Near East Areas, and in the Light of the Recommendation of the General Assembly of the United Nations Regarding the Partition of Palestine" at paras. 27, 31–31 (19 Jan. 1948), *reprinted in* M.J. Cohen, *The Rise of Israel: The American Trusteeship Proposal 1948* at 12–22 (Garland, 1987). Interestingly, the Memorandum also recommended against referring the matter to the International Court of Justice, as "the fundamental issue, that is, whether the two communities will cooperate to make the partition plan effective, is not a proper question for the Court." *Id.* at para. 33. The following week, however, Dean Rusk, the future Secretary of State and then a high-ranking official in the Department, criticized the Policy Planning Staff's memorandum, asking "What events have occurred which create a 'new situation' with respect to the action taken by the General Assembly on Palestine? Were not the considerations discussed in the attached paper known at the time of the decision to support the plan of the UNSCOP majority? At what point or points can it be reasonably concluded that the situation in Palestine will render impossible the implementation of the General Assembly resolution?" FRUS, 867N.01/2–648, Memorandum (Top Secret) by Dean Rusk to the Under Secretary of State (26 Jan. 1948). Within days both George Kennan and Loy Henderson responded in writing with their own criticisms of Rusk's analysis. Henderson's memorandum borrowed heavily from Kennan's, suggesting a coordinated effort by the two officials to undermine the President's prior decision to support partition. *See* FRUS, PPS Files, Lot 64 D 563, Memorandum (Top Secret) by the Director of the Policy Planning Staff to the Under Secretary of State (29 Jan. 1948); FRUS, 867N.01/2–648, Memorandum (Top Secret) by the Director of the Office of Near Eastern and African Affairs to the Director of the Office of United Nations Affairs (6 Feb. 1948).

64 "Samuel Kopper, FRAMCO Aide, Dies," *New York Times*, 5 June 1957 at 35.

65 FRUS, 501.BB Palestine/1–2748, Memorandum (Top Secret) by Mr. Samuel K. C. Kopper of the Office of Near Eastern and African Affairs, "The Partition of Palestine and United States Security" at 31 (27 Jan. 1948).

66 United Nations, S/614, Letter from Secretary-General to President, Security Council (2 Dec. 1947).

67 United Nations, S/PV.222, Palestine Question/GA Resolution 181, "Future Government of Palestine" – Security Council meeting – Verbatim record (9 Dec. 1947) (emphasis added).

68 *Id.*

69 *But see* United Nations, A/AC.21/13, United Nations Palestine Commission, Relations between The United Nations Commission and the Security Council, Working Paper Prepared by the Secretariat (3 Feb. 1948) ("The phrase 'being seized of the question' was interpreted by the President of the Security Council to mean that 'the matter remains on the agenda, available for discussion at the request of any member or members at any time'"). The Working Paper went on to note, however, that the *Trieste* precedent provided authority for the Security Council to exercise control of the Palestine situation: "In the case of the Free Territory of Trieste, which presents some similar aspects to the present case, the Security Council answered the question in the affirmative ... Under the Peace Treaty with

Italy, various responsibilities were assigned to the Security Council with regard to the Free Territory of Trieste, and as a result, the Council of Foreign Ministers requested the Security Council to adopt the three instruments relating to the administration of the Free Territory and to accept the responsibilities devolving upon it under the same instruments. During the discussion in the Security Council, a legal objection was raised by the Australian representative whether the Security Council has the power to accept new responsibilities and further, whether it had the power to assume functions having no direct connection with the maintenance of international peace and security. At the 91st meeting of the Security Council, a statement of the Secretary-General was read regarding the legal issues raised by the representative of Australia. According to the statement, the words of Article 24 'primary responsibility for the maintenance of international peace and security' coupled with the phrase 'acts on their behalf' constitute a grant of power sufficiently wide to enable the Security Council to approve the documents in question and to assume responsibilities arising therefrom." The five-member Palestine Commission, chaired by Karel Lisicky of Czechoslovakia and containing delegates from Bolivia, Denmark, Panama and the Philippines, was formed to oversee the implementation of Resolution 181(II) during the transition period until the formal termination of the Mandate. The Palestine Commission reported directly to the Security Council, bypassing the General Assembly. *Id.*, *see also* United Nations, A/AC.21/SR.1, Summary Record of the First Meeting of the Palestine Commission (9 Jan. 1948).

70 Elaraby, *op. cit.* at 107.

71 United Nations, A/AC.21/W.2, Working Paper, General Assembly, United Nations Palestine Commission (9 Jan. 1948).

72 "Text of the British Statement on Palestine, Chronicling History and Policy of the Mandate," *New York Times*, 14 May 1948 at 4 ("When this advance party had visited Palestine and seen for themselves the conditions prevailing there, the Commission reported to the Security Council that they would be unable to carry out their task without the assistance of armed forces, which the Security Council declined to provide. It then became obvious that the Commission would not themselves be able to arrange for the transfer of the functions exercised by the Central Government and steps were accordingly taken to devolve upon local authorities those functions which could appropriately be assumed by them").

73 United Nations A/AC.21/9, S/676, Para. I(3)(C) (16 Feb. 1948).

74 United Nations Security Council, S/691 (5 Mar. 1948).

75 Z. Elipeleg, *Why Was "Independent Palestine" Never Created?*, Jerusalem Quarterly, 50 at 3–22 (1989).

76 M. Tessler, *A History of the Israeli-Palestinian Conflict* at 261 (Indiana Univ. Press, 2009).

77 Central Intelligence Agency, ORE-748, *Possible Developments in Palestine* (Secret) at 1 (1948).

78 R. Yitzhak, *Transjordan's Occupation of Jerusalem in the 1948 War*, Israel Affairs, 25:2 at 308–09 (2019); C. Sykes, *Crossroads to Israel: 1917–1948* at 333, 337–39 (Indiana Univ. Press, 1965); B. Morris, *The Birth of the Palestinian Refugee Problem, 1947–1949* at 29 (Cambridge Univ. Press, 1987); E. Karsh, *Palestine Betrayed* at 100 *et seq.* (Yale Univ. Press, 2010); M.J. Cohen, *Palestine and the Great Powers, 1945–1948* at 302–03 (Princeton Univ. Press, 1982); Radosh and Radosh, *op. cit.* at 280; M. Maoz, *The UN Partition Resolution of 1947: Why Was It Not Implemented?*, Palestine-Israel Journal of Politics, Economics, and Culture, 9:4 at 18–19 (2002).

79 J. Nevo, *The Arabs of Palestine, 1947–48: Military and Political Activity*, Middle Eastern Studies, 23:1 at 14–15 (1987) ("From his Cairo residence, the president

of the AHC, al-Hajj Amin al-Husayni, promised a swift Arab offensive in order to make maximum military gains which would make the Arabs the leading power in the country to whom the British would delegate the reins of authority when they departed. Al-Hajj Amin also sought to secure his own position as the unchallenged leader of the Palestinian Arabs and to guarantee his nomination as the head of the Palestinian state, once military successes ensured its foundation"); Penkower, *op. cit.* at 521 (the Palestinian Arabs "launched a civil war" in response to the UN's offer of the two-state solution).

80 Central Intelligence Agency, CIA-RDP82-00457R000300140006-1, "Mufti's Declarations on Palestine Situation" (Secret) (27 Jan. 1947) (reporting on meeting "last November" [1946] between the Mufti and Afif Tibi, the owner of the Lebanese newspaper *al-Yawm*).

81 KV2/2091, Report No. 82 (28 July 1947) (relaying information received from sources on 17 July 1947).

82 KV2/2091, *Extract from Account forwarded by S.I.S. re Palestine – Political. The Arab "National Conference" at Haifa* (29 July 1947).

83 KV2/2091, C.S. 808/2, Memorandum (Top Secret) from Officer Administering the Government of Palestine to Secretary of State for the Colonies (23 Sept. 1947) enclosing 21 Sept. 1947 Report (Top Secret) regarding unofficial meeting between Palestine Mandatory police officials with Mufti in Cairo (9 Oct. 1947).

84 "Zionists Ask U.N. to Pass New Plan; Arabs Inflamed," *New York Times*, 2 Sept. 1947 at 1. The article quoted Ghory threatening that if the General Assembly were to accept the Special Committee's partition recommendation, "the Arabs will oppose it by every means at their disposal."

85 FRUS, 501.BB Palestine/10–1647, Letter from Emil Ghory, Arab Higher Committee, to United States Consul General, Jerusalem (3 Oct. 1947).

86 G. Bilainkin, "The Man Who May Lead the Holy War," *Sunday Despatch* (12 Oct. 1947).

87 "Jamal: We Must Foil Partition," *Palestine Post*, 27 Oct. 1947 at 1.

88 KV2/2091, *Extract (Secret) from Report No. 95 re the Arabs and Palestine* (4 Nov. 1947).

89 United Nations, A/AC.21/6, United Nations Palestine Commission, Communication from the Representative of the Arab Higher Committee for Palestine (19 Jan. 1948); *see also* "Arabs Refuse to Cooperate," *The Times*, 20 Jan. 1948 at 3; "Arabs Again Shun Any Partition Aid," *New York Times*, 20 Jan. 1948 at 4. The Palestine Commission notified the Security Council, in its first monthly report to the Council, of the Arab Higher Committee's refusal to cooperate and its rejection of General Assembly Resolution 181(II). The Commission noted, "No further communication has been addressed to or received from the Arab Higher Committee by the Commission. The Commission will, at the appropriate time, set forth in a separate document its views with regard to the implementations of this refusal by the Arab Higher Committee." United Nations, A/AC.21/7, United Nations Palestine Commission, First Monthly Progress Report to the Security Council (29 Jan. 1948).

90 Granados, *op. cit.* at 271.

91 United Nations Archives, S-0472-0090-0018-00001, Letter from I. Nakhleh, Representative of the Arab Higher Committee, to Secretary General (6 Feb. 1948).

92 *Id.* (Emphasis added).

93 Central Intelligence Agency, ORE-748, *Possible Developments in Palestine* (Secret) at 1 (1948).

94 *Id.*; *see also* A. Shlaim, *The Rise and Fall of the All-Palestine Government in Gaza*, Journal of Palestine Studies, 20:1 at 38 (1990).

95 J. Nevo, *King Abdallah and Palestine: A Territorial Ambition* at 176 (St. Martin's Press, 1996).

96 FO 371/68368, K. Buss Minute (13 Feb. 1948), *reprinted in* Toye and Seay, *op. cit.* Vol. 2 at 104.
97 United Nations, S/775, Letter from Jamal Husseini, Arab Higher Committee, to Secretary-General regarding Questions Submitted by the Security Council (24 May 1948).
98 KV2/2091, Intelligence Repot No. 114 (Secret), *Palestine: The Mufti's Preparations for Guerilla War* (17 Aug. 1948); *see also* KV2/2091, SIME/P.F.1415/B.1, Despatch (Secret) to Director General, London, from E. Richardson, *Activities of the Mufti* (18 Aug. 1948) (enclosing Report No. 2813, *Palestine: Political Activities of the Mufti*, 31 July 1948).
99 United Nations, A/C.1/SR.207, Continuation of the discussion on the Progress Report of the United Nations Mediator on Palestine (22 Nov. 1948).
100 N. Magally, *The Position of the Arab Leadership vis-à-vis the Partition Plan: The Crime and Its Punishment*, in R. Gavison (ed.), *The Two-State Solution: The UN Partition Resolution of Mandatory Palestine* at 38–39 (Bloomsbury Academic Press, 2013).
101 *Palestine: Termination of the Mandate, Statement Prepared for Public Information by the Colonial Office and the Foreign Office* at 2 (15 May 1948).
102 A. Bell and E. Kontorovich, *Palestine, Uti Possidetis Juris, and the Borders of Israel*, Arizona Law Review, 58, 633–92 at 683 (2016) (Mandate terminated by operation of law as of midnight 14/15 May 1948). Some scholars, however, argue the Mandate was never formally terminated and survives as an international legal instrument to this day. Although the legal ramifications of such a claim are not clear, those who make the argument believe it means Israel had no legal basis upon which to sever itself from the Mandate and declare its independence.
103 United Nations General Assembly, A/RES/181(II), *Plan of Partition with Economic Union*, para. A1 (29 Nov. 1947).
104 FRUS, E. Epstein, as Agent of the Provisional Government of Israel, to President Truman (14 May 1948).
105 G. Watson, *The Oslo Accords: International Law and the Israeli-Palestinian Peace Agreements* at 25 (Oxford Univ. Press, 2000).
106 Israel Declaration of Independence, Provisional Government of Israel Official Gazette: No. 1 at 1 (14 May 1948), https://m.knesset.gov.il/en/about/pages/declaration.aspx (last accessed 5 Feb. 2023). During the May 1949 General Assembly debate regarding Israel's proposed admission to the United Nations as a member state, the Cuban Ambassador characterized noted Resolution 181 as "in a sense, Israel's birth certificate in that it legalized the existence of Israel." United Nations, Official Records of The Third Session of the General Assembly, 207th Plenary Meeting (11 May 1949, Statement of Cuban Ambassador Ramón Zaydín).
107 Letter from Moshe Sharett, Minister for Foreign Affairs of the Provision Government of Israel, to United Nations Secretary General Trygve Lie, UN File No. 1204-1-21, UN Archives S0472, Box 98, File 14 (29 Nov. 1948).
108 J. Crawford, *The Creation of States in International Law* (2nd ed.) at 434 (Oxford Univ. Press, 2006).
109 J. Stone, *Israel and Palestine: Assault on the Law of Nations* at 61 (John Hopkins Univ. Press, 1981).
110 Y. Shany, *Legal Entitlements, Changing Circumstances and Intertemporality: A Comment on the Creation of Israel and the Status of Palestine*, Israel Law Review, 49:3 at 391, 408 (2016).
111 Bell and Kontorovich, *op. cit.* at 637–38, 681–82 (2016).
112 J. Crawford, *Brownlie's Principles of Public International Law* (9th ed.) at 224 (Oxford Univ. Press, 2019).

113 *Id.*
114 *Frontier Dispute (Burkina Faso/Mali)*, Judgment, I.C.J. Reports 1986, 554 at 565–66 paras. 20–23 (22 Dec. 1986).
115 *Id. at* 565 para. 22 (22 Dec. 1986).
116 *Id.* at 566, para. 23.
117 *Id.* at 568, para. 30.
118 *Id.* at 565, para. 20; see also Conference on Yugoslavia Arbitration Commission, Opinion No. 3 at para. 2 (1992), opinion reported in A. Pellet, *The Opinions of the Badinter Arbitration Committee: A Second Breath for the Self-Determination of Peoples*, European Journal of International Law, 3 at 178, 185 (1992).
119 *El Salvador/Honduras*, ICJ Reports, 1992 351, 387 at para. 42 (11 Sept. 1992).
120 *Frontier Dispute (Burkina Faso/Mali)*, Judgment, I.C.J. Reports 1986, at 554, 566–67, paras. 25–26 (22 Dec. 1986); *see also* Conference on Yugoslavia Arbitration Commission, Opinion No. 2 at para. 1 (1992) ("whatever the circumstances, except where the states concerned agree otherwise, the right to self-determination must not involve changes to existing frontiers existing at the time of independence (*uti possidetis juris*) except where the states concerned agree otherwise."), reported in A. Pellet, *The Opinions of the Badinter Arbitration Committee: A Second Breath for the Self-Determination of Peoples*, European Journal of International Law, 3 at 178, 183–84 (1992); *see also* M. Shaw, *International Law* (9th ed.) at 451 (2021).
121 Bell and Kontorovich identify various scholars who would apply the *uti possidetis juris* doctrine in favor of Palestinian sovereignty over the West Bank, or perhaps the entire area of the Mandate, including J. Salmon, *Declaration of the State of Palestine*, Palestine Yearbook of International Law, 5 at 48, 53 (1989) (denying Israeli claims based on uti possidetis but using the doctrine to favor Palestinian claims); G. Naldi, *The Peaceful Settlement of Disputes in Africa and Its Relevance to the Palestinian/Israeli Peace Process*, Palestine Yearbook of International Law, 10 at 27, 40 (1998–1999) (arguing uti possidetis juris would confer Palestinian sovereignty over "all the Palestinian territories Israel has occupied since 1967, including East Jerusalem."); I. Scobbie and S. Hibbin, Research Paper, *The Israel-Palestine Conflict in International Law: Territorial Issues* (SOAS Sch. L., Research Paper No. 02/2010, 2009), http://ssrn.com/abstract=1621382 (arguing *uti possidetis juris* would require transferring the borders of the Palestine Mandate to a future Palestinian Arab state).
122 Y.Z. Blum, *The Missing Reversioner: Reflections on the Status of Judea and Samaria*, Israel Law Review, 3 at 279, 287 (1968).

10

THE "ALL-PALESTINE GOVERNMENT," 1948

Background

Once the surrounding Arab States invaded the newly declared State of Israel on 15 May 1948, King Abdullah moved swiftly to supplant the Mufti as the supreme authority over the Palestinian Arab population. The Palestinian Arabs had still taken no steps to create a functioning government in the area of Palestine the General Assembly had offered them in Resolution 181(II).

Instead, the Palestinians and their Arab supporters did everything possible to prevent the UN from implementing the two-state solution. The UN Palestine Commission reported to the Security Council in February 1948 that "Powerful Arab interests, both inside and outside Palestine, are defying the resolution of the General Assembly and are engaged in a deliberate effort to alter by force the settlement envisaged therein."[1]

An Egyptian newspaper columnist harshly criticized the Palestinian Arab leadership in a surprisingly candid August 1948 editorial for failing to establish a government for their portion of Palestine, dismissing Palestinian excuses as without merit:

> The Arab-controlled part of Palestine has no government to administer its affairs. The Jews were wiser than the Arabs in this respect. They hastened to form a government as soon as the U.N. Assembly voted for partition ... Palestine, however, is still without an Arab government. It may be argued that the establishment of an Arab government in Palestine was delayed because the Jews drove several hundred thousand Palestinian Arabs out of their homes, and because the Arab governments wanted to avoid disputes among themselves over this matter. *Both excuses are silly.*[2]

DOI: 10.4324/9781032686561-13

But the Mufti began planning a year earlier under Egyptian sponsorship to set up a "government" to rule *all* of Palestine. The Beirut newspaper *Al Naha* reported in August 1947 that the Mufti had rented space in an Egyptian hotel, where he intended to establish a Palestinian Arab government in exile.[3] Nevertheless, the Arab League in December 1947 voted down a motion to allow the Mufti to set up his own government for Palestine.[4]

In late January 1948 MI-6 reported the Mufti wanted to establish a symbolic Palestinian Arab government for all of Palestine, with the Mufti at its head.[5] In early January 1948 Syria, Egypt, and Saudi Arabia proposed the creation of an "Administrative Apparatus" (consisting of a national council, an executive council and a president), but not an independent government, to assume some measure of administrative responsibility for Palestine upon the British departure from the country. But Jamal Husseini clarified this did not mean the Palestinian Arabs were forming a functioning government.[6]

The British Ambassador in Beirut speculated the Palestinian Arabs believed they needed to set up a "government in exile" as a way to preserve their legal position.[7] Jamal Husseini confirmed this when he told an American official in Amman that a "government" would be formed only on paper, to preserve Palestinian claims to the *entirety* of Palestine, and to show the Arab League the Mufti was determined to oppose King Abdullah's designs on the West Bank.[8]

Significantly, however, the Palestinian Arabs never asserted a formal reservation of rights to the portion of Palestine the United Nations had allocated to them for statehood in Resolution 181(II). Instead, the Palestinian Arabs laid claim to *all* of Palestine. In so doing, the Palestinian Arabs purported to preserve the *same* legal arguments the United Nations had *already* rejected; namely, that the United Nations lacked authority to adopt the partition resolution; that the partition resolution itself was illegal; and that the Palestinian Arabs therefore were entitled to sovereignty over the *entirety* of Palestine.

Formation of the "All-Palestine Government"

By July 1948 the Arab League, led by Egypt, was pushing back on King Abdullah's effort to claim the Arab portions of Palestine for Jordan. The Arab League thus revived the idea of a Palestinian Arab "Administration" to govern the entire country, including the area comprising the nascent State of Israel.[9] The League's Political Committee adopted a Resolution on 8 July 1948 (the last day of the first truce of the 1948–1949 war) approving the establishment of a "provisional civil administration" for those portions of Palestine the Arab armies had thus far captured, "until all of Arab Filastin is included."[10]

But the provisional civil administration never came into existence. The Mufti objected to the Political Committee's resolution, as it gave the

Palestinian Arabs no authority over political or military issues. On 8 September 1948 the Mufti wrote that he was working on obtaining an amendment to the Resolution.[11] That effort apparently bore fruit, as the Arab League on 22 September 1948 approved the conversion of the Palestinian civil administrative council into a "government" for all of what had been Mandatory Palestine.[12]

Accordingly, the Arab Higher Committee announced on 23 September 1948 that with the Arab League's approval, it would establish a government in Gaza to rule *all* of Palestine, in violation of the General Assembly's two-state solution.[13]

On 30 September–1 October 1948 the Mufti and approximately 150 of his followers met in Gaza "in an atmosphere of festivity" and proclaimed the establishment of the "Palestinian National Council" and the formation of the "All Palestine Government."[14] The "National Council" elected the Mufti as "President," who in turn appointed his cousin Jamal Husseini as "Foreign Minister."[15] Ahmed Hilmi Pasha, a Palestinian banker, was appointed "Prime Minister."[16]

The "Council" issued the "Palestine Declaration of Independence," asserting sovereignty over *all* of Palestine, including the new State of Israel, with the borders designated as "Syria and Lebanon in the north, Transjordan in the east, the Mediterranean Sea in the west and Egypt in the south" and Jerusalem designated as its capital.[17] The British Ambassador to Jordan, Sir Alec Kirkbride, bluntly characterized the "government" as a "farce" and its members as "a collection of stooges."[18]

The Arab League offered symbolic support to the Mufti, with Syria successfully lobbying all member states except Jordan and Yemen to recognize the All Palestine Government.[19] But as with most Middle East politics, the undercurrent of conflicting and complex rivalries created even further ambiguity. Egypt, for example, joined the Arab League vote supporting the establishment of a Palestinian Arab government, but conditioned its support on the Mufti having no role in that government.[20] Even more significantly, according to the British Ambassador in Cairo, Egypt's vote had been given *without* King Farouk's consent.[21]

In any event, the Mufti's focus was not on preserving legal claims to Palestine, but on working in tandem with Egypt to create "a focal point of opposition to Abdullah and ... frustrating [Abdullah's] ambition to federate the Arab regions of Palestine with Transjordan."[22] The Lebanese Foreign Minister noted the "Gaza Government was set up as opposition to Abdullah.... popular reaction is that other Arabs wish to thwart Abdullah's ambitions for federation of Arab regions with Transjordan; [and] concomitant tacit recognition of Israel."[23] Abu-Odeh (1999) described the Gaza Government as "subservient to Egypt" and "an Egyptian ploy designed to prevent Jordan's annexation of Palestinian territory."[24]

The U.S. State Department responded swiftly to the formation of the "All-Palestine Government," instructing every American Ambassador in the Middle East to contact their host governments and notify them the United States opposed the Declaration as "prejudicial to the successful solution of the Palestine problem."[25]

Britain also opposed the creation of the All Palestine Government, conducting a "harsh, unremitting campaign" against the Mufti in tandem with Jordan.[26] The Foreign Office sent a cable marked "most immediate; secret" to its Ambassador in Cairo instructing him to "do whatever you can to prevent Arab Governments deciding to recognize so-called [All-Palestine] Arab Government."[27] British diplomats also worked to persuade countries outside the Arab bloc not to recognize the Mufti's Gaza-based "government."[28]

Collapse of the "All-Palestine Government"

The All-Palestine "government" proved to be nothing more than an illusory, paper government. It controlled no territory, employed no people, mustered no army, exercised no functions, provided no public services, collected no revenue, and largely vanished one month after it was established. It boasted only one actual achievement, managing to print about 14,000 "passports," a symbol of a would-be "government" that never became a reality. In a final humiliation, the Egyptian government announced in 1962 that it had discovered "irregularities" in the production of the All-Palestine Government passports and thus would no longer recognize their validity.[29]

Significantly, the All Palestine Government failed to attract any support from the Palestinian public. Plascov (1981) described Palestinian mistrust of the so-called government, blaming many of its leaders for neglecting them, lacking confidence in the government's ability to help them, and feeling betrayed by the corrupt lifestyle its officials enjoyed.[30]

As Shlaim (1990) noted:

> [T]he contrast between the pretensions of the All-Palestine Government and its capability quickly reduced it to the level of farce. It claimed jurisdiction over the whole of Palestine, yet it had no administration, no civil service, no money, nor real army of its own ... Ostensibly the embryo for an independent Palestinian state, the new government, from the moment of its inception, was thus reduced to the unhappy role of a shuttlecock in the ongoing power struggle between Cairo and Amman.[31]

As early as 7 October 1948, less than one week after the government had been formed, the Egyptians expelled the Mufti from Gaza and took him by force to Cairo, where he was placed under house arrest and forbidden from engaging in any political activity.[32]

On 29 October 1948 the British Consulate in Jerusalem notified London the Gaza "government" had collapsed less than one month after it had been created. The Consulate noted there had been "a perceptible movement towards King Abdullah" among the Palestinian Arab population.[33] Every remaining member of the Gaza "government" abandoned the Mufti and took new positions in Egypt, Jordan, Lebanon, and Saudi Arabia.[34] Jamal Husseini even spoke of agreeing to serve under King Abdullah.[35] The "All Palestine Government" vanished "under the weight of its own impotence."[36]

British Intelligence prepared an extensive report in March 1949 regarding the "All Palestine Government." The report noted the so-called government existed only on paper, and only briefly. The "government" exercised no authority, ruled no territory, and held no legal status.[37] It aspired to rule all of Palestine, in violation of Resolution 181(II). No international organizations, including the United Nations, recognized the "All Palestine Government."[38]

According to the British Intelligence report, the nominal head of the government, Hilmi Pasha, was ready to defect to King Abdullah along with several other members of the government, as the Mufti "keeps everything under his own control." The report also noted the Mufti had embezzled the funds received from Arab states.[39] Hilmi Pasha had concluded the Gaza Government "could not carry on any longer, i.e., they have created a state without financial resources and that now is the time to face facts and call it a failure."[40]

The Mufti, still bitter over Abdullah's victory over him, briefly floated the idea of forming another government in Gaza in October 1949, this time aimed at ruling only the West Bank (then occupied by Jordan) and Gaza (occupied by Egypt).[41] The idea failed to rally pan-Arab support, as "it was obvious that Gaza could only go to Egypt and eastern Palestine to Jordan, while any remnant of Galilee that could be rescued should be attached to Syria."[42] A British military official based in Jerusalem described the idea of a new Mufti-led Palestinian government as a "ridiculous plan" and a "bluff."[43]

The original "All Palestine Government" continued to exist solely on paper from a new base in Cairo, until the 1952 overthrow of King Farouk.[44]

Implications for the Palestinian Legal Case Today

Some Palestinian legal scholars argue the Palestinians achieved statehood with the formation and brief existence of the "All-Palestine Government" in Gaza in October 1948. This argument cannot be taken seriously.

First, the Mufti's effort to form a government (even if only on paper) to "rule" all of Palestine constituted a violation of United Nations Resolution 181(II), as the General Assembly had already rejected Arab statehood in all of Palestine in favor of the two-state solution.[45]

Second, the Palestinians lacked any legal basis to assert sovereignty beyond the areas the United Nations had allocated to them in Resolution 181(II).

Moreover, the Palestinian renunciation of the two-state solution arguably deprived them of any legal basis to assert sovereignty over *any* portion of Palestine in October 1948, five months *after* the Mandate had ended.

Third, the All-Palestine Government never acquired any of the internationally legally required attributes of statehood, as will be discussed in Chapter 19. It controlled no territory. It did not conduct foreign relations.

Fourth, the All-Palestine Government did not even enjoy recognition from the people it purported to govern, as they were already preparing to name Jordan's King Abdullah as their new, post-Mandate ruler.

Therefore, the brief existence on paper of the "All Palestine Government" in the fall of 1948 carries no legal weight in assessing modern-day Palestinian claims of statehood.

Notes

1 United Nations A/AC.21/9, S/676, Para. I(3)(C) (16 Feb. 1948).

2 Central Intelligence Agency, RDP83-00415R001300100016-8, A. Kader al Mazny, editorial in *Al Assas* (22 Aug. 1948) (U.S. Embassy translation, Cairo) (emphasis added); *see also* R. Khalidi, *The Palestinians and 1948: The Underlying Causes of Failure*, in E. Rogan and A. Shlaim (eds.), *The War for Palestine: Rewriting the History of 1948* at 12–36 (Cambridge Univ. Press, 2001) (noting the Palestinian Arabs were plagued by "poor political calculations ... disorganization, confusion and leaderless chaos").

3 KV2/2091, Dispatch (Secret) SIME/P1415/Blb from S.I.M.E General Headquarters, Middle East Land Forces to Director General, London, *The Mufti* (14 Aug. 1947). Jamal Husseini publicly denied the rumors that the Mufti intended to set up a Palestinian Arab government in exile. *Id.* By early September the Mufti himself had also indicated he had no intention of establishing a Palestinian Arab government in Egypt. KV2/2091, Intelligence Report No. 80, *Palestine. The Mufti and the Arab Resistance* at 1 (2 Sept. 1947).

4 J. Nevo, *King Abdallah and Palestine: A Territorial Ambition* at 97 (St. Martin's Press, 1996).

5 KV2/2091, *Extract from M.I.6. Report re Palestine – Arab Dissensions* (27 Jan. 1948).

6 Nevo (1996), *op. cit.* at 28.

7 FO 371/68376, Telegram (Secret) No. 688 from British Embassy, Beirut to Foreign Office (21 Sept. 1948), *reprinted in* P. Toye and A. Seay, *Israel: Boundary Disputed with Arab Neighbours, 1946–1964*, Vol. 2 at 187–90 (Archive Editions, 1995) (noting motivations for creating Palestinian Arab "government" included the desire to "safeguard the Arab juridical position, i.e. their claim to sovereignty over the whole of Palestine," but also identifying intra-Arab disputes between Abdullah and the Mufti, and Abdullah and the Arab League, as more important factors in the move to create a Palestinian Arab "government.").

8 FRUS, 867N.01/9–2648, Telegram No. 65 from Amman (26 Sept. 1948).

9 A. Sela, *Transjordan, Israel and the 1948 War: Myth, Historiography and Reality*, Middle Eastern Studies, 28:4 at 668 (1992); A. Shlaim, *The Rise and Fall of the All-Palestine Government in Gaza*, Journal of Palestine Studies 20:1, 37–53 at 39 (1990).

10 M. Shemesh, *The Palestinian National Revival: In the Shadow of the Leadership Crisis*, 1937–1967 at 45–46 (Indiana Univ. Press, 2018).

11 *Id.* at 46 and n.6.
12 Shlaim, *op. cit.*, at 29–30.
13 *Id.* at 40; Shemesh (2018), *op. cit.* at 48 ("The emphasis on 'All-Palestine' was meant to express rejection of the division of Filastin and preservation of its unity.").
14 Shemesh (2018), *op. cit.* at 48–49.
15 *Id.* at 30; *see also* Shlaim, *op. cit.* at 42–43 (1990); FRUS, Telegram from U.S. Embassy, Cairo to Acting Secretary of State (2 Oct. 1948) (emphasis added).
16 A. Abu-Odeh, *Jordanians, Palestinians & the Hashemite Kingdom in the Middle East Peace Process* at 44 (U.S. Institute of Peace, 1999); Nevo (1996), *op. cit.* at 159.
17 Nevo (1996), *op. cit.* at 160–61, 165; Shemesh (2018), *op. cit.* at 49–50.
18 A. Kirkbride, *From the Wings: Amman Memoirs 1947–1951* at 58–59, 66 (Frank Cass & Co. Ltd., 1976).
19 Cypher Telegram No. 726 (Secret) from British Embassy, Beirut to Foreign Office, London (2 Oct. 1948), *reprinted in* Toye and Seay, *op. cit.* Vol. 2 at 323 ("the Syrian Minister for Foreign Affairs was in Cairo for the purpose of securing immediate simultaneous recognition by all Arab states of Mufti-headed Palestine Government"); Nevo (1996), *op. cit.* at 161.
20 Shemesh (2018), *op. cit.* at 51–52.
21 KV2/2091, Telegram No. 1405 (Secret) from British Embassy, Cairo to Foreign Office (8 Oct. 1948).
22 Shlaim, *op. cit.* at 40; for a different perspective, *see* W. Salem, *Legitimization or Implementation: On the UN Partition Plan*, Palestine-Israel Journal of Politics, Economics and Culture, 9:4 at 10 (2002) (arguing the formation of the All-Palestine Government is evidence of the Palestinian Arab willingness to "deal pragmatically with the results of partition"); see also K. Katz, *Jordanian Jerusalem: Holy Places and National Spaces* at 51 (Univ. Press of Florida, 2005) ("The APG was not a solute on to the Palestine problem it aimed merely to provide a façade of Palestinian rule, albeit under Egyptian military control.")
23 FRUS, 867N.01/10–148, Telegram No. 498 (1 Oct. 1948).
24 Abu-Odeh, *op. cit.* at 44.
25 FRUS, 501.BB Palestine/10–248: Circular telegram (Secret) from the Acting Secretary of State to Certain Diplomatic Offices (2 Oct. 1948).
26 Shemesh (2018), *op. cit.* at 54–55.
27 Cypher Telegram No. 1672 (Most Immediate; Secret) from Foreign Office to British Embassy, Cairo (2 Oct. 1948), *reprinted in* Toye and Seay, *op. cit.* Vol. 2 at 325.
28 Abu-Odeh, *op. cit.* at 44.
29 Shemesh (2018), *op. cit.* at 155.
30 A. Plascov, *The Palestinian Refugees in Jordan, 1948–1957* at 9 (Frank Cass & Co. Ltd., 1981).
31 Shlaim, *op. cit.* at 43; *see also* Plascov, *op. cit.* at 8 ("This Egyptian-sponsored government, whose 'jurisdiction' encompassed a tiny enclave around the town of Gaza, had, in practice, no budget or army. The puppet government had no 'country' to govern and existed only on paper. The whole attempt proved to be a farce ...").
32 Shemesh (2018), *op. cit.* at 52.
33 FO 371/68643, Telegram No. 578 (Secret) from Acting British Consul General, Jerusalem to Foreign Office (29 Oct. 1948), *reprinted in* Toye and Seay, *op. cit.* Vol. 2 at 203–05.
34 Shemesh (2018), *op. cit.* at 63.
35 Plascov, *op. cit.* at 8–9 nn.19–22 (identifying various prominent Mufti associates who defected to the Jordanians less than one month after the founding of the All-Palestine Government).

36 Shlaim, *op. cit.* at 50; Elipeleg, *op. cit.*
37 Central Intelligence Agency, 51966ec8993294098d50a4bf, "Haj Amin al-Husseini, Mufti of Jerusalem, Biographic Sketch No. 60" (Confidential, prepared by Department of State) at 5 (10 Apr. 1951) ("A so-called Palestine Arab Government was set up in Gaza in September 1948 ... The Gaza Arab Government existed for a time, on paper only, and then folded its tents"); M. Shemesh, *The Palestinian National Revival: In the Shadow of the Leadership Crisis, 1937–1967*, at 56 (Indiana Univ. Press, 2018). The British Government reacted to the formation of the supposed Palestinian Government by flatly refusing to recognize "this so-called government." FRUS, 867N.01/10-748, Telegram No. 4423 (7 Oct. 1948). A British official reported during a formal visit to Gaza in June 1949 that he "heard no mention of the 'Gaza Government' which had a fleeting existence toward the end of last year." FO 371/75342, Letter (Confidential) from E. Troutbeck, British Middle East Office, Cairo, to Bevin (16 June 1949), *reprinted in* Toye and Seay, *op. cit.* Vol. 2 at 601.
38 For a more sympathetic view of the All-Palestine Government, *see* I. Al-Shuaibi, *The Development of Palestinian Entity-Consciousness: Part I*, Journal of Palestine Studies, 9:1, 67–84 at 72 (1979) ("[T]he Arab states' enthusiasm for the government gradually waned, and the Arab League did not invite it to attend its subsequent meetings. The Egyptian government, although the principal backer of the All Palestine Government, would not allow it to perform its tasks in the Gaza Strip, which was then controlled by the Egyptian army.").
39 KV2/2091, SIME/SF.2119/B.1 (Secret) (29 Mar. 1949) (enclosing CX Report No. 1399, Palestine, Political, *The Present Position of the Gaza Government*, 5 Mar. 1949). The report attached copies of "passports" issued by the "All Palestine Government."
40 *Id.*
41 Cypher Telegram No. 500 (Confidential) from Kirkbride (Amman) to Foreign Office (4 Oct. 1949), *reprinted in* Toye and Seay, *op. cit.* Vol. 2 at 472.
42 Despatch No. 65 (Confidential) from Kirkbride (Amman) to Bevin (4 Oct. 1949) (noting Jordan, Syria and Lebanon all regarded any new attempt to set up an independent government for Arab Palestine as "folly"); *reprinted in* Toye and Seay, *op. cit.* Vol. 2 at 473–74.
43 29/DO/49, Despatch (Secret and Personal) from Major V.P. Rich (Military Liaison Office, British Consulate-General, Jerusalem) to Major C de B Lisle, War Office, London, para. 6 (16 Oct. 1949), *reprinted in* Toye and Seay, *op. cit.* Vol. 2 at 475–78.
44 Plascov, *op. cit.* at 9.
45 See, e.g., V. Kattan, *The False Premise Sustaining Israel's West Bank Claim – Part II*, Opinio Juris (8 Apr. 2019), http://opiniojuris.org/2019/04/08/the-false-premise-sustaining-israels-west-bank-claim-part-ii/ (last accessed 24 Jan. 2023).

11

THE FORGOTTEN OCCUPATION OF THE WEST BANK – JORDAN, 1948–1967

Introduction

The 1948–1949 Arab-Israeli war ended via armistice agreements. As a result of those agreements, one portion of Mandate Palestine, including approximately half the area the United Nations General Assembly had recommended in Resolution 181(II) for the Palestinian Arab State, had become the sovereign territory of the new State of Israel. Jerusalem, which the UN had recommended for designation as a separate entity under international control, ended up a divided city, with Israel soon afterward declaring the western portion of the city its capital.

For the next two decades, Jordan occupied the West Bank and East Jerusalem, while Egypt occupied the Gaza Strip.

The modern Palestinian narrative completely ignores those non-Israeli occupations, both of which lasted from 1948 to 1967. Instead, the Palestinian narrative of occupation begins either in 1948, describing the State of Israel itself as Palestinian territory occupied by Zionist colonial settlers, or beginning in June 1967, with the onset of Israeli occupation of the West Bank and the Gaza Strip.[1] In either event, as Mishal (1996) notes, "only after the Six-Day War was the term 'Palestinians' reborn in the political dictionary of many countries, having been dead since the 1948 Arab-Israeli War."[2]

The narrative also neglects the very important legal facts regarding Palestinian waivers of West Bank and Gaza sovereignty and Palestinian acquiescence in Jordanian annexation and Egyptian rule.

The Jordanian and Egyptian "forgotten occupations" are therefore highly relevant to any analysis of the merits of the modern-day Palestinian legal case.

DOI: 10.4324/9781032686561-14

The West Bank: Abdullah Takes Control

King Abdullah publicly opposed Resolution 181(II) and Jewish statehood anywhere in Palestine, even as he negotiated in private with the Zionists over the possibility of agreeing to some form of Jewish statehood in a portion of Palestine.[3]

But Abdullah conducted no such negotiations with the Mufti, whom he viewed as a greater threat to his kingdom than the Zionists. Abdullah strongly rejected the possibility of a Mufti-led Palestine on Transjordan's western border. Instead, Abdullah, consistent with his broader territorial ambitions, laid claim to the areas the United Nations had designated west of the Jordan River for the Palestinian Arab State.[4] Abdullah "was determined to occupy the area assigned to the new Arab state, prevent its coming into being, and make it part of his kingdom."[5]

The bitter rivalry between Abdullah and the Mufti continued both before and after Israel's May 1948 declaration of statehood. The Arab League was suspicious of Abdullah's territorial designs but reluctant to break openly with Transjordan.[6] The League thus offered half-hearted support for the Mufti.

Nevo (1996) described the situation during the spring of 1948:

> In some areas, the King and the Mufti vied for influence. Yet, without the backing of the Arab League, which even refused to let the AHC (Arab Higher Committee)-sponsored national committees in the various Palestinian towns take control of the places evacuated by the British, the local Arab leadership could do very little against Abdallah's mounting influence. The presence of the Arab Legion on the one hand and the growing number of Arab settlements lost to the Jews on the other, caused more and more inhabitants to turn to Abdallah and not to the AHC as their potential saviour.[7]

Nevo notes that "between January and March 1948, many Palestinians approached Abdallah to seek his intervention."[8] Nevo also describes how the Palestinian Arab military setbacks in the spring of 1948 led the local, "practically leaderless" Palestinian Arabs to look to Abdullah and the Arab Legion for protection and for provision of basic services.[9]

The United Nations Mediator Count Folke Bernadotte, in his posthumously published memoir, characterized Palestinian national aspirations in 1948 in less than optimistic terms:

> The Palestine Arabs have at present no will of their own. Neither have they ever developed any specifically Palestinian nationalism. The demand for a separate Arab State in Palestine is consequently relatively weak. It would seem as though in existing circumstances most of the Palestinian Arabs would be quite content to be incorporated in Trans-Jordan.[10]

Abdullah's popularity among most (but not all) Palestinian Arabs improved rapidly in the weeks and months following Israel's declaration of independence:

> Apart from his traditional supporters, the Nashashibis and the other anti-Husayni factions, he [Abdullah] now became popular with wider circles: mayors, *mukhtars*, merchants and members of the middle class whose primary concern was order and stability and who eschewed radical change.[11]

The British commander of the Arab Legion, John Bagot Glubb, "even managed to cajole the chieftains of the main Bedouin tribes of Hebron and Beersheba districts into signing a petition asking Abdallah to take over Palestine as soon as the British had left."[12]

Most West Bank Palestinian Arab civil society leaders ignored the Mufti's October 1948 Gaza-based "All-Palestine" government, deciding instead their best hope lay in pledging loyalty to King Abdullah and submitting to Transjordanian rule.

The Amman Conference, October 1948

On 1 October 1948, the same day the Mufti and his small group of followers declared their new government in Gaza, Abdullah convened a competing group of several thousand Palestinian Arabs in Amman under the banner of the "First Palestinian National Congress."[13] Some of those present were cajoled into attending or otherwise expected to do so.[14] Others attended willingly, including prominent Palestinians such as Jaffa Mayor Yusuf Haykal. Nablus Mayor Sulayman Tuqan, who had rejected the Mufti's offer of a "ministerial" position in the "All-Palestine" Government, also attended the Amman Conference.

The Palestinian delegates in Amman made no secret of their support for King Abdullah and their desire for the West Bank to merge into Transjordan rather than attain independent statehood. Several of the delegates visited the King to express their loyalty:

> The Hashemite Propaganda Association, headed by Ali Khalaf and composed of local mayors and notables from the Ramallah area, also came to see Abdullah. They called him 'Saviour of Palestine' and trusted that he would solve the Palestinian problem by peace or war, and regard the inhabitants of Jordan and Palestine as one nation to be led by one leader. A similar delegation came from Abd al-Karim al-Alami, the 'Ramleh-Lydda representative.' The Jaffa refugees in Ramallah also told the Military

> Governor there that they gave the King full authority to represent them. Delegates from Jerusalem, Ramallah, Deir Ghassanah, Amwas, Hebron, Bethlehem and Bayt Jala followed suit ... contrary to the widely-held belief outside Jordan, those representatives did reflect the feelings of a large segment of the population.[15]

The Amman delegates adopted a resolution objecting to the formation of the "All Palestine Government" and declaring their loyalty to King Abdullah. The delegates affirmed Transjordan and Palestine constituted a single territorial and political entity.[16] The delegates gave the King "unrestricted power" to speak for and act on behalf of the Palestinian Arabs "in any way" he saw fit.[17]

In the weeks following the formation of the Mufti's "All-Palestine Government," King Abdullah received a stream of petitions from West Bank notables, including from Ramallah, Ramleh-Lydda, Jerusalem, Hebron, Bethlehem, Beit Jala, and elsewhere, all asking him to rule over the Palestinian Arabs and to deal with their situation in any way he deemed appropriate.[18] Those petitions reflected the feelings of a "large segment" of the Palestinian population that their best hopes lay with absorption into Transjordan rather than independent statehood.[19]

In addition, as mentioned above, several members of the All-Palestine Government and other followers of the Mufti, including the Mayors of Bethlehem, Nablus, and Hebron, quickly defected to Abdullah less than a month after the "All-Palestine Government" had been formed.[20] The Mufti and his few remaining loyalists fled to Cairo following Israeli military gains in the Negev in the fall of 1948.[21]

The Acting British Consul General in Jerusalem cabled London on 29 October 1948 to report the All-Palestine Arab Government's "hasty withdrawal from Gaza." The cable further noted:

> The political trimmers in Palestine – and for lack of any clear indication on the future of Arab Palestine, there are many – are coming to the conclusion that the likelihood of the establishment of an independent Arab State here is receding while union with Transjordan appears more probable and, perhaps, more profitable. There has, therefore, been a perceptible movement towards King Abdullah.[22]

Sir Alec Kirkbride, the British Ambassador in Amman, cabled London on 2 November 1948 and reported the various Palestinian delegations who had visited Transjordan in recent days "would now be graciously pleased to permit the Transjordan authorities to earn their support to the scheme to unite Arab areas of Palestine with Transjordan."[23]

On 15 November 1948 Abdullah visited East Jerusalem, where the Bishop of the Coptic Church crowned him "King of Palestine." The Jewish Telegraphic Agency described the "coronation" as a "political coup" for Abdullah, who received both Muslim and Christian well-wishers during his visit.[24] Although the coronation was not well publicized locally, word spread and within a short time more Palestinian delegations traveled to Amman to pledge loyalty to the King. Several Palestinian groups held public gatherings in Amman asking Abdullah to annex the Arab portion of Palestine.[25]

The Jericho Conference, December 1948

On 1 December 1948 approximately 3,000 Palestinian Arabs met in Jericho to formalize their allegiance to King Abdullah.[26] The United States Ambassador in Amman described the delegates as "far more representative of Palestine Arabs than [the] Gaza Government."[27] The delegates included prominent Palestinians who had deserted the Mufti. Hebron Mayor Muhammad Ali al-Ja'abri, a former Mufti ally and member of the October 1948 Palestinian National Council, served as lead organizer of the Jericho Conference. Others abandoning the Mufti included the prominent Palestinian lawyer Auni Bey Abdul Hadi, the Mufti's cousin Mussah Abdallah al-Husayni of Jerusalem, and Haifa-based lawyer Fu'ad Atallah.[28]

The Jericho delegates included a wide swath of Palestinian society, including Bedouins, urban and rural inhabitants, rich and poor, Christians and Muslims. Fully aware the Mufti's Gaza-based paper government had been a failure, the delegates chose Transjordanian rule. They denounced the Mufti's "All Palestine Government." They called for the unification of Arab Palestine (by which they meant the West Bank and East Jerusalem) with Transjordan, referring to both as part of "Greater Syria," "Southern Syria," and "Natural Syria," and "as a whole and indivisible entity." They pledged fealty to Abdullah and recognized him as "King of all Palestine." They granted Abdullah full authority to act on their behalf.[29] In so doing, they explicitly waived any claims to independent Palestinian statehood in the West Bank, including East Jerusalem.

The final version of the Jericho Resolutions, issued on 2 December 1948 after revisions in response to objections from Abdullah to the original version, read as follows:

1 The Congress expresses its non-confidence in the AHC [Arab Higher Committee] and calls to elect a new Committee.
2 The Gaza [All-Palestine] Government does not represent the Arabs of Palestine.
3 Palestine and Transjordan will be united to create the 'Arab Hashemite Kingdom,' with Abdallah as its King.

4 Palestinian representatives will be co-opted into the Transjordanian parliament.
5 The Congress empowers Abdallah to solve the Palestine problem in any way he considers proper. The Congress also asks the King to promptly execute these resolutions.[30]

Abbasi noted the Jericho conference reflected the overwhelming Palestinian preference for King Abdullah and absorption into Transjordan rather than attempting to exist as an independent country under the Mufti's leadership:

> At the beginning of December 1948 the Jericho Conference, chaired by the Mayor of Hebron, Sheikh Mahmud Ja'bari, was held in the presence of delegations from most of the cities in the West Bank, including Jerusalem, Hebron, Bethlehem, Ramallah, and with the participation of representatives of the military authorities, officers of the Legion, Members of the High Muslim Council, tribal chiefs, and hundreds of leaders and heads of the Palestinian people besides many others. This conference adopted a series of resolutions, the most important being the demand that King Abdullah should unite the West Bank with the Kingdom of Jordan and be recognized as the king of both banks. 8 The resolution by these leaders and others was not only due to the friendship and historical alliance between them and the Hashemite crown, but was also the result of the total collapse of the Palestinian leadership under Hajj Amin Husseini during the 1948 war. This leadership had tried to continue ruling through all kinds of measures, especially after the establishment of the 'All Palestine Government', but it did not win the confidence of the public, some of whom regarded Abdullah as redeemer and savior, and Hajj Amin as an irresponsible adventurer.[31]

The President of the Jericho Conference, Mohamed Ali al Ja'abari, summarized the Conference's decisions in a 4 December 1948 letter to Kirkbride. Ja'abari noted "the conference decided that Palestine and the Transjordan Hashemite Kingdom should combine into the kingdom and that His Majesty King Abdulla ibn Hussein should be acknowledged as constitutional King of Palestine."[32]

Kirkbride sent a confidential report regarding the Jericho Conference to Foreign Secretary Ernest Bevin on 8 December 1948.[33] Kirkbride said 3,000 delegates attended the conference, "larger and more representative of the Arabs of Palestine" than the 1 October Amman conference. Kirkbride noted many former "erstwhile" supporters of the Mufti attended and were "co-operating actively" with the other Palestinian delegates. Kirkbride rejected claims that Abdullah had stage-managed the proceedings to create the pretext for his eventual annexation of Arab Palestine:

> While the promoters have been encouraged and assisted by King Abdullah and the Government of Transjordan, the initiative came from the Palestinians and the movement does indicate a growing volume of dissatisfaction amongst them with ... their old leaders in general and the Mufti in particular ...[34]

The U.S. Ambassador in Amman corroborated Kirkbride's assessment of the Jericho Conference in a secret cable to Washington several days later. He reported "several thousand" Palestinian delegates had attended, including "numerous delegations including mayors of Hebron, Bethlehem, Ramallah, Arab Legion Military Governor General and military governors [of] all districts, and other notables."[35] The Ambassador noted that "although usual jealousies and frictions were apparent during meeting, it is believed of significance, particularly in light recent developments in UN political committee, as King may regard resolution as his mandate from Palestine Arabs."[36]

In January 1949 two additional key Mufti supporters defected to Abdullah – Kamil Arakat, former commander of *Al-Futuwwah*, the Mufti's youth organization, and Munir Abu Fadhal, commander of the Mufti's *Jihad* squadrons.[37]

Annexation Begins

Abdullah announced several days following the Jericho Conference that he would accept the request from the Palestinian Arab delegates and "proclaim the annexation of Arab Palestine to Transjordan."[38]

Both Abdullah and a broad range of West Bank Palestinian leaders moved swiftly to merge the West Bank into Transjordan. On 14 December 1948, a group of Palestinians representing 57 villages from the Lydda-Ramallah regions met and authorized a delegation to visit Amman to thank Abdullah for his efforts on behalf of those residing in the "western part of his Kingdom."

Kirkbride reported to London in a 14 December 1948 cable that "practically all" the population of Hebron and Nablus now supported unification with Transjordan.[39]

On 26 December 1948, a group of Palestinians from Ramallah and the surrounding villages expressed their support for the outcome of the Jericho Conference and condemned "the falsified and distorted propaganda" coming from Egypt and other Arab League members who opposed Abdullah's territorial ambitions in Palestine and Syria.[40]

On 28 December 1948, a conference took place in Nablus under the leadership of Mayor Suleiman Tuqan.[41] Approximately 500 Palestinians from the northern area of the West Bank attended the conference. The delegates passed nine resolutions, including one calling for the unification of Palestine and Transjordan under King Abdullah's rule. The delegates then proceeded to Amman in a 100-car caravan to urge Abdullah to annex Arab Palestine.[42]

Abdullah, for his part, appointed a new Mufti on 20 December 1948 to replace Haj Amin al Husseini, who by this time was under house arrest in Cairo.[43] Abdullah also disbanded the Arab Higher Committee and other similar groups. He appointed governors for Ramallah and the northern districts, Jerusalem, and Hebron, all reporting directly to the Jordanian Interior Minister in Amman. Abdullah issued various directives to unify the East and West Banks, abolishing the border between the two sides, and extending Jordanian administrative, legal, and financial control over the West Bank.[44]

On 6 January 1949 Abdullah decreed the Palestinian Arabs in the West Bank and all Palestinians living abroad would become Jordanian nationals with full citizenship, receiving Jordanian passports and the right to vote and serve in government.[45] Abdullah toured Hebron, Ramallah, Bethlehem, Nablus and Jerusalem in December 1948 and January 1949 to shore up support for unification.

Although not every Palestinian supported the King, even those less enthusiastic "would rather become Jordanian citizens, with full civil and political rights as soon as possible, than remain with an unclear personal status ..."[46]

Abdullah took additional steps during 1949 and 1950 to complete the *de jure* consolidation of Arab Palestine into the Hashemite Kingdom. Jordanian military governors (later replaced by civilian governors) relocated from the East Bank to the West Bank and took over the administration of Palestinian towns. Militias loyal to the Mufti were disbanded. The legal systems of the East and West Banks were merged. Customs and travel controls were eliminated at all crossing points along the Jordan River.

In May 1949 Abdullah appointed three Palestinians to the Jordanian cabinet – Musa Nasir (Communications), Khulusi al-Khayri (Agriculture and Commerce), and Ruhi Bey 'Abd al-Hadi (later Pasha) (Foreign affairs).[47] Many other Palestinians served in high-level positions in the Jordanian government, including in the ministries of Agriculture, Economics, Education, Development and Foreign Affairs, as well as high-level judicial positions.[48] Palestinians were also appointed to important ambassadorial posts. Dr. Yusuf Haykal Bey, the former Mayor of Jaffa, became the first-ever Jordanian Ambassador to the United States. Former Jaffa Mayor Edmond Bey Rock was appointed Jordan's ambassador to Italy.

The British Government strongly supported Abdullah's annexation of the West Bank, believing it represented the best outcome for Britain, the Jordanians, and the Palestinian Arabs. A Foreign Office minute from October 1949 explained the advantages of annexation:

> The Jordan Government is anxious to proceed with the formal annexation of central Arab Palestine. There is no doubt, as has been pointed out by H.M. Minister at Amman and H.M. Consul General at Jerusalem, that such a step is most desirable from a purely local point of view. It would

> greatly reduce the dangers of the ex-Mufti's renewed activities, strengthen the Arab position vis-à-vis that of Israel over Jerusalem, provide an opportunity to redress the present maladministration in Arab Palestine (due partly to the temporary and uncertain character of the present regime) and be a considerable step forward towards the stability necessary for a final settlement.[49]

The United States Government also supported annexation. The Acting Secretary of States sent a top secret cable to U.S. Ambassador Wells Stabler in Amman in early January 1949 advising "most satisfactory solution disposition greater part Arab Palestine would be incorporate[ed] in Transjordan. Therefore Dept approves principle underlying Jericho resolutions."[50]

Kirkbride cabled the Foreign Office on 25 February 1949 to report "Transjordan is gradually assuming a more direct control over ... Arab areas of Palestine and this process seems to meet with the approval of the great majority of the inhabitants of those areas."[51] On 1 March 1949 Kirkbride reported "the absorption of Arab areas of Palestine by Transjordan is taking place fairly painlessly."[52]

In October 1949 the Foreign Office Research Department in London prepared a secret memorandum entitled "The Union of the Kingdom of Jordan and Arab Palestine."[53] The memorandum summarized the various expressions of Palestinian Arab support for Jordanian annexation, while also acknowledging many Palestinians were less than enthusiastic about Abdullah:

> Inside Palestine many genuine expressions of the desire for unification with Jordan have been given – by the Jericho and Nablus Congresses of December 1948, ... by the demonstrations of loyalty to King Abdullah during his tours of the area ... and by many other Arab organizations and conferences, the majority of which favour union to some extent, even if only as a step toward pan-Arab union, and not from any friendly feeling towards Jordan or Abdullah.[54]

In mid-October 1949, while the Foreign Office was preparing its analysis, a British Military official in Jerusalem reported to the War Office in London that Abdullah had just visited Jerusalem, Nablus, Hebron, Ramallah, and Jenin. The report noted prominent and ordinary Palestinians rushed "to meet him, see him, applaud him and pay him flowery compliments, only to return to their houses to talk hate of him. These people certainly know which side their bread is buttered."[55] The military official speculated the Palestinian desire for union with Jordan was driven by the desire to "Palestinianize" Jordan: "in two or three years, he thinks he will be able to infiltrate the Jordanian Government and run affairs to suit the Palestinians."[56]

April 1950 Jordanian Parliamentary Elections

Elections were held for a new and enlarged Jordanian parliament on 11 April 1950. Palestinian candidates and voters participated actively in the electoral process. Hoping to play a major role in running the newly unified country, Palestinians campaigned on the slogan "Yes to the union [with Jordan], no to the peace with Israel."[57]

More than 300,000 people were eligible to vote in the April 1950 election, slightly more than half of whom resided in the West Bank. More than 120 candidates vied for 40 seats, 20 to represent the West Bank and 20 the East Bank. The West Bank Palestinians were equally represented with the East Bank Transjordanians, with 20 seats allocated to each.

The American Embassy in Amman reported the Transjordanian Prime Minister, Said Pasha Mufti, "confirmed general opinion approximately 60% registered voters eastern Jordan and 65% in western participated April 11 elections. This widely and I believe accurately interpreted as constituting plebiscite union issue."[58]

Kirkbride cabled London on 15 April 1950 with his analysis of the significance of the Parliamentary elections. He noted, "all but a very small percentage of the inhabitants of the area to be united with Jordan have voted for the union." He explained

> the election ... of deputies to a common Parliament is in itself an act of union and the subsequent declaration in that Parliament is nothing more than a formal ratification of that act. The Union therefore has been effected.

Kirkbride concluded by again emphasizing the "great majority" of the West Bank population preferred waiving independence and sovereignty in favor of Jordanian annexation.[59]

Annexation Approved

On 24 April 1950, every member of the newly elected Jordanian parliament voted in favor of unifying the East and West Banks of the kingdom and changing the name of the country from "Transjordan" to the "Hashemite Kingdom of Jordan." Parliament also abolished the word "Palestine" and replaced it with the official designation "West Bank of the Hashemite Kingdom of Jordan."[60] The Parliamentary resolution reiterated the Palestinian and pan-Arab goal of eliminating Israel, even though Israel and Jordan had just signed an Armistice Agreement three weeks earlier (3 April 1949) ending the 1948–1949 war.

The Parliamentary resolution read in part as follows:

> In confirmation of the confidence of the nation and in recognition of the good efforts for the realization of national aspirations exerted by His Majesty Abdullah Ben-el-Husein, King of the Hashemite Kingdom of the Jordan, and in accordance with the right of self-determination, the existing situation of the two banks of the Jordan, the eastern and western, their national, physical, geographical unity and the necessities of their common interests, the Jordan Parliament, representing both banks, decides on this day, Monday, April the 24th, 1950, and declares the following:

1 Approval is granted to complete unity between the two banks of the Jordan, the eastern and western, and their amalgamation in one single state—the Hashemite Kingdom of Jordan, under the crown of His Hashemite Majesty, King Abdullah Ben-el-Husein, the Exalted. This will be upon the basis of Parliamentary Constitutional rule and complete equality in the rights and duties of all the citizens.
2 Arab rights in Palestine shall be protected. Those rights shall be defended with all possible legal means and this unity shall in no way be connected with the final settlement of Palestine's just cause within the limits of national hopes, Arab cooperation, and international justice.[61]

The language in the last quoted paragraph was intended to preserve Palestinian Arab claims to the entirety of the former Palestine Mandate, rather than just the areas the United Nations had allocated for Arab statehood in Resolution 181(II). Significantly, the Palestinian members of the Jordanian Parliament never proposed any legislation during the two decades of Jordanian occupation to confer independent statehood on the West Bank.

The Jordanian government moved ahead with annexation, establishing a commission in 1950 to unify the East and West Bank legal systems. The government also established the Jordanian dinar as the official currency for the unified kingdom.[62]

On 9 May 1950, the Jaffa Refugee Committee in Nablus issued a proclamation responding to Arab League criticism of the annexation. The Committee rebuked the League, saying "we now prefer to be the masters of our fate and decide ourselves on our destiny ... and we want our beloved King Abdullah ... to accept our acceptance."[63]

In December 1950 Abdullah appointed the prominent anti-Mufti Palestinian Arab and former Jerusalem Mayor Raghib al-Nashashibi to the ministerial-level post of Custodian of the Holy Places in East Jerusalem and the Old City. Al-Nashashibi wrote to the King accepting the appointment and expressing his "profound" loyalty to the King.[64]

Although the Arab League opposed Jordan's purported annexation of the West Bank, there were pockets of support from some Arab countries, especially Iraq. For example, the Iraqi Newspaper *Al Ittihad ad-Disturi* explained its support for annexation in a 19 May 1950 article:

> In 1949, it was unanimously decided by the Political Committee of the Arab League that since those parts of Palestine left in Arab hands could not possibly become an independent state, it was advisable for the Arab areas of Palestine to join the adjacent Arab states. Moreover, the Political Committee also decided that in the event that the UN Conciliation Commission should inquire as to the future disposition of Arab Palestine, the unanimous Arab reply would be that the issue was strictly the concern of the Arabs. The Jordanian representative was designated spokesman for all the Arab states. The Political Committee's designation of the Jordanian representative as the spokesman ... indirectly recognized the fact that the future disposition of the Arab parts of Palestine was the primary concern of Jordan. Jordan has annexed Arab Palestine only after the people of that area had voice their desire to join Jordan in order to eliminate the threat of Zionist expansion.[65]

Ongoing Unification Post-Abdullah

Abdullah's assassination on 20 July 1951 by a suspected acolyte of the Mufti at the al-Aqsa Mosque in Jerusalem did not slow Arab Palestine's absorption into Jordan.[66] As Katz (2006) notes, Amman continued to cement the annexation, including issuing the "Unity" postage stamp in 1952. The stamp pictured the Nabatean Treasury in Petra together with the Dome of the Rock in Jerusalem, the two "most famous architectural inheritances from each bank of the newly unified kingdom."[67]

Abu-Odeh (1999) offers a more complete picture of the socio-economic integration of the West and East Banks and Palestinian life under Jordanian occupation, including the transfer of East Bank Jordanian citizens to the occupied West Bank:

> The pronounced similarity in culture made it easy for the Jordanians and Palestinians to communicate and act as one people. Almost in no time, the Jordanian and Palestinian intelligentsia shared membership in the same political parties. Intermarriages, which had occurred before the unification, continued on a larger scale. Close relationships of all kinds were established ... Civil servants from the West Bank were appointed on the East Bank and vice versa. The Transjordanian families of some of the military and police moved to the West Bank, where their units were deployed.[68]

To be sure, Palestinian support for Abdullah was neither unanimous nor entirely enthusiastic. Some historians (including some Israeli historians) have questioned the authenticity of the October 1948 Amman and December 1948 Jericho conferences, noting the Jordanian authorities bused in some of the delegates and otherwise engineered the proceedings to look as if they reflected genuine Palestinian "support" for Abdullah.[69]

Moreover, Palestinian dissatisfaction with the Jordanian regime was evident following annexation.[70] The West Bank population was larger, more educated, more entrepreneurial, and more urbane than their east bank counterparts.[71] Some West Bank Palestinians felt they should have received more than 50% representation in the Jordanian parliament, as that number was disproportionate to their larger population relative to the East Bank. The Palestinians were unhappy about the downgrading of Jerusalem, formerly the capital of Mandate Palestine, to a peripheral role in favor of Amman as the capital of the unified kingdom.[72]

Many Palestinians also felt the Amman authorities favored the East Bank in allocating economic and other resources.[73] Abdullah even refused to permit the opening of a four-year university in the West Bank.[74] The Palestinians also opposed Abdullah's willingness to negotiate the April 1949 armistice with Israel instead of pursuing the destruction of the Jewish State.[75]

The Amman government, aware of the undercurrents of dissatisfaction, created a vast security apparatus in the West Bank to monitor potential anti-regime activity. As Shemesh (2018) notes:

> All the important dignitaries of the West Bank, especially those suspected of acting against the regime, were subjected to strict surveillance and monitoring. These dignitaries were primarily concentrated in Nablus ... The regime imposes strict censorship over mail and placed wiretaps on the telephone conversations of political activists in the West bank ... Publications critical of the regime that were sent to Jordan were confiscated before they could reach their destination.[76]

But even at the height of their frustration with Jordanian rule, the Palestinians never advocated secession from Jordan. Nor did the Palestinians *ever* demand their own independent state in the West Bank and Gaza during the two decades of Jordanian and Egyptian rule. Although we do not have the benefit of polling data or a formal plebiscite to ascertain the precise levels of Palestinian support, opposition, or apathy regarding unification with Jordan, the contemporaneous diplomatic cable traffic from British and American officials in Amman demonstrates Palestinian support for Jordanian unification far exceeded Palestinian support for self-determination in the West Bank and Gaza. The robust levels of Palestinian participation in the April 1950 parliamentary election also evidences Palestinian support for unification with Jordan.

As Plascov (1981) notes, "the West Bankers' protest against the regime's discriminatory policy throughout the 1950s did not call for separation from the East Bank, but rather for a change in policy."[77] Likewise, Plascov explains how the Palestinians

> willingly took part in the offered process of integration, voting and being elected to Parliament, serving in the rapidly expanding Jordanian administration, and in effect carrying out the policy which aimed at thwarting any Palestinian, or for that matter, refugee political separateness.[78]

Mainstream Palestinian leaders viewed themselves as *Jordanian* politicians.[79] And Palestinians living abroad "coveted" the far more comfortable life their brethren enjoyed under Jordanian rule.[80]

Indeed, although there were some efforts among Palestinians during the 1950s, especially those living abroad, to galvanize support during the Jordanian occupation for some form of Palestinian national movement,[81] the emphasis was always on liberating "occupied Palestine" – destroying the State of Israel and replacing it with a Palestinian Arab state – but *not* establishing a Palestinian State in either the areas the United Nations had allocated for that purpose in Resolution 181(II), or in the remaining uncaptured portion of those areas in the West Bank and Gaza. As Plascov (1981) notes, "up to the 1960s the Palestinians could not and did not try to organize themselves as a distinct group, concentrating rather on their integration into the Hashemite Kingdom of Jordan."[82]

Mishal (1996) describes the Palestinian acceptance of Jordanian rule during 1949-1967 as grounded in "conditional legitimacy."[83] Mishal characterizes the Palestinian attitude toward Jordanian rule as "ambivalent." Nevertheless, Mishal concedes "the Palestinians were willing to accept Jordanian rule as long as they could play a part in the definition of political goals and in the allocation of resources."[84]

However, the Jordanian and Palestinian political goals sometimes stood in conflict. For the Jordanians, the primary goal was to "gain the loyalty of and control over the Palestinians in order to integrate the West Bank into the Kingdom of Jordan."[85] For the Palestinians, "recovery of Palestine from the Jews and the establishment of Palestinian or Arab rule over the entire territory of Palestine became the central political dream of many Palestinians."[86] The West Bank Palestinians and the occupying Jordanians reconciled their conflicting goals through compromise and cooperation. The irony, according to Mishal (1996), was that "the prolonging of existence between the two banks fostered patterns of relations in which *recognition of the transitoriness of the arrangements paradoxically contributed to their persistence.*"[87]

But even after two decades of unification, by 1967 "the West Bank bore few signs of Jordanization." Mishal (1978) described the West Bank population's "floating identities" during the years of Jordanian occupation, ranging from Jordanian to Pan-Arab, to Pan-Islamic, to Palestinian, with no single identity emerging as dominant.[88] West Bankers viewed the Jordanians "more as occupiers than countrymen."[89] Nevertheless, it was only after Israel replaced Jordan and Egypt as the occupant of the West Bank and Gaza in June 1967 that the Palestinians refocused their efforts on West Bank/Gaza statehood.

The Legality of Jordan's Annexation of the West Bank

Jordan's military invasion of the newly declared State of Israel in May 1948 violated Article 2(4) of the United Nations Charter, prohibiting "the threat or use of force against the territorial integrity or political independence of any State, or in any other manner inconsistent with the Purposes of the United Nations." Although some historiography has attempted to explain the military invasion of the nascent Jewish State as an expression of Palestinian and broader Arab dissatisfaction with the "injustice" of the General Assembly's November 1947 two-state solution, international law permits no such justification for launching war and committing the crime of aggression.

As Blum (1968) noted, "It must, therefore, be concluded that the armed intervention of the various Arab States –including Transjordan – was a violation of international law. Its real aim was of course to crush by military force the newly-established State of Israel."[90]

By the time the Israel-Jordan Armistice Agreement ending the 1948–1949 war was signed at Rhodes on 3 April 1949, Israel had expanded its territory into roughly half the area the United Nations had allocated for the Palestinian Arab State in Resolution 181. The Palestinians were not a party to the armistice agreement, having ceded any standing with their decision to abandon statehood in favor of Transjordanian rule at the Jericho Conference four months earlier.

The Israel-Jordan Armistice Agreement stated in Article 2(2) that "no provision of this Agreement shall in any way prejudice the rights, claims, and positions of either Party hereto in the ultimate peaceful settlement of the Palestine question, the provisions of this Agreement being dictated exclusively by military considerations." Blum (1968) argues the Armistice Agreement froze the rights and claims of the parties as they existed on the day the agreement was signed. Accordingly, neither party could undertake any unilateral act to alter or purport to improve their rights as they existed as of the date the Agreement was signed, and for as long as the Agreement remained in effect.

Therefore, Blum argues, Jordan's purported annexation of the West Bank violated Article 2(2) and thus was void under international law. As Blum notes, "just as annexation of occupied territory by a belligerent occupant is obviously prohibited before the cease-fire or the armistice, it is equally prohibited, under international law, after the cease-fire or armistice, as long as this remains in force."[91]

On 11 May 1949, five weeks following the Israel-Jordan Armistice Agreement, the United Nations granted full membership to Israel. The General Assembly did not require Israel to withdraw to the lines demarcated in Resolution 181, thereby implicitly recognizing Israel's borders as including the Arab-designated areas Israel had captured during the 1948–1949 war.[92] The United Nations Security Council reiterated this implicit recognition 18 years later in Resolution 242, which called for Israel to withdraw from "territories occupied in the *recent* conflict," meaning the June 1967 Six-Day War, but *not* from Arab-allocated territories captured in the 1948–1949 war.[93]

Significantly, Abdullah's purported annexation of the West Bank did not encompass the Arab-allocated areas Israel had captured in the 1948–1949 war. Indeed, Abdullah accepted those areas as falling on the Israeli side of the "Green Line" in the 3 April 1949 Armistice Agreement.

Nor did Abdullah's purported annexation of the West Bank lawfully transfer West Bank sovereignty to Jordan. Scholars have differed over the precise legal characterization of Jordan's status as the occupant of the West Bank and East Jerusalem from 1948 to 1967. Most scholars agree, however, that Jordan never acquired sovereignty over the West Bank and East Jerusalem during its two decades of occupation. E. Lauterpacht (1968), for example, rejected any Jordanian claim to sovereignty over the West Bank and East Jerusalem as entirely without legal justification.[94]

Blum (1968) argues Jordan was at most a belligerent occupant of the West Bank and East Jerusalem between 1948 and 1967:

> [T]he Kingdom of Jordan never acquired the status of a legitimate sovereign over Judea and Samaria and enjoyed at the most the rights of a belligerent occupant there ... It would seem to follow that, in a case like the present where the ousted State never was the legitimate sovereign, those rules of belligerent occupation directed to safeguarding that sovereign's reversionary rights have no application.[95]

Gerson (1973) takes a different approach. He contends the Palestinian Arabs, as a matter of law, did not formally cede whatever sovereign claim they may have had as to the Arab portions of Palestine to Jordan at the 1 December 1948 Jericho Conference. Gerson argues that even if "the decision to merge expressed at the Jericho Conference represented in fact the free choice of the West Bank inhabitants, it would still remain questionable whether that decision indicated an intent wholly and irrevocably to transfer such sovereign rights."[96]

Therefore, Gerson (1973, 1978) disagreed with Blum's characterization of Jordan as a "belligerent occupant." At most, according to Gerson, Jordan's legal status in the West Bank between 1948 and 1967 was more akin to a "trustee-occupant" than a belligerent occupant.

Palestinian and International Acquiescence in Jordan's Occupation

Throughout the two decades of Jordan's forgotten occupation of the West Bank, neither the Palestinians nor the United Nations ever raised the sorts of objections that have been leveled repeatedly against the subsequent Israeli occupation. The United Nations, for example, never convened the General Assembly or the Security Council between 1948 and 1967 to discuss Jordan's occupation of the West Bank. Although only Britain and Pakistan formally recognized Jordan's annexation of the West Bank, no meaningful objections were raised to the annexation once it became a fait accompli in mid-1950. Britain went so far as to extend the protective umbrella of the Anglo-Jordanian defense treaty to the West Bank.[97]

Nor did the Palestinians or the United Nations ever condemn the relocation of Jordanian citizens to homes in the West Bank, as they repeatedly have done regarding Israeli relocations to the West Bank after June 1967. To be sure, Jordan did not construct any settlements in the West Bank between 1949 and 1967, and the number of Jordanians who relocated to the West Bank was far lower than the number of Israelis who relocated to the West Bank after 1967. But if the current Palestinian legal argument regarding the Fourth Geneva Convention's prohibition in Article 49, paragraph 6 of the Occupying Power's deportation or transfer "of its own civilian population into the territory it occupies" applies to Israeli relocations to the West Bank, then it would have applied equally to Jordanian relocations to the West Bank between 1948 and 1967, as the prohibition makes no distinction based on the quantum of relocation activity or the creation of settlements. Indeed, it could be argued that building settlements in unpopulated areas constitutes a lesser form of relocation activity (as it does not involve the risk of displacing the local population from their existing homes), than sending people to live in existing towns and cities, as Jordan did. In any event, no one ever raised the issue during the two decades of Jordanian occupation.

Moreover, neither the Palestinians nor the United Nations ever criticized Jordan's treatment of the West Bank Palestinians. Jordan's policy of favoring the East Bank over the West Bank provoked no protest from the international community. Nor did the presence of Jordan's secret police and security agencies in the West Bank stir any criticism.

The Palestine issue simply vanished from the international community's agenda between 1952 and 1967. Even the 4-1/2-month temporary Israeli occupation of the Gaza Strip during the 1956–1957 Sinai War failed to spark any calls for Palestinian self-determination in Gaza or the West Bank. The contemporaneous documents reveal the world community in early 1957 was focused on returning the Gaza Strip to Egypt, together with a newly-established United Nations buffer force in the area. Neither the Palestinians nor anyone else advocated Palestinian statehood in Gaza and the West Bank at that time.

Indeed, it is not at all farfetched to speculate that absent Israel's replacement of Jordan as the occupant in June 1967, the West Bank Palestinians today would still be living under Jordanian rule, with little or no support from the United Nations or anyone else for Palestinian statehood in the West Bank.

Implications for the Palestinian Legal Case Today

The Palestinians rejected the one-state solution in May 1939 and the two-state solution in November 1947. The Palestinians asked Abdullah in late 1948 to annex the West Bank, waiving statehood in favor of merging into Transjordan. Thus, rather than accept the General Assembly's offer of *statehood*, the Palestinians opted for *statelessness* under Jordanian occupation/annexation.

Neither the Palestinians nor the United Nations raised any legal objections to Jordan's occupation and the various activities associated with that occupation, including the relocation of some Jordanians from the East to the West Bank.

Israel's replacement of Jordan as the occupant of the West Bank in June 1967 changed nothing as a matter of international law. Sovereignty over the West Bank remained in abeyance during the Jordanian occupation, and it has continued in abeyance under the Israeli occupation. There was no "state of Palestine" during the Jordanian occupation, nor has the Israeli occupation given rise to such a state today.

The Palestinian legal position regarding occupation has been inconsistent. The Palestinians accepted Jordanian occupation/annexation, but now they reject Israeli occupation. They rejected the two-state solution for decades, but now they want the two-state solution. They accepted the relocation of east bank Jordanians, but now they argue the relocation of Israelis violates international law.

These inconsistencies undermine the modern Palestinian legal narrative invoking "injustice," "victimhood," and alleged violations of Palestinian self-determination. Palestinian advocates and their supporters should be required to explain and reconcile these inconsistencies in the proceedings before the International Court of Justice (ICJ) and the International Criminal Court (ICC).

But all this begs the question regarding the legal ramifications of the Palestinian rejection of the United Nations' offer of the two-state solution in November 1947. Regardless of the extent to which the Palestinians were in favor, opposed, or apathetic about Jordanian unification, the Palestinians could have obtained statehood in an area *twice the size* of today's West Bank and Gaza if they had simply said yes to the two-state solution the United Nations offered in November 1947.

Notes

1 S. Mishal, *West Bank/East Bank: The Palestinians in Jordan, 1949–1967* at 2 (Yale Univ. Press, 1978) ("Palestinian desires for a 'homeland' did not become the major political issue in the Middle East until the late 1960s").
2 *Id.* at xi.
3 See generally A. Shlaim, *Collusion Across the Jordan: King Abdullah, the Zionist Movement and the Partition of Palestine* (Columbia Univ. Press, 1988).
4 *See* KV2/2091, Intelligence Report (Secret) No. 111, *Palestine: Activities of the Mufti* (15 Dec. 1947) (Mufti instigated a "whispering campaign through paid agents" against King Abdullah, portraying the King "as a monster waiting and planning to pounce on Palestine and occupy it when the British withdraw"); A. Plascov, *The Palestinian Refugees in Jordan, 1948–1957* at 1 (Frank Cass & Co. Ltd., 1981).
5 Plascov, *op. cit.* at 5.
6 *See, e.g.*, Cypher Telegram No. 227 from Sir Alec Kirkbride, British Ambassador, Amman to Foreign Office (16 Apr. 1948), *reprinted in* P. Toye and A. Seay, *Israel: Boundary Disputes with Arab Neighbours 1946–1964* Vol. 2 at 292–93 (Archive Editions, 1995). (quoting Azzam Pasha, Secretary General of the Arab League as saying "Palestine must be taken over as a whole and remain an Arab State. There must be no acceptance by Transjordan of partition.").
7 J. Nevo, *King Abdallah and Palestine: A Territorial Ambition* at 122–23 (St. Martin's Press, 1996).
8 *Id.* at 126.
9 *Id.* at 124–25, 127.
10 F. Bernadotte, *To Jerusalem* at 113 (Hodder and Stoughton, 1951).
11 *Id.* at 126.
12 *Id.* at 125.
13 K. Katz, *Jordanian Jerusalem: Holy Places and National Spaces* at 52 (Univ. Press of Florida, 2005); Nevo (1996), *op. cit.* at 162 ("media estimations varied between 5,000 and 10,000 participants, although other sources suggested a much smaller number"); Plascov, *op. cit.* at 11–12.
14 Plascov, *op. cit.* at 11.
15 *Id.* at 12 (citations omitted).
16 A. Shlaim, *The Rise and Fall of the All-Palestine Government in Gaza*, Journal of Palestine Studies, 20:1 at 44 (1990a); Z. Elipeleg, *Why Was "Independent Palestine" Never Created?* Jerusalem Quarterly, 50, 3--22 (1989). Elipeleg, *op. cit.*
17 Nevo (1996), *op. cit.* at 163.
18 *Id.* at 165.
19 Plascov, *op. cit.* at 12.
20 Cypher Telegram No. 578 from Acting British Consul General, Jerusalem to Foreign Office (29 Oct. 1948), *reprinted in* Toye and Seay, *op. cit.* Vol. 2 at 203–05 (noting the former Mayor of Bethlehem, "a staunch supporter of the mufti, had gone to Amman to spy out the land on his own behalf," and the Mayor of Nablus had also paid a visit to King Abdullah in the wake of the "present discomforture [sic] of the Gaza Government."); Plascov, *op. cit.* at 12.
21 *Id.*
22 Cypher Telegram No. 578 from Acting British Consul General, Jerusalem to Foreign Office (29 Oct. 1948), *reprinted in* Toye and Seay, *op. cit.* Vol. 2 at 203–05.
23 Telegram No. 4 (Secret) from British Ambassador, Amman to Foreign Office (2 Nov. 1948), *reprinted in* Toye and Seay, *op. cit.* Vol. 2 at 205–07.
24 Jewish Telegraphic Agency, *Daily News Bulletin*, 16 Nov. 1948 at 4.
25 Nevo (1996), *op. cit.* at 167.
26 A. Shlaim, *The Politics of Partition: King Abdullah, the Zionists and Palestine, 1921–1951* at 257 (Columbia Univ. Press, 1990b).

27 FRUS 867N.01/12–248, Telegram No. 138 (Secret) from U.S. Ambassador Wells Stabler to the Acting Secretary of State (2 Dec. 1948).
28 Nevo (1996), *op. cit.* at 169.
29 FRUS 867N.01/12–448: Telegram No. 140 (Confidential), U.S. Ambassador Wells Stabler to the Acting Secretary of State (4 Dec. 1948); A. Sela, *Transjordan, Israel and the 1948 War: Myth, Historiography and Reality*, Middle Eastern Studies, 28:4 at 672 (1992); see also FO 371/68644, Letter from Mohamed Ali al Ja'bari, President of the Second Arab Palestinian Conference to British Ambassador Sir A. Kirkbride, British Embassy, Amman (4 Dec. 1948), *reprinted in* Toye and Seay, *op. cit.* Vol. 2 at 208–09 (enclosing document entitled "Decisions Taken by 2d Arab Palestinian Conference held at Jericho on the 1st of December, 1948," including "the Conference decides that Palestine and the Hashemite Kingdom of Transjordan should be incorporated into one Kingdom and acknowledges his Majesty King Abdulla ibn Hussein as the Constitutional King of Palestine"). This gave Abdullah political cover to move ahead with attempting to annex the West Bank, as it had been the view previously that so long as Abdullah was aiming at fighting the Jews he could count on "a large measure of support in the Arab world," but if his true aim were to take control of the Arab-designated portions of Palestine, then "his action will be interpreted as personal aggrandizement and will isolate him from his neighbours and from Arab opinion generally." FO 371/68364, H. Beeley Minute, para. 4 (6 Jan. 1948), *reprinted in* Toye and Seay, *op. cit.* Vol. 2 at 100–01; *see also* E. Wright, *Abdallah's Jordan: 1947–1951*, Middle East Journal, 5:4, 439–60 at 446 (1951); *see also* Plascov, *op. cit.* at 13.
30 Nevo (1996), *op. cit.* at 170.
31 Mustafa Abbasi, *The Education System in East Jerusalem during the Period of Jordanian Rule, 1948–1967*, Journal of Politics and Law, 6 at 174, 176 (2013).
32 Letter from Mohamed Ali al Ja'bari, President of the 2d Arab Palestinian Conference to Sir Alec Kirkbride, British Minister, Amman (4 Dec. 1948), *reprinted in* Toye and Seay, *op. cit.* Vol. 2 at 208–09.
33 S/1136/48, Report No. 84 (Confidential) from British Legation, Amman to Ernest Bevin, Secretary of State for Foreign Affairs (8 Dec. 1948), *reprinted in* Toye and Seay, *op. cit.* Vol. 2 at 211–12.
34 *Id.* para. 3.
35 FRUS 867N.01/12–448: Telegram No. 140 (Confidential), U.S. Ambassador Wells Stabler to the Acting Secretary of State (4 Dec. 1948).
36 *Id.*
37 Wright, *op. cit.* at 447.
38 FO 371/68644, Telegram (Confidential) No. 5566 from British Embassy, Washington to Foreign Office (7 Dec. 1948), *reprinted in* Toye and Seay, *op. cit.* Vol. 2 at 210. The Jordanian Parliament ratified the Jericho resolutions on 7 and 13 Dec. 1948. A. Abu-Odeh, *Jordanians, Palestinians and The Hashemite Kingdom in the Middle East Peace Process* at 45 (United States Institute of Peace Press, 1999).
39 Cypher Telegram No. 952 (Secret) from Kirkbride to Foreign Office (14 Dec. 1948), *reprinted in* Toye and Seay, *op. cit.* Vol. 2 at 216–17.
40 Plascov, *op. cit.* at 15 and accompanying n. 37.
41 Plascov, *op. cit.* at 13.
42 Telegram No. 714 from Sir H. Dow, British Consulate, Jerusalem to Foreign Office, London (30 Dec. 1948), *reprinted in* Toye and Seay, *op. cit.* Vol. 2 at 242.
43 Nevo (1996), *op. cit.* at 193.
44 Katz, *op. cit.* at 52–53. The legal, administrative and financial relationship continued until 31 July 1988, when King Hussein announced Jordan's decision to terminate its administrative and legal ties to the West Bank; *see also* Nevo (1996), *op. cit.* at 193–94; Mishal, *op. cit.* at 5–9.

45 C. Bailey, *Jordan's Palestinian Challenge 1948–1983: A Political History* at 2 (Westview Press, 1984); Nevo (1996), *op. cit.* at 193–94. In December 1949 the Jordanian Parliament passed *Additional Law No. 56*, granting Jordanian passports to Palestinian refugees as well. Plascov, *op. cit.* at 44–45. In February 1954 the Jordanian Parliament granted citizenship to all Palestinian refugees. *Id.* at 47.
46 Nevo (1996), *op. cit.* at 193.
47 Katz, *op. cit.* at 53; L. Gandolfo, *Palestinians in Jordan: The Politics of Identity* at 10 (I.B. Tauris, 2012); Mishal, *op. cit.* at 8; Abu-Odeh, *op. cit.* at 55–56.
48 Mishal, *op. cit.* at 8.
49 J.G.T. Sheringham Minute (14 Oct. 1949), *reprinted in* J. Priestland (ed.), *Records of Jerusalem, Vol. 5: 1946–1949* at 605–07 (Archive Editions, 2002). Bevin emphasized several months later in a secret cable to the British UN delegation the Government's desire "for the realisation at the earliest possible moment ... of the formal union of Central Arab Palestine with Jordan." Cypher Telegram (Secret) No. 3620 from Bevin to UK delegation to United Nations, *reprinted in* J. Priestland (ed.), *Records of Jerusalem, Vol. 5: 1946–1949* at 626–28 (Archive Editions, 2002). The United States Government agreed with Britain in late 1949 to "accept the principle of a union of Arab Palestine with Jordan. Cypher Telegram No. 5415, from British Embassy Washington DC to Foreign Office (18 Nov. 1949), *reprinted in* J. Priestland (ed.), *Records of Jerusalem, Vol. 5: 1946–1949* at 642–44 (Archive Editions, 2002).
50 FRUS 867N.01/12–2848, Telegram (Top Secret) from the Acting Secretary of State to Ambassador Wells Stabler (3 Jan. 1949).
51 Cypher Telegram No. 103 (Confidential) from Kirkbride (Amman) to Foreign Office (25 Feb. 1949), *reprinted in* Toye and Seay, *op. cit.* Vol. 2 at 613–14.
52 Cypher Telegram No. 113 (Important and Confidential) from Amman to Foreign Office (1 Mar. 1949), *reprinted in* J. Priestland (ed.), *Records of Jerusalem, Vol. 5: 1946–1949* at 519 (Archive Editions, 2002).
53 FO 371/75287, Memorandum (Secret), *The Union of the Kingdom of Jordan and Arab Palestine*, Research Department, Foreign Office (Oct. 1949), *reprinted in* Toye and Seay, *op. cit.* Vol. 2 at 362–68.
54 *Id.* para. 2.
55 29/DO/49, Despatch (Secret and Personal) from Major V.P. Rich (Military Liaison Office, British Consulate-General, Jerusalem) to Major C de B Lisle, War Office, London, para. 3 (16 Oct. 1949), *reprinted in* Toye and Seay, *op. cit.* Vol. 2 at 475–78.
56 *Id.* at para. 4.
57 Abu-Odeh, *op. cit.* at 51.
58 FRUS, 611.84/4–1750, Telegram No. 72 (Secret) from the Minister in Jordan (Drew) to the Secretary of State (17 Apr. 1950).
59 Cypher Telegram No. 146 from Kirkbride (Amman) to Foreign Office (15 Apr. 1950), *reprinted in* Toye and Seay, *op. cit.* Vol. 4 at 189–90.
60 Telegram No. 160 from Kirkbride (Amman) to Foreign Office (25 Apr. 1950), *reprinted in* Toye and Seay, *op. cit.* Vol. 4 at 197–98.
61 FRUS, 684.85/4–2550: Telegram No. 82 from the Minister in Jordan (Drew) to the Secretary of State (25 Apr. 1950).
62 Mishal, *op. cit.* at 6–7.
63 Plascov, *op. cit.* at 16.
64 *Id.* at 76.
65 Central Intelligence Agency, Report No. 00-W-11528, *Iraqi Government and Press Stand on Jordan's Annexation of Arab Palestine* (9 June 1950).
66 *See* ET 1942/66, Despatch No. 140 from Kirkbride (Amman) to K. Younger, Foreign Office (London), Events Leading up to the Murder of King Abdullah (17 Sept. 1951).

67 *Id.* at 58.
68 Abu-Odeh, *op. cit.* at 111.
69 *See, e.g.*, Plascov, *op. cit.* at 12–13.
70 M. Shemesh, *The Palestinian National Revival: In the Shadow of the Leadership Crisis, 1937–1967* at 172 (Indiana Univ. Press, 2018) (describing a 26 July 1952 memorandum from 15 Palestinian members of the Jordanian House of Representatives to Prime Minister Tawfik Abu al-Huda listing a variety of grievances, including economic issues and the downgraded status of Jerusalem relative to Amman).
71 Mishal, *op. cit.* at 3–4.
72 Plascov, *op. cit.* at 38.
73 *Id.* at 37; *see also* Abu-Odeh, *op. cit.* at 60; Plascov, *op. cit.* at 36–37; Shemesh (2018), *op. cit.* at 166–73.
74 Bir Zeit University was only a junior college offering a two-year program during the Jordanian occupation. In 1972, while under Israeli occupation, Bir Zeit converted from a junior college to a university offering four-year degrees. A. Gerson, *Israel the West Bank and International Law* at 177 (Frank Cass & Co. Ltd., 1978).
75 Nevo (1996), *op. cit.* at 194–95; Mishal, *op. cit.* at 35–37.
76 Shemesh (2018), *op. cit.* at 167–68.
77 Plascov, *op. cit.* at 39.
78 *Id.* at 160–61.
79 Abu-Odeh, *op. cit.* at 57, 104–07.
80 *Id.* at 110.
81 *Id.* at 71.
82 Plascov, *op. cit.* at 40.
83 Mishal, *op. cit.* at 22 *et seq.*
84 *Id.* at 16.
85 *Id.*
86 Mishal, *op. cit.* at 112.
87 *Id.* at 115 [emphasis in original].
88 Mishal, *op. cit.* at 74 *et seq.*
89 Gandolfo, *op. cit.* at 17.
90 Y.Z. Blum, *The Missing Reversioner: Reflections on the Status of Judea and Samaria*, Israel Law Review, 3:2, 279–301 at 287 (1968).
91 *Id.* at 289.
92 United Nations General Assembly Resolution 273, A/RES/273(III) (11 May 1949). The resolution "noted" both Resolutions 181 and 194 regarding the internationalization of Jerusalem, as well as comments Israeli Ambassador Abba Eban had made pledging Israel's support for humanitarian efforts regarding Palestinian refugees. But the operative clauses of Resolution 273 imposed no conditions or prerequisites on Israel's admission as a member state. Thus, the Resolution said The General Assembly "1. *Decides* that Israel is a peace loving State which accepts the obligations contained in the Charter and is able and willing to carry out those obligations; 2. *Decides* to admit Israel to membership in the United Nations."
93 United Nations Security Council, S/RES/242, para. 1(i) (22 Nov. 1967).
94 E. Lauterpacht, *Jerusalem and the Holy Places* at 47 (Anglo-Israel Association, 1968).
95 Blum, *op. cit.* at 283, 292, 293.
96 A. Gerson, *Trustee-Occupant: The Legal Status of Israel's Presence in the West Bank*, Harvard International Law Journal, 14 at 37–38 (1973).
97 Hansard, HC Deb. 27 Apr. 1950, vol. 474, cols. 1137–39 (speech by Kenneth Younger, Minister of State at the Foreign Office).

12

THE FORGOTTEN OCCUPATION OF THE GAZA STRIP – EGYPT, 1948–1967

Introduction

The Gaza Strip is a small geographic area, comprising roughly 141 square miles along the Mediterranean coastline southwest of Tel Aviv. The Gaza Strip was part of the Palestine Mandate, but it came under Egyptian military occupation following the outbreak of the 1948–1949 war.

In August 1948 the Egyptian Government issued Ministerial Order Number 274, empowering an Egyptian Administrator-General with all the powers formerly wielded by the British High Commissioner for Palestine.[1]

The February 1949 Israel-Egypt Armistice Agreement left Gaza under Egyptian military occupation.[2] The Egyptian occupation continued until June 1967, except for approximately 18 weeks between 29 October 1956 and 11 March 1957, when Israel temporarily supplanted Egypt as Gaza's occupant during the Suez/Sinai War.[3]

Unlike Jordan's policy of unification with the West Bank, Egypt never annexed Gaza, preferring to position itself as a temporary trustee or guardian of the local population until such time as the State of Israel could be destroyed and replaced with an Arab State.

Jordanian and Israeli Designs on Gaza

Jordan harbored its own early designs over Gaza in quest of access to the Mediterranean. Jordanian Prime Minister Tewfik Pasha advised the members of the Palestine Conciliation Commission at a February 1949 meeting in Jericho of Jordan's desire to obtain control of Gaza. Sir Alec Kirkbride, the British Ambassador in Amman, quoted the Prime Minister saying "[i]t was

DOI: 10.4324/9781032686561-15

essential that Transjordan plus Arab Palestine should have a Mediterranean port and Gaza was the most obvious site. He wished to warn everybody that all the influence and strength of Transjordan would be used to secure this."[4]

Kirkbride's report also described an interesting side conversation between Tewfik Pasha and the Turkish member of the Conciliation Commission:

> After the meeting the Turkish member remarked in private that as far as he could judge the majority of the Palestine Arabs wanted union with Transjordan and asked if the Prime Minister thought a plebiscite would give a majority in favour of union. The Prime Minister replied that he was convinced that a majority would be secured and that he would welcome a plebiscite.[5]

In response to Kirkbride's report, the Foreign Office noted,

> Gaza is not merely a bargaining demand, but that the Transjordan Government will really do all they can to secure a port. This would, of course, suit us very well, but it seems almost impossible that the Transjordan Government could bring it off.[6]

The Israelis also floated the idea in mid-1949 of taking control of Gaza. The Foreign Office's reaction was mildly favorable, on condition Israel make territorial compensation "for other areas held by Israel but not allotted to her under the 1947 [United Nations partition] Plan." The Foreign Office added that "Arab Palestine should be formally incorporated in Jordan."[7]

Neither the Jordanian nor Israeli designs on Gaza came to fruition. The Gazan Palestinians therefore remained under Egyptian occupation until June 1967, just as they later would live under Israeli occupation from June 1967 until Israel's unilateral withdrawal in September 2005.

The Forgotten Egyptian Occupation

Egypt wanted to maintain the Gaza Strip as part of the future Arab state that would encompass all of Mandate Palestine once the new State of Israel could be destroyed. Egypt therefore decided not to annex the Gaza Strip, but it nevertheless exercised total control over the local population to protect Egypt's own interests.[8]

The Egyptian occupiers imposed a series of harsh edicts during the subsequent two decades severely restricting the local inhabitants' freedom. These included a nighttime curfew (expanded in 1962 to dawn to dusk), limits on Gazan fishing rights, tariffs on Gazan exports, and strict entry and exit controls.[9]

Gazans were also required to obtain permission to cross the border into Egypt. They were permitted to remain in Egypt for only a limited time unless they received additional approval to extend their stay.[10]

The Egyptian security services established and maintained a "wide and deep" presence throughout the Gaza Strip.[11] Egyptian police actively surveilled potential dissident groups in Gaza, including the Muslim Brotherhood, communists, and others.[12]

Ilana Feldman (2015), in her study of Egyptian policing and surveillance practices in Gaza, noted the extensive reach of Egyptian surveillance into the everyday life of Gaza's population. Feldman also documented the Egyptian practice of fomenting suspicion to keep the local population from forming any organized opposition to Egyptian rule:

> The extensive security apparatus developed to police the Gaza Strip during the Egyptian Administration was guided by intersecting concerns about national interest, social propriety, and everyday illegality. In pursuit of security in these areas, the police extended their reach across the public domain into many aspects of private life. In this process, Palestinians were identified as, at once, security threats and vulnerable subjects who needed protection. And both threat and protection seemed to require expansive policing. That this police practice – with its heavy surveillance, emphasis on informing, and often severe punishments – exerted a repressive influence on life in Gaza is beyond dispute.[13]

Egyptian control of Gazan life also extended to the economic sector. Egypt nationalized Gazan assets in 1961, pursuant to financial laws applicable throughout Egypt.[14]

Despite the repressive nature of the Egyptian occupation, the local population expressed little desire for self-rule in Gaza prior to 1967. Although the Mufti had selected Gaza as the base for his short-lived "All Palestine Government" in October 1948, the local population and local leaders were largely uninterested in self-determination. J.M. Troutbeck, a Cairo-based British official, traveled through Gaza in June 1949, the first time any British official had visited Gaza since the end of the Mandate. Troutbeck reported hearing "no mention ... of the so-called 'Gaza Government' which had a fleeting existence towards the end of last year."[15]

In August 1950 the British Embassy in Cairo reported to London regarding a conversation with the Mayor of Gaza City. The Mayor said his first choice for Gaza's future would be annexation by Jordan. His second choice would be annexation by Egypt. He said nothing about an independent Palestinian State.[16] Indeed, Gazan leaders asked Egypt in late 1948, and again following the formation of the United Arab Republic in 1958, to annex and absorb them, but the Egyptians decided they did not need to do so to run Gaza's affairs.[17]

In early 1951 British authorities in Cairo inquired about the legal status of Gaza. The Legal Counsellor at the British Embassy in Cairo, Murray Graham, prepared a short minute summarizing his analysis. First, Graham noted no one possessed sovereignty over Gaza. Neither the Arab States nor the Arab League had the legal right to control Gaza, nor did Israel. Second, Graham said the United Nations failed to preserve any rights to Gaza (or indeed to any portion of the former Palestine Mandate) after the Mandate ended on 14 May 1948. The Mandate did not revert to the United Nations, and thus the United Nations "do not possess any legal rights of control" over Gaza. Third, although Egyptian military forces had occupied Gaza, that occupation did not vest sovereignty in Egypt. Finally, therefore, Murray concluded that no one possessed sovereignty over Gaza as of early 1951.[18]

The Legal Adviser to the Foreign Office concurred with Graham's conclusions. The Legal Adviser agreed

> it would be difficult for making out a good legal case for holding that the control over the areas included in the Palestine mandate has passed to the United Nations ... there are no good legal grounds for holding that on the dissolution of the League [of Nations] such sovereignty would automatically have passed to the United Nations.

Therefore, the Legal Adviser concluded, "the Gaza area is at present *res nullius*."[19] The Foreign Secretary reiterated this view in the House of Commons in March 1957, saying "The facts about the Gaza strip seem to me to be these. No country has legal sovereignty."[20] That conclusion remains as true today as it was in 1950.

Egyptian policy in Gaza was to stimulate Palestinian resentment of both Israel and Jordan. This was especially true after a rise in nationalist sentiment in Gaza following Israel's four-month occupation of the Strip during the 1956–1957 Sinai War.[21] The result was that Gaza, far more than the West Bank, became a "hotbed" of Palestinian nationalism after the 1956–1957 war. But that manifestation of Palestinian nationalism was completely focused on destroying the State of Israel, not on obtaining Palestinian statehood in the Gaza Strip and the West Bank. Moreover, in contrast to the stirrings in Gaza after the 1956–1957 war, the West Bank Palestinians continued during those later years of occupation to feel "more comfortable" living as Jordanian citizens under Jordanian rule.[22]

To that extent, therefore, Gaza under Egyptian occupation served as an "experimental laboratory" for Palestinian national aspirations. The first step was the promulgation of a symbolic "constitution" for the Gaza Strip in 1962.[23] But as Shemesh (2018) notes, the 1962 "constitution" actually cemented Egyptian control over Gaza rather than accord any political or legal rights to the local population:

> In actuality, the Egyptian Governor ruled the Gaza Strip as if it were an Egyptian territory in every sense. Although the three authorities of the

> state (judicial, legislative and executive) were established in accordance with the constitution as an expression of Palestinian autonomy, in practice the constitution enabled Egypt to continue governing Gaza as if it were Egyptian territory, with the residents having minimal governmental participation and no real authority ... Gaza's governor was indeed called a 'governor general,' but in practice he was a military governor in every sense. The executive authority was subordinate to him... The heads of the Executive Council's administrative body (its various departments) were typically officers appointed by the Egyptian minister of war ...[24]

Palestinian and International Acquiescence in Jordan's Occupation

During the nearly two decades of Egyptian occupation of Gaza, the local population never demanded Egypt's withdrawal, nor did they ever demand statehood in Gaza and the West Bank. The United Nations never passed any resolutions calling for Egypt's withdrawal from Gaza or statehood for the Palestinians in Gaza and the West Bank. Nor did any international groups, non-governmental organizations, or the international media ever demand Egypt's withdrawal from Gaza or statehood for the Palestinians. Nor did the Palestinians or anyone else ask the International Court of Justice to rule on the legality of Egypt's occupation of Gaza.

Interestingly, Israel's withdrawal from Gaza following its temporary occupation during the 1956–1957 war did not give rise to any calls from Palestinian or international leaders for Palestinian independence in Gaza. Instead, the United Nations and the international community focused attention on establishing the United Nations Emergency Force (UNEF) in Gaza as a peacekeeping force, alongside the restoration of Egypt's "legal right" to reoccupy Gaza based on the February 1949 Israel-Egypt armistice agreement.

The UN, in contrast to its position today that the Palestinians are entitled to statehood in the Gaza Strip and the West Bank, insisted in 1957 that Egypt enjoyed sole legal rights over Gaza. For example, in a meeting at the U.S. Department of State in late February 1957, Israeli Ambassador Abba Eban reported United Nations Secretary-General Dag Hammarskjöld had

> made clear that he could not limit Egypt's rights [in Gaza] as they were defined by the Armistice Agreement and by the resolutions of the General Assembly; that Egypt retained the rights which they had before and that any arrangements made would depend upon Egypt's consent.[25]

Several days later Secretary-General Hammarskjöld said "we do not question Egyptians' legal right" to reoccupy Gaza.[26]

But Secretary-General Hammarskjöld was less certain regarding the legal basis for establishing any sort of the UN presence in Gaza above and beyond UNRWA's ongoing humanitarian work on behalf of Palestinian refugees who had fled there during the 1948-1949 war. In an early March 1957 meeting with U.S. Ambassador Henry Cabot Lodge, Jr., Secretary-General Hammarskjöld expressed concern that the United Nations lacked a strong legal theory for entering Gaza:

> Hammarskjold outlined three current theories regarding UN's legal status in Gaza upon Israel's withdrawal:
>
> 1 The extreme Israel stand was that Gaza would be given to the UN by Israeli occupation force. This implied that Israel would delegate to the UN re Gaza authority stemming from such occupation (Israel contended that Armistice Agreement—at least insofar as it applied to Gaza—was dead). As a result, the UN could not permit anything in Gaza that Israel would not have permitted. In Hammarskjold's opinion, to accept this thesis would be to legalize Israel's claims to occupation of Gaza and at the same time annul Armistice Agreement.
> 2 UK/French theory, which Dixon (UK) had expounded to him today, was that "UN would be in Gaza because UN had decided to be there." Hammarskjold has pointed out to Dixon undesirable precedents such thesis established. For instance, if Algeria or Kashmir or some other disputed area could not be agreed upon, the UN could under this theory decide to take it over. Dixon had immediately reacted that such legal theory would be unacceptable. Hammarskjold had replied to Dixon that if the General Assembly could not take such action, neither could Secretary-General.
> 3 Third, and only tenable theory in SYG's opinion, was that the UN's legal status for activities in Gaza stemmed from the Armistice Agreement. It followed from such thesis that the extent of the UN's activity there depended upon Egypt's agreement. It was also clear that Egypt would not permit UN activities in Gaza to go so far as to give rise to the appearance that Egypt had given up its rights in Gaza.[27]

Hammarskjöld explained, therefore, that he would aim to establish a UN administration "in Gaza, not of Gaza."[28] Ultimately, UNEF replaced the Egyptian army as the primary military force in Gaza, but Egypt continued to exercise a tight grip on policing and surveillance of the local population until the June 1967 war.[29]

Implications for the Palestinian Legal Case Today

Egypt's nearly two-decade occupation of Gaza has been forgotten by today's advocates for the Palestinian legal case, just as with Jordan's occupation of the West Bank during those same years. The modern narrative of Gazan and West Bank occupation tends to begin with the events of June 1967, as if the

Gaza Strip and the West Bank had somehow been free of occupation prior to the Israeli takeover of the areas in the Six-Day War.

As will be discussed in Chapter 17, even after Israel's full withdrawal from the Gaza Strip in September 2005 and Hamas' forcible takeover in June 2007, many (including at least one prominent Israeli legal scholar) claim Israel still "occupies" the Gaza Strip under their interpretations of international law and the Oslo Accords. As will also be discussed in Chapter 17, the better view under international law is that the Gaza Strip has not been occupied by *anyone* except the Palestinians themselves since 2005, including Hamas since 2007.

Notes

1 R. Shehadeh, *From Occupation to Interim Accords: Israel and the Palestinian Territories* at 77 (Kluwer Law International, 1997).
2 United Nations S/1264, *Cablegram Dated 23 February 1949 from the Acting Mediator to the Secretary-General Transmitting the Text of an Armistice Agreement between Egypt And Israel* (23 Feb. 1949).
3 M. Fry and M. Hochstein, *The Forgotten Middle Eastern Crisis of 1957: Gaza and Sharm-el-Sheikh*, The International History Review, 15:1 at 46–83 (1993).
4 Cypher Telegram No. 83 from Sir A. Kirkbride to Foreign Office (12 Feb. 1949), *reprinted in* J. Priestland (ed.), *Records of Jerusalem, Vol. 5: 1946–1949* at 491 (Archive Editions, 2002).
5 *Id.*
6 E2073, J.G.S. Beith minute (15 Feb. 1949), *reprinted in* J. Priestland (ed.), *Records of Jerusalem, Vol. 5: 1946–1949* at 487 (Archive Editions, 2002).
7 Cypher Telegram No. 7008, Foreign Office to British Embassy, Washington (12 July 1949), *reprinted in* J. Priestland (ed.), *Records of Jerusalem, Vol. 5: 1946–1949* at 544–45 (Archive Editions, 2002).
8 I. Feldman, *Governing Gaza: Bureaucracy, Authority, and the Work of Rule: 1917–1967* at 19 (Duke Univ. Press, 2008).
9 M. Shemesh, *The Palestinian National Revival: In the Shadow of the Leadership Crisis, 1937–1967* at 152–53, 159 (Indiana Univ. Press, 2018).
10 A. Abu-Odeh, *Jordanians, Palestinians and The Hashemite Kingdom in the Middle East Peace Process* at 102–03 (United States Institute of Peace Press, 1999).
11 I. Feldman, *Police Encounters: Security and Surveillance in Gaza under Egyptian Rule* at 24, 27 (Stanford Univ. Press, 2015).
12 Shemesh (2018), *op. cit.* at 154.
13 Feldman (2015), *op. cit.* at 144–45.
14 *Id.* at 158.
15 FO 371/75342, Despatch No. 22 (Confidential) from J.M. Troutbeck to Foreign Office (16 June 1949); *reprinted in* P. Toye and A. Seay, *Israel: Boundary Disputes with Arab Neighbours 1946–1964* Vol. 2 at 601–05 (Archive Editions, 1995).
16 FO 371/82256, from British Embassy, Amman to Foreign Office (6 Aug. 1950), cited in Feldman (2008), *op. cit.* at 8 n.31.
17 A. Plascov, *The Palestinian Refugees in Jordan, 1948–1957* at 8, nn.17–18 (Frank Cass & Co. Ltd, 1981); Shemesh (2018), *op. cit.* at 153–54 (describing multiple Gazan pleas to the Egyptian government for annexation).

18 Despatch (Top Secret and Personal) from T. Rapp (British Embassy, Cairo) to R.J. Bowker, Foreign Office (12 Feb. 1951) enclosing Minute prepared by Murray Graham, Legal Counsellor (26 Jan. 1951), *reprinted in* Toye and Seay, *op. cit.* Vol. 5 at 3–4.

19 JE 1082/1, Despatch (Secret) from R.J. Bowker (Foreign Office) to T. Rapp (Cairo) (13 Mar. 1951), *reprinted in* Toye and Seay, *op. cit.* Vol. 5 at 5.

20 Hansard, HC Deb., vol. 566, cc1317-1439 at 1320 (14 Mar. 1957).

21 *See generally* N. Masalha, *The 1956–57 Occupation of the Gaza Strip: Israeli Proposals to Resettle the Palestinian Refugees*, British Journal of Middle Eastern Studies, 23:1 at 55–68 (1996); Feldman (2008), *op. cit.* at 26 n.102.

22 Abu-Odeh, *op. cit.* at 108–09.

23 M. Shemesh, *The Palestinian Entity, 1959–1974: Arab Politics and the PLO* (2nd ed.) at 5 (Frank Cass Ltd., 1996).

24 Shemesh (2018), *op cit.* at 157.

25 FRUS, Department of State, Central Files, 674.84A/2–2657 (Confidential) *Memorandum of a Conversation*, Department of State, Washington (26 Feb. 1957); see also FRUS, Department of State, Central Files, 674.84A/3–1357 (Confidential) *Memorandum of a Conversation*, Department of State, Washington (13 Mar. 1957) (State Department Legal Adviser Herman Phleger insisted, "An Egyptian return to Gaza would in itself be no violation of the Armistice Agreement.").

26 FRUS, Telegram 615 from Lodge to Department of State, Central Files, 674.84A/3–1257 (12 Mar. 1957).

27 FRUS, Department of State, Central Files, 684A.86/3–557 (Confidential, Priority), *Telegram from the Mission at the United Nations to the Department of State* (5 Mar. 1957).

28 *Id.*

29 Feldman (2015), *op. cit.* at 34–35.

13

THE ORIGINAL PLO CHARTER, MAY 1964

During the late 1950s and early 1960s, Egypt and various Palestinian intellectuals began discussing the notion of a Palestinian "entity" (*al-kiyan al-filastini*).[1] The "entity" was not intended to become a government-in-exile or an independent state in the West Bank and Gaza, nor in the areas the United Nations had allocated for the Palestinian Arab State in Resolution 181. Rather, the "entity" would serve as a conceptual device for framing the Palestinians as an organized people whose voice would be heard both in the Arab world and globally.[2]

The Magazine *Filastinuna* described the aspirational, imagined nature of the Palestinian entity in the following terms in a 1961 editorial:

> [A] revolutionary entity that is neither subservient, nor submissive nor directed ... an entity that restores hope, assurance and a conscious revolutionary spirit ... an entity deriving from the very essence of the Palestinian people, their disaster and their living conscience ... But that an entity should be established at the decision of a certain Arab state, or that certain Arab fronts should agree to revive a stunted and puny entity that would give Palestine to the Jews, and then wash their hands of the consequences – this shall never be. The Palestinian people ... demands an entity that is free, non-aligned and not directed, so that they may be able to prepare themselves for the battle for freedom.[3]

Egypt took the lead in supporting the notion of a Palestinian "entity," but did so in the service of the purely Egyptian interest of weakening Jordan's primacy in Palestinian affairs.[4] Ahmed Shukheiry, a Palestinian lawyer based in Cairo, was elected as "Representative of Filastin" at a September

DOI: 10.4324/9781032686561-16

1963 meeting of the Arab League Council. No Palestinians were involved in selecting Shukheiry as their ostensible representative.

Shukheiry, careful not to risk confrontation with the Jordanian government, emphasized the Palestinian entity would serve the symbolic purpose of galvanizing Palestinian, Jordanian, and pan-Arab support for destroying Israel. The Entity would also, according to Shukheiry, provide a platform for creating a Palestine National Fund to raise money for Palestinian refugees and to finance armed attacks against Israel.[5]

The desire to form a Palestinian entity led eventually to the founding of the Palestine Liberation Organization (PLO) in May 1964 at a gathering at the Intercontinental Hotel in East Jerusalem under Shukheiry's leadership.[6] The delegates approved a Charter expressing the organization's *raison d'etre* and its political goals, including the destruction of the State of Israel.[7]

Significantly, however, the PLO Charter explicitly reaffirmed the December 1948 Jericho Conference waiver of sovereignty and statehood in the West Bank. The Charter also extended the express waiver to Gaza. Article 24 of the Charter proclaimed, "This Organization does not exercise *any* regional sovereignty over the West Bank in the Hashemite Kingdom of Jordan, [or] the Gaza Strip."[8] The British Ambassador to Jordan reported to London that the delegates to the PLO's founding conference resolved "not to exercise sovereignty on the West Bank, in the Gaza Strip, or the Himmeh area."[9]

This language, unthinkable for the Palestinians and their supporters to embrace today, reflected the official PLO position from the time of the organization's founding in May 1964 until the Charter was amended in July 1968 to seek statehood in the West Bank and the Gaza Strip, more than one year following the Six-Day War.

Moreover, the original PLO Charter said *nothing* about establishing a Palestinian State in the West Bank and Gaza Strip. The "Palestine" it aimed to "liberate" was the State of Israel, whose destruction was the PLO's primary objective. The Charter was vague regarding whether the West Bank would become part of post-liberation Palestine, or remain under Jordanian rule.[10]

Abu-Odeh (1999) notes that the founding of the PLO in May 1964 had little impact on the by-then "entrenched" West Bank Palestinian attachment to Jordan. That sense of attachment, according to Abu-Odeh, continued for two decades beyond Israel's replacement of Jordan as the occupant following the June 1967 Six-Day War:

> The PLO came into existence at a crucial point in the all-encompassing process of integration between the West Bank and the East Bank. Palestinian instrumental attachment to the Jordanian state was already established. This attachment was manifested in Palestinian acceptance of the laws and regulations of their state, their 'entanglement in social roles,'

> and commitment to the state's 'institutional arrangements and operating values' ... Furthermore, this instrumental attachment was developing into sentimental attachment within large Palestinian sectors. Already large segments had identified themselves as Jordanians both technically and emotionally ... Instrumental attachment was not affected [by the formation of the PLO] and persisted as strongly as it had before, even for two decades following the occupation of the West Bank by Israel in 1967.[11]

The language in the original PLO Charter severely undermines the current Palestinian legal claim of sovereignty over the West Bank and Gaza. Indeed, in the months preceding the formation of the PLO, Shukheiry assured Jordan's King Hussein he had *no* intention of seeking Palestinian statehood in the West Bank. As the British Ambassador to Jordan noted in a report to London in February 1964:

> Shukheiry's first statement on arriving in Amman was that there was no question of creating a Palestine Republic as this would be meaningless, nor was there any intention of attempting to establish a form of Palestinian territorial sovereignty ... he added that the creation of a Palestinian government was not desirable, as this would not serve the Palestinian cause.[12]

The PLO's formation had no legal effect on West Bank and Gaza sovereignty, which continued in abeyance after Israel replaced Jordan and Egypt as the occupant in June 1967. Jordan's subsequent termination of its legal and administrative relationship with the West Bank in July 1988 had no legal effect either, as Jordan never possessed sovereignty over those areas, and thus could not lawfully transfer sovereignty to anyone else.[13] Sovereignty has remained in abeyance until the present day.[14]

Notes

1 I. Al-Shuaibi, *The Development of Palestinian Entity-Consciousness: Part I*, Journal of Palestine Studies, 9:1, 67–84, at 79–84 (1979).

2 M. Shemesh, *The Palestinian Entity, 1959–1974: Arab Politics and the PLO* (2nd ed.) at 1 (Frank Cass Ltd., 1996).

3 *Id.* at 83–84, quoting from *Filastinuna*, No. 18 (4th year), July 1961.

4 I. Al-Shuaibi, *The Development of Palestinian Entity-Consciousness: Part II*, Journal of Palestine Studies, 9:2, 50–70, at 51 (1980).

5 FO 371/175562, E1075/2, Despatch (Confidential) from British Embassy, Amman to Foreign Office, London (26 Feb. 1964); *see also* S. Mishal, *West Bank/East Bank: The Palestinians in Jordan, 1949–1967* at 77 (Yale Univ. Press, 1978).

6 For more detail regarding the background and organization of the conference, *see* M. Shemesh, *The Palestinian National Revival: In the Shadow of the Leadership Crisis, 1937–1967* at 225–34 (Indiana Univ. Press, 2018).

7 Palestinian National Charter (28 May 1964). The following provisions of the Charter not only call for the elimination of the State of Israel but also sound many

of the same legal arguments and legal framing that continue to the present day among some Palestinian advocates and their supporters:

"Article 14. The liberation of Palestine from an Arab viewpoint, is a national duty. Its responsibilities fall upon the entire Arab Nation, Governments and peoples, the Palestinian people being in the foreground. For this purpose the Arab Nation must mobilize its military spiritual and material potentialities, specifically, it must give to the Palestinian Arab people all possible support and backing and place at its disposal all opportunities and means to enable them to perform their roles in liberating their homeland.

Article 15. The liberation of Palestine, from a spiritual view point, prepares for the Holy Land, an atmosphere of tranquility and peace, in which all the Holy Places will be safeguarded, and the free worship and visit to all will be guaranteed, without any discrimination of race, colour, tongue, or religion. For all this, the Palestinian people look forward to the support of all spiritual forces in the world.

Article 16. The liberation of Palestine from an international view point is a defensive act necessitated by the demands of self-defense as stated in the charter of the United Nations. That is why the people of Palestine desiring to befriend all nations that love freedom, justice, and peace, is looking forward to their support in restoring the legitimate situation to Palestine, establishing peace and security in its territory, and enabling its people to exercise national sovereignty and freedom.

Article 17. The Partitioning of Palestine in 1947 and the establishment of Israel are illegal and false regardless of the loss of time, because they were contrary to the wish of the Palestine people and their natural right to its homeland, and in violation of the basic principles embodied in the charter of the United Nations, foremost among which is the right to self-determination.

Article 18. The Balfour Declaration, the Mandate system, and all that has been based upon them are considered fraud. The claims of historic and spiritual ties, ties between Jews and Palestine are not in agreement with the facts of history or with the true basis of sound statehood. Judaism because it is a divine religion is not a nationality with independent existence. Furthermore, the Jews are not one people with an independent personality because they are citizens of the countries to which they belong.

Article 19. Zionism is a colonialist movement in its inception, aggressive and expansionist in its goals, racist and segregationist in its configurations and fascist in its means and aims. Israel in its capacity as the spearhead of this destructive movement and the pillar of colonialism is a permanent source of tension and turmoil in the Middle East in particular and to the international community in general. Because of this, the People of Palestine are worthy of the support and sustenance of the community of nations.

Article 20. The causes of peace and security and the needs of right and justice demanded from all nations, in order to safeguard true relationships among peoples, and to maintain the loyalty of citizens to their homeland, to consider Zionism an illegal movement and to outlaw its presence and activities.

Article 21. The Palestine people believe in the principle of justice, freedom, sovereignty, self-determination, human dignity, and the right of people to practice these principles. It also supports all international efforts to bring about peace on the basis of justice and free international cooperation.

Article 22. The People of Palestine believe in peaceful coexistence on the basis of legal existence, for there can be no coexistence with aggression, nor can there be peace with occupation and colonialism."

8 Palestinian National Charter, Art. 24 (28 May 1964) [emphasis added]. The Charter was amended in July 1968 to replace Article 24 with language claiming sovereignty over the entirety of Mandate-era Palestine.

9 FO 371/175562, E1075/2, Despatch (Confidential) from British Embassy, Amman to Foreign Office, London (3 June 1964).
10 A. Abu-Odeh, *Jordanians, Palestinians and The Hashemite Kingdom in the Middle East Peace Process* at 108 (United States Institute of Peace Press, 1999).
11 *Id.* at 112.
12 *Id.*
13 *Speech by King Hussein on Jordan's Separation from West Bank* (31 July 1988), 28 I.L.M. 1637 (1988). Regarding the status of West Bank sovereignty, for a pro-Palestinian view *see* United Nations A/CN.4/557, V. Rodríguez Cedeño, Special Rapporteur, *Unilateral Acts of States (Eighth Report)* at para. 53 (2005) ("The question arises whether the King of Jordan was competent to act at the international level and to formulate the waiver on behalf of Jordan. It is significant that the Constitution of Jordan prohibits any act related to the transfer of territory, so that it would appear that the King exceeded his authority. However, that did not prevent the waiver from producing legal effects, and in fact a transfer of the territory of the West Bank to the State of Palestine actually took place").
14 M. Shaw, *The League of Nations Mandate System and the Palestine Mandate: What Did and Does It Say About International Law and What Did and Does It Say About Palestine*, Israel Law Review, 49 at 287, 304 (2016); *but see* N. Erakat, *Justice For Some: Law and the Question of Palestine* at 80–81 (Stanford Univ. Press, 2019) ("Palestinians had successfully inscribed their right to self-determination in the White Paper of 1939, in the UN Partition Plan (1947), and in the UN draft Trusteeship Agreement (1948). Thus, when the British Mandate for Palestine expired in May 1948, sovereignty vested in the people of Palestine"). As discussed above in chapter 9, Bell and Kontorovich, contend Israel inherited the boundaries of the entirety of Mandate Palestine as of the moment the Mandate ended on 15 May 1948. They rely on the doctrine of *Uti Possidetis Juris*, arguing the boundaries of Mandate Palestine automatically became the boundaries of the new State of Israel at the moment of Israel's independence on 15 May 1948, because Israel was the only State to emerge from the Mandate, and because as of the moment of the Mandate's termination no one else claimed sovereignty over the areas of Palestine the United Nations had allocated to the Arabs. A. Bell and E. Kontorovich, *Palestine, Uti Possidetis Juris, and the Borders of Israel*, Arizona Law Review, 58, 633–92, at 688 (2016).

14

THE OSLO ACCORDS, 1993–1995

Introductory Note

The Oslo Accords represented a dramatic breakthrough in relations between Israel and the Palestinians. Following months of intensive, arms-length negotiations, in which the Palestinian delegation argued over every word and every punctuation mark,[1] Israel and the Palestine Liberation Organization (PLO) solemnly agreed in writing, witnessed by the United States and the Russian Federation,

> to put an end to decades of confrontation and conflict, recognize their mutual legitimate and political rights, and strive to live in peaceful coexistence and mutual dignity and security and achieve a just, lasting and comprehensive peace settlement and historic reconciliation through the agreed political process.[2]

Israel agreed to recognize the PLO as the representative of the Palestinian people, to withdraw its military forces from Gaza and the main Palestinian towns in the West Bank, beginning with Jericho, and to accord the Palestinians a large measure of autonomy in the Palestinian-populated areas of the West Bank and Gaza Strip through the establishment of the Palestinian Authority as a transitional self-governing entity. The PLO agreed to recognize Israel's existence and its right to live in peace and security, to renounce terrorism, and to amend its Charter to remove the language calling for Israel's destruction.

The Oslo Accords comprise several documents signed between 1993 and 1995, the result of long and intense negotiations between the Israelis and the Palestinians.[3]

DOI: 10.4324/9781032686561-17

The Accords began with an exchange of letters dated 9 September 1993 between PLO Chairman Yasser Arafat, Norwegian Foreign Minister Johan Jergen Holst, and Israeli Prime Minister Yitzhak Rabin.[4] Four days later, the parties signed the *Declaration of Principles on Interim Self-Government Arrangements* (sometimes referred to as "Oslo I").[5] Next came the May 1994 *Gaza-Jericho Agreement*,[6] followed by the August 1994 *Agreement on Preparatory Transfer of Powers and Responsibilities*.[7] The parties signed the *Israeli-Palestinian Interim Agreement on the West Bank and the Gaza Strip* (sometimes referred to as "Oslo II") in September 1995.[8]

Several follow-on agreements form a package of understandings to implement the Oslo II Interim Agreement, including the 1997 *Protocol Concerning the Redeployment in Hebron*,[9] the 1997 *Note for the Record* prepared by the American diplomat Dennis Ross,[10] the 1998 *Wye River Memorandum*,[11] and the 1999 *Sharm el-Sheikh Memorandum*.[12]

The Palestinians agreed in Oslo II to the division of the West Bank into three separate areas. The arrangement remains in place until the present day. Area "A" comprises roughly 18% of the West Bank, consisting of the major Palestinian towns such as Ramallah, Bethlehem, Jericho, Nablus, Qalqilya, Jenin, Tulkarem, and most of Hebron. The Palestinian Authority received civic autonomy in Area A.

The Palestinians also received civic autonomy in the second area, known as Area "B," comprising smaller towns, villages and certain rural areas and amounting to approximately 22% of the West Bank.

Area "C" comprises the remaining 60% of the West Bank, including the Jewish settlements. The Palestinians conceded Area C would remain under exclusive Israeli control pending the outcome of future permanent status negotiations.

The Palestinians also agreed in Oslo II that the issue of Israeli settlements in the West Bank would be deferred to the permanent status negotiations. In the meantime, Israel

> shall continue to carry ... the responsibility for overall security of Israelis and Settlements, for the purpose of safeguarding their internal security and public order, and will have *all* the powers to take the steps necessary to meet this responsibility.[13]

Regarding the Gaza Strip, the Palestinians agreed in the Oslo Accords that Israel would retain control over the Gaza Strip's major roads, its borders with Israel and Egypt, and its territorial waters and airspace. Israel also retained control of its then-existing settlements in the Gaza Strip. Israel also retained responsibility for overall security authority over the entire Gaza Strip. The arrangements regarding the Gaza Strip became moot following Israel's September 2005 withdrawal from Gaza, eventually resulting in Hamas taking control of the entire Gaza Strip in 2007, where it remains in power as of this writing.

Both the Palestinians and Israel also agreed in Oslo II they were preserving their respective claims pending the outcome of the contemplated permanent status negotiations. Those negotiations were supposed to have occurred by 2000, but have not yet concluded. In the meantime, the Accords continue governing the status of the West Bank.

Overview of Key Provisions of the Oslo Agreements

The Rabin-Arafat-Holst Exchange of Letters (9 September 1993)

Following months of intense negotiations, the process of reducing the Oslo Accords to writing began with an exchange of three letters between PLO Chairman Yasser Arafat, Israeli Prime Minister Yitzhak Rabin, and Norwegian Foreign Minister Johan Jorgen Holst. Arafat wrote separate letters to Rabin and Holst. Rabin responded with a letter to Arafat.

In his letter to Rabin, Arafat, on behalf of the PLO and the Palestinian people, confirmed several commitments to Israel.

First, the PLO for the first time in its history recognized "the right of the State of Israel to exist in peace and security."

Second, the PLO committed itself to "a peaceful resolution of the conflict."

Third, the PLO committed itself to resolving through negotiations "all outstanding issues relating to permanent status."

Fourth, the PLO pledged to renounce "terrorism and other acts of violence" to "prevent all PLO elements and their personnel" from violating this pledge, and to "discipline violators."

Fifth, Arafat pledged to submit to the Palestinian National Council proposed amendments to the Palestinian Covenant to delete any provisions denying Israel's right to exist.

In his separate letter to Norwegian Foreign Minister Holst, Arafat confirmed he would include the following in his public statements:

> In light of the new era marked by the signing of the Declaration of Principles, the PLO encourages and calls upon the Palestinian people in the West Bank and Gaza Strip to take part in the steps leading to the normalization of life, rejecting violence and terrorism, contributing to peace and stability and participating actively in shaping reconstruction, economic development and cooperation.

In his response to Arafat, Prime Minister Rabin confirmed Israel's decision to move ahead with the Oslo Accords was expressly contingent on the commitments Arafat had made. Thus, Rabin wrote, "in light of the PLO commitments included in your letter, the Government of Israel has decided to recognize the PLO as the representative of the Palestinian people and commence negotiation with the PLO within the Middle East peace process."

Declaration of Principles (13 September 1993)

Four days following the 9 September 1993 exchange of letters, the PLO and Israel signed the Declaration of Principles on Interim Self-Governing Arrangements (the "DOP").

The preamble to the DOP stated as follows:

> The Government of the State of Israel and the PLO team (in the Jordanian-Palestinian delegation to the Middle East Peace Conference) (the "Palestinian Delegation"), representing the Palestinian people, agree that it is time to put an end to decades of confrontation and conflict, recognize their mutual legitimate and political rights, and strive to live in peaceful coexistence and mutual dignity and security and achieve a just, lasting and comprehensive peace settlement and historic reconciliation through the agreed political process.

The substantive provisions of the DOP include the following agreements:

First, the parties agreed to establish a transitional Palestinian Interim Self-Government Authority, which became known as the "Palestinian Authority" or "PA." The parties also agreed to establish an elected Council for West Bank and Gaza Palestinians for a transitional period not to exceed five years (Art. I).

The five-year deadline was later extended, and as of today neither the Israelis nor the Palestinians have revoked the Oslo Accords. Moreover, the Oslo Accords contain no provisions limiting their duration or allowing the parties to withdraw from the agreements.[14] Although the "transitional period" described in Article I of the DOP was to last for a period not exceeding five years, Sabel (2022) notes that both sides "have acquiesced in the considerable extension of the period."[15] Nor do the Accords contain any escape clauses or any firm deadlines for completing negotiations.

Second, the parties agreed to pursue a permanent settlement of the conflict based on United Nations Security Council Resolutions 242 and 338. (Art. I).

Resolution 242 (November 1967) provides, in part:

> The Security Council ... [a]ffirms that the fulfilment of Charter principles requires the establishment of a just and lasting peace in the Middle East which should include the application of both the following principles: (i) 'Withdrawal of Israel armed forces from territories occupied in the recent conflict; (ii) Termination of all claims or states of belligerency and respect for and acknowledgement of the sovereignty, territorial integrity and political independence of every State in the area and their right to live in peace within secure and recognized boundaries free from threats or acts of force.'[16]

Resolution 338 (October 1973) provides, in part:

> The Security Council 1. Calls upon all parties to the present fighting to cease all firing and terminate all military activity immediately, no later than 12 hours after the moment of the adoption of this decision, in the positions they now occupy; 2. Calls upon the parties concerned to start immediately after the cease-fire the implementation of Security Council resolution 242 (1967) in all of its parts; 3. Decides that, immediately and concurrently with the cease-fire, negotiations shall start between the parties concerned under appropriate auspices aimed at establishing a just and durable peace in the Middle East.[17]

Third, the parties agreed the Palestinians would conduct free elections under "agreed supervision and international observation" for a governing Palestinian Council (Art. III.1).

Fourth, the parties agreed that "Jurisdiction of the [Palestinian] Council will cover the West Bank and Gaza Strip territory, except for issues that will be negotiated in the permanent status negotiations" (Art. IV). Thus, the Palestinians gained no interim jurisdiction over any portion of Jerusalem, as Jerusalem was deferred to the permanent status negotiations.

Fifth, the parties agreed that the West Bank and Gaza would be viewed as "a single territorial unit" (Art. IV).

Sixth, the parties agreed on a list of issues to be negotiated as part of a future permanent status agreement, including Jerusalem, refugees (not just Palestinian refugees), settlements, security arrangements, borders, relations and cooperation with other neighbors, and "other issues of common interest" (Art. V.3).

The Agreed Minutes to the DOP expressly state that the Palestinian Council will have jurisdiction over the West Bank and Gaza Strip, "*except* for issues that will be negotiated in the permanent status negotiations: Jerusalem, settlements, military locations, and Israelis."[18] Thus, the DOP expressly permits the Israeli occupation of all areas except parts of the Gaza Strip and Jericho, and the Israeli settlements, to remain in place pending the culmination of a future permanent status agreement. The DOP contains no language freezing the existing settlements as of September 1993, nor does the DOP place any limitations on increasing the size of existing settlements or building new settlements.

Seventh, Israel agreed to withdraw immediately from Jericho and from the vast majority of the Gaza Strip, other than areas of Gaza populated at that time by Israeli settlers. The Palestinians would immediately assume control in Jericho and Gaza for education and culture, health, social welfare, direct taxation, and tourism. Israel would retain responsibility for the overall security of Israelis in the West Bank and the Gaza Strip (Art. VI).

Eighth, the parties agreed to establish a Joint Israeli-Palestinian Liaison Committee to deal with issues requiring coordination and other matters (Art. X).

Ninth, the parties agreed upon a specific and binding Dispute Resolution process. That process requires in the first instance that any disputes be resolved by negotiations within a Joint Israeli-Palestinian Liaison Committee. If the dispute cannot be resolved by negotiations within the Joint Liaison Committee, then the next step would be to resolve the dispute "by a mechanism of conciliation to be agreed upon by the parties." Should that not produce a resolution, then the final avenue would be for the parties to mutually agree to submit the dispute to an Arbitration Committee to be established by the parties themselves. There is no language in the DOP permitting either party to commence (or to ask others to commence) legal proceedings before the International Court of Justice, the International Criminal Court, or any other external body (Art. XV).

Gaza-Jericho Agreement (4 May 1994)

The Preamble to the Gaza-Jericho agreement of May 1994 begins with a series of recitals, including the parties' reaffirmation of the commitments they made to each other in the 9 September 1993 exchange of letters. The recitals also reaffirm the parties' intention that the future permanent status negotiations would lead to the eventual implementation of UN Security Council resolutions 242 and 338.

The substantive provisions of the Gaza-Jericho Agreement include the following:

First, the parties agreed that Israel would "withdraw" its military forces from the Gaza Strip and Jericho areas by redeploying its forces to areas of Israeli settlements and a military installation area along the Egyptian border of the Gaza Strip, with a temporary international presence (Arts. II, XXI).

Second, the agreement formally created the Palestinian Authority as the governing body for the portions of the Gaza Strip and Jericho transferred to Palestinian control. But the agreement states the Palestinian Authority would not have jurisdiction over "foreign relations, internal security and public order of Settlements and the Military Installation Area and Israelis, and external security" (Art. V.1). The agreement goes on to say that "Israel has authority over the Settlements, the Military Installation Area, Israelis, external security, internal security and public order of Settlements, the Military Installation area and Israelis" (Arts. V.1 and V.3).

Third, the Palestinians agreed in Article VI.2 that other than limited interactions with donor countries for economic aid, the Palestinian Authority

> will not have powers and responsibilities in the sphere of foreign relations, which sphere includes the establishment abroad of embassies, consulates

> or other types of foreign missions or posts or permitting their establishment in the Gaza Strip or the Jericho Area, the appointment of or admission of diplomatic and consular staff, and the exercise of diplomatic functions.

This language, which the Palestinians negotiated for and agreed to, demonstrates the parties agreed the Palestinians were not obtaining statehood by virtue of the agreement, and that in fact and in law statehood was expressly precluded prior to the completion of permanent status negotiations, and entirely dependent on the outcome of those negotiations.

Fourth, the parties reiterated the dispute resolution provisions of the DOP (Art. XVII). They also agreed on a separate and specific dispute resolution process for instances in which Israel believed that proposed Palestinian Authority legislation would exceed the PA's jurisdiction or otherwise conflict with the provisions of the Gaza-Jericho Agreement. In such an event, the matter would be referred to a joint Legislation Subcommittee. If the Subcommittee is unable to agree within 15 days, then the dispute would be referred to a "Board of Review" comprising two judges, one from each side, to determine whether the proposed legislation dealt "with a security issue which falls under Israel's responsibility, that it does not seriously threaten other Israeli interests protected by this Agreement, and that the entry into force of the legislation could not cause irreparable damage or harm." If not, then the legislation would enter into force. If the judges cannot agree, then the matter would be referred to the Joint Israeli-Palestinian Liaison Committee as set forth in the DOP (Arts. VII.5–7).

Fifth, the parties agreed that Israel and the Palestinian Authority would "seek to foster mutual understanding and tolerance and shall accordingly refrain from incitement, including hostile propaganda, against each other" (Art. XII).

Sixth, the parties agreed to take "all measures necessary in order to prevent acts of terrorism" against each other (Art. XVIII).

Seventh, the parties (in language especially relevant after Hamas took more than 200 hostages during its 7 October 2023 terror attacks against Israel), the parties agreed that "The Palestinian Authority shall cooperate with Israel by providing all necessary assistance in the conduct of searches of Israel within the Gaza Strip and the Jericho Area for missing Israelis, as well as by providing information about missing Israelis" (Art. XIX).

Eighth, Israel agreed to release approximately 5,000 Palestinian prisoners as a confidence-building measure (Art. XX).

Ninth, again in language especially haunting in light of the 7 October 2023 Hamas terror attacks, the parties agreed that "the security fence erected by Israel around the Gaza Strip shall remain in place" (Art. XXIII.4).

Tenth, the parties agreed that

> Nothing in this Agreement shall prejudice or preempt the outcome of the negotiations on the interim agreement or on the permanent status to be conducted pursuant to the Declaration of Principles. Neither Party shall be deemed, by virtue of having entered into this Agreement, to have renounced or waived any of its existing rights, claims or positions.
>
> *(Art. XXIII.5)*

Finally, the parties reiterated their prior agreements that the Gaza Strip and the Jericho Area shall be deemed to be an integral part of the West Bank and the Gaza Strip, and that the status of those areas "shall not be changed for the period of this Agreement" (Art. XXIII.7).

Agreement on Preparatory Transfer of Powers (29 August 1994)

As with the Gaza-Jericho Agreement, the August 1994 Agreement on Preparatory Transfer of Powers began with a series of recitals, including the parties' reaffirmation of the commitments they made to each other in the 9 September 1993 exchange of letters. The recitals also reaffirm the parties' intention that the future permanent status negotiations would lead to the eventual implementation of UN Security Council resolutions 242 and 338.

The key substantive provisions of the Preparatory Agreement include the following:

First, the parties agreed Israel would transfer to the Palestinian Authority responsibility in the West Bank for education and culture, health, social welfare, tourism, direct taxation, and value-added taxation on local production (Art. II.1).

Second, the parties confirmed that the Palestinian Authority was not receiving any powers or responsibilities over Jerusalem, settlements, military locations, and Israelis (Art. III).

Third, the parties refined the dispute resolution process for Israeli objections to proposed Palestinian Authority legislation, eliminating the judicial review board established in the Gaza-Jericho Agreement, and instead referring disputes to the Legislative Subcommittee. If the dispute could not be resolved within 30 days, then it would be referred to the Joint Liaison Committee for resolution within 30 days (Art. VII.3–7).

Fourth, the agreement contained the same language as the Gaza-Jericho Agreement indicating the parties were reserving all their positions, that the Gaza Strip and the Jericho Area continue to be an integral part of the West Bank and the Gaza Strip, and that the status of those areas would not be changed for the period of the Agreement (Art. XIII.3–5).

Israeli-Palestinian Interim Agreement on the West Bank and Gaza Strip (28 September 1995)

This agreement began with a more detailed preamble than the Gaza-Jericho and Preparatory Transfer agreements. The Preamble reaffirms the parties' desire to "put an end to decades of confrontation and to live in peaceful coexistence." It then declares that the "peace process and the new era it has created ... are irreversible." The Preamble also reaffirmed the parties' commitments to each other in the 9 September 1993 exchange of letters, and reiterated "their mutual commitment to act ... immediately, efficiently and effectively against acts or threats of terrorism, violence or incitement."

The key substantive provisions of the Interim Agreement include the following:

First, the Agreement spelled out in detail the mechanics of the Palestinian Government for the West Bank and Gaza Strip, including holding elections for the Palestinian Council and other governance arrangements (Arts. I–IX).

The Palestinians agreed their Government would be barred from conducting foreign relations (Art. IX.5):

a In accordance with the DOP, the Council will not have powers and responsibilities in the sphere of foreign relations, which sphere includes the establishment abroad of embassies, consulates or other types of foreign missions and posts or permitting their establishment in the West Bank or the Gaza Strip, the appointment of or admission of diplomatic and consular staff, and the exercise of diplomatic functions.

b Notwithstanding the provisions of this paragraph, the PLO may conduct negotiations and sign agreements with states or international organizations for the benefit of the Council in the following cases only

   1 economic agreements ...
   2 agreements with donor countries for the purpose of implementing arrangements for the provision of assistance to the Council;
   3 agreements for the purpose of implementing the regional development plans ... and
   4 cultural, scientific and educational agreements.

c Dealings between the Council and representatives of foreign states and international organizations, as well as the establishment in the West Bank and the Gaza Strip of representative offices ... for the purpose of implementing the agreements referred to in subparagraph 5.b above, *shall not be considered foreign relations.*[19]

The ban on conducting foreign relations meant, as a matter of international law, that the Palestinians were conceding that they had not obtained statehood as a result of the Interim Agreement. Moreover, by negotiating for and agreeing to this language, the Palestinians further conceded they would not obtain statehood unless and until statehood could be achieved as a result of a future permanent status agreement.

Second, the Agreement reiterated the prior statement of the parties that the West Bank and Gaza Strip constitute a single territorial unit (Art. XI.1).

Third, in one of the most significant elements of all the Oslo-related documents, the parties agreed to divide the West Bank into three areas – A, B, and C. Areas A and B comprised roughly 40% of the West Bank, including all Palestinian populated areas. Area A included the main Palestinian cities in the West Bank, and area B the smaller towns and rural areas. Area C comprised the remaining approximately 60% of the West Bank, including Israeli settlements and non-populated areas. The parties agreed that the Israeli army would remain in the West Bank but would redeploy to specified military areas (Art. XI.2).

The Palestinians and their supporters have for the past decade pointed to the division of the West Bank into three separate areas as evidence of Israeli "apartheid," without mentioning that this division reflects *exactly* what the Palestinians themselves bargained for in the Interim Agreement.

Fourth, the agreement set forth the responsibilities of the Palestinian police force to be established in Areas A and B (Arts. XII–XIV).

Fifth, the parties agreed in Article XIV.4 that except for the arms needed for the Palestinian police force and the Israeli military,

> no organization, group of individual in the West Bank and the Gaza Strip shall manufacture, sell, acquire, possess, import or otherwise introduce into the West Bank or the Gaza Strip any firearms, ammunition, weapons, explosives, gunpowder or any related equipment.

The Palestinians began violating this provision before the ink had even dried on the agreement, and have continued violating it ever since.

Sixth, the parties again agreed to take all measures necessary to prevent terrorism and hostilities against each other and to take legal measures against offenders (Art. XV).

The Palestinian Authority's longstanding "pay for slay" policy, rewarding terrorists and their families with "pensions," clearly violates this provision.

Seventh, Israel once again agreed to release Palestinian prisoners and detainees as a "confidence building measure" (Art. XVI).

Eighth, the parties agreed the West Bank and Gaza would be deemed single territorial unit (Art. XVII.1).

Ninth, the parties agreed the Palestinians would have jurisdiction over the West Bank and Gaza, *except* "issues that will be negotiated in the permanent status negotiations: Jerusalem, settlements, specified military locations, refugees, borders, foreign relations and Israelis" (Art. XVII.1.a; Art. XXXI.5).

As Watson (2000) noted, "the Oslo Accords did not establish a right to return or repossession, or even specify whether the question of refugees covers displaced Jews as well as displaced Palestinians."[20]

Tenth, the Interim Agreement incorporated the same three-step dispute resolution process as initially described in the DOP (Art. XXI).

This was the fourth time in the last two years that the Palestinians had agreed to language limiting their rights in the event of a dispute and precluded them from initiating or asking others to initiate litigation at the International Court of Justice or anywhere else on their behalf.

Eleventh, both sides agreed to devote their educational systems to achieving peace between the Israeli and Palestinian peoples, and to "refrain from the introduction of any motifs that could adversely affect the process of reconciliation" (Art. XXII.2).

Twelfth, the parties again agreed to "cooperate by providing each other with all necessary assistance in the conduct of searches for missing persons and bodies of persons which have not been recovered, as well as by providing information about missing persons" (Art. XXVIII.1).

Thirteenth, the Gaza-Jericho Agreement and the Preparatory Transfer Agreement were deemed no longer valid and superseded by the Interim Agreement (Art. XXXI.1).

Fourteenth, the agreement contained the same language as the Gaza-Jericho Agreement indicating the parties were reserving all their positions, that the Gaza Strip and the Jericho Area continue to be an integral part of the West Bank and the Gaza Strip, and that the status of those areas would not be changed for the period of the Agreement (Art. XXXI.6–8).

Just as the parties had done with the DOP, they, along with the United States and the Russian Federation, formally submitted the Interim Agreement to the Secretary General of the United Nations and requested the agreement be made an official record of the General Assembly and the Security Council.[21]

The Interim Agreement contained various annexes. Annex III delineates 40 categories of powers and areas of responsibility of the Palestinian Authority and the allocation of powers and responsibilities between Israel and the Palestinian Authority. Annex V, the Protocol on Economic Relations, contains provisions on banking, taxation, labor, agriculture, industry, tourism, and insurance.

Lapidoth (2001) summarized the respective Israeli and Palestinian commitments in the Interim Agreement:

> In a nutshell, Israel was obliged, under the various agreements to redeploy its forces, to permit a 'safe passage' by Palestinians between the Gaza Strip

and the West Bank, to negotiate with them on the construction of a sea port and air ports, to cooperate on security matters and on passage from the Gaza Strip to Egypt as well as from the West Bank to Jordan, to cooperate on economic issues and to share certain tax and tariff revenue with the Palestinian authority. In addition, Israel was to respect internationally accepted norms of human rights and to release Palestinian prisoners in accordance with an agreed schedule. The Palestinians, for their part, were obliged to amend the Palestinian National Covenant and remove its anti-Israel provisions, to combat terrorism, to transfer terror suspects to Israel, and to cooperate with Israel on security matters as well as in the sphere of economics, legal, and other civilian matters. They were to meet regularly with the Israeli side on security matters. They too committed themselves to the protection of human rights. Incitement to hatred was strictly forbidden.[22]

Protocol Concerning the Redeployment in Hebron (15 January 1997)

The Hebron Protocol dealt specifically with the redeployment of the Israeli military away from the Palestinian-populated areas of Hebron ("Area H-1") to focus on protecting nearby Israeli settlers ("Area H-2").

First, the Protocol reiterated the parties' prior commitments to prevent terrorism and violence (Art. 2.b).

Second, the parties next agreed to various security arrangements, a division of responsibility over certain areas, as well as joint mobile patrols in other areas of Hebron (Art. 4).

Third, the parties also agreed that Jewish Holy Sites in and near Hebron would fall under the protection of the Palestinian police, who would ensure "free, unimpeded, and secure" Jewish access to those sites (Art. 6.b).

Fourth, the parties further agreed on a variety of measures to maintain "normal life" in the Old City of Hebron (Art. 7).

Fifth, the parties agreed on the specific division of responsibility for Area H-2. In general, the Palestinians received civil powers and responsibilities, except for Israelis and their property (Art. 10.b).

Sixth, the Palestinians agreed to coordinate with the Israelis regarding activities in area H-2 that could impact the daily life of Israelis living in Area H-2.

Note for the Record (15 January 1997)

Israeli Prime Minister Benjamin Netanyahu and PLO Chairman Yasser Arafat met with the American envoy Dennis Ross on 15 January 1977 and requested Ross prepare a note for the record, summarizing what had been agreed during the meeting.

First, the parties reaffirmed their commitment to implement the 28 September 1995 Interim Agreement.

Second, the Israelis reaffirmed their commitments regarding military redeployment, prisoner releases, and a variety of minor issues, which the Israelis had not yet completely fulfilled.

Third, the Palestinians reaffirmed their commitments to finalize the revisions to the Palestine National Charter (which as of January 1997 still called for the destruction of Israel); to fight terror and prevent violence, incitement, and hostile propaganda (all of which were still ongoing).

Wye River Memorandum (23 October 1998)

Following negotiations under the auspices of the US President Bill Clinton, the parties signed the Wye River memorandum, containing the following substantive provisions:

First, the parties agreed that Israel would transfer 13% of Area C to the Palestinians, with 1% earmarked for Area A and the remaining 12% for Area B (Para. I.A).

Second, a committee would be formed to facilitate further Israeli military deployments pursuant to the Interim Agreement (Para. I.B).

Third, the parties agreed that "it is in their vital interests to combat terrorism" (Para. II). The memorandum dealt with the terrorism issues in extraordinary detail, beginning with the following statement (once again, both sides signed the memorandum after negotiating for the following language):

> [T]he struggle against terror and violence must be comprehensive in that it deals with terrorists, the terror support structure, and the environment conducive to the support of terror. It must be continuous and constant over a long-term, in that there can be no pauses in the work against terrorists and their structure. It must be cooperative in that no effort can be fully effective without Israeli-Palestinian cooperation and the continuous exchange of information, concepts, and actions.

Fourth, the parties agreed that the Palestinian side would be responsible for implementing various security, security cooperation, and related issues, including the following:

- The Palestinians agreed to outlaw and combat terrorist organizations and "make known its policy of zero tolerance for terror." The Palestinians agreed to develop a work plan to implement this commitment. The work plan would be shared with the United States. Thereafter, "implementation will begin immediately to ensure the systematic and effective combat of terrorist organizations and their infrastructure."

- The Palestinians agreed to form a US-Palestinian committee that would meet biweekly "to review the steps being taken to eliminate terrorist cells and the support structure that plans, finances, supplies, and abets terror. In these meetings, the Palestinian side will inform the United States fully of the actions it has taken to outlaw all organizations (or wings of organizations, as appropriate) of a military, terrorist, or violent character and their support structure and to prevent them from operating in areas under its jurisdiction." The Palestinians further agreed to apprehend terror suspects and to prosecute and punish all persons involved in acts of violence and terror.
- The Palestinians agreed to criminalize the importation, manufacturing or unlicensed sale, acquisition or possession of firearms, ammunition, or weapons in areas under Palestinian jurisdiction. The Palestinians further agreed to the creation of a US-Palestinian-Israeli committee to assist and enhance cooperation in preventing the smuggling or other unauthorized introduction of weapons or explosive materials into areas under Palestinian jurisdiction.
- The Palestinians further agreed to issue a decree prohibiting all forms of incitement to violence or terror, and establishing mechanisms for acting systematically against all expressions or threats of violence or terror.

Fifth, the parties agreed to improve their security cooperation, including the Palestinians providing the Israelis with the names of all Palestinian police officers (Paras. II.B; II.C.1).

Sixth, the Palestinians agreed to implement the long-delayed commitment to remove the language from their Charter calling for the destruction of Israel (Para. II.C.2).

Seventh, the parties agreed to undertake further work to implement their prior agreements regarding economic development in the West Bank and the Gaza Strip; safe passage between the West Bank and the Gaza Strip; and developing the Port of Gaza.

Eighth, the parties agreed to "immediately resume permanent status negotiations on an accelerated basis and will make a determined effort to achieve the mutual goal of reaching an agreement by May 4, 1999" (Para. IV).

Ninth, the parties agreed that "neither side shall initiate or take any step that will change the status of the West Bank and the Gaza Strip in accordance with the Interim Agreement" (Para. V).

Sharm el-Sheikh Memorandum (4 September 1999)

The "Sharm el-Sheikh Memorandum on Implementation Timeline of Outstanding Commitments of Agreements Signed and the Resumption of Permanent Status Negotiations" reiterated the parties' desire to implement the

September 1995 Interim Agreement and all other agreements since the September 1993 exchange of letter.

First, the parties agreed to resume the Permanent Status negotiations "in an accelerated manner" (Para. 1a).

Second, the parties reaffirmed their understanding that the negotiations on the Permanent Status will lead to the implementation of Security Council Resolutions 242 and 338 (Para 1b).

Third, the parties agreed to conclude a comprehensive agreement on all Permanent Status issues within one year from the resumption of the Permanent Status negotiations (Para. 1d).

Fourth, the Israelis agreed to transfer additional portions of Area C to Areas A and B (Para. 2).

Fifth, the Israelis agreed to additional prisoner releases (Para. 3).

Sixth, the Israelis agreed to take steps to facilitate safe passage between the Gaza Strip and the West Bank (Para. 5).

Seventh, the parties agreed to take steps to facilitate and enable the construction of the Gaza Sea Port (Para. 6).

Eighth, the parties agreed to take steps to ensure "the immediate, efficient and effective handling of any incident involving a threat or act of terrorism, violence or incitement, whether committed by Palestinians or Israelis" (Para. 8a).

Ninth, the parties agreed that "neither side would initiate or take any step that will change the status of the West Bank and the Gaza Strip in accordance with the Interim Agreement" (Para. 10).

Legal Implications of the Oslo Accords

Summary

The Oslo Accords are enormously significant from a legal perspective. They constitute the legally binding documents governing all aspects of the Israeli-Palestinian dispute. The parties committed themselves to the Middle East peace process. They agreed to resolve every issue in the dispute through negotiation, including the most difficult permanent status issues.

The Oslo Accords continue in full force and effect today. They remain legally binding on both the Israelis and the Palestinians, despite the moribund political process and long delay in completing the permanent status negotiations. Neither party has formally abrogated the Accords. The dispute resolution provisions preclude the parties from initiating litigation before the international courts (or asking others to do so on their behalf), consistent with their repeated and legally binding commitments to each other to resolve *all* issues in the conflict through negotiation.

The Palestinians knowingly, voluntarily, and willingly signed the Oslo Accords, which they negotiated vigorously over a long period following the

1991 Madrid Conference. No one forced or coerced the Palestinians to sign the agreements. The Palestinians knew exactly what they were doing, as Abu Mazen confirmed in his memoir of the negotiations.

The Oslo Accords deal comprehensively with the entire set of issues dividing the parties, addressing some on an interim basis, while reserving others for later negotiations toward a permanent status agreement intended to implement UN Security Council Resolutions 242 and 338.

During the interim phase, Israel would withdraw from most of the Gaza Strip and Jericho, and from almost half the West Bank (Areas A and B). The Palestinians agreed Israel would retain exclusive control of the remainder of the West Bank (Area C). The Palestinians agreed the Israeli settlements and settlers could remain in Area C during the interim period, pending a permanent status deal. The Palestinians obtained no commitments from Israel to refrain from building new settlements or expanding existing settlements during the interim period.

The PLO gained Israeli recognition as the representative of the Palestinian people. The Palestinians negotiated for the right to create a Palestinian Authority to govern themselves in Areas A and B, plus the Gaza Strip and Jericho, through a Palestinian Council to be elected democratically. The Council would be responsible for civic affairs in the areas from which Israel would withdraw. The Palestinians agreed Israel would remain responsible for Israelis, Israeli property, and overall military security in both the West Bank and the Gaza Strip.

The Palestinians further committed themselves to recognizing Israel's right to exist in peace and security. The Palestinians also agreed to renounce terrorism, violence, and incitement. They agreed to stop teaching their children to hate Jews and Israelis.

The Palestinians agreed that "permanent status" issues such as Jerusalem, borders, refugees, and the final status of Israeli settlements would be reserved for later negotiation. The Palestinians obtained *no* promises or guarantees of future statehood. Nor did they obtain any commitments regarding the borders of a potential future Palestinian state or other non-state entity. Both sides reserved their rights regarding all issues, agreeing "[n]either Party shall be deemed, by virtue of having entered into this Agreement, to have renounced or waived any of its existing rights, claims or positions."[23]

The Palestinians also committed themselves to pursue their claims *solely* through diplomacy and negotiation. The Palestinians further agreed to limit themselves to a very specific dispute resolution process, a process that did not allow either party to initiate litigation, or to ask others to initiate litigation on their behalf.

Both sides additionally agreed not to initiate or take any steps that would change the status of the West Bank and the Gaza Strip.

The political situation and the division of land and responsibility in the West Bank today reflect *exactly* what the Palestinians bargained for at Oslo, no more and no less. The Palestinians enjoy full civic autonomy in Areas A and B of the West Bank. Hamas captured control of the Gaza Strip in June 2007, less than two years following Israel's complete withdrawal from the area in September 2005. Some commentators make the illogical argument that Israel continued to "occupy" the Gaza Strip after withdrawing from it. Perhaps those commentators would be willing to acknowledge that the devastating October 2023 Hamas attack on Israel undermines any such claims of ongoing Israeli occupation.

Are the Oslo Accords Legally Binding?

The question whether the Olso Accords are legally binding on both the Israelis and Palestinians requires an analysis of two issues. First, did the PLO have the legal capacity to enter into an agreement with Israel, meaning the agreement would bind both the PLO and Israel as a matter of international law? Second, even if the PLO had such capacity, do the Oslo Accords constitute either a treaty or another type of international agreement that legally binds the parties?

Malanczuk (1996) addressed the question whether the parties had the legal capacity to enter into an international agreement. Israel, of course, could do so in its capacity as a State. But what about the PLO, which was not a State?

Malanczuk argued the PLO had gained acceptance globally as a national liberation movement, and as such it could be deemed a "partial subject of international law." Thus, Malanczuk contended that "as a partial subject of international law, the PLO is not equal to a state, but that does not affect the validity of a treaty it concludes with a state."[24]

Interestingly, Malanczuk did not rely on the parties' commitments to each other in the 9 September 1993 exchange of letters. Nevertheless, it could also be argued that Rabin's confirmation in his letter to Arafat of the Israeli government's recognition of the PLO as the representative of the Palestinian people further vested the PLO with the capacity to enter into a binding agreement with Israel under international law.

Watson (2000) agreed with Malanczuk's conclusion that the PLO had the capacity to enter into a legally binding agreement with Israel. Watson characterized the PLO as a "subject," rather than a "partial subject" of international law.[25]

Corten and Klein (2011) also viewed the PLO as a non-state actor, yet sufficiently vested with the legal capacity to enter into a binding treaty-type arrangement with Israel: "Insurrectional movements regarded as belligerents have the capacity to conclude treaties ... groups known as national liberation movements have the capacity to conclude treaties."[26]

Sabel (2022) took a somewhat different approach, characterizing the PLO as "sub-state actor" which at the time of signing the Accords did not control any territory. Sabel instead prefers to ground the legal status of the Oslo Accords on the notion of *unilaterality*, based on Israel's decision to be bound by the Accords, but only to the extent the PLO complies with its own obligations under the Accords.[27] Sabel nevertheless concluded that "both Israel and the PLO intended the DOP to be a binding legal instrument."[28]

Blum (1994), however, questioned whether the PLO, which he characterized as a "non-state" actor, had sufficient legal capacity to bind Israel:

> It has been asserted that the recognition of the PLO by the United Nations as a 'national liberation movement' and as 'the representative of the Palestinian people' has transformed it into a subject (albeit a unique one) of international law and hence one capable of concluding international agreements. Without going into the rather vexed question as to whether such movements are indeed subjects of international law, suffice it say here that even if one is prepared to recognize their status as such, it does not necessarily follow that agreements entered by them become international agreements; partial and limited subjects of international law logically have only partial capacities under that law.[29]

Despite Blum's concerns, the majority view holds the PLO, whether characterized as a "sub-state actor," a "subject" of international law, or a "partial subject" of international law, indeed had the capacity to enter into an international agreement with the Government of Israel in the form of the Oslo Accords.

The next step is to determine whether the Oslo Accords are legally binding on both parties.

The Accords cannot be characterized as comprising a formal "treaty." Article 2(1)(a) of the 1969 Vienna Convention on the Law of Treaties defines "treaty" solely as "an international agreement concluded *between States*." The Oslo Accords represented an agreement not between states but between a state (Israel) and a subject or partial subject of international law (the PLO). Therefore, the Oslo Accords cannot be characterized as a "treaty."

Nevertheless, the Oslo Accords should still be deemed binding on both parties under international law.

The analysis begins with Article 3 of the Vienna Convention on the Law of Treaties. Article 3 anticipated situations such as the Oslo Accords, in which international agreements might not rise to the level of a treaty, but should still be viewed as legally binding on the parties:

> The fact that the present Convention does not apply to international agreements concluded between States and other subjects of international

> law or between such other subjects of international law, or to international agreements not in written form, shall not affect: (a) the legal force of such agreements; (b) the application to them of any of the rules set forth in the present Convention to which they would be subject under international law independently of the Convention; (c) the application of the Convention to the relations of States as between themselves under international agreements to which other subjects of international law are also parties.[30]

The language of Article 3 applies directly to the Oslo Accords. The Accords were "international agreements concluded between States and other subjects of international law." Thus, the Accords are infused with legal force. Accordingly, the Accords are subject to "the application ... of any of the rules set forth in the present Convention to which they would be subject under international law independently of the Convention."

The most important such rule can be found in Article 26 of the Vienna Convention, embodying the customary international law principle of *pacta sunt servanda*. Article 26 declares that "[e]very treaty in force is binding upon the parties to it and must be performed by them in good faith."

Shaw (2021) describes *pacta sunt servanda* as "arguably the oldest principle of international law."[31] Thus, under Article 3 of the Vienna Convention, the principle of *pacta sunt servanda* applies to the Oslo Accords as a rule to which the Accords "would be subject under international law independently of the Convention."

Watson (2000) also viewed the Oslo Accords as legally binding. While the Accords could not be characterized as forming a "treaty," given that the Accords did not constitute an agreement "between states," the Accords nevertheless were binding international instruments:

> Most of the Accords have the formal attributes of binding instruments; they are styled 'agreements' and 'protocols,' they are structures like treaties, and they contain mandatory rather than permissive language. Even the somewhat less formal instruments – the Note for the Record and the Wye River Memorandum – still clearly reflect an intent to be legally bound. It appears, then, that the Oslo Accords are legally binding international agreements. Thus there is a legal basis for the assertion that the Oslo process is 'irreversible.' Whether there is a practical basis for that assertion is more a question of political will. Conversely, there is no basis for the claim that the Accords are non-binding 'political' documents.[32]

Therefore, because both parties had the legal capacity to enter into the Oslo Accords, and because the Accords represent a valid and legally binding international agreement between the parties, both sides are legally bound to comply with the Accords.

Did the Oslo Accords Grant or Promise Statehood to the Palestinians?

The Palestinians obtained no commitments in the Oslo Accords from Israel regarding future Palestinian statehood. Indeed, the Palestinians agreed during the interim period that the newly-created Palestinian Authority would forego important attributes of statehood and sovereignty, including the ability to enter into treaty relations with other states. Nothing in the Accords contains any promise or guarantee of eventual Palestinian statehood, reserving the final status of the West Bank and Gaza Strip for future permanent status negotiations.

Benvenisti (1993), in an early commentary on the DOP, argued Israel implicitly recognized Palestinian self-determination by agreeing to language acknowledging the "political rights" of the Palestinians:

> [T]hough the Declaration itself does not recognize the PLO as the representative of a State, the Israeli recognition of the Palestinian people does constitute an implied recognition of the right of that people to determine freely its political status, and to pursue freely its economic, social, and cultural development. Indeed, the Declaration explicitly recognizes the right of the Palestinian people 'to govern themselves' in the West Bank and Gaza strip ... One can argue that the consequence of recognizing the Palestinian people and its right to govern itself in the West Bank and Gaza is recognition in principle of the right of this people to establish a state in these areas if it so desires. In light of this recognition, the Declaration is an agreement between two equal subjects of international law.[33]

If Benvenisti is correct, then the Palestinians can hardly be heard to complain that Israel has denied their right to self-determination. If Benvenisti is incorrect, then at worst the Oslo Accords created the *opportunity* for the Palestinians to pursue their self-determination claims as part of the permanent status negotiations.

Becker (1998) took a different view than Benvenisti. Becker noted the Oslo Accords represented a "watershed" in Israeli-Palestinian relations, but did *not* confer any guarantee of future statehood on the Palestinians:

> The Oslo Accords represent a watershed in Israeli-Palestinian relations because they express an agreement between the principal parties that their claims to self-determination are not absolute but relative notions. The Palestinians have legally accepted Israel's right to exist within secure and recognized boundaries. For its part, Israel has acknowledged the existence of the Palestinian people with certain rights to self-determination. The precise limits of these rights are as yet undefined. Admittedly, international political pressure, agreement or Palestinian unilateral acts may lead to the creation of a Palestinian state, *but legally this need not be the result.*[34]

Did the Oslo Accords Prohibit New or Expanded Israeli Settlements in Area C?

The Palestinians explicitly agreed in the Oslo Accords that the Israeli settlements and settlers could remain in Area C during the interim period, pending a permanent status deal.

But what about Israel expanding existing settlements and/or building new settlements, as it has done throughout the decades since Oslo? As noted above, the Oslo Accords forbid both parties from initiating or taking "any steps that would change the status of the West Bank and the Gaza Strip." However, that same provision also says no such steps may be taken that would change the status quo "in accordance with the interim agreement." What exactly does this mean as applied to Israel's construction of new settlements and expansion of existing settlements since Oslo?

The Palestinians, of course, would argue that any new settlement construction or expansion of existing settlements violates the Oslo Accords by changing the "status" of the "West Bank." Watson (2000) agrees, noting:

> Only an exceedingly formalistic reading of the word 'status' would permit Israel to construct vast new settlements under the pretense that they were prompting no change in 'status' of the territories. Not every enhancement of existing settlements changes the status' of the territories, but expansion of existing settlements on to new land does tend to change the 'status' of that land.[35]

The Palestinians have also argued, somewhat bizarrely, that Israel's unilateral withdrawal from the Gaza Strip in 2005 also breached the Israeli obligation not to change the status quo in the Gaza Strip beyond the requirements of the Gaza-Jericho Agreement and the Interim Agreement.

Notwithstanding Watson's argument, the better reading of the language barring any changes to the "status quo" would focus on the status quo *as defined in the Oslo Accords*. The language of the Accords states that "neither side shall initiate or take any step that will change the status of the West Bank and the Gaza Strip *in accordance with the Interim Agreement*." Thus, the best reading of this provision is that it bans any steps by either party to expand the geographic size of the areas assigned to them or to encroach on the geographic areas assigned to the other party.

Thus, for example, Israel would be prohibited from expanding the geographic size of Area C by encroaching on Areas A and/or B. Likewise, the Palestinians would be prohibited from trying to expand the geographic size of Areas A and B by encroaching on Area C.

However, nothing in the Interim Agreement can be read as forbidding the expansion of existing settlements or the construction of new settlements *within* Area C. Such activity would not constitute a change to "the status of the West Bank and the Gaza Strip *in accordance with the Interim*

Agreement." That is because nothing in the Interim Agreement can be read as precluding Israel from expanding existing settlements or building new settlements within Area C. The same holds true for Palestinian construction activity in Areas A and B.

On the other hand, in recent years the Palestinian Authority has initiated hundreds of building projects in Area C. The Palestinian leadership has declared the construction activity represents an effort to "change the facts on the ground" by creating geographic continuity with Palestinian towns and cities in Areas A and B.[36] This effort to "change the facts on the ground" by launching construction projects in Area C clearly violates the ban on initiating or taking "any steps that would change the status of the West Bank." The construction projects also directly breach the provisions of the Interim Agreement assigning Area C exclusively to the Israelis pending the outcome of the permanent status negotiations.

Therefore, the language the Palestinians negotiated for at Oslo contained no express or implied commitments from Israel to refrain from building new settlements or expanding existing settlements during the interim period. Nor do the Accords contain any express or implied language permitting Palestinian construction activity in Area C.

Significantly, as the Palestinian legal expert Raja Shehadeh (1997) has noted, the framework agreement for the interim stage, reached as part of the 1993 Oslo DOP, "did not limit Israel's ability to expand the settlements and create more facts on the ground."[37] Indeed, Shehadeh admits the Palestinian negotiators were well aware of Israeli plans to expand the settlements, yet they signed the DOP and the Interim Agreement anyway.

Did the Oslo Accords End the Israeli Occupation of the West Bank and the Gaza Strip?

Benvenisiti raised the possibility that the Declaration of Principle had changed the legal status of the West Bank and Gaza by transferring "effective control" from Israel to the Palestinians, meaning those areas could no longer be deemed under Israeli occupation within the meaning of the 1907 Hague Regulations.[38] Benvenisti noted, however, that the opposite could also be true:

> [I]t should be emphasized that the phrasing of the Declaration may also be interpreted to support the reverse stance, as the Palestinian authority's lack of jurisdiction over matters of external security and foreign relations denies the Palestinian entity the conventional indicators of independence, as described under the Montevideo formula. This interpretation is supported by the emphasis on the transfer of authority from the IDF to the Palestinian authority, (rather than assigning original powers in the Declaration),

> and by the wording of Article 6 of Annex 11, which provides that in the interim period, the status of the Gaza strip and the Jericho area will remain unchanged, and will continue to be an integral part of the West Bank and the Gaza Strip.[39]

Watson (2000), writing several years after Benvenisti and analyzing both the DOP and the ensuing Oslo agreements, concluded Israel would be deemed the occupant of Area C under the "effective control" test of the 1907 Hague Regulations. However, Watson also concluded that under those same regulations Israel would no longer be deemed the occupant of Areas A and B:

> [I]t seems fair to conclude that Israel still does occupy Area C, since it has not withdrawn its military forces from that Area. That the PA exercises civilian functions there is not dispositive, since Area C is sparsely populated and is not the focus of Palestinian civilian administration, and the PA lacks civil authority over land-related matters there. Area B, however, is probably not 'occupied' territory because Israel has withdrawn from it and because the PA exercises substantial civilian control there. It is true that Israel continues to patrol Area B, and that it maintains responsibility for external security, but it no longer maintains a permanent military presence in that area, nor is it the sole civilian administrator. Likewise, Area A would no longer seem to be occupied territory: Israel has withdrawn from it, and the PA authority there is at its maximum. That Israel maintains responsibility for external security is not, in itself, enough to rise to the level of 'occupation,' which implies day-to-day control on the ground.[40]

Watson's conclusion that Israel no longer occupies Areas A and B applies with even greater force to the Gaza Strip, from which Israel withdrew completely in 2005. This issue is discussed further in Chapter 17.

Have the Parties Breached and/or Revoked the Oslo Accords?

The Preamble to the Interim Agreement proclaims that "the peace process and the new era that it has created, as well as the new relationship established between the two Parties as described above, are irreversible."

Nevertheless, since Oslo both parties have repeatedly accused each other of breaching the Accords. The Palestinians claim Israel has violated its commitment not to change the *status quo* in the West Bank by expanding existing settlements and building new settlements. The Palestinians also argue Israel breached its obligation to maintain the *status quo* in the Gaza Strip when it withdrew unilaterally in 2005. Further, the Palestinians argue Israel delayed the implementation of various military redeployments during the mid- and late 1990s.

The Israelis, for their part, have accused the Palestinians of breaching the Accords in a variety of ways. The Palestinians have repeatedly violated their commitment to renounce violence. In September 2000 the Palestinian leadership launched the so-called "second intifada." During the ensuing five years, a wave of suicide bombings and other attacks claimed more than 1,000 Israeli lives.[41]

Israel also alleges the Palestinian Authority has violated its commitment to renounce terrorism by rewarding terrorists who kill Israelis with "pensions," otherwise known as the "pay for slay" program, which continues to the present day. The PA has also continued teaching hatred of Israelis and Jews to Palestinian schoolchildren.

Watson (2000) also noted Yasser Arafat's disturbing rhetoric in the mid-1990s, when he compared the Oslo Accords to treaties made and thereafter abrogated by the Prophet Mohammed, such as the "covenant the Prophet Mohammed made with the tribe of Kureish, a treaty he broke when the time was right, when that tribe became weak. He then proceeded to slaughter them."[42]

The Israelis, however, have also acknowledged and praised the PA's occasional security cooperation as an example of Palestinian compliance with the Accords.

The breaches on both sides could give rise to a claim by either party under Article 60(1) of the Vienna Convention to terminate or suspend the Oslo Accords in part or in full based on a "material breach" by the other party. Article 60(3) defines "material breach" as "(a) a repudiation of the treaty not sanctioned by the present Convention; or (b) the violation of a provision essential to the accomplishment of the object or purpose of the treaty."

Significantly, however, neither side has invoked Article 60 or otherwise abrogated the Oslo Accords as of the present date. Shaw (2021) noted that "[s]ince neither side has to date denounced the Oslo Accords and succeeding instruments, they remain in effect."[43]

However, as Benvenisti (1993) explained, even if one or both of the parties were to invoke Article 60(1) and seek to suspend or terminate the Accords, under Article 70 the termination or suspension would not, "affect any right, obligation or legal situation of the parties created through the execution of the treaty prior to its termination," such as the mutual recognition reflected in the DOP and the 9 September 1993 exchange of letters. And the creation of "a Palestinian entity, with defined borders and broad jurisdiction ... in the Gaza Strip and Jericho."[44]

Impact of the Oslo Accords on Pending Litigation at the International Court of Justice

On 30 December 2022, the United Nations General Assembly adopted Resolution 77/247.[45] Running nearly nine single-spaced pages, the Resolution – which makes no mention of the Oslo Accords – recites a litany of criticisms of Israel, culminating in a request to the ICJ to render an advisory opinion on the following two questions:

a What are the legal consequences arising from the ongoing violation by Israel of the right of the Palestinian people to self-determination, from its prolonged occupation, settlement, and annexation of the Palestinian territory occupied since 1967, including measures aimed at altering the demographic composition, character and status of the Holy City of Jerusalem, and from its adoption of related discriminatory legislation and measures?
b How do the policies and practices of Israel referred to ... above affect the legal status of the occupation, and what are the legal consequences that arise for all States and the United Nations from this status?

The ICJ ordered state parties to file opening briefs on 25 July 2023 and responsive briefs on 25 October 2023 (the ICJ did not extend the deadline following Hamas's horrific 7 October 2023 terror attack against Israel.) Although only states are allowed to file briefs, the ICJ permitted the Organization for Islamic Cooperation to file briefs but refused the same courtesy to the World Jewish Congress.

The ICJ has scheduled public hearings to commence 19 February 2024.

Jurisdictional Issues

The first question implicated by the Oslo Accords is whether the dispute resolution provisions either deprive the ICJ of jurisdiction or provide a "compelling" basis for the court to exercise its discretion not to render an advisory opinion.

Article 37 of the ICJ statute provides as follows:

> Whenever a treaty or convention in force provides for reference of a matter to a tribunal to have been instituted by the League of Nations, or to the Permanent Court of International Justice, the matter shall, as between the parties to the present Statute, be referred to the International Court of Justice.[46]

The Oslo Accords contain no provision allowing the parties (or anyone acting at their request) to initiate litigation at the ICJ, or to seek external adjudication of disputes. Moreover, the dispute resolution provisions of the Oslo Accords contain no language conferring jurisdiction on the ICJ to intervene in the Israeli-Palestinian dispute.

Instead, the parties negotiated for and agreed to comply with a binding Dispute Resolution process. That process requires in the first instance that any disputes be resolved by negotiations within a Joint Israeli-Palestinian

Liaison Committee. If the dispute cannot be resolved by negotiations within the Joint Liaison Committee, then the next step would be to resolve the dispute "by a mechanism of conciliation to be agreed upon by the parties." Should that not produce a resolution, then the final avenue would be for the parties to mutually agree to submit the dispute to an Arbitration Committee to be established by the parties themselves. In no event, however, do the Oslo Accords permit either party to commence (or to ask others to commence) legal proceedings before the International Court of Justice or any other external body.

In other contexts involving dispute resolution clauses, the ICJ has taken jurisdiction under Article 37 only where the parties specifically agreed to confer jurisdiction on the court. For example, in the *Maritime Delimitation and Territorial Questions between Qatar and Bahrain* case, the parties initially agreed on a binding dispute resolution process before the King of Saudi Arabia. Subsequently, however, the parties agreed in an exchange of letters to submit their dispute to the ICJ. Qatar eventually asked the ICJ to take jurisdiction.

Bahrain objected, contending the exchange of letters did not give rise to any binding legal obligation to consent to ICJ jurisdiction. Bahrain further argued that even if the exchange of letters did rise to the level of a binding agreement between the two countries, the ICJ's jurisdiction could not be invoked unilaterally by Qatar without Bahrain's consent. The ICJ rejected both arguments. It accepted jurisdiction of the issues Qatar had raised and allowed both parties the opportunity to submit their entire dispute to the ICJ.[47]

In *Cameroon v. Nigeria*, the ICJ noted that in ordinary circumstances,

> [n]either in the Charter nor otherwise in international law is any general rule to be found to the effect that the exhaustion of diplomatic negotiations constitutes a precondition for a matter to be referred to the Court. No such precondition was embodied in the Statute of the Permanent Court of International Justice ...[48]

However, the court also stated that parties are free to constrain the court's jurisdiction by specifying alternative means of resolving their disputes, which is exactly what the Israelis and Palestinians did in the dispute resolution provisions of the Oslo Accords. Thus, the court said:

> A precondition of this type may be embodied and is often included in compromissory clauses of treaties. It may also be included in a special agreement whose signatories then reserve the right to seise the Court only after a certain lapse of time ... Finally, States remain free to insert into their optional declaration accepting the compulsory jurisdiction of the Court

> a reservation excluding from the latter those disputes for which the parties involved have agreed or subsequently agree to resort to an alternative method of peaceful settlement.

Here, by contrast, the Israelis and Palestinians have *never* agreed in any of the Oslo documents or any subsequent agreements to submit disputes to the ICJ. Given the broad scope of the Oslo Agreements, covering the entire set of issues dividing the parties, there is no legal basis for the ICJ to accept the General Assembly's request to render an advisory opinion addressing *any* of those issues.

The ICJ, however, previously disregarded the Oslo Accords when it intervened in the Israeli-Palestinian dispute at the request of the UN General Assembly. Israel had constructed a separation barrier along the West-Bank Israel border, and in some portions of Area C of the West Bank, to protect itself following a wave of deadly terrorist incursions from the West Bank during the so-called Second Intifada between 2001 and 2003.

In December 2003 the UN General Assembly adopted a resolution asking the ICJ to render an advisory opinion regarding "the legal consequences arising from the construction of the wall being built by Israel ... in the Occupied Palestinian Territory, including in and around East Jerusalem."[49]

The ICJ issued the *Wall* Advisory Opinion only a few months later, in July 2004.

The ICJ began by rejecting a variety of serious challenges to its jurisdiction. The court also rejected various requests that it should exercise its discretion not to intervene in the dispute.

First, the court noted it had never in its entire history refused a request from the United Nations to render an advisory opinion, proclaiming "[t]he present Court has never, in the exercise of this discretionary power, declined to respond to a request for an advisory opinion."[50]

The court acknowledged the language of Article 65(1) of the ICJ Statute, providing "[t]he Court *may* give an advisory opinion," meaning "the Court has a discretionary power to decline to give an advisory opinion even if the conditions of jurisdiction are met." Nevertheless, the court explained that "only 'compelling reasons' should lead the Court to refuse" to render an advisory opinion, and that it had never in its history found a compelling reason in any case to decline jurisdiction.

The court rejected all the objections to its jurisdiction to render an advisory opinion regarding the legality of the separation barrier. One such objection noted that if the court were to intervene in the dispute it would disrupt the diplomatic process envisioned in the 2003 "Roadmap for Peace," a document prepared by the "Quartet," consisting of representatives of the United States of America, the European Union, the Russian Federation and the United Nations.

The court acknowledged the United Nations Security Council had endorsed the Roadmap on 19 November 2003 in Resolution 1515, calling on the Israeli and Palestinians "to fulfil their obligations under the Roadmap in cooperation with the Quartet and to achieve the vision of two States living side by side in peace and security."

But the court nevertheless brushed aside the objection as not providing a "compelling" basis to exercise its discretion under Article 65(1) to decline to render the advisory opinion:

> The Court is conscious that the "Roadmap", which was endorsed by the Security Council ... constitutes a negotiating framework for the resolution of the Israeli-Palestinian conflict. It is not clear, however, what influence the Court's opinion might have on those negotiations: participants in the present proceedings have expressed differing views in this regard. The Court cannot regard this factor as a compelling reason to decline to exercise its jurisdiction.[51]

Significantly, the ICJ never mentioned the dispute resolution provisions in the DOP. Thus, the *Wall* opinion cannot be viewed as having any precedential impact on jurisdictional objections based on the dispute resolution provisions of the Oslo Accords.

If the ICJ decides it has jurisdiction over the issues raised in the General Assembly's December 2022 request for an Advisory Opinion, the question arises whether *any* international parties in the future would include dispute resolution language in their agreements. What would be the point of doing so, if the court could intervene whenever the General Assembly or even one of the parties themselves ask the court to do so?

Substantive Issues

The substantive issues raised by the General Assembly's request to the ICJ should be resolved consistently with the positions the Palestinians themselves took when they negotiated the Oslo Accords.

First, the General Assembly resolution asks the ICJ to determine "the legal consequences arising from the ongoing violation by Israel of the right of the Palestinian people to self-determination." The premise of this question is factually and legally incorrect.

There is no "ongoing violation by Israel of the right of the Palestinian people to self-determination." That is because the Palestinians themselves negotiated for and agreed in writing in the Oslo Accords that they would obtain *civic autonomy* – but *not* self-determination – in Areas A and B of the West Bank and in the Gaza Strip during the interim period, prior to the completion of the permanent status negotiations. Thus, the Palestinians knowingly, voluntarily, and willingly agreed to *defer* their self-determination claims until the permanent status negotiations. Moreover, the Palestinians signed the Oslo Accords despite the complete absence in the Accords of any promise or guarantee of future statehood.

In this context, it must be mentioned again how intensely the Palestinians negotiated at Oslo. As Mahmoud Abbas described in his account of the negotiations, the Palestinian delegation gave

> attention to every word, sentence and expression. It was even necessary to scrutinize every comma and full stop so that we could eliminate the likelihood of fatal pitfalls occurring in the future ... the DOP documents were reviewed by our legal consultant, Taher Shash, whom we had sent to Oslo for this purpose just before they were initialed on 20 August 1993.[52]

The Palestinians argue self-determination is a core international legal norm, so fundamental that it cannot be negotiated away. The Palestinians rely on the language in the ICJ's 2004 *Wall* advisory opinion, where the court said:

> As regards the principle of the right of peoples to self-determination, the Court observes that the existence of a 'Palestinian people' is longer in issue. Such existence has moreover been recognized by Israel in the exchange of letters of 9 September 1993 between Mr. Yasser Arafat, President of the Palestine Liberation Organization (PLO) and Mr. Yitzhak Rabin, Israeli Prime Minister. In that correspondence, the President of the PLO recognized "the right of the State of Israel to exist in peace and security" and made various other commitments. In reply, the Israeli Prime Minister informed him that, in the light of those commitments, "the Government of Israel has decided to recognize the PL0 as the representative of the Palestinian people". The Israeli-Palestinian Interim Agreement on the West Bank and the Gaza Strip of 28 September 1995 also refers a number of times to the Palestinian people and its "legitimate rights" [citation omitted.] The Court considers that those rights include the right to self-determination, as the General Assembly has moreover recognized on a number of occasions ... .[53]

Thus, the Palestinians would argue their right to immediate self-determination trumps the *deferred possibility* of self-determination which they knowingly, voluntarily and willingly accepted Oslo. But that argument makes no sense, as it would render the Oslo Accords meaningless. Moreover, as Watson (2000) noted,

> the problem with this argument is that the content of the right of self-determination is indeterminate. In particular, there is little consensus on

> what, if any, remedy exists for impingement of a people's right of self-determination ... this variegated practice might lead one to concludes that there is no meaningful right of self-determination at all.[54]

Shaw (2021), writing more recently, explained that self-determination continues to evolve as a principle of international law. However, the precise nature and scope of the right have yet to be clearly defined. Although the UN has taken a very broad view of self-determination as a "right of all peoples," Shaw criticized that formulation as unworkable, and argued instead that self-determination as a legal principle must be defined by reference to colonially defined territories:

> If this is so, then all peoples would become thereby to some extent subjects of international law as the direct repositories of international rights, and if the definition of 'people' used was the normal political-sociological one, a major rearrangement of international law perceptions would have been created. In fact, that has not occurred and an international law concept of what constitutes a people for these purposes has been evolved, so that the 'self' in question must be determined within the accepted colonial territorial framework.[55]

Shaw's formulation does not apply neatly to the West Bank and Gaza Strip, as those areas never constituted a distinct, "colonially defined territorial unit."[56] The only such unit was the area comprising the Palestine Mandate. The United Nations General Assembly offered significant portions of that area – larger than the modern-day West Bank and Gaza Strip – to the Palestinians for self-determination in November 1947, but the Palestinians flatly rejected the offer. The Palestinians again rejected self-determination in December 1948, when they asked King Abdullah at the Jericho Conference to annex the West Bank. And they expressly disclaimed sovereignty over the West Bank and the Gaza Strip in the May 1964 PLO Covenant. All these prior acts undermine the modern-day Palestinian claim to self-determination in the same areas.

Moreover, UN Security Council Resolution 242 did not address the issue of Palestine, nor recognize a Palestinian right of self-determination. Cassese (1995), however, notes the United Nations in the ensuing years gradually proclaimed the existence of Palestinian "rights to self-determination," but "without specifying how this right should be implemented."[57]

This shift occurred without any legal or historical basis. The mere fact that the pro-Palestinian bloc at the UN mustered the votes to endorse this shift should be viewed as nothing more than an attempt to alter international law and history by administrative fiat.

In any event, the most important legal point is that the Palestinians negotiated at Oslo for no more than the *possibility* of future self-determination. Cassese (1995) reads the DOP very broadly, arguing it recognized "internal" self-determination, based on the establishment of the Palestinian Council. However, Cassese admits the DOP makes no provision for "external" self-determination:

> How will the right to external self-determination be exercised? The Declaration simply states that 'permanent status' of the West Bank and the Gaza Strip shall be the subject of negotiations between Israel and the 'Palestinian people representatives' and that the negotiations must start as soon as possible ... This means that the determination of the *international status* of the of the Palestinian territories currently occupied by Israel will be the subject of negotiations between the democratically elected Palestinians and the Israeli authorities ... Everything is left to the agreement of these two parties. In particular, the declaration does not spell out the possible final options: independent statehood free from any military or territorial servitudes; independent statehood subject to a set of servitudes or disabilities in favour of Israel (e.g., right of passage for Israeli troops or nationals, Israeli jurisdiction over Israeli settlements, the maintenance of Israeli military bases, the obligation for the Palestinians not to militarize certain areas, etc.); free integration into another State; or free association with another State. Nor does the Declaration specify whether the Palestinians will have to hold a referendum or plebiscite on the matter.[58]

The Oslo Accords remain in full force and effect. Thus, there are no "legal consequences" arising from the absence of self-determination during the interim period, even though the interim period has lasted longer than originally contemplated.

The Accords contemplate the Palestinians will be able to negotiate for the *possibility* of self-determination during the permanent status negotiations. Rather than asking the ICJ to intervene and disrupt the Oslo process, the General Assembly should instead encourage and offer good faith assistance to the parties to pursue the process consistent with the Oslo Accords, the Roadmap, and Security Council Resolutions 242 and 338.

Second, the General Assembly resolution asks the ICJ to determine the legal consequences arising from Israel's "prolonged occupation, settlement and annexation of the Palestinian territory occupied since 1967." The Oslo Accords once again determine the answers to this question. The Palestinians knowingly, voluntarily, and willingly agreed to *allow* the occupation to continue until such time as a permanent status deal would be reached. The Palestinians further agreed the settlements could remain in place pending the completion of the permanent status negotiations. Although the time frame to conclude the permanent status negotiations has run longer than originally contemplated, neither party has rescinded or revoked the Accords based on the lapse of time, or indeed on any other basis.

The concept of "prolonged" occupation is unknown to international law. The Hague Regulations of 1907 and the Fourth Geneva Convention of 1949 set forth the legal framework for maintaining the *status quo ante* of occupied territory until such time as a peace agreement or other means of ending the occupation may be reached. But neither instrument sets forth any time limit for occupation. Moreover, Security Council Resolution 242, which called for Israel to withdraw from territories "occupied in the recent conflict," placed no time frame or deadline for *when* the withdrawal should occur.

Nevertheless, Palestinian advocates in recent years have argued without citing any legal authority (other than arguments made by other Palestinian advocates) that any occupation exceeding ten years should be regarded as presumptively unlawful. For example, a recent UN publication, written for the purpose of influencing the ICJ's advisory ruling regarding the "prolonged occupation" argument, declared:

> [T]he present study highlights the positions of leading authorities on international law which consider that the practice of 'prolonged occupation' has related to occupations of no more than four or five years in length, such as Germany's four-year occupation of Belgium during World War I, or Germany's five-year occupation of Norway in World War II. Former United Nations Special Rapporteur Michael Lynk observes that modern occupations compliant with the principles of occupation law 'have not exceeded 10 years, including the American occupation of Japan, the Allied occupation of western Germany and the American-led occupation of Iraq.'[59]

But Lynk's statement and the General Assembly's reference to "prolonged" occupation completely ignores the UN's tolerance of Turkey's nearly 50-year occupation of Northern Cyprus, which Turkey invaded without provocation on 20 July 1974. The Security Council requested Turkey's withdrawal from Cyprus in Resolution 360 (16 August 1974), but since then neither the Security Council nor the General Assembly have demanded Turkey's withdrawal or otherwise condemned the occupation or described it as "prolonged."[60]

The UN likewise has never condemned Morocco's nearly 50-year occupation of most of the Western Sahara as "prolonged," and the Arab League recognizes Moroccan sovereignty over the occupied territory. Although the General Assembly condemned the Moroccan occupation in Resolution 35/19

(11 November 1980), neither it nor the Security Council has condemned the occupation since then.

Third, the General Assembly's December 2022 reference to "annexation of occupied Palestinian territory" is unclear. The only territories Israel annexed following the June 1967 war were the Golan Heights in 1981, formally part of Syria. Israel also annexed East Jerusalem and the Old City in 1980. But East Jerusalem and the Old City were never "Palestinian" territory. From the 1840s onward Jews comprised the largest identifiable population group in Jerusalem. The United Nations November 1947 partition plan called for the internationalization of Jerusalem. No part of the city was allocated to the proposed Palestinian state.

Following the 1948–1949 war Israel retained West Jerusalem and Jordan seized control of East Jerusalem and the Old City. Israel declared West Jerusalem its capital in 1950. Jordan held the West Bank and East Jerusalem until losing the areas to Israel in the June 1967 war.

Significantly, from 1948 to 1967 the Palestinians never laid claim to any portion of Jerusalem. Following the June 1967 War, the UN Security Council adopted Resolution 242, demanding Israel withdraw only "from territories occupied in the recent conflict," meaning East Jerusalem and the Old City. Implementing Resolution 242 would have meant returning East Jerusalem and the West Bank to Jordan, *not* the Palestinians. In the Oslo Accords, the PLO obtained no interim rights over East Jerusalem. The PLO agreed to defer any discussion of Jerusalem to the permanent status negotiations.

Moreover, the Israel-Jordan peace treaty of 1994 acknowledged Jordanian, but not Palestinian rights at the Muslim Holy sites in Jerusalem. The Treaty takes note of "the present special role of the Hashemite Kingdom of Jordan in Muslim Holy shrines in Jerusalem."[61] The Jordanian role was reaffirmed in a March 2023 Joint Communique issued by Israel, Jordan, Egypt, the United States and even the Palestinian Authority reiterating their "commitment of upholding unchanged the historic status quo at the Holy Sites in Jerusalem, both in word and in practice, and ... the importance of the Hashemite Custodianship/special role of the Hashemite Kingdom of Jordan."[62]

Therefore, it is fair to ask exactly how and when did East Jerusalem and the Old City morph into "Palestinian" territory? Interestingly, in 1979 the UN Security Council in Resolution 446 (22 March 1979) referred solely to "*the Arab territories* occupied since 1967, including Jerusalem." The following year, in Resolution 478 (22 August 1980), the Security Council added the word "Palestinian," modifying the formulation to read, "*the Palestinian and other Arab territories* occupied since June 1967, including Jerusalem." By December 2016, the Security Council in Resolution 2334 (23 December

2016) had dropped the word "Arab" and modified the formulation yet again to refer to "*the Palestinian territory* occupied since 1967, including East Jerusalem." But the mere change in formulation conferred no legal rights on the Palestinians regarding East Jerusalem.

Fourth, the General Assembly resolution asks the ICJ to determine the legal consequences arising from "measures aimed at altering the demographic composition, character, and status of the Holy City of Jerusalem, and from its adoption of related discriminatory legislation and measures."

The sweeping language of the General Assembly's request regarding Jerusalem is highly troubling. The reference to the "Holy City of Jerusalem" appears to encompass the entirety of the city, including West Jerusalem. Furthermore, what exactly is meant by the phrase "measures aimed at altering the demographic composition, character, and status of the Holy City of Jerusalem, and from its adoption of related discriminatory legislation and measures"? The Resolution nowhere provides any specificity regarding any such measures or legislation.

Moreover, the Palestinians obtained no concessions from Israel in the Oslo Accords that would impact Israel's sovereignty over West Jerusalem. Significantly, in recent years the Palestinian Authority has repeatedly laid claim only to East Jerusalem, despite their lack of any legal basis for so doing.

Furthermore, the Palestinians agreed at Oslo that the status of Jerusalem would be reserved for future negotiations as part of the eventual permanent status talks. Jerusalem will be the most sensitive and protracted issue for the final rounds of the permanent status negotiations. Jerusalem holds intense religious and emotional attachment for Muslims, Christians and Jews. The Temple Mount has been a flashpoint for decades. If there were ever a "compelling" reason for the ICJ to exercise its discretion and decline to issue an advisory opinion, surely it must be to avoid interfering in and expressing its own view regarding the permanent status of Jerusalem.

Therefore, the ICJ should refrain from stepping in and advising the United Nations regarding the permanent status of Jerusalem.

Unfortunately, however, the ICJ can be expected to disregard all the above arguments and simply adopt the position of the United Nations Committee on the Inalienable Rights of the Palestinian People, which concluded its recent report with the following diatribe against Israel:

> Whether the occupation is illegal *ab initio* or subsequently becomes illegal, the consequences should be the immediate, unconditional and total withdrawal of Israel's military forces; the withdrawal of colonial settlers; the repeal of all discriminatory laws; and the dismantling of the military administrative regime; with clear instructions that withdrawal for breach of an internationally wrongful act is not subject to negotiation. Full and commensurate reparations should be accorded to the affected Palestinian individuals, corporations and entities, for the generational harm caused

by Israel's land and property appropriations, house demolitions, pillage of natural resources, denial of return, and other war crimes and crimes against humanity orchestrated for the colonialist, annexationist aims of an illegal occupant.[63]

Concluding Comments

The Palestinians are legally bound by their agreements at Oslo. Unfortunately, they have spent most of the decades since Oslo undermining those agreements, except for their occasional security cooperation with Israel in portions of the West Bank.

The Palestinians knowingly and voluntarily agreed when they negotiated and signed the Oslo Accords that they would be legally barred from litigating against Israel at the international courts; from objecting to Israeli settlements in Area C, including expanding existing settlements and building new settlements; from initiating construction activity in Area C; from tacitly or expressly condoning terrorism and violence against Israel; from arguing that the mere duration of the Israeli occupation of portions of the West Bank is illegal; from laying claim to any portion of Jerusalem, except as part of their negotiation position during the permanent status process; from obtaining statehood during the ongoing interim period; and from using any means other than diplomacy to achieve their aspirations.

From the Israeli perspective, it is fair to ask whether the Palestinians can ever be trusted or relied upon to uphold their end of any future agreements that might be negotiated between the parties, especially the permanent status agreements contemplated by the Oslo Accords. As Shaw (2021) noted in his discussion of customary international law, "in the absence of a certain minimum belief that states will perform their treaty obligations in good faith, there is no reason for countries to enter into such obligations with one another."[64]

Shehadeh (1997) blames the significant Palestinian legal concessions at Oslo on the Palestinian political leadership's overarching goal of securing Israeli political recognition of the PLO above all other objectives. Shehadeh laments the lack of "clear strategy" for the Palestinians from a legal perspective. Shehadeh admits the Palestinians obtained no Israeli concessions regarding the West Bank settlements and other key issues. Shehadeh blames the Palestinian delegation for not doing enough to involve the Palestinian legal team in the negotiations.[65] As noted above, however, Mahmoud Abbas brought a Palestinian lawyer to Oslo to review and make changes to the draft documents.

The bottom line is that even if some Palestinians do not like the deal Arafat and Abbas negotiated and signed on their behalf at Oslo, they are still legally bound to comply. Palestinian leaders have had three decades to demonstrate their faithfulness to the principle that parties must respect their international agreements. Unfortunately, their failure to do so calls into question their willingness to abide by any future agreements with Israel.

Notes

1 M. Abbas, *Through Secret Channels* at 161–62 (Garnet, 1997) (the Palestinian delegation gave "attention to every word, sentence and expression. It was even necessary to scrutinize every comma and full stop so that we could eliminate the likelihood of fatal pitfalls occurring in the future ... the DOP documents were reviewed by our legal consultant, Taher Shash, whom we had sent to Oslo for this purpose just before they were initialed on 20 August 1993.").
2 *Declaration of Principles on Interim Self-Government Arrangements, Israel-Palestine Liberation Organization*, 13 Sept. 1993, 32 I.L.M. 1525 (1993).
3 Abbas, *op cit.* (describing intensity of negotiations from the Palestinian perspective); Y. Beilin, *Touching Peace: From the Oslo Accord to a Final Agreement* (Weidenfeld & Nicolson, 1995) (same, but from the Israeli perspective).
4 Letter from Yasser Arafat, Chairman, Palestine Liberation Organization, to Yitzhak Rabin, Prime Minister of Israel (9 Sept. 1993), https://www.un.org/unispal/document/auto-insert-205528/#:~:text=LETTER%20FROM%20YASSER%20ARAFAT%20TO%20PRIME%20MINISTER%20RABIN%3A&text=In%20firm%20conviction%20thereof%2C%20I,Council%20Resolutions%20242%20and%20338 (last accessed 30 Sept. 2023); Letter from Yitzhak Rabin, Prime Minister of Israel to Yasser Arafat, Chairman, Palestine Liberation Organization (9 Sept. 1993), https://www.un.org/unispal/document/auto-insert-205528/#:~:text=LETTER%20FROM%20YASSER%20ARAFAT%20TO%20PRIME%20MINISTER%20RABIN%3A&text=In%20firm%20conviction%20thereof%2C%20I,Council%20Resolutions%20242%20and%20338 (last accessed 30 Sept. 2023).

Letter from Yasser Arafat, Chairman, Palestine Liberation Organization, to Johan Jorgen Holst, Foreign Minister of Norway, https://www.un.org/unispal/document/auto-insert-205528/ (last accessed 21 Oct. 2023).
5 *Declaration of Principles on Interim Self-Government Arrangements, Israel-Palestine Liberation Organization*, 13 September 1993, 32 I.L.M. 1525 (1993).
6 *Agreement on the Gaza Strip and the Jericho Area*, 4 May 1994, 33 I.L.M. 622 (1994).
7 *Agreement on Preparatory Transfer of Powers and Responsibilities*, 29 Aug. 1994, 34 I.L.M. 455 (1994).
8 *The Israeli-Palestinian Interim Agreement on the West Bank and Gaza Strip*, 28 Sept. 1995, 36 I.L.M. 551 (1997).
9 *Protocol Concerning the Redeployment in Hebron, Israel-Palestine Liberation Organization*, 15 Jan. 1997, 36 I.L.M. 650 (1997).
10 *Note for the Record* (15 Jan. 1977), reprinted in G. Watson, *The Oslo Accords: International Law and the Israeli-Palestinian Peace Agreements* at 375–76 (Oxford Univ. Press, 2000), Appendix G.
11 *Wye River Memorandum*, 23 Oct. 1998, 37 I.L.M. 1251 (1998).
12 *The Sharm el-Sheikh Memorandum on Implementation Timeline of Outstanding Commitments of Agreements Signed and the Resumption of Permanent Status Negotiations*, 4 Sept. 1999, 38 I.L.M. 1465 (1999).
13 Oslo Interim Agreement, Arts. XVII(1)(a)(settlements to be deferred to permanent status negotiations), XXXI(5)(same), and XII(1)(Israel responsible for security of settlements and settlers)[emphasis added].
14 Sabel, *op. cit.* at 281.
15 *Id.*
16 United Nations Security Council, S/RES/242 (22 Nov. 1967).
17 United Nations Security Council, S/RES/338 (22 Nov. 1973).
18 *Declaration of Principles on Interim Self-Government Arrangements, Israel-Palestine Liberation Organization, 13 September 1993*, Agreed Minutes, Part B, Art. IV.1, 32 I.L.M. 1525 (1993).

19 *Israeli-Palestinian Interim Agreement on the West Bank and the Gaza Strip*, Article IX (5), 37 ILM (1997) 551 (8 Sept. 1995) [emphasis added].
20 Watson (2000), *op. cit.* at 284–85.
21 Letter dated 27 Dec. 1995 from the Permanent Representatives of the Russian Federation and the United States of America to the United Nations addressed to the Secretary-General; Letter dated 28 Dec. 1995 from the Permanent Representative of Israel to the United Nations addressed to the Secretary-General; Letter dated 19 Dec. 1995 from the Permanent Observer of Palestine to the United Nations addressed to the Secretary-General, available at https://www.un.org/unispal/document/auto-insert-185434/ (last accessed 29 Oct. 2023).
22 R. Lapidoth, *Israel and the Palestinians: Some Legal Issues*, Die Friedens-Warte, 76:2/3, 211–240 at 221 (2001).
23 *Agreement on Preparatory Transfer of Powers and Responsibilities* (29 Aug. 1994), Art. Xiii.3, 34 I.L.M. 455 (1994); *Israeli-Palestinian Interim Agreement on the West Bank and Gaza Strip* (28 Sept. 1995), Art. XXXI.6, 36 I.L.M. 551 (1997).
24 P. Malanczuk, *Some Basic Aspects of the Agreements between Israel and the PLO from the Perspective of International Law*, European Journal of International Law, 7:4, 485–500 at 489 (1996).
25 Watson, *op. cit.* at 101–02 ("the Oslo Accords are legally binding international agreements. Thus, there is a legal basis for the assertion that the Oslo process is 'irreversible.' ... Conversely, there is no basis for the claim that the Accords are non-binding 'political' documents.").
26 O. Corten and P. Klein (eds.), *The Vienna Convention on the Law of Treaties: A Commentary* (Vol. I) at 75 (Oxford Univ. Press, 2011).
27 R. Sabel, *International Law and the Arab-Israeli Conflict* at 272–75 (Cambridge Univ. Press, 2022).
28 *Id.* at 12.
29 Y. Blum, *From Camp David to Oslo*, Israel Law Review, 28:2–3, 211–235 at 212 (1994).
30 Vienna Convention on the Law of Treaties, 23 May 1969, UN Doc. A/CONF.39/27, Art. 3(a).
31 M. Shaw, *International Law* (9th ed.) at 788 (Cambridge Univ. Press, 2021).
32 Watson (2000), *op. cit.* at 101–02.
33 E. Benvenisti, *The Israeli-Palestinian Declaration of Principles: A Framework for Future Settlement*, European Journal of International Law, 4:4, 542–554 at 543–44 (1993).
34 T. Becker, *Self-Determination in Perspective: Palestinian Claims to Statehood and the Relativity of the Right to Self-Determination*, Israel Law Review, 32:2, 301–354, at 352 (1998) (emphasis added).
35 Watson (2000), *op. cit.* at 135.
36 A. Binyamin, Y. Admoni and Y. Hemo, *The War of Attrition, The Palestinian Authority's Program for Establishing a De Facto State in Judea and Samaria: Report on Land Status in Judea and Samaria* (Oct. 2022), https://www.regavim.org/wp-content/uploads/2022/10/War-of-Attrition-2022.pdf (last accessed 28 Oct. 2023).
37 R. Shehadeh, *From Occupation to Interim Accords: Israel and the Palestinian Territories* at 27 (Kluwer Law International, 1997). Shehadeh argues the Palestinian negotiators lacked a "clear strategy" at Oslo to leverage global sympathy and internal Israeli opposition to the settler movement. *Id.* at. 129–31.
38 Convention Respecting the Laws and Customs of War on Land, with Annex of Regulations, 18 Oct. 1907, TS 539. Article 42 of the Hague Regulations states, "Territory is considered occupied when it is actually placed under the authority of the hostile army. The occupation applies only to the territory where such authority is established, and in a position to assert itself." For further discussion of the Hague Regulations, see chapter 15 infra.

39 *Id.* at 548.
40 Watson (2000), *op. cit.* at 176.
41 B. Rubin, *Israel, Occupied Territories*, Max Planck Encyclopedias of International Law, para. 34 (2009).
42 Watson (2000), *op cit.* at 59, citing E. Wachsman, "Too Much in Return for Nothing," Jerusalem Post, 13 Dec. 1996.
43 Shaw (2021), *op. cit.* at 216. For a somewhat different view, *see* Rubin, *op. cit.* at para. 31 ("The Interim Agreement is part of a process that envisaged a development on the permanent status agreement within five years. The fact that this time frame has long expired may give rise to the contention that the Accords also expired at the end of the five-year period. Another legal argument would be that by now the Oslo Accords have lost their validity due to frequent violations from both sides. It is also arguable that the Accords have simply lost their political purpose and agreements of that kind, whether or not they are formally in force, are significant only as long as they are still on course towards achieving their political purpose.").
44 Benvenisti, *op. cit.* at 545.
45 United Nations, A/RES/77/247 (30 Dec. 2022).
46 Statute of the International Court of Justice, Art. 37, https://www.icj-cij.org/statute (last accessed 29 Oct. 2023).
47 *Maritime Delimitation and Territorial Questions between Qatar and Bahrain, Jurisdiction and Admissibility - Judgment*, I.C.J. Reports 1994, 112 at 121–25 (1 July 1994).
48 *Land and Maritime Boundary between Cameroon and Nigeria, Preliminary Objections, Judgment*, I.C.J. Reports 1998, pp. 275, 302–03 para. 56.
49 United Nations, A/RES/ES-10/14 (8 Dec. 2003).
50 *Legal Consequences of the Construction of a Wall in the Occupied Palestinian Territory*, Advisory Opinion, I.C.J. Reports 2004, 136, para. 44.
51 *Id.*, para. 53.
52 Abbas, *op. cit.* at 161–62.
53 ICJ *Wall* Advisory Opinion, *op. cit.* at 182–83 para. 118, citing *East Timor (Portugal v. Australia)*, Judgment, I.C.J. Reports 1995, 102, at para. 29.
54 Watson (2000), *op. cit.* at 270–71.
55 Shaw (2021), *op. cit.* at 233.
56 *Id.* at 234 ("To summarize: the principle of self-determination provides that the people of the colonially defines territorial unit in question may freely determine their own political status.").
57 A. Cassese, *Self-Determination of Peoples: A Legal Reappraisal* at 239 (Cambridge Univ. Press, 1995).
58 *Id.* at 244–45.
59 United Nations Committee on the Exercise of the Inalienable Rights of the Palestinian People, *Study on the Legality of the Israeli occupation of the Occupied Palestinian Territory, including East Jerusalem* at 8 (2023), https://www.un.org/unispal/document/ceirpp-legal-study2023/ (last accessed 30 Oct. 2023).
60 The Security Council in Resolution 541 (18 Nov. 1983) rejected Turkey's effort to declare the independence of Northern Cyprus but did not explicitly call for Turkey's withdrawal from the Island. No states currently recognize Northern Cyprus as a separate state, but several states maintain informal relations with the entity, and the Organization for Islamic Cooperation has granted it observer status.
61 Israel-Jordan Peace Treaty, UNTS 35325, Art. 9(2) (26 Oct. 1994).
62 *Joint Communique from the March 19 meeting in Sharm El Sheikh* (19 Mar. 2023), https://www.state.gov/joint-communique-from-the-march-19-meeting-in-sharm-el-sheikh/.
63 See n. 51, supra, at 102.
64 Shaw (2021), *op. cit.* at 788–89.
65 Shehadeh, *op. cit.* at 128–31.

PART III

Assessing the Palestinian Legal Case

The West Bank and the Gaza Strip

15

IS ISRAEL'S OCCUPATION OF THE WEST BANK ILLEGAL?

Introductory Comment

Israel engaged in a lawful act of anticipatory self-defense against Egypt in June 1967, following Egyptian threats to destroy Israel and various actions to make good on that threat, including closing the Straits of Tiran and expelling the United Nations Emergency Force (UNEF) from the Sinai area. Jordan responded to the events in Egypt by launching an unprovoked and illegal military assault against Israel, even though Israel had twice urged Jordan not to attack. Israel lawfully defended itself against the unprovoked Jordanian attack, capturing the West Bank and East Jerusalem in the ensuing war.

No one possessed sovereignty over the West Bank as of June 1967. Israel has occupied the West Bank ever since. Israel has applied the law of belligerent occupation to the West Bank on a *de facto* basis, without conceding the territory belongs to Jordan or the Palestinians as a matter of law.

Israel formally annexed East Jerusalem and the Old City in 1980, when the Knesset passed a Basic Law declaring "Jerusalem, complete and united, is the capital of Israel."[1]

Initial Occupation: Anticipatory Self-Defense and the Six-Day War

Arab Threats to Destroy Israel

The months of May and June 1967 were among the most consequential in the history of the Israeli-Palestinian conflict. On 14 May 1967, Egypt moved four brigades to the Israeli border, in response to Egyptian Field Marshal Abd al-Hakim Amer issuing Battle Order No. 1, ordering the army to raise

DOI: 10.4324/9781032686561-19

"the level of preparedness to full alert for war."[2] Three days later, Syrian forces massed in attack formations along the Golan Heights.

On 18 May 1967, Egypt's President Gamal Abdel Nasser expelled the UNEF from the Sinai Peninsula, removing the international community's protective buffer since the end of the 1956-57 Suez War. With UNEF gone, the Egyptian Army stood less than 50 miles from Tel Aviv.

On 18 May 1967, the "Voice of the Arabs" radio program in Egypt proclaimed:

> The Zionist barrack in Palestine is about to collapse and be destroyed. Every one of the hundred million Arabs has been living for the past nineteen years on one hope – to live to see the day Israel is liquidated...There is no life, no peace nor hope for the gangs of Zionism to remain in the occupied land ... As of today, there no longer exists an international emergency force to protect Israel ... The sole method we shall apply against Israel is a total war which will result in the extermination of Zionist existence.

On 19 May 1967 Cairo Radio proclaimed "It is our chance, Arabs, to direct a blow of death and annihilation to Israel, and all its presence in our Holy Land. It is a war for which we are awaiting and in which we will triumph."

On 22 May 1967 Egypt closed the Straits of Tiran, declaring that "under no circumstances will we allow the Israeli flag to pass through the Aqaba Gulf." Closing the Straits, Israel's only outlet to the Indian Ocean, constituted a *casus belli* for Israel. Cairo Radio announced the same day that "the Arab people is firmly resolved to wipe Israel off the map." Five days later Nasser declared, "our basic objective will be the destruction of Israel."

On 30 May 1967 Nasser signed a defense pact with Jordan's King Hussein. Nasser proclaimed "the armies of Egypt, Jordan, Syria and Lebanon are poised on the borders of Israel ... the Arabs are arranged for battle, the critical hour has arrived." The next day, Iraq moved troops and armor to Jordan.

In response to the steady escalation of Egyptian, Syrian, Iraqi, and Jordanian military threats and Egypt's closure of the Straits, Israel launched a preemptive strike against Egypt, destroying most of the Egyptian Air Force on the morning of 5 June 1967.

Jordanian troops opened fire and dropped bombs on Israeli positions in Jerusalem, Netanya, and elsewhere on the morning of 5 June, despite two separate Israeli pleas to Jordan not to attack.[3]

Two days later Israel captured East Jerusalem and broke the blockade of Straits of Tiran. By 8 June Israel had captured the entire West Bank. On 10 June Israel captured the Golan Heights.

Self-Defense Against Jordan

Article 2(4) of the United Nations Charter obligates nations to "refrain in their international relations from the threat or use of force against the territorial integrity or political independence of any State, or in any other manner inconsistent with the purposes of the United Nations."

Jordan violated Article 2(4) and the April 1949 armistice agreement when it launched an unprovoked military attack against Israel on 5 June 1967, even after Israel had twice urged Jordan to refrain from launching war.

Article 51 of the Charter sets forth a self-defense exception to the rule against armed aggression, providing, "Nothing in the present Charter shall impair the inherent right of individual or collective self-defense if an armed attack occurs against a Member of the United Nations." Israel acted fully within its rights in responding militarily to Jordan's attacks, especially given the warnings Israel had conveyed to Jordan to stay out of the war.

Therefore, as discussed below, Israel acquired possession of the West Bank and East Jerusalem as the result of a lawful act of self-defense against Jordan's unprovoked attack on Israel.

Anticipatory Self-Defense Against Egypt

Israel also acted in lawful self-defense against Egypt, in response to Egypt's hostile action in closing the Straits of Tiran, ejecting the UNEF peacekeepers from the Sinai Peninsula, and threatening to attack Israel. Nevertheless, questions have arisen as to whether those Egyptian actions violated Article 2(4) of the UN Charter and triggered Israel's Article 51 self-defense rights; or, assuming Egypt had not yet crossed the line and violated Article 2(4), whether Israel had the right to launch a preemptive strike against the Egyptian Air Force as a legitimate act of "anticipatory self-defense."

International custom and practice have long permitted anticipatory self-defense in circumstances where an armed attack appears imminent. The concept derives from the so-called "*Caroline* Doctrine." The *Caroline* was a privately owned American steamboat attempting to transport supplies to Canadian insurgents. A British force intercepted the *Caroline* in United States waters on 29 December 1837. The British force fired on the *Caroline*, forcibly seized it, set it on fire, and sent it plunging over Niagara Falls. Two Americans died in the attack.[4]

Britain, in an exchange of letters with US Secretary of State Daniel Webster, defended the attack on the *Caroline* as a justified act of self-defense or self-preservation. Webster, however, rejected Britain's assertion of a broad, peremptory right of anticipatory self-defense. He argued Britain had failed to demonstrate the *Caroline* posed an "instant, overwhelming [threat], and leaving no choice of means, and no moment for deliberation." Webster emphasized Britain had failed to demonstrate any necessity for the attack. Nor had Britain acted in proportion to whatever threat it perceived from the *Caroline's* activity.[5]

Webster's formulation, which left open the possibility of anticipatory self-defense in certain circumstances, became known as the "*Caroline* doctrine." Rogoff and Collins (1990) describe the doctrine as follows:

> [U]se of force by one nation against another is permissible as a self-defense action only if force is both necessary and proportionate. The first of these conditions, necessity, means that resort to force in response to an armed attack, *or the imminent threat of an armed attack*, is allowed only when an alternative means of redress is lacking. The second condition, proportionality, is linked closely to necessity in requiring that a use of force in self-defense must not exceed in manner or aim the necessity provoking it.[6]

Britain reasserted the *Caroline* doctrine many years later in the 1893 *Fur Seal Arbitration*. Britain argued anticipatory self-defense could be justified in emergency situations, "when there is no time for deliberation, no time for contrivance, no time for warning, no time for diplomatic expostulation."[7]

The early commentator Westlake (1904) endorsed the legality of anticipatory self-defense. Westlake argued a state has the legal right to use force

> by preventive means if in its conscientious judgment necessary, against attack by another State, threat of attack, or preparations or other conduct from which an intention to attack may reasonably be apprehended. In doing so it will be acting in a manner intrinsically defensive even though externally aggressive.[8]

A later commentator (Ross, 1947) explained:

> Even internal law recognizes that acts committed in self-defense to avert an illegitimate act which has 'commenced' or is impending are 'legitimate.' In this situation it would evidently be impossible to expect that the party attacked should wait and try to obtain his rights by asserting them before the courts. The same must be all the more valid in International Law where there is no organized administration of justice to turn to.[9]

Bowett (1958), in his treatise on self-defense and international law, urged a broad interpretation of the right of anticipatory self-defense:

> [T]he right [of self-defense] under traditional international law, has always been 'anticipatory,' that is to say its exercise was valid against imminent

> as well as actual attacks or dangers ... No state can be expected to await an initial attack which, in the present state of armaments, may well destroy the state's capacity for further resistance and so jeopardize its very existence.[10]

Quigley (2002/2003, 2013), however, rejects the *Caroline* doctrine as a basis for anticipatory self-defense, arguing the doctrine recognizes solely the defense of necessity.[11]

Anticipatory Self-Defense Against Egypt: The United Nations Charter

As noted above, the reference to "inherent" rights of self-defense would suggest Article 51 was not intended to supersede preexisting customary international law, including the *Caroline* doctrine.[12]

Bowett (1958) noted the interpretational difficulty that would arise if Article 2(4) were construed to limit the Article 51 right to self-defense solely to situations where an actual armed attack first occurred:

> [T]he question of who decides when an armed attack occurs ... a question determined by the Charter, loses any special significance, for the right of self-defense is not confined to that eventuality. The question is in fact a broader one as to who decides, in the first place, whether the occasion has arisen which justifies the exercise of the right of self-defense. In the nature of things this must be a decision for the state invoking the right, but this does not imply that the states unilaterally determines the legality of the action as is taken, for this final decision ought properly to be made by an impartial body and not by the parties concerned.[13]

Bowett offered as one example Pakistan's defense of its 1950 invasion of Kashmir as a legitimate exercise of the right of anticipatory self-defense against the possibility of an Indian invasion.[14]

Thus, Article 51 permits both actual self-defense in response to an armed attack, such as Jordan's 5 June 1967 attack against Israel, and anticipatory self-defense when such an attack reasonably appears imminent. Article 51 therefore does not require the party invoking self-defense to wait until the first bomb has been dropped on its people or territory.

Rogoff and Collins (1990) likewise argue the word "inherent" in Article 51 of the United Nations Charter incorporates and refines prior international law, including the *Caroline* Doctrine:

> It is clear that nations faced with a perceived danger of immediate, large-scale attack cannot be expected to passively await the attack. It is equally clear that the international community cannot accept a rule that allows

> anticipatory strikes in the absence of a clear and impending attack. The great value of the Caroline doctrine is that it allows use of force only in situations in which the imminence of attack is so clear and the danger is so great that defensive action is absolutely necessary.[15]

The Attorney General of the United Kingdom agreed with this view in answering a question during a House of Lords debate in April 2004:

> It is argued by some that the language of Article 51 provides for a right of self-defence only in response to an actual armed attack. However, it has been the consistent position of successive United Kingdom Governments over many years that the right of self-defence under international law includes the right to use force where an armed attack is imminent. It is clear that the language of Article 51 was not intended to create a new right of self-defence. Article 51 recognises the inherent right of self-defence that states enjoy under international law. That can be traced back to the "Caroline" incident in 1837... . It is not a new invention. The charter did not therefore affect the scope of the right of self-defence existing at that time in customary international law, which included the right to use force in anticipation of an imminent armed attack.[16]

Brownlie, however, disputes the legality of anticipatory self-defense:

> It can only be concluded that the view that Article 51 does not permit anticipatory action is correct and that the arguments to the contrary are either unconvincing or based on inconclusive pieces of evidence ... the beginning of an armed attack is a condition precedent for resort to force in self-defense. Anticipatory self-defense is unlawful; an attack must have commenced.[17]

Nevertheless, Brownlie concedes that "[p]reventive action in case of actual and imminent breaches of neutrality has been lawful until very recently and is still lawful in the opinion of a substantial number of jurists."[18]

Self-Defense, Anticipatory Self-Defense and the Six-Day War

Israeli Foreign Minister Golda Meir gave notice in a 1 March 1957 speech to the United Nations that any future "interference, by armed force, with ships of the Israeli flag exercising free and innocent passage in the Gulf of Aqaba and through the Straits of Tiran" would be treated as an act of war. Egypt's President Nasser, however, in his own speech ten days later (11 March 1957) rejected Meir's position.[19]

Scholars, therefore, have differed on whether Egypt's closure of the Straits of Tiran on 22 May 1967 provided a reasonable basis for Israel to invoke the right of self-defense or anticipatory self-defense.[20]

Some scholars argue Israel was not dependent on navigation through the Straits, and used the closing of the Straits as a pretext for launching the June 1967 war. Others have noted Israel could reasonably argue the closing of the Straits, with the resulting blockade of the Israeli port of Eilat, by itself constituted an act of "force" by Egypt in violation of Article 2(4) of the United Nations Charter and the January 1949 armistice agreement, thereby permitting Israel immediately to invoke its actual (rather than anticipatory) self-defense rights under Article 51.[21]

Regardless how important the Straits were to Israeli navigation, as a matter of law Egypt's unilateral decision to deny Israel access to the Straits posed a threat to Israel. Some nevertheless argue Israel was the aggressor in the June 1967 war, and it violated Article 2(4) of the United Nations Charter when it fired the first shot against the Egyptian air force. But the United Nations itself overwhelmingly rejected two post-war resolutions (one Soviet, the other Albanian) in June and early July 1967 that would have condemned Israel as the aggressor.[22]

The Security Council also implicitly recognized several months later in Resolution 242 that Israel had acted lawfully when it launched the first strike in the June 1967 war, as the Security Council affirmed "the necessity for guaranteeing freedom of navigation through international waterways in the area."[23]

In any event, the other threatening moves Egypt, Syria, Iraq, and Jordan made toward Israel during May 1967 provided more than adequate justification for Israel to protect itself by striking first. As Shaw (2021) has noted, a series of activities forming part of a sequence or chain of events may be taken into account, rather than just the immediate and most recent provocation, in justifying the use of anticipatory self-defense.[24]

Israel could reasonably have viewed the Egyptian, Iraqi and Syrian troop movements, the Egypt–Jordan defense pact, and Cairo's announcement that the Egyptian, Iraqi, Syrian, Lebanese, and Jordanian armies were on the verge of launching war as constituting imminent threats to the country justifying the anticipatory use of force to defend itself.

As Gerson (1978) noted:

> Israel's right of passage through the Straits of Tiran was guaranteed by international law. Closure of the Straits, in itself, may or may not have been sufficient justification for initiating a general war under the terms of the Charter ... But in the instant case it was not only closure of an international waterway that occurred, but also the issuance of credible threats of 'all out' war against the target state, should it attempt to secure its right of free

> passage by either a forceful opening or reprisals. In such a situation where closure is coupled with a threat of war, it is submitted that international law allows the blockaded state, upon exhaustion of peaceful avenues for redress [which Israel had attempted unsuccessfully to do], to resort to war ... maintenance of the status quo was equivalent to slow strangulation.[25]

Moreover, the 1948 precedent supported Israel's apprehensions of imminent attack. The same four neighboring Arab countries – Egypt, Jordan, Lebanon, and Syria – plus Iraq and Saudi Arabia, had all threatened war for months following the United Nations November 1947 partition vote. Those nations made good on those threats when they launched military attacks against Israel immediately following the 14 May 1948 Israeli declaration of independence.

Given the 1948 precedent, combined with the Arab threats and war preparations during May 1967, Israel's apprehension of an imminent Arab attack was well-founded. Israel, therefore, had more than ample basis under both Article 51 of the United Nations Charter and the customary international law doctrine of anticipatory self-defense to strike first in June 1967.

As Schwebel (1970) argued:

> The facts of the June, 1967, "Six Day War" demonstrate that Israel reacted defensively against the threat and use of force against her by her Arab neighbors. This is indicated by the fact that Israel responded to Egypt's prior closure of the Straits of Tiran, its proclamation of a blockade of the Israeli port of Elath, and the manifest threat of the U.A.R.'s use of force inherent in its massing of troops in Sinai, coupled with its ejection of UNEF. It is indicated by the fact that, upon Israeli responsive action against the U.A.R., Jordan initiated hostilities against Israel. It is suggested as well by the fact that, despite the most intense efforts by the Arab states and their supporters, led by the Premier of the Soviet Union, to gain condemnation of Israel as an aggressor by the hospitable organs of the United Nations, those efforts were decisively defeated. The conclusion to which these facts lead is that the Israeli conquest of Arab and Arab-held territory was defensive rather than aggressive conquest.[26]

Quigley disagrees, advancing a classic form of unsupported lawfare argumentation by claiming Israel's June 1967 leaders "are individually responsible for the crime of aggression" against Egypt.[27]

The better view, is that Israel's preemptive strike against Egypt on 5 June 1967 was lawful and justified under Article 51 of the United Nations Charter and longstanding international legal notions of the right of states to invoke anticipatory self-defense when faced with imminent attack.[28]

Israel replaced Jordan as the occupant of the West Bank and East Jerusalem in a lawful exercise of self-defense under Article 51 of the Charter, in response to Jordan's unprovoked military attacks against Israel. Moreover, Israel replaced Egypt as the occupant of the Sinai Peninsula and the Gaza Strip through the lawful exercise of either self-defense under Article 51 or anticipatory self-defense under Article 51 and customary international law.

As Higgins (1970) argued:

> There is nothing in either the Charter or general international law which leads one to suppose that military occupation, pending a peace treaty, is illegal ... The law of military occupation, with its complicated web of rights and duties, remains entirely relevant, and until such time as the Arab nations agree to negotiate a peace treaty, Israel is in legal terms entitled to remain in the territories she now holds.[29]

United Nations Security Council Resolution 242

On 22 November 1967, the United Nations Security Council unanimously adopted Resolution 242, calling for a return to the *status quo ante* and various protections for all parties. The key language included the following:

> The Security Council ... Affirms that the fulfilment of Charter principles requires the establishment of a just and lasting peace in the Middle East which should include the application of both the following principles: (i) Withdrawal of Israel armed forces *from territories occupied in the recent conflict*; (ii) Termination of all claims or states of belligerency and respect for and acknowledgement of the sovereignty, territorial integrity and political independence of every State in the area and their right to live in peace within secure and recognized boundaries free from threats or acts of force; ... Affirms further the necessity (a) For guaranteeing freedom of navigation through international waterways in the area; (b) For achieving a just settlement of the refugee problem; (c) For guaranteeing the territorial inviolability and political independence of every State in the area through measures including the establishment of demilitarized zones.[30]

Huber (2021) explained the drafting process that led to the final language of Resolution 242:

> In direct response to the 1967 war, several draft resolutions circulated. The "three power draft" by India, Mali, and Nigeria stated that the "occupation or acquisition of territory by military conquest is inadmissible under the Charter of the United Nations and consequently Israel's armed forces should withdraw from all the territories occupied as a result of the recent conflict" (UNSC 2007). In stark contrast to this draft, the one presented by the US called for the "withdrawal of armed forces from occupied

> territories." A last-minute Soviet draft called for a withdrawal to the lines preceding the outbreak of hostilities. The UK then produced a draft that tried to bridge these differences and became the basis of Resolution 242, the land for peace resolution adopted under Chapter VI of the UN Charter, which asserts "the inadmissibility of the acquisition of territory by war" and calls for the withdrawal of Israeli armed forces from territories ("the territories" in the French version) occupied in recent conflict, and respect for the sovereignty, territorial integrity, and political independence of every state in the area and the right to live in peace within secure and recognized boundaries.[31]

Huber further noted that Resolution 242 conditioned Israel's withdrawal "from territories" on Arab recognition of Israel's right to exist. Huber also concedes the Resolution "implicitly made the 1949 armistice agreements borders Israel's borders." Nor does the Resolution say anything regarding the Palestinians.

Resolution 242 has gained broad acceptance internationally, and among Israel and the Arab world, including the Palestinian Authority. Nevertheless, the language of Resolution 242 creates ambiguity regarding the legality of Israel's replacement of Jordan and Egypt as occupant of the West Bank and Gaza Strip.

First, the language of Resolution 242 only requires Israel to withdraw "from territories," but not from "the territories" or "all territories" occupied in the June 1967 conflict. The omission of "the" and "all" therefore must be viewed as deliberate.[32] Thus, an argument can be made that Resolution 242 requires Israeli withdrawal from merely some, but *not* all territories captured in the June 1967 war. If that is the correct interpretation, then arguably Israel has *already* complied with Resolution 242, given that it has withdrawn from the entire Sinai Peninsula, the entire Gaza Strip, and portions of the West Bank and Golan Heights.[33]

As Lapidoth (1992) explained:

> The interpretation according to which the Resolution does not call for a full withdrawal of all Israeli forces from all the territories occupied in 1967 is also in line with pronouncements by various diplomats who were involved in the adoption of the Resolution and in its interpretation.39 The gist of the withdrawal clause is that '[w]hen peace is made, the Resolution calls for Israeli withdrawal to 'secure and recognized' boundaries.'[34]

In a later article, Lapidoth (2011) explained, "[t]he English version of the withdrawal clause requires only "withdrawal from territories," not from "all" territories, nor from "the" territories."[35] This interpretation, oddly enough, finds support in the Arab League's Khartoum Resolutions of 1 September 1967.[36] Those resolutions are remembered for the League's "no peace with Israel, no recognition of Israel, no negotiations with it." But the League also called upon Israel to withdraw only "from the Arab lands which have been occupied *since the aggression of June 5*," meaning *not* from West Jerusalem or any lands Israel had captured in prior conflicts, such as the Arab-designated areas it captured in the 1948–1949 war. Indeed the League rejected the Palestinian delegation's request for language that would have reached back prior to June 1967.[37]

Second, although Resolution 242 calls for Israel to withdraw from territories "occupied in the recent conflict," it places no time frame or deadline for *when* the withdrawal should occur. This language, as noted in Chapter 14, undermines the argument that Israel's occupation of the West Bank is illegal based solely on its "prolonged" duration.

Third, Resolution 242 has often been described as the first articulation of the "land for peace" formulation, because the "withdrawal from territories" language appears prior to the "peace" language. But despite the sequential wording, the Resolution does not specify whether withdrawal must precede peace, or whether peace must precede withdrawal, or whether the two events must occur simultaneously. Indeed, a reasonable argument could be made, especially in light of the Arab League's "three nos" at Khartoum that pre-dated Resolution 242 by almost three months, that withdrawal need not occur until the other conditions specified in the Resolution have also occurred, especially

> [t]ermination of all claims or states of belligerency and respect for and acknowledgement of the sovereignty, territorial integrity and political independence of every State in the area and their right to live in peace within secure and recognized boundaries free from threats or acts of force.

Accordingly, a reasonable argument could be made that Resolution 242 contemplated "peace for land," rather than "land for peace." Under this interpretation, the requirement for Israeli withdrawal from the West Bank, therefore, would not be triggered until *all* surrounding Arab countries terminate the state of belligerency with Israel. Unfortunately, that has not yet occurred, as Lebanon, Syria, Iraq, and Saudi Arabia remain averse to making peace with Israel. Therefore, Israel's legal obligation under Resolution 242 to withdraw has not yet arisen.[38] As Gerson (1978) notes:

> A lawful entrant has a right of occupation ... pending conclusion of a peace treaty or its functional equivalent. Any other rule would impose no sanction on aggressive behavior and thus defeat the basic quest of international law, or any law, in distinguishing lawful from unlawful behavior.

> A rule or policy requiring lawful entrants to relinquish gains in bargaining power gained in reacting against unlawful behavior would condone aggression and penalize defensive action.[39]

The Israeli Occupation: Lawful "Belligerent Occupation," or Outright Illegal?

The 1907 Hague Regulations and the 1949 Geneva Convention

Under international law, a party who militarily occupies part or all of another country's territory is deemed a "belligerent occupant." As Shaw (2021) explains:

> The military occupation of enemy territory is termed 'belligerent occupation' and international law establishes a legal framework concerning the legal relations of occupier and occupied. There are two key conditions for the establishment of an occupation in this sense: first, that the former government is no longer capable of publicly exercising its authority in the area in question; and secondly, that the occupying power is in a position to substitute its own authority for that of the former government.[40]

The law of belligerent occupation is embodied primarily in two international instruments. The first instrument comprised the annex to the Hague Convention (II) of 1899. That Convention was revised in the 1907 Hague Convention (IV) on Land Warfare. The accompanying Regulations to the 1907 Convention (Articles 42–56) address the definition of occupation and the international humanitarian law norms relative to occupied territories.[41]

The second international instrument addressing the law of belligerent occupation is the Fourth Geneva Convention on the Protection of Civilian Persons in Time of War. Article 49 of that Convention says, "[t]he Occupying Power shall not deport or transfer parts of its own civilian population into the territory it occupies."

The law of belligerent occupation is part of the law of international armed conflict and international humanitarian law. International humanitarian law was once viewed as reflecting only the Geneva Conventions, but more recently is acknowledged as encompassing both "Geneva Law" and "Hague Law." As the ICJ explained in the *Nuclear Weapons* Advisory Opinion, the two branches "have become so closely interrelated that they are considered to have gradually formed one single complex system, known today as international humanitarian law."[42]

The basic purpose of both the Hague Regulations and Article 49 of the Fourth Geneva Convention is to ensure the occupant preserves, to the extent reasonably possible and consistent with military necessity and self-defense, the pre-war status of the occupied areas until such time as a final resolution of the conflict is reached. As the ICJ noted in its 2004 Advisory Opinion regarding the Israel-West Bank Wall of Separation (the *Wall* Advisory Opinion):

> Whilst the drafters of the Hague Regulations of 1907 were as much concerned with protecting the rights of a State whose territory is occupied, as with protecting the inhabitants of that territory, the drafters of the Fourth Geneva Convention sought to guarantee the protection of civilians in time of war, regardless of the status of the occupied territories.[43]

Thus, for example, Article 43 of the Hague Regulations provides:

> The authority of *the legitimate power* having in fact passed into the hands of the occupant, the latter shall take all the measures in his power to restore, and ensure, as far as possible, public order and safety, while respecting, unless absolutely prevented, the laws in force in the country.[44]

Therefore, the Hague Regulations are intended to preserve, as far as possible, the pre-war status of territories under belligerent occupation. The regulations contemplated the ousted party would retain sovereignty over the occupied territory. The regulations thus were intended to ensure sovereignty did not pass from the ousted party to the occupying party. As Gerson (1978) notes, the "primary interests sought to be protected in the Hague Regulations were those of the ousted power."[45] Thus, the predominant theme "was the provisional character of the occupation, wherein the ousted power retains sovereignty, his authority being merely in a state of abeyance."[46]

Notwithstanding the above principles, the law of belligerent occupation does not regard such occupation as illegal. Instead, occupation is viewed as a temporary condition, usually ending with a peace treaty or other restoration of the status quo ante.[47] Graber (1949) argues "occupation is a merely a matter of fact which gives authority to the occupant because he has the physical force to exercise it. But the occupant is not rightfully substituted for the legal sovereign."[48]

Applicability of the Hague Regulations and the Geneva Convention to the West Bank and Gaza

The Jordanian and Egyptian Occupations, 1948–1967. Article 43 of the Hague Regulations applies to occupations where "[t]he authority of *the legitimate power* ... [has] passed into the hands of the occupant." The Fourth Geneva Convention applies only to situations involving "partial or total occupation *of the territory of a High Contracting Party.*"

As discussed in Chapter 4, the last party to have any claim of sovereignty over the West Bank and Gaza Strip was the Ottoman Empire, which ruled the area from 1517 to 1917. Although Britain defeated the Empire and ousted it from Palestine in December 1917, sovereignty did not pass to the United Kingdom.

The Hague Regulations would have applied to Palestine during Britain's military occupation between 1917 and 1923. Turkey retained sovereignty over Palestine during those years of British occupation, until Turkey formally relinquished sovereignty in the 1923 Treaty of Lausanne. But no one replaced Turkey as sovereign. The League of Nations did not gain sovereignty over Palestine. Nor did the League purport to confer sovereignty on Britain in its capacity as Mandatory for Palestine, or on anyone else.

The United Nations eventually offered sovereignty to the Arabs and Jews over separate portions of Palestine in November 1947. The Jews accepted; the Arabs rejected. The 1949 armistice agreement did not confer sovereignty over the West Bank on Jordan. Nor did sovereignty over the West Bank pass to Jordan as a result of Jordan's occupation and purported annexation between 1948 and 1967. The June 1967 war changed nothing, as Israel did not acquire sovereignty over the West Bank when it replaced Jordan as the occupant. Nor did Israel acquire sovereignty over the Gaza Strip when it replaced Egypt as the occupant between 1967 and 2005.

Thus, from the moment Turkey signed the Treaty of Lausanne until today, the West Bank and Gaza Strip have existed in a sovereignty vacuum.

Therefore, Jordan could not be said to have displaced a "legitimate power," or to have partially or totally occupied the territory "of a High Contracting Party" when it occupied the West Bank between 1948 and 1967. Accordingly, neither the 1907 Hague Regulations nor the 1949 Geneva Convention would have applied to the Jordanian occupation of the West Bank between 1948 and 1967, nor would the occupation have been deemed a "belligerent occupation" subject to the rules of those international legal instruments.

Gerson (1973) takes a different view of Jordan's status in the West Bank between 1948 and 1973, choosing to characterize Jordan not as a belligerent occupant but instead as a "trustee-occupant," based on the Palestinian Arabs' request for and/or consent to Jordanian occupation. In that capacity, Jordan would not have been constricted by the Hague Regulations and the Geneva Convention, and would have enjoyed more power to make changes to West Bank laws and institutions.[49] Gerson further argues Israel should be viewed as a successor trustee-occupant, having stepped into Jordan's shoes in June 1967.[50]

The Israeli Occupation. When Israel in June 1967 replaced Jordan as the occupant of the West Bank, Israel had not displaced either a "legitimate power" or acquired the territory of a High Contracting Party. Thus, neither the 1907 Hague Regulations nor the 1949 Geneva Convention would seem to apply to Israel's occupation, just as neither instrument had previously applied to the Jordanian occupation.

On the other hand, if Israel were deemed a belligerent occupant subject to the requirements of both international legal instruments, then the same would have been true of the prior Jordanian occupation, unless Gerson's characterization of the Jordanian occupation as merely that of a "trustee-occupant" is correct.

Therefore, it is at best unclear whether the Hague Regulations and Article 49 of the Fourth Geneva Convention apply to Israel's occupation of the West Bank, as the area had not been captured from a sovereign party.

As Blum (1968) noted:

> The legal standing of Israel in the territories in question is thus that of a State which is lawfully in control of territory in respect of which no other States can show a better title. Or, if it is preferred to state the matter in terms of belligerent occupation, then the legal standing of Israel in the territories in question is at the very least that of a belligerent occupant of territory in respect of which Jordan is not entitled to the reversionary rights of a legitimate sovereign.[51]

Israel, for its part, has never admitted the *de jure* application of either the Hague Regulations or the Fourth Geneva Convention to the West Bank, although it has applied the international humanitarian law norms of both conventions on a *de facto* basis to the West Bank and Gaza Strip, even following Israel's 2005 unilateral withdrawal from Gaza.[52] As the Israel Supreme Court stated in the *Alfei Menashe* case:

> The legal meaning of this view is twofold: first, Israeli law does not apply in these areas. They have not been "annexed" to Israel. Second, the legal regime which applies in these areas is determined by public international law regarding belligerent occupation [citation omitted.] In the center of this public international law stand the ... Hague Regulations. These regulations are a reflection of customary international law. The law of belligerent occupation is also laid out in ... the Fourth Geneva Convention. The State of Israel has declared that it practices the humanitarian parts of this convention. In light of that declaration on the part of the government of Israel, we see no need to reexamine the government's position.[53]

Dinstein (2019), however, rejects the official Israeli interpretation of the Geneva Convention as inapplicable on a *de jure* basis to Israel's occupation of the West Bank. Dinstein's analysis begins with the "shall also" clause of the second paragraph of Article 2:

> The Convention *shall also apply to all cases of partial or total occupation of the territory of a High Contracting Party*, even if the said occupation meets with no armed resistance.

Dinstein argues the "shall also" clause renders the Convention applicable to Israel on a *de jure* basis, noting,

> [t]he general rule is stated in the first paragraph (which does not include the words 'territory of a High Contracting Party'), and the second paragraph (which does) relates only to the exceptional scenario of an occupation that meets with no armed resistance.[54]

The ICJ agreed with Dinstein in the *Wall* Advisory Opinion:

> The object of the second paragraph of Article 2 is not to restrict the scope of application of the Convention, as defined by the first paragraph, by excluding therefrom territories not falling under the sovereignty of one of the contracting parties. This interpretation reflects the intention of the drafters of the Fourth Geneva Convention to protect civilians who find themselves, in whatever way, in the hands of the occupying Power.[55]

Dinstein further notes that despite the ICJ's harsh criticism in the *Wall* Advisory Opinion of some of Israel's actions during the occupation, the Court conspicuously 'refrained from characterizing the Israeli occupation as "illegal."'[56] Indeed, as Dinstein accurately observes, the "legality" of occupation does not depend on the legality or illegality of the events giving rise to the occupation. Even an unlawful use of force resulting in an occupation binds the occupier to observe the norms of the Hague Regulations and the Fourth Geneva Convention.

Both the Israeli government and the Israel Supreme Court have treated Israel's status in the West Bank as that of a *de facto* belligerent occupant.[57] The government has also voluntarily observed the humanitarian norms of the 1949 Geneva Conventions and the Hague Regulations.[58]

As the Legal Advisor to the Foreign Office noted in a 1980 memorandum, "we would prefer not to refer to the 'illegal occupation' of Arab territories in so far as this might imply that the Israeli occupation has from the outset been or is in itself illegal."[59]

Kretzmer (2012) describes the early views of the Israel military and legal establishments following the June 1967 war regarding the status of the West Bank:

> In a military order promulgated by the military commanders of the various fronts when the IDF forces entered the [occupied territories] in 1967, military tribunals were established to try local residents accused of security offences. That military order stated expressly that the military courts were to apply the provisions of the Fourth Geneva Convention, thus reflecting the view of army lawyers that all the territories were subject to the law of

> belligerent occupation. However, soon after the 1967 War ended, voices were heard both in political quarters and among a number of academic lawyers in Israel that the West Bank and the Gaza Strip, both of which had been part of British Mandatory Palestine, should not be regarded as occupied territories. Under the influence of these voices, a few months after the war ended the military commanders made an amendment to the military order, deleting the provision that mentioned the Fourth Geneva Convention. The Government of Israel adopted the position that the status of the West Bank and Gaza was unclear and that in all events it was questionable whether the Fourth Geneva Convention applied there. At the same time the government declared that the IDF would respect the humanitarian provisions of the Convention.[60]

Moreover, as noted above regarding Resolution 242's lack of a deadline, the mere temporal duration of Israel's occupation does not render it "illegal." The UN General Assembly in Resolution 77/247 (30 December 2022) referred to Israel's "prolonged" occupation as creating a legal issue. But the Hague Regulations place no time limit on occupation. In addition, the UN has never condemned Turkey's nearly 50-year occupation of Northern Cyprus as "prolonged." The Security Council requested Turkey's withdrawal from Cyprus in Resolution 360 (16 August 1974), but since then neither the Security Council nor the General Assembly have demanded Turkey's withdrawal or otherwise condemned the occupation or described it as "prolonged."[61]

The UN likewise has never condemned Morocco's nearly 50-year occupation of most of the Western Sahara as "prolonged," and the Arab League recognizes Moroccan sovereignty over the occupied territory. Although the General Assembly condemned the Moroccan occupation in Resolution 35/19 (11 November 1980), neither it nor the Security Council has condemned the occupation since then.

Assessment

Israel replaced Jordan as the occupant of the West Bank in a lawful act of self-defense following Jordan's unprovoked and illegal military attack against Israel on 5 June 1967. Israel also replaced Egypt as the occupant of the Gaza Strip in June 1967 as the result of the lawful exercise of anticipatory self-defense. Israel's subsequent occupation of both the West Bank and Gaza Strip was lawful. Even if Israel's preemptive use of force in June 1967 against Egypt were somehow deemed unlawful, that would not vitiate the legality of Israel's occupation of the West Bank.

Israel's precise status as occupant and the related questions regarding the applicability of the 1907 Hague Regulations and 1949 Geneva Convention are not free from doubt. Neither Jordan nor Egypt enjoyed sovereignty over the West Bank and Gaza Strip. Thus, Israel cannot be said to have captured those territories from a legitimate sovereign. Accordingly, the Hague Regulations most likely do not apply. Moreover, the Palestinians themselves were not a "High Contracting Party" to the 1949 Geneva Convention, meaning the provisions of that instrument likewise are not applicable.

Nevertheless, Israel has chosen to observe the humanitarian provisions of both international instruments on a voluntary basis. Accordingly, Israel may or may not be deemed a "belligerent occupant" of the West Bank. As for the Gaza Strip, from which Israel withdrew completely in 2005, a debate has ensued – as discussed in Chapter 17 – regarding whether Israel continues to "occupy" the area, but even if Israel can still be characterized as a "constructive occupant" of Gaza, it is unclear whether it is now or ever was a "belligerent occupant" bound by the Hague Regulations and the Geneva Convention.

During the years of the Jordanian and Egyptian occupations (1948–1967), no one – not the United Nations, nor the international NGO community, nor the Palestinians themselves – ever mentioned the Hague Regulations or the Fourth Geneva Convention. King Abdullah purported to annex the West Bank, eliminated the border, merged the legal systems of both banks of the Jordan, and granted Jordanian citizenship to the residents of the West Bank. Jordanians from the East Bank relocated to the West Bank. Yet during the two decades of the Jordanian occupation, no one ever accused Jordan of violating the 1907 Hague Regulations or Article 49 of the Fourth Geneva Convention. The same was true of the Egyptian occupation of the Gaza Strip.

Although no one in the international community paid much attention to international law during the Jordanian and Egyptian occupations between 1948 and 1967, international law suddenly attracted enormous attention when Israel replaced Jordan and Egypt as the occupant in June 1967.

Palestinian advocates and their supporters argue today that Israel's ongoing occupation of the West Bank is "illegal." But if the Jordanian and Egyptian occupations of those areas between 1948 and 1967 were lawful under international law, then Israel's subsequent occupations were equally lawful, especially because both occupations resulted from Israel's legitimate exercise of its rights to self-defense and anticipatory self-defense.

Notes

1 Basic Law: *Jerusalem, Capital of Israel*, No. 980 of the 23rd Av, 5740 (5 Aug. 1980), 186; the Bill and an Explanatory Note were published in *Hatza'ot Chok* No. 1464 of 5740, 287. Amendment no. 1 was passed by the Knesset on the 29th Heshvan 5761 (27 Nov. 2000) and published in *Sefer Ha-Chukkim* No. 5762, 28.

2 The timeline in the following sentences is derived from *Six-Day War Comprehensive Timeline* (1 May 2007), https://web.archive.org/web/20070518044748/http://www.sixdaywar.co.uk/timeline.htm (last accessed 6 Dec. 2023).

3 On the morning of 5 June 1967, Israeli Prime Minister Levi Eshkol transmitted through the Chief of Staff of the UN Truce Supervision Organization, Norwegian Lt. General Odd Bull, a message to King Hussein asking Jordan to refrain from hostilities. The message read, "We are engaged in defensive fighting on the Egyptian sector, and we shall not engage ourselves in any action against Jordan, unless Jordan attacks us. Should Jordan attack Israel, we shall go against her with all our might." *See also* FRUS, Telegram 208049 (5 June 1967) ("Israeli Representative here asks us to convey earnest desire of his government not do any harm to Jordan. They hope that hostilities between the two countries can be avoided or kept to a minimum") and State Department Historian's footnote to Telegram 208049 ("Telegram 523 from USUN, June 5, reported that UN Under Secretary Ralph J. Bunche had informed Goldberg of a report by UNTSO Chief of Staff Lieutenant General Odd Bull that he had conveyed an Israeli message to King Hussein that no action would be taken against Jordan unless Jordan started it, in which case Israel would hit back hard (*Id.* Office of the Executive Secretariat, Middle East Crisis Files, 1967, Entry 5190, Arab-Israeli Crisis, Box 6, Chron, USUN) Telegram 1106 from Amman, August 26, reports that King Hussein told Burns he received two messages from the Israelis on June 5, the first through General Bull that morning, after the Jordanian Air Force had already taken off against Israel, and the second through the U.S. Embassy that evening (*Id.*, RG 59, Central Files 1967–69, POL 15-1 JORDAN)").

4 M. Rogoff and E. Collins Jr., *The Caroline Incident and the Development of International Law*, Brooklyn Journal of International Law, 16, 493–528 at 494–95 (1990).

5 *Id.* at 497–98.

6 *Id.* at 498 (emphasis added); *see also* R. Jennings, *The Caroline and McLeod Cases*, American Journal of International Law, 32:1 at 82–99 (1938).

7 *Fur Seal Arbitration* (U.S. v. Gr. Brit.), Proceedings of the Tribunal of Arbitration at 299 (1893).

8 J. Westlake, *International Law, Part I: Peace* (Cambridge Univ. Press, 1904); *see also* E. Root, *The Real Monroe Doctrine*, The American Journal of International Law, 8:3, 427–42 at 432 (1914).

9 A. Ross, *A Textbook of International Law* (Longmans, Green, 1947).

10 D.W. Bowett, *Self-Defense in International Law* at 187–90, 191–92 (Praeger, 1958).

11 J. Quigley, *The Six-Day War and Israeli Self-Defense: Questioning the Legal Basis for Preventive War* at 158 (Cambridge Univ. Press, 2013); J. Quigley, *The United Nations' Response to Israel's Seizure of the West Bank and Gaza Strip*, The Palestine Yearbook of International Law, XII at 145–64 (2002/2003).

12 M. Shaw, *International Law* (9th ed.) at 994 (Cambridge Univ. Press, 2021).

13 Bowett (1958), *op. cit.* at 193.

14 United Nations, S/PV.464, Security Council Official Records, 464th Meeting (8 Feb. 1950) (statement of Mohammed Zafrulla Khan, Pakistani Ambassador to the United Nations).

15 Rogoff and Collins Jr., *op. cit.* at 506.

16 HL Deb., Vol. 660, cols. 356–76 at 370 (21 Apr. 2004) (response of the Attorney General, Lord Goldsmith).

17 *Id.* at 244, 266.

18 I. Brownlie, *The Use of Force in Self-Defense*, British Year Book of International Law, 37, 183–268 at 226 (1961).

19 E. Barak, *Between Reality and Secrecy: Israel's Freedom of Navigation through the Straits of Tiran, 1956–1967*, Middle East Journal, 61:4, 657–79 at 657–58 (2007).

20 *See, e.g.*, Barak, op. cit. (arguing that both Israel and Egypt retreated from their opposing 1957 regarding the Straits over the next decade, creating some ambiguity regarding the extent to which a closure of the Straits would have provided a reasonable basis for Israel to invoke the right of anticipatory self defense).
21 See, e.g., Shaw (2021), *op. cit.* at 999 ("It could, of course, also be argued that the Egyptian blockade itself constituted the use of force, thus legitimizing Israeli actions without the need for 'anticipatory' conceptions of self-defense, especially when taken together with other events."). At 999 n. 100 Shaw cites various authorities for the proposition that anticipatory self-defense forms part of the customary international law of self-defense.
22 E. Lautepacht, *Jerusalem and the Holy Places* at 11 n.1 (Anglo-Israel Association, 1968).
23 United Nations Security Council, S/RES/242 (22 Nov. 1967).
24 Shaw, *op. cit.* at 1003.
25 A. Gerson, *Israel the West Bank and International Law* at 72–73 (Frank Cass, 1978).
26 S. Schwebel, *What Weight to Conquest?*, American Journal of International Law, 64:2, 344–47 at 346 (1970).
27 Quigley (2002/2003), *op. cit.* at 155.
28 For a contrary view, *see* Quigley (2013), *op. cit.*
29 R. Higgins, *The Place of International Law in the Settlement of Disputes by the Security Council*, American Journal of International Law, 64, 1–18 at 8 (1970).
30 United Nations Security Council, S/RES/242 (22 Nov. 1967).
31 D. Huber, *The International Dimension of the Israel-Palestinian Conflict: A Post-Eurocentric Approach* at 127 (SUNY Press, 2021).
32 Gerson (1978), *op. cit.* at 76.
33 E. Kontorovich, *Resolution 242 Revisited: New Evidence on the Required Scope of Israeli Withdrawal*, Chicago Journal of International Law, 16:1, 127–150 at 130 (2015). *But see, e.g.,* G. Perry, *Security Council Resolution 242: The Withdrawal Clause*, The Middle East Journal, 31:4 at 413–33 (1977) (arguing Resolution 242 requires Israel to withdraw from "all" territories occupied in the Six Day War); McHugo, *op. cit.* (withdrawal must be from "all" territories). For a contrary view, *see* M. Lynk, *Conceived in Law: The Legal Foundations of Resolution 242*, Journal of Palestine Studies, 37:1 at 7–23 (2007) (arguing that the "withdrawal" provision, when read together with the "inadmissibility" provision require Israeli withdrawal from "all" territories Israel acquired in the June 1967 war).
34 R. Lapidoth, *Security Council Resolution 242 at Twenty Five*, Israel Law Review, 26:3, 295–318, at 310 (1992).
35 R. Lapidoth, *The Misleading Interpretation of UN Security Council Resolution 242 (1967)*, Jewish Political Studies Review, 23:3/4, 7–17, at 12 (2011).
36 Fourth Arab League Summit, Khartoum Resolutions (29 Aug.–1 Sept. 1967), https://ecf.org.il/media_items/513 (last accessed 12 Nov. 2023).
37 Y. Meital, *The Khartoum Conference and Egyptian Policy after the 1967 War: A Reexamination*, Middle East Journal, 54:1, 64–82 at 80 (2000).
38 For a contrary view, *see* D. McDowall, *Clarity or Ambiguity? The Withdrawal Clause of UN Security Council Resolution 242*, International Affairs, 90:6, 1367–81 at 1379 (2014) (arguing the "inadmissibility" clause of Resolution 242 should be read together with the "withdrawal" clause to conclude that immediate Israeli withdrawal was the intended outcome).
39 Gerson (1978), *op. cit.* at 75.
40 Shaw (2021), *op. cit.* at 1039.
41 *Convention Respecting the Laws and Customs of War on Land*, Oct. 18, 1907, 36 Stat. 2277, 1 Bevans 631 (entered into force Jan. 26, 1910).

42 *Legality of the Threat or Use of Nuclear Weapons*, Advisory Opinion, I.C.J. Reports 1996, 226, 256 at para. 75 (8 July 1996).
43 *Legal Consequences of the Construction of a Wall in the Occupied Palestinian Territory*, Advisory Opinion, I.C.J. Reports 2004, p. 136, 175 at para. 95 (9 July 2004).
44 *Convention Respecting the Laws and Customs of War on Land, with Annex of Regulations*, 18 Oct. 1907, TS 539 [emphasis added].
45 Gerson (1978) *op. cit.* at 10.
46 *Id.* at 9.
47 D. Graber, *The Development of the Law of Belligerent Occupation, 1863–1914: A Historical Survey* at 56 (Columbia Univ. Press, 1949).
48 *Id.* at 58.
49 A. Gerson, *Trustee-Occupant: The Legal Status of Israel's Presence in the West Bank*, Harvard International Law Journal, 14:1 at 39–40 (1973).
50 Gerson (1978), *op. cit.* at 80–82. Gerson concedes this point has become moot in light of Israel's *de facto* observance of the Hague Regulations in the West Bank and Gaza Strip.
51 Blum, *op. cit.* Y.Z. Blum, *The Missing Reversioner: Reflections on the Status of Judea and Samaria*, Israel Law Review 3:2, 279–301 (1968).
52 Y. Dinstein, *The International Law of Belligerent Occupation (2nd ed.)* at 28 (Cambridge University Press, 2019).
53 HCJ 7957/04 *Mara'abe v. The Prime Minister of Israel* at para. 14 (15 Sept. 2005).
54 Y. Dinstein, *The International Law of Belligerent Occupation (2nd ed.)* at 25 (Cambridge Univ. Press, 2021).
55 *Advisory Opinion on Legal Consequences of the Construction of a Wall in the Occupied Palestinian Territory*, 2004 ICJ Rep. 136, 175 at para. 95 (9 July 2004).
56 Dinstein (2021), *op. cit.* at 2–3, citing R. Sabel, *Book Review*, Israel Law Review, 42 at 628, 631 (2009).
57 *See, e.g.*, *Ajuri v. IDF Commander*, HCJ 7015/02 para. 22 (3 Sept. 2002); *Beit Sourik Village Council v. Government of Israel*, HCJ 2056/04 at para. 1 (30 May 2004) ("Since 1967, Israel has been holding the areas of Judea and Samaria in belligerent occupation"); *Gaza Beach Regional Council v. Knesset of Israel*, HCJ 1661/05, at paras. 76–77 (2005) (holding the High Court of Justice and every Israeli government since 1967 had accepted the "framework of belligerent occupation"), cited in D. Kretzmer, *The Law of Belligerent Occupation in the Supreme Court of Israel*, International Review of the Red Cross, 94:885 at 210 n.14 (2012).
58 Kretzmer, *op. cit.* at 213 ("without ever ruling positively that the Fourth Geneva Convention applies in the [occupied territories] or that all its provisions are part of customary law, relating to provisions of the Fourth Geneva Convention has become part of the Court's standard practice.").
59 FCO 93/2621, Memorandum (Confidential) from J. Siddle to D.A. Anderson, para. 3 (24 July 1980).
60 Kretzmer, *op. cit.* 207–36 at 209–10.
61 The Security Council in Resolution 541 (18 Nov. 1983) rejected Turkey's effort to declare the independence of Northern Cyprus, but did not explicitly call for Turkey's withdrawal from the Island. No states currently recognize Northern Cyprus as a separate state, but several states maintain informal relations with the entity, and the Organization for Islamic Cooperation has granted it observer status.

16

ARE ISRAELI SETTLEMENTS IN THE WEST BANK ILLEGAL?

Introduction

Israeli settlement activity in the West Bank started modestly in the immediate aftermath of the Six-Day War. In the late 1960s the government approved a small number of settlements in locations deemed to be of military and strategic importance, such as Kfar Etzion. Eventually, however, the settlement project expanded dramatically, motivated by those who viewed the West Bank (Judea and Samaria) and its multitude of biblical sites as part of as Israel's religio-national patrimony.

Gerson (1978) described the early competing interests in Israel regarding settlement activity:

> Those in the political community openly opposed to settlement argued that settlement would create vested interests and imply annexation, both of which would make more difficult, if not impossible, the task of negotiating a settlement ... The middle course chosen favored paramilitary settlement, mostly along the frontier, while opposing the purchase and settlement of West Bank land by Israeli nationals ... Before long, however, the Israeli Government was to succumb to the pressures for allowing civilian settlement and land purchase.[1]

As of 31 December 2021, there were 132 Israeli settlements in the West Bank. The settlers comprised 14% of the entire West Bank population (451,700 out of 3,267,704), and approximately 5% of the total Israeli population (451,700 out of 9,289,800). Approximately half the settlers (230,000) lived in ten

DOI: 10.4324/9781032686561-20

settlements in East Jerusalem. An estimated 3,000 additional settlers lived in compounds inside nine Palestinian Arab neighborhoods in East Jerusalem.[2]

The Palestinians conceded in the Oslo Accords that the settlements could remain in Area C, pending final resolution in the permanent status negotiations. The Palestinians and the international community nevertheless unanimously view the settlements as constituting an obstacle to peace. Most of the international community and the ICJ also view the settlements as illegal. For example, the United Nations' Security Council declared in Resolution 2334 (23 December 2016) that the settlements are a "flagrant violation of international law." The ICJ also declared the settlements illegal in the *Wall* opinion, even though the issue had not even been raised in the General Assembly's request for an advisory opinion.

But are the settlements truly unlawful under international law? The facts and law are more complex than would appear at first glance.

Applicable International Law

The Fourth Geneva Convention provides in Article 49, paragraph 6 that "[t]he Occupying Power shall not deport or transfer parts of its own civilian population into the territory it occupies."[3] The purpose of Article 49(6) is to prevent the occupying power from displacing the population of the occupied territory with its own nationals.

Lapidoth (2001) has noted the Israeli legal view that Article 49(6)

> [P]revents the deportation and transfer of civilians to the occupied territory but it does not deal with the voluntary movement of individuals who do not displace the local inhabitants. This interpretation is based on the plain meaning of the words and on the legislative history of the provision: it was adopted soon after World War II, in 1949, in order to pre vent the recurrence of mass transfers of civilians against their will for the purpose of displacing the population of the occupied territory, by the Nazis during the war.[4]

The Rome Statute of the International Criminal Court incorporates and expands this language in Article 8(2)(b)(viii), criminalizing

> The transfer, directly or indirectly, by the Occupying power of parts of its own civilian population into the territory it occupies, or the deportation or transfer of all or parts of the population of the occupied territory within or outside this territory.[5]

The Rome Statute's expansion of Article 49(6) resulted from lobbying by Palestinians and their supporters and was intended to create the possibility of an international criminal prosecution of Israeli nationals for settlement activity in the West Bank. Shaw (2021), however, notes the additional provisions, including the "directly or indirectly" language, do not reflect customary international law.[6]

Those who argue the settlements are illegal rely on Article 49 to support their claim. On the surface, the language would seem to bar settlement activity sponsored, encouraged, or facilitated by the Israeli government However, a closer reading of Article 49(6) suggests it would only be triggered only if the settlers had *displaced* the local population, which has not occurred.[7]

Thus, Article 49(6) does not prohibit private transactions between West Bank sellers or lessors and Israeli buyers or lessees resulting in Israelis relocating to the West Bank.[8] As Dinstein (2019) notes:

> If individual Israeli settlers have gained ownership of real estate in the West Bank, their private transaction should not have any impact on any final status agreement regarding the future of the area. Once the occupation is over, these settlers – if they choose to remain in the formerly occupied territory (and if the final status agreement allows them to do so) – may have to live under a new flag. 'In principle, there should be a symmetry between Israel and its neighbours. Israel has a large Arab minority which enjoys civil rights within it. Why shouldn't Jews be allowed to live in neighbouring Arab countries?"[9]

Kontorovich (2018) notes Article 49(6) reflected a new development in international law when it was adopted in 1949, and did not reflect longstanding international law or prior state practice. Thus, Kontorovich argues, the scope and extent of Article 49(6) must be determined by reference to subsequent state practice in the international arena post-1949, including various examples of occupation and accompanying settlement activity that have received less attention than Israel's occupation of the West Bank, but that nonetheless are relevant to the proper interpretation of Article 49(6).

Based on his study of other post-1949 occupations (Indonesia-East Timor, Morocco-Western Sahara, Turkey-Northern Cyprus, Syria-Lebanon, Vietnam-Cambodia, Armenia-Azerbaijan, Russia-Georgia, and Ukraine) Kontorovich concludes "there is no basis to assume ... that a state's mere "encouragement" of civilian settlers is enough to bring the state within the purview of Article 49(6)."[10]

Kontorovich also argues Article 49(6) cannot be read as broadly as the international community has applied it in the Israeli context:

> [O]utside the context of Israel, Article 49(6) is not invoked by the international community in reaction to settlement enterprises in occupied territories. The most striking thing about the state practice is the ubiquity

> of settlement activity and the accompanying international acquiescence. Large-scale settlement activity appears to be an almost inevitable accompaniment of all but the briefest occupations of contiguous territory. Most of the examined settlement movements into occupied territory have proved demographically significant. The arrival of settlers has in the case studies here typically been accompanied by a similarly large-scale expulsion or departure of the prior population. Vietnam and Israel appear to be among the unusual exceptions in which prior populations remained intact.[11]

Also relevant here, but not mentioned by Kontorovich or any other scholars, are the "forgotten occupations" of the West Bank and Gaza Strip between 1949 and 1967. As discussed in Chapter 11, during the Jordanian occupation of the West Bank between 1948 and 1967, a small number of Jordanians settled in the West Bank at the behest of the Jordanian government, and a larger number of West Bank residents relocated to the East Bank. Egyptian officers and espionage agents likewise relocated to the Gaza Strip between 1949 and 1967. None of this resettlement/relocation activity generated a single Article 49(6) objection from the Palestinian leadership in the West Bank, the United Nations, or the international community.

Nevertheless, Article 49(6) formed the basis for United Nations Security Council Resolution 2334 of 23 December 2016. That resolution declared, "the establishment by Israel of settlements in the Palestinian territory occupied since 1967, including East Jerusalem, has no legal validity and constitutes a flagrant violation under international law."[12] The UN's singular focus on the alleged illegality of Israeli settlements cannot be reconciled with the UN's silence and presumed acquiescence in the other ongoing occupations and accompanying settlement activity Kontorovich has identified.

In contrast to Resolution 2334, Watson (2000) offers a more nuanced perspective regarding the legality of Israeli settlements:

> Israel's arguments against the applicability of the Fourth Geneva Convention are hardly frivolous, as has sometimes been suggested, but the better view is that the Convention is applicable to all the territories occupied in 1967. Israel is right that some voluntary, purely private settlement in the West Bank might be permissible under Article 49 of the Convention. But state-sponsored and -subsidized settlement does begin to look like an impermissible 'transfer' of civilians to occupied territory, a violation of Article 49.[13]

Some on the Israeli side question whether the Fourth Geneva Convention applies to territory over whom no one has sovereignty, such as the West Bank and the Gaza Strip. By its terms, the Fourth Geneva Convention applies solely to "cases of partial or total occupation *of the territory of a High Contracting*

Party."[14] As discussed above, sovereignty over the West Bank and Gaza has remained in abeyance or suspension ever since the end of World War I. Thus, neither the West Bank nor Gaza qualify under the Fourth Geneva Convention as "territory *of* a High Contracting Party." Therefore, it could be argued Article 49(6) has no applicability to the West Bank or the Gaza Strip.[15]

Gerson (1978) drew a distinction between the political and legal viability of the settlements:

> Israeli settlement aroused, among all segments of West Bank society, deep resentment and distrust of Israeli authorities. The escalation of private land transactions and the campaign to legalize these purchases only accentuated Arab fears. Although the land transactions appear, in fact, to have been the product of free [and lawful] bilateral bargaining, the sale of Arab land to an Israeli Jew was fundamentally different from the sale of Arab land to an Arab or a foreign investor ... Nevertheless, in the perspective if contemporary international law, Israel's land acquisition and settlement policy was not unlawful as it neither aimed for, nor neared, a stage involving displacement of the existing population as a prelude to annexation.[16]

Benvenisti (2012), however, argues the settlements might be legal only if Israel were to claim and establish sovereignty over the West Bank, but Israel thus far has not done so. Although Israel preserved its claims to the West Bank in the 1949 Armistice Agreement with Jordan[17] and in the 1995 Oslo Interim Agreement,[18] Israel thereafter never formally asserted sovereignty over the West Bank. Absent a claim of sovereignty, Benvenisti argues, the settlements cannot be justified either under Article 49(6) or the Hague Regulations.

The Israeli Supreme Court and Settlements

The Israeli Supreme Court, which has stood for decades as a bulwark of the country's democracy, has accepted hundreds of cases from West Bank litigants challenging the existence of settlements and many other practices during the occupation. Both Palestinian and Israeli lawyers have represented West Bank clients before the High Court throughout the entirety of the nearly six decades of occupation, a phenomenon unique in the annals of belligerent occupation.

The Israeli Supreme Court's decisions in cases challenging the legality of settlements reflect the importance of an independent judiciary. The Court has sometimes ruled in favor of the settlers and has sometimes ruled against them. The same is true regarding other occupation-related issues that have been brought before the Court, such as the legality of the route traversed by certain sections of the Wall of Separation, the legality of house demolitions, etc.

In adjudicating legal challenges to Israeli settlements during the 1970s, the Israeli Supreme Court did not view Article 49(6) as forming part of customary international law. The adoption of Article 49(6) in 1949 represented an *innovation* rather than a *codification* of longstanding international custom and practice. Nevertheless, the Israeli Supreme Court has treated Article 49(6) as applicable on a *de facto* basis to Israel.[19] The Court has tended to draw a distinction between settlement activity serving a military or security objective, versus settlements built solely to serve civilian interests. The Court also has not hesitated to rule against Israeli civilian settlements encroaching on privately owned Palestinian land in the West Bank.

For example, Dinstein (2019) notes that in the *Beth El* and *Matityahu* cases (both decided in 1979), the Court upheld the legality of the settlements at issue because they were deemed to comprise part of Israel's security belt. In the *Elon Moreh* case, however, the Court found the settlement lacked the requisite security function, and ordered it dismantled. More recently, the Court ordered both the Amona settlement (2017) and a new neighborhood in Beth El (2012) dismantled. The Court has also emphasized the temporary nature of the settlements, even as it has sidestepped requests to rule on the legality of the entire settlement enterprise, characterizing such requests as involving nonjusticiable political questions best left to the Oslo-contemplated permanent status negotiations between the Israelis and Palestinians.[20]

The Oslo Accords and Israeli Settlements

The subject of Israeli settlements was addressed in both the 1993 Oslo Declaration of Principles and the 1995 Oslo Interim Agreement. In the Agreed Minutes to the Declaration of Principles, the parties explicitly deferred four issues for later permanent status negotiations, including settlements. As Shehadeh (1997) has noted, the framework agreement for the interim stage, reached as part of the 1993 Declaration of Principles, "did not limit Israel's ability to expand the settlements and create more facts on the ground."[21] Indeed, Shehadeh admits the Palestinian negotiators were well aware of Israeli plans to expand the settlements, yet they signed the Declaration of Principles and the Interim Agreement anyway.

The 1995 Oslo Interim Agreement also addressed Israeli settlements in the West Bank. The Palestine Liberation Organization (PLO) and Israel agreed to defer the settlements issue to the permanent status negotiations. In the meantime, the PLO agreed to ongoing exclusive Israeli control over Area C, including full Israeli responsibility for the overall security of Israelis and settlements, including "all the powers to take the steps necessary to meet this responsibility."[22] Subsequent Palestinian efforts to seek United Nations resolutions and international judicial rulings against the legality of the settlements contradict the PLO's willingness at Oslo to negotiate over the settlements at a later date.

The PLO agreed in Oslo that the issue of Israeli settlements would be one of the subjects of the contemplated permanent status negotiations. The PLO's agreement to negotiate regarding the settlements undermines their more recent claim that the settlements are illegal are non-negotiable.

The PLO also agreed at Oslo to allow Israel to take all steps necessary to protect Israelis and Israeli settlements, thereby providing a legal justification for Israel to construct a security barrier, otherwise known as the Wall of Separation, to protect Israelis living both inside Israel proper and in West Bank settlements from Palestinian terror attacks.

The Palestine Mandate and Israeli Settlements

As discussed in Chapter 19, some Palestinian advocates (such as Dugard, 2014) argue the Palestine Mandate somehow remains in effect today as a matter of international law.[23] They argue the United Nations never formally terminated the Mandate, and that Britain's unilateral termination of the Mandate on 14/15 May 1948 had no legal force. They further argue Resolution 181(II) lacked legal force, as it represented merely a recommendation of the General Assembly; whereas the Mandate, which the League of Nations Council (roughly equivalent to the United Nations Security Council) approved unanimously in July 1922, reflected an expression of international law.

The better argument is that the Mandate came to an end on 14/15 May 1948.[24] But if the Mandate indeed remains in force today, then Article 49(6) would be moot. Instead, *all* Israeli settlements in the West Bank would be legal under Article 6 of the Mandate, which required Britain to facilitate "close settlement" throughout Palestine by Jews immigrating from around the world:

> The Administration of Palestine, while ensuring that the rights and position of other sections of the population are not prejudiced, shall facilitate Jewish immigration under suitable conditions and shall encourage, in co-operation with the Jewish agency referred to in Article 4, *close settlement by Jews on the land*, including State lands and waste lands not required for public purposes. [Emphasis added.]

The term "the land" in Article 6 is not limited geographically, and thus would have included *all* land within the borders of Mandatory Palestine, including the West Bank.

Moreover, as discussed in Chapter 9, Israel has a credible (but admittedly not iron-clad) argument that, as the only state to have emerged from the Mandate, it inherited the borders of the Mandate under the doctrine of *uti possidetis juris* when it declared its independence on 14 May 1948. Thus, the settlements could also be deemed legal as they fall within Israel's *uti possidetis* borders, which include the West Bank.

Legality of the Wall of Separation: The Israeli Supreme Court

Following a wave of terror attacks by West Bank Palestinians against Israeli civilians inside Israel during the Second Intifada (2000–2002), the Israeli government began building a security barrier separating the West Bank from Israel and surrounding Israeli settlements in the West Bank. The barrier proved remarkably effective at stemming the number of attacks, and undoubtedly saved many lives on both sides of the Wall – on the Israeli side by reducing such attacks, and on the Palestinian side by reducing Israel's military operations in response to such attacks.

The separation barrier was comprised mainly of so-called "smart-fencing," equipped with electronic sensors and other measures to detect infiltration into Israel from the West Bank. In some areas, however, the barrier consisted of a large wall formed from concrete slabs.

In certain instances, the separation barrier encroached on Palestinian land. In those instances the owners were offered compensation. The encroachments were not significant but caused inconvenience and disruption to a small number of West Bank farmers and other Palestinians.

A variety of Palestinian plaintiffs brought an action before the Israeli Supreme Court challenging the legality of a 40-kilometer portion of the Wall northwest of Jerusalem. The Supreme Court, in the landmark 2004 *Beit Sourik* ruling, declared a 30 km portion of the challenged area to have been constructed illegally on Palestinian land and ordered the government to relocate that portion of the Wall.

The Court noted that Israel, as the occupying power, had the right to construct the Wall for security reasons, but only in proportion to the legitimate security needs of the state balanced against the rights of Palestinian impacted by the Wall:

> We accept that the military commander cannot order the construction of the separation fence if his reasons are political. The separation fence cannot be motivated by a desire to 'annex' territories to the State of Israel. Indeed, the military commander of territory held in belligerent occupation must balance between the needs of the army on one hand, and the needs of the local inhabitants on the other. In the framework of this delicate balance, there is no room for an additional system of considerations, whether they be political considerations, the annexation of territory, or the establishment of the permanent borders of the state.[25]

The Court further noted the 30-kilomoter segment of the Wall encroaching on Palestinian land might have been lawful had it comported with the principle of proportionality, but in this instance the Wall's impact on the West Bank plaintiffs was disproportionate to Israel's security needs:

> The injury caused by the separation fence is not restricted to the lands of the inhabitants and to their access to these lands. The injury is of far wider a scope. It strikes across the fabric of life of the entire population. In many locations, the separation fence passes right by their homes. In certain places (like Beit Sourik), the separation fence surrounds the village from the west, the south, and the east.[26]

The ruling stirred controversy in Israel and criticism of the Supreme Court. However, as Justice Aharon Barak explained in the ruling, Israel's dedication to the rule of law was paramount:

> Our task is difficult. We are members of Israeli society. Although we are sometimes in an ivory tower, that tower is in the heart of Jerusalem, which is not infrequently hit by ruthless terror. We are aware of the killing and destruction wrought by terror against the state and its citizens. As any other Israelis, we too recognize the need to defend the country and its citizens against the wounds inflicted by terror. We are aware that in the short term, this judgment will not make the state's struggle against those rising up against it easier. But we are judges. When we sit in judgment, we are subject to judgment. We act according to our best conscience and understanding. Regarding the state's struggle against the terrorism that rises up against it, we are convinced that at the end of the day, a struggle according to the law will strengthen her power and her spirit. There is no security without law. Satisfying the provisions of the law is an aspect of national security ... Only a separation fence built upon a foundation of law will grant security to the state and its citizens. Only a separation route based on the path of law, will lead the state to the security so yearned for.[27]

Prime Minister Sharon immediately ordered the army to comply with the Supreme Court's decision and revise the route for the Wall accordingly.

Legality of the Wall of Separation and Israeli Settlements: The ICJ 2004 Advisory Ruling

Several days after the Israeli Supreme Court's decision in the *Beit Sourik* case, the ICJ issued its sweeping Advisory Opinion in the *Wall* case. The General

Assembly had previously requested the ICJ render an advisory opinion addressing the following question:

> What are the legal consequences arising from the construction of the wall being built by Israel, the occupying Power, in the Occupied Palestinian Territory, including in and around East Jerusalem, as described in the report of the Secretary-General, considering the rules and principles of international law, including the Fourth Geneva Convention of 1949, and relevant Security Council and General Assembly resolutions?[28]

The ICJ issued an advisory opinion in July 2004 declaring the portions of the Wall built on West Bank land (including Area C) to be illegal. The court exceeded the narrow question presented to it regarding the legal consequences of the Wall, as it also declared Israeli settlements in the West Bank illegal.

Jurisdiction

The court began by brushing aside jurisdictional objections to its role in the case. The General Assembly had requested the Advisory Opinion, according to the court, to aid the General Assembly in obtaining "enlightenment as to the course of action it should take" regarding the Israeli-Palestinian dispute.[29] Certain parties suggested the court should decline to take jurisdiction because the General Assembly had already declared the construction of the Wall illegal. Moreover, the General Assembly had already determined the legal consequences by demanding that Israel stop and reverse its construction. Nevertheless, the court insisted on taking the case anyway, noting somewhat disingenuously that "the General Assembly has not yet determined all the possible consequences of its own resolution."[30]

The court based its decision to accept jurisdiction on the "factual record" supplied by the United Nations,[31] plus the long history of Israel-related General Assembly resolutions.

The court rejected challenges to its jurisdiction based on the political question doctrine, even though the Palestinians had previously committed themselves in the Oslo Accords to negotiation rather than litigation. The court further characterized the matter as stemming from the United Nations' decades-long interest in the Palestine issue, beginning with the Mandate and extending through Resolution 181, including the implications of the dispute for international peace and security. The court completely ignored the Palestinian rejections of both the Mandate and Resolution 181 and the multiple Palestinian waivers of statehood and sovereignty, preferring instead to emphasize the "realization of the inalienable rights of the Palestinian people."[32]

Applicability of Fourth Geneva Convention

The court next found the provisions of the Fourth Geneva Convention applied to the West Bank. The court reached this result simply by noting both Israel and Jordan were parties to the Convention, and thus Israel was bound to follow the Convention once it captured the West Bank from Jordan:

> In view of the foregoing, the Court considers that the Fourth Geneva Convention is applicable in any occupied territory in the event of an armed conflict arising between two or more High Contracting Parties. Israel and Jordan were parties to that Convention when the 1967 armed conflict broke out. The Court accordingly finds that that Convention is applicable in the Palestinian territories which before the conflict lay to the east of the Green Line and which, during that conflict, were occupied by Israel, there being no need for any enquiry into the precise prior status of those territories.[33]

The problem with the court's ruling on this point is that Jordan itself never held sovereignty over the West Bank. No countries, except Pakistan and the United Kingdom, recognized Jordan's purported annexation of the West Bank. Moreover, the ICJ itself referred to the West Bank as occupied "Palestinian" territory, not as occupied "Jordanian" territory.

Indeed, no one has ever possessed sovereignty over the West Bank and the Gaza Strip since the end of World War I. Therefore, when Israel captured the West Bank from Jordan, it did not seize "the territory *of* a High Contracting Party," as the West Bank had never been Jordan's sovereign territory. Moreover, the court completely failed to acknowledge that during the two decades of Jordanian occupation of the West Bank, the Palestinians never raised a single objection to the transfer of Jordanian civilians to homes in West Bank towns, presenting a higher risk of displacing the local population than Israeli settlements built away from Palestinian towns and villages.

Next, in a brief discussion, the court made the sweeping statement that "the Israeli settlements in the Occupied Palestinian Territory (including East Jerusalem) have been established in breach of international law." The issue of settlements was not before the Court, but it reached out anyway and condemned them as unlawful:

> [S]ince 1977, Israel has conducted a policy and developed practices involving the establishment of Settlements in the Occupied Palestinian Territory, contrary to the terms of Article 49, paragraph 6, just cited. The Security Council has thus taken the view that such policy and practices "have no legal validity." ... The Court concludes that the Israeli settlements in the

> Occupied Palestinian Territories (including East Jerusalem) have been established in breach of international law.[34]

The court offered no factual or legal basis for its conclusion, or for its characterization of East Jerusalem as "Palestinian territory." This issue is addressed further in Chapter 20.

The court also ignored history in its discussion of freedom of access to Holy Sites. The court noted that by signing the Israel-Jordan Armistice Agreement of 3 April 1949, "Israel thus undertook, as did Jordan, to guarantee freedom of access to the Holy Places. The Court considers that this undertaking by Israel has remained valid for the Holy Places which came under its control in 1967."[35]

But the court completely ignored Jordan's refusal to allow Jews to visit the Wailing Wall during the entire two decades of Jordanian occupation of the Old City of Jerusalem between 1948 and 1967, in violation of Jordan's obligations under the 3 April 1949 Armistice Agreement to guarantee free access for members of all religions to the Holy Places under Jordanian control.

The court also rejected Israel's security reasons for establishing the wall, again based on the "factual" record submitted to it by the Secretary General, and with no meaningful discussion:

> To sum up, the Court, from the material available to it, is not convinced that the specific course Israel has chosen for the wall was necessary to attain its security objectives. The wall, along the route chosen, and its associated régime gravely infringe a number of rights of Palestinians residing in the territory occupied by Israel, and the infringements resulting from that route cannot be justified by military exigencies or by the requirements of national security or public order. The construction of such a wall accordingly constitutes breaches by Israel of various of its obligations under the applicable international humanitarian law and human rights instruments. The Court has thus concluded that the construction of the wall constitutes action not in conformity with various international legal obligations incumbent upon Israel.[36]

The court did not stop there, also rejecting any notion that the wall could be justified based on the doctrines of self-defense or necessity under Article 51 of the United Nations Charter.[37]

The ICJ also ignored Justice Barak's recent ruling in the *Beit Sourik* case. The ICJ paid no heed to the Israeli Supreme Court Court's analysis distinguishing those sections of the Wall that could remain from those that needed to be moved.

In his dissenting opinion, Judge Buergenthal of the ICJ chastised the Court for its dismissiveness of the legitimate security concerns that motivated Israel to construct the wall:

> [T]he Court fails to address any facts or evidence specifically rebutting Israel's claim of military exigencies or requirements of national security ... the Court barely addresses the summaries of Israel's position on this subject that are attached to the Secretary-General's report and which contradict or cast doubt on the material the Court claims to rely on. Instead, all we have from the Court is a description of the harm the wall is causing and a discussion of various provisions of international humanitarian law and human rights instruments followed by the conclusion that this law has been violated. Lacking is an examination of the facts that might show why the alleged defenses of military exigencies, national security or public order are not applicable to the wall as a whole or to the individual segments of its route. The Court says that it 'is not convinced' but it fails to demonstrate why it is not convinced, and that is why these conclusions are not convincing.[38]

Dinstein (2021) criticized the ICJ opinion for lumping together all Israeli settlements, rather than distinguishing purely private from government-sponsored or financed activity:

> [T]he crucial reference to 'transfer' in the text of Article 49 (sixth paragraph) requires some calibration where the Occupying Power gives the settlements no backing at all. The 'one-size-fits all' panoramic view of settlements in the West Bank is incompatible with the Geneva limitation of the prohibition to those settlements that can be subsumed under the heading of a 'transfer.' It is easy to understand the condemnation of settlers who come to live in an occupied territory under the cloak of a Government-coordinated (and subsidized) scheme, by dint of official organization or institutional inducement (the paramount manifestation of which is the offer of public land by the military government for the purposes of the settlement and the building of supportive infrastructure). However, the chorus of recriminations against Israeli settlements disregards two (by no means trivial) categories of settlements in the West Bank: (a) So-called 'outposts', set up by private Israeli individuals acting without official support, and frequently against the policy of the Government of the day, having purchased the land for full market value from those vested with valid title to it (provided that the purchase transaction is not fictitious); and (b) Israeli nationals who repossess private land owned by their (Jewish) families and registered in their names since the days of the British Mandate or even the Ottoman Empire (or persons who have purchased such land from

> the rightful owners) ... From the perspective of the Geneva Convention, when settlers act entirely on their own initiative; when they do not arrogate to themselves land belonging to others or requisitioned from its rightful owners; and when they do not benefit from any overt or covert governmental backing ... neither the letter nor the spirit of Article 49 (sixth paragraph) comes into play.[39]

The ICJ very likely will reach the same result in response to the General Assembly's December 2022 request for yet another advisory opinion regarding Israel's presence in the West Bank and Jerusalem. The ICJ will likely ignore the Oslo Accords and issue a broad ruling condemning Israel's alleged denial of Palestinian self-determination, including denouncing all settlement activity in the West Bank. It will also likely condemn Israel's presence in East Jerusalem and the Old City. It will, as it did in the *Wall* opinion, likely characterize East Jerusalem as "occupied Palestinian territory," without explaining how and when East Jerusalem's status morphed from the UN's longstanding position that Jerusalem should be an internationalized separate entity.

Assessment

Israeli settlement activity in the West Bank has expanded beyond the original focus on defensive outposts. The settlements, as the parties agreed in the Oslo Accords, will need to be addressed in any permanent status deal between the Israelis and Palestinians. Israel previously demonstrated a willingness to dismantle settlements when it withdrew from the Sinai Peninsula between 1979 and 1982, and when it withdrew from the Gaza Strip in September 2005, but doing the same today in the West Bank (especially those ringing Jerusalem) will be far more difficult.

But the legal status of the settlements presents a closer question under international law, deserving much more careful analysis than the ICJ's summary disposition of the issue in the 2004 *Wall* advisory opinion. The settlements violate no one's sovereignty, because no one has held sovereignty over the West Bank since the end of World War I. The Fourth Geneva Convention likely does not apply on a *de jure* basis to the West Bank, because no one with sovereignty over the West Bank was a "High Contracting Party" to the convention. Nor have any Palestinians been displaced from their existing homes by the settlements. Finally, and most importantly, the Palestinians themselves conceded in the Oslo Accords that the settlements could remain in Area C under Israeli protection, pending final resolution in the permanent status negotiations.

The political and legal aspects of the settlements should therefore be decoupled and treated separately. The Palestinian political argument against the settlements is much better than their argument. The final outcome, therefore, should be left to diplomacy, not litigation.

Notes

1 A. Gerson, *Israel The West Bank and International Law* at 136 (Frank Cass & Co. Ltd., 1978).
2 European Union, Office of the European Union Representative (West Bank and Gaza Strip, UNRWA), *2021 Report on Israeli settlements in the Occupied West Bank, including East Jerusalem* (20 July 2022), https://www.eeas.europa.eu/sites/default/files/documents/EU%20Settlement%20Report%202021.pdf (last accessed 9 Jan. 2023).
3 *Convention (IV) Relative to the Protection of Civilian Persons in Time of War*, Geneva, 75 U.N.T.S. 287.Art. 49. (12 Aug. 1949).
4 R. Lapidoth, *Israel and the Palestinians: Some Legal Issues*, Die Friedens-Warte, 76:2/3, 211–40 at 227–28 (2001).
5 Rome Statute of the International Criminal Court, https://www.icc-cpi.int/sites/default/files/RS-Eng.pdf (last accessed 25 Feb. 2023).
6 M. Shaw, *International Law* (9th ed.) at 370 n.276 (Cambridge Univ. Press, 2021).
7 E. Benvenisti, *The International Law of Occupation* (2nd ed.) at 240 (Oxford Univ. Press, 2012) (describing, but not agreeing with, an Israeli argument that the settlements do not implicate Article 49(6) because "Arab inhabitants have not been displaced by Israeli settlements").
8 In the *I.G. Farben* trial at Nuremberg, the Military Tribunal discussed the scope of Article 49 and held it did not bar private transactions: "We look in vain for any provision in the Hague Regulations which would justify the broad assertion that private citizens of the nation of the military occupant may not enter into agreements respecting property in occupied territories when consent of the owner is, in fact, freely given." *United States v. Krauch, et al.*, Case No. 6 (United States Military Tribunal, Nuremberg), Judgment of the Tribunal at 76–77 (29 July 1948), https://digitalcommons.law.uga.edu/cgi/viewcontent.cgi?article=1007&context=nmt6 (last accessed 14 Jan. 2023).
9 Y. Dinstein, *The International Law of Belligerent Occupation* (2nd ed.) at 261 (Cambridge Univ. Press, 2021), quoting R. Gavison, *Legal Systems and Public Attitudes during Negotiations towards Transition from Conflict to Reconciliation: The Middle East, 1992– 1994*, The Arab-Israeli Accords: Legal Perspectives at 21, 41–42.
10 E. Kontorovich, *Unsettled: A Global Study of Settlements in Occupied Territories*, Journal of Legal Analysis, 9:2, 285–350 at 294 (2018).
11 *Id.* at 336.
12 United Nations, S/RES/2334 (23 Dec. 2016) The resolution passed as a result of the United States' decision in the waning days of the Obama Administration to abstain rather than exercise its veto power, as had previously occurred under both Democratic and Republican administrations to prevent similar resolutions from passing. The Resolution's characterization of East Jerusalem as "occupied Palestinian territory" bears close scrutiny. The designation contravenes the United Nations' original position in General Assembly Resolution 181, and many resolutions thereafter, that Jerusalem should be treated as aseparate entity under international control, not as "Israeli" or "Palestinian." This issue will be explored further in Chapter 20.
13 G. Watson, *The Oslo Accords: International Law and the Israeli-Palestinian Peace Agreements* at 141 (Oxford Univ. Press, 2000).
14 *Id.* Art. 2.
15 All Israeli settlements in Gaza were evacuated and dismantled in September 2005. "On this day in 2005: Israel completes disengagement from the Gaza Strip," Jerusalem Post (13 Sept. 2021) ("Over 9,000 Israeli citizens living in 25 settlements

were evicted from the Gaza Strip and northern Samaria in the West Bank as part of the plan, with Israel withdrawing all of its forces from Gaza.").

16 Gerson (1978), *op. cit.* at 171–72, 173.

17 Israel-Jordan Armistice Agreement, *op. cit.*, Art. II(2) (3 Apr. 1949) ("It is also recognized that no provision of this Agreement shall in any way prejudice the rights, claims and positions of either Party hereto in the ultimate peaceful settlement of the Palestine question, the provisions of-this Agreement being dictated exclusively by military considerations.").

18 Oslo Interim Agreement, *op. cit.*, Art. XXXI(6) (28 Sept. 1995) ("Nothing in this Agreement shall prejudice or preempt the outcome of the negotiations on the permanent status to be conducted pursuant to the DOP [1993 Declaration of Principles]. Neither Party shall be deemed, by virtue of having entered into this Agreement, to have renounced or waived any of its existing rights, claims or positions.").

19 HCJ 390/79, *Dweikat et al., v. Government of Israel et al.* (22 Oct. 1979) (unofficial translation).

20 Y. Dinstein, *The International Law of Belligerent Occupation (2nd ed.)*, at 261–66 (Cambridge University Press, 2019).

21 R. Shehadeh, *From Occupation to Interim Accords: Israel and the Palestinian Territories* at 27 (Kluwer Law International, 1997). Shehadeh argues the Palestinian negotiators lacked a "clear strategy" at Oslo to leverage global sympathy and internal Israeli opposition to the settler movement. *Id.* at 129–31.

22 Oslo Interim Agreement, Arts. XVII(1)(a)(settlements to be deferred to permanent status negotiations), XXXI(5)(same), and XII(1)("Israel shall continue to carry ... the responsibility for overall security of Israelis and Settlements, for the purpose of safeguarding their internal security and public order, and will have *all* the powers to take the steps necessary to meet this responsibility.") [emphasis added].

23 *See* J. Dugard, *A Tale of Two Sacred Trusts: Namibia and Palestine*, in T. Maluwa (ed.), *Law, Politics and Rights: Essays in Memory of Kader Asmal* at 287 (Martinus Nijhoff, 2014).

24 Watson (2000), *op. cit.* at 25.

25 *Beit Sourik Village Council v. Government of Israel and Commander of the IDF Forces in the West Bank*, HCJ 2056/ 04, para. 27 (30 June 2004).

26 *Id.* para. 94.

27 *Id.* para. 86.

28 United Nations, General Assembly Resolution A/RES/ES-10/14 (12 Dec. 2003).

29 *Legal Consequences of the Construction of a Wall in the Occupied Palestinian Territory*, Advisory Opinion, I. C. J. Reports 2004, 136, 158 at para. 47 (9 July 2004).

30 *Id.* at 163, para. 62.

31 Dinstein notes several flaws in the court's recitation of the facts, including overstating the portion of the wall encroaching on Palestinian land at 16%, when the actual figure was 5%. The court also treated the wall as a permanent fixture, ignoring that Israel had previously rerouted portions of the wall, and completely ignoring the Israeli Supreme Court's *Beit Sourik* ruling from a few days earlier, requiring the rerouting of 30 kilometers of the wall. Dinstein (2019), *op. cit.* at 270–71. Thus, the court proclaimed, with no evidentiary support, that "whilst the Court notes the assurance given by Israel that the construction of the wall does not amount to annexation and that the wall is of a temporary nature ... it nevertheless cannot remain indifferent to certain fears expressed to it that the route of the wall will prejudge the future frontier between Israel and Palestine, and the fear that Israel may integrate the settlements and their means of access. The Court considers that the construction of the wall and its associated régime create a "fait

accompli" on the ground that could well become permanent, in which case, and notwithstanding the formal characterization of the wall by Israel, it would be tantamount to de facto annexation." *Legal Consequences of the Construction of a Wall in the Occupied Palestinian Territory*, Advisory Opinion, I. C. J. Reports 2004, 184 at para. 121 (9 July 2004). Dinstein notes that in subsequent years, "Time and again, proceedings before the [Israeli Supreme] Court led to the re-drawing of the routes of large segments of the security barrier, in some instances more than once." Dinstein (2019), *op. cit.* at 279.

32 *Id.* at 158–59, para. 49.
33 *Id.* at 177, para. 101.
34 *Legal Consequences of the Construction of a Wall in the Occupied Palestinian Territory*, Advisory Opinion, ICJ Reports 2004, 136, 183–84 para. 120 (9 July 2004).
35 *Id.* at 189, para. 129.
36 *Id.* at 193–93, paras. 137–38.
37 *Id.* at 195, para. 142.
38 Id. at 243–44, para. 7 (dissenting opinion of Judge Buergenthal).
39 Dinstein (2019), *op. cit.* at 259–61.

17

IS THE GAZA STRIP "OCCUPIED"?

Introduction

Israel occupied the Gaza Strip twice. The first occupation occurred for a brief period during the 1956–1957 Suez/Sinai war. The second occupation began following the June 1967 Six Day War and lasted until the Israeli government voted in February 2005 to unilaterally disengage from the territory. The Disengagement Plan stipulated that all Israeli settlements in Gaza and the Israeli-Palestinian Erez Industrial Zone would be dismantled, military bases removed, and all 9,000 Israeli settlers be relocated away from Gaza.[1]

Israel implemented the Disengagement Plan in September 2005 and withdrew completely from Gaza. Israel continued to control Gaza's airspace, territorial maritime area, and the northern and eastern borders with Israel. Egypt controls Gaza's southern border with Egypt.

Nevertheless, Palestinian legal advocates argue Israel continues to "occupy" Gaza by exercising "effective control," within the meaning of the 1907 Hauge Regulations, and therefore remains bound to comply with and liable for any violations of international law. Even if Israel no longer exercised effective control directly over Gaza after its 2005 withdrawal, Palestinian advocates claim Israel still maintains a chokehold on Gaza's borders, airspace, and maritime activity, as well as Gaza's supply of infrastructural necessities such as heating oil, drinking water, telecommunications, and sewage. Therefore, Israel's ongoing involvement with Gaza constitutes indirect, functional, and/or potential "effective control," thereby rendering Gaza still under Israeli occupation.

Some pro-Palestinian frame entrepreneurs characterize Gaza as the "largest open-air prison in the world," notwithstanding the dismantling of all

DOI: 10.4324/9781032686561-21

Israeli settlements, the forcible eviction of settlers, and the total withdrawal of Israeli armed forces in September 2005. For example, John Dugard, the former United Nations Special Rapporteur for the Occupied Territories, has employed the "prison" frame:

> Statements by the Government of Israel that the withdrawal ended the occupation of Gaza are grossly inaccurate. Even before the commencement of "Operation Summer Rains," following the capture of Corporal Gilad Shalit, Gaza remained under the effective control of Israel. This control was manifested in a number of ways. Israel retained control of Gaza's air space, sea space and external borders, and the border crossings of Rafah (for persons) and Karni (for goods) were ultimately under Israeli control and remained closed for lengthy periods. In effect, following Israel's withdrawal, Gaza became a sealed off, imprisoned, and occupied territory.[2]

But Gaza could just as easily and far more accurately be described as the world's largest terrorist base. Hamas, Palestinian Islamic Jihad, and other terrorist groups have fired thousands of rockets into Israel since Israel's 2005 withdrawal, hardly evidence of Israel's ongoing "effective control" or occupation of the Gaza Strip. The horrific Hamas invasion of southern Israel on 7 October 2023 proved that the Gaza Strip indeed is the world's largest terrorist base.

Does Israel Continue to Exercise "Effective Control" over Gaza?

As discussed in Chapter 3, the Palmer-Uribe Commission determined that Israel's naval blockade of the Gaza Strip satisfied the requirements of international law as a valid self-defense measure against unprovoked and unlawful Hamas rocket attacks on Israeli civilian targets. The question for purposes of this chapter is whether the legal blockade amounts to Israel exercising "effective control" of the Gaza Strip, such that Israel should still be deemed to be occupying the Strip as a matter of international law.

Relevant International Legal Principles

Article 42 of the Hague Regulations of 1907 provides that "a territory is considered occupied when it is actually placed under the authority of the hostile army" and that "[t]he occupation extends only to the territory where such authority can be established and can be exercised."[3]

Article 42 of the Hague Regulations is identical to Article 1 of the Brussels Code of 1874. Graber (1949) noted that "as far as the international codes are concerned, the definition of the nature of occupation has not changed since the Brussels code of 1874."[4]

The Brussels Code reflected the work of an international conference in Brussels in the summer of 1874, representing the first international effort to codify the laws of war, including the laws of belligerent occupation. The conference resulted in the drafting of a code containing 56 articles, 17 of which dealt with belligerent occupation. While the "Brussels Code" never attained treaty status, it later served as a template for the Hague Regulations and the military manuals of several countries.[5]

International law has subsequently considered occupation to hinge on whether the purported occupant exercises "effective control" over the occupied area. As Jennings and Watts (2008) note:

> Theory and practice agree upon the rule that occupation is effected through taking possession of, and establishing an administration over, territory in the name of, and for, the acquiring state.1 Occupation thus effected is real occupation, and, in contradistinction to fictitious occupation, is named effective occupation. Possession and administration are the two essential facts that constitute an effective occupation. The territory must really be taken into possession by the occupying state ... This – at least for considerable and habitable areas – normally involves a settlement on the territory, accompanied by some formal act which announces both that the territory has been taken possession of and that the possessor intends to keep it under his sovereignty. After having taken possession of a territory, the possessor must establish some kind of administration thereon which shows that the territory is really governed by the new possessor. If, within a reasonable time after the act of taking possession, the possessor does not establish some responsible authority which exercises governing functions, there is then no effective occupation, since in fact no sovereignty is exercised by any state over the territory.[6]

In the so-called *Hostages* case, for example, the United States Military Tribunal at Nuremburg after World War II provided a further definition of "occupation:"

> The term invasion implies a military operation while an occupation indicates the exercise of governmental authority to the exclusion of the established government. This presupposes the destruction of organised resistance and the establishment of an administration to preserve law and order. To the extent that the occupant's control is maintained and that of the civil government eliminated, the area will be said to be occupied.[7]

In *Democratic Republic of Congo v. Uganda* the ICJ considered whether Uganda had placed any portion of Congo under its effective control for purposes of being deemed an occupant under Article 43 of the Hague Regulations. The Court first set forth the relevant test under the Hague Regulations:

> The Court observes that, under customary international law, as reflected in Article 42 of the Hague Regulations of 1907, territory is considered to be occupied when it is actually placed under the authority of the hostile army, and the occupation extends only to the territory where such authority has been established and can be exercised [citation omitted]. In order to reach a conclusion as to whether a State, the military forces of which are present on the territory of another State as a result of an intervention, is an "occupying Power" in the meaning of the term as understood in the jus in bello, the Court must examine whether there is sufficient evidence to demonstrate that the said authority was in fact established and exercised by the intervening State in the areas in question. In the present case the Court will need to satisfy itself that the Ugandan armed forces in the DRC were not only stationed in particular locations but also that they had substituted their own authority for that of the Congolese Government.[8]

The Court then focused on the Ituri area, where it found:

> General Kazini, commander of the Ugandan forces in the DRC, created the new 'province of Kibali-Ituri' in June 1999 and appointed Ms Adèle Lotsove as its Governor. Various sources of evidence attest to this fact, in particular a letter from General Kazini dated 18 June 1999, in which he appoints Ms Adèle Lotsove as "provisional Governor" and gives suggestions with regard to questions of administration of the new province ... The Court thus concludes that Uganda was the occupying Power in Ituri at the relevant time.[9]

No such circumstances have existed in the Gaza Strip since Israel's 2005 withdrawal. There can be no comparison between Israel's role in Gaza post-2005 with Egypt's military occupation of Gaza between 1949 and 1967, with its attendant curfews, human rights violations, property expropriations and other abuses.

Garber (1949) notes the leading international law authorities in the 19th century disagreed as to whether the physical presence of troops was an essential condition for belligerent occupation, but those debates usually occurred in the context of determining whether the occupying power could continue to exercise control after withdrawing its troops, rather than the occupied party insisting that a state of occupation should be deemed to continue despite the withdrawal of troops.[10]

Dinstein (2019) identified two "cumulative conditions" for belligerent occupation:

> (i) the authority by the Occupying Power must be established; and (ii) the Occupying Power must be able to ('can') exercise that authority. In other words, belligerent occupation pertains only to that area in which the Occupying Power is actually exercising its authority and is capable of doing so.[11]

Shany (2005) describes the three-prong test under Article 42 of the Hague Regulations for determining whether occupation exists: first, actual presence of hostile forces in the territory; second, such forces have the potential to exercise effective powers of government in the area; and third, the legitimate government is incapable of exercising effective powers of government or otherwise to exercise its sovereign authority over the territory.[12]

Samson (2010) states the test somewhat differently: first, whether the territory is actually placed under the authority of the hostile army, and such authority has been established and can be exercised; second, whether the state in power exercises the functions of government in such territory; *and* third, whether the occupier's authority exists in exclusion of the established government. Samson contends all three prongs of the test must be met before a party can be characterized as an "occupier."[13]

The International Tribunal for the Former Yugoslavia applied a narrower test in the *Naletilic* case, holding "The law of occupation only applies to those areas actually controlled by the occupying power and ceases to apply where the occupying power no longer exercises an actual authority over the occupied area."[14]

Application of The Effective Control Test to the Gaza Strip

The Palestinian Authority governed the Gaza Strip from September 2005 until June 2007, when Hamas violently overthrew it. Hamas has remained in uncontested control ever since. Hamas' brutal rule tolerates no opposition or dissent from the local population. Anyone suspected of collaborating with Israel is likely to be tried before Hamas-run courts and sentenced to death.

Hamas' complete and unchallenged authority over the Gaza Strip since June 2007 belies any claim that Israel continues to exercise "effective control" over the area. Hamas has repeatedly conducted military parades through Gaza's cities without Israeli interference. Hamas has amassed an enormous arsenal of weaponry. Hamas conceals rocket launchers in schools, hospitals, and United Nations (UNRWA) facilities, using innocent Gazans – including children, the sick and the elderly – as human shields against Israeli counterattacks. Hamas constructed hundreds of kilometers of tunnels for the sole purpose of serving its terror agenda against Israel.

Nevertheless, Palestinian supporters argue Israel still exercises "effective control" over the Gaza Strip, for the following reasons: first, Israel patrols Gaza's territorial waters and maintains exclusive control in the air space over Gaza. Second, Israel controls the entire Israeli border with Gaza and the border crossings. Third, Israel controls Egypt's border with Gaza, including the Rafah border crossing. Fourth, Israel supplies Gaza with electricity, fuel, telecommunications services, water, and sewage removal and is said to "control" the administration of these services in Gaza. Fifth, Israel maintains a population registry of Gazans and collects, on behalf of the Palestinian Authority, taxes on goods bound for Gaza passing through Israeli ports and, therefore, "controls" Gaza's tax system and population registry. Sixth, Israel reserves the right to re-enter Gaza for "self-defense." Seventh, Israel has the ability and *potential* to exert power over Gaza.[15]

Samson (2010) argues that none of the above items satisfies any element of the three-prong test for declaring that Israel exercises "effective control" over Gaza.[16] For example, the Gaza Strip is not "under the authority" of the Israeli Army. Moreover, Israel does not exercise any governmental functions in the Gaza Strip. Finally, Israel's authority does not supplant or exist to the exclusion of the established government in Gaza. Depending on the outcome of Israel's military response to the Hamas invasion of 7 October 2023, these conclusions may need to be revisited, although at the time of publication of this study, there was no indication that Israel intended to reoccupy the Gaza Strip.

Darcy and Reynolds (2010) summarized the debate regarding whether Israel continues to maintain effective control over Gaza after the 2005 withdrawal:

> On the one hand, it is clear that Israel no longer maintains a fixed military presence in the Gaza Strip, it is not fully administering or governing the territory and there may be some doubt as to whether the control exercised over Gaza is 'effective', given the launching of rocket attacks by Palestinian armed groups into Israel. It could be argued that since the seizure of control by Hamas in June 2007, it is they who exercise effective control on the ground in Gaza and for Israel to reassert control would require a major ground offensive involving the likelihood of numerous casualties. On the other hand, Israel continues to exercise considerable control over this relatively small geographical area, through the control of airspace, coastal waters and borders, and through the dependence of Gaza's population and economy on Israel.[17]

While Gaza depends on Israel for certain infrastructural needs, and while Hamas lacks control of Gaza's airspace, this is far from sufficient to deem Israel in "effective control" of Gaza. Gaza also relies heavily on financial backers such as Qatar, but no one would claim Doha enjoys effective control over Gaza. Nor could anyone credibly claim Iran exercises effective control over Gaza, notwithstanding Tehran's enormous influence with Hamas and Palestinian Islamic Jihad in Gaza. Nor could anyone argue that Egypt, Gaza's former occupant and southern neighbor, exercises "effective control."

Nor does Israel's naval blockade constitute "effective control." The United States did not have "effective control" of Cuba during the 1962 blockade any more than Israel has such control over Gaza today. The Israeli blockade has proven ineffective in stopping the flow of enormous quantities of weapons through the porous Egyptian border in southern Gaza. The Israeli blockade was similarly ineffective in preventing thousands of Hamas terrorists from invading Israel from the land, air, and sea on 7 October 2023.

Israel may be stronger militarily than Hamas, but that is far from a sufficient basis to satisfy the requirements of Article 42. Samson (2010) notes that between Israel and Hamas, the latter satisfies the effective control test and the former does not:

> Furthermore, the exercise of 'some' power does not give rise to an occupation. The Hague Regulations are triggered when the invader's functional control on the ground outruns the existing authority's formal control over the territory. The provisions define an occupier as possessing actual control that is adverse to the territory's official legal status. The language of Article 43 of the Hague Regulations, which states that "[t]he authority of the legitimate power having in fact passed into the hands of the occupant," indicates that the invader must have a monopoly or near-monopoly on the use of force, as well as the ability to govern the civilian population.180 All other things being equal, Hamas, as the dominant political party of the Palestinian Authority and the governmental authority in Gaza since its takeover in June 2007, has a far greater "ability" to exercise control over Gaza than Israel does ... In addition, if there were ever an airtight case that Israel does not have any real ability to rule over Gaza, it would be evidenced by the fact that after Hamas won control over the Palestinian Authority and took command of Gaza in 2007, ejected the Fatah party from the Gaza Strip – an act that Israel did not support. The ability or potential to exercise authority over Gaza satisfies no part of the "effective control" test. While potential for control may demonstrate the possibility of occupation, occupation will only exist when there is an actual fulfillment of the three requirements comprising "effective control" under international law.[18]

Shany (2012), notes the "binary" and "dichotomous" nature of the effective control construct does not fit neatly into the Gaza fact pattern.[19] He therefore argues Gaza is not occupied within the meaning of Article 42 of the Hague Regulations, but neither is it an independent state:

> Israel exerts some control over the Gaza Strip, which falls short of the level of control typically associated with occupiers under the classic occupation paradigm, (and, certainly, falls short of the level of control Israel held in Gaza before 1994). At the same time, some control is also exercised by the Palestinian government in Gaza (previously, the P.A. now, the Hamas), which seems to fall short of the degree of control exercised by an independent government over its territory.[20]

The Supreme Court of Israel stated in a 2008 ruling that the Gaza Strip is controlled not by Israel, but "by a murderous terrorist organization, that works unceasingly to harm the State of Israel and its residents, and violates every possible principle of international law in its violent activities, indiscriminately targeting all civilians – men, women and children."[21] Unfortunately that remains the situation as of the present day, as exemplified most horrifically by the Hamas invasion and ensuing massacres, rapes, sexual violence and kidnappings of 7 October 2023.

Benvenisti (2012) notes that Israel's failure to regain control of the Gaza Strip after the heavy fighting in 2008–2009 "demonstrated that Israel was no longer exercising effective control in Gaza."[22] Subsequent clashes including the 2021 Israel-Gaza fighting reaffirm the legal strength of Benvenisti's conclusion.

Darcy and Reynolds (2010) concluded that Gaza poses a unique situation under international humanitarian law. While the situation is not free from doubt, they argued (as of 2010) that Gaza remained under occupation:

> While events in Gaza have departed from traditional conceptions of warfare and occupation, and international humanitarian law's own limitations have been exposed by the many grey areas that arise in its application therein, sufficient clarity is retained when it comes to the effective control exercised by Israel over the Gaza Strip in order to categorize the territory as occupied.[23]

Writing in late 2005 shortly following Israel's withdrawal from Gaza, Shany concluded Israel lacked effective control, and thus no longer met the Article 42 definition of occupant:

> [A]lthough it is undeniable that Israel retains some powerful points of leverage over the lives of Palestinians in Gaza, it would seem difficult to maintain that such leverage enables Israel to effectively govern Gaza, i.e., to effectively control day-to-day life in the area. Furthermore, following the opening of the Rafah crossing between Gaza and Egypt (accompanied by a loose monitoring arrangement designed to alleviate some of Israel's security and trade-related concerns), Israel lost its ultimate control over

movement to and from Gaza. As a result, its power to influence events in Gaza through 'siege policies' has been significantly reduced ... At the same time, it should be noted that the PA employs tens of thousands of government officials and security personnel, who assume the daily functions of government in Gaza. While the PA's actual exercise of control might be unsatisfactory or even inefficient, it still is arguably in a much better position than Israel to exercise such authority, i.e., its potential for effective control is considerably greater. Hence, it is perhaps more reasonable to view the Gaza Strip even under the expansive approach as an area over which the preponderance of authority now rests with the PA.[24]

The Oslo Accords and Gaza

Some commentators argue Israel's withdrawal from Gaza did not legally terminate the occupation, given that the withdrawal occurred unilaterally and not pursuant to an agreement with the Palestinians. This claim is based on language in the Oslo 1995 Interim Agreement. Article XXXI(7) states, "neither side shall initiate or take any step that will change the status of the West Bank and Gaza Strip pending the outcome of the permanent status negotiations."

It seems far-fetched to argue that Israel's unilateral withdrawal from Gaza would be the sort of "change in status" the Oslo Accords were intended to prevent. It could far more credibly be argued that Hamas' forcible takeover of Gaza in 2007 and expulsion of the Palestinian Authority constituted a violation of the no change in status provisions of the Oslo Accords, even if Israel's withdrawal in 2005 set in motion the chain of events leading to the Hamas takeover.

Dinstein (2021) further argues the Israeli withdrawal from Gaza should be regarded not as ending the occupation but rather as a "redeployment within the single Palestinian occupied territory," given the language in Articles XI(1) and XXXI(8) of the Oslo Interim Agreement, stating Israel and the Palestinian Authority "view the West Bank and the Gaza Strip as a single territorial unit, the integrity and status of which will be preserved during the interim period."[25] Thus, Dinstein argues, the Hamas takeover of Gaza was legally insignificant as it did not undermine the "single territory" concept the Israelis agreed to in Oslo.

But this too seems far-fetched. First, the "single territory" concept had nothing to do with ascertaining "effective control" for purposes of applying Article 42 of the Hague Regulations. Instead, as the prominent Palestinian lawyer Raja Shehadeh (1997) has noted, the purpose for the single territory provision was to hedge against Israel's insistence on excluding the issues of Jerusalem, settlements, military locations, etc. from the scope of the Oslo Interim Agreement and reserving those issues for the permanent status negotiations.[26] In so doing, Shehadeh argues, "the Palestinians were hoping to be able to argue that the two Palestinian areas of the West Bank and Gaza should be linked and that Israeli settlements break the areas' integrity and violate this provision."[27]

Second, the Palestinians never passed legislation implementing the Interim Agreement. Nor did the Palestinians take any steps after Oslo to merge the preexisting separate legal systems in the West Bank and Gaza or to bring the two areas together socially and economically.[28] Thus, the "single territory" language may be moot.

Moreover, the Oslo Accords treated Gaza and the West Bank as one entity because the drafters contemplated both areas would be under the control of a *single* ruler, the Palestinian Authority. It would have made no sense for Israel to have agreed to the "single territory" language had it known in 1995 that a violent civil war in Gaza would result in its political and functional separation from the West Bank a little more than a decade later.

Moreover, characterizing Israel's full withdrawal from Gaza as merely a redeployment within the "one Palestine" construct elevates form over substance. If, for example, Israel had withdrawn completely from the West Bank but continued to occupy the Gaza Strip, or even a tiny portion of the Strip, then by Dinstein's logic the West Bank would still be considered "occupied." That outcome does not make sense, nor does it appear to comport with the intent and logic behind the Oslo Accords.[29]

What Is Gaza's Legal Status Today?

International law, as Shany (2012) notes, has not developed the flexibility to deal with a situation as unique as Gaza:

> Indeed, it appears as if the application of Article 42 – especially in accordance with the restrictive interpretation given to it by the ICJ in *Armed Activities* [Congo v. Uganda] – may lead to a potentially unjust result: Israel might be released from its legal obligations vis-a-vis Gaza notwithstanding its overwhelming economic, military, and political might and clear ability to influence the living conditions in Gaza. At the same time, applying an excessively liberal version of the effective control test to the situation in Gaza can also produce an awkward outcome: Israel may be required to assume the full responsibilities of an occupier without having the material ability to do so (in fact, it may even be legally barred by virtue of the Oslo Accords, if they are still valid, from exercising many of the powers of an occupier).[30]

Perhaps a more accurate description of Gaza's unique legal status would be to acknowledge that ever since Israel's withdrawal in 2005, the Gaza Strip has existed in *legal limbo* – neither occupied nor under anyone's sovereignty. The local inhabitants live as virtual hostages under the iron-fisted rule of Hamas, an outlawed terrorist organization that overran the area in June 2007, seizing control from the Palestinian Authority in a brief but bloody civil war. Gaza's secession from the Palestinian Authority and the West Bank has left the area as a rump territory, a terrorist base for launching rockets and other attacks on Israel and Israeli civilians, demonstrated most horrifically during the 7 October 2023 massacres, pillaging, rapes, and hostage taking of innocent Israelis and others.

Gaza therefore has no current legal status at all. Hamas lacks international standing and legitimacy. The Palestinian Authority has no administrative role in Gaza. No countries recognize its existence as a stand-alone entity. No one has sovereignty. The best description of the Gaza Strip, therefore, is that of a land in legal purgatory.

Notes

1 The Israeli Foreign Ministry published the Gaza Disengagement Plan on its website on 20 Apr. 2005, https://www.gov.il/en/Departments/General/israel-s-disengagement-plan-renewing-the-peace-process-apr-2005 (last accessed 12 Apr. 2024).
2 *Report of the Special Rapporteur on the Situation of Human Rights in the Palestinian Territories Occupied since 1967*, Implementation of G.A. Res. 601251 of Mar. 15, 2006, 76, U.N. Doc. A/HRC/4/17 (2007).
3 *Hague Convention (IV) Respecting the Laws and Customs of War on Land and Its Annex: Regulations Concerning the Laws and Customs of War on Land* (18 Oct. 1907), https://www.refworld.org/docid/4374cae64.html (last accessed 15 Jan. 2023).
4 D. Graber, *The Development of the Law of Belligerent Occupation, 1863–1914: A Historical Survey* at 61 (Columbia Univ. Press, 1949).
5 E. Benvenisti, *The Origins of the Concept of Belligerent Occupation*, Law and History Review, 26:3 at 621–48 (2008).
6 R. Jennings and A. Watts, *Oppenheim's International Law: Vol. 1, Peace* (9th ed.) at 688–89 (1996).
7 *United States of America v. List et al.*, 8 Law Reports of Trials of Major War Criminals 38, 55–56 (United Nations War Crimes Commission 1949).
8 *Armed Activities on the Territory of the Congo (Democratic Republic of the Congo v. Uganda)*, Judgment, I.C.J. Reports 2005, 168, 230, para. 173 (19 Dec. 2005).
9 *Armed Activities on the Territory of the Congo (Democratic Republic of the Congo v. Uganda)*, Judgment, I.C.J. Reports 2005, 168, 230–31, paras. 175, 178 (19 Dec. 2005).
10 Graber, *op. cit.* at 55–65; 265 (discussing the example of the German insistence that it continued to exercise rights as an occupant of the French village of L'Isle Adam even after German troops withdrew).
11 Y. Dinstein, *The International Law of Belligerent Occupation (2nd ed.)* at 43 (Cambridge University Press, 2019).
12 Y. Shany, *Faraway, So Close: The Legal Status of Gaza after Israel's Disengagement*, Yearbook of International Humanitarian Law, 8, 369–83 at 370, 376 (2005).

13 E. Samson, Is Gaza Occupied? Redefining the Legal Status of Gaza under International Law, American University Law Review, 25, 915-67 at 934–35.
14 *Prosecutor v. Naletilic*, ICTY Case No. IT-98-34-T, Judgment, Trial Chamber, p. 74, para. 218 (31 Mar. 2003).
15 Samson, op. cit. at 933–34.
16 *Id.*
17 S. Darcy and J. Reynolds, *An Enduring Occupation: The Status of the Gaza Strip from the Perspective of International Humanitarian Law*, Journal of Conflict & Security Law, 15:2, 211–43 at 227 (2010).
18 Samson, *op. cit.* at 960–61. For a detailed "dismantling" of the effective control arguments raised against Israel, *see id.* at 935–61; *but see* R. Bachmutsky, *Otherwise Occupied: The Legal Status of the Gaza Strip 50 Years after The Six-Day War*, Virginia Journal of International Law, 57:2, 413–54 at 453 (2018) (arguing that "although Israel lost effective control of Gaza in September 2005, it has gradually regained it as a result of its armed conflict with Hamas").
19 Y. Shany, *Binary Law Meets Complex Reality: The Occupation of Gaza Debate*, Israel Law Review, 41:1–2 at 68–86 (2012).
20 *Id.* at 77.
21 H.C. 9132/07, *Al-Basyuni v. Prime Minister*, para. 22 (30 Jan. 2008) (unofficial translation).
22 E. Benvenisti, *The International Law of Occupation* (2nd ed.) at 211–12 (Oxford Univ. Press, 2012).
23 Darcy and Reynolds, *op. cit.* at 243.
24 Shany (2005), *op. cit.* at 382–83.
25 Oslo Interim Agreement, *op. cit.*, Art. XXXI(7) and (8); Y. Dinstein, *The International Law of Belligerent Occupation* (2nd ed.) at 297–98 (Cambridge Univ. Press, 2021).
26 R. Shehadeh, *From Occupation to Interim Accords: Israel and the Palestinian Territories* at 18 (Kluwer Law International, 1997), citing Oslo Accords, *Agreed Minutes to the Declaration of Principles on Interim Self-Government Arrangements*, 32 I.L.M. 1525 Article IV, para. 1 (13 Sept. 1993).
27 Shehadeh, *op. cit.* at 18–19.
28 *Id.* at 152, 168.
29 Dinstein notes both the United Nations Security Council in 2009 and the Israeli Supreme Court in 2007 continued to view Gaza and the West Bank as a single entity following Hamas' forcible expulsion of the Palestinian Authority. But those pronouncements express the aspirational view that at some future point the West Bank and Gaza might yet reconcile their political differences and reunite as a single entity, and do not negate the fact that Israel no longer exercises effective control over Gaza. Dinstein (2021), *op. cit.* at 298, citing HCJ 11120/05 etc., *Hamdan et al. v. Commander of Southern Region* (7 Aug. 2007) and United Nations Security Council, S/RES/1860 (8 Jan. 2009).
30 Shany (2012), *op. cit.* at 84.

PART IV

Assessing the Palestinian Legal Case

Statehood

18

ARE THE PALESTINIANS LEGALLY ENTITLED TO STATEHOOD?

Introduction

After initially rejecting the existence of Palestine as a political entity, the Palestinians subsequently rejected and renounced multiple offers of statehood. Those rejections and renunciations, which the Palestinians made knowingly, voluntarily, and willingly, amounted to *implicit waivers* of sovereignty over the West Bank and Gaza.

The Palestinians *explicitly* reaffirmed those implicit waivers of sovereignty twice following Israel's declaration of independence. The first explicit waiver occurred at the Jericho Conference in December 1948, when the Palestinian Arabs pledged their loyalty to King Abdullah and expressly waived West Bank sovereignty in favor of Jordan.

The second explicit waiver was codified in Article 24 of the original May 1964 Palestinian National Charter. The Charter reaffirmed the Palestinian Arabs' renunciation of General Assembly Resolution 181(II) and called for the destruction of the State of Israel.[1] The Charter also specifically recognized *Jordanian* sovereignty over the West Bank, and explicitly *disclaimed* Palestinian Arab sovereignty over both the West Bank and the Gaza Strip. Article 24 declared, "This Organization does not exercise *any* regional sovereignty over the West Bank in the Hashemite Kingdom of Jordan, [or] the Gaza Strip."[2] The Charter said *nothing* about establishing a Palestinian State in the West Bank and Gaza Strip.

The Palestinians acted consistently with those implied and express waivers from 1949 to 1967. During those nearly two decades, when Jordan occupied and purported to annex the West Bank and Egypt occupied the Gaza Strip,

DOI: 10.4324/9781032686561-23

the Palestinians *never* sought or demanded statehood in the West Bank and Gaza.[3] The Arab League, which objected to Jordan's annexation of the West Bank, never called for Palestinian statehood there either, preferring instead to view Jordan as the *de facto* ruler of Palestine until Israel's destruction could be achieved.[4]

Today, however, the Palestinians insist they are legally entitled to the *same* outcome they renounced and waived for decades: statehood in the West Bank and Gaza. The Palestinians reversed their legal position more than one year after the June 1967 war, and have demanded statehood in the West Bank and Gaza ever since.

Ironically, in September 2022 Palestinian Authority President Mahmoud Abbas presented to the United Nations "a formal request to implement General Assembly Resolution 181, which formed the basis for the two-state solution in 1947,"[5] the *same* Resolution the Palestinians had renounced and rejected for decades.

The Palestinian Arab longstanding rejection of the two-state solution undermines their modern-day legal argument that they now are legally entitled to the same outcome. If anyone caused a legal wrong to the Palestinians, it was their own leadership for renouncing and waiving separate offers of statehood from Britain in July 1937 and May 1939, and especially from the United Nations in the November 1947 two-state solution embodied in Resolution 181(II).

The Palestinian Arabs did not just reject the United Nations' 29 November 1947 two-state solution; they deliberately *renounced* the United Nations' offer of statehood in areas of Palestine specifically allocated to them. The Palestinian Arabs punctuated their renunciation by launching a violent and bloody war. Moreover, the Palestinian Arabs *continued* renouncing the two-state solution for more than four decades after rejecting the United Nations' original offer.

Under international law, "[t]itle to territory – or a claim to it – may be abandoned. The consequence of abandonment is that the territory either becomes *res nullius* or falls under another state's sovereignty."[6] The related concept of "renunciation" in international law refers to the "unequivocal" or "deliberate" abandonment of rights.[7]

As a matter of international law, a strong argument can be made that the Palestinian Arab renunciation of the United Nations' November 1947 offer of statehood constituted a renunciation and waiver of Palestinian sovereignty over the Arab-designated portions of Palestine. The Palestinian Arabs reiterated and expressly reaffirmed that waiver at the Jericho Conference in December 1948, and again in the original May 1964 PLO Charter.

This argument, of course, does not preclude a *political* settlement of the conflict under which the Palestinians will receive statehood in the West Bank and Gaza Strip. The Oslo Accords offer the possibility, but no guarantee, of that outcome. But the Palestinians have a weak *legal entitlement* to statehood.[8]

The multiple Palestinian renunciations and waivers of sovereignty, as a matter of international law, arguably give rise to Israeli claims of *estoppel* regarding two distinct Palestinian territorial claims. First, the Palestinian Arabs are unquestionably estopped from reclaiming the portions of land the United Nations had allocated to them in Resolution 181(II), but which the Israelis captured during the 1948–1949 war.

Sovereignty over the Arab-allocated areas remained in abeyance during the war, due to the Palestinian Arab rejection of Resolution 181. Those areas belonged to no one as of the moment Israel captured portions of them in the 1948–1949 war.

E. Lauterpacht (1968) contends Israel gained sovereignty over those captured areas, as "Israel acquired a valid title to ... those parts of Palestine *outside* the area allotted to the Jewish State, which Israeli forces were compelled to occupy by way of self-defensive measures during the fighting of 1948-1949."[9] As Lauterpacht further explains:

> [T]he defensive measures adopted by the Israeli forces could not be limited to the area allocated to Israel in the Partition Plan. The Arabs by attacking the Jews outside the area of the Jewish State [in Jerusalem] and by forcibly rejecting the internationalization of Jerusalem were themselves responsible for the first Israeli expansion beyond the Partition boundaries. By provoking this Israeli movement outside the boundaries of the Jewish State, the Arabs themselves legitimized the process by which Israel filled the vacancy in sovereignty in the areas which, in order to save their kin, the Israeli forces were obliged to defend and therefore to occupy.[10]

Moreover, Jordan accepted in the 3 April 1949 Armistice Agreement the "Green Line" as encompassing the Arab-allocated areas Israel had captured in the 1948–1949 war. The Palestinians had pledged loyalty to Jordan four months earlier at the Jericho Conference, meaning they were legally bound by Jordan's agreement to the armistice lines as well. This supports Crawford's (2006) argument that Israel's original territory "was its armistice territory, not the partition territory."[11]

Second, the Palestinian Arabs might also be estopped as a legal matter, but not precluding a political settlement, from claiming statehood in the remaining areas allocated to them in Resolution 181(II), known colloquially as the West Bank and Gaza Strip.

Waiver, Estoppel, and Acquiescence in International Law

Estoppel is a general principle of international law providing "that international jurisprudence has a place for some recognition of the principle that a State cannot blow hot and cold."[12] Estoppel expresses the international legal principle that a party in an international lawsuit "is bound by its previous acts or attitude when they are in contradiction with its claims in the litigation."[13]

Judge Spender, in his dissenting opinion in the *Temple of Preah Vihear* case, explained estoppel as follows:

> The principle [of estoppel] operates to prevent a State contesting before the Court a situation contrary to a clear and unequivocal representation previously made by it to another State, either expressly or impliedly, on which representation the other State was, in the circumstances, entitled to rely and in fact did rely, and as a result the other State has been prejudiced or the State making it has secured some benefit or advantage for itself.[14]

The Permanent Court of Arbitration defined estoppel under international law in the *Chagos Marine Protected Area (Mauritius v. United Kingdom)* arbitral award:

> The principle [of estoppel] stems from the general requirement that States act in their mutual relations in good faith and is designed to protect the legitimate expectations of a State that acts in reliance upon the representations of another.[15]

The purpose of the estoppel principle is to promote stability and certainty in international relations. Admittedly, the international courts have rarely invoked estoppel to resolve international legal disputes. Nevertheless, the estoppel principle reflects the important international legal norm that prevents a state from benefiting by changing its position after another state previously acted in reliance on the state's original position. As Judge Alfaro explained in his separate opinion in the *Temple of Preah Vehar* case:

> Whatever term or terms be employed to designate this principle such as it has been applied in the international sphere, its substance is always the same: inconsistency between claims or allegations put forward by a State, and its previous conduct in connection therewith, is not admissible . . . Its purpose is always the same: a State must not be permitted to benefit by its own inconsistency to the prejudice of another State ... the State must not be allowed to benefit by its inconsistency when it is through its own

> wrong or illegal act that the other party has been deprived of its right or prevented from exercising it ... Finally, the legal effect of the principle is always the same: the party which by its recognition, its representation, its declaration, its conduct or its silence has maintained an attitude manifestly contrary to the right it is claiming before an international tribunal is precluded from claiming that right.[16]

Judge Alfaro also quoted approvingly Lauterpacht's view that estoppel

> is a precept of fair dealing inasmuch as it prevents states from playing fast and loose with situations affecting others; and it is in accordance with equity inasmuch as it protects a State from the contingency of incurring responsibilities and expense, in reliance on the apparent acquiescence of others, and being subsequently confronted with a challenge on the part of those very States.[17]

Estoppel derives from the common law notion that when a party acts to its detriment in reliance on the statement or conduct of another party, the other party may not later change its position and assert a different state of affairs.[18] The International Law Commission notes "the most characteristic element of estoppel is not the conduct of the State, but rather the confidence that is created in the other State."[19]

The Permanent Court of Arbitration discussed the meaning of estoppel in international law in a recent dispute between the United Kingdom and Mauritius:

> Estoppel is a general principle of law that serves to ensure, in the words of Lord McNair, 'that international jurisprudence has a place for some recognition of the principle that a State cannot blow hot and cold – *allegans contraria non audiendus est*.' The principle stems from the general requirement that States act in their mutual relations in good faith and is designed to protect the legitimate expectations of a State that acts in reliance upon the representations of another. The principle as it exists in international law was well summarized by Judge Spender in the *Temple of Preah Vihear*: the principle [of estoppel] operates to prevent a State contesting before the Court a situation contrary to a clear and unequivocal representation previously made by ... either expressly or impliedly, on which representation the other State was, in the circumstances, entitled to rely and in fact did rely, and as a result the other State has been prejudiced or the State making it has secured some benefit or advantage for itself.[20]

The Court also noted the requirement for the party asserting estoppel to establish detrimental reliance on the estopped party's conduct:

> Further to this jurisprudence, estoppel may be invoked where (a) a State has made clear and consistent representations, by word, conduct, or silence; (b) such representations were made through an agent authorized to speak for the State with respect to the matter in question; (c) the State invoking estoppel was induced by such representations to act to its detriment, to suffer a prejudice, or to convey a benefit upon the representing State; and (d) such reliance was legitimate, as the representation was one on which that State was entitled to rely.[21]

The Palestinians, although not a "state," clearly and consistently rejected statehood on multiple occasions, including when the British offered them statehood in 1937 and again in 1939, and when the United Nations offered statehood in 1947. The Mufti, in his capacity as the Palestinian leader and head of the Arab Higher Committee, acted with both actual and apparent authority in rejecting and renouncing each of those offers of statehood. Israel, for its part, relied on the Mufti's rejections and renunciations as reflecting the official Palestinian position.[22]

In the *North Sea Continental Shelf* case, involving a dispute between Denmark, the Netherlands and the Federal Republic of Germany over the delimitation of the North Sea continental shelf, the International Court of Justice emphasized the need for the party claiming estoppel to demonstrate "past conduct, declarations, etc., which not only clearly and consistently evinced acceptance of that régime, but also had caused Denmark or the Netherlands, in reliance on such conduct, detrimentally to change position or suffer some prejudice."[23]

The International Tribunal for the Law of the Sea said the following regarding estoppel in the *Dispute concerning Delimitation of the maritime boundary in the Bay of Bengal (Bangladesh/Myanmar)*:

> In international law, a situation of estoppel exists when a State, by its conduct, has created the appearance of a particular situation and another State, relying on such conduct in good faith, has acted or abstained from an action to its detriment. The effect of the notion of estoppel is that a State is precluded, by its conduct, from asserting that it did not agree to, or recognize, a certain situation.

Wass (2015) offers a related definition:

> Estoppel exists when a party, including a state, has created the appearance of a particular situation and another party, relying on such conduct

in good faith, has acted or abstained from an action to its detriment. The doctrine has long been recognised as a general substantive principle of international law, and is entwined in international jurisprudence with the doctrine of acquiescence, which exists when a state has waived a right by remaining silent in circumstances that called for a reaction. Both doctrines derive from the principle that a state should not be permitted to 'blow hot and cold.'[24]

The estoppel principle recognizes States must act in their mutual relations in good faith. Good faith ordinarily implies consistency. The principle exists to protect the reasonable expectations of a State acting in reliance on the express or implied representations of another party. Bowett (1957) noted the rule precluding inconsistent positions means "a party will be estopped from taking up a position on the facts of an issue inconsistent with that he has previously taken up on the same issue."[25]

MacGibbon (1958) noted that:

> Underlying most formulations of the doctrine of estoppel in international law is the requirement that a State ought to be consistent in its attitude to a given factual or legal situation. Such a demand may be rooted in the continuing need for at least modicum of stability and for some measure of predictability in the pattern of State conduct. It may be, and often is, grounded on considerations of good faith.[26]

Pan (2017), however, argues the consistency requirement can sometimes be taken too far. For example, if a state had for decades opposed banning nuclear weapons, adhering strictly to the consistency requirement would mean the state could not change its position and vote to ban such weapons.[27]

Silence can give rise to estoppel, as the International Court of Justice recognized in a dispute between the United States and Italy, noting "it cannot be excluded that an estoppel could in certain circumstances arise from a silence when something ought to have been said."[28]

The concept of prejudice or detrimental reliance is best viewed in the face of silence, in the words of Judge Fitzmaurice in his separate opinion in the *Temple of Preah Vihear* case, as existing when the conduct or silence of one party "brought about a change in the *relative positions* of the parties, worsening that of the one, or improving that of the other, or both."[29]

Estoppel is sometimes conflated with the related concept of acquiescence in international law. Acquiescence ordinarily operates where one party is silent in the face of circumstances where it otherwise would or should have been expected to speak. Pan (2017) offers a further description of the distinction between estoppel and acquiescence:

> While acquiescence and estoppel are often employed in parallel, the meaning of acquiescence is a silence when something ought to have been said … Literally, acquiescence is a description of a situation in legal language or a "qualified inaction." By contrast estoppel is a legal principle meaning that when a certain situation meets the requirements, it would entail legal effects, viz. the State is precluded from changing its position.[30]

In the *Costa Rican-Nicaragua Boundary* case, Nicaragua argued the treaty of 1858 defining its boundary with Costa Rica was not binding. The Arbitrator rejected Nicaragua's claim, noting Nicaragua had acquiesced for at least a decade to the treaty's validity. "The Government of Nicaragua was silent when it ought to have spoken," wrote the arbitrator, and "so waived the objection now made."[31]

Jennings (1963), however, urged caution in approaching the principle of estoppel in international law. Thus, it is necessary to analyze separately the West Bank from the Arab-allocated areas that fell into Israeli hands in the 1948–1949 war and were subsumed into Israel pursuant to the Israel-Jordan armistice agreement of 3 April 1949. First, we examine the 2,500 square miles of such area lost to Israel in the 1948–1949 War. Second, we examine the remaining 2,200 square miles (the West Bank), occupied by Jordan from 1948 to 1967, as well as the Gaza Strip (135 square miles), occupied by Egypt from 1948 to 1967 (and Israel from 1967 to 2005).[32]

Areas of Arab-Allocated Palestine Lost to Israel in the 1948–1949 War

The concepts of waiver, estoppel, and acquiescence apply squarely to the Palestinian Arab implied and express multiple renunciations of sovereignty over the areas of Palestine the United Nations allocated to them in Resolution 181(II). The Palestinian Arabs would argue against estoppel by asserting Israel did not rely to its detriment on the Palestinian rejection of Resolution 181(II). Thus, the Palestinians would claim estoppel is inapplicable, and thus they are not precluded from asserting sovereignty over the portions of Arab-designated Palestine lost to Israel in the 1948–1949 war.

On the other hand, Israel could argue it indeed relied to its detriment on the Palestinian rejection of the two-state solution. Israel did so by capturing control during the 1948–1949 war of certain areas the United Nations had previously allocated for the Palestinian Arab State. The United Nations implicitly recognized those boundaries when it extended membership to Israel in May 1949.

The Palestinians also recognized those boundaries in former PLO Chairman Yassir Arafat's 9 September 1993 letter to then-Israeli Prime Minister Yitzhak Rabin, in which Arafat in his capacity as Chairman of the PLO accepted "the right of the State of Israel to exist in peace and security." Arafat's letter also said the PLO accepted United Nations Security Council Resolutions 242 and 338. This is highly significant, as both Resolutions implicitly recognize Israeli sovereignty over the Arab-allocated areas captured in the 1948–1949 war.

In any event, the Palestinians not only renounced the United Nations' offer of statehood on 29 November 1947 but punctuated their renunciation by starting a war. Those acts, as a matter of law, arguably constituted the deliberate *abandonment* of statehood in the Arab-allocated portions of Palestine. Moreover, the Palestinian Arabs never asserted a reservation of rights as to the areas of Palestine the United Nations had allocated to them for statehood. Indeed, the Palestinians expressly rejected statehood in those areas, demanding *all* of Palestine, or nothing. In so doing, the Palestinian Arabs waived their claim to sovereignty over those areas of Palestine.[33]

As Judge Alfaro noted in a different context:

> The reasoning used and the jurisprudence developed as regards the subject of failure to protest is also applicable in the case of failure to reserve rights of which a State is legally possessed and which it is entitled to claim or exercise in due course. Such failure may be and has been interpreted as a waiver of such rights.[34]

In the *Land and Maritime Boundary* case involving Cameroon, Nigeria, and Equatorial Guinea,[35] the International Court of Justice noted Nigeria had failed to raise any objections to the exclusion of the Bakassi Peninsula in Lake Chad from Nigeria's sovereign territory at the time it gained independence. Nigeria's silence was deemed acquiescence to the boundary and its later objections came too late.

Following the Israel-Jordan armistice agreement of 3 April 1949 and up to the present day, the Palestinian Arabs failed to reserve *any* rights regarding the Arab-designated areas of Palestine lost to Israel in the 1948–1949 war. Israel relied on that failure by quickly incorporating those areas into the country. As noted above, the United Nations recognized those areas as part of Israel's sovereign territory on several occasions, including most significantly in Security Council Resolution 242 of November 1967, which called on Israel to withdraw "from territories occupied *in the recent* [June 1967] conflict," but not from the territories it captured and controlled during and after the 1948–1949 war, including West Jerusalem.[36] The internationally recognized borders of the state of Israel therefore include the 1948–1949 captured lands, and the Palestinians would be hard-pressed to lay claim to those areas today.

The Palestinian Arab failure to reserve their rights regarding the areas lost to Israel in the 1948–1949 war constituted a waiver by the Palestinian Arabs and estopped them from attempting to reclaim those areas later. Moreover, the ongoing Palestinian acquiescence in Israel's possession and incorporation of those areas within the sovereign borders of Israel also gave rise to Israeli rights of *prescription*. As MacGibbon (1957) noted,

> historic, prescriptive and customary rights share a common process of development which involves, on the one hand, the constant assertion of the right in question and, on the other hand, consent or acquiescence in that assertion on the part of the affected States.[37]

These facts demonstrate the Palestinian Arabs abandoned and waived sovereignty over the Arab-allocated areas Israel captured in the 1948–1949 war, and that Israel has possessed sovereignty over those areas ever since.[38]

The International Court of Justice considered a similar situation in the *Minquiers and Ecrehos* case,[39] where it awarded sovereignty over disputed "islets and rocks" to the United Kingdom based on French acquiescence in allowing Jersey authorities to administer the areas and incur the expenses of the installation and upkeep of slip-ways, buoys, marks, beacons and other works from which navigation could benefit. The legal advisor to the British Foreign Office, future ICJ Judge Sir Gerald Fitzmaurice, argued France had abandoned title to the disputed territory:

> [B]y letting another country assume and carry out for many years all the responsibilities and expenses in connection with the territory concerned. Could any thing be imagined more obviously amounting to acquiescence, that is in effect abandonment? Such a course of action, or rather inaction, disqualifies the country concerned from asserting the continued existence of the title.[40]

Salmon (1989), writing in support of Palestinian statehood, argued the Arab-allocated areas Israel captured in the 1948–1949 war should be regarded as Palestinian land to be included in a future Palestinian state. But Salmon also concedes the possibility of estoppel, admitting "third parties do not appear to have protested at the actual situation resulting from Israel's 1948 to 1949 conquests and Jordan's annexation except as regards Jerusalem as a *corpus separatum*."[41]

The Palestinians have no legal claim today to the 50% of Arab-designated Palestine lost to Israel in the 1948–1949 war. The Palestinian Arabs rejected the United Nations' offer of statehood, started a war, and lost half their designated territory. Israel incorporated that territory into its sovereign borders in reliance on the Palestinians' waiver, estoppel, and/or acquiescence to Israel's possession of those areas. Israel thereafter invested billions to upgrade the areas' infrastructure and otherwise fully incorporate the areas into Israel. Proving Palestinian waiver and Israeli detrimental reliance on that waiver would be an easy lift, and any judicial tribunal would be hard-pressed to make any decision other than the Palestinians are now estopped from laying claim to the Arab-allocated areas lost to Israel in the 1948–1949 war.

Remaining Arab-Allocated Areas: The West Bank and Gaza

But does the above analysis also apply to the other 50% of the areas the United Nations allocated to the Palestinian Arabs in Resolution 181, but that were captured by Jordan (the West Bank and East Jerusalem) and Egypt (Gaza) during the 1948–1949 war? If not, then what is the legal distinction between the two sets of territory?

From 1948 until at least June 1967 the Palestinian Arabs acquiesced in the Egyptian occupation of the Gaza Strip and the Jordanian occupation of the West Bank and East Jerusalem, renouncing statehood in both areas. Mishal (1978) describes Palestinian acquiescence to Jordanian rule in the West Bank as ambivalent, based on a willingness to grant Jordan "conditional legitimacy" in the West Bank.[42] Nevertheless, the fact of Palestinian acquiescence in Jordanian rule cannot be disputed.

The Palestinians in more recent years have walked back their previous rejections of West Bank and Gaza sovereignty, reversing their prior renunciations and arguing they now are *legally* entitled to statehood in the West Bank and the Gaza Strip. Some Palestinian commentators, such as Burghis-Kasthala (2014) even rely on Resolution 181(II) – the *same* Resolution they renounced in November 1947 – as providing the legal basis for Palestinian sovereignty over the West Bank and Gaza today:

> It is no wonder, then, that by 1947 when the newly established UN GA weighed the fate of the territory and its people that partition along ethnic lines was favoured by many. In spite of the Partition Plan's lack of implementation as a result of the breakout of hostilities in 1948 and the concomitant Israeli declaration of statehood, this blueprint is seized on by Palestinians today as its promise of 44 per cent of the territory is far more generous that what has now become the default two-state boundary: those territories first occupied by Jordan (the West Bank) and Egypt (Gaza) in 1948/1949 and then taken over by Israel in 1967 until the present day.[43]

The Palestinian "reverse renunciation" has prompted criticism from some legal scholars. Stone (1981) recounted in his study of international law and the

Israeli-Palestinian conflict how the Palestinian position regarding Resolution 181(II) had flip-flopped over the decades, originally renouncing the Resolution and violating its terms when they thought they could drive the Jews out of Palestine by force, and decades later embracing the same Resolution as the legal basis for their claims of statehood in the West Bank.

Accordingly, Stone argues, the Palestinian Arabs renounced and lost their legal entitlement to the Arab portions of Palestine, and therefore have no ongoing legal basis for claiming statehood.[44] Stone contends that under international principles of equity, the Palestinian Arabs *forfeited* their rights under Resolution 181(II):

> Their position resembles that of a party to a transaction who has unlawfully repudiated the transaction, and comes to court years later claiming that selected provisions of it should be meticulously enforced against the wronged party. It also resembles that of a party who has by unlawful violence willfully destroyed the subject-matter that is the 'fundamental basis' on which consent rested, and now clamors to have the original terms enforced against the other party ... the Partition Resolution and Plan, since they were prevented by Arab rejection and armed aggression from entering into legal operation, could not thereafter carry any legal effects ... [45]

Stone also addressed the waiver and estoppel issues.[46] Invoking longstanding international legal notions of equity, Stone argued the Palestinian Arabs, by virtue of their rejection of the United Nations' offer of statehood in November 1947, became legally estopped from changing course and claiming statehood thereafter:

> Such claimants do not come with 'clean hands' to seek equity; their hands indeed are mired by their lawlessly violent bid to destroy the very resolution and plan from which they now seek equity. They may also be thought by their representations concerning these documents, to have led others to act to their own detriment, and thus to be debarred by their own conduct from espousing, in pursuit of present expediencies, positions they formerly so strongly denounced.[47]

Stone further argues the Palestinian Arab rejection of Resolution 181(II) and resort to war frustrated the implementation of Resolution 181(II) and thus rendered it legally null. Crawford notes that subsequent events in Palestine caused the United Nations to abandon the partition plan and the Resolution to lapse.[48]

Soroczyński (2017) has described how the Palestinians themselves have acquiesced to Israel's borders, including the Arab-designated portions of Palestine that Israel captured during the 1948–1949 war:

> [A]pplying on behalf of Palestine for membership in the United Nations in September 2011, in his statement before the General Assembly, President Abbas informed the delegates that he had 'submitted to Secretary-General Ban Ki-Moon an application for the admission of Palestine as a full Member of the United Nations on the basis of the 4 June 1967 borders, with Al-Quds Al-Sharif as its capital.' As this initiative had failed, the following year Palestine successfully attempted to obtain the non-member observer state status in the UN, and in his speech preceding the voting on the matter President Abbas stressed again that '[w]e will accept no less than the independence of the State of Palestine, with East Jerusalem as its capital, on all the Palestinian territory occupied in 1967'... In the light of the analysis presented above no serious doubts seem to rise from the fact that that Israel's sovereignty over the areas situated between the partition lines and the pre-1967 lines has been universally accepted.[49]

Gerson (1973), however, takes a somewhat different view. Gerson argues the Palestinian Arabs, by rejecting partition and demanding statehood over the *entirety* of Palestine, did not necessarily renounce sovereignty over the portions of Palestine allocated to them in Resolution 181(II). Essentially, Gerson argues that rejecting half a loaf and demanding everything, but then later accepting the original half a loaf after all, should not preclude the Palestinians' legal claims today:

> [S]overeignty in the West Bank vested in the Palestinian Arabs in 1947. Their rejection of the Partition Plan represented a denial of its limitation rather than a renunciation *in toto*. Subsequent loss of title could be accomplished only in a manner similar to the traditional modes applicable to sovereign states – cession, prescription, or *debellatio*. In the context of a people possessing sovereign rights, the latter two modes can be said to have occurred when no attempt at the exercise of sovereignty is made when an opportunity to do so exists.[50]

Strawson (2010), however, agrees with the argument that by choosing to wage war against Resolution 181(II), the Palestinians waived sovereignty over the portions of Palestine allocated to them. "It was ironic," Strawson notes, "that just at the moment the United Nations recognized the Arab people of Palestine's right to self-determination, their representatives were to reject it."[51]

Karsh (2014) summarized the Palestinian Arabs' repeated rejections of opportunities for statehood throughout the 20th and early 21st centuries:

> For nearly a century, Palestinian leaders have missed no opportunity to impede the development of Palestinian civil society and the attainment of

> Palestinian statehood. Had Hajj Amin Husseini chosen to lead his constituents to peace and reconciliation with their Jewish neighbors, the Palestinians would have had their independent state over a substantial part of mandate Palestine by 1948, if not a decade earlier, and would have been spared the traumatic experience of dispersal and exile. Had Arafat set the PLO from the start on the path to peace and reconciliation instead of turning it into one of the most murderous and corrupt terrorist organizations in modern times, a Palestinian state could have been established in the late 1960s or the early 1970s; in 1979, as a corollary to the Egyptian-Israeli peace treaty; by May 1999, as part of the Oslo process; or at the very latest, with the Camp David summit of July 2000. Had Abbas abandoned his predecessors' rejectionist path, a Palestinian state could have been established after the Annapolis summit of November 2007, or during President Obama's first term after Benjamin Netanyahu broke with the longstanding Likud precept by publicly accepting in June 2009 the two-state solution and agreeing to the establishment of a Palestinian state.[52]

Sir Alec Kirkbride, the British Ambassador to Jordan, best summarized the weakness in the Palestinian legal case in an April 1949 cable to London, when he wrote, "It is typical of the Palestinians to fail to realise that an offer refused in [November] 1947 has become a mere pipe-dream in 1949."[53]

Self-Determination and Palestinian Statehood

Even though the Palestinians have little or no legal claim to statehood under international law, it could be argued that Palestinian rights to statehood arise separately under modern international legal notions of the right to self-determination.

In the *East Timor* case the ICJ described the nature of the right to self-determination:

> [T]he right of peoples to self-determination, as it evolved from the Charter and from United Nations practice, has an *erga omnes* character, is irreproachable. The principle of self-determination of peoples has been recognized by the United Nations Charter and in the jurisprudence of the Court [citations omitted]; it is one of the essential principles of contemporary international law.[54]

Becker (1998), however, cautions that self-determination itself must be viewed as a relative right, not as an absolute right, as it can pit the interests of established states against communities wishing to secede.[55] Becker offers various examples in support of his argument, including the Kurdish claim to self-determination, which "has remained unanswered primarily because

Kurdish self-determination would threaten the national and political interests of Turkey, Iran, Iraq and Syria."[56]

The Arab nations in May 1948 justified their invasion of Israel as necessary to protect the Palestinian Arab right to self-determination. The Palestinians and the surrounding Arab countries rejected the two-state solution and instead insisted the Palestinian Arab right to self-determination extended to the entirety of Mandate Palestine, in direct defiance of Resolution 181(II).

But as E. Lauterpacht (1968) notes, the Arab argument ignores that Resolution 181(II),

> far from being a denial of the right of self-determination, was in fact a direct application of the principle. The Jews were not to determine the future of the Arabs, nor were the Arabs to determine the future of the Jews. Each group was to determine its own future. This the Jews subsequently did. The Arabs of Palestine did not ...[57]

Scholars agree that as of 1947 self-determination had not yet gained recognition as part of customary international law. The Arab invasions and attempts to the destroy the new State of Israel were illegal under any view of international law as of 1947, and would be just as illegal today if the Arab countries were to launch was against Israel on behalf of alleged Palestinian self-determination rights "from the River to the Sea."

The question arises, however, whether in the modern era the Palestinian Arabs, despite having rejected the United Nations' offer of statehood in 1947, and subsequently reaffirming those rejections in the 1948 Jericho Conference and the 1964 original PLO Charter, remain legally entitled to statehood in the West Bank and Gaza based solely on the right to self-determination. A corollary question concerns whether the Palestinian right to self-determination was *already* fulfilled in 1923, when Britain partitioned the original area of the Palestine Mandate pursuant to Article 25 to create Transjordan in eastern Palestine, reserving western Palestine for the Jewish National Home.

The United Nations never mentioned Palestinian rights of self-determination during the forgotten Jordanian and Egyptian occupations of 1949–1967. Following the Six-Day war the Security Council adopted Resolution 242, but that resolution says nothing about self-determination rights for the Palestinians.

But that began to change following the 1973 Yom Kippur War. In 1974 the General Assembly adopted Resolution 3236 (XXIX), in which it referred to "the inalienable rights of the Palestinian people in Palestine, including the right to self-determination without external interference."[58]

The Palestine National Council thereafter invoked the right to self-determination in its 15 November 1988 Declaration of Independence.[59] Cassese

(1995) argues the Palestinians can assert rights of self-determination, given the majority of world opinion and state practice supporting such a claim.[60]

Cassese also rejects objections to Palestinian self-determination based on Blum's "missing reversioner" theory:

> The response to this objection is that self-determination is not contingent on sovereignty; it is a concept geared to peoples, not to sovereign legal titles. To put it differently, in the case of controversy over a territory, its legal determination focuses on the wishes of the people concerned; by the same token, it subordinates the issue of who is the holder of sovereign title. The crucial matter for the rules on self-determination is that the State that wields effective authority over a territory, whatever its legal entitlement, should grant the population concerned the possibility of freely choosing its international (and internal) status.[61]

Cassese concedes the Oslo 1993 Declaration of Principles does not explicitly mention Palestinian self-determination, but he argues that at least "internal" self-determination can be inferred from various provisions in the Declaration of Principles. Regarding "external" self-determination, Cassese states, "it can be safely asserted that, although in an oblique and roundabout way, the Declaration is grounded upon, and logically presupposes, the idea of the final attainment by Palestinians of external self-determination."[62]

But Cassese acknowledged the ambiguities in the Oslo Accords left open various potential forms of self-determination, including several falling well short of full-fledged Palestinian statehood.[63]

Quigley (1996) supports Cassese's rejection of the missing reversioner concept:

> Some have contested the 'void of sovereignty' argument on the ground that no such void existed. The mandate arrangement involved a trust relationship, in which Great Britain filled a role analogous to what, in domestic law, would be called a trustee, while the community of citizens (all citizens of Palestine, whether Arab or Jew) was the beneficial title holder. Thus, upon Britain's departure, the previously divided title automatically became unitary in the hands of the community of citizens. Thus, there was no 'void of sovereignty,' rather the assertion of sovereignty by the (minority) Jewish community amounted to an infringement on the rights of the lawful putative sovereign.[64]

Becker (1998) offered the most accurate assessment of Palestinian rights to self-determination. Becker noted the Palestinians certainly meet the test of a distinct "people," the first requirement to qualify for self-determination.

But Becker noted that in other respects the Palestinian claim to statehood via self-determination falls short:

> United Nations organs initially related to the Palestinians merely as refugees and Security Council Resolution 242 of 1967, and resolutions preceding it, made no reference to a Palestinian right to self-determination. It was only since 1969 that the rights of the Palestinian people to self-determination have been repeatedly endorsed by the General Assembly. However, Assembly Resolutions notwithstanding, it would seem that Palestinian claims to self-determination are not consistent with any category of external self-determination accepted under customary law. The Israel-Palestinian conflict represents so unique and complex a situation in international law that it is doubtful that any established category of customary self-determination relates directly to it.[65]

Thus, Becker argues, Palestinian self-determination rights in the West Bank and Gaza Strip must be balanced on a relative basis against Israel's right to self-determination, and its right to protect its territorial integrity and its people from potential threats posed by a future Palestinian entity. The Gaza experience post-2005 has confirmed what Becker wrote in 1998, as Israel has faced intermittent Hamas rocket attacks ever since disengaging from Gaza, culminating in the horrific massacres, rapes, sexual violence, and hostage-takings of 7 October 2023.

Therefore, Becker argues:

> The doctrine of relative self-determination under international treaty law does not allow Israel to deny Palestinian rights to self-determination but neither does it guarantee that Palestinian self-determination in the territories will take the form of independent statehood. There seems to be general agreement in the international community that Palestinian self-determination could be implemented in the occupied territories while taking Israeli security concerns into account so that the sovereign integrity of Israel would be safeguarded.194 There is also widespread consensus that after years of conflict this balance should be reached by peaceful negotiation between all concerned parties.[66]

Assessment

The Palestinians have a strong political case for statehood in the West Bank and Gaza Strip, but their legal case is weak. The Palestinians waived and renounced statehood in those same areas for decades, hoping instead their Arab neighbors would destroy the Jewish State. When that dream led to disaster in June 1967, the Palestinians eventually reversed course and demanded statehood in the West Bank and Gaza.

However, the historical Palestinian position bears legal consequences relevant to their change of position today. The Palestinians are certainly estopped from laying claim today to the areas they lost to Israel in the 1948-49 war. The Palestinians failed to preserve their legal claims to those areas. Israel relied on Palestinian silence, as well as near-unanimous international recognition of the April 1949 Green Line borders.

The Palestinians may also be estopped from legal rights to statehood in the West Bank and Gaza Strip, but that presents a much closer question as a legal matter, even though as a political matter it may well represent the best and fairest outcome to the conflict.

Notes

1 Palestinian National Charter, Preamble and Art. 2 (28 May 1964).
2 *Id.* Art. 24 (emphasis added).
3 A. Abu-Odeh, *Jordanians, Palestinians and The Hashemite Kingdom in the Middle East Peace Process* at 105 (U.S. Institute of Peace Press, 1999).
4 A. Plascov, *The Palestinian Refugees in Jordan, 1948–1957* at 15 (Frank Cass & Co. Ltd., 1981).
5 WAFA, English edition, official PA news agency (23 Sept. 2022).
6 K. Parlett, *State Conduct in Territorial Disputes Beyond Effectivites: Recognition, Acquiescence, Renunciation and Estoppel*, in M. Kohen and M. Hebie (eds.), *Research Handbook on Territorial Disputes in International Law* at 183 (Edward Elgar, 2018).
7 L. Oppenheim and H. Lauterpacht, *International Law: A Treatise*, Vol. I (7th ed.) at 875 (Longmans, Green, 1948); *see also Case of Certain Norwegian Loans*, Judgment of July 6, 1957, I.C.J. Reports 1957, 9, 26 (express abandonment of known rights constitutes waiver under international law); *Armed Activities on the Territory of the Congo (Democratic Republic of the Congo v. Uganda)*, Judgment, I.C.J. Reports 2005, 168, para. 293 ("waivers or renunciations of claims or rights must either be express or unequivocally implied from the conduct of the State alleged to have waived or renounced its right ... [s]imilarly, the International Law Commission ... points out that '[a]lthough it may be possible to infer a waiver from the conduct of the States concerned or from a unilateral statement, the conduct or statement must be unequivocal'").
8 Indeed, it was not until the signing of the Oslo Accords that the PLO formally accepted the existence of Israel and refocused its aspirations for sovereignty on the West Bank and Gaza Even then, however, the Palestinians agreed that most of the West Bank (Area C) would remain under Israeli control, and they acknowledged Israel was reserving all rights regarding the final status of the West Bank, Gaza and East Jerusalem.
9 H. Lauterpacht, *Sovereignty over Submarine Areas* at 44 (British Yearbook, 1950) [emphasis in original].
10 *Id.* at 45.
11 J. Crawford, *The Creation of States in International Law* (2nd ed.) at 434 (Oxford Univ. Press, 2006).

12 *Chagos Marine Protected Area Arbitration (Mauritius v. UK)*, Permanent Court of Arbitration, 172, para. 435 (2015), quoting A.D. [Lord] McNair, *The Legality of the Occupation of the Ruhr*, British Year Book of International Law, 5 at 17, 35 (1924); *see also Dispute Concerning Delimitation of the Maritime Boundary between Bangladesh and Myanmar in the Bay of Bengal (Bangladesh/Myanmar)* (Judgment), ITLOS 4, 42 para. 124 (2012) ("in international law, a situation of estoppel exists when a State, by its conduct, has created the appearance of a particular situation and another State, relying on such conduct in good faith, has acted or abstained from an action to its detriment. The effect of the notion of estoppel is that a State is precluded, by its conduct, from asserting that it did not agree to, or recognize, a certain situation.").

13 *Temple of Preah Vihear (Cambodia v. Thailand)*, I.C.J. Reports, 1962, p. 6 at 39 (Separate Opinion of Vice-President Alfaro).

14 *Id.* at 143–44 para. 101 (Dissenting Opinion of Judge Spender).

15 *Chagos Marine Protected Area Arbitration (Mauritius v. UK)*, Permanent Court of Arbitration, 174, para. 438 (2015); *see also North Sea Continental Shelf (Germany/Denmark)*, ICJ Reports 1969, 26, para. 30 ("Having regard to these considerations of principle, it appears to the Court that only the existence of a situation of estoppel could suffice to lend substance to this contention, that is to say if the Federal Republic were now precluded from denying the applicability of the conventional regime, by reason of past conduct, declarations, etc., which not only clearly and consistently evinced acceptance of that regime, but also had caused Denmark or the Netherlands, in reliance on such conduct, detrimentally to change position or suffer some prejudice.").

16 *Id.* at 40.

17 *Id.* quoting Lauterpacht, *op.cit.*

18 R.Y. Jennings, *The Acquisition of Territory in International Law* at 58–60 (Manchester Univ. Press, 1963).

19 International Law Commission, *First Report of Special Rapporteur Victor Rodrígues Cedeño on Unilateral Acts of States*, A/CN.4/486, in *Yearbook of the International Law Commission*, vol. 2 at 250, para. 200 n.4 (1998), quoted in A. Kulick, *About the Order of Cart and Horse, Among Other Things: Estoppel in the Jurisprudence of International Investment Arbitration Tribunals*, European Journal of International Law, 27:1 at 108 (2016).

20 *In The Matter of The Chagos Marine Protected Area Arbitration* (Mauritius v. U.K, Case No. 2011-03) Award, Permanent Court of International Arbitration, para. 435 (18 Mar. 2015).

21 *Id.* paras. 436–38; *see also* Land and Maritime Boundary between Cameroon and Nigeria, Preliminary Objections, Judgment, I. C. J. Reports 1998, pp. 275, 303–04 para. 57 ("It would further be necessary that, by relying on such an attitude, Nigeria had changed position to its own detriment or had suffered some prejudice.").

22 The question whether Israel suffered any "detriment" by relying on the Palestinian waivers of sovereignty over the West Bank and Gaza is complex. Unquestionably Israel made significant financial investments to absorb the areas of Palestine the Arabs lost in the 1948-49 war. Whether the same analysis applies to the areas Israel captured in the June 1967 war presents a more difficult question.

23 *North Sea Continental Shelf, Judgment* (Federal Republic of Germany v. Denmark; Federal Republic of Germany v. Netherlands), 1969 I.C.J. Reports 3, 26 (1969).

24 J. Wass, *Jurisdiction by Estoppel and Acquiescence in International Courts and Tribunals*, The British Yearbook of International Law, 86:1, 155–95 at 155 (2017).
25 D.W. Bowett, *Estoppel before International Tribunals and Its Relation to Acquiescence*, British Yearbook of International Law, 33 at 176 (1957).
26 I.C. MacGibbon, *Estoppel in International Law*, The International and Comparative Law Quarterly, 7:3, 468–513 at 468–69 (1958).
27 K. Pan, *A Re-Examination of Estoppel in International Jurisprudence*, Chinese Journal of International Law, 16:4, 751–86 at 757–58 (2017).
28 *Elettronica Sicula S.p.A. (ELSI) (US v. Italy)*, ICJ Reports 1989, 44, para. 54.
29 *Temple of Preah Vihear (Cambodia v. Thailand)*, I.C.J. Reports, 1962, p. 6, 61 (Separate Opinion of Judge Fitzmaurice).
30 Pan, *op. cit.* at 773–74.
31 Reports of International Arbitral Awards, *Award in Regard to the Validity of the Treaty of Limits between Costa Rica and Nicaragua of 15 July 1858*, Decision of 26 July 1899, Volume XXVIII, 189–236 at 202–03.
32 Square mileage numbers are from S. Mishal, *West Bank/East Bank: The Palestinians in Jordan, 1949–1967* at 2 (Yale Univ. Press, 1978).
33 R.W. Ash, *Is Palestine a State: A Response to Professor John Quigley's Article, the Palestine Declaration to the International Criminal Court*, Rutgers Law Record, 36 at 198 (2009).
34 *Temple of Preah Vihear (Cambodia v. Thailand)*, I.C.J. Reports, 1962, p. 6, 41 (Separate Opinion of Vice-President Alfaro).
35 *Land and Maritime Boundary (Cameroon v. Nigeria: Equatorial Guinea intervening)*, ICJ Reports 2002, 341–42 para. 52; 409–411, paras. 213–14.
36 United Nations, S/242 (22 Nov. 1967); G. Watson, *The Oslo Accords: International Law and the Israeli-Palestinian Peace Agreements* at 268 (Oxford Univ. Press, 2000) ("Resolution 242 implicitly acknowledges Israel's sovereignty over West Jerusalem, since it calls only for withdrawal from 'territories occupied' in the 1967 War.").
37 I.C. MaGibbon, *Customary International Law and Acquiescence*, British Year Book of International Law, 33, 115–45, at 119 (1957).
38 *But see* J. McHugo, *Resolution 242: A Legal Reappraisal of the Right-Wing Israeli Interpretation of the Withdrawal Phrase with Reference to the Conflict between Israel and the Palestinians*, The International and Comparative Law Quarterly, 51:4, 851–81 at 880 (2002) (Discussing the interplay between the "inadmissibility" clause of Security Council Resolution 242 and the Arab designated areas of Palestine Israel captured in the 1948–1949 war, and noting "However, if any validity is to be attributed to the designation of the territories occupied in 1967 as 'disputed territories', Israel should be aware that the territory on the Israeli side of the 1949 Armistice Lines must ipso jure be treated as 'disputed'. Israeli title can only be perfected through the final peace settlement envisaged by Resolution 242 and subsequent resolutions, which alone can establish 'secure and recognised boundaries'. Failing this, Israel will always be exposed to a risk that claims may be brought for the territories which Israel took in 1948–9.")
39 *The Minquiers and Ecrehos Case*, Judgment of 17 Nov. 1953, I.C. J. Reports 1953, p. 47.
40 I.C.J. Oral Pleadings, *The Minquiers and Ecrehos Case* at 351 (United Kingdom/France).
41 J. Salmon, *Declaration of the State of Palestine*, The Palestine Yearbook of International Law, V at 48–82, 58–59 (1989).
42 Mishal, *op.cit.* at 22–23.

43 M.L. Burgis-Kasthala, Overstating *Palestine's UN Membership Bid? An Ethnographic Study on the Narratives of Statehood*, European Journal of International Law, 25:3, 677–701 at 681 (2014).
44 Salmon, *op. cit.* at 65.
45 *Id.*; *see also* D. Benoliel and R. Perry, *Israel, Palestine and the ICC*, Michigan Journal of International Law, 32:1 at 73–127 (2010) (arguing neither the West Bank nor Gaza are "states" under international law).
46 J. Stone, *Israel and Palestine: Assault on the Law of Nations* at 64 (The Johns Hopkins Univ. Press, 1981).
47 *Id.*
48 *Id.*
49 R. Soroczyński, *Acquisition of Title to Territory in the Aftermath of the Use of Force in the United Nations Era: The case of the State of Israel*, Revue Québécoise De Droit International/Quebec Journal of International Law/Revista Quebequense de Derecho Internacional, 30:1, 65–88 at 82 (2017).
50 A. Gerson, *Trustee-Occupant: The Legal Status of Israel's Presence in the West Bank*, Harvard International Law Journal, 14 at 35–36 (1973).
51 J. Strawson, *Partitioning Palestine: Legal Fundamentalism in the Palestinian-Israeli Conflict* at 102 (Pluto Press, 2010) (emphasis added).
52 E. Karsh, *Palestinian Leaders Don't Want an Independent State*, Middle East Quarterly, 21:3 at 11 (2014).
53 Cypher Telegram No. 232 (Confidential) from Kirkbride (Amman) to Foreign Office (23 Apr. 1949); *reprinted in* P. Toye and A. Seay, *Israel: Boundary Disputes with Arab Neighbours 1946–1964* Vol. 2 at 622 (Archive Editions, 1995).
54 *East Timor (Portugal v. Australia)*, Judgment, I.C.J. Reports 1995, 90, 102 para. 29 (30 June 1995).
55 T. Becker, *Self-Determination in Perspective: Palestinian Claims to Statehood and the Relativity of the Right to Self-Determination*, Israel Law Review, 32:2 at 301–54 (1998). Becker offers various examples in support of his argument, including the Kurdish claim to self-determination, which "has remained unanswered primarily because Kurdish self-determination would threaten the national and political interests of Turkey, Iran, Iraq and Syria."
56 *Id.* at 322.
57 Lauterpacht, *op. cit.* at 18.
58 United Nations General Assembly, A/RES/3226(XXIX) para. 1 (22 Nov. 1974).
59 Palestine National Council, *Declaration of Independence*, U.N. Doc. A/43/827, S/20278 (15 Nov. 1988).
60 A. Cassese, *Self-Determination of Peoples: A Legal Reappraisal* at 240 (Cambridge Univ. Press, 1995); *see also* H.B. Talal, *Palestinian Self-Determination: A Study of the West Bank and Gaza Strip* (Quartet, 1981).
61 Cassese, *op.cit.* at 242.
62 *Id.* at 243–44.
63 *Id.* at 245.
64 J. Quigley, *Sovereignty in Jerusalem*, Catholic University Law Review, 45 at 765, 768 (1996).
65 Becker, *op. cit.* at 342.
66 *Id.* at 346.

19

IS PALESTINE ALREADY A "STATE"?

Introductory Comments

Despite rejecting the two-state solution in November 1947 and for decades afterward, the Palestinians have reversed course in more recent years, arguing Palestine is already a "state" entitled to all the legal rights and privileges of statehood under international law.

Benoliel and Perry (2012) note that

> [t]o qualify as a state, a political entity must have a legal order that is distinct from other states and the capacity to act as it wishes within the limits of international law, without direct or indirect subordination to the will of another state or a group of states.[1]

The Palestinians fail this test for many reasons, perhaps most especially because the PLO willingly agreed in the Oslo Accords that it would not obtain statehood, if at all, until a permanent status agreement would be reached with Israel at some future date.

The Palestinians take a contradictory position regarding their status as a "state." On one hand, they claim they are already a state for various purposes, such as accession to the Rome Statute of the International Criminal Court. On the other hand, they claim they are not yet a state, and demand they be granted statehood. Indeed, the linchpin of Palestinian transformational legal framing ever since Oslo has focused on achieving international recognition of its "statehood:"

DOI: 10.4324/9781032686561-24

> Palestine's admission into the UN would, in Abbas' view, transform the Israeli-Palestinian conflict into a matter of one UN member state violating the sovereign rights of another. That could give the Palestinians access to various international forums and mechanisms, such as the UN's human rights bodies, the International Court of Justice, and even the International Criminal Court, and offer them new avenues to seek redress.[2]

For the past several decades, therefore, Palestinian lawyers and their supporters have argued Palestine has *already* evolved into statehood, even though they cannot pinpoint precisely *when* that occurred. Moreover, Palestinian claims that they have already achieved statehood cannot be reconciled with the facts on the ground, including the ongoing lawful Israeli military occupation of the West Bank, and the presence, whether legal or not, of tens of thousands of Israeli settlers in the West Bank.

Palestinian legal claims to statehood are based on a variety of theories as to when statehood arose. Some argue Palestine achieved proto-statehood long ago when the League of Nations granted Britain the Mandate to administer the country until the local population would be able to rule itself.[3] Others argue statehood arrived when the Mufti established the Gaza-based "All Palestine Government" in the fall of 1948. Still others point to the Palestine Liberation Organization's declaration of statehood in late 1988 following King Hussein's renunciation of Jordan's legal and administrative role in the West Bank.[4] All Palestinian supporters agree Palestine today should be regarded as a sovereign state, because the vast majority of countries around the world have accorded some form of recognition to the "State of Palestine."

Other scholars disagree, arguing Palestine has never attained statehood, and is not a state today. For example, Crawford (2006) noted Palestine failed to achieve statehood as a matter of international law after its unilateral declaration of statehood in 1988, and again after entering into the Oslo Accords with Israel.[5]

Moreover, Palestine cannot be regarded as a state *today*, because the Palestinians themselves have participated in multiple diplomatic initiatives over the past several decades with the stated goal of achieving Palestinian statehood at a *future* date. As Shaw (2011) notes:

> In the case of the Palestine, not only has no clear and formal claim to statehood been made, but also statements have been made continually declaring that the aim of the peace process is to establish a state of Palestine. This goes hand in hand with the explicit nature of the many instruments signed from the Declaration of Principles in 1993 onwards between the

relevant parties, and witnessed by leading members of the international community, and indeed with the whole tenor of international documents.[6]

The better view under international law is that Palestine, considering the West Bank and the Gaza Strip as a single entity pursuant to the Oslo Accords, is not a "state" but merely a non-state "subject of international law."[7]

The *Montevideo* Criteria

The disagreement regarding the "statehood of Palestine" depends on whether the Palestinians can prove they meet all four of the traditional four criteria for statehood under Article 1 of the 1933 *Montevideo Convention on the Rights and Duties of States*: (1) a permanent population, (2) a defined territory, (3) government, and (4) the capacity to enter into relations with another State (often read in tandem with the third element).[8] It is generally agreed these conditions represent customary international law.[9]

Population

This is the only element of the Montevideo test the Palestinians can satisfy, as there is a permanent, stable, and growing population in both the West Bank and the Gaza Strip.

Defined Territory

The Palestinians fail this element of the *Montevideo* test, as the West Bank is not a "defined territory." The Palestinians agreed in the Oslo Accords to the division of the West Bank into three separate areas. Area A comprises roughly 18% of the West Bank, consisting of the major Palestinian towns such as Ramallah, Bethlehem, Jericho, Nablus, Qalqilya, Jenin, Tulkarem, and most of Hebron. The Palestinian Authority received civic autonomy in Area A. The second area, known as Area B, comprises smaller towns and certain rural areas under the joint control of Israel and the PA, amounting to approximately 22% of the West Bank. The Palestinian Authority also received civic autonomy in Area B. Area C, which the PLO conceded would remain under exclusive Israeli control pending a permanent status agreement, contains the remaining 60% of the West Bank and tens of thousands of Israeli settlers.

Significantly, both the Palestinians and Israel agreed in the Oslo Interim Agreement (1995) that both sides were preserving all claims to the West Bank and Gaza pending the permanent status negotiations, contemplated to occur by the year 2000.[10] The mutual reservation of rights plus the Palestinian concessions in Area C constituted an implicit Palestinian acknowledgment that the Palestinian Authority lacks possession of a "defined territory."

Government

The Palestinians also cannot show they exercise governmental authority and effective control over the West Bank.[11] The West Bank remains under Israeli military occupation, although Areas A and B are largely autonomous and mainly under the control of Palestinian Authority security forces. The Palestinians, however, willingly agreed at Oslo they would have no jurisdiction over Area C. Tens of thousands of Israelis live in the West Bank in towns and settlements in Area C, not subject to Palestinian governmental authority. The Palestinians further agreed in the Oslo Accords that Israel would retain exclusive legal authority over Israel nationals and Israeli settlements in the West Bank during the interim period.[12]

Moreover, control of Palestine is fragmented. The PA has civic autonomy in Areas A and B of the West Bank. Hamas, on the other hand, has held absolute control over Gaza's population since overthrowing the PA in June 2007, although that is likely to change following Israel's military response to the 7 October 2023 Hamas terrorist invasion of southern Israel.[13]

Significantly, not a single country has recognized the Gaza Strip as an independent "state." As Benoliel and Perry (2010) noted:

> No state or important international organization has recognized a Hamas-based Palestinian state in the Gaza Strip. Such status most probably was never acquired by Hamas following its forcible assumption of power in the Strip in defiance of Palestinian Authority hegemony and of the Oslo peace process at large. Neither does the international community recognize the Hamas government, although it was democratically elected. Hence, the Gaza Strip cannot be deemed an independent state under this theory.[14]

The PA and Hamas have each established their own "ministries." Each maintains separate armed units. A potential Pakistan-Bangladesh style split seems as likely as reconciliation and unity among the competing Palestinian factions.

Foreign Relations

As discussed in Chapter 14, the Palestinians voluntarily agreed in the Oslo Interim Agreement that they would be barred from conducting foreign relations prior to reaching a permanent status deal with Israel. That agreement remains legally binding, even though the PA has subsequently signed a wide variety of international agreements in its capacity as a non-state "subject of international law" under Article 3(a) of the Vienna Convention on the Law of Treaties. But the PA's actions in that capacity do not suffice to meet the *Montevideo* test for conducting foreign relations, given the PA's express agreement at Oslo not to conduct such relations.

Moreover, both Shany (2010)[15] and Watson (2000)[16] have noted Oslo's severe limitations on the Palestinian Authority's ability to conduct foreign relations as a major factor in concluding Palestine fails the foreign relations element of the *Montevideo* test for statehood. Even the International Criminal Court, in its controversial 2021 split decision in favor of Palestine's "accession" to the Rome Statute, nevertheless found Palestine lacked the capacity to enter into treaty relations.[17]

The Palestinians fail the second, third, and fourth requirements of the *Montevideo* test for statehood. Crawford (1990), writing prior to the Oslo Accords, also rejected the Palestinian claim to have met the *Montevideo* criteria:

> Even applying the Montevideo Convention, in a relatively superficial way, in accordance with its terms, it is difficult to see how Palestine could constitute a state. Its whole territory is occupied by Israel, which functions as a government in the territory. The Palestine Liberation Organization has never functioned as a government in respect of the occupied territories. But the Montevideo Convention treats statehood essentially as an existing state of affairs, as a matter of fact as much as a matter of law. And as a matter of fact, notwithstanding that allegiance, neither the PLO nor the Palestine National Council has been in a position to exercise the whole range of governmental powers within the territory concerned. That they may have a right to do so – or, more accurately, that the Palestinian people may have a right to choose a representative authority to govern themselves – is beside the point, from the perspective of the Montevideo formula.[18]

Moreover, the historical facts demonstrate the Palestinian Arabs have never satisfied the *Montevideo* test. They rejected statehood over all of Palestine when the British Government offered it to them in the 1939 White Paper. They renounced statehood over a portion of Palestine when the British Government offered it to them in 1937, and again when the United Nations offered it to them in 1947.

Furthermore, during the 45 years between the Palestinian pledge of loyalty to King Abdullah in December 1948 and the September 1993 Oslo Declaration of Principles, the Palestinians never revoked their renunciation of Resolution 181(II) and the two-state solution. Nor did they attempt to create a state in the Jordanian-occupied West Bank and East Jerusalem or the Egyptian-occupied Gaza Strip between 1948 and 1967. The United Nations lost interest as well during the period between 1952 and 1967. Those years saw a "shift away from international recognition of Palestinian Arab Nationhood."[19]

Circumventing *Montevideo*

Palestinian advocates nevertheless offer a broad variety of arguments in support of their claim that Palestine is *already* a State. Knowing they cannot satisfy the *Montevideo* criteria, those advocates have proposed new formulae to replace *Montevideo* as the appropriate test for statehood.

For example, some Palestinian advocates have urged replacing *Montevideo* with other theories for determining statehood, such as the "declaratory" theory and/or the "constitutive/recognition" theory. Other advocates urge replacing *Montevideo* with a far more elastic "functional equivalent" test, designed to make it as easy as possible for Palestine to qualify for statehood.[20]

The *declaratory* theory holds that statehood may be recognized based on another State's willingness to engage in diplomatic relations with the emerging State. The theory posits that an entity may be defined as a "state" if it meets certain structural criteria, even if it is not recognized as such by other states. "Recognition, therefore, is only declaratory of an existing fact."[21]

The *constitutive* theory requires formal recognition from other states. "The controversy," according to Ronen (2014), "revolves on whether recognition, as a legal concept, should be perceived as a requisite for the existence of a state (constitutive) or whether it merely acknowledges an existing situation (declaratory)."[22]

Proponents of the "functional" theory argue the ICC may treat Palestine as a "state" to fulfill the purposes and objectives of the court. Thus, they argue, the court should be free, under the *kompetenz-kompetenz* principle, to treat Palestine as a "state" for purposes of applying the Rome Statute.[23] Soler (2019) offers the following definition of the principle:

> The ultimate power possessed by courts is the *compétence de la compétence* doctrine. The *kompetenz-kompetenz* doctrine allows court to assess, to determine and restrict their own jurisdictional competence. It is hence the very same courts which determine their own jurisdictional competence and the limits to be imposed there upon. Such inherent powers could be exercised for various reasons, such as the right and power to adjudicate. Inherent powers are 'powers that are not expressly conferred on them by the terms of their statutes and rules of procedure,' these being their constitutive instruments, 'but which are nonetheless necessary for the performance of their functions.'[24]

Soler adds that *kompetenz-kompetenz* can only be invoked in cases where the court already has jurisdiction, and "cannot be exercised by courts which want or vaunt the right to enjoy (assume) jurisdiction."[25]

Shaw (2011) criticized the functional approach as a "teleological" argument designed to achieve statehood for Palestine where the text of the Rome Statute permitted no such outcome:

> The whole teleological argument revolves around two essential points: first, that the term 'state' in Article 12(3) is inherently ambiguous, and, secondly, that the interpretation of that term in the light of the objects and purpose of the Rome Statute led inexorably to the conclusion that such term must be understood to include entities that are clearly not states in public international law ... It is, of course, necessary that the [Rome] Statute be interpreted in a way that fulfils its objectives, but such objectives do not include re-interpretation of clear terms ... The teleological approach to treaty interpretation does not give free reign to the interpreter to alter the clear meaning of terms.[26]

When did Palestine Achieve Statehood?

Palestinian advocates have offered a range of inconsistent theories to pinpoint precisely *when* Palestine achieved statehood. Quigley (2010), for example, argues Palestine achieved at least "provisional statehood" as early as mid-1919, pursuant to Article 22 of the Covenant of the League of Nations, which conferred sovereignty on the people of Palestine, who at that time were overwhelmingly Arab.[27]

But Quigley's view has little or no support, even among Arab experts. For example, the Crown Prince of Jordan, His Royal Highness Hassan bin Talal (1979), rejected Quigley's argument:

> It would seem, therefore, that nothing in the Mandate for Palestine conferred territorial sovereignty over any part of Palestine, including Jerusalem, upon the Council of the League, the League itself, the Mandatory, or upon the Arab or Jewish communities comprising the inhabitants of the mandated area. During the existence of the Mandate, i.e., until May 14, 1948, territorial sovereignty was in abeyance or suspense.[28]

Crawford (2007) also rejects Quigley's view, arguing the Mandate system did not confer sovereignty on the mandated territories or their inhabitants:

> The notion of 'sovereignty' then was inapplicable to the system of Mandates and Trusteeships, according to the received view. Nevertheless writers tended to be internally consistent in their approaches to the questions of sovereignty, termination and revocation— deducing, for example, the existence of a power of revocation from the location of a residual sovereignty in the League or the United Nations, or conversely the impossibility of revocation from the existence of sovereignty 'subject to the Mandate' in the Mandatory. Neither approach is satisfactory. The implications to be drawn from the creation and structure of the two systems are not usefully summarized one way or another by the concept of sovereignty, which, if anything, would be a conclusion from the power of revocation rather than its premise.[29]

Others argue statehood arose later, when the Mufti established the sham Gaza-based "All-Palestine Government" in October 1948.[30] But as discussed in Chapter 10, that "government" was nothing more than an empty shell.

Still others argue statehood arose when the United Nations Security Council adopted Resolutions 242 and 338 after the June 1967 and October 1973 Arab-Israeli wars; or when Jordan renounced its legal and administrative ties to the West Bank in 1988; or when the Palestine Liberation Organization unilaterally declared Palestinian "statehood" in 1988; or when the Israelis agreed to limited Palestinian autonomy in Area A of the West Bank in the 1994 Oslo Accords; or when the United Nations General Assembly granted Palestine non-member "observer state" status in 2012 and 2024; or when the majority of United Nations member states subsequently recognized the "State of Palestine."

The ambiguity in the Palestinian position regarding *when* statehood arose became a key issue in a landmark 2005 case before the United States Court of Appeals for the First Circuit. The PLO had been named as a defendant in a tort lawsuit in the United States. The PLO moved to dismiss the case, arguing it was a "state" and therefore entitled to sovereign immunity. The court rejected the PLO's argument. In so doing, the court focused on the PLO's inability to prove when it had supposedly achieved statehood:

> [I]t is hard to pin down exactly when or how the defendants assert that Palestine achieved statehood. At various points in their briefs, they hint at three possibilities: (i) the period from the beginning of the mandate through the 1967 Arab-Israeli war; (ii) the period from the end of that war up until the creation of the Palestinian Authority (1994); and (iii) the period from 1994 forward ... the defendants have not carried their burden of showing that Palestine satisfied the requirements for statehood under the applicable principles of international law at *any* point in time.[31]

Saed (2019) nevertheless argues Palestine has achieved "abstract statehood" by virtue of its broad, although not unanimous, international recognition.[32] Other scholars argue the General Assembly's grant of "non-member observer State status" in Resolution 67/19 (29 November 2012) somehow equated to a legal grant of "statehood."[33] Ronen (2014) argues the Resolution accorded statehood to Palestine by virtue of the broad international consensus in support of recognition:

> [T]he recognition of the state of Palestine by UNGA Resolution 67/19 encompasses the international recognition of territory belonging to that state, notwithstanding the absence of Israeli consent (of whatever meaning) with respect to that territory ... there is without doubt an overwhelming international consensus on the right of the Palestinians to self-determination in the West Bank and Gaza Strip, which through UNGA Resolution 67/19 has been realised through an acknowledgement of statehood.[34]

Still others contend many countries and international organizations have accorded various forms of *de facto* recognition to "Palestine," thereby amounting to a collective recognition of Palestinian statehood. These scholars further argue that nothing subsequent to the issuance of the Covenant of the League of Nations and the Mandate deprived the Palestinian Arabs of their putative statehood, at least as to the portions of Palestine (the West Bank, Gaza, and East Jerusalem) they continue claiming today.[35]

The Palestinians more recently have implemented a strategy to achieve "statehood" unilaterally, by self-acclamation. The strategy emerged on 30 November 1988 with the Palestine National Council's adoption of a "Declaration of Independence," proclaiming their "statehood."[36] The United Nations General Assembly, completely siding with the Palestinian cause since the late 1960s, recognized the Declaration and replaced the designation "Palestine Liberation Organization" with "Palestine."[37]

In December 2012 the United Nations General Assembly gave the Palestinian effort a huge boost, adopting Resolution 67/19 and elevating the Palestinian territories to the Vatican-like status of "non-member observer state."[38] More than 100 countries currently recognize the "State of Palestine."

Statehood Not Yet Achieved

Despite those developments, the legal reality is that Palestine to this day has *never* achieved statehood. Although modern-day Palestine possesses far more attributes of proto- or quasi-statehood than did the Mufti's short-lived "All Palestine Government," Palestine still falls well short of statehood. Palestine enjoys "observer status" at the United Nations. It has overseas "missions" and "ambassadors" and a national flag – all symbols of *aspirational* but not *actual* statehood.

Moreover, neither the Palestinian Authority, Hamas, Israel, Jordan or Egypt holds sovereignty over the West Bank or the Gaza Strip. Indeed, no one has held sovereignty over those areas since Turkey renounced its claims to Palestine in the 1923 Treaty of Lausanne.[39]

Stone (1981) notes that if the Palestinian Arabs had accepted Resolution 181, then both the Jews and Palestinian Arabs would have obtained sovereignty in the areas allocated to them. However, Stone argues, when the Arabs rejected the partition resolution and launched war, "[t]here was in fact no such agreement, no such effect in vesting and delimiting titles, and no such entities as the proposed Arab state and *corpus separatum* [internationalized Jerusalem] came into being in fact or in law."[40]

The 1949 armistice agreements froze sovereignty in the West Bank and the Gaza Strip. Thus, both Gaza and the West Bank as early as 15 May 1948 – and certainly by April 1949 – existed with sovereignty suspended or in abeyance.[41] Jordan did not acquire sovereignty when it "annexed" the

West Bank and occupied it between 1949 and 1967. Nor did Egypt gain or even assert sovereignty over Gaza between 1949 and 1967.[42]

Instead, Jordan and Egypt occupied the West Bank and Gaza from 1949 to 1967. In June 1967 Israel replaced Jordan as the occupant of the West Bank, and from June 1967 to September 2005 Israel replaced Egypt as the occupant of the Gaza Strip. Jordan's subsequent termination of its legal and administrative ties with the West Bank in 1988 had no legal effect, as Jordan never possessed sovereignty over those areas, and thus could not lawfully transfer sovereignty to anyone else. Nor did Israel's unilateral withdrawal from the Gaza Strip in September 2005, ending Israel's status as a "belligerent occupant," have any effect on Gaza's ongoing status as a legal non-entity.[43]

Assessment

To this day, sovereignty over the West Bank and the Gaza Strip has not been resolved conclusively as a matter of international law. No one has legal title to either area.

The most that can be said regarding sovereignty over the areas Israel has occupied since 1967 is that *neither* the Palestinian Arabs *nor* Israel can establish, as a purely legal matter, a perfected claim to sovereignty. The Palestinian Authority maintains civilian control over Area A, but Israel continues to exercise military control over Area A, thereby precluding a finding of Palestinian *effective* control over Areas A and B as a matter of international law.

Moreover, the Palestinian Authority has no control over Area C. Nor can Palestinian efforts to change the facts on the ground by mounting illegal construction projects in Area C pave the way for Palestinian statehood as a matter of international law.

As Ronen (2021) aptly noted, "One cannot hold that Palestine has sufficient control over a territory to be regarded as a state, and at the same time that Israel has sufficient control to be regarded as an occupant in the same territory."[44] Even Palestinian frame entrepreneurs prefer to characterize the West Bank as not under effective Palestinian control, but instead controlled by Israel through South-African style apartheid practices.

Israel, for its part, has never formally asserted sovereignty over any portion of the West Bank or the Gaza Strip (notwithstanding proposals floated in 2019–2020 to annex portions of the West Bank, including the Jordan Valley and the Israeli settlements), except for Greater Jerusalem and the Old City, where the Israeli claim to sovereignty is arguably stronger than the Palestinian claim, as discussed below in Chapter 20.

Israel remains a belligerent occupant of the West Bank, whereas Gaza has lived under the non-sovereign control of Hamas since mid-2007. In that regard, Hamas – at least prior to October 2023 – could have made a stronger claim of statehood in the Gaza Strip than the PA could have made for the

West Bank, although the Hamas claim still would not have passed the *Montevideo* test. Ironically, Palestinian frame entrepreneurs continually undermine any claim of Gazan statehood by arguing the area is not under Palestinian control, but instead is "the world's largest open air prison" and remains under Israeli "occupation."

This *legal* outcome, however, does not preclude the Palestinians from arguing, as a *political* matter, their entitlement to statehood in the West Bank and Gaza Strip. But such statehood may arise only from a negotiated political settlement with Israel, not as the result of any Palestinian legal claim to the same United Nations offer of sovereignty they renounced in November 1947. Palestinian statehood in the West Bank and Gaza Strip can and should be resolved through diplomatic negotiation, *not* adversarial litigation.

Notes

1 D. Benoliel and R. Perry, *Israel, Palestine and the ICC*, Michigan Journal of International Law, 32:1, 73–127 at 92 (2010).
2 K. Elgindy, *Palestine Goes to the UN: Understanding the New Statehood Strategy*, Foreign Affairs, 90:5 at 107 (2011); *see also* N. Erakat, *Justice for Some: Law and the Question of Palestine* at 221–22 (Stanford Univ. Press, 2019) (explaining ulterior legal motives for Palestinian efforts to achieve "statehood").
3 *See, e.g.*, V. Kattan, *From Co-Existence to Conquest: International Law and the Origins of the Arab-Israeli Conflict, 1891–1949* at 133–40 (Pluto Press, 2009).
4 *Speech by King Hussein on Jordan's Separation from West Bank* (31 July 1988), 28 I.L. M. 1637 (1988). For a pro-Palestinian view regarding the status of West Bank sovereignty, *see* United Nations A/CN.4/557, V. Rodríguez Cedeño, Special Rapporteur, *Unilateral Acts of States (Eighth Report)* at para. 53 (2005) ("The question arises whether the King of Jordan was competent to act at the international level and to formulate the waiver on behalf of Jordan. It is significant that the Constitution of Jordan prohibits any act related to the transfer of territory, so that it would appear that the King exceeded his authority. However, that did not prevent the waiver from producing legal effects, and in fact a transfer of the territory of the West Bank to the State of Palestine actually took place").
5 J. Crawford, *The Creation of States in International Law* (2nd ed.) at 448 (Clarendon Press, 2006); *see also* note 162 *supra*.
6 M. Shaw, *The Article 12(3) Declaration of the Palestinian Authority, the International Criminal Court and International Law*, Journal of International Criminal Justice, 9:2, 301–24 (2011).
7 G. Watson, *The Oslo Accords: International Law and the Israeli-Palestinian Peace Agreements* at 58 (Oxford Univ. Press, 2000). Eyal Bevenisti (1993) noted some scholars had been willing to acknowledge that insurgent movements, especially those signing peace agreements with the governments they had fought against, could possibly be recognized as "subjects of international law." E. Benvenisti, *The Israeli-Palestinian Declaration of Principles: Framework for Future Settlement*, European Journal of International Law, 4:4, 542–54 at 544–45 (1993).
8 Montevideo Convention, Art. I (1933). The United States standard for determining statehood is set forth in the Restatement (Third) of Foreign Relations, deeming a state to be "an entity that has a defined territory and a permanent population, under the control of its own government, and that engages in, or has the capacity to engage in, formal relations with other such entities." *Restatement (Third) of*

Foreign Relations § 201 (1987). Some recent scholarship has questioned the ongoing validity of the four *Montevideo* criteria as determinants of statehood. *See, e.g.*, J. Crawford, *The Creation of States in International Law* at 47 (Oxford Univ. Press, 1979); T. Grant, *Defining Statehood: The Montevideo Convention and Its Discontents*, Columbia Journal of Transnational Law, 37:2, 403–45 (1999).

9 R. Lapidoth, *When Is an Entity Entitled to Statehood?*, Israel Journal of Foreign Affairs, 6:3, 77–81 at 77–78 (2012).

10 *Oslo II*, Art. XXXI.6 ("Nothing in this Agreement shall prejudice or preempt the outcome of the negotiations on the permanent status to be conducted pursuant to the DOP. Neither Party shall be deemed, by virtue of having entered into this Agreement, to have renounced or waived any of its existing rights, claims or positions.").

11 Y. Ronen, *Israel, Palestine and the ICC – Territory Uncharted but not Unknown*, Journal of International Criminal Justice, 12:1, 7–25, at 13 (2014), quoting Crawford, *op. cit.* at 48.

12 *Israeli-Palestinian Interim Agreement on the West Bank and the Gaza Strip*, Article XVII (2), 37 ILM (1997) 551 (8 Sept. 1995).

13 Shaw (2011), *op. cit.* at 307–08 (PA's lack of control over Gaza undermines "the necessary criterion of effective government" for statehood).

14 Benoliel and Perry, *op. cit.* at 101.

15 Y. Shany, *In Defence of Functional Interpretation of Article 12(3) of the Rome Statute: A Response to Yael Ronen*, Journal of International Criminal Justice, 8:2, 329–43 at 340–41 (2010).

16 Watson (2000), *op. cit.* at 70–71.

17 International Criminal Court, *Situation in the State of Palestine*, ICC-01/18, para. 108 (5 Feb. 2021) ("The Court is not constitutionally competent to determine matters of statehood that would bind the international community. In addition, such a determination is not required for the specific purposes of the present proceedings or the general exercise of the Court's mandate.").

18 J. Crawford, *The Creation of the State of Palestine: Too Much Too Soon*, European Journal of International Law, 1, 307–13, at 308–09 (1990); *see also* R. Jennings and A. Watts (eds.), *Oppenheim's International Law, Vol. I: Peace* (9th ed.) at 131 n.2 (Longman, 1996) (rejecting statehood status for Palestine due to the lack of defined territory and the lack of governing authority over the West Bank).

19 O. Dajani, *Stalled between the Seasons: The International Legal Status of Palestine during The Interim Period*, Denver Journal of International Law and Policy, 26 at 40 (1997).

20 *See generally* E. Kontorovich, *Israel/Palestine – The ICC's Uncharted Territory*, Journal of International Criminal Justice, 11 at 979 (2013).

21 Benoliel and Perry, *op. cit.* at 102.

22 Ronen, *op. cit.* at 12; *see also* D. Benoliel and R. Perry, *Israel, Palestine and the ICC*, Michigan Journal of International Law, 32:1, 73–127 at 82 (2010) (criticizing the constitutive theory as "overly subjective and hence practically insufficient vis-a-vis the Palestinian statehood case.").

23 *See* S. Adem, *Palestine and the International Criminal Court* at 55–76 (Springer, 2019); Crawford, *op. cit.* at 17–25; Brownlie, *op. cit.* at 91–93; Oppenheim and Lauterpacht, *op. cit.* at 120–34.

24 C. Soler, *The Exercise of Kompetenz-Kompetenz in the Determination of Presumptive Jurisdiction*, in *The Global Prosecution of Core Crimes under International Law*, 587–96 at 588 (T.M.C. Asser Press, 2019).

25 *Id.*

26 Shaw (2011), *op. cit.* at 311–14.

27 J. Quigley, *The Statehood of Palestine: International Law in the Middle East Conflict* (Cambridge Univ. Press, 2010).

28 H. Bin Talal, *A Study on Jerusalem* at 17 (Longman, 1979).

29 Crawford (2006), *op. cit.* at 573.

30 V. Kattan, "A Critical Assessment of the Government of Israel's Memorandum to the ICC – Part I," Blog (30 Jan. 2020), https://www.ejiltalk.org/a-critical-assessment-of-the-government-of-israels-memorandum-to-the-icc-part-i/ (last accessed 12 Apr. 2024). ("Although the APG did not last a long time, it was sufficiently 'sovereign' to have proclaimed independence, drafted a constitution, issued passports, and established diplomatic relations with the Arab League and with other Arab states."). As already demonstrated in this study, the Palestinian "government" in Gaza was nothing more than a paper creation, exercising no governmental authority at all. The fact that it managed to print a few hundred passports is meaningless for purposes of satisfying the *Montevideo* criteria.

31 *Ungar v. Palestine Liberation Organization*, 402 F.3d 274, 289, 292 (1st Cir. 2005) (emphasis added).

32 Adem, *op. cit.* at 68.

33 United Nations, General Assembly Resolution 67/19, (A/67/L.28 and Add.1), *Status of Palestine in the United Nations* (29 Nov. 2012) ("The General Assembly ... "*Decides* to accord to Palestine non-member observer State status in the United Nations, without prejudice to the acquired rights, privileges and role of the Palestine Liberation Organization in the United Nations as the representative of the Palestinian people, in accordance with the relevant resolutions and practice.").

34 Ronen, *op. cit.* at 12, 14.

35 *See, e.g.*, Quigley (2010), *op. cit.*; F. Boyle, *The Creation of the State of Palestine*, European Journal of International Law 1 at 301 (1990); *but see* Crawford (1990), *op. cit.* (criticizing Boyle's argument for Palestinian statehood as "weak and unconvincing. Indeed, it is weaker and more unconvincing than it need have been, having regard to some of the post-1945 developments, and in particular to the case of Guinea Bissau. But if that case is to be justified on the premise '*nasciturus pro jam natus habetur*,' the fact remains that a real State of Palestine is by no means yet assured. For a Palestinian State to be properly described as '*nasciturus*,' what is needed is statesmanship on all sides, and respect for the rights of the peoples and states of the region. The manipulation of legal categories is unlikely to advance matters").

36 United Nations General Assembly, A/43/827, Palestine Declaration of Independence (18 Nov. 1988).

37 United Nations General Assembly, Resolution 43/177, UN Doc. A/RES/43/177 (15 Dec. 1988); *see also* Adem, *op. cit.* at 62. Adem concedes, however, that "it is difficult to reach a definite conclusion on the statehood of Palestine on a mere reliance on the declaration of independence and the engagement of Palestine with international law and organisations." *Id.* at 64; V. Tsilonis, *The Jurisdiction of the International Criminal Court* at 56 (Springer, 2019) ("the term 'State' has for each international organisation and court a 'variable geometry,' that is, a constantly changing definition; a fact which undoubtedly proves that the term 'State' does not have such a strictly defined meaning from a legal perspective as one would initially think").

38 United Nations, UNGA A/RES/67/19 "Status of Palestine in the United Nations" (4 Dec. 2012). The General Assembly upgraded Palestine's "observer status" on 10 May 2024 and requested the Security Council consider granting Palestine full membership, even though the United States vetoed a similar request three weeks earlier, on 18 April 2024.

39 *British Empire, France, Italy, Japan, Greece, &c., and Turkey: Treaty of Peace, signed at Lausanne, July 24, 1923*, League of Nations Treaty Series, Vol. XXVIII, Nos. 1, 2, 3 and 4 (1924).

40 *Id.* at 62–63; *see also* Shany, *op. cit.* at 403 (Resolution 181(II) lapsed and fell into "desuetude"); *but see* A. Gerson, *Trustee-Occupant: The Legal Status of Israel's Presence in the West Bank*, Harvard International Law Journal, 14 at 35–36 (1973) (arguing the Palestinian Arabs received sovereignty over the areas the UN had allocated to them by operation of law immediately upon the adoption of Resolution 181(II)).

41 The Jordan-Israel armistice agreement contained language expressly preserving both parties' rights and claims to the West Bank and East Jerusalem. The Israel-Egypt Armistice Agreement provided, "It is not the purpose of this Agreement to establish, to recognize, to strengthen, or to weaken or nullify, in any way, any territorial, custodial or other rights, claims or interests which may be asserted by either Party in the area of Palestine or any part or locality thereof covered by this Agreement." Israel-Egypt Armistice Agreement, United Nations Treaty Series No. 654, Art. IV.2 (24 Feb. 1949). Likewise, the Jordan-Israel Armistice Agreement provided, "No provision of this Agreement shall in any way prejudice the rights, claims and positions of either Party hereto in the ultimate peaceful settlement of the Palestine question." United Nations Treaty Series No. 656, Art. II.2 (3 Apr. 1949); *see also* United Nations Security Council, S/1302/REV.1 1/, cablegram from the United Nations Acting Mediator to the Secretary-General transmitting the text of the General Armistice Agreement between the Hashemite Jordan Kingdom and Israel, Art. II.2 (3 Apr. 1949). The British Government also took the legal position that the Arab renunciation of Resolution 181(II) would result in the Arab-allocated areas of Palestine becoming a "'no man's land' on and after May 15." 867N.01/5–248, L. Henderson, Memorandum (Top Secret), "British-American Cooperation with Regard to Palestine" at 3–4 (2 May 1948).

42 A. Sharon, *Why Is Israel's Presence in the Territories Still Called "Occupation"?* Jewish Political Studies Review, 23:3/4 at 46 (2011) (Egypt claimed sovereignty over the Sinai Peninsula but not Gaza).

43 *Ahmad et al. v. Prime Minister*, Israel Supreme Court (sitting as the High Court of Justice), HCJ 9132/07 (30 Jan. 2008) at 8, para. 12 ("The State argued before us that it acts according to the rules of international law and respects its humanitarian obligations under the laws of warfare. According to counsel for the State, these are limited obligations, derived from the state of warfare in existence between the State of Israel and the Hamas organization that controls the Gaza Strip, and from the need to prevent harm to the civilian population caught in the area of the hostilities. In this context, we note that since September 2005, Israel no longer has effective control over what takes place within the territory of the Gaza Strip. The military government that previously existed in that territory was abolished by means of a decision of the government, and Israeli soldiers are not present in that area on a permanent basis and do not direct what occurs there. In these circumstances, under the international law of occupation, the State of Israel has no general obligation to care for the welfare of the residents of the Strip").

44 Y. Ronen, *Palestine in the ICC: Statehood and the Right to Self-Determination in the Absence of Effective Control*, Journal of International Criminal Justice, 18:4, 947–66 at 957 (2021).

PART V

Assessing the Palestinian Legal Case

Jerusalem

20
WHO OWNS JERUSALEM?

Introductory Comment

The legal status of Jerusalem is the most difficult knot to untangle in the entire Israeli-Palestinian conflict. Britain conquered Jerusalem in December 1917. The League of Nations awarded the Palestine Mandate to Great Britain in July 1922, but Britain never acquired sovereignty over Jerusalem.

The United Nations General Assembly in the 29 November 1947 partition resolution called for Jerusalem to become a separate entity under international authority. The UN did not allocate *any* portion of Jerusalem to the Palestinian Arabs. By the end of the 1948–1949 war, Israel controlled West Jerusalem. Jordan controlled East Jerusalem and the Old City. The United Nations did nothing to implement or enforce the proposal to internationalize Jerusalem, and it dropped the issue entirely between 1952 and 1967.

Following the 1948–1949 war, the international community refused to recognize Israeli sovereignty over West Jerusalem, which Israel proclaimed as its capital in 1950. Over time, however, several countries decided to move their embassies from Tel Aviv to Jerusalem, and by late May 1967, more than 20 countries had done so.

Meanwhile, no country except Pakistan recognized Jordanian sovereignty over East Jerusalem and the Old City between 1948 and 1967. Jordan kept Amman as its capital, relegating Jerusalem to second-class status. During the years of Jordanian occupation, the Palestinians never asserted any claims of sovereignty over Jerusalem. Nor did the UN during those years ever characterize any portion of Jerusalem as "occupied Palestinian territory."

Israel captured the West Bank, East Jerusalem, and the Old City following Jordan's unprovoked attack against Israel in June 1967. Israel acted lawfully

DOI: 10.4324/9781032686561-26

in self-defense. Five months later, the UN Security Council in Resolution 242 called for Israel to withdraw "from territories occupied in the recent conflict," meaning only East Jerusalem and the Old City. The Security Council thereby implicitly recognized Israel's sovereignty over West Jerusalem.

Although Israeli diplomats argued during the early 1950s that the Old City should be internationalized, Israel changed its position after capturing the Old City from Jordan in June 1967. Israel subsequently passed legislation declaring all of Jerusalem its capital.

Arab and Palestinian commentators, on the other hand, insist Resolution 242 obligates Israel to withdraw completely from East Jerusalem, including the Old City. The Palestinians have also left open the possibility of laying claim to West Jerusalem. Thus, for example, two weeks after Jordan renounced its administrative links to the West Bank in October 1988, the PLO proclaimed the State of Palestine with "Jerusalem" as its capital, without specifying which areas of Jerusalem.[1]

In any event, Jerusalem will be the most sensitive and protracted issue for the final rounds of the permanent status negotiations, if those negotiations ever occur.

Lapidoth (2001) explained the complex interplay of religio-nationalist issues involved in determining Jerusalem's legal status:

> The international community has not recognized Israeli de jure sovereignty in Jerusalem, although in practice Israeli's control over the western neighbourhoods has been accepted, in particular the applicability of Israeli law and jurisdiction. Most states, as well as the UN organs, however, consider the eastern parts as occupied territory. There are at least four components to the Jerusalem problem: 1. The national aspirations: Israelis and Palestinians have conflicting claims to sovereignty. Israel claims sovereignty over the whole city, and the Palestinians have a similar claim, at least over the eastern neighbourhoods of the city. 2. The religious aspect: Some of the most sacred places according to Judaism, Christianity and Islam are located in the city. These places are holy to many millions of people who do not live in the city nor in the area. 3. The demography: The population of Jerusalem is very heterogeneous, and hence special solutions are needed for the municipal management. 4. The periphery: Whatever solution is reached with regard to borders, Jerusalem will be between Israel and the Palestinian entity. The relationship between the city and its periphery requires special arrangements. In the above-mentioned Declaration of Principles on Interim Self-Government Arrangements of 1993 Israel and the Palestinians dealt, although to a very limited extent, with Jerusalem. Jerusalem was not to be included in the interim arrangements – a concession by the Palestinians – and, on the other hand, Israel conceded that the city would be one of the subjects to be dealt with in the framework of the negotiations on the 'permanent status negotiations.'[2]

The Crown Prince of Jordan, Hassan bin Talal, offered the following advice many years ago to lawyers seeking to parse the legal issues regarding Jerusalem:

> The literature on the political, religious and historical claims to Jerusalem considerably exceeds the writing of jurists about the validity of such claims. All too frequently much of the literature is markedly partial. This makes it the more necessary that the lawyer should approach the legal issues concerning Jerusalem with the maximum amount of detachment that he can bring to bear in order to counterbalance the partisan nature of the political polemic and the dogmatic quality of much of the religious debate.[3]

This chapter has been written in that spirit.

Relevant History

Ottoman Rule (1517–1917)

History records the ancient presence of both Israelite (later Jewish) and non-Israelite peoples in the areas including modern-day Israel, the West Bank, Gaza, and Jordan. King David conquered Jerusalem from the Jebusites in 1055 BCE. Thereafter Jerusalem stood for centuries as the center of Jewish life and religious observance, and later as a Holy City for Christians and Muslims too.

Following the Roman conquest in 70 A.D., a small number of Jews remained more or less continuously in Jerusalem, Tzfat, Hebron, and Tiberias, including after the Muslim conquest in the first half of the 7th century. Except for a period during the Crusader wars, Jerusalem remained under Muslim rule until the end of World War I, including the last 400 years (1517–1917) under Ottoman rule.

Jerusalem remained a backwater during Ottoman times, although it enjoyed special status as an independent *Sanjak* reporting directly to the Sultanate. In the wake of the Crimean War, the European powers took an interest in Jerusalem. The March 1856 Treaty of Paris accorded special recognition to Christian rights at Jerusalem's Holy sites, providing for a *Status Quo* regime that has prevailed to this day.[4]

From the 1840s onward Jews comprised the largest identifiable population group in Jerusalem.

World War I to 1948

Britain ousted the Ottoman Empire from the Middle East near the end of World War I. General Edmund Allenby marched into Jerusalem in December 1917, reading a proclamation announcing Britain's intention to enforce the *Status Quo* at the Holy sites and to guarantee freedom of religion and free access.

The British military administration left Jerusalem in July 1920 with the arrival of High Commissioner Sir Herbert Samuel, who established his headquarters in Jerusalem. In July 1922, the League of Nations appointed Britain as mandatory. The situation remained that way until Britain handed the Palestine file to the UN in early 1947, culminating in the General Assembly's recommendation for the two-state solution in November 1947, with Jerusalem to remain a separate entity under international control.

United Nations Partition Plan

The UN's 29 November 1947 partition plan envisioned the internationalization of Jerusalem:

> The City of Jerusalem shall be established as a corpus separatum under a special international regime and shall be administered by the United Nations. The Trusteeship Council shall be designated to discharge the responsibilities of the Administering Authority on behalf of the United Nations.[5]

The plan provided that after ten years under international control,

> the whole scheme shall be subject to examination by the Trusteeship Council in the light of experience acquired with its functioning. The residents of the City shall be then free to express by means of a referendum their wishes as to possible modifications of regime of the City.[6]

The UN defined Jerusalem's boundaries very broadly, encompassing not just the city itself but also

> the surrounding villages and towns, the most eastern of which shall be Abu Dis; the most southern, Bethlehem; the most western, Ein Karim (including also the built-up area of Motsa); and the most northern Shu'fat, surrounding suburbs, and even extending south to include Bethlehem.[7]

1948–1967

As discussed in Chapter 9, the Jews accepted the UN partition plan, including the internationalization of Jerusalem. However, the Palestinians rejected the plan and launched a civil war. Israel declared its independence on 14 May 1948 several hours prior to Britain's withdrawal from the country. The armies of every surrounding Arab nation plus Iraq immediately invaded the nascent Jewish State, joining the Palestinians in their attempt to destroy Israel.

The General Assembly adopted a Resolution on 14 May 1948 dissolving the Palestine Commission established as part of Resolution 181(II) and appointing a mediator to

> (i) Arrange for the operation of common services necessary to the safety and well-being of the population of Palestine; (ii) Assure the protection of the Holy Places, religious buildings and sites in Palestine; and (iii) Promote a peaceful adjustment of the future situation of Palestine.[8]

The Security Council appointed Count Folke Bernadotte of Sweden to serve as the Mediator.

Meanwhile, the Israeli and Jordanian military forces were engaged in an intense battle for Jerusalem. On 27 May 1948, William Burdett, the American Vice Consul in Jerusalem, cabled Washington with an update on the battle. Burdett described the situation of the Jerusalem Jewish population in bleak terms, noting "Arabs are preparing for a long siege of Jewish Jerusalem in hope starving inhabitants into submission."[9] The Jews surrendered the Old City of Jerusalem the next day to the Jordanian Legion.

On 28 June 1948 Bernadotte offered his initial "suggestions" to the Jews and Arabs to resolve the conflict. He proposed that Palestine, as originally defined in the League of Nations Mandate, meaning both Transjordan and Cisjordan, "form a Union comprising two members, one Arab and one Jewish." The Jews would receive the entire Western Galilee region. The Arabs would receive the entire (and far larger) Negev region. The most important and controversial suggestion, however, involved Jerusalem, which Bernadotte proposed be deemed entirely "Arab territory, with municipal autonomy for the Jewish community and special arrangements for the protection of the Holy Places."[10]

On 11 July 1948, James McDonald, the United States Consul General in Jerusalem (and soon to be the first-ever U.S. Ambassador to Israel) reported to Washington that the Israelis, who had initially accepted the UN proposal to internationalize Jerusalem, had changed their position in light of the Jordanian attack on Jerusalem:

> Cynical attitude towards United Nations and increasing demand for incorporation new Jerusalem within state of Israel now apparent here. Immediately following May 14 projected international status for Jerusalem was accepted by Jewish officials and people but prior beginning truce and during cease-fire noticeable shift in attitude occurred which will probably be accentuated with resumption fighting ... Jews justify claim to Jerusalem by pointing to failure United Nations take effective action protect city or establish government. Maintain Israel forces only ones which have defended city from Moslems and now in fact occupy most of city.[11]

On 15 July 1948, the United Nations Security Council adopted Resolution 54. The Security Council appeared to back away from the United Nations' prior position that Jerusalem should be internationalized, as it instructed Bernadotte

> to continue his efforts to bring about the demilitarization of the City of Jerusalem, *without prejudice to the future political status of Jerusalem*, and to assure the protection of and access to the Holy Places, religious buildings and sites in Palestine.[12]

On 2 August 1948 Israeli Prime Minister David Ben-Gurion signed Decree Law No. 12, establishing military rule in Jerusalem and extending Israeli law to West Jerusalem.[13] The new law further provided that the law in force in the State of Israel should also apply to any part of Palestine that the Minister of Defense would designate by proclamation as under occupation of the Israel Defense Forces. By this time both the Israeli and Transjordanian governments were focused on consolidating their hold on the areas of Jerusalem they controlled.[14]

On 4 August 1948, McDonald cabled Washington, indicating some optimism regarding a possible Jewish-Arab agreement to accept the UN's internationalization proposal for Jerusalem:

> Consul General most desirous information on current thinking in Department re future Jerusalem. It has worked on assumption Department envisages eventual internationalization Jerusalem as provided for in November 29 resolution both to facilitate over-all permanent solution Palestine problem and to preserve city sacred to Christians, Jews and Moslems. Consul General feels even at this late stage acquiescence both sides in internationalization can be obtained provided definite policy announced by United Nations (strongly tracked by United States) and concrete energetic action taken.[15]

But McDonald's optimism was short-lived. On 12 August 1948, McDonald reported to Washington regarding a conversation he had the previous day with Golda Myerson (Meir), Israel's Ambassador-designate to the Soviet Union:

> Internationalization Jerusalem is definitely impossible now and Jews will never agree accepting it. If Jerusalem does not become all Jewish city Israel might consent to partition on following lines. New Jerusalem to be part of Israel. Old city to be considered a museum and be given some sort of international status under the United Nations. Allocation of some small area outside of old city to Arabs might be given consideration.[16]

On 1 September 1948, the State Department cabled McDonald with instructions regarding a variety of issues, including Jerusalem. The Department indicated its willingness to accept a joint Arab-Jewish solution for Jerusalem that did not involve internationalization, so long as access to the Christian Holy Sites were protected:

> Since Jerusalem is such a bone of contention between Arabs and Jews and is focal center of Christian interest in Palestine, we believe that it should form international enclave along lines recommended by GA resolution of Nov. 29, 1947, or by Trusteeship Council in its meetings in April and May, 1948. Any other arrangement satisfactory to both Jews and Arabs would, however, be acceptable to us, provided guarantees were given for access to and safety of holy places.[17]

On 8 September, McDonald reported that Ben Gurion and Israeli Foreign Minister Moshe Sharett had expressed flexibility regarding Jerusalem, especially the Old City which was then under Jordanian control:

> Prime Minister observed that at least US suggestions admitted of some flexibility. Jerusalem, he stated, meant more to Jews than Paris to French or London to British. He asked, however, did our suggestion envisage Jewish corridor to Jerusalem which he declared was absolutely vital? He observed reflectively that the people of Israel had right to all of western Palestine but that personally in order get agreement with Arabs on Jerusalem he would recommend sacrifice of much that was dear to Israel for the sake of real peace with Arabs. Shertok interrupted to say that his personal opinion was that Old City might be internationalized and a portion of New City be given to Arabs under some mutually acceptable partition agreement. Prime Minister and Shertok feel this suggestion can be further examined.[18]

On 11 September 1948 Abba Eban, at that time serving as Israel's Ambassador to the UN, spoke in Tel Aviv. Eban said several United Nations delegates who had supported the internationalization of Jerusalem as part of Resolution 181(II) now admitted the project was "dead," and that the UN had proven itself unable to handle the situation.[19]

By 28 September 1948 McDonald reported the Israeli government "might agree to partition of new city Jerusalem between Arabs and Jews and might suggest internationalization of old city within walls."[20] But the Secretary General of the Arab League, Azzam Pasha, had already rejected any solution for Jerusalem other than complete Arab control over the entire city.[21]

On 16 November 1948 the U.S. National Security Council prepared a top secret report discussing "the type of United Nations police force for Jerusalem which the United States could accept if Jerusalem is placed under United Nations control."[22] The report noted

> the present session of the United Nations General Assembly ... may recommend for Jerusalem an international regime under UN control. The Department of State is of the opinion that this Government must in one form or another support a proposal to establish a United Nations police force in Jerusalem.[23]

On 30 November 1948 the Israelis and Jordanians agreed to a ceasefire in Jerusalem, leaving each in control of their respective areas of the City.

In December 1948 the Palestinian Arabs asked King Abdullah to annex the West Bank, choosing Jordanian rule over self-determination. Abdullah later did so, laying claim to East Jerusalem and the Old City.

Meanwhile, the UN continued to push for Jerusalem to be internationalized, adopting Resolution 194 on 11 December 1948.[24] Among other things, Resolution 194 created the Palestine Conciliation Commission (PCC). The United States, France, and Turkey were named as standing members.

Two days later, the American Consul General in Jerusalem, William Burdett, secretly proposed partitioning Jerusalem "into permanent Arab and Jewish areas," the former becoming part of Transjordan and the latter part of Israel.[25] American policy toward Jerusalem, which to this point had consistently favored internationalization, began to fray.

Jordan and Israel, already entrenched in their respective areas of Jerusalem, worked to undermine any PCC effort to internationalize Jerusalem. As Ben-Dror (2015) explained:

> Passage of Resolution 194 gave Israel and Jordan a shared interest in frustrating the internationalisation project. That same month they launched talks on a comprehensive settlement with special attention to Jerusalem. In these negotiations, both sides displayed unprecedented flexibility regarding the city in the hope of achieving a bilateral arrangement that would make it difficult to establish an international regime. From the outset, each agreed to oppose internationalisation and preferred to split Jerusalem between them.[26]

On 13 January 1949, Burdett again advocated partitioning rather than internationalizing Jerusalem, cabling Washington regarding an Israeli initiative to divide Jerusalem between Israel and Jordan. Burdett acknowledged such a settlement would run counter to Resolution 181s recommendation that Jerusalem be internationalized, but he argued peace would be preferable to internationalization:

> Settlement above basis might involve renunciation principle international city as called for by GA resolution but both French Consul General and I believe clause could be included in agreement between PGI and

> Transjordan to effect agreement would not prejudice any action by UN to internationalize entire area. Even if not acceptable consider establishment peace by agreement more important than internationalization Jerusalem.[27]

But the State Department rejected partition, while leaving open the possibility that internationalization might take a different form than envisioned by some countries:

> US cannot therefore support any arrangements which would purport to authorize estab[lishment] of Israeli or TJ [Transjordanian] sovereignty over parts of Jerusalem ... Arrangements re Jerusalem agreed upon by Israel and Transjordan should be of provisional character and subject to approval by GA. However, GA could be expected view with much sympathy any proposal re Jerusalem mutually accepted by Arabs and Jews even though direct responsibility of U.N. thereunder might be less extensive than certain U.N. Delegations have thought necessary.[28]

Burdett, however, continued insisting partition represented the best possibility for peace. He sought to placate Foggy Bottom by describing partition as without prejudice to the eventual internationalization of the City. Thus, in late January 1949, he cabled Washington:

> Believe agreement should follow lines Dayan suggestions, avoiding references sovereignty, and prefacing agreement with stipulation it is without prejudice international status city as provided GA resolution. Agreement would have object achieving peace and demilitarization city and would be signed directly between parties. It is recognized immediate agreement establishing demarcation line between Arab and Jewish areas and postponing question internationalization may result in intervening period being utilized to make ultimate agreement on internationalization more difficult. However, absence of any agreement now would have same result, present opportunity for peaceful settlement in city would be forfeited and permanent retention by Jews of Arab areas now held would become most likely. US Del and Consulate General, therefore, believe every effort should be exerted reach agreement now delineating Arab-Jewish area and demilitarizing city.[29]

Meanwhile, on 17 January 1949, the British Consul General in Jerusalem wrote to the Foreign Office recommending the British Government accept the inevitability of a Jerusalem divided between Israel and Jordan. Although it might have been possible to achieve the internationalization of Jerusalem as late as June 1948, the situation had changed so dramatically in the intervening months that it was now "almost certain that [an] international state of Jerusalem will never be born."[30]

By February 1949, events on the ground had rendered internationalization moot. On 1 February 1949, the Israeli Government declared an end to the military government it had established over Jerusalem in August, 1948, replacing it with civilian administration over the City. Burdett reported the development to Washington:

> At its meeting yesterday the Cabinet decided to terminate the military governorship of Jerusalem and to institute in that city governmental arrangements obtaining in other parts of the State of Israel. 'On the 2nd of August, 1948, the Government proclaimed that all laws of the State of Israel apply to the area of Jerusalem under Israeli occupation, and in view of the conditions prevailing at the time, the Government then deemed it necessary to establish the military governorship in the city.' Initial local public reaction is that announcement tantamount to annexation Jewish sections city Jerusalem to State of Israel.[31]

The State Department reacted quickly, instructing U.S. diplomats in Israel the following day not to attend the opening of the Israeli constituent assembly in Jerusalem in "view US position in support UNGA decision re internationalization Jerusalem."[32]

Meanwhile, Israel and Transjordan were moving ahead with secret negotiations to achieve an armistice. McDonald reported to Washington on 3 February that King Abdullah was "opposed to the internationalization of whole or part Jerusalem, favors partition, with old and portion of new city assigned Transjordan and rest to Israel, both portions remaining under some form United Nations supervision."[33]

On 3 April 1949 Israel and Jordan signed an Armistice Agreement, brokered by the Acting UN Mediator Ralph Bunche. The Agreement left Israel in control of West Jerusalem, while Jordan controlled East Jerusalem and the Old City.[34] The armistice agreement fixed the boundaries of each side's presence in Jerusalem as those agreed upon in the 30 November 1948 cease-fire agreement.

The armistice agreement required Jordan to guarantee free access to the Holy Places, but Jordan thereafter refused to allow any Jews to visit the Wailing Wall, a blatant violation of both the armistice agreement and the *status quo* that had prevailed during four centuries of Ottoman Turkish rule and three decades of British rule. Not surprisingly, neither the General Assembly nor the Security Council ever called on Jordan to permit Jewish access to the Wailing Wall.

In September 1949, the PCC recommended Jerusalem be divided into two demilitarized areas, one under Israeli control and the other under Jordanian control. A supreme council would be appointed and made up of 14 members, four of them UN representatives with wide powers. The UN would be responsible for protecting the Holy Sites.

Ultimately, however, on 9 December 1949, the General Assembly adopted Resolution 303, reflecting an Australian proposal to internationalize Jerusalem. The General Assembly returned to the original internationalization proposal of Resolution 181, reiterating:

> [I]ts intention that Jerusalem should be placed under a permanent international regime, which should envisage appropriate guarantees for the protection of the Holy Places, both within and outside Jerusalem and to ... request for this purpose that the Trusteeship Council at its next session, whether special or regular, complete the preparation of the Statute of Jerusalem ... and, without prejudice to the fundamental principles of the international regime for Jerusalem set forth in General Assembly resolution 181 (II) introducing therein amendments in the direction of its greater democratization, approve the Statute, and proceed immediately with its implementation. The Trusteeship Council shall not allow any actions taken by any interested Government or Governments to divert it from adopting and implementing the Statute of Jerusalem.[35]

On 23 January 1950 Israel proclaimed Jerusalem as its capital city, and announced it was relocating the Knesset from Tel Aviv to Jerusalem.[36] On 4 May 1952 Israel moved its Foreign Ministry to Jerusalem.[37]

Although the UN Trusteeship Council prepared a draft statute in 1950 for Jerusalem, from 1952 until the Six Day War in 1967, no significant debates occurred at the UN regarding the Palestinians, the West Bank, or Jerusalem.[38] Lauterpacht concluded that by 1952 the UN had abandoned the provisions of Resolution 181 regarding the internationalization of Jerusalem:

> From 1952 to 1967 the question of Jerusalem was conspicuous only by its absence from discussion in the U.N. During those fifteen years, the matter was never referred to in the General Assembly ... For all practical purposes, the idea of internationalizing Jerusalem was forgotten. Moreover, the members of the U.N. showed no concern whatsoever about the protection of the Holy Places.[39]

Thereafter and until June 1967 Jerusalem remained a divided city. East Jerusalem and the Old City did not fare well under Jordanian occupation. Heimann (2015) described the contrast between Israel's efforts to modernize West Jerusalem and Jordan's neglect of East Jerusalem between 1948 and 1967:

> In the period 1948-67, Jerusalem was a divided city. Israel controlled the southern and western neighbourhoods and part of the city's commercial centre. The Jordanians controlled the northern and eastern neighbourhoods and the Old City between the walls. The Jordanian section was

> larger than the Israeli section. On the other hand, Israeli Jerusalem was more densely populated; in 1967 the Jerusalem's Jewish population was 199,000 compared with 66,000 in Arab Jerusalem. One reason for the demographic difference was the different importance ascribed to the city by Israel and Jordan. The Israeli authorities regarded Jerusalem as the historic capital of the new state and went to great pains to strengthen it. They sent many new immigrants to live in the city and most government ministries were transferred there. One reason for this was to encourage ministry staff to relocate from Tel-Aviv. The Jordanian government ascribed no such importance to Jerusalem. King Abdullah made the strategic decision to strengthen Hashemite Amman's status as Jordan's capital at the expense of Palestinian Jerusalem, so that the latter suffered from lack of investment.[40]

Abbasi (2013) further described Jordan's second-class treatment of Jerusalem during those years:

> [I]in spite of all the rapid Jordanian measures to integrate the two banks, and the efforts to restore life in Jerusalem to their normal lines of conduct, post-war Jerusalem was transformed from a central capital city into a border city divided between two hostile states. While the western part of the city became the capital of the State of Israel, and was given special attention by the Israeli government, the eastern part was mired in a difficult economic and social situation ... the Hashemite regime treated the city which had been the stronghold of his rival, the Mufti, with a certain suspicion, and regarded it as a center of opposition to his plans. This attitude towards the city became even more ingrained after the murder of king Abdullah in the al-Aqsah mosque on July 20, 1951.[41]

As noted above, no one acquired sovereignty over Jerusalem during the period between the end of World War I and the termination of the British Mandate in 1948. As Cassese (1981) has argued:

> It is not disputed that from 1517-1917 Jerusalem was under the exclusive control and indeed the sovereignty of the Ottoman Empire. Similarly, no one questions the fact that in the period from 1917 to 1947 Jerusalem was actually controlled by the United Kingdom, first as a military occupant (during and after the first World War) then, since 1922, as the mandatory power under the League of Nations system. During those thirty years the United Kingdom did not possess, however, sovereign rights over the City. Although opinions on the general question where sovereignty in respect of the mandated city lay differ widely, in the case of Jerusalem the better

view seems to be that 'if the test of sovereignty rests in determining who had the power to dispose of any part of a territory under the Mandate, the answer is that sovereignty lay in the League and the administering authority acting jointly.'[42]

Post-1967

Jordan attacked Israel without provocation on 5 June 1967, even after Israel had conveyed two messages to King Hussein asking him not to enter the war that had begun between Israel and Egypt/Syria.[43] Jordan attacked anyway, hoping to destroy Israel together with Egypt, Syria and Iraq. Israel lawfully defended itself against the Jordanian onslaught in full conformity with Article 51 of the UN Charter. By the time the fighting ended on 10 June 1967, Israel had captured East Jerusalem and the Old City.

On 27 June 1967 the Israeli Knesset amended the Law and Administrative Ordinance of 1948 to apply Israeli law to East Jerusalem.[44] The Knesset also enacted a law to protect free access to the Holy Places.[45]

The Israeli government since 1967 has allowed the Jordanian *Wakf* authorities to administer the Old City's Muslim Holy Sites and the Christian authorities to administer their Holy Sites, while Israeli authorities have remained responsible for overall security. Jewish visitation atop the Temple Mount is permitted, but Jewish prayer is strictly prohibited consistent with the principles of the longstanding *status quo*.

Israel's approach stands in stark contrast with Jordan's outright ban on Jewish visits to the Wailing Wall during the nearly two decades of Jordanian rule in Jerusalem, in violation of both the *status quo* and the Israel-Jordan Armistice Agreement of 3 April 1949.

The Israel-Jordan Peace Treaty of 1994 recognizes "the present special role of the Hashemite Kingdom of Jordan in Muslim Holy shrines in Jerusalem."[46] As recently as March 2023 the Israelis, Jordanians, Palestinians, and Egyptians issued a Joint Communique together with the United States reiterating their "commitment of upholding unchanged the historic status quo at the Holy Sites in Jerusalem, both in word and in practice, and reaffirmed in this context the importance of the Hashemite Custodianship/special role of the Hashemite Kingdom of Jordan."[47] This language, of course, is inconsistent with the UN/International Court of Justice (ICJ) characterization of East Jerusalem and the Old City as occupied "Palestinian" territory.

The UN, for its part, rejected Israel's post-June 1967 legislative actions regarding Jerusalem. On 4 July 1967, the General Assembly adopted Resolution 2253, declaring the Israeli legislation "invalid" and calling upon Israel "to rescind all measures already taken and to desist forthwith from taking action which would alter the status of Jerusalem."[48] The General Assembly adopted Resolution 2254 ten days later, reiterating its request that Israel "rescind all measures already taken and to desist forthwith from taking any action which would alter the status of Jerusalem."[49]

The Security Council adopted Resolution 242 on 22 November 1967, calling upon Israel to "withdraw from territories occupied in the recent conflict" meaning East Jerusalem and the West Bank, but not West Jerusalem.[50] Thus, Resolution 242 implicitly recognized Israeli sovereignty over West Jerusalem. Furthermore, the phrase "from territories" could be read as applicable to either "all" territories or only "some" territories. If the latter interpretation is correct, then Israel would have a valid argument that it is not required to withdraw from certain portions of the West Bank and/or East Jerusalem.

Moreover, implementing Resolution 242 would have meant returning East Jerusalem and the West Bank to *Jordan*, not the Palestinians. Nothing in Resolution 242 recognizes any Palestinian legal claim to either the West Bank or East Jerusalem. This language also contradicts the more recent UN/ICJ characterization of East Jerusalem and the Old City as occupied "Palestinian" territory.

Over the next several years, the Security Council adopted additional resolutions, each of which declared invalid the Israeli legislative changes impacting East Jerusalem and the Old City and demanded Israel rescind all such measures.[51]

Mallison and Mallison (1981) discussed the various post-1967 General Assembly and Security Council resolutions regarding Jerusalem, particularly the ambiguous language regarding the "legal status" of the city. The Mallisons argued that the best reading of the UN resolutions reflects a commitment to the original November 1947 proposal to internationalize Jerusalem:

> Thus there is apparent lack of clarity in the post 1967 General Assembly resolutions and in the Security Council resolutions as to whether the status of Jerusalem referred to in particular instances is the legal status of the corpus separatum provided for in General Assembly resolutions 181, 194 and 303, and in the specific reference to the 'legal status' in Security Council resolution 252, or the factual status of the pre-June 1967 divided City. However, in examining the Security Council resolutions along with those of the General Assembly, it appears that there is, at the least, an intent to preserve the principle of the *corpus separatum* even though these resolutions, following the intense hostilities of June 1967, put special emphasis upon the post-1967 Israeli actions.[52]

But as noted above, the Mallisons' interpretation cannot be squared with the language of Resolution 242, which required Israel to withdraw only from areas occupied in the "recent conflict," meaning the June 1967 war, thereby implicitly recognizing Israeli pre-June 1967 sovereignty over West Jerusalem.

For the first several years following the June 1967 war, Israel repeatedly insisted its actions in Jerusalem did not constitute formal annexation. However, in July 1980 the Knesset did exactly that when it enacted the "Basic Law – Jerusalem:"

> 1. Jerusalem, complete and united, is the capital of Israel. 2. Jerusalem is the seat of the President of the State, the Knesset, the Government and the Supreme Court. 3. The Holy Places shall be protected from desecration and any other violation and from anything likely to violate the freedom of access of the members of the different religions to the places sacred to them or their feelings towards those places. 4. (a) The Government shall provide for the development and prosperity of Jerusalem and the well-being of its inhabitants by allocating special funds, including a special annual grant to the Municipality of Jerusalem (Capital City Grant) with the approval of the Finance Committee of the Knesset. (b) Jerusalem shall be given special priority in the activities of the authorities of the State so as to further its development in economic and other matters. (c) The Government shall set up a special body or special bodies for the implementation of this section. 5. The jurisdiction of Jerusalem includes, as pertaining to this basic law, among others, all of the area that is described in the appendix of the proclamation expanding the borders of municipal Jerusalem beginning the 20th of Sivan 5727 (June 28, 1967), as was given according to the Cities' Ordinance. 6. No authority that is stipulated in the law of the State of Israel or of the Jerusalem Municipality may be transferred either permanently or for an allotted period of time to a foreign body, whether political, governmental or to any other similar type of foreign body. 7. Clauses 5 and 6 shall not be modified except by a Basic Law passed by a majority of the members of the Knesset.[53]

Israel has taken the position ever since that united Jerusalem comprises the capital city of Israel. The international community rejects Israel's claim to East Jerusalem and the Old City. The Palestinian Legislative Council went even further in 2002 when it adopted the *Law of the Capital*, defining "Jerusalem" (potentially including West Jerusalem) as the capital of the Palestinian State.[54]

Thus, it is necessary to analyze separately the legal status of West and East Jerusalem.

Legal Status of West Jerusalem

Israeli Arguments Regarding West Jerusalem

Israel has an extremely strong claim to sovereignty over West Jerusalem.

Lapidoth (1996 and 2011b) identified four different and conflicting theories regarding the legal status of Jerusalem.[55]

First, some argue Israel lawfully acquired sovereignty in 1948. When Britain terminated the Mandate and left Palestine at midnight on 14/15 May 1948, a vacuum of sovereignty arose which could be validly filled only by lawful action. Israel acquired control of West Jerusalem in 1948 in a lawful act of self-defense after the Jordanian Legion invaded the Jewish State without legal justification. Israel therefore was lawfully entitled to fill the sovereignty vacuum and thereby became the lawful sovereign over West Jerusalem.

Giladi (1999) explained the "vacuum of sovereignty" argument regarding West Jerusalem. Giladi noted that those who argue in favor of Israeli sovereignty over West Jerusalem contend that Resolution 181(II) was a mere recommendation, and the United Nations itself abandoned internationalization after 1952. Once Britain terminated the Palestine Mandate on 14 May 1948, sovereignty was left in a legal vacuum. Giladi continued:

> Only a party acting lawfully could have filled this vacuum. The invasion of the Arab States into Palestine contravened rules of international law pertaining to legal use of force. None of these States – and Jordan especially – could have therefore legally invoked title in Jerusalem. Israel, on the other hand, was acting in lawful self-defense. As such, it could fill the vacuum in sovereignty and so it acquired valid title in Jerusalem.[56]

Second, according to Lapidoth, others argue that sovereignty over Jerusalem was suspended following Britain's ouster of the Ottoman Empire at the end of World War I. Sovereignty remained suspended throughout the years of the British Mandate and continued in suspense even after Britain's departure and the 1948–1949 war. Therefore, even as of today sovereignty over all of Jerusalem should be deemed suspended until a comprehensive settlement is reached.

Third, many Palestinian advocates argue the Palestine Mandate conferred "legal sovereignty" over the whole of Palestine including Jerusalem, and that grant of sovereignty remains legally valid today.

Fourth, other Palestinian supporters argue the status of Jerusalem is still subject to the UN November 1947 partition resolution. Therefore, international law should still regard all of Jerusalem as subject to the General Assembly's recommendation that it be treated as a separate entity under international control and administered by the United Nations.

Gruhin (1980) disagreed with the last point, noting the UN's abandonment of the internationalization plan left it to Israel and Jordan to determine sovereignty over Jerusalem, at least between 1948 and 1967:

> The United Nations terminated the Palestine Mandate only in respect to the area of Palestine that became Israel and the Arab state. Its intent was to extend the Palestine Mandate over Jerusalem, and it attempted to do

> so by placing Jerusalem under a new Mandate of Trusteeship. As a result, the Palestinians and Jews still retained contingent rights in Jerusalem. Although the United Nations was unable to effectuate the trusteeship, its future intent to establish Jerusalem as an international city was enough to prevent a suspended sovereignty from vesting in either the Arab or Jewish State. When it abandoned that intent in 1952, there was no further encumbrance on the vesting of sovereignty over Jerusalem. The United Nations, in effect, left it to the two states to determine the future sovereign of Jerusalem.[57]

By 1967, 23 countries maintained their embassies in West Jerusalem, representing 40% of all foreign missions in Israel. However, this did not, as Golani (1999) noted, imply legal recognition of Israeli sovereignty over West Jerusalem:

> In fact, though, the countries in question did not recognize Jerusalem's status de jure, but merely made what they considered a technical adjustment to the place where the Israeli government sat. As of 1967, no country was ready to offer juridical recognition of Israel's presence in West Jerusalem ... This complex reality was reflected both in general statements, especially in relation to the ongoing deliberations at the United Nations, and over ostensibly small matters, which gave expression to Israel's problematic status – from the international standpoint – in Jerusalem. Thus, for example, following an accident that was caused by a driver from the Belgian consulate in Jerusalem in August 1952, the Belgian government stated that it was willing to acknowledge its responsibility and reach a compromise regarding suitable compensation. However, should its position be rejected, 'the possibility must be considered of advancing the argument that Israeli law does not apply in Jerusalem.' This trivial matter was discussed by the forum of the consular staff in Jerusalem, and some viewed it as an opportunity to address the 'question of the applicability of Israeli law to international Jerusalem.'[58]

Today, most of the international community does not recognize Israeli sovereignty over West Jerusalem, as nearly every country with whom Israel maintains diplomatic relations has chosen to locate its embassy in Tel Aviv. However, as Lapidoth (2011b) noted:

> Despite this non-recognition of Israeli sovereignty, most States have nevertheless accepted the de facto applicability of Israeli law, and none has so far demanded that the laws of occupation, including the 1949 Fourth Geneva Convention Relative to the Protection of Civilian Persons in Time of War, be applied. The European Union supports the idea that Jerusalem is

> still subject to the corpus separatum status. Thus in 1999 the Ambassador of the Federal Republic of Germany (at that time holding the presidency of the EU) wrote in a diplomatic note: … The EU reaffirms its known position concerning the specific status of Jerusalem as a corpus separatum …[59]

Watson (2000), however, dismissed the lack of foreign embassies in West Jerusalem as relevant in determining Israel's claim to sovereignty over that portion of the City. Instead, Watson argued that Israel has a powerful legal claim to sovereignty over West Jerusalem:

> As to West Jerusalem, Israel's claim is very strong. West Jerusalem has been a part of the State of Israel since its inception; it has had a Jewish majority since the nineteenth century; and states have *de facto* acquiesced in Israeli sovereignty over West Jerusalem. It is true that many states still decline to move their embassies there, but this posture reflects concern over recognizing Israel's sovereignty over East Jerusalem, not West Jerusalem. As for the United Nations, Resolution 242 implicitly acknowledges Israel's sovereignty over West Jerusalem, since it calls only for withdrawal from 'territories occupied' in the 1967 War. Even the PLO does not vigorously press a claim to the western sector of the city.[60]

Watson's view, perhaps somewhat surprisingly, finds support in the Arab Peace Initiative (API) of March 2002, adopted at the Arab Summit in Beirut based on a Saudi Arabian proposal. The API called for "[t]he acceptance of the establishment of a sovereign independent Palestinian state on the Palestinian territories occupied since June 4, 1967, in the West Bank and Gaza Strip, *with East Jerusalem* as its capital."[61] Thus, the API recognizes West Jerusalem as belonging to Israel.

Sabel (2022) offers a different argument in support of Israeli sovereignty over West Jerusalem. Sabel contends Israeli sovereignty has been established via the international legal concept of "prescription," or "the continuous and peaceful display of territorial sovereignty."[62] The Permanent Court of International Arbitration discussed the concept in the *Island of Palmas* case:

> Titles of acquisition of territorial sovereignty in present-day international law are either based on an act of effective apprehension, such as occupation or conquest, or, like cession, presuppose that the ceding and the cessionary Powers or at least one of them, have the faculty of effectively disposing of the ceded territory. In the same way natural accretion can only be conceived of as an accretion to a portion of territory where there exists an actual sovereignty capable of extending to a spot which falls within its sphere of activity. It seems therefore natural that an element which is essential for the constitution of sovereignty should not be lacking

> in its continuation. So true is this, that practice, as well as doctrine, recognizes—though under different legal formulae and with certain differences as to the conditions required—that the continuous and peaceful display of territorial sovereignty (peaceful in relation to other States) is as good as a title ... The principle that continuous and peaceful display of the functions of State within a given region is a constituent element of territorial sovereignty is not only based on the conditions of the formation of independent States and their boundaries (as shown by the experience of political history) as well as on an international jurisprudence and doctrine widely accepted; this principle has further been recognized in more than one federal State, where a jurisdiction is established in order to apply, as need arises, rules of international law to the interstate relations of the States members.[63]

Palestinian Arguments Regarding West Jerusalem

Some Palestinian advocates argue sovereignty in Jerusalem is exclusively Palestinian. They contend Resolution 181(II) had no impact on Palestinian legal title to Jerusalem. Therefore, Israel does not possess sovereignty over West Jerusalem but instead should be regarded as an occupying power. Moreover, they argue the UN's post-1967 resolutions do not implicitly recognize Israeli sovereignty in West Jerusalem.

Giladi (1999) noted that some Palestinian advocates view Resolution 181(II) as still legally binding. They contend Israel's original acceptance of the resolution bound Israel to concede the internationalization of Jerusalem, and precluded Israel from later changing its position and arguing it had acquired sovereignty over West Jerusalem. The problem with this approach, however, is that those who rely on Resolution 181(II) to argue against Israeli sovereignty over *West* Jerusalem would be bound by the same argument regarding Palestinian claims of sovereignty over *East* Jerusalem.

Moreover, this approach ignores that Israel acquired sovereignty over West and East Jerusalem as the result of Jordan's unprovoked and unlawful military attacks in May 1948 and June 1967. In both instances, Israel acted fully within its self-defense rights under Article 51 of the UN Charter. The territory Israel acquired in those acts of self-defense had not previously been under anyone else's sovereignty, and therefore Israel was legally entitled to claim sovereignty for itself.

Quigley (1996) nevertheless insists Israel lacks sovereignty over West Jerusalem and anywhere else over the area comprising mandatory Palestine:

> States recognizing Israel have not recognized Israeli sovereignty over either the western or eastern sector of Jerusalem, despite nearly half a century of Israeli control in West Jerusalem, and nearly thirty years in East Jerusalem.

> Regarding West Jerusalem, states maintaining diplomatic relations with Israel have avoided locating their embassies there, placing them instead in Tel Aviv, precisely because they consider the status of Jerusalem to be undetermined. As for East Jerusalem, objection to Israel's control is exhibited through collective criticism of Israel at the United Nations. There was no void of sovereignty in Palestine because, during the mandate period, the community of citizens of Palestine held sovereignty subject to Great Britain's administration. A community under a League mandate was deemed to be a subject of international law with a legal interest in the territory that was separate from that of the mandatory power. In Palestine under the mandate, the inhabitants carried Palestine citizenship. When Britain withdrew, the community of citizens was entitled to exercise its latent sovereignty. The majority of that community of citizens was represented by a United Nations recognized political organization, the Arab Higher Committee, which asserted a right to establish a government for Palestine. Separate from rights stemming from the mandate arrangement, the community of citizens of Palestine enjoyed a right to sovereignty by virtue of the self-determination principle. The analysis the International Court of Justice used in the *Western Sahara* case would lead to a conclusion that the community of citizens of Palestine, predominantly Arab, but with a Jewish minority, had a right to sovereignty based on its connection to the territory, and on the principle of self-determination.[64]

Quigley's analysis relies on the ICJ's *Western Sahara* decision, but that reliance is misplaced. The ICJ there dealt with conflicting Moroccan and Mauritanian claims to the Western Sahara region following the end of Spanish colonization. The key issue was whether the record demonstrated "any tie of territorial sovereignty between the territory of *Western Sahara* and the Kingdom of Morocco or the Mauritanian entity."[65] The ICJ answered the question by concluding

> the Court has not found legal ties of such a nature as might affect the application of resolution 1514 (XV) in the decolonization of Western Sahara and, in particular, of the principle of self-determination through the free and genuine expression of the will of the peoples of the Territory.[66]

Western Sahara involved a situation entirely different from the Palestine Mandate. As noted in Chapter 5, the Mandate in its preambulatory clauses confirmed the League's legal recognition of the right of the Jewish people to reconstitute their homeland in Palestine. No parallel rights, nor any other political rights, were extended to the Arab population of Palestine.

Moreover, as the ICJ noted in the *South West Africa* case, the only legal rights derived from the post-World War I mandates were those expressly granted by the mandate instruments themselves. Thus, Quigley's assertion that the Palestine Mandate can be construed as granting sovereignty to the "community of citizens of Palestine," despite the absence of any such provision in the Mandate, cannot be sustained. As the ICJ noted:

> [T]he principle of the sacred trust has no residual juridical content which could, so far as any particular mandate is concerned, operate per se to give rise to legal rights and obligations outside the system as a whole; and, within the system equally, such rights and obligations exist only in so far as there is actual provision for them. Once the expression to be given to an idea has been accepted in the form of a particular régime or system, its legal incidents are those of the régime or system. It is not permissible to import new ones by a process of appeal to the originating idea – a process that would, *ex hypothesi*, have no natural limit.[67]

Cassese (1981) nevertheless agreed with Quigley, questioning whether Israel ever acquired sovereignty over West Jerusalem.[68]

First, Cassese argued that even if the nascent State of Israel had been acting in self-defense during the 1948–1949 war, that alone would not have given Israel the right to claim sovereignty over any portions of Jerusalem it retained as of the end of hostilities.

Second, Cassese contended the UN Charter does not permit the acquisition of sovereignty through conquest. Cassese posited the illogical notion that noted Israel would only have been able to claim sovereignty over West Jerusalem if Israel previously had undisputed sovereignty over West Jerusalem prior to the expiration of the British Mandate, meaning prior to Israel's very existence.[69]

Third, Cassese argued the UN's inaction regarding Jerusalem after 1952 can only be interpreted to mean the UN accepted and acquiesced in Jordanian and Israeli *de facto* control of Jerusalem, but not either party's claim of legal title:

> The granting of a legal title, or, to be more precise, the turning of de facto authority into fully-fledged sovereignty, could not be brought about by mere silence ... how could one assume that the UN has expressed its consent on such a complex and explosive matter by merely *keeping silent*? At least a *tacit manifestation of consent through conclusive acts* would have been necessary.[70]

Fourth, Cassese argues most governments only accorded *de facto* recognition to Jordanian and Israeli claims to Jerusalem and located their embassies in Tel Aviv.

Di Marco (2018) agreed with Cassese's point:

> The legal status of Jerusalem is also unclear if we consider the status of foreign consulates: 'According to international law, a consul can fulfil his functions only once he gets an *exequatur* from the country where he is to serve. The *exequatur* means that the government allows this person to fulfil his consular functions. The consuls stationed in Jerusalem do not apply for an *exequatur* because their countries don't want to recognize Israeli sovereignty over West or East Jerusalem. Despite the fact that they have not submitted their letters of appointment, Israel grants them consular privileges. Officially they do not have any contacts with the Israeli Foreign Ministry other than the Department of Ceremonies.'[71]

Fifth, Cassese argues that after the Six-Day war, 20 countries co-sponsored an unsuccessful General Assembly resolution reviving the idea of Jerusalem as a separate entity under international control. Thus, "the attitude taken by the aforementioned States only confirms that U.N. inaction cannot be taken to mean tacit acceptance of sovereignty over Jerusalem."[72]

Sixth, Cassese conceded the UN resolutions adopted after the Six-Day war (including Security Council Resolution 242, and other resolutions discussing Jerusalem) do not call for internationalization. Nevertheless, he argued that does not mean the UN had abandoned the idea. "[T]his inference could be warranted only if there were conclusive evidence that such was the intention of the General Assembly and the Security Council."[73]

Seventh, Cassese argued the UN has "not eventually acquiesced in the alleged acquisition of Israeli sovereignty over Jerusalem, neither in Western Jerusalem nor, and the more so, in the Eastern part of the City."[74]

Eighth, Cassese argued that under international law, Israel only exercises de facto control over Jerusalem. In addition, Israel's control over East Jerusalem "is in breach of the international rules on military occupation, because it goes much beyond the limits assigned to the powers of a military occupant."[75]

Conclusion: Israel Possesses Full Sovereignty Over West Jerusalem

Notwithstanding the arguments of Cassese, Quigley, and others, the Israeli legal claim to West Jerusalem is overwhelming. West Jerusalem has been under undisputed Israeli control since 1948. Israel has maintained its capital there since 1950. The UN abandoned the internationalization proposal in 1952 and took no action thereafter to implement it. The Security Council implicitly recognized Israeli sovereignty over West Jerusalem in Resolution 242. The Arab League implicitly recognized Israeli sovereignty over West Jerusalem in the Arab Peace Initiative. No one else can support a claim superior to or even remotely close to the Israeli claim.

East Jerusalem and the Old City

Introductory Comments and Summary of Arguments

Walid Khalidi (1978) described the deep emotional attachment of the Arabs to East Jerusalem:

> Without East Jerusalem there would be no West Bank. It is the navel, the pivotal link between Nablus to the north and Hebron to the south. Together with its Arab suburbs it is the largest Arab urban concentration on the West Bank. It is the former capital of the sanjak (district) of Jerusalem under the Ottomans, as well as of mandatory Palestine. The highest proportion of the Palestinian professional elite under occupation resides in it. It is the site of the holiest Muslim shrines on Palestinian soil. Muslims first turned to it in prayer before they turned to Mecca. Toward it – the Prophet Muhammed journeyed on his mystical nocturnal flight and from it he ascended to within "two bow-lengths" of the Throne of God. It is the fountainhead and focus of Sufism – the deepest spiritual tradition of Islam. Within its precincts are buried countless generations of Muslim saints and scholars, warriors and leaders. It evokes the proudest Palestinian and Arab historical memories. It contains the oldest religious endowments of the Palestinians, their most prestigious secular institutions, the cumulative and priceless patrimony of a millennium and a quarter of residence. Architecturally it is distinctively Arab. In ownership and property, it is overwhelmingly so. It is the natural capital of Arab Palestine.[76]

Lapidoth (1996) identified four prevailing and conflicting opinions on the legal status of East Jerusalem during the period 1948–1967.[77]

First, some argue that between 1948 and 1967 East Jerusalem existed under a vacuum of sovereignty. Britain, which never had sovereignty, withdrew from Palestine on 14/15 May 1948. Jordan launched an unprovoked attack against Israel in violation of Article 4(2) of the UN Charter, and ended up occupying East Jerusalem. Because Jordan committed an illegal act of aggression, it did not obtain legal title to or sovereignty over East Jerusalem.

Second, similar to the parallel Palestinian argument regarding West Jerusalem, the Mandate granted the Palestinians sovereignty over the whole of Palestine, including East and West Jerusalem.

Third, others argue Jordan lawfully acquired sovereignty over East Jerusalem, based on the exercise of the right of self-determination by the inhabitants, as expressed in the resolutions they adopted at the December 1948 Jericho Conference requesting Jordanian annexation of the West Bank and East Jerusalem.

Fourth, still others argue Resolution 181(II) continues to require the internationalization of both East and West Jerusalem.

Lapidoth (2011b) also analyzed the various conflicting arguments regarding post-1967 sovereignty over East Jerusalem.[78]

First, some Israeli supporters argue Israel occupied East Jerusalem in a lawful act of self-defense following the unprovoked Jordanian military attack on Israel on 5 June 1967. Therefore, Israel had the lawful right to fill the gap in sovereignty that had prevailed in East Jerusalem since the end of World War I.

Second, other Israeli supporters, especially Yehuda Z. Blum, argue that Jordan never enjoyed sovereignty over East Jerusalem between 1948 and 1967, having occupied it illegally as a result of its unlawful aggression in May 1948. Thus, Israel has the strongest relative title to the area in the absence of a lawful "sovereign reversioner."

Third, Palestinian advocates argue the June 1967 war had no impact on Palestinian sovereignty over the whole of Palestine.

Fourth, other Palestinian supporters argue that if Jordan acquired sovereignty over East Jerusalem in 1948 by virtue of the principle of self-determination based on the Palestinian resolutions adopted at the December 1948 Jericho conference requesting Jordanian annexation, then Israel's status in East Jerusalem post-1967 is that of a lawful belligerent occupant, but not the lawful sovereign.

Fifth, if, as the Arab States claim (with no basis in fact or law) that Israel and not Jordan was the aggressor in June 1967, then Israel's status in East Jerusalem since then has been that of an illegal occupant.

Sixth, still others argue, just as they did for the pre-1967 period, that Resolution 181(II) continues to require the internationalization of both East and West Jerusalem.

Giladi (1999) summarized the various arguments regarding legal claims to East Jerusalem:

> Due to the different historical circumstances in which it came under Israeli control, the legal status of East Jerusalem has to be distinguished from that of West Jerusalem. Still, some of the views are similar. Thus, there is the argument that the vacuum in sovereignty created with the termination of the British Mandate could not be filled by Jordan during its de facto control of East Jerusalem – Jordan having made recourse to unlawful use of armed force in 1948. Israel, by acting in self-defense in 1967, filled this vacuum and acquired title either because of the legality of its actions or because it had better relative title to the territory in question. Another view is that the Palestinian people enjoy exclusive sovereignty over all parts of Palestine – including East and West Jerusalem, while others refer to the continued validity of the internationalization scheme under Resolution 181(II). Last, there is the view that postulates Jordanian sovereignty

based on exercise of self-determination by West Bank dignitaries on the occasion of the Palestine Congress convened by King Abdulla in Jericho on 1 December 1948.[79]

Israeli Legal Arguments Regarding East Jerusalem

Despite the undeniably strong Palestinian religious and emotional ties to East Jerusalem, the Palestinian legal claim of sovereignty over East Jerusalem is demonstrably weak. The Israeli case for sovereignty over East Jerusalem is also weaker than the solid Israeli legal claim to West Jerusalem, but it nevertheless is stronger than the Palestinian claim.

As noted earlier, Britain did not possess sovereignty over any portion of Palestine during the post-World War I and Mandate years, including East Jerusalem and the Old City. Nor did Jordan gain sovereignty when it occupied and purported to annex East Jerusalem after invading Israel in May 1948. Furthermore, the Palestinians expressly waived sovereignty over the West Bank, including East Jerusalem at the Jericho Conference in December 1948 and again in Article 24 of the original PLO Charter of May 1964. The question therefore arises whether Israel gained sovereignty over East Jerusalem following the unprovoked Jordanian military attack of 5 June 1967, resulting in Jordan's loss of East Jerusalem and the Old City to Israel.

Hirsch (2005) described the Israeli legal argument for sovereignty over East Jerusalem:

> Following the 1948 war, Jordan controlled the West Bank, including Jerusalem's Old City but it did not acquire legal sovereignty because its occupation lacked legal justification. The armistice lines that were drawn in the 1949 agreement between Israel and Jordan were not intended to be final borders. The Armistice Agreement stated explicitly that its provisions would not prejudice the rights and claims of the two parties. The annexation of East Jerusalem (together with the West Bank) in 1950 to Jordan constituted a violation of international law and was invalid. The provisions of the Armistice Agreement remained in force until the Six-Day War. This approach further argues that Jordan violated the Armistice Agreement materially by its act of aggression against Israel at the beginning of the 1967 war. This gave Israel the right to consider the Armistice Agreement as terminated, and it so declared. Israel captured East Jerusalem in June 1967 in the course of a lawful act of self-defense (after the Jordanian attack) and acquired sovereign title there. The difference between Lauterpacht's position and that taken by Blum and Schwebel is that Lauterpacht holds that Israel seized East Jerusalem legally and therefore had the right to/fill the vacuum in sovereignty, while Blum and Schwebel

examine post-1967 legal situation by comparing the rights of Israel and Jordan to East Jerusalem and concluding that Israel acquired sovereignty in this area since it has a better title in that territory.[80]

E. Lauterpacht (1968) has argued that Jordan's occupation of the Old City from 1948 to 1967 was unlawful, based on Jordan's violation of Article 2(4) of the United Nations Charter when its army invaded Palestine in May 1948:

> Thus Jordan's occupation of the Old City – and indeed of the whole area west of the Jordan River – entirely lacked legal justification; and being defective in this way could not form any basis for Jordan validly to fill the sovereignty vacuum in the Old City. Jordan's prolonged *de facto* occupation of the Old City was protected exclusively by the Armistice Agreement which prohibited Israel from initiating action to displace Jordan; and Jordan's occupation could last no longer than the protection thus afforded. This bulwark was abandoned when Jordan destroyed the Armistice Agreement by its attack on Israeli Jerusalem on 5th June 1967.[81]

Berkovitz (1998) made a similar argument to Lauterpacht:

> [U]pon the termination of the British Mandate, a 'vacuum in sovereignty' was created over Palestine, including Jerusalem, which should have been filled upon Jerusalem turning into an international city in accordance with the UN Partition Plan. Accordingly, the conquest of east Jerusalem by Jordan in May 1948 was an unlawful act of aggression, which did not confer any rights upon Jordan, as was evidenced by the fact that apart from Pakistan, no country in the world (and no Arab country) officially recognized the lawfulness of Jordan's rule over east Jerusalem. As opposed to Jordan, Israel captured east Jerusalem within the framework of a lawful act of self-defence during the Six Day War, following the shelling of western Jerusalem by Jordan (Jordan ignored Israel's pronouncements that the latter had no intention of attacking Jordan, and disregarded Israel's requests that Jordan also refrain from attacking her). Thus, Israel acquired the sovereignty over east Jerusalem in a lawful manner, and in any event Israel's rights in this part of the city are superior to the rights of Jordan.[82]

Gerson (1978) argued that Israel's legal claims to East Jerusalem and the West Bank are fundamentally identical:

> No valid distinction appears to exist between the legitimacy of Israeli claims to sovereignty over the West Bank and those made in regard to East Jerusalem. Both seem to stand or fall on the same merits. One searches in vain in the academic literature and history of diplomatic debates on the issue for

any thesis advancing the claim that Israeli claims to sovereignty over East Jerusalem are doctrinally distinct from those pertaining to the West Bank.[83]

In the *Jamait Askan* case, the Supreme Court of Israel drew a distinction between East Jerusalem and the remainder of the West Bank post-1967:

> In the Six-Day War, 'East' Jerusalem, Judea and Samaria were occupied by the Israel Defence Force. In 'East' Jerusalem, 'the law, jurisdiction and administration of the State' were applied ... The approach concerning Judea and Samaria was different. The law, jurisdiction and administration of Israel were not applied in Judea and Samaria ... Judea and Samaria are held by Israel by way of military occupation or 'belligerent occupation'. In the area, a military government was established, headed by a military commander. The powers and authority of the military commander are nourished by the rules of public international law concerning belligerent occupation.[84]

Dinstein argued that although Israel's extension of its law to East Jerusalem following the June 1967 war might not have constituted annexation, Israel eventually annexed East Jerusalem when the Knesset enacted the 1980 "Basic Law:"

> The phrase 'law, jurisdiction and administration' [in the 1967 law] per se need not be construed as an outright annexation. Indeed, in the context of Jerusalem – a single city, divided by Israel's War of Independence in 1948 and reintegrated as an outcome of the Israeli victory in 1967 – an 'administrative union of East and West Jerusalem' made pragmatic sense. But this was not the end of the road. In 1979, the Knesset enacted 'Basic Law: Jerusalem, Capital of Israel', which (eschewing the term annexation) expressly proclaims that 'Jerusalem, complete and united, is the capital of Israel'. Given that the entire city – 'complete and united' – is declared to be the capital of Israel, there cannot be a shred of doubt that the Knesset considered East Jerusalem annexed ... The view that East Jerusalem was annexed has been upheld by the Supreme Court of Israel, both before and after the adoption of the Basic Law ... [85]

Lapidoth (2011b) noted the Israeli judiciary recognized "at first somewhat hesitantly, that the eastern sectors of Jerusalem have become part of the State of Israel" after June 1967.[86]

Lapidoth explained further:

> The differences among the various opinions on the status of Jerusalem can explain the controversy over the question whether Israelis may build houses and neighbourhoods in east Jerusalem. According to the attitude

> of the government of Israel, since Israel was entitled to fill the sovereignty gap at the departure of Great Britain, Israeli law, jurisdiction and administration apply lawfully to the whole city ... Others claim that east Jerusalem is an occupied territory and therefore subject to the Fourth 1949 Geneva Convention.[87]

Palestinian Legal Arguments Regarding East Jerusalem

Palestinian supporters offer a variety of objections to Israeli assertions of sovereignty over East Jerusalem. Draper (1981), for example, contends Israel acquired East Jerusalem through the exercise of force. Even if such use of force was justified, that did not give Israel any lawful right to annex East Jerusalem:

> The Israeli contention that the absence of Jordanian sovereignty in the East City and environs, before June, 1967, negates a belligerent Occupant status for Israel after that date, is not tenable. An exercise of self-defence is not a basis for legal title to territory. The legal instruments governing belligerent occupation are not rendered inapplicable because there is no 'missing reversioner' entitled to territorial sovereignty. The present situation is that the City has been illegally annexed by Israel. The annexation has not only been recognized, but has been considered invalid by the international community.[88]

Quigley (1996) rejected any Israeli claim of sovereignty over either the West Bank or East Jerusalem:

> As territory taken during hostilities, the West Bank is under a regime that in international law is termed belligerent occupation. Belligerent occupation yields no sovereignty. This result follows regardless of whether the belligerent power's use of force was aggression or lawful defense. Thus, even if one were to consider Israel to have acted defensively in its use of force against Egypt, and hence against Jordan, it would not acquire sovereign rights in East Jerusalem.[89]

Cattan (1981) also flatly rejects Israeli sovereignty over both West and East Jerusalem. In so doing, he mischaracterizes the legal significance of the events of 1948. Moreover, he asserts the spurious claim that the Jewish people did not originate in ancient Israel. This claim has reemerged in recent years as a key element of the Palestinian effort to deny Jewish indigeneity and rights of self-determination in their ancient homeland:

> From 1948 until 1967 Jerusalem was occupied by Israel, which held modern Jerusalem, and by Jordan, which held the Old City. Both states

> annexed the section which they controlled. These two annexations, however, cannot be equated. Israel's annexation was a flagrant violation of international law carried out by an occupying power against the will of the original inhabitants. Jordan's action was not, strictly speaking, an annexation by an occupying power, but was, in fact, the result of the union of Jordan and Palestine which was carried out in accordance with a resolution adopted on April 24, 1950 in Amman by a national assembly composed of an equal number of Palestinians and Jordanians. In June 1967, Israel captured and annexed the Old City and since that date it has been in occupation of the entire City of Jerusalem. Israel's annexation of Jerusalem, whether its modern section or the Old City, was made under the pretext of a historic or biblical right to restore the capital of the Jewish kingdom of David and Solomon which existed some thirty centuries ago. This claim is fallacious. First, the Jews of the twentieth century who emigrated to Palestine during the British Mandate or since the establishment of Israel are in many cases not the descendants of the biblical Israelites, but are converts to Judaism who have exploited religion for political and nationalistic purposes. Joseph Reinach, a French politician of Jewish origin, has explained that very few of today's Jews have any connection with Palestine and that the great majority of Russian and Polish Jews – who incidentally constituted the majority of immigrants to Palestine during the British Mandate – descend from the Khazars, a Tartar people of southern Russia who were converted in a body to Judaism at the time of Charlemagne.[90]

Significantly, however, former Jordanian Crown Prince Hassan Bin Talal (1979) disagreed with both Quigley and Cattan, conceding that neither Israel nor Jordan

> had acquired territorial sovereignty over the area of Jerusalem under its control by the outbreak of the war in June 1967. During that period, 1949–1967, both States were in effective control of their respective areas as military occupants with an Armistice Agreement binding them.[91]

Hirsch (2005) reviewed the Palestinian legal arguments regarding their claims to both West and East Jerusalem:

> Henry Cattan holds that sovereignty over all of Palestine, including Jerusalem, accrued to the Palestinian people already in the Mandate period, and this situation remained unchanged after the 1947 UN General Assembly 'Partition Resolution', the 1948 War, and Six-Day War. The unification measures undertaken by Jordan in 1950 did not impair the sovereignty of the Palestinian people over the Eastern part of Jerusalem. The decision of the Jordanian parliament in 1950 stated that the rights of the Palestinians would be reserved

and the unification would not prejudice the rights in the final settlement of the Palestine question. In Cattan's view, the legislative steps undertaken by Israel after the Six-Day War are an attempt to annex East Jerusalem and UN bodies have declared several times that those measures violate international law and have no legal validity. International law does not permit the acquisition of territory through the use of force, and the international community has refused to recognize Israel's annexation of East Jerusalem. Thomas and Sally Mallison also maintain that sovereignty over East Jerusalem resides in the Palestinian people. Their view emphasizes that the Palestinian people has the right of self-determination, which includes the right to sovereignty ... and East Jerusalem should be placed under the control of the Palestinian state.[92]

The UN/ICJ Position Regarding East Jerusalem

The United Nations' characterizations of the legal status of Jerusalem are inconsistent and confusing. In Resolution 181(II) the General Assembly recommended that Jerusalem be declared an internationalized separate entity, under no nation's sovereignty. On that basis, the UN to the present day denies Israeli sovereignty over West Jerusalem and has urged UN member states not to locate embassies there.[93] In other resolutions the UN has declared that Jerusalem's status remains legally unresolved and can only be resolved through final status negotiations.

However, regarding East Jerusalem, ever since the June 1967 war, the UN has abandoned internationalization, choosing instead to characterize East Jerusalem as occupied Arab territory, and in more recent years as occupied *Palestinian* territory. Apparently, the UN has already resolved sovereignty over East Jerusalem (including the Old City) in favor of the Palestinians.

The evolution of East Jerusalem from "Arab" to "Palestinian" territory can be traced through a series of UN resolutions since 1967. Security Council Resolution 242 made no reference to any "Palestinian" territory, either in the West Bank or Jerusalem. Security Council Resolution 446 (22 March 1979) referred to "Arab" Jerusalem ("*the Arab territories* occupied since 1967, including Jerusalem"). The following year, in Resolution 478 (22 August 1980), the Security Council added the word "Palestinian," modifying the formulation to read, "*the Palestinian and other Arab territories* occupied since June 1967, including Jerusalem."

The ICJ continued this evolution in the 2004 *Wall* Advisory opinion, where it characterized East Jerusalem as "occupied Palestinian territory" and the Israeli inhabitants residing in East Jerusalem as "Israeli settlers" living in settlements "established in breach of international law."[94]

By December 2016, the Security Council in Resolution 2334 (23 December 2016) had dropped the word "Arab," referring solely to "*the Palestinian territory* occupied since 1967, *including East Jerusalem.*"

On 30 November 2017 the United Nations General Assembly adopted a resolution rejecting Israeli sovereignty over any portion of Jerusalem (West, East, and the Old City).[95] The resolution expressed "grave concern" regarding "the further isolation of the city *from the rest of the Occupied Palestinian Territory*."

But less than one month later (22 December 2017), the General Assembly adopted an "emergency resolution" condemning the Trump Administration's decision to move the U.S. Embassy from Tel Aviv to West Jerusalem in compliance with longstanding U.S. law. That Resolution, unlike the November 2017 resolution, stresses that "Jerusalem is a *final status issue to be resolved through negotiations*."[96]

Exactly how and when did East Jerusalem and the Old City morph into "Palestinian" territory? There exists no legal basis for this conclusion. Or, if East Jerusalem is Palestinian territory, then why is West Jerusalem not Israeli territory?

The drafting changes in the UN resolutions mentioned above and the ICJ's characterization in the *Wall* Advisory opinion conferred no legal rights on the Palestinians regarding East Jerusalem. Moreover, the Palestinians voluntarily agreed in the Oslo Accords that they would *not* obtain jurisdiction over *any* portion of Jerusalem (including East Jerusalem and the Old City) unless and until they and the Israelis were to agree otherwise in the eventual permanent status negotiations. Specifically, the Palestinians knowingly and voluntarily agreed that "[j]urisdiction of the [Palestinian] Council will cover West Bank and Gaza Strip territory, except for issues that will be negotiated in the permanent status negotiations," including Jerusalem.[97]

However, as Sabel (2022) has noted, the issue cuts both ways: Israel's agreement to use the word "Jerusalem" in the Declaration of Principles, rather than the more limited term "East Jerusalem," "opens up the possibility of a demand that negotiations deal with the future of the City as a whole."[98] This view, however, overlooks the provisions of the Oslo Accords committing the parties to implement Security Council Resolution 242, which implicitly recognized Israeli sovereignty over West Jerusalem.

Unfortunately, the General Assembly's December 2022 resolution asking the ICJ to render an Advisory Opinion muddled the Jerusalem issue yet again. The resolution asked the ICJ to determine the legal consequences arising from "measures aimed at altering the demographic composition, character, and status of the Holy City of Jerusalem, and from its adoption of related discriminatory legislation and measures."[99] The reference to the "Holy City of Jerusalem" appears to encompass the entirety of the city, including West Jerusalem. The language could also be read as limited to East Jerusalem or solely to the Old City, which the Palestinians claim belongs to them, despite any sound legal basis for such a claim.

Conclusion: Neither Party Has Sovereignty Over East Jerusalem, But Israel's Claim Is Superior

Both Israel and the Palestinians claim ownership of East Jerusalem. These claims are relatively new, as neither party controlled East Jerusalem at any time prior to 1967, nor did Jerusalem belong to anyone else before 1967. The UN designated East Jerusalem as part of the internationalized greater Jerusalem area 20 years earlier in November 1947, but it took no action to implement its decision, and it dropped the matter 5 years later.

Jordan illegally laid claim to East Jerusalem after invading Israel in violation of international law in May 1948. Jordan remained there until June 1967 at the request of the Palestinians themselves, who urged King Abdullah to annex the West Bank (including East Jerusalem) at the Jericho Conference in December 1948. The Palestinians reiterated their abdication of sovereignty over the West Bank (including East Jerusalem) in Article 24 of the original May 1964 PLO Covenant.

Israel replaced Jordan as the occupant of the West Bank and East Jerusalem in June 1967, following Jordan's second unprovoked and illegal military attack against Israel since May 1948. However, the Palestinians did not assert any claim to the West Bank or East Jerusalem until several years later. By that time Israel had extended its legal system to East Jerusalem and fully unified the two halves of the city. Israel eventually annexed East Jerusalem with the Knesset's passage of the 1980 Basic Law and its subsequent amendments.

The PLO knowingly, voluntarily and willingly agreed in the Oslo Accords that Jerusalem's final disposition would be the subject of future permanent status negotiations. The PLO obtained no concessions from Israel in the Oslo Accords regarding either Jerusalem's interim or permanent status.

This background demonstrates that between Israel and the Palestinians, neither party has a perfected claim of legal title to East Jerusalem. Watson (2000) identified similar arguments to those Giladi had covered earlier:

> As to East Jerusalem, opinion ranges from the view that Israel occupied East Jerusalem in 1967 and is now entitled to fill a vacuum in sovereignty that had existed there earlier; that Israel has the strongest relative title to East Jerusalem, since Jordan was never a legitimate sovereign; the view that sovereignty is in suspension, awaiting final settlement; the view that the Partition Resolution still governs; and the view that the Palestinians have legal sovereignty over East Jerusalem.[100]

But Watson further argued:

> Israel's claim to East Jerusalem, however, is weaker. East Jerusalem was not part of the State of Israel at its inception; though it now houses a

> Jewish majority, its demographic history is much more Arab than is the case in the western sector; and while it was acquired in a war of self-defence, conquest even in self-defence does not necessarily confer territorial sovereignty.[101]

The Israeli position, at least regarding the Old City, has changed over time. Israeli diplomats proposed long ago that the Old City be internationalized, but changed their position after Israel captured the area in June 1967. For example, in early May 1949, Israeli Ambassador to the UN Abba Eban expressed Israel's willingness in a speech to the General Assembly to accept the internationalization of the Old City. Eban said, "the government of Israel advocated the establishment by the United Nations of an international regime with full juridical status for Jerusalem concerned exclusively with the control and protection of the holy places, and would co-operate with such a regime."[102]

The former Israeli Foreign Ministry Legal Advisor, Professor Robbie Sabel, recently conceded Israel's claim to East Jerusalem is weaker than its claim to West Jerusalem: "There is, however, no international acquiescence to Israeli sovereignty in East Jerusalem and it would not be correct to deduce that 'prescription' applies to Israeli jurisdiction in East Jerusalem."[103]

But the Palestinian claim to East Jerusalem is weaker than the Israeli claim. Watson (2000) listed the following serious weaknesses in the Palestinian legal claim to East Jerusalem:

> [T]he Palestinian claim to East Jerusalem also has its weaknesses. Even if East Jerusalem is occupied territory, that does not necessarily imply any ultimate conclusion about territorial sovereignty. The mixed demographic makeup of East Jerusalem suggests that Jews as well as Arabs have rights of self-determination there. Moreover, there has never been a Palestinian state there (or anywhere else). Even the UN Partition Plan did not call for Palestinian sovereignty over East Jerusalem, but rather a *corpus separatum*. Likewise, Resolution 242 called for Israeli withdrawal from 'territories' occupied in the 1967 War, but it apparently did not call for withdrawal from *all* territories.[104]

Further, an argument can be made that Israel's annexation of East Jerusalem and the Old City did not violate international law. Under the traditional view, a state acting consistent with its right to self-defense under Article 51 of the UN Charter – as Israel did when Jordan attacked without provocation on 5 June 1967 – may lawfully annex the territory of the aggressor State to protect against future aggression.

As Hofmann (2020) noted, the traditional view was that the prospect of annexation would also help deter aggressor states from launching war.[105]

But Hofmann has also explained that the traditional view of annexation no longer conforms to modern state practice and principles of international law. Hofmann notes, for example, that the UN Security Council rejected the notion that Iraq should not lose any of its territory as the result of its unprovoked August 1990 invasion of Kuwait.[106] However, Hofmann also notes the UN has not passed a single resolution since 1965 regarding China's purported annexation of Tibet in 1951.

In any event, the situation regarding East Jerusalem is different. Jordan *never* had sovereignty over the West Bank, or over East Jerusalem and the Old City. Jordan's predecessor Britain did not have sovereignty either, and Turkey renounced sovereignty in the 1923 Treaty of Lausanne. The question, therefore, is whether Israel lawfully acquired sovereignty over East Jerusalem after capturing it in a lawful war of self-defense in 1967, and thereafter extending its law and taking a multitude of other steps to unify it with West Jerusalem.

Watson (2000) concluded that neither the Israelis nor the Palestinians have a perfected claim to East Jerusalem. Accordingly, the UN/ICJ characterization of East Jerusalem as "occupied Palestinian territory" lacks any legal basis:

> The weaknesses in each party's claim to East Jerusalem lend support to intermediate theories of sovereignty over East Jerusalem, such as the theory that sovereignty there is suspended pending a final settlement ... Applying these standards to East Jerusalem, it would appear that the law of self-determination does not demand any particular solution ... East Jerusalem includes both a substantial Arab and a substantial Jewish population, and the Old City obviously houses places of enormous importance to both sides. Self-determination might take the form of full Palestinian sovereignty in East Jerusalem ... but it might not have to take that form ... In sum, a final status agreement conferring upon Israel sovereignty over East Jerusalem would not deprive Palestinians there of their self-determination, as long as the agreement was freely negotiated and so long as the agreement fully protected the civil and political rights of Palestinians there. It is quite improbable that such an agreement would be invalid for coercion or duress.[107]

Cassese (1981), writing more than a decade prior to the Oslo Accords, argued the UN remains responsible for determining Jerusalem's legal status. Cassese contended that

> Because of the 18 April 1946 League of Nations resolution, and because the UK relinquished power over Palestine on 14 May 1948, the UN's

> consent must still be obtained for anyone who wants to claim sovereignty over Jerusalem ... If this is so, it follows that it is ultimately for the United Nations, Israel and Jordan to make arrangements for the international status of Jerusalem.[108]

The better view is that the UN lacks the legal power to award sovereignty over any portion of post-Mandate Palestine, including any portion of Jerusalem. The termination of the Mandate on 14 May 1948, together with the UN's failure to implement Resolution 181, deprived the UN of jurisdiction over post-Mandate questions of sovereignty. The Security Council, of course, retains its authority under Article VII of the United Nations Charter over threats to peace and acts of aggression, but those powers do not extend to determining sovereignty over post-Mandate Palestine, including any portion of Jerusalem.

In 1952 the legal advisor to the British Foreign Office, Sir Gerald Fitzmaurice, noted

> Jerusalem is quite definitely *not* de jure under UN control and never has been. Moreover the original UN resolution of 1947 about internationalization is dead and has no operative force and I doubt if any of these resolutions [pertaining to Jerusalem] are relevant.[109]

This view is supported by the Oslo Accords, where the Palestinians agreed to negotiate with Israel to determine the final status of Jerusalem. Nothing in the Accords designates East Jerusalem as "occupied" or as "Palestinian." Moreover, both the Palestinians and the Israelis have continued to recognize Jordan's special role with respect to the Muslim Holy sites in East Jerusalem.

In the final analysis, the Palestinian legal claim to East Jerusalem is weak. The Israeli legal claim is stronger, but not absolute.

Perhaps DiMarco (2018) said it best:

> To conclude, there are many opinions about the legal status of Jerusalem. As I said at the beginning of my short dissertation, the opinion on who Jerusalem really belongs to depends on the political, historical and religious context. And if it so difficult to identify who it belongs to, maybe it is because it doesn't belong to a single group. It never did. And the history of the UN Resolutions, of the wars between peoples and of the colonial powers demonstrates this. Everyone wants Jerusalem.[110]

As Sabel (2022) concluded, "It appears that international law may help buttress solutions [for Jerusalem] but, unfortunately, international law holds no magic answers or golden key."[111]

Notes

1 Palestinian Declaration of Independence, Palestine National Council 19th Session Algiers (15 Nov. 1988), https://www.palquest.org/en/historictext/9673/palestinian-declaration-independence (last accessed 17 Nov. 2023).
2 R. Lapidoth, *Israel and the Palestinians: Some Legal Issues*, Die Friedenswarte, 76:2/3, 211–40, at 223–24 (2001).
3 H. Bin Talal, *A Study on Jerusalem* at 3 (Longman, 1979).
4 Article IX of the treaty recognized the rights of the Christian population of the Ottoman Empire and reaffirmed the Sultan's 1852 *Firman* reinforcing the *status quo* at the Christian Holy Sites in Jerusalem and Bethlehem. Treaty of Paris (30 Mar. 1856).
5 United Nations General Assembly Resolution 181, *op. cit.*, Part III (A).
6 *Id.* Part III (D).
7 *Id.* Part III (B).
8 United Nations General Assembly, Res. 186 (S-2) (14 May 1948).
9 FRUS, 867N.01/5–2748, Telegram No. 767 (Confidential) from Burdett to Secretary of State (27 May 1948).
10 FRUS, *Text of Suggestions Presented by Count Bernadotte, at Rhodes, to the Two Parties* (28 June 1948). Bernadotte modified his proposal for Jerusalem three months later, writing to the Secretary General in September 1948 that "The City of Jerusalem, which should be understood as covering the area defined in the resolution of the General Assembly of 29 November, should be treated separately and should be placed under effective United Nations control with maximum feasible local autonomy for its Arab and Jewish communities, with full safeguards for the protection of the Holy Places and sites and free access to them, und for religious freedom." United Nations A/648, *Progress Report of the United Nations Mediator on Palestine Submitted to the Secretary-General for Transmission to the Members of the United Nations in pursuance of paragraph 2, part II, of resolution 186 (S-2) of the General Assembly of 14 May 1948*, General Assembly Official Records: Third Session, Supplement No. 11 (Sept. 1948). Bernadotte also proposed transferring the Negev region to Transjordan in exchange for Israel receiving the entire Galilee region. Bernadotte's proposals were published 16 Sept. 1948. Jewish terrorists assassinated Bernadotte in Jerusalem the following day, 17 Sept. 1948. United Nations Secretary General Trygve Lie appointed the American diplomat Ralph Bunche to succeed Bernadotte as mediator.
11 FRUS, 501.BB Palestine/7–1148, Telegram No. 1061 (Confidential) from MacDonald to Secretary of State (11 July 1948).
12 United Nations Security Council, S/902, Res. 54 para. 6 (15 July 1948) (emphasis added).
13 See FRUS, 867N.01/8–348, Telegram No. 37 from the Acting Special Representative of the United States in Israel (Knox) to the Secretary of State (3 Aug. 1948).
14 A. Ilan, *Bernadotte in Palestine, 1948: A Study in Contemporary Humanitarian Knight-Errantry* at 165–66 (MacMillan, 1989).
15 FRUS, 501.BB Palestine/8–448, Telegram No. 1157 (Secret and Urgent) from McDonald to Secretary of State (4 Aug. 1948).
16 FRUS, 501.BB Palestine/8–1248, Telegram No. 1190 (Secret) from Macdonald to the Secretary of State (12 Aug. 1948). On 23 August McDonald reported to the State Department that Israeli Foreign Minister Moshe Shertok told him Israel might still consider internationalization or partition of Jerusalem. FRUS 867N.01/8–2348, Telegram (Secret and Urgent) No. 67 from McDonald to Secretary of State (23 Aug. 1948).
17 FRUS, 501.BB Palestine/9–148, Telegram No. 72 (Top Secret and Urgent) from the Secretary of State to McDonald (1 Sept. 1948).

18 FRUS, 501.BB Palestine/9–948, Telegram (Top Secret and Urgent) No. 98 from McDonald to Secretary of State (9 Sept. 1948).

19 FRUS, 501.BB Palestine/9–1248, Telegram No. 1274 from Macdonald to Secretary of State (12 Sept. 1948).

20 FRUS, 501.BB Palestine/9–2848, Telegram No. 151 (Secret and Urgent) from McDonald to Secretary of State (28 Sept. 1948). Two days later the State Department drafted but did not send a telegram to McDonald reiterating the State Department's view that Jerusalem should be internationalized. 501. BB Palestine/9–3048, Draft Telegram (Secret and Urgent) to the Special Representative of the United States in Israel (McDonald) (30 Sept. 1948) ("As for pretensions of PGI to the extension of its authority to include the greater part of Jerusalem, US Government is convinced that recommendations of Mediator which are in effect identical to those recommended by UN GA in its resolution of Nov. 29, 1947, afford most equitable settlement of Jerusalem problem. This Government, while sympathetic to views of both Arab and Jewish Governments regarding their respective communities in the Holy City, nevertheless must look to worldwide interest in preservation of Jerusalem and its ready access to persons of all three religious faiths who regard Jerusalem as a central and symbolic point. Accordingly, this government does not believe that PGI should control part of Jerusalem or that it should have a corridor to that city. Conclusions in Bernadotte Plan specifically providing for right of unimpaired access to Jerusalem by rail, road and air would seem in our opinion to obviate any need for a Jewish corridor").

21 FRUS, 501.BB Palestine/9–2548, Telegram No. 1392 (Secret) from the U.S. Ambassador in Egypt (Griffis) to the Acting Secretary of State (25 Sept. 1948).

22 FRUS, 501.BB Palestine/11–1648, NSC 27/3, Report (Top Secret) by the National Security Council on Provision of a Police Force for Jerusalem (16 Nov. 1948).

23 *Id.*

24 United Nations General Assembly, A/RES/194 (11 Dec. 1948).

25 FRUS, 501.BB Palestine/12–1348, Telegram No. 1530 (Secret) from Burdett to the Acting Secretary of State (13 Dec. 1948).

26 E. Ben-Dror and A. Ziedler, *Israel, Jordan, and their Efforts to Frustrate the United Nations Resolutions to Internationalise Jerusalem*, Diplomacy & Statecraft, 26, 636–58 at 639 (2015).

27 FRUS, 867N.01/1–1349, Telegram No. 35 (Secret and Urgent) from Burdett to the Secretary of State (13 Jan. 1949).

28 FRUS, 501.BB Palestine/1–1849, Telegram No. 35 (Secret) from the Acting Secretary of State to the Consulate General in Jerusalem (19 Jan. 1949).

29 FRUS, 501.BB Palestine/1–2949, Telegram No. 78 (Secret and Urgent) from Burdett to the Secretary of State (29 Jan. 1949).

30 Cypher Telegram (Immediate and Secret) No. 57 from British Consulate, Jerusalem to Foreign Office (17 Jan. 1949), *reprinted in* P. Toye and A. Seay, *Israel: Boundary Disputes with Arab Neighbours 1946–1964* Vol. 2 at 495–96 (Archive Editions, 1995).

31 FRUS, 867N.01/2–149, Telegram No. 94 (Confidential and Urgent) from Burdett to the Secretary of State (1 Feb. 1949). According to the State Department Historian, "Israeli Foreign Minister Shertok informed McDonald of this action and explained, 'to avoid international misunderstanding,' that it 'was administrative and not annexation of Jerusalem.'" Citing FRUS 867N.01/2–149, Telegram No. 78 (1 Feb. 1949).

32 FRUS, 501.BB Palestine/2–249, Telegram No. 62 (Confidential) from Secretary of State to Burdett (2 Feb. 1949).

33 FRUS, 867N.01/2–349, Telegram No. 88 (Top Secret) from McDonald to the Secretary of State (3 Feb. 1949).

34 Hashemite Jordan Kingdom-Israel General Armistice Agreement, 3 Apr. 1949, Art. V(b), reproduced in R. Lapidoth and M. Hirsch (eds.), *The Jerusalem Question and Its Resolution: Selected Documents*, 33–41 at 35 (Martinus Nijhoff, 1994).
35 United Nations General Assembly, A/RES/303 (9 Dec. 1949).
36 Records of Knesset Proceedings, Vol. 4 (2d Sess.) p. 603, reproduced in R. Lapidoth and M. Hirsch (eds.), *The Jerusalem Question and Its Resolution: Selected Documents* at 105 (Martinus Nijhoff, 1994) ("Whereas, on the establishment of the State of Israel, Jerusalem once again became its capital").
37 *Aide Memoir* Delivered by the United States Embassy at Tel Aviv to the Israel Government concerning the Removal of the Israel Ministry of Foreign Affairs to Jerusalem (9 July 1952), M. Whiteman, Digest of International Law, Vol. 1 at 594–95 (1963), reproduced in R. Lapidoth and M. Hirsch (eds.), *The Jerusalem Question and Its Resolution: Selected Documents* at 155 (Martinus Nijhoff, 1994).
38 United Nations A/1286, Question of An International Regime for the Jerusalem Area and Protection of The Holy Places, Special Report of the Trusteeship Council (1950); United Nations T/592, Statute for Jerusalem (T/564, approved by the Trusteeship Council, 4 Apr. 1950).
39 E. Lauterpacht, *Jerusalem and the Holy Places* at 33, 36 (1968); *see also* A. Gerson, *Israel the West Bank and International Law* at 212 (Frank Cass & Co. Ltd., 1978) ("since 1950, the international community has essentially abandoned internationalization as a viable solution to the political status of Jerusalem.").
40 G. Heimann, *The Struggle between the United States and Israel over Recognition for Jerusalem as Israel's Capital, 1952–67*, The International History Review, 37:4, 790–808 at 792–93 (2015).
41 M. Abbasi, *The Education System in East Jerusalem during the Period of Jordanian Rule, 1948–1967*, Journal of Politics and Law, 6 at 174, 176–77 (2013).
42 A. Cassese, *Legal Considerations on the International Status of Jerusalem*, in H. Kochler (ed.), *The Legal Aspects of the Palestine Problem with Special Regard to the Question of Jerusalem* at 144 (William Braumuller, 1981).
43 On the morning of 5 June 1967, Israeli Prime Minister Levi Eshkol transmitted through the Chief of Staff of UNTSO, Norwegian Lt. General Odd Bull, a message to King Hussein asking Jordan to refrain from hostilities. The message read, "We are engaged in defensive fighting on the Egyptian sector, and we shall not engage ourselves in any action against Jordan, unless Jordan attacks us. Should Jordan attack Israel, we shall go against her with all our might." *See also* FRUS, Telegram 208049 (5 June 1967) ("Israeli Representative here asks us to convey earnest desire of his government not do any harm to Jordan. They hope that hostilities between the two countries can be avoided or kept to a minimum") and State Department Historian's footnote to Telegram 208049 ("Telegram 523 from USUN, June 5, reported that UN Under Secretary Ralph J. Bunche had informed Goldberg of a report by UNTSO Chief of Staff Lieutenant General Odd Bull that he had conveyed an Israeli message to King Hussein that no action would be taken against Jordan unless Jordan started it, in which case Israel would hit back hard (Ibid., Office of the Executive Secretariat, Middle East Crisis Files, 1967, Entry 5190, Arab-Israeli Crisis, Box 6, Chron, USUN) Telegram 1106 from Amman, August 26, reports that King Hussein told Burns he received two messages from the Israelis on June 5, the first through General Bull that morning, after the Jordanian Air Force had already taken off against Israel, and the second through the U.S. Embassy that evening (Ibid., RG 59, Central Files 1967–69, POL 15–1 JORDAN)".).
44 Law and Administration Ordinance (Amendment No. 11) Law, 5727-1967, addition of section 11(b) ("The law, jurisdiction and administration of the State shall extend to any area of Eretz Israel designated by the Government by order."),

reproduced in R. Lapidoth and M. Hirsch (eds.), *The Jerusalem Question and Its Resolution: Selected Documents* at 167 (Martinus Nijhoff, 1994).

45 Protection of Holy Places Law, Laws of the State of Israel, Vol. 21, 5727-1966/7, p. 76 reproduced in R. Lapidoth and M. Hirsch (eds.), *The Jerusalem Question and Its Resolution: Selected Documents* at 169 (Martinus Nijhoff, 1994).

46 Israel-Jordan Peace Treaty, UNTS 35325, Art. 9(2) (26 Oct. 1994).

47 *Joint Communique from the March 19 meeting in Sharm El Sheikh* (19 Mar. 2023), https://www.state.gov/joint-communique-from-the-march-19-meeting-in-sharm-el-sheikh/ (last accessed 22 Nov. 2023).

48 United Nations General Assembly, A/RES/2253 (4 July 1967).

49 United Nations General Assembly, A/RES/2254 (14 July 1967).

50 United Nations Security Council, S/RES/242 (22 Nov. 1967).

51 *See, e.g.*, Security Council Resolution 252 (21 May 1968):

Reaffirming that acquisition of territory by military conquest is inadmissible, 1. Deplores the failure of Israel to comply with the General Assembly resolutions mentioned above; 2. Considers that all legislative and administrative measures and actions taken by Israel, including expropriation of land and properties thereon, which tend to change the legal status of Jerusalem are invalid and cannot change that status; 3. Urgently calls upon Israel to rescind all such measures already taken and to desist forthwith from taking any further action which tends to change the status of Jerusalem;

Security Council Resolution 267 (3 July 1969):

Reaffirming the established principle that acquisition of territory by military conquest is inadmissible, 1. Reaffirms its resolution 252 (1968); 2. Deplores the failure of Israel to show any regard for the resolutions of the General Assembly and the Security Council mentioned above; 3. Censures in the strongest terms all measures taken to change the status of the City of Jerusalem; 4. Confirms that all legislative and administrative measures and actions taken by Israel which purport to alter the status of Jerusalem, including expropriation of land and properties thereon, are invalid and cannot change that status; 5. Urgently calls once more upon Israel to rescind forthwith all measures taken by it which may tend to change the status of the City of Jerusalem, and in future to refrain from all actions likely to have such an effect; 6. Requests Israel to inform the Security Council without any further delay of its intentions with regard to the implementation of the provisions of the present resolution; 7. Determines that, in the event of a negative response or no response from Israel, the Security Council shall reconvene without delay to consider what further action should be taken in this matter;

Security Council Resolution 298 (25 Sept. 1971):

Reaffirms its resolutions 252 (1968) and 267 (1969); 2. Deplores the failure of Israel to respect the previous resolutions adopted by the United Nations concerning measures and actions by Israel purporting to affect the status of the City of Jerusalem; 3. Confirms in the clearest possible terms that all legislative and administrative actions taken by Israel to change the status of the City of Jerusalem, including expropriation of land and properties, transfer of populations and legislation aimed at the incorporation of the occupied section, are totally invalid and cannot change that status; 4. Urgently calls upon Israel to rescind all previous measures and actions and to take no further steps in the occupied section of Jerusalem which may purport to change the status of the City or which would prejudice the rights of the inhabitants and the interests of the international community, or a just and lasting peace.

Security Council Resolution 465 (1 Mar. 1980), para. 5:

Determines that all measures taken by Israel to change the physical character, demographic composition. institutional structure or status of the Palestinian and other Arab territories occupied since 1967, including Jerusalem, or any part thereof have no legal validity and that Israel's policy and practices of settling parts of its population and new immigrants in those territories constitute a flagrant violation of the Geneva Convention relative to the Protection of Civilian Persons in Time of War and also constitute a serious obstruction to achieving a comprehensive, just and lasting peace in the Middle East.

52 S. Mallison and T.W. Mallison, The Jerusalem Problem in International Public Law: Juridical Status and a Start Towards Solution, in H. Kochler (ed.), *The Legal Aspects of the Palestine Problem with Special Regard to the Question of Jerusalem* at 107 (William Braumuller, 1981).

53 Jerusalem, Basic Law, Passed by the Knesset on the 17th Av, 5740 (30th July, 1980) and published in Sefer Ha-Chukkim No. 980 of the 23rd Av, 5740 (5 Aug. 1980), p. 186; the Bill and an Explanatory Note were published in Hatza'ot Chok No. 1464 of 5740, p. 287. Amendment no. 1 was passed by the Knesset on the 29th Heshvan 5761 (27 Nov. 2000) and published in Sefer Ha-Chukkim No. 5762, p. 28, reproduced in R. Lapidoth and M. Hirsch (eds.), *The Jerusalem Question and its Resolution: Selected Documents* at 322 (Martinus Nijhoff, 1994). The last two clauses of the Law were added in November 2000. The new restrictions were adopted because the Knesset wanted to make sure Prime Minister Ehud Barak would not reach an agreement with the Palestinians against the will of the majority in the Knesset. *See* Lapidoth (2011), *op. cit.* at 17.

54 M.L. DiMarco, *The Legal Status of Jerusalem in the State of Israel*, Rivista Telematica, Stato, Chiese e Pluralismo Confessionale, 27:1–12 at 8 (2018).

55 R. Lapidoth, *Jerusalem: Some Jurisprudential Aspects*, Catholic University Law Review, 45, 661–86 at 672 (1996); R. Lapidoth, *Jerusalem – Some Legal Issues*, in R. Wolfrum (ed.), *The Max Planck Encyclopedia of Public International Law* at 21 (Oxford Univ. Press, 2011b).

56 R. Giladi, *Practice and Case Law of Israel in Matters Related to International Law*, Israel Law Review, 33:1, 106–38 at 109 (1999).

57 M.I. Gruhin, *Jerusalem: Legal & Political Dimensions in a Search for Peace*, Case Western Reserve Journal of International Law, 12:1, 169–214 at 206 (1980).

58 M. Golani, *Jerusalem's Hope Lies Only in Partition: Israeli Policy on the Jerusalem Question, 1948–67*, International Journal of Middle East Studies, 31:4, 577–604 at 585–86 (1999).

59 Lapidoth, *op. cit.* at 22.

60 Watson (2000), *op. cit.* at 268.

61 Arab Peace Initiative (27 Mar. 2022), https://www.kas.de/c/document_library/get_file?uuid=a5dab26d-a2fe-dc66-8910-a13730828279&groupId=268421 (last accessed 16 Nov. 2023).

62 R. Sabel, *International Law and the Arab-Israeli Conflict* at 367 (Cambridge Univ. Press, 2022).

63 *Island of Palmas (Miangas), United States v. Netherlands*, Reports of International Arbitral Awards Recueil Des Sentences Arbitrales, 2 U.N. Rep. Intl. Arb. Awards 829–71 at 839–40 (Perm. Ct. Arb. 1928) (4 Apr. 1928).

64 J. Quigley, *Sovereignty in Jerusalem*, Catholic University Law Review, 45, 765–80 at 777–78 (1996).

65 *Western Sahara*, Advisory Opinion, 1.C.J. Reports 1975, 12, 68 at para. 262.

66 *Id.*

67 *South West Africa*, Second Phase, Judgment, I.C.J. Reports 1966, pp. 6, 35 at para. 54.

68 Cassese (1981), *op. cit.* at 147–52.

69 *Id.* at 146.

70 *Id.*

71 M.L. DiMarco, *The Legal Status of Jerusalem in the State of Israel*, Rivista Telematica, Stato, Chiese e Pluralismo Confessionale, 27:1–12 at 9 (2018).
72 Cassese (1981), *op. cit.* at 146.
73 *Id.*
74 *Id.*
75 *Id.*
76 W. Khalidi, *Thinking the Unthinkable: A Sovereign Palestinian State*, Foreign Affairs, 56:4, 695–713 at 705 (1978).
77 R. Lapidoth, *Jerusalem: Some Jurisprudential Aspects*, Catholic University Law Review, 45, 661–86 at 673–74 (1996).
78 Lapidoth (2011b), *op.cit.* at 22–23.
79 R.M. Giladi, *Practice and Case Law of Israel in Matters Related to International Law*, Israel Law Review, 33:1 at 106–38 (1999).
80 M. Hirsch, *The Legal Status of Jerusalem following the ICJ Advisory Opinion on the Separation Barrier*, Israel Law Review, 38 at 298, 300 (2005).
81 Lauterpach (1968), *op. cit.* at 47.
82 S. Berkovitz, *The Holy Places in Jerusalem: Legal Aspects*, Rivista di Studi Politici Internazionali, 65:3 (259), 403–15 at 405 (1998).
83 Gerson (1978), *op. cit.* at 213–14.
84 HCJ 393/ 82, *Jamait Askan et al. v. IDF Commander of Judea and Samaria et al.*, 37(4) PD 785 at para. 10, unofficial translation at https://hamoked.org/items/160_eng.pdf (last accessed 5 Jan. 2023).
85 Y. Dinstein, *The International Law of Belligerent Occupation* (2nd ed.) at 22–23 (Cambridge University Press, 2019).
86 Lapidoth, *op.cit.* at 24–25.
87 *Id.* at 14.
88 G.I.A.D. Draper, *The Status of Jerusalem as a Question of International Law*, in H. Kochler (ed.), *The Legal Aspects of the Palestine Problem with Special Regard to the Question of Jerusalem* at 163 (William Braumuller, 1981).
89 J. Quigley, *Sovereignty in Jerusalem*, Catholic University Law Review, 45 at 765, 774 (1996).
90 H. Cattan, *The Status of Jerusalem under International Law and United Nations*, Journal of Palestine Studies, 10:3, 3–15 at 10–11 (1981).
91 Bin Talal, *op cit.* at 27.
92 M. Hirsch, *The Legal Status of Jerusalem following the ICJ Advisory Opinion on the Separation Barrier*, Israel Law Review, 38 at 298, 301–02 (2005).
93 *See, e.g.*, United Nations Security Council Res. 478, para. 5(b) (20 Aug. 1980) (calling on "states that have established diplomatic missions at Jerusalem to withdraw such missions from the Holy City").
94 *Wall* Advisory Opinion, paras. 78, 84, 120.
95 United Nations General Assembly, Resolution A/RES/72/15, *Jerusalem* (30 Nov. 2017).
96 United Nations General Assembly, Resolution ES-10/19, *Status of Jerusalem* (22 Dec. 2017).
97 A/48/486, S/26560, *Declaration of Principles on Interim Self-Government Arrangements*, paras. IV, V(3) (13 Sept. 1993).
98 Sabel (2022), *op. cit.* at 377.
99 United Nations, A/RES/77/247 para. 18(a) (22 Dec. 2022).
100 Watson (2000), *op. cit.* at 26.
101 *Id.* at 268.
102 GAOR, 3rd Sess., part 2, 1949, Ad Hoc Political Committee, 45th meeting, May 5, 1949 (A/818), 230–36, reproduced in R. Lapidoth and M. Hirsch (eds.), *The Jerusalem Question and Its Resolution: Selected Documents*, 43–48 at 48 (Martinus Nijhoff, 1994).

103 Sabel (2022), *op. cit.* at 373.
104 Watson (2000), *op. cit.* at 269.
105 R. Hofmann, *Annexation*, Max Planck Encyclopedia of Public International Law, para. 23 (2020).
106 *Id.* para. 24 (2020), citing UN Security Council, S/RES/686 (1991).
107 Watson (2000), *op. cit.* at 269, 272.
108 Cassese (1981), *op. cit.* at 144, 152.
109 FO 371/98488, Sir Gerald Fitzmaurice Minute (18 June 1952).
110 M.L. Di Marco, *The Legal Status of Jerusalem in the State of Israel.* Rivista Telematica, Stato, Chiese e Pluralismo Confessionale, 27:1–12 at 11 (2018).
111 Sabel (2022), *op. cit.* at 379.

CONCLUSION

The Palestinians have chosen to pursue litigation and lawfare for the last three decades after signing the Oslo Accords, rather than the negotiations to which they committed themselves. Therefore, it is entirely fair to ask whether the Palestinians have a meritorious *legal* case, as separate and distinct from their *political* case. As this study has shown, the answer is a resounding no.

The legal analysis requires applying the relevant facts and history to the applicable principles of international law. The historical facts are often overlooked when assessing the merits of the Palestinian legal case. But those facts are extremely important.

The Palestinians rejected various offers of statehood in all or part of Palestine on multiple occasions between the 1930s and 1960s. In May 1939 they rejected a British offer of future statehood over the entirety of Palestine. In November 1947 they rejected the United Nations' offer of statehood in an area larger than today's West Bank and Gaza Strip. In December 1948 they explicitly waived West Bank sovereignty when they asked Jordan to annex the area. They reiterated that explicit waiver in the original PLO Charter of May 1964, declaring, "this organization does not exercise any regional sovereignty over the West Bank in the Hashemite Kingdom of Jordan, [or] on the Gaza Strip."

Moreover, the Palestinians acquiesced in Jordanian and Egyptian occupation of the West Bank and Gaza between 1948 and 1967, never seeking statehood during those years, and never raising any legal objections to the Jordanian and Egyptian occupations. Nor did the United Nations or the ICJ ever condemn the Jordanian and Egyptian occupations and demand statehood for the Palestinians during those years.

DOI: 10.4324/9781032686561-27

The June 1967 Six-Day War marked a dramatic change. Arab armies massed along Israel's borders in late May 1967, answering Nasser's rallying cry to reprise the 1948–1949 war and destroy Israel for good. Israel struck Egypt first in a lawful exercise of anticipatory self-defense. Jordan then launched an unprovoked and unlawful attack against Israel despite two Israeli pleas to stay out of the conflict.

This was the second time since 1948 that Jordan had violated international law by launching war against Israel. Israel lawfully exercised its self-defense rights on both occasions. By the end of the 1948–1949 war, Israel had obtained control of West Jerusalem and portions of the areas the UN had previously allocated for the future Arab State. By the end of the June 1967 war, Israel had replaced Jordan as the occupant of the West Bank and East Jerusalem, and Egypt as the occupant of the Gaza Strip.

On 22 November 1967 the United Nations Security Council adopted Resolution 242, demanding Israel withdraw "from territories occupied in the recent conflict," but not from *all* territories, nor from any other territories acquired *prior* to the June 1967 war, such as West Jerusalem or the Arab-designated areas captured during the 1948–1949 war. Notably, even the Arab League, at their 1 September 1967 conference in Khartoum, Sudan called only for Israeli withdrawal from "the Arab lands which have been occupied since the aggression of June 5," and not from any lands Israel had captured in prior conflicts. Nor did the Khartoum Resolutions call for a Palestinian state in the West Bank and the Gaza Strip. Instead, the Arab League swore "no peace with Israel, no recognition of Israel, no negotiations with it."

Moreover, Resolution 242 did not specify a deadline for withdrawal. Indeed, the text of Resolution 242 failed to specify whether Israel must withdraw first, or the Arabs must make peace first, or territorial withdrawal and peace must occur simultaneously. Thus, the Resolution, commonly interpreted as requiring Israel to withdraw first ("land for peace"), could just as easily be read to require the Arabs to make peace first, as a precondition for Israeli withdrawal ("peace for land"). A strong argument can be made that the latter interpretation should control, given the Resolution post-dated by only a few weeks the Arab summit in Khartoum and the "three nos."

Before long, however, the United Nations turned dramatically against Israel. Despite the United Nations' failure during the years of Jordanian and Egyptian occupation of the West Bank and the Gaza Strip to demand statehood for the Palestinians, by the late 1960s the General Assembly had elevated the issue to the top of its agenda, where it has remained ever since.

Indeed, the United Nations in recent decades has focused disproportionality on the Israeli-Palestinian conflict. The infamous 1975 "Zionism is Racism" resolution (later repealed)[1] marked a low point for the UN's anti-Israeli bias, which has only intensified since then. In 2022, the General Assembly adopted 28 resolutions criticizing various countries around the world. Fifteen of those resolutions were aimed at Israel. Only six resolutions were directed at Russia, which had launched a full-scale war against Ukraine in February 2022, provoking the most serious threat to global peace since the end of World War II.

The same attitude toward Israel pervades other United Nations agencies. For example, between 2006 and 2022 the United Nations Human Rights Council adopted 99 resolutions against Israel, more than the rest of the world combined.[2]

The Palestinians have capitalized on this dynamic and poured enormous resources into their lawfare/litigation campaign. The latest Palestinian legal effort bore fruit in December 2022, when the United Nations General Assembly voted to seek an Advisory Opinion from the International Court of Justice regarding the legality of Israel's "prolonged occupation" and its activities in Jerusalem.[3]

The General Assembly's action represents the latest example of Palestinian efforts to use the law to gain leverage and influence international opinion in the conflict. The Palestinians and their supporters argue Israel's occupation of the West Bank is illegal; that Israeli settlements in the West Bank are illegal; that Israel's presence in East Jerusalem and the Old City violates international law; and that the Gaza Strip, from which Israel withdrew completely in 2005, and from where a horrifically bloody surprise attack was launched against Israel on 7 October 2023, nevertheless remains "occupied."

The Palestinians and their supporters further argue they are *legally entitled* to sovereignty and statehood in the West Bank and Gaza. They also argue, in the alternative, that Palestine has *already* achieved statehood/sovereignty over the West Bank and Gaza.

This study, however, has shown the Palestinian legal case, as opposed to its political case, is demonstrably weak, for at least the following reasons:

First, the Oslo Accords undermine every aspect of the Palestinian legal case. The Oslo Accords are enormously significant from a legal perspective. They constitute the legally binding documents governing all aspects of the Israeli-Palestinian dispute. The parties committed themselves to the Middle East peace process. They agreed to resolve *every* issue in the dispute through negotiation, including the most difficult permanent status issues.

The Oslo Accords continue in full force and effect today. They remain legally binding on both the Israelis and the Palestinians, despite the moribund political process and long delay in completing the permanent status negotiations. Neither party has formally abrogated the Accords. The dispute resolution provisions preclude the parties from initiating litigation before the international courts (or asking others to do so on their behalf), consistent with their repeated and legally binding commitments to each other to resolve *all* issues in the conflict through negotiation.

The Palestinians knowingly, voluntarily, and willingly signed the Oslo Accords, which they negotiated vigorously over a long period following the

1991 Madrid Conference. No one forced or coerced the Palestinians to sign the agreements. The Palestinians knew exactly what they were doing, as Mahmoud Abbas confirmed in his memoir of the negotiations.

The Oslo Accords comprehensively address the entire set of issues dividing the parties, addressing some on an interim basis, while reserving others for eventual permanent status negotiations intended to implement UN Security Council Resolutions 242 and 338.

During the interim phase, Israel would withdraw from most of the Gaza Strip and Jericho, and from almost half the West Bank (Areas A and B). The Palestinians agreed Israel would retain exclusive control of the remainder of the West Bank (Area C). The Palestinians agreed the Israeli settlements and settlers could remain in Area C during the interim period, pending a permanent status deal. The Palestinians obtained no commitments from Israel to refrain from building new settlements or expanding existing settlements during the interim period.

The PLO gained Israeli recognition as the representative of the Palestinian people. The Palestinians negotiated for the right to govern themselves in Areas A and B, plus the Gaza Strip and Jericho, through a Palestinian Council to be elected democratically. The Council would be responsible for civic affairs in the areas from which Israel would withdraw. The Palestinians agreed Israel would remain responsible for Israelis, Israeli property, and overall military security in both the West Bank and the Gaza Strip.

The Palestinians further committed themselves to recognizing Israel's right to exist. The Palestinians also agreed to renounce terrorism, violence, and incitement. They agreed to stop teaching their children to hate Jews and Israelis.

The Palestinians agreed that "permanent status" issues such as Jerusalem, borders, refugees, and the final status of Israeli settlements would be reserved for later negotiation. The Palestinians obtained no promises or guarantees regarding any of the permanent status issues, including Palestinian statehood.

Both sides reserved their rights regarding all issues, agreeing "[n]either Party shall be deemed, by virtue of having entered into this Agreement, to have renounced or waived any of its existing rights, claims or positions."[4]

The Palestinians also committed themselves to pursue their claims *solely* through diplomacy and negotiation. The Palestinians further agreed to limit themselves to a very specific dispute resolution process, a process that did not allow either party to initiate litigation, or to ask others to initiate litigation on their behalf.

Both sides additionally agreed not to initiate or take any steps that would change the status of the West Bank and the Gaza Strip.

The division of land and responsibility in the West Bank and East Jerusalem today reflects *exactly* what the Palestinians bargained for at Oslo, no more and no less. The Palestinians enjoy full civic autonomy in the Areas A and B of the West Bank.

Hamas has controlled the Gaza Strip since June 2007, following Israel's complete withdrawal from the area in September 2005. Some commentators make the illogical argument that Israel continued to "occupy" the Gaza Strip after withdrawing from it. Perhaps those commentators would be willing to acknowledge that the devastating October 2023 Hamas attack on Israel belies any such claims of ongoing Israeli occupation.

Second, the early 20th-century Palestinian position negating the existence of "Palestine" as a recognized geopolitical entity undermines the 21st-century Palestinian legal claim regarding the longstanding and consistent desire of the Palestinian people for statehood and sovereignty.

Moreover, the Mufti's 1929 concession that the Mandate granted no political rights to the Palestinian Arabs flatly contradicts the arguments of some Palestinian lawyers today that the Mandate somehow remains in effect and that it grants rights of sovereignty and statehood to the Palestinian Arabs.

Third, the Palestinians' current quest for statehood is inconsistent with their prior multiple rejections of the same outcome. Their repeated implied and expressed rejections of statehood and sovereignty carry legal consequences for the legal claims they assert today. For example, a strong argument can be made that the Palestinians are estopped under international law from laying claim to West Jerusalem and to the portions of Palestine that the General Assembly had recommended for Palestinian statehood but that were lost to Israel in the 1948–1949 war. An argument could also be made, although not as strong, that the implicit and explicit Palestinian waivers of sovereignty over the West Bank, East Jerusalem, and the Gaza Strip estop the Palestinians from asserting sovereignty over those same areas today.

Fourth, the Palestinian rejections of offers of statehood in July 1937 and May 1939 from Britain and in November 1947 from the United Nations, plus their pledges of loyalty to King Abdullah in 1948 and 1950, and the language in Article 24 of the original May 1964 PLO Charter expressly disavowing sovereignty over the West Bank and Gaza all contradict their current legal position.

Fifth, the Palestinians never sought statehood in the West Bank and the Gaza Strip between 1949 and 1967, when they acquiesced in Jordan's purported annexation and Egypt's military occupation. While there was some discontent among West Bank Palestinians living as Jordanian citizens during those years, the vast majority accepted Jordanian rule without objection. The same was true for Gazans living under Egyptian occupation. To the extent there were any stirrings of Palestinian nationalism between 1949 and 1967, they were directed at destroying Israel rather than seeking Palestinian statehood in the West Bank and Gaza. It was only well after June 1967, when

Israel replaced Jordan and Egypt as the occupying power, that the Palestinians changed course and demanded statehood in the West Bank and Gaza.

Today, however, the Palestinians have come full circle, repeatedly invoking the injustice/victimhood narrative and lawfare to demand the very same outcome they rejected from the 1930s until the late 1960s – statehood in a portion of the former mandatory Palestine.

Sixth, sovereignty over the West Bank and Gaza has remained suspended or in abeyance since the end of World War I. Israel's presence in the West Bank resulted from a lawful exercise of self-defense against Jordan in early June 1967. Israel's continued occupation of the West Bank comports with more than a century of international laws of occupation. Nevertheless, neither Israel nor the Palestinians today possess legal title to the West Bank and Gaza Strip. Moreover, despite Palestinian efforts to characterize East Jerusalem as occupied "Palestinian" territory (which they never did during the two decades of Jordanian occupation between 1948 and 1967), East Jerusalem's legal status has never been conclusively resolved since Britain ousted Turkey from Palestine at the end of World War I.

Seventh, Palestine has not yet achieved statehood. Admittedly, many countries have accorded some form of recognition to the "State of Palestine," but that alone does not satisfy the traditional international law test for determining the existence of statehood. At most, Palestine is an *aspirational state* whose final status can only be determined through negotiation and diplomacy rather than litigation.

Eighth, the Palestine Mandate no longer carries any legal force. Britain terminated the Mandate on 14 May 1948. At that moment the post-World War I international control of Palestine through the League of Nations and its successor the United Nations also ended, thereby depriving the United Nations of legal authority thereafter to reallocate or determine sovereignty over any portion of post-Mandate Palestine.[5] Subsequent United Nations actions (as recently as May 2024) purporting to grant Palestine the status of a "state" for purposes of participating in various United Nations agencies and committees do not satisfy international legal requirements for conferring Palestinian Arab sovereignty over the West Bank and Gaza.

Finally, the international courts should decline to intervene in the inherently political, non-justiciable issues in the Israeli-Palestinian conflict. The courts lack the authority to determine sovereignty over the West Bank, East Jerusalem, and Gaza. Shaky Palestinian legal claims based on "rights," "victimhood" and "injustice" should not obfuscate the reality that the conflict is inherently political and must be resolved by diplomats through negotiation – as the Palestinians solemnly promised to do in the Oslo Accords – and not by lawyers and judges through litigation.

Nevertheless, Palestinian frame entrepreneurs have brilliantly exploited the world community's disregard for the historical facts and the associated legal consequences, successfully positioning Palestinian nationalism at the center of the global social justice movement. The Palestinian political case for statehood is stronger than its legal case, yet the Palestinians in recent years have shunned diplomacy and the peace process in favor of transformational legal framing and lawfare. While this effort has garnered broad support from social justice entrepreneurs and the international courts, there is little chance the Palestinians will be able to convert these successes into achieving the *political* goal of Palestinian statehood.

And therein lies the greatest irony of all: the conflict, inherently political and non-legal in nature, must be resolved through political, *not* legal means. If the Palestinian Arabs deserve statehood in the West Bank and Gaza, despite rejecting and waiving it at every prior opportunity, then it is not because they have any *legal* right to it, but instead because the two-state solution continues to represent the most viable long-term *political* outcome for all stakeholders in the conflict. But the Palestinian insistence on invoking transformational legal framing and the "victimhood" narrative has become so overwhelmingly identified with the Palestinian national movement that little or no room remains for serious discussion of the future task of state-building.

This study concedes the Palestinians have a strong *political* claim against the Israeli occupation and settlements, and an even stronger *political* claim for Palestinian statehood in the West Bank and the Gaza Strip. The Palestinian political case finds support in the aspirations of the Palestinian people for self-determination in the West Bank and Gaza Strip. The diplomatic process envisioned at Oslo three decades ago will hopefully lead someday to two states living side-by-side in peace.

The two-state solution would also serve the long-term national security interests of Israel and Jordan to stabilize the West Bank, and the parallel security interests of Israel and Egypt to stabilize the Gaza Strip. In the wake of the October 2023 war, any future Palestinian state will need to be completely demilitarized and rendered incapable of harming its Israeli neighbor. The diplomatic process has taken much longer than anyone had anticipated, but it remains the process to which the parties committed themselves at Oslo three decades ago.

The Mufti's failure to embrace the two-state solution in 1947–1948 and engage in state-building and peaceful coexistence rather than violence and bloodshed proved catastrophic for the Palestinian people. That failure of Palestinian leadership in 1947 was the true *Nakba*.

Unfortunately, modern-day Palestinian leaders, like the Mufti before them, have opted for conflict *perpetuation* through lawfare and violence, rather than conflict *resolution* through negotiation.

If the goal of the two-state solution is ever to be realized, then the Palestinians must abide by the legally binding pledges they made at Oslo. They must reject violence and terrorism. They must stop paying rewards to terrorists for killing Israelis. They must stop teaching Jew hatred to their children. They must instead pursue their politically legitimate goals through statecraft and diplomacy. The Israelis, for their part, despite the horrors of the Hamas massacre, must also return to the Oslo process and engage constructively with responsible, peace-seeking Palestinians.

There is no other way.

Notes

1 UN A/RES/3379 (10 Nov. 1975), *repealed*, UN A/RES/46/86 (16 Dec. 1991).
2 UN Watch, https://unwatch.org/2022-2023-unga-resolutions-on-israel-vs-rest-of-the-world/ (last accessed 5 Feb. 2023).
3 United Nations General Assembly, A/77/247, *Israeli Practices and Settlement Activities Affecting the Rights of the Palestinian People and Other Arabs of the Occupied Territories*, para. 18 (30 Dec. 2022). The General Assembly approved the Resolution by a vote of 87 in favor and 26 against, with 53 abstentions.
4 *Agreement on Preparatory Transfer of Powers and Responsibilities* (29 Aug. 1994), Art. Xiii.3, 34 I.L.M. 455 (1994); *Israeli-Palestinian Interim Agreement on the West Bank and Gaza Strip* (28 Sept. 1995), Art. XXXI.6, 36 I.L.M. 551 (1997).
5 *Palestine, Termination of the Mandate, 15th May 1948*, Statement Prepared for Public Information by the Colonial Office and the Foreign Office (15 May 1949).

BIBLIOGRAPHY

Abbas, M. (1997). *Through Secret Channels*. Reading: Garnet.

Abbasi, M. (2013). The Education System in East Jerusalem during the Period of Jordanian Rule, 1948–1967. *Journal of Politics and Law*, 6:4, 174–86.

Abu-Odeh, A. (1999). *Jordanians, Palestinians and The Hashemite Kingdom in the Middle East Peace Process*. Washington, DC: United States Institute of Peace Press.

Adelman, H. (2009). Research on the Ethics of War in the Context of Violence in Gaza. *Journal of Academic Ethics*, 7:1–2, 93–113.

Adem, S. (2019). *Palestine and the International Criminal Court*. Berlin: Springer.

Akram, S., et. al. (eds.). (2011). *International Law and the Israeli-Palestinian Conflict: A Rights-Based Approach to Middle East Peace*. Abingdon and Oxon: Routledge.

Alimi, E. (2007). *Israeli Politics and the First Palestinian Intifada: Political Opportunities, Framing Processes and Contentious Politics*. London and New York: Routledge.

Allen, L.A. (2017). Determining Emotions and the Burden of Proof in Investigative Commissions in Palestine. *Comparative Studies in Society and History*, 59:2, 385–414.

Allena, P. and Keller, A. (2006). *What Is a Just Peace?* Oxford: Oxford University Press.

Al-Omar, A.K. (ed.). (1999). *The Memoirs of Al-Haj Mohammed Amin Al-Husseini*. Damascus: Al-Ahly Press.

Al-Shuaibi, I. (1979). The Development of Palestinian Entity-Consciousness: Part I. *Journal of Palestine Studies*, 9:1, 67–84.

Al-Shuaibi, I. (1980). The Development of Palestinian Entity-Consciousness: Part II. *Journal of Palestine Studies*, 9:2, 50–70.

Amar-Dahl, T. (2017). *Zionist Israel and the Question of Palestine: Jewish Statehood and the History of the Middle East Conflict*. Berlin: DeGruyter.

Anderson, B. (1983). *Imagined Communities: Reflections on the Origin and Spread of Nationalism*. London and New York: Verso.

Andrews, F. (1931). *The Holy Land Under Mandate*. Westport: Hyperion.

Antonius, G. (1939). *The Arab Awakening: The Story of the Arab National Movement*. Forest Grove: Allegro.

Ash, R.W. (2009). Is Palestine a State: A Response to Professor John Quigley's Article, the Palestine Declaration to the International Criminal Court. *Rutgers Law Record*, 36, 186–200.

Bachmutsky, R. (2018). Otherwise Occupied: The Legal Status of the Gaza Strip 50 Years after the Six-Day War. *Virginia Journal of International Law*, 57:2, 413–54.

Bailey, C. (1984). *Jordan's Palestinian Challenge, 1948–1983: A Political History*. Boulder and London: Westview Press.

Bakan, A. and Abu-Laban, Y. (2009). Palestinian Resistance and International Solidarity: The BDS Campaign. *Race & Class*, 51:1, 29–54.

Baker, A. (2012). Is Jerusalem Really Negotiable? An Analysis of Jerusalem's Place in the Peace Process. *Jewish Political Studies Review*, 24:3/4, 72–95.

Barak, E. (2007). Between Reality and Secrecy: Israel's Freedom of Navigation through the Straits of Tiran, 1956–1967. *Middle East Journal*, 61:4, 657–79.

Barghouti, O. (2011). *BDS: The Global Struggle for Palestinian Rights*. Chicago: Haymarket Press.

Barghouti, O. (2014). Opting for Justice: The Critical Role of Anti-Colonial Israelis in the Boycott, Divestment, And Sanctions Movement. *Settler Colonial Studies*, 4:4, 407–12.

Barghouti, O. (2015). Upholding International Law, Asserting Palestinian Rights, in A. Imseis (ed.), *The Palestine Yearbook of International Law* (Birzeit University Institute of Law 2013–2014), pp, 15–40. Leiden: Brill Nijhoff.

Barnidge, R. (2016). Palestinian Engagement with The International Criminal Court: From Preliminary Examination to Investigation? *The Journal of the Middle East and Africa*, 7:2, 109–23.

Bartal, S. (2017). *The Peel Commission Report of 1937 and the Origins of the Partition Concept*. Jerusalem: Jerusalem Center for Public Affairs.

Baumgart-Ochse, C. (2017). Claiming Justice for Israel/Palestine: The Boycott, Divestment, Sanctions (BDS) Campaign and Christian Organizations. *Globalizations*, 14:7, 1172–87.

Becker, A. (1988). *The United Nations and Israel: From Recognition to Reprehension*. Lexington: Lexington Books.

Becker, T. (1998). Self-Determination in Perspective: Palestinian Claims to Statehood and the Relativity of the Right to Self-Determination. *Israel Law Review*, 32:2, 301–54.

Beckerman, C. (2020). *Unexpected State, British Politics and the Creation of Israel*. Bloomington: Indiana University Press.

Beilin, Y. (1999). *Touching Peace: From the Oslo Accord to a Final Agreement*. London: Weidenfeld & Nicolson.

Bell, A. and Kontorovich, E. (2016). Palestine, Uti Possidetis Juris, and the Borders of Israel. *Arizona Law Review*, 58, 633–92.

Ben-Bassat, Y. (2013). *Petitioning the Sultan: Protests and Justice in Late Ottoman Palestine 1865–1908*. London and New York: I.B. Tauris.

Ben-Dror, E. (2007). The Arab Struggle Against Partition: The International Arena of Summer 1947. *Middle Eastern Studies*, 43:2, 259–93.

Ben-Dror, E. (2008). Ralph Bunche and the Establishment of Israel. *Israel Affairs*, 14:3, 519–37.

Ben-Dror, E. (2014). The Success of the Zionist Strategy vis-a-vis UNSCOP. *Israel Affairs*, 20:1, 19–39.

Ben-Dror, E. and Ziedler, A. (2015). Israel, Jordan, and their Efforts to Frustrate the United Nations Resolutions to Internationalise Jerusalem. *Diplomacy & Statecraft*, 26, 636–658.

Benoliel, D. (2012). Israel and the Palestinian State: Reply to Quigley. *University of Baltimore Journal of International Law*, 1, 1–57.

Benoliel, D. and Perry, R. (2010). Israel, Palestine and the ICC. *Michigan Journal of International Law*, 32:1, 73–127.

Bentwich, N. (1929). Judicial Interpretation of the Mandate for Palestine. *Zeitschrift für Ausländisches Öffentliches Recht und Völkerrecht*, 1:1, 212–22.

Bentwich, N. (1932). *England in Palestine*. London: Kegan Paul.

Bentwich, N. and Bentwich, H. (1965). *Mandate Memories 1918–1948*. New York: Schocken.

Benvenisti, E. (1993). The Israeli-Palestinian Declaration of Principles: Framework for Future Settlement. *European Journal of International Law*, 4:4, 542–54.

Benvenisti, E. (2008). The Origins of the Concept of Belligerent Occupation. *Law and History Review*, 26:3, 621–48.

Benvenisti, E. (2012). *The International Law of Occupation* (2nd ed.). Oxford: Oxford University Press.

Benvenisti, E. (2017). An Article that Changed the Course of History. *Israel Law Review*, 50:3, 269–98.

Berkovitz, S. (1998). The Holy Places in Jerusalem: Legal Aspects. *Rivista di Studi Politici Internazionali*, 65:3(259), 403–15.

Berkowitz, S. (2018). *The Status of Jerusalem in International and Israeli Law*. Jerusalem: Jerusalem Center for Public Affairs.

Bernadotte, F. (1951). *To Jerusalem*. London: Hodder and Stoughton.

Bethell, N. (1979). *The Palestine Triangle: The Struggle for the Holy's Land, 1935–1948*. New York: G.P. Putnam's Sons.

Bin Talal, H. (1979). *A Study on Jerusalem*. London and New York: Longman.

Bin Talal, H. (1981). *Palestinian Self-Determination: A Study of the West Bank and Gaza Strip*. New York and London: Quartet Books.

Bishara, A. (2003). House and Homeland: Examining Sentiments About and Claims to Jerusalem and Its Houses. *Social Text*, 21:2, 141–62.

Blizzard, E. (2017). Peace Journalism in Palestine's BDS Campaign. *Peace Review: A Journal of Social Justice*, 29:4, 467–74.

Blum, S. (2019). Between the Lion Cub of Judea and the British Lion: Cause Lawyers, British Rule and National Struggle in Mandatory Palestine. *Comparative Legal History*, 7:1, 2–36.

Blum, Y.Z. (1968). The Missing Reversioner: Reflections on the Status of Judea and Samaria. *Israel Law Review*, 3:2, 279–301.

Blum, Y.Z. (1974). *The Juridical Status of Jerusalem*. Jerusalem: Leonard David Institute for International Relations.

Blum, Y.Z. (1994). From Camp David to Oslo. *Israel Law Review*, 28:2–3, 211–35.

Blum, Y.Z. (2018). The Status of Judea and Samaria Revisited: A Response to Eyal Benvenisti. *Israel Law Review*, 51:2, 165–68.

Bosco, D. (2016). Palestine in the Hague: Justice, Geopolitics, and the International Criminal Court. *Global Governance*, 22, 155–71.

Boustany, W.F. (1936). *The Palestine Mandate Invalid and Impracticable: A Contribution of Arguments and Documents Towards the Solution of the Palestine Problem.* Beirut: American Press.

Bowett, D.W. (1957). Estoppel before International Tribunals and Its Relation to Acquiescence. *British Year Book of International Law*, 33, 176–202.

Bowett, D.W. (1958). *Self-Defense in International Law*. New York: Praeger.

Boyle, F. (1990). The Creation of the State of Palestine. *European Journal of International Law*, 1:1, 301–06.

Bracka, J. (2021). False Messiah? The ICC in Israel/Palestine and the Limits of International Criminal Justice. *Vanderbilt Journal of Transnational Law*, 54:2, 283–342.

Breger, M. and Ahimeir, O. (2002). *Jerusalem: A City and Its Future*. Syracuse: Syracuse University Press.

Brierly, J.L. (1955). *The Law of Nations: An Introduction to the International Law of Peace* (5th ed.). Oxford: Oxford University Press.

Brownlie, I. (1961). The Use of Force in Self-Defense. *British Year Book of International Law*, 37, 183–268.

Brownlie, I. (1973). *Principles of Public International Law* (2nd ed.). Oxford: Oxford University Press.

Bullock, A. (1983). *Ernest Bevin: Foreign Secretary: 1945–1951*. New York and London: W.W. Norton & Co.

Burgis-Kasthala, M.L. (2014). Overstating Palestine's UN Membership Bid? An Ethnographic Study on the Narratives of Statehood. *European Journal of International Law*, 25:3, 677–701.

Calame, J. and Charlesworth, E. (2009). *Divided Cities: Belfast, Beirut, Jerusalem, Mostar and Nicosia*. Philadelphia: University of Pennsylvania Press.

Cammarata, M. (2010). *La Palestina del Mandato nell'Editoria Italiana, 1918–1939*. Trieste: Edizioni Universita di Trieste.

Caplan, N. (1978). *Palestine Jewry and the Arab Question, 1917–1925*. London: Frank Cass.

Caplan, N. (1983). *Futile Diplomacy: Early Arab-Zionist Negotiation Attempts, 1913–1931*. London: Frank Cass.

Cassese, A. (1981). Legal Considerations on the International Status of Jerusalem, in H. Kochler (ed.), *The Legal Aspects of the Palestine Problem with Special Regard to the Question of Jerusalem*, pp.144–153. Vienna: William Braumuller.

Cassese, A. (1995). *Self-Determination of Peoples: A Legal Reappraisal*. Cambridge: Cambridge University Press.

Cattan, H. (1969). *Palestine, the Arabs and Israel: The Search for Justice*. London and New York: Longmans.

Cattan, H. (1973). *Palestine and International Law: The Legal Aspects of the Arab-Israeli Conflict* (2nd ed.). London and New York: Longmans.

Cattan, H. (1981). The Status of Jerusalem under International Law and United Nations. *Journal of Palestine Studies*, 10:3, 3–15.

Cattan, H. (2000). *Jerusalem*. London: Saqi Books.

Clancy, P. and Falk, R. (2021). The ICC and Palestine: Breakthrough and End of the Road?, *Journal of Palestine Studies*, 50:3, 56–68.

Clarno, A. (2017). *Neoliberal Apartheid: Palestine/Israel and South Africa after 1994*. Chicago and London: University of Chicago Press.

Cohen, H. (2008). *Army of Shadows: Palestinians and Collaboration with Zionism, 1917–1948*. Berkeley, Los Angeles and London: University of California Press.
Cohen, H. (2011). *The Rise and Fall of Arab Jerusalem: Palestinian Politics and the City Since 1967*. London and New York: Routledge.
Cohen, H. (2015). *Year Zero of the Arab Israeli Conflict: 1929*. Detroit: Wayne State University Press.
Cohen, M. and Freilich, C. (2018). War by Other Means: The Delegitimisation Campaign Against Israel. *Israel Affairs*, 24:1, 1–25.
Cohen, M.J. (1973). Appeasement in the Middle East: The British White Paper on Palestine. *The Historical Journal*, 16:3, 571–96.
Cohen, M.J. (1976). The British White Paper on Palestine, May 1939. Part II: The Testing of a Policy, 1942–1945. *The Historical Journal*, 19:3, 727–57.
Cohen, M.J. (1978). *Palestine: Retreat from the Mandate, the Making of British Policy, 1936–45*. New York: Holmes and Meier.
Cohen, M.J. (1979). The Genesis of the Anglo-American Committee on Palestine, November 1945: A Case Study in the Assertion of American Hegemony. *The Historical Journal*, 22:1, 185–207.
Cohen, M.J. (1982). *Palestine and the Great Powers, 1945–1948*. Princeton: Princeton University Press.
Cohen, M.J. (ed.). (1987a). *The Rise of Israel*. New York and London: Garland.
Cohen, M.J. (1987b). *The Origins and Evolution of the Arab-Zionist Conflict*. Berkeley, Los Angeles and London: University of California Press.
Cohen, M.J. (1990). *Truman and Israel*. Berkeley: University of California Press.
Cohen, M.J. (2014). *Britain's Moment in Palestine: Retrospect and Perspectives, 1917–48*. Abingdon, Oxon and New York: Routledge.
Corn, G. (2020). The Essential Link between Proportionality and Necessity in the Exercise of Self-Defense, in C. Kreß and R. Lawless (eds.), *Necessity and Proportionality in International Peace and Security Law*, pp. 79–112. Oxford: Oxford University Press.
Corten, O. and Klein, P. (eds.). (2011). *The Vienna Convention on the Law of Treaties: A Commentary* (Vol. I). Oxford: Oxford University Press.
Cover, R. (1983). Nomos and Narrative. *Harvard Law Review*, 97:1, 4–69.
Crawford, J. (1990). The Creation of the State of Palestine: Too Much Too Soon. *European Journal of International Law*, 1:1, 307–13.
Crawford, J. (2006). *The Creation of States in International Law* (2nd ed.). Oxford: Oxford University Press.
Crawford, J. (2019). *Brownlie's Principles of Public International Law* (9th ed.). Oxford: Oxford University Press.
Cust, L.G.A. (1927). *Jerusalem, The Status Quo, Its Origin and History Till the Present Time*. Jerusalem: High Commission. Chancellor Papers, MSS. Brit. Emp. S.284, Box 24/2. Bodleian Libraries, Oxford.
Dajani, O. (1997). Stalled between the Seasons: The International Legal Status of Palestine during the Interim Period. *Denver Journal of International Law and Policy*, 26, 27–92.
Darcy, S. and Reynolds, J. (2010). An Enduring Occupation: The Status of the Gaza Strip from the Perspective of International Humanitarian Law. *Journal of Conflict & Security Law*, 15:2, 211–43.

Davis, A. (2016). *Freedom Is a Constant Struggle: Ferguson, Palestine, and the Foundations of a Movement*. Chicago: Haymarket Books.

De Blois, M. (2016). The Unique Character of the Mandate for Palestine. *Israel Law Review*, 49:3, 365–89.

De Blois, M. and Tucker, A. (2018). *Israel on Trial: How International Law is Being Misused to Delegitimize the State of Israel*. The Hague: The Hague Initiative for International Cooperation.

Dershowitz, A. (2011). *Countering Challenges to Israel's Legitimacy*. Jerusalem: Jerusalem Center for Public Affairs.

Destani, B. (ed.). (2004). *The Zionist Movement and the Foundation of Israel, 1839–1972*. Cambridge: Archive Editions.

de Waart, P.J. (2005). International Court of Justice Firmly Walled in the Law of Power in the Israeli-Palestinian Peace Process. *Leiden Journal of International Law*, 18:3, 467–88.

Di Marco, M.L. (2018). The Legal Status of Jerusalem in the State of Israel. *Rivista Telematica, Stato, Chiese e Pluralismo Confessionale*, 27, 1–12.

Dinstein, Y. (2019). *The International Law of Belligerent Occupation* (2nd ed.). Cambridge: Cambridge University Press.

Draper, G.I.A.D. (1981). The Status of Jerusalem as a Question of International Law, in H. Kochle (ed.), *The Legal Aspects of the Palestine Problem with Special Regard to the Question of Jerusalem*, pp. 154–163. Vienna: William Braumuller.

Dresner, C. and Litvinoff, B. (eds.). (1978). *The Letters and Papers of Chaim Weizmann*. New Brunswick: Transaction.

Dugard, J. (2013). Palestine and the International Criminal Court: Institutional Failure or Bias. *Journal of International Criminal Justice*, 11, 563–70.

Dugard, J. (2014). A Tale of Two Sacred Trusts: Namibia and Palestine, in T. Maluwa (ed.), *Law, Politics and Rights: Essays in Memory of Kader Asmal*, pp. 287–305. Leiden: Martinus Nijhoff.

Dumper, M. and Larkin, C. (2012). The Politics of Heritage and the Limitations of International Agency in Contested Cities: A Study of the Role of UNESCO in Jerusalem's Old City. *Review of International Studies*, 38, 25–52.

Elaraby, N. (1968). Some Legal Implications of the 1947 Partition Resolution and the 1949 Armistice Agreements. *Law and Contemporary Problems*, 33:1, 97–109.

Elaraby, N. (2017). Palestine and the Law of Nations. *Cairo Review of Global Affairs*, 27, 47–57.

Elgindy, K. (2011). Palestine Goes to the UN: Understanding the New Statehood Strategy. *Foreign Affairs*, 90:5, 102–13.

Elipeleg, Z. (1989). Why Was "Independent Palestine" Never Created? *Jerusalem Quarterly*, 50, 3–22.

Elipeleg, Z. (2009). *Through the Eyes of the Mufti: The Essays of Haj Amin Al Husseini Translated and Annotated*. London: Valentine Mitchell.

Emmett, C.F. (1996). The Capital Cities of Jerusalem. *Geographical Review*, 86:2, 233–58.

Epstein, L. (2016). *The Dream of Zion: The Story of the First Zionist Congress*. Lanham: Rowman & Littlefield.

Erakat, N. (2019). *Justice For Some: Law and the Question of Palestine*. Stanford: Stanford University Press.

Esco Foundation for Palestine. (1947). *Palestine, A Study of Jewish, Arab and British Policies*. New Haven: Yale University Press.

Evatt, H.G. (1949). *The Task of Nations*. New York: Duell, Sloan and Pearce.

Feinberg, N. (1970). *The Arab-Israel Conflict in International Law: A Critical Analysis of the Colloquium of Arab Jurists in Algiers*. Jerusalem: Magnes Press.

Feldman, I. (2008). *Governing Gaza: Bureaucracy, Authority, and the Work of Rule: 1917–1967*. Durham and London: Duke University Press.

Fischbach, M. (2018). *Black Power and Palestine: Transnational Countries of Color*. Stanford: Stanford University Press.

Friedman, I. (1970). The McMahon-Hussein Correspondence and the Question of Palestine. *Journal of Contemporary History*, 5:2, 83–122.

Friedman, I. (1973). *The Question of Palestine, 1914–1918: British-Arab-Jewish Relations*. New York: Schocken.

Friedman, I. (1973). The Response to the Balfour Declaration. *Jewish Social Studies*, 35:2, 105–24.

Friedman, I. (1999). *Palestine, A Twice Promised Land? The British, the Arabs and Zionism 1915–1920*. New Brunswick: Transaction.

Friesel, O. (2016). Israel's 1967 Governmental Debate about the Annexation of East Jerusalem: The Nascent Alliance with the United States, Overshadowed by "United Jerusalem." *Law and History Review*, 34:2, 363–92.

Fry, N. and Hochstein, M. (1993). The Forgotten Middle Eastern Crisis of 1957: Gaza and Sharm-el-Sheikh. *The International History Review*, 15:1, 46–83.

Galnoor, I. (1991). Territorial Partition of Palestine: The 1937 Decision. *Political Geography Quarterly*, 10:4, 382–404.

Galnoor, I. (2009). The Zionist Debates on Partition (1919–1947). *Israel Studies*, 14:2, 74–87.

Gamson, W. (1992). *Talking Politics*. Cambridge: Cambridge University Press.

Gandolfo, L. (2012). *Palestinians in Jordan: The Politics of Identity*. London and New York: I.B. Tauris.

Garcia Granados, J. (1948). *The Birth of Israel: The Drama as I Saw It*. New York: Alfred A. Knopf.

Gardiner, R. (2015). *Treaty Interpretation* (2nd ed.). Oxford and New York: Oxford University Press.

Gavison, R. (ed.). (2013). *The Two-State Solution: The UN Partition Resolution of Mandatory Palestine*. New York and London: Bloomsbury Academic Press.

Gerber, H. (2008). *Remembering and Imagining Palestine: Identity and Nationalism from the Crusades to the Present*. Houndmills and Basingstoke: Palgrave Macmillan.

Gerson, A. (1973). Trustee-Occupant: The Legal Status of Israel's Presence in the West Bank. *Harvard International Law Journal*, 14, 1–49.

Gerson, A. (1978). *Israel The West Bank and International Law*. London: Frank Cass & Co. Ltd.

Ghandour, Z. (2010). *A Discourse on Domination in Mandate Palestine: Imperialism, Property and Insurgency*. Abingdon and Oxon: Routledge.

Giladi, R.M. (1999). Practice and Case Law of Israel in Matters Related to International Law. *Israel Law Review*, 33:1, 106–38.

Gilbert, M. (1996). *Jerusalem in the Twentieth Century*. New York: John Wiley & Sons.

Gilbert, M. (2008). *The Routledge Historical Atlas of Jerusalem* (4th ed.). Abingdon, Oxon and New York: Routledge.

Gilbert, M. (2012). *The Routledge Atlas of the Arab-Israeli Conflict* (10th ed.). Abingdon, Oxon, and New York: Routledge.

Glick, E. (1959). Latin America and the Palestine Partition Resolution. *Journal of Inter-American Studies*, 1:2, 211–22.

Goda, N. et al. (2015). *To the Gates of Jerusalem: The Diaries and Papers of James G. McDonald, 1945–1947*. Bloomington: Indiana University Press.

Goda, N. et al. (eds.) (2017). *Envoy to the Promised Land: The Diaries and Papers of James G. McDonald, 1948–1951*. Bloomington: Indiana University Press.

Golani, M. (1999). Jerusalem's Hope Lies Only in Partition: Israeli Policy on the Jerusalem Question, 1948–67. *International Journal of Middle East Studies*, 31:4, 577–604.

Golani, M. (2013). *Palestine between Politics and Terror*. Waltham: Brandeis University Press.

Goldmann, N. (1969). *The Autobiography of Nahum Goldmann: Sixty Years of Jewish Life*. New York: Holt, Rinehart and Winston.

Graber, D. (1949). *The Development of the Law of Belligerent Occupation, 1863–1914: A Historical Survey*. New York: Columbia Univ. Press.

Grant, T. (1999). Defining Statehood: The Montevideo Convention and its Discontents. *Columbia Journal of Transnational Law*, 37:2, 403–45.

Grantham, D. (2019). Argentina, the Arab World, and the Partition of Palestine, 1946–1947. *Journal of Global South Studies*, 36:1, 88–115.

Graves, P. (1923). *Palestine, the Land of Three Faiths*. London: J. Cape.

Gribetz, L. (1930). *The Case for the Jews: An Interpretation of their Rights Under the Balfour Declaration and the Mandate for Palestine*. New York: Bloch.

Grief, H. (2008). *The Legal Foundation and Borders of Israel Under International Law*. Jerusalem: Mazo.

Gruhin, M.I. (1980). Jerusalem: Legal & Political Dimensions in a Search for Peace. *Case Western Reserve Journal of International Law*, 12:1, 169–214.

Hahn, P. (2004). *Caught in the Middle East: U.S. Policy toward the Arab-Israeli Conflict, 1945–1961*. Chapel Hill and London: University of North Carolina Press.

Haim, Y. (1978). Zionist Attitudes toward Partition, 1937–1938. *Jewish Social Studies*, 40:3, 303–20.

Handmaker, J. (2015). Taking Academic Freedom Seriously: Exploring the Legal and Moral Underpinnings of BDS, in A. Imseis (ed.), *The Palestine Yearbook of International Law* (Birzeit University Institute of Law 2013–2014), pp. 101–114. Leiden: Brill Nijhoff.

Harpaz, G. (2015). When Does a Court Systematically Deviate from Its Own Principles? The Adjudication by the Israel Supreme Court of House Demolitions in the Occupied Palestinian Territories. *Leiden Journal of International Law*, 28:1, 31–47.

Hatoum, N.A. (2017). Framing Visual Politics: Photography of the Wall in Palestine. *Visual Anthropology Review*, 33:1, 18–27.

Hattis, S. (1970). *The Bi-National Idea in Palestine during Mandatory Times*. Haifa: Shikmona.

Heidborn, A. (1908). *Manuel de Droit Public et Administratif de l'Empire Ottoman*. Vienna: C.W. Stern.

Heimann, G. (2015). The Struggle between the United States and Israel over Recognition for Jerusalem as Israel's Capital, 1952–67. *The International History Review*, 37:4, 790–808.

Herscho, T. (2006). *Le Grand Mufti de Jérusalem en France: Histoire d'une Evasion.* Controverses: Revue d'Idees 1.

Herscho, T. (2008). France and the Partition Plan: 1947–1948. *Israel Affairs*, 14:3, 486–98.

Higgins, R. (1970). The Place of International Law in the Settlement of Disputes by the Security Council. *American Journal of International Law*, 64:1, 1–18.

Hirsch, M. (2005). The Legal Status of Jerusalem Following the ICJ Advisory Opinion on the Separation Barrier. *Israel Law Review*, 38:1–2, 298–315.

Hirsch, M., Housen-Couriel, D. and Lapidoth, R. (eds.). (1995). *Whither Jerusalem? Proposals and Positions Concerning the Future of Jerusalem.* The Hague, London and Boston: Martinus Nijhoff Publishers.

Holder, W.E. (1972). 1971 Advisory Opinion of the International Court of Justice on Namibia (South West Africa). *Federal Law Review*, 5:1, 115–24.

Hollis, R. (2016). Palestine and the Palestinians in British Political Elite Discourse: From 'The Palestine Problem' to 'The Two-State Solution.' *International Relations*, 30:1, 3–28.

Horowitz, D. (1953). *State in the Making.* New York: Alfred A. Knopf.

Huber, D. (2021). *The International Dimension of the Israel-Palestinian Conflict: A Post-Eurocentric Approach.* Albany: State University of New York Press.

Hughes, M. (2010). From Law and Order to Pacification: Britain's Suppression of the Arab Revolt in Palestine, 1936–39. *Journal of Palestine Studies*, 39:2, 6–22.

Huneidi, S. (1998). Was Balfour Reversible, The Colonial Office and Palestine, 1921–23. *Journal of Palestine Studies*, 27:2, 23–41.

Huneidi, S. (2001). *A Broken Trust: Herbert Samuel, Zionism and the Palestinians.* New York: I.B. Tauris.

Hurevitz, J.C. (1976). *The Struggle for Palestine.* New York: Schocken Books.

Husseini, H. (2008). A "Middle Power" in Action: Canada and the Partition of Palestine. *Arab Studies Quarterly*, 30:3, 41–55.

Iglesias Velasco, A. (1999). El Estatuto Jurídico-Internacional de Jerusalén. *Revista CIDOB d'Afers Internacionals*, 48, 75–87.

Imseis, A. (2003). On the Fourth Geneva Convention and the Occupied Palestinian Territory. *Harvard International Law Journal*, 44:1, 65–138.

Imseis, A. (2021). The United Nations Plan of Partition for Palestine Revisited: On the Origins of Palestine's International Legal Subalternity. *Stanford Journal of International Law*, 57:1, 1–54.

Israeli, R. (2002). *Jerusalem Divided: The Armistice Regime, 1947–1967.* London: Frank Cass & Co.

Jager, E. (2018). *The Balfour Declaration: Sixty Seven Words, One Hundred Years of Conflict.* Jerusalem: Geffen.

Jeffries, J.M.N. (1938). *Palestine: The Reality.* London: Longmans, Green.

Jennings, R.Y. (1938). The Caroline and McLeod Cases. *American Journal of International Law*, 32:1, 82–99.

Jennings, R.Y. (1963). *The Acquisition of Territory in International Law.* Manchester: Manchester University Press.

Jennings, R.Y. and Watts, A. (eds.). (1996). *Oppenheim's International Law, Vol. I: Peace* (9th ed.). London and New York: Longman.

Jones, A.P. (1979). *Britain and Palestine, 1914–1948: Archival Sources for the History of the British Mandate*. Oxford: Oxford University Press for the British Academy.

Jones, M. (1986). *Failure in Palestine: British and United States Policy after the Second World War*. London: Bloomsbury.

Ju'Beh, N. (2001). Jewish Settlement in the Old City of Jerusalem after 1967. *Palestine-Israel Journal of Politics, Economics, and Culture*, VIII:1, 48–54.

Karsh, E. (1999). The Collusion That Never Was: King Abdallah, the Jewish Agency and the Partition of Palestine. *Journal of Contemporary History*, 34:4, 569–85.

Karsh, E. (2008). Zionism and the Palestinians. *Israel Affairs*, 14:3, 355–73.

Karsh, E. (2010). *Palestine Betrayed*. New Haven: Yale University Press.

Karsh, E. (2014). Palestinian Leaders Don't Want an Independent State. *Middle East Quarterly*, 21:3, 1–11.

Kattan, V. (2009). *From Coexistence to Conquest: International Law and the Origins of the Arab-Israeli Conflict 1891–1949*. New York: Pluto.

Kattan, V. (2014). The Implications of Joining the ICC after Operation Protective Edge. *Journal of Palestine Studies*, 44:1, 61–73.

Katz, K. (2005). *Jordanian Jerusalem: Holy Places and National Spaces*. Gainesville: University Press of Florida.

Kedourie, E. (1976). *In the Anglo-Arab Labyrinth: The McMahon-Husayn Correspondence and Its Interpretations 1914–1939*. London and Portland: Frank Cass.

Kedourie, E. and Haim, S. (eds.). (1982). *Zionism and Arabism in Palestine and Israel*. Abingdon and Oxfordshire: Frank Cass.

Keiler, J.F. (2009). The End of Proportionality. *Parameters*, 39:1, 53–64.

Kelsen, H. (1951). *The Law of the United Nations: A Critical Analysis of Its Fundamental Problems*. London: Stevens & Sons.

Khader, N. (2014). Interview with Noura Erakat: Framing the Palestinian Narrative. *Journal of Palestine Studies*, 44:1, 106–17.

Khalidi, W. (1978). Thinking The Unthinkable: A Sovereign Palestinian State. *Foreign Affairs*, 56:4, 695–713.

Khalidi, W. (1984). *Before Their Diaspora: A Photographic History of the Palestinians 1876–1948*. Washington, DC: Institute for Palestine Studies.

Kirkbride, A. (1976). *From the Wings: Amman Memoirs 1947–1951*. London: Frank Cass & Co. Ltd.

Kittrie, O. (2016). *Lawfare: Law as a Weapon of War*. New York: Oxford University Press.

Klein, M. (2001). *Jerusalem: The Contested City*. London: Hurst & Co.

Klieman, A. (ed.) (1987). *The Rise of Israel: A Documentary Record from the Nineteenth Century to 1948*. New York: Garland.

Knoops, G.-J.A. (2009). The Duality of the Proportionality Principle within Asymmetric Warfare and Ensuing Superior Criminal Responsibilities. *International Criminal Law Review*, 9:3, 501–29.

Knoops, G.-J.A. and Zwart, T. (2015). The Flotilla Case before the ICC: The Need to Do Justice While Keeping Heaven Intact. *International Criminal Law Review*, 15:6, 1069–97.

Kochler, H. (ed.) (1981). *The Legal Aspects of the Palestine Problem with Special Regard to the Question of Jerusalem*. Vienna: William Braumuller.

Kohen, M. and Hebie, M. (2018). *Research Handbook on Territorial Disputes in International Law*. Cheltenham: Edward Elgar.

Kontorovich, E. (2013). Israel/Palestine – The ICC's Uncharted Territory. *Journal of International Criminal Justice*, 11:5, 979–99.

Kontorovich, E. (2014). When Gravity Fails: Israeli Settlements and Admissibility at the ICC. *Israel Law Review*, 47:3, 379–99.

Kontorovich, E. (2015). Resolution 242 Revisited: New Evidence on the Required Scope of Israeli Withdrawal. *Chicago Journal of International Law*, 16:1, 127–50.

Kontorovich, E. (2018). Unsettled: A Global Study of Settlements in Occupied Territories. *Journal of Legal Analysis*, 9:2, 285–350.

Kramer, G. (2008). *A History of Palestine: From the Ottoman Conquest to the Founding of the State of Israel*. Princeton and Oxford: Princeton University Press.

Kretzmer, D. (2012). The Law of Belligerent Occupation in the Supreme Court of Israel. *International Review of the Red Cross*, 94:885, 207–36.

Kretzmer, D. and Ronen, Y. (2021). *The Occupation of Justice: The Supreme Court of Israel and the Occupied Territories* (2nd ed.). Oxford: Oxford University Press.

Kulick, A. (2016). About the Order of Cart and Horse, among Other Things: Estoppel in the Jurisprudence of International Investment Arbitration Tribunals. *European Journal of International Law*, 27:1, 107–28.

Kuper, L. (1990). Theological Warrants for Genocide: Judaism, Islam and Christianity. *Terrorism and Political Violence*, 2:3, 351–79.

Lapidoth, R. (1992). Security Council Resolution 242 at Twenty Five. *Israel Law Review*, 26:3, 295–318.

Lapidoth, R. (1996). Jerusalem: Some Jurisprudential Aspects. *Catholic University Law Review*, 45, 661–86.

Lapidoth, R. (2001). Israel and the Palestinians: Some Legal Issues. *Die Friedens-Warte*, 76:2/3, 211–40.

Lapidoth, R. (2005). The Advisory Opinion and the Jewish Settlements. *Israel Law Review*, 38:1–2, 292–97.

Lapidoth, R. (2011a). The Misleading Interpretation of UN Security Council Resolution 242 (1967). *Jewish Political Studies Review*, 23:3/4, 7–17.

Lapidoth, R. (2011b). Jerusalem – Some Legal Issues, in R. Wolfrum (ed.), *The Max Planck Encyclopedia of Public International Law*, pp. 7–35. Oxford: Oxford University Press.

Lapidoth, R. (2012). When Is an Entity Entitled to Statehood? *Israel Journal of Foreign Affairs*, 6:3, 77–81.

Lapidoth, R. and Hirsch, M. (eds.). (1992). *The Arab-Israeli Conflict and Its Resolution: Selected Documents*. Dordrecht, Boston and London: Martinus Nijhoff Publishers.

Lapidoth, R. and Hirsch, M. (eds.). (1994). *The Jerusalem Question and its Resolution: Selected Documents*. Dordrecht, Boston and London: Martinus Nijhoff Publishers.

Laurens, H. (2002). *La Question du Palestine*. Paris: Fayard.

Lautepacht, E. (1968). *Jerusalem and the Holy Places*. London: Anglo-Israel Association.

Lee, H. (2016). Defining State for the Purpose of the International Criminal Court: The Problem Ahead After the Palestine Decision. *University of Pittsburgh Law Review*, 77:3, 345–84.

Lemire, V. (2011). The Awakening of Palestinian Hydropolitical Consciousness: The Artas Jerusalem Water Conflict of 1925. *Jerusalem Quarterly*, 48, 31–53.

Lesch, A.M. (1979). *Arab Politics in Palestine, 1917–1939: The Frustration of a Nationalist Movement*. Ithaca: Cornell University Press.

Likhovski, A. (2006). *Law and Identity in Mandate Palestine*. Chapel Hill: University of North Carolina Press.

Litvinoff, B. and Rose, N. (eds.). (1980). *The Letters and Papers of Chaim Weizmann, Series A, Letters*. Rutgers: Transaction; Jerusalem: Israel Universities Press.

Loevy, K. (2016). Reinventing a Region (1915–22): Visions of the Middle East in Legal and Diplomatic Texts Leading to the Palestine Mandate. *Israel Law Review*, 49:3, 309–37.

Long, C.W.R. (2018). *The Palestinians and British Perfidy: The Tragic Aftermath of the Balfour Declaration of 1917*. Brighton, Portland and Toronto: Sussex.

Louis, W. and Stookey, R. (eds.). (1986). *The End of the Palestine Mandate*. Austin: University of Texas Press.

Lundsten, M.E. (1978). Wall Politics: Zionist and Palestinian Strategies in Jerusalem, 1928. *Journal of Palestine Studies*, 8:1, 3–27.

Lustick, I. (2000). Yerushalayim and al-Quds: Political Catechism and Political Realities. *Journal of Palestine Studies*, 30:1, 5–21.

Lynk, M. (2007). Conceived in Law: The Legal Foundations of Resolution 242. *Journal of Palestine Studies*, 37:1, 7–23.

MacGibbon, I.C. (1957). Customary International Law and Acquiescence. *British Year Book of International Law*, 33, 115–45.

MacGibbon, I.C. (1958). Estoppel in International Law. *The International and Comparative Law Quarterly*, 7:3, 468–513.

Malanczuk, P. (1996). Some Basic Aspects of the Agreements between Israel and the PLO from the Perspective of International Law. *European Journal of International Law*, 7:4, 485–500.

Mallison, S. and Mallison, T.W. (1981). The Jerusalem Problem in International Public Law: Juridical Status and a Start Towards Solution, in H. Kochle (ed.), *The Legal Aspects of the Palestine Problem with Special Regard to the Question of Jerusalem*. Vienna: William Braumuller.

Mallison, S. and Mallison, T.W. (1984). *The Juridical Basis for Palestinian Self-Determination*. The Palestine Yearbook of International Law, al-Shaybani Society of International Law Ltd.

Mallison, T.W. and Mallison, S. (1974). The Role of International Law in Achieving Justice and Peace in Palestine-Israel. *Journal of Palestine Studies*, 3:3, 77–87.

Mallison, T.W. and Mallison, S. (1986). *The Palestine Problem: International Law and World Order*. Harlow: Longman.

Mandel, D. (2004). *H.G. Evatt and the Establishment of Israel: The Undercover Zionist*. London: Frank Cass.

Mann, P. (1975). *Ralph Bunche: UN Peacemaker*. New York: Coward, McCann & Geoghegan.

Manusama, K. (2013). Lawfare in the Conflict between Israel and Palestine. *Amsterdam Law Forum*, 5:1, 121–24.

Maoz, M. (2002). The UN Partition Resolution of 1947: Why Was It Not Implemented? *Palestine-Israel Journal of Politics, Economics, and Culture*, 9:4, 15–30.

Marlowe, J. (1959). *The Seat of Pilate: An Account of The Palestine Mandate*. London: Cresset Press.

Masalha, N. (1996). The 1956–57 Occupation of the Gaza Strip: Israeli Proposals to Resettle the Palestinian Refugees. *British Journal of Middle Eastern Studies*, 23:1, 55–68.

Mattar, P. (1992). *The Mufti of Jerusalem: Haj Amin al Husseini and the Palestinian National Movement*. New York: Columbia University Press.

Matthew, W. (2014). *The Palestine Deception, 1915–1923: The McMahon-Hussein Correspondence, the Balfour Declaration, and the Jewish National Home*. Washington, DC: Institute for Palestine Studies.

Mazzawi, M. (1997). *Palestine and the Law: Guidelines for the Resolution of the Arab-Israeli Conflict*. Reading: Garnet.

McDonald, J. (1951). *My Mission in Israel*. New York: Simon and Schuster.

McDowall, D. (2014). Clarity or ambiguity? The Withdrawal Clause of UN Security Council Resolution 242. *International Affairs*, 90:6, 1367–81.

McHugo, J. (2002). Resolution 242: A Legal Reappraisal of the Right-Wing Israeli Interpretation of the Withdrawal Phrase with Reference to the Conflict between Israel and the Palestinians. *The International and Comparative Law Quarterly*, 51:4, 851–81.

McMahan, J. (2020). Necessity and Proportionality in Morality and Law, in C. Kreß and R. Lawless (eds.), *Necessity and Proportionality in International Peace and Security Law*, pp. 1–38. Oxford: Oxford University Press.

McMahon, S. (2014). The Boycott, Divestment, Sanctions Campaign: Contradictions and Challenges. *Race & Class*, 55:4, 65–81.

Meital, Y. (2000). The Khartoum Conference and Egyptian Policy after the 1967 War: A Reexamination. *Middle East Journal*, 54:1, 64–82.

Miller, R. (2010). *Britain, Palestine and Empire: The Mandate Years*. Farnham: Ashgate.

Mishal, S. (1978). *West Bank/East Bank: The Palestinians in Jordan, 1949–1967*. New Haven and London: Yale University Press.

Monk, D.B. (2002). *An Aesthetic Occupation: The Immediacy of Architecture and the Palestine Conflict*. Durham and London: Duke University Press.

Montefiore, S. (2011). *Jerusalem*. New York: Alfred A. Knopf.

Montell, J. (2016). Learning from What Works: Strategic Analysis of the Achievements of the Israel-Palestine Human Rights Community. *Human Rights Quarterly*, 38:4, 928–68.

Moore, J.N. (1974). *The Arab-Israeli Conflict*. Princeton: Princeton University Press.

Morris, B. (1987). *The Birth of the Palestinian Refugee Problem, 1947–1949*. Cambridge: Cambridge University Press.

Mourad, A., Koltun-Fromm, N. and Der Matossian, B. (eds.). (2019). *Routledge Handbook on Jerusalem*. London and New York: Routledge.

Muslih, M. (1988). *The Origins of Palestinian Nationalism*. New York: Columbia University Press.

Nasrallah, R. (2002). The Road to Partition. *Palestine-Israel Journal of Politics, Economics & Culture*, 9:4, 58–66.

Nevo, J. (1987). The Arabs of Palestine, 1947-48: Military and Political Activity. *Middle Eastern Studies*, 23:1, 3–38.

Nevo, J. (1996). *King Abdallah and Palestine: A Territorial Ambition*. New York: St. Martin's Press.

Omer, A. (2009). 'It's Nothing Personal:' The Globalisation of Justice, the Transferability of Protest, and the Case of the Palestine Solidarity Movement. *Studies in Ethnicity and Nationalism*, 9:3, 497–518.

Oppenheim, B. and Lauterpacht, H. (eds.). (1955). *International Law: A Treatise* (8th ed.). London: Longman, Green.

Orzeck, R. (2015). The Jewish Agency's Case Before the UNSCOP: Image and Discourse. *Jerusalem Quarterly*, 63/64, 7–23.

Ovendale, R. (1989). *Britain, the United States, and the End of the Palestine Mandate:1942–1948*. Woodbridge and Wolfeboro: Royal Historical Society, Boydell Press.

Palestine Partition (Woodhead) Commission. *Report*, Command Paper 5854 (Nov. 1938).

Palestine Royal Commission. *Report*, Command Paper 5479 (Jul. 1937).

Pan, K. (2017). A Re-Examination of Estoppel in International Jurisprudence. *Chinese Journal of International Law*, 16:4, 751–86.

Pappe, I. (2004). *A History of Modern Palestine: One Land, Two Peoples*. Cambridge: Cambridge University Press.

Pappe, I. (2015). The Framing of the Question of Palestine by the Early Palestinian Press: Zionist Settler-Colonialism and the Newspaper Filastin, 1912–1922. *Journal of Holy Land and Palestine Studies*, 14:1, 59–81.

Pellet, A. (1992). The Opinions of the Badinter Arbitration Committee: A Second Breath for the Self-Determination of Peoples. *European Journal of International Law*, 3, 178–85.

Penkower, M.N. (2019). *Palestine to Israel, Mandate to State, 1945–1948, Volume I: Rebellion Launched*. New York: Touro University Press.

Perry, G. (1977). Security Council Resolution 242: The Withdrawal Clause. *The Middle East Journal*, 31:4, 413–33.

Peteet, J. (2016). Language Matters: Talking about Palestine. *Journal of Palestine Studies*, 45:2, 24–40.

Plascov, A. (1981). *The Palestinian Refugees in Jordan, 1948–1957*. London: Frank Cass & Co. Ltd.

Porath, Y. (1974). *The Emergence of the Palestinian-Arab National Movement, 1918–1929*. London and Portland: Frank Cass.

Porath, Y. (1977). *The Palestinian Arab National Movement: From Riots to Rebellion, 1929–1939*. London: Routledge.

Priestland, J. (ed.). (2002). *Records of Jerusalem 1917–1971*. Cambridge: Cambridge University Press, Archive Editions.

Quigley, J. (1990). *Palestine and Israel, A Challenge to Justice*. Durham and London: Duke University Press.

Quigley, J. (1996). Sovereignty in Jerusalem. *Catholic University Law Review*, 45:3, 765–80.

Quigley, J. (2005). *The Case for Palestine: An International Law Perspective*. Durham: Duke University Press.

Quigley, J. (2009). Palestine Statehood: A Rejoinder to Professor Robert Weston Ash. *Rutgers Law Record*, 36, 257–63.

Quigley, J. (2010). *The Statehood of Palestine: International Law in the Middle East Conflict.* Cambridge: Cambridge University Press.

Quigley, J. (2011). Palestine is a State: A Horse with Black and White Stripes is a Zebra. *Michigan Journal of International Law*, 32:4, 749–64.

Radosh, R. and Radosh, A. (2009). *A Safe Haven, Harry S. Truman and the Founding of Israel.* New York: Harper Collins.

Regan, B. (2017). *The Balfour Declaration: Empire, the Mandate and Resistance in Palestine.* London and New York: Verso.

Reiter, Y. (2017). *Contested Holy Places in Israel-Palestine: Sharing and Conflict Resolution.* Abingdon, Oxon and New York: Routledge.

Rempel, T. (1997). The Significance of Israel's Partial Annexation of East Jerusalem. *Middle East Journal*, 51:4, 520–34.

Rettig, E. and Avraham, E. (2016). The Role of Intergovernmental Organizations in the "Battle over Framing:" The Case of the Israeli–West Bank Separation Barrier. *International Journal of Press/Politics*, 21:1, 111–33.

Reynold, N. (2014). *Britain's Unfulfilled Mandate for Palestine.* Lanham: Lexington Books.

Rizk, E. (1968). *The Palestine Question, Seminar of Arab Jurists on Palestine, Algiers, 22–27 July, 1967.* Beirut: Institute for Palestine Studies.

Roberts. N. (2017). *Islam Under the Palestine Mandate: Colonialism and the Supreme Muslim Council.* London and New York: I.B. Tauris.

Robinson, J. (1947). *Palestine and the United Nations.* Washington, DC: Public Affairs Press.

Rogoff, M.A. and Collins, E. (1990). The Caroline Incident and the Development of International Law. *Brooklyn Journal of International Law*, 16:3, 493–528.

Ronen, Y. (2014). Israel, Palestine and the ICC - Territory Uncharted but not Unknown. *Journal of International Criminal Justice*, 12:1, 7–25.

Ronen, Y. (2014). Recognition of the State of Palestine: Still Too Much Too Soon? in C. Chinkin and F. Baetens (eds.), *Sovereignty, Statehood and State Responsibility: Essays in Honour of James Crawford*, pp. 229–247. Cambridge: Cambridge University Press.

Ronen, Y. (2021). Palestine in the ICC: Statehood and the Right to Self-Determination in the Absence of Effective Control. *Journal of International Criminal Justice*, 18:4, 947–66.

Roosevelt, K. (1948). The Partition of Palestine: A Lesson in Pressure Politics. *The Middle East Journal*, 2:1, 1–16.

Root, E. (1914). The Real Monroe Doctrine. *The American Journal of International Law*, 8:3, 427–42.

Rose, N. (1986). *Chaim Weizmann: A Biography.* New York: Viking Penguin.

Ross, N. (1947). *A Textbook of International Law.* London: Longmans, Green.

Royal Institute of International Affairs. (1946). *Great Britain and Palestine, 1915–1945.* Welwyn Garden City: Broadwater Press.

Sabel, R. (2005). The Status of the Territories: The International Court of Justice Decision on The Separation Barrier and the Green Line. *Israel Law Review*, 38, 316–78.

Sabel, R. (2022). *International Law and the Arab-Israeli Conflict.* Cambridge: Cambridge University Press.

Said, E. (1979a). *The Question of Palestine*. New York: Random House.

Said, E. (1979b). Zionism from the Standpoint of Its Victims. *Social Text*, 1, 7–58.

Said, E. (1994). *The Politics of Dispossession: The Struggle for Palestinian Self-Determination, 1969–1994*. New York: Pantheon Books.

Sakran, S. (2020). *The Legal Consequences of Limited Statehood: Palestine in Multilateral Frameworks*. London and New York: Routledge.

Salem, W. (2002). Legitimization or Implementation: On the UN Partition Plan. *Palestine-Israel Journal of Politics, Economics and Culture*, 9:4, 7–14.

Salmon, J. (1989). Declaration of the State of Palestine. *The Palestine Yearbook of International Law*, V, 48–82.

Samson, E. (2010). Is Gaza Occupied? Redefining the Legal Status of Gaza under International Law. *American University International Law Review*, 25, 915–67.

Samuel, M.T. (2014). Punitive House Demolitions in the West Bank: The Hague Regulations, Geneva Convention IV, and a Jus Cogens Bypass. *Berkeley Journal of Middle Eastern and Islamic Law*, 6:1, 1–24.

Scham, P. et al. (2002). Roundtable Discussion: Narratives of 1948. *Palestine - Israel Journal of Politics, Economics, and Culture*, 9:4, 22–38.

Schwebel, S. (1979). The Effect of Resolutions of the U.N. General Assembly on Customary International Law. *Proceedings of the Annual Meeting (American Society of International Law)*, 73, 301–09.

Segev, T. (1999). *One Palestine, Complete: Jews and Arabs Under the British Mandate*. New York: Henry Holt & Co.

Segev, T. (2005). *1967: Israel, The War, and The Year that Transformed the Middle East*. New York: Henry Holt & Co.

Segev, T. (2019). *A State at Any Cost: The Life of David Ben-Gurion*. New York: Farrar, Straus and Giroux.

Sela, A. (1992). Transjordan, Israel and the 1948 War: Myth, Historiography and Reality. *Middle Eastern Studies*, 28:4, 632–88.

Seller, M. (1968). Isaac Leeser's Views on the Restoration of a Jewish Palestine. *American Jewish Historical Quarterly*, 58:1, 118–35.

Shahar, I. (2015). *Legal Pluralism in the Holy City: Competing Courts, Forum Shopping, and Institutional Dynamics in Jerusalem*. Farnham: Ashgate.

Shalakany, A.A. (2002). Privatizing Jerusalem or an Investigation into the City's Future Legal Stakes. *Leiden Journal of International Law*, 15:2, 431–44.

Shamir, R. (1990). "Landmark Cases" and the Reproduction of Legitimacy: The Case of Israel's High Court of Justice. *Law and Society Review*, 24:3, 781–806.

Shany, Y. (2005). Faraway, So Close: The Legal Status of Gaza after Israel's Disengagement. *Yearbook of International Humanitarian Law*, 8, 369–83.

Shany, Y. (2010). In Defence of Functional Interpretation of Article 12(3) of the Rome Statute: A Response to Yael Ronen. *Journal of International Criminal Justice*, 8:2, 329–43.

Shany, Y. (2012). Binary Law Meets Complex Reality: The Occupation of Gaza Debate. *Israel Law Review*, 41:1–2, 68–86.

Shany, Y. (2016). Legal Entitlements, Changing Circumstances and Intertemporality: A Comment on the Creation of Israel and the Status of Palestine. *Israel Law Review*, 49:3, 391–408.

Sharon, A. (2011). Why Is Israel's Presence in the Territories Still Called "Occupation"? *Jewish Political Studies Review*, 23:3/4, 40–64.

Shaw, M. (2011). The Article 12(3) Declaration of the Palestinian Authority, the International Criminal Court and International Law. *Journal of International Criminal Justice*, 9:2, 301–24.

Shaw, M. (2016). The League of Nations Mandate System and the Palestine Mandate: What Did and Does It Say About International Law and What Did and Does It Say About Palestine. *Israel Law Review*, 49:3, 287–308.

Shaw, M. (2021). *International Law* (9th ed.). Cambridge: Cambridge University Press.

Shehadeh, R. (1997). *From Occupation to Interim Accords: Israel and the Palestinian Territories*. London: Kluwer Law International.

Shemesh, M. (1996). *The Palestinian Entity, 1959–1974: Arab Politics and the PLO* (2nd ed.). London: Frank Cass Ltd.

Shemesh, M. (2018). *The Palestinian National Revival: In the Shadow of the Leadership Crisis, 1937–1967*. Bloomington: Indiana University Press.

Shepherd, N. (2000). *Ploughing Sand: British Rule in Palestine, 1917–1948*. New Brunswick: Rutgers University Press.

Sherman, A.J. (1997). *Mandate Days: British Lives in Palestine, 1918–1948*. London: Thames and Hudson.

Shindler, C. (2009). Opposing Partition: The Zionist Predicaments after the Shoah. *Israel Studies*, 14:2, 88–104.

Shlaim, A. (1988). *Collusion Across the Jordan: King Abdullah, the Zionist Movement and the Partition of Palestine*. New York: Columbia University Press.

Shlaim, A. (1990a). The Rise and Fall of the All-Palestine Government in Gaza. *Journal of Palestine Studies*, 20:1, 37–53.

Shlaim, A. (1990b). *The Politics of Partition: King Abdullah, the Zionists and Palestine, 1921–1951*. New York: Columbia University Press.

Shorrock, W. (1976). *French Suspicion of British Policy in Syria, 1900-1914*, Journal of European Studies 6:23, 190-208.

Shragai, N. (2015). *Jerusalem: Delusions of Division*. Jerusalem: Jerusalem Center for Public Affairs.

Shuqair, R. (1996). *Jerusalem: Its Legal Status and the Possibility of a Durable Settlement*. Ramallah: Al Haq.

Sicker, M. (2000). *Pangs of the Messiah, The Troubled Birth of the Jewish State*. Westport: Praeger.

Sidebotham, H. (1937). *Great Britain and Palestine*. London: MacMillan & Co.

Silverburg, R. (ed.). (2001). *Palestine and International Law: Essays on Politics and Economics*. London: McFarland & Co.

Sobel, R. (2011). The Campaign to Delegitimize Israel with the False Charge of Apartheid. *Jewish Political Studies Review*, 23, 18–31.

Soler, C. (2019). *The Exercise of Kompetenz-Kompetenz in the Determination of Presumptive Jurisdiction, in The Global Prosecution of Core Crimes under International Law*. The Hague: T.M.C. Asser Press.

Soroczyński, R. (2017). Acquisition of Title to Territory in the Aftermath of the Use of Force in the United Nations Era: The case of the State of Israel. *Revue Québécoise de Droit International / Quebec Journal of International Law / Revista Quebequense de Derecho Internacional*, 30:1, 65–88.

Sosebee, S. (1991). Seeds of a Massacre: Israeli Violations at Haram al-Sharif. *American-Arab Affairs*, 36, 104–116.

Sperber, J. (2015). BDS, Israel, and the World System. *Journal of Palestine Studies*, 45:1, 8–23.

Stone, J. (1981). *Israel and Palestine: Assault on the Law of Nations*. Baltimore and London: The Johns Hopkins University Press.

Stover, W. and Mankaryous, M. (2008). Sovereignty Over Jerusalem: A Legal Solution to a Disputed Capital. *International Journal on World Peace*, 25:4, 115–36.

Stoyanovksy, J. (1928). *The Mandate for Palestine: A Contribution to The Theory and Practice of International Mandates*. London: Longmans, Green.

Strawson, J. (2010). *Partitioning Palestine: Legal Fundamentalism in the Palestinian-Israeli Conflict*. London: Pluto Press.

Susser, A. (2018). The Historical Linkage: Israel's Legitimacy and the Idea of Partition. *Israel Studies*, 23:3, 216–27.

Sykes, C. (1965). *Crossroads to Israel: 1917–1948*. Bloomington: Indiana University Press.

Terry, P. (2018). Britain in Palestine (1917–1948) - Occupation, the Palestine Mandate, and International Law. *University of Bologna Law Review*, 2:2, 187–251.

Tessler, M. (2009). *A History of The Israeli-Palestinian Conflict*. Bloomington: Indiana University Press.

Teveth, S. (1985). *Ben-Gurion and the Palestinian Arabs: From Peace to War*. Oxford and New York: Oxford University Press.

Teveth, S. (1987). *Ben-Gurion: The Burning Ground, 1886–1948*. Boston: Houghton, Mifflin.

Thomas, J. (2020). The Intersection of Palestine with Ferguson, Missouri. *Journal of Ecumenical Studies*, 55:1, 82–90.

Toye, P. (ed.). (1989). *Palestine Boundaries 1833–1947*. Cambridge: Cambridge University Press, Archive Editions.

Toye, P. and Seay, A. (eds.). (1995). *Israel: Boundary Disputes with Arab Neighbours 1946–1964*. Cambridge: Archive Editions.

Trachtman, J. (2016). Integrating Lawfare and Warfare. *Boston College International and Comparative Law Review*, 39:2, 267–82.

Truman, H. (1956). *Memoirs, Volume Two: Years of Trial and Hope*. New York: Doubleday.

Tsilonas, V. (2019). *The Jurisdiction of the International Criminal Court*. Berlin: Springer.

Urquhart, B. (1993). *Ralph Bunche: An American Life*. New York: W.W. Norton.

Van Steenburgh, R. (2012). Proportionality Under Jus Ad Bellum and Jus In Bello: Clarifying Their Relationship. *Israel Law Review*, 45:1, 107–24.

Vareilles, G. (2010). *Les Frontieres de la Palestine, 1914–1947*. Paris: L'Harmattan.

Vidmar, J. (2013). Palestine and the Conceptual Problem of Implicit Statehood. *Chinese Journal of International Law*, 12, 19–41.

Voltolini, B. (2016). Non-State Actors and Framing Processes in EU Foreign Policy: The Case of EU–Israel Relations. *Journal of European Public Policy*, 23:10, 1502–19.

Wallach, Y. (2020). *A City in Fragments: Urban Text in Modern Jerusalem*. Stanford: Stanford University Press.

Wass, J. (2017). Jurisdiction by Estoppel and Acquiescence in International Courts and Tribunals. *The British Yearbook of International Law*, 86:1, 155–95.

Wasserstein, B. (1978). *The British in Palestine: The Mandatory Government and the Arab-Jewish Conflict, 1917–1929*. London: Royal Historical Society.

Watson, G. (2000). *The Oslo Accords: International Law and the Israeli-Palestinian Peace Agreements*. Oxford: Oxford University Press.

Watson, G. (2018). The Balfour Declaration in International Law. *Journal of Levantine Studies*, 8:1, 101–20.

Weiler, J.H.H. (2013). Differentiated Statehood? "PreStates"? Palestine@the UN. *European Journal of International Law*, 24:1, 1–11.

Weizmann, C. (1949). *Trial and Error: The Autobiography of Chaim Weizmann*. New York: Harper & Bros.

Wells-Greco, M. (2010). Operation 'Cast Lead': Jus in Bello Proportionality. *Netherlands International Law Review*, 57:3, 397–422.

Werner, W. (2010). Historical and Semiotic Origins of "Lawfare:" The Curious Career of Lawfare. *Case Western Reserve Journal of International Law*, 43:1/2, 61–72.

Wheatley, N. (2015). Mandatory Interpretation: Legal Hermeneutics and the New International Order in Arab and Jewish Petitions to the League of Nations. *Past and Present*, 227:1, 205–48.

Whitman, C. (2013). Palestine's Statehood and Ability to Litigate in the International Court of Justice. *California Western International Law Journal*, 44, 73–112.

Wilmshurt, E., et. al. (2006). The Chatham House Principles of International Law on the Use of Force in Self-Defence. *The International and Comparative Law Quarterly*, 55:4, 963–72.

Wilson, E. (1973). The Palestine Papers, 1943–1947. *Journal of Palestine Studies*, 2:4, 33–54.

Wilson, E. (1979). *Decision on Palestine: How the U.S. Came to Recognize the State of Israel*. Stanford: Hoover Institution Press.

Worster, W. (2011). The Exercise of Jurisdiction by the International Criminal Court Over Palestine. *American University International Law Review*, 26:5, 1153–209.

Wright, E. (1951). Abdallah' s Jordan:1947–1951. *Middle East Journal*, 5:4, 439–60.

Wright, Q. (1923). Sovereignty of the Mandates. *The American Journal of International Law*, 17:4, 691–703.

Wright, Q. (1930). *Mandates under the League of Nations*. Chicago: University of Chicago Press.

Yitzhak, R. (2019). Transjordan's Occupation of Jerusalem in the 1948 War. *Israel Affairs*, 25:2, 307–17.

Yusuf, M. (2002). The Partition of Palestine (1947) - An Arab Perspective. *Palestine - Israel Journal of Politics, Economics, and Culture*, 9:4, 39–49.

Ze'evi, D. (1996). *An Ottoman Century: The District of Jerusalem in the 1600s*. Albany: State University of New York Press.

Zimmermann, A. (2013). Palestine and the International Criminal Court Quo Vadis: Reach and Limits of Declarations under Article 12(3). *Journal of International Criminal Justice*, 11:2, 303–30.

Zipperstein, S. (2020). *Law and the Arab-Israeli Conflict: The Trials of Palestine*. London and New York: Routledge.

Zipperstein, S. (2022). *Zionism, Palestinian Nationalism and the Law: 1939–1948*. London and New York: Routledge.

INDEX

Note: **Bold** page numbers refer to tables and page numbers followed by "n" denote endnotes.